MAGILL'S
SURVEY
OF
CINEMA

MAGILL'S SURVEY OF CINEMA

English Language Films

SECOND SERIES
VOLUME 3
HAN-LUC

Edited by

FRANK N. MAGILL

Associate Editors

STEPHEN L. HANSON

PATRICIA KING HANSON

SALEM PRESS
Englewood Cliffs, N.J.

LIBRARY OF CONGRESS CATALOG CARD NUMBER: 81-84330

Complete Set: ISBN 0-89356-230-0
Volume 3:   ISBN-0-89356-233-5

.

PRINTED IN THE UNITED STATES OF AMERICA

LIST OF TITLES IN VOLUME THREE

MAGILL'S
SURVEY
OF
CINEMA

THE HANGING TREE

Released: 1959
Production: Martin Jurow and Richard Shepherd for Warner Bros.
Direction: Delmer Daves
Screenplay: Wendell Mayes and Halsted Welles; based on a novelette of the
    same name by Dorothy M. Johnson
Cinematography: Ted McCord
Editing: Owen Marks
Music: Max Steiner
Song: Mack David and Jerry Livingston
Running time: 106 minutes

> *Principal characters:*
> Doc Joe Frail .... Gary Cooper
> Elizabeth Mahler .... Maria Schell
> Frenchy Plante .... Karl Malden
> Rune .... Ben Piazza
> Grubb .... George C. Scott

The Hanging Tree is a thoughtful, unvarnished Western which exhibits many of the classic traits associated with the genre—notably that of the mysterious stranger attempting to hide his past, the unbridled greed that accompanies gold fever, and the hanging tree itself—long an imposing symbol of frontier justice. Adapted from Dorothy M. Johnson's novelette, which received the Spur Award from the Western Writers of America, *The Hanging Tree* presents real, sometimes unlikable characterizations against the rugged setting of a gold mining camp in the 1870's.

The story line involves a frontier doctor who is as cynical as he is compassionate and equally skilled with both scalpel and gun. Doc Frail (Gary Cooper), who has hung up his shingle on the outskirts of Skull Creek, a Montana mining camp, is a laconic loner known for his poker skills and fast gun. In dispensing medicine, Frail can be both greedy and kind. To those without money, there are no fees, but Frail has no qualms about asking high prices from those who can pay. Through town gossip, it is revealed that Frail, who has been moving from frontier town to frontier town, is attempting to escape his reputation. Back in his home state of Missouri, Frail killed his brother after finding him with his wife; later, Frail's wife committed suicide. Before riding away, an embittered Frail burned his home to the ground. He now seemingly has no need for personal relationships.

As with many other films within this genre, outsiders do invade his life. The first is a would-be sluice robber who is shot, although never seen, by an angry mob of prospectors. After taking the bullet out of Rune (Ben Piazza), who has called himself a "wood's colt," indicating he has no home, the doctor pockets the tell-tale bullet and threatens to use the bullet as evidence against Rune unless the youth agrees to become his manservant. Rune has no choice but to obey. Eventually, he comes to sense the doctor's need for companionship, despite Frail's attempts to keep his distance from any possible friendship.

The doctor's detached demeanor falters when he treats Elizabeth (Maria Schell), a young woman who has been blinded by the sun after wandering for days in the wilderness. A Swiss immigrant, she was aboard a stagecoach with her father when bandits attacked. The only survivor, she was thrown clear of the wreckage. She is rescued from her wanderings by Frenchy (Karl Malden), a vociferous and rather lecherous prospector who seems to look upon the girl as his property. Indeed, after locating the girl, Frenchy victoriously parades her before the other miners. She is a pathetic sight: she is almost in shock, her clothes are in tatters, and she has been severely sunburned, bruised, and blinded. Because she requires constant medical care, she is taken to Doc Frail's cabin. There, she begins to show signs of improvement.

In her disturbed state, Elizabeth is also in need of friendship and support. In a touching scene, the blind girl, who is becoming more attractive-looking with each day, clings desperately to the doctor's strong hands. Frail will not allow himself to feel affection for the grateful girl, but he is concerned for her health. After becoming convinced that her blindness is due to shock from witnessing the murder of her father, he turns to unorthodox treatment. Taking her to the edge of a cliff, he forces her to look down. Insisting that her eyes are physically healed, the doctor maintains that if she still cannot see it is because she refuses to see "things as they are." His treatment is successful. Following her cure, an indebted Elizabeth stays on at Frail's cabin, where she cooks and cleans. Although she becomes increasingly fond of him, he will not declare any feeling for her. The living arrangement comes to an end after town gossip increases and Elizabeth is verbally assaulted. As a result she moves into her own cabin, but she is still determined to repay Doc Frail. The best way to do so, she surmises, is with her own grubstake, but her efforts to solicit grubstake funds prove futile until Frail anonymously provides the money. Elizabeth then takes Rune and Frenchy as partners.

Working alongside Rune and Frenchy in the muddy riverbeds, Elizabeth discovers that the work is back-breaking and filthy. Although their spirits grow downcast, they are revived—for obvious reasons—when they uncover a glory hole in the aftermath of a dramatic storm. The hole is uncovered when a gnarled old tree is toppled, and its roots are discovered to be entangled with nuggets. The entire community is excited by the discovery, and the frenzy grows after Frenchy invites the entire town to the saloon, where he buys bottles instead of glasses. Inevitably, the mood grows dangerous, particularly after a massive bonfire is lit in the town's main street. Frenchy, propelled by the excitement and his new lofty status, leaves the saloon and breaks into Elizabeth's cabin, where he attempts to rape her. The assault is interrupted by the arrival of Frail, who finds a bloodied Elizabeth lying unconscious on the floor with a drunken Frenchy standing over her. Drawing his gun, Frail begins shooting. After driving Frenchy to the edge of a nearby cliff, Frail empties his gun into the prospector, then uses his foot to lift the body and send it toppling over the cliff.

Grubb (George C. Scott), a zealot whose faith-healing tactics had previously agitated Frail, now leads the angered, drunken miners in an assault on the doctor. He is swiftly carried to the camp's hanging tree, and the noose is lowered around his neck. The frenzied crowd's excitement changes direction, however, when Elizabeth confronts them. With Rune at her side, she offers the miners her nuggets. Met by a stifled response and with Rune's agreement, she next offers them the deed to their mine in exchange for Frail's life. As one of the miners loudly proclaims, Elizabeth is trying to buy Frail's life because she loves him, while Rune is declaring his friendship for the man who blackmailed him. During the film's final moments, Elizabeth and Doc Frail embrace, with Rune at their side. Dominating the scene is the now life-giving hanging tree.

Although 1959 was marked by the blockbuster spectacular *Ben-Hur*, the low-key *The Hanging Tree* proved to be one of the year's sleepers. All exteriors were shot in a mining camp built near Yakima, Washington, and the location filming, enhanced by the breathtaking mountain landscapes, greatly add to the rustic flavor of the Technicolor production. Cinematography by Ted McCord, who had also filmed *East of Eden* (1955) and *The Treasure of the Sierra Madre* (1948), is top-notch. Performances are effective: Cooper is a perfect choice for the role of the tight-lipped doctor, and Schell is excellent in a role that deviates from her usual parts, particularly since her character toils alongside the men, thus denying a glamorous appearance. As Frenchy, Malden provides an enthusiastically menacing portrayal that marked the first of his screen villains. The role of the crazed Grubb also provided Scott with a memorable and highly dramatic film debut.

Critics of the day were generally enthusiastic about this literate Western, although some were upset by the film's "phychological" implications, such as the doctor's unorthodox treatment of Elizabeth's blindness. The film's song, a powerful ballad sung by Marty Robbins (written by Mack David and Jerry Livingston), proved popular and garnered an Academy Award nomination. The film's rather unexpected popularity resulted from many facets, including a superb production crew which included composer Max Steiner. Skillfully bringing all the elements together was director Delmer Daves. Daves's Westerns, as first evidenced by *Broken Arrow* in 1950, are marked by social realism and a personal rather than epic stature. The still-effective *The Hanging Tree* typifies Daves's quality-minded thought-provoking approach.

Pat H. Broeske

THE HAPPIEST DAYS OF YOUR LIFE

Released: 1950
Production: Sidney Gilliat and Frank Launder for British Lion
Direction: Frank Launder
Screenplay: Frank Launder and John Dighton; based on the play of the same name by John Dighton
Cinematography: Stan Pavey
Editing: Oswald Hafenrichter
Title design: Ronald Searle
Running time: 91 minutes

Principal characters:

Wetherby Pond	Alastair Sim
Muriel Whitchurch	Margaret Rutherford
Miss Harper	Bernadette O'Farrell
Richard Tassell	John Bentley
Miss Gossage	Joyce Grenfell
Victor Hyde-Brown	Guy Middleton
Arnold Billings	Richard Wattis
Rainbow	Edward Rigby
Anthony Ramsden	Arthur Howard
Reverend Birch	Stringer Davis
Angela	Patricia Owens
Conrad Matthews	John Turnbull
Monsieur Jove	Percy Walsh
Miss Jezzard	Muriel Aked
Doctor Collett	Laurence Naismith
Sir Angus McNally	Kenneth Downey
Edwin	Harold Goodwin
Mr. West	Russell Waters

British comedies gained wider popularity in America during the 1950's with Alec Guinness and Peter Sellers films being among the frontrunners. Paving the way from the beginning of the decade were such "delicious" (one of the favorite words used by critics to describe such fare) gems as *The Happiest Days of Your Life*. This film concerns the age-old conflict between the sexes but changes it into a boys-against-girls story. The formula was later used with even better results for the outrageous St. Trinian's comedies of the 1950's and 1960's, using much of the same talent for tales of a girls' school in which wildness seemed to be the major subject in the curriculum. The St. Trinian's films were based on the cartoons of Ronald Searle, whose work also adorns the title cards for *The Happiest Days of Your Life*.

Director and coscreenwriter Frank Launder had a long and prosperous collaboration with Sidney Gilliat, beginning with a writing partnership and eventually expanding into producing feature films under the name Individual Films. Launder later directed *Lady Godiva Rides Again* (1951), which satirizes beauty contests; two very funny Bill Travers films, *Geordie* (or *Wee Geordie*, 1955) and *The Bridal Path* (1959); and the St. Trinian's epics. As a writer and director, Gilliat strayed from the comic mold a little more than his partner, doing *State Secret* (or *The Great Manhunt*, 1950), a suspense drama with a good share of laughs; the musical *The Story of Gilbert and Sullivan* (1953); and a crime drama, *Fortune Is a Woman* (*She Played with Fire*, 1957). Gilliat also directed such fine comedies as *Left Right and Centre* (1959) with Alastair Sim and *Only Two Can Play* (1961) with Sellers.

Sim, who had been playing middle-aged oddballs in films since 1935 (when, at thirty-five, he was prematurely bald and looked much older), continued to appear in Launder-Gilliat productions, including *The Belles of St. Trinian's* (1954), first in that series, and *Blue Murder at St. Trinian's* (1957). Margaret Rutherford worked extremely well with Sim in *The Happiest Days of Your Life*, but went on her own to win greater fame as the embodiment of Agatha Christie's Miss Marple and to win an Academy Award for Best Supporting Actress for her performance in *The V.I.P.s* (1963).

Joyce Grenfell, the British comedienne, also known on American television, has a nice supporting role, but is unable to do much with it since her opportunities are limited. Even the nominal romantic interest, between John Bentley and Bernadette O'Farrell (later the original Maid Marian in the *Robin Hood* television series), is almost nonexistent. As Billings, Richard Wattis has a particularly funny role, disdainful as he always is but somehow much more likable. Arthur Howard, strongly resembling his late, more famous actor-brother Leslie, is the typical absent-minded professor, and Rutherford's husband Stringer Davis is seen in the minor role of the Reverend Birch. Also in the cast are two actors who later became well-known figures in films, an unbilled George Cole is the junior assistant caretaker and pretty young Canadian actress Pat Owens, who portrays the saucy schoolgirl Angela. As Patricia Owens, she later had a Hollywood career and would appear in many films of the 1950's and 1960's including *Island in the Sun* (1957), *Sayonara* (1957), and *Hell to Eternity* (1960).

Although the opportunities are inherent in the story for a very risqué approach, Launder, Gilliat, and collaborating screenwriter John Dighton, on whose play the film was based, never give in to temptation. The setting is fall, 1949, although it could easily be sometime during World War II because many films set in that era reflect wartime emergencies which have caused drastic adjustments in people's lives. Richard Tassell (John Bentley), a handsome young English master, arrives at Nutbourne College, an all-boys' school, just before the new term is to begin, and is met at the station by the math teacher.

Caustic Arnold Billings (Richard Wattis) introduces Richard to his new colleagues after remarking that janitor Rainbow (Edward Rigby) really runs the place and that "you'll loathe it." Victor Hyde-Brown (Guy Middleton), nicknamed Whizzo, is the playboy and gambler who is sports master, seemingly in his spare time; Anthony Ramsden (Arthur Howard) is the science master who is constantly preoccupied; Conrad Matthews (John Turnbull) functions as second master; and Monsieur Jove (Percy Walsh) is the French master, always sleeping, possibly in self-defense. Finally, there is head master Wetherby Pond (Alastair Sim), who has endured fifteen years at Nutbourne. At a rare tea for his professors, Pond happily announces that he may be transferred to Harlingham after the board of governors pays Nutbourne a visit. He urges everyone to straighten out, including Billings, who has a penchant for football pools.

Rainbow says that 217 trunks are in the driveway, one hundred of them rerouted from St. Swithin's. "This is what comes of nationalizing the railroads," observes Pond, who then makes plans to put up the extra students for a night. Heading purposefully toward the school are Muriel Whitchurch (Margaret Rutherford), her staff, and the pupils of St. Swithin's, an all-girls' institute. While Pond and his staff are busy upstairs, Miss Whitchurch and her group arrive below. When sports mistress Miss Gossage (Joyce Grenfell) loudly hits a gong to attract their attention, it prompts Whitchurch to remark, "Just a tap. You're not introducing a film." (This is a sly reference to the famed J. Arthur Rank trademark.)

Inspecting the premises, Miss Whitchurch purses her lips at the school motto, "Guard Thine Honor." When Pond finally learns the truth, that an all-girls' school is to be billeted with his students because of a Ministry error, he accuses the Ministry of being guilty of an appalling sexual aberration. Aware of the gender of the Nutbourne enrollment, Miss Whitchurch is phoning the Ministry when Pond angrily snatches the phone from her hands. The two school heads confer, after which the girls arrive and the household staff leaves. Introduced to Richard, Miss Harper (Bernadette O'Farrell), St. Swithin's English and history mistress, is immediately infatuated, as is he. Pond, hoping to cut off an invasion, orders the dormitory to be locked, but finds he and his masters have been locked in the common room. The girls do take over the dorm, as the Nutbourne boys bicycle onto the grounds and observe Whizzo climbing out a window to unlock the others.

The boys sleep in the gym, the male teachers in the barn, and Pond in a tub. As he rises, the familiar theme music from *The Third Man* (1949) can be heard briefly. Having taken charge, Whitchurch orders her students to prepare breakfast; one boy says about the food, "Please, sir, I don't want anymore." Billings and Gossage are assigned to censor the mail for any embarrassing information the students may be passing to their parents, she liking her proximity to him better than he does. The girls' eurhythmics beat makes it hard for the boys to study, and Miss Whitchurch frowns on the

Tassell-Harper liaison as well as Hyde-Brown's accompanying the girls of the botany class. Timid Miss Jezzard (Muriel Aked) tells her superior that five parents are planning to visit, so Whitchurch persuades Pond to hide the boys and turn the grounds into a female institute for the afternoon. She informs Pond of her influence with the board of governors and he, on his way to the Ministry, discovers three of the governors at the train station about to pay their respects the same day.

Billings arrives to chauffeur the governors—Dr. Collett (Laurence Naismith), Sir Angus McNally (Kenneth Downey), and the Reverend James Rich (Stringer Davis)—and Pond, in a roundabout fashion, to Nutbourne. Once back at the school, Pond agrees with Miss Whitchurch that split-second timing and cooperation can save them and prevent the two groups from ever meeting. One student, however, Angela Parry (Pat Owens), turns up in every class to which the parents are escorted, causing some confusion. Rainbow and assistant Edwin (Harold Goodwin) put up and take down the goalposts, depending upon who is on the field.

Collett leaves Pond's tour group, and the split-second timing collapses when the governors run into the girls. On the field, both student bodies engage in a free-for-all, while a woeful Pond looks on, saying "Instead of lacrosse, it's la double cross." Finally Ministry division manager West (Russell Waters) arrives to inform everyone that a coed school will replace the St. Swithin's girls, and he is followed by an even wilder group of mixed students. In the final scene, Tassell and Harper kiss as Pond and Whitchurch make plans to go to Tanganyika. Following the end credits, Rainbow and Edwin are observed in a state of collapse on the field.

John Cocchi

THE HARDER THEY COME

Released: 1973
Production: Perry Henzell for New World
Direction: Perry Henzell
Screenplay: Perry Henzell and Trevor D. Rhone
Cinematography: Peter Jasson
Editing: John Victor Smith, Seicland Anderson, and Richard White
Running time: 93 minutes

Principal characters:

Ivan Martin	Jimmy Cliff
Elsa	Janet Barkley
Jose	Carl Bradshaw
Pedro	Ras Daniel Hartman
Hilton	Bobby Charlton
Preacher	Basil Keane
Detective Ray Jones	Winston Stona

The Harder They Come stands as one of the most remarkable films of the 1970's for a variety of reasons. It was the first feature film to be made in Jamaica by Jamaicans, and the plot centered on that Caribbean island's two most prominent exports—marijuana and reggae music. All of the characters speak English, but so much of the dialogue is rendered in a dense (if melodic) island accent that its distributor saw fit to add subtitles when the film was released in the United States.

Perhaps unsurprisingly, in its initial run, *The Harder They Come* was less than successful with American audiences. It did, however, attract a hard core of devotees; and soon word of mouth plus the growing popularity of reggae music brought the film an expanded audience. *The Harder They Come* became a staple on college campuses and at revival theaters throughout the country.

The film's story is an old one—country boy comes to the city to make his fortune, but falls in with the wrong crowd and meets an untimely end—but Perry Henzell, the film's producer, director, and coscenarist, brings it to life. Henzell and Trevor D. Rhone have combined elements of the career of a legendary Jamaican outlaw of the 1950's with incidents from the life of their star, reggae singer Jimmy Cliff. The outlaw—named Rhygin—was a gunman in the Kingston ghetto; he was famous not only for his crimes but also for the way he publicly taunted his police pursuers. Naturally, when they finally caught up with him, they were not inclined to be merciful, and he died in a hail of police bullets.

Cliff's contributions to the story line were economic rather than criminal. He had been a "successful" recording artist on the island for a decade, and was one of the foremost practitioners of reggae, a unique blend of New

Orleans piano rock-and-roll and traditional Caribbean calypso. Some understanding of reggae music in its social context is essential to an understanding of *The Harder They Come*; therefore, a word of explanation is in order. When the music began to evolve in the early 1960's (it was first called "ska," then "rock steady," and finally reggae), its only distinctive characteristic was its beat. By 1970, however, the lyrics had taken an apocalyptic turn, offering visions of political revolution and religious armageddon. Jamaica's economy had gone bad, and as society failed them, the island's poor flocked in increasing numbers to Rastafarianism, a back-to-Africa cult that worshiped Ethiopian Emperor Haile Selassie as the living God, advocated the sacramental use of marijuana (or ganja, as it was known on Jamaica), and looked to the island's reggae musicians to spread their gospel.

Indeed, for much of the population, there appeared to be only two ways to escape their grinding poverty: join the illegal ganja trade, or become a musician. As Jimmy Cliff and a host of other aspirants discovered, the latter course was not all it was supposed to be. The music industry on the island was rigidly controlled by the owners of a handful of studios, who were disinclined to share their profits with their musicians.

Into this milieu wanders the film's protagonist Ivan Martin (Jimmy Cliff), who has come to Kingston from the country to become a singer. He is quickly tricked out of his few possessions by one of the ghetto's hordes of con artists and is forced to take a job as a handyman at a small pentecostal church for room and board. He does his singing in the church's choir, where he meets and woos Elsa (Janet Barkely), a pretty young ward of the Preacher (Basil Keane).

Although he means no harm, Ivan is a wild and ambitious young man, and his recklessness in pursuit of what he imagines will be musical glory often ends up hurting those around him, as well as himself. He seduces Elsa and talks her into helping him use the church as a rehearsal hall, but when the Preacher catches him in this desecration, he punishes Elsa along with Ivan.

Undeterred, Ivan wangles a tryout at a local recording studio, where he sings "The Harder They Come," which he has written himself. The lyrics are full of defiance: "The oppressors are trying to keep me down, trying to drive me underground . . . as sure as the sun will shine, I'm gonna get my share now, what's mine—and then the harder they come, the harder they fall, one and all!" The producer, a burly man named Hilton (Bobby Charlton), is impressed with the song, but less so with the brash Ivan. He offers the boy twenty dollars for the complete rights to the record. Stunned, Ivan refuses.

Ivan's troubles suddenly multiply. Thrown out by the Preacher (who evidently had his own lustful designs on Elsa), he gets into a fight with the Preacher's assistant and cuts him badly. Ivan is apprehended and receives an excruciating public flogging. After he recovers, he begins hanging out with Jose (Carl Bradshaw), a ghetto hustler who is a middleman in the local ganja trade, which is controlled by the chief of detectives, Ray Jones (Winston Stona). Jose and Ivan attend a Sergio Leone-Clint Eastwood spaghetti Western, where the first hint of Ivan's taste for guns and violence is revealed. The rapture in his eyes as he watches Eastwood slaughter his opponents foreshadows Ivan's own destruction at the film's end.

Ivan and Elsa move into a suffocating one-room flat, where Elsa looks for work while Ivan (having swallowed his pride and taken the twenty dollars from Hilton) struts his stuff as the neighborhood's newest star. Jose introduces him to Pedro (Ras Daniel Hartman), a devout Rastafarian and low-level ganja runner, and Ivan joins the ganja trade as Pedro's partner.

It should be noted here that Henzell offers no condemnation of the ganja trade *per se*. Pedro, in fact, is a benevolently spiritual character who wishes no one harm, even under extreme provocation. The other ganja traders are portrayed in much the same light: they are decent working folk who are simply trying to feed their families. As one of the characters notes, the island's whole economy is based on marijuana; without it, there would be chaos.

Neither is it Henzell's intention to turn his film into a parable of the white exploitation of blacks. Where blacks are exploited in *The Harder They Come*, it is by other blacks. Indeed, whites are virtually absent from the film. Instead, Henzell takes Jamaica's social, political, and economic plight as a given, and the effect is to personalize the film. In any society, Henzell is saying, there are people (such as Elsa and Pedro) who are drawn to good works, and others (such as Jose, Hilton, and ultimately Ivan) who are leeches and predators.

Ivan acquires a motorcycle and a brace of pistols; he is making a relatively good living as a courier in the drug trade, but, characteristically, he is not satisfied. When he declines to pay Jose his weekly kickback, Jose goes to Detective Jones, who orders his police to teach Ivan a lesson. Bullets fly, and Ivan kills one of the policemen. When he shoots his way out of another police ambush, he becomes a ghetto legend. Ivan is delighted—he is finally famous.

Ivan taunts the police at their inability to apprehend him, leaving notes in abandoned hideouts and sending snapshots of himself in gunslinger poses to the newspapers. The notoriety even boosts the sales of his record. Most of the ganja traders support Ivan, at least initially. They admire his bravado and have no particular love for Jose and his superiors. When Detective Jones flexes his muscles by shutting down the ganja trade entirely, however, their enthusiasm diminishes in direct proportion to the growth of their hunger. Finally only Pedro remains loyal.

The film's denouement takes place on a deserted beach on Jamaica's shoreline. Pedro has arranged for a boat to take Ivan to Cuba, but Ivan, wounded in a previous encounter with the police, misses the rendezvous. Meanwhile, Elsa, who, as the forgotten woman, has grown closer to Pedro and his son, resolves to end the whole affair by informing on Ivan. The police close in, and Ivan, with visions of Clint Eastwood dancing in his mind, charges the waiting machine guns. He dies with his record at the top of the charts.

On a technical level, parts of *The Harder They Come* betray its Third World origins. The photography is sometimes grainy, and the editing is rough compared to the seamless product turned out by American studios. In a very real sense, however, this raggedness works to the film's advantage: it lends an air of verisimilitude to the film, giving it a documentary quality that ends up drawing the audience into the film rather than putting it off.

Another important factor in the film's success is its cast. Cliff's range as an actor is doubtless limited, but he captures perfectly Ivan's fierce joy in his music and does a creditable job at portraying the young man's mean streak as well. No doubt he is acting out the settling of some old music business scores, but whatever his internal motivation, his performance is unforgettable. Barkley as Elsa delivers a poignant performance in a role that is surprisingly well rounded, given the generally misogynistic ambiance of the part of Jamaican culture that inspired the film. Elsa has a carnal side as well as a spiritual side—part of her was attracted to Ivan, after all—and Barkley shows us both. Among the supporting cast, Charlton stands out as the beefy and imperious Hilton, czar of the local reggae scene; he seems to enjoy his role thoroughly. Hartman is a striking Pedro, with his long hair matted into the dreadlocks style; Bradshaw is appropriately sleazy as Jose; and Keane is righteously indignant as the Preacher. Clearly, Henzell's vision is the guiding force of the film. His direction, although it lacks a Hollywood polish, is just right for the subject at hand, as critics generally agreed. Some of the film's images remain indelible: the ecstasy of the parishioners at the pentecostal service, Ivan driving a stolen white Cadillac across a golf course, and, most of all, the music. Henzell collected much of the best Jamaican music of the day to provide the film's heartbeat, and made it an organic part of the narrative. Aside from Cliff's "The Harder They Come" and the Maytals' "Sweet and Dandy" (both scenes from Hilton's recording studio), the music seems to come from everywhere—transistor radios in the streets, bars, from the air itself. There is not a bad song in the film, but two in addition to those noted above deserve special mention: the Melodians' hypnotic and mystical "Rivers of Babylon," and the Maytals' grimly rollicking "Pressure Drop."

Ironically, *The Harder They Come*'s most enduring contribution may well have been its sound track album, which did much better business than the film itself. The sound track spearheaded the subtle but pervasive spread of Jamaican rhythms into popular music in the decade after the film was released. One can only hope that the film that started it all will eventually attain similar recognition.

Robert Mitchell

THE HARDER THEY FALL

Released: 1956
Production: Philip Yordan for Columbia
Direction: Mark Robson
Screenplay: Philip Yordan; based on the novel of the same name by Budd Schulberg
Cinematography: Burnett Guffey
Editing: Jerome Thoms
Running time: 108 minutes

Principal characters:
Eddie Willis .... Humphrey Bogart
Nick Benko .... Rod Steiger
Beth Willis .... Jan Sterling
Toro Moreno .... Mike Lane
Buddy Brannen .... Max Baer
George .... Jersey Joe Walcott

In the tradition of fight films, which usually focus on the fighter as protagonist, *The Harder They Fall* is atypical. Unlike *Body and Soul* (1947), *Champion* (1949), or *Rocky* (1977), this film is not a character study nor does it ever allow the audience the pleasure of vicariously sharing the triumphs of a boxer as he rises to the top. *The Harder They Fall* is a study of corruption within the fight game and has an unyielding harshness in exposing a machine of deceit in which each individual has a place, and in which the fighter himself is more spectacle than man. The duped Toro Moreno is not the principal character (although he is an effectively realized presence as played by the hulking and somber Mike Lane), and the carnival atmosphere in which he is "sold" is reminiscent of nothing so much as the carnival which goes up during the rescue of the ill-fated Leo in Billy Wilder's *Ace in the Hole* (1951).

Toro is imported from South America by a fight promoter, Nick Benko (Rod Steiger), to be developed into a money-making contender, but although he looks and believes himself to be formidable, Toro is really awkward, has a "glass jaw," and "could not punch his way out of a paper bag." Backed by an efficient team of experts both in and out of the ring, Toro becomes a popular contender, unaware that Benko is having all of his fights fixed. A former sports writer, Eddie Willis (Humphrey Bogart), whom Benko has hired as a publicist, initially has misgivings about selling this sham of a boxer; but he throws himself into his work on the theory that Toro, too, will receive a substantial share of the money for which they are all working. Ultimately, Toro must fall from innocence and subsequently take a terrible beating from the champion, Buddy Brannen (Max Baer), the only fighter he has been up against who cannot be fixed. When Willis goes to Benko to collect Toro's share of the money, however, he finds that Benko has cheated him out of almost all of it. Remorseful over his involvement, Willis gives Toro his own share, twenty-six thousand dollars, and puts him on a plane to Argentina. Ignoring threats from Benko, he then begins an exposé of the syndicate and its power over boxing in America.

If there is a protagonist in this socially conscious drama, it is Eddie Willis, and the audience is immediately alerted to his relative moral superiority by the casting of the role. Bogart had much earlier established an image in most of his classic films—that of the hard-shelled idealist who ultimately turns out to be a white knight in black armor. In *The Harder They Fall*, his last film, Bogart looks more world-weary than ever (perhaps the result of his illness), and the film's responsiveness to the audience's faith in his essential integrity adds much feeling to the final sequences. This is an excellent example of the idolization of a star adding dimension and meaning to a film.

With the exception of Willis, the major characters are either ruthless and unsympathetic manipulators like Benko or pathetic fools like Toro. Willis' wife Beth (Jan Sterling), although she is intelligent and sympathetic, has only a marginal role in the story, while Toro's trainer, George (Jersey Joe Walcott), although he appears at times to be a sensitive man, never reproaches himself for his self-demeaning participation in the elaborate setup. The film's strongest and most characteristic scenes are of confrontations between callous men, relentlessly planning strategies and proclaiming their self-interest without pretense. Benko is continually in a rage over his associates' mistakes and weaknesses. His egotism, which is often the dramatic focus of individual scenes, gives these scenes forcefulness and intensity.

The unsparing cynicism and appealing lack of sentimentality in the film are visually enhanced by effective direction, cinematography, and editing. The characteristic sharp black-and-white contrasts of the 1950's are persistent in the texture of the film, giving an impression of vivid realism to the scenes in the ring, in the dressing rooms, and in the hotel suites and streets of the small towns through which Toro is paraded with his *entourage*. Director Mark Robson's work on the film reflects his early experience as an editor in the almost musical precision with which he realizes a succession of short scenes which build dramatically to convey the unsparing manipulation of Toro, his opponents, and the public.

The film reflects credit most of all on Philip Yordan, who not only wrote it but also served as its producer. Yordan is one of the great screenwriters of the modern cinema and has never received the attention or honors which he deserves. He has the ability to create highly unusual relationships in conventional genre films, as in *The Big Combo* (1955), in which Jean Wallace spends most of the time mesmerized by her attachment to the "bad" gangster, Richard Conte, while the "good" cop, Cornel Wilde, pathetically carries a torch for her. Yordan has the insight to create an offbeat romance between the puritanical plantation owner Charlton Heston and the "fallen woman" Eleanor Parker in *The Naked Jungle* (1954), so that when the ants attack there are intimations that they are the physical manifestation of Heston's own neurotic self-destructiveness. Yordan's special gifts are displayed in the reflective and sensitive war film *Men in War* (1957), which suggests the complexity of its characters with a minimum of dialogue. At the same time, Yordan can write very beautiful dialogue, as in the celebrated central love scene between Joan Crawford and Sterling Hayden in *Johnny Guitar* (1954), in which the two characters express their romantic bitterness in mocking phrases which both conceal and reveal their true feelings. Yordan benefited from the artistic personalities of the directors of these films, especially Nicholas Ray and Anthony Mann, for whom he had a special regard; but even in the work of less imaginative collaborators, Yordan's gift for subtly poeticizing his material is always evident.

The Harder They Fall is one of the most striking examples of this gift. The source material is in some ways narrow, highly explicit in its social concerns and moral themes, and very much of its time. The stylistic richness of Yordan's writing lifts the film above these liabilities, with the result that it retains a surprising power on repeated viewings.

Blake Lucas

HARRY AND TONTO

Released: 1974
Production: Paul Mazursky for Twentieth Century-Fox
Direction: Paul Mazursky
Screenplay: Paul Mazursky and Josh Greenfield
Cinematography: Michael Butler
Editing: Richard Halsey
Running time: 115 minutes

Principal characters:
Harry	Art Carney (AA)
Shirley	Ellen Burstyn
Sam Two Feathers	Chief Dan George
Jessie	Geraldine Fitzgerald
Eddie	Larry Hagman
Burt	Phil Bruns
Ginger	Melanie Mayron
Hooker	Barbara Rhoades
Norman	Joshua Mostel

Harry and Tonto is something of an updated sequal to Vittorio DeSica's masterpiece, *Umberto D* (1955). That film, which was the story of an old man who is ultimately thrown out of his apartment for lack of money, ends with the man facing the remainder of his life with only his faithful dog as a companion. *Harry and Tonto* begins when a man in his seventies, Harry (Art Carney), is forced out of his New York apartment building with only his cat, Tonto, as his companion. Urban renewal has precipitated the destruction of Harry's apartment in order to make way for a parking lot. Obstinately fighting eviction to the end, Harry is forcibly carried out of his one-room apartment by the police while he is still sitting in his favorite easy chair. From then on, Harry begins his picaresque adventures, meeting all sorts of people and experiencing freedom on a trip across the United States. Harry misses his dead wife Annie, but he optimistically begins the journey with Tonto, his best friend and confidant.

At first Harry's son Burt (Phil Bruns) tries to convince Harry to move in with his family in the suburbs, but Harry has no desire to live there, so he decides to fly to Los Angeles, where another son, Eddie (Larry Hagman), now lives. Harry cannot get a flight, however, because the airline will not go out of its way for cats; and because his driver's license expired ten years earlier, Harry and Tonto continue their trip by bus. They decide to stop in Chicago to visit Harry's daughter Shirley (Ellen Burstyn), who is a lonely and cynical bookstore owner, toughened and embittered by four failed marriages.

When Harry finally arrives in Los Angeles, he and Tonto visit the other son, Eddie, who is a stereotype of a Southern California swinger who lives in a singles' complex replete with sauna. We discover, however, that Eddie is only pretending to be a successful bachelor; actually, he is a man with no direction in life who even needs to borrow money from his father. The three children, although young, are confused and unhappy, whereas Harry, who is old, has now found a new independence which brings his life purpose. His odyssey from New York to Los Angeles has shown him that it is his vital spirit that is important, not the past.

The story would seem to be fairly predictable and ordinary, but the screenplay and the acting add the dimension needed to make the film a gem. Carney is wonderful as the cranky, bursitis-suffering Harry. Although Carney was actually much younger than Harry in the film, he makes Harry "a character" without being a caricature. Additionally, the other members of the cast, who are virtually all supporting players, give dimension to their roles. While Harry and Tonto are on their journey, they meet many interesting people, all of whom represent different elements of society and illustrate some things that are wrong with it. Harry is old, but willing to accept the idiosyncrasies of the people he meets. Thus, he does not judge Ginger (Melanie Mayron), the sixteen-year-old runaway, but merely spends a platonic night with her in a motel. Neither does he judge a hooker (Barbara Rhoades) who offers her services to him explaining that she has had previous experience with men of his age.

Although he used to be a professor of Shakespeare, Harry seems to get along fine with the oddballs he meets on the road. He also seems to be the only one who can understand his plump grandson Norman (Joshua Mostel), who is interested in brown rice, yoga, and Zen, and who has taken a solemn vow of silence. Harry is flexible enough to accept Norman's silence early in the film, just is he is able to accept the senility of Jessie (Geraldine Fitzgerald), his first love, whom he visits in a nursing home later on. Jessie was once a beautiful woman and used to dance with Isadora Duncan; now she is senile and cannot even remember Harry's name.

The various characters add color to the film and illuminate varied aspects of our society, but it is Harry who is the center of attention and dominates the film. Carney won an Academy Award for *Harry and Tonto*, one of his first films. Although he had been a successful television actor for years, playing Ed Norton on *The Honeymooners* with Jackie Gleason, he had been in only a handful of films before *Harry and Tonto*. This was also his first starring role in a motion picture, although he had built up a considerable reputation as a lead actor on Broadway even while he was performing on *The Honeymooners*. Since the film, Carney has starred and costarred in several films, most notably *The Late Show* (1977) and *House Calls* (1978). He has a sardonic appeal which is equally pleasing in comic or dramatic roles, and often, as in *Harry and Tonto*, the blending of the two elements produces effective characterizations.

There are a number of well-known actors in small roles in the film, most notably Ellen Burstyn, who won an Oscar for Best Actress the same year as *Harry and Tonto* for *Alice Doesn't Live Here Anymore*. Chief Dan George is also very good as Sam Two Feathers, an Indian herbal medicine man whom Harry meets in jail. Two Feathers is a 106-year-old man who, like Harry, refuses to give up, and is thrown into jail in Las Vegas for practicing medicine without a license. Of the rest of the cast, only Hagman as Eddie and Fitzgerald as Jessie are well-known names. Some minor roles are acted by people of interest to the audience, such as Mostel, who is comedian Zero Mostel's son, Sally Marr, who is Lenny Bruce's mother, as a cat lover, and director Paul Mazursky as a male hustler. Mazursky seems to favor these little "in" jokes and bits of casting and they are frequently evident in his films.

Although *Harry and Tonto* is basically a comedy rather than a social message film, it does offer some insights into the condition of old people in the United States. The opening montage of elderly people (not actors) sitting on city benches makes its own subtle statement about the plight of the elderly. Additionally, Harry's strength and dignity, even after the death of his beloved Tonto, show what inner reserves people can have if they are able to maintain their own sense of dignity.

Leslie Taubman

THE HARVEY GIRLS

Released: 1946
Production: Arthur Freed for Metro-Goldwyn-Mayer
Direction: George Sidney
Screenplay: Edmund Beloin, Nathaniel Curtis, Harry Crane, James O'Hanlon, and Samson Raphaelson, with additional dialogue by Kay Van Riper; based on the book of the same name by Samuel Hopkins Adams
Cinematography: George J. Folsey
Editing: Albert Akst
Song: Harry Warren and Johnny Mercer, "On the Atchison, Topeka and the Santa Fe" (AA)
Running time: 101 minutes

> *Principal characters:*
> Susan Bradley .... Judy Garland
> Ned Trent .... John Hodiak
> Judge Sam Purvis .... Preston Foster
> Alma .... Virginia O'Brien
> Deborah .... Cyd Charisse
> Em .... Angela Lansbury
> H. H. Hartsey .... Chill Wills
> Sonora Cassidy .... Marjorie Main
> Chris Maule .... Ray Bolger

George Sidney's place in the rank of directors of musicals is clearly below that of such luminaries as Busby Berkeley or Vincente Minnelli. Nevertheless, he has brought some memorable moments to the screen in films such as *Anchors Aweigh* (1945), *Annie Get Your Gun* (1950), *Bye Bye Birdie* (1963), and *The Harvey Girls*. In *The Harvey Girls*, Sidney is blessed with wonderful songs by Harry Warren and Johnny Mercer and by the ineffable presence of Judy Garland in the lead. The music and the star, however, occasionally fall victim to a script that is totally unimaginative. The result is a film that mirrors Sidney's career: uneven, but with moments of brilliance.

Harvey Girls were young (and sometimes not so young) women who were recruited by Fred Harvey to staff his chain of restaurants strung throughout the American frontier along the route of the famous Atchison, Topeka and Santa Fe railroad. As the film opens, a trainload of Harvey Girls are heading toward Sand Rock, Arizona, to help open Harvey's latest dining room. Their motto is: "Where Harvey Girls appear, civilization is not far behind."

The film's star is Judy Garland, who plays Harvey Girl Susan Bradley, a prettier than usual mail order bride. She intends to marry one H. H. Hartsey, who placed an advertisement for a wife in an Ohio newspaper read by Susan. Susan is befriended by Alma (Virginia O'Brien) and Deborah (Cyd Charisse)—a farm girl and a would-be dancer, respectively—who have joined the Harvey organization in their quest for love and adventure.

Far and away the film's finest sequence comes when the train arrives in Sand Rock and the assembled cast breaks into Warren and Mercer's Academy Award-winning song "On the Atchison, Topeka and the Santa Fe." The song introduces the townsfolk and the Harvey Girls to one another, thus advancing the plot. The tune was an instant classic, and Sidney's staging matched the brightness of the melody. While there is a great deal of movement in this scene, however, Sidney never allows things to get out of control. It is a *tour de force*.

Unfortunately, at this point the plot, which is the weakest part of the film, begins to thicken. H. H. Hartsey (Chill Wills) turns out to be a nervous yokel who is as afraid of Susan Bradley as she is of him, and they quickly agree to terminate their "relationship." Hartsey reveals that a local saloon operator named Ned Trent (John Hodiak) wrote his flowery proposal as a joke. Furious, Susan corners Trent in his Alhambra Saloon and publicly denounces him. The sparks that fly from this encounter inevitably kindle the flame of romance in their hearts, and the rest of the film is an overly melodramatic account of their courtship, lightened only by a few excellent musical sequences.

"The Train Must Be Fed" is a witty and well-staged exposition of the Harvey philosophy, performed by Sonora Cassidy (Marjorie Main) and the girls in ensemble. "It's a Big Wide World," sung by Garland, O'Brien, and Charisse (whose voice was dubbed by Betty Russell), relates the three women's struggles to find true love—a quest which O'Brien further explicates later in the delightful "The Wild Wild West," in which she bemoans the lack of romantic action on the part of the he-men on the frontier, especially her love interest, Chris Maule (Ray Bolger).

Sidney is at his best in these scenes. He is at his worst when the music stops and the melodrama resumes. Trent's two-faced partner, Judge Sam Purvis (Preston Foster), and his wicked henchmen try to burn out the Harvey House, pegging it as competition for the Alhambra. Trent's growing affection for Susan tempers his own ruthlessness, however, and he decides to leave town with his other paramour, a dancehall girl named Em (Angela Lansbury), but finally opts to remain in Standing Rock and marry Susan. The story ends as the two meet in a running embrace.

Garland does her best with Susan Bradley, and she has her moments. She projects spunk, intelligence, and, of course, a good singing voice; but the script (a large team effort by Edmund Beloin, Nathaniel Curtis, Harry Crane, James O'Hanlon, and Samson Ralpaelson, with additional dialogue by Kay Van Riper) does not give her much with which to work. The rest of the cast is in much the same boat: they are ultimately defeated by the script. Perhaps O'Brien fares best; her wry, down-home wit and mannerisms work against the script's strained seriousness to good effect.

Sidney's ultimate problem in *The Harvey Girls* is that his script and his music simply did not go together. Warren and Mercer wrote bouncy, terrifically hummable tunes that unfortunately were out of place in the stock Western script. Since the music is better than the script, it would have made sense to come up with a different story line.

Still, it is possible to be too critical of *The Harvey Girls*. The film was quite popular in its day and merits our attention even now. At its best—particularly in the "On the Atchison, Topeka and the Santa Fe" scene, for which the film will ultimately be remembered—it is very good indeed. It is also one of the best-loved of all the "big" M-G-M musicals and is frequently shown on television.

Robert Mitchell

A HATFUL OF RAIN

Released: 1957
Production: Buddy Adler for Twentieth Century-Fox
Direction: Fred Zinnemann
Screenplay: Michael V. Gazzo and Alfred Hayes; based on the play of the
  same name by Michael V. Gazzo
Cinematography: Joe MacDonald
Editing: Dorothy Spencer
Music: Bernard Herrmann
Running time: 109 minutes

Principal characters:
Celia Pope .... Eva Marie Saint
Johnny Pope .... Don Murray
Polo Pope .... Anthony Franciosa
John Pope, Sr. .... Lloyd Nolan
Mother .... Henry Silva
Chuch .... Gerald O'Loughlin
Apples .... William Hickey

Drug addiction has never been a very useful subject for Hollywood since
it lacks the histrionic possibilities of alcoholism and psychological disorders,
and there is not much chance for a realistically happy ending. In the mid-
1950's, however, when the problem first really burst upon the American public
and when Hollywood's Production Code loosened enough to actually permit
mention of the subject onscreen, there was a quick rash of exploratory dramas,
all tautly enlightening and harrowingly detailed and none very popular. The
most praiseworthy of these and, also, the most highly praised in its own time,
was *A Hatful of Rain*. It was initially a 1955 Broadway play by Michael V.
Gazzo (who is better known today as a character actor specializing in such
ethnic oriented roles as a traitorous Mafioso lieutenant in *The Godfather,
Part II*, 1974). Gazzo's play probingly detailed the grim difficulties imposed
on a lower-middle-class Italian household when a young husband, Johnny
Pope (Don Murray) becomes a heroin addict as a result of becoming hooked
on morphine while recovering from Korean War wounds in a GI hospital.
His addiction has caused him to lose laborer's job after laborer's job, hindered
his efforts to improve his education, and led him to roam the streets at night
looking for a fix. This, in turn, causes his sweetly concerned but not overly
intelligent wife, Celia (Eva Marie Saint), to become convinced that he is
seeing another woman. Meanwhile, his frantic older brother, Polo (Anthony
Franciosa), is supplying him with the money he had intended to loan to their
father (Lloyd Nolan) to help him set up a small business. The father is
exceedingly small-minded and blames his son bitterly for not having the money

to give him. Additionally, Polo not so secretly is in love with Johnny's despairing and noticeably pregnant wife.

It is to Gazzo's credit that he manages to draw these unwieldy strands together. He suggests, for example, that in the father's gruff obtuseness and detached *machismo* lie the real seeds of his son's addiction. He builds this idea through a number of powerful scenes to an inevitible conclusion. The now fully aware wife, with her husband's permission, calls the authorities to have him sent away for a cure that may well not work. It was a realistic conclusion to a drama of fine individual moments but also of numerous fits, starts, and breaks in continuity that many observers felt belied the place where it had been nurtured and somewhat developed: the Actors Studio. Staffed almost completely with Actors Studio graduates and performed very much in the Method manner, it soon became the most acclaimed example of what that much-maligned school could produce.

Twentieth Century-Fox producer Buddy Adler saw the play and, confident that all Production Code difficulties could be met, bought the film rights. He had long been searching for another project for himself and director Fred Zinnemann. The two had already been responsible for the Oscar-winning *From Here to Eternity* (1954). Zinnemann thought it all over and flew to New York to work with Gazzo on the script. As might be expected, Zinnemann had his own views on the work. "This is not a case of history of a dope addict," he told one interviewer. "We're concerned with a family, nice people, who love one another and are suddenly confronted with a terrible revelation, a real problem . . . this is the real poignancy of a life cut short." To give the story more universal appeal, Zinnemann and Gazzo dropped any ethnic orientation and changed the family's social rank to housing development status (since *Marty* in 1955, Italian ghetto dwellers had become somewhat clichéd anyway). To give the story more realism, Zinnemann and Murray, who was to play the addict, spent a month working with the Narcotics Squad. "We didn't just want to see how these people looked," Zinnemann said. "Or how they acted when they needed the drug or took the drug. We tried to find out about their emotions—why they took drugs, how it felt to crave it, the land of relief that drugs gave them." Zinnemann and Murray even "roamed the streets between nine at night and five in the morning . . . when these poor people come to life and died all over again."

For further authenticity, Zinnemann did something that even in 1957 was still a bit rare. He went on location, shooting for two winter weeks on Manhattan's Lower East Side because "I wanted to shoot the exteriors in the worst possible New York weather—rain, fog, snow. And the interiors in impossibly cramped settings that would create a sense of intimacy with the people who lived in that crowded flat." This same quest also led Zinnemann to settle on a cast of New Yorkers to play the roles. Only Nolan, as the irascible father, had more of a Hollywood background than a Broadway one. Murray was a

New Yorker recently risen to film prominence in *Bus Stop* (1956) and *Bachelor Party* (1957); Saint, cast as Celia, the wife, had won an Oscar for *On The Waterfront* (1953), another film with strong Actors Studio connections, and had played the wife in *A Hatful of Rain* when it was still an Actors Studio project. From the original Broadway cast itself, Zinnemann chose Franciosa to repeat his part as the brother, Polo. If the cast shared a New York City authenticity, however, they also possessed an apple-cheeked wholesomeness, a middle-America charm that Zinnemann planned to use for its ironic effect.

Zinnemann seemed to see the conflict as similar to those in such films as *High Noon* (1952), *The Search* (1948), and *From Here to Eternity*. In these films, as well as in Zinnemann's later works, his characters were torn by an unexpected outside force that had slowly made them examine themselves and come to a moral decision. The sheriff in *High Noon* has to stand up to a sudden menace but finds that the very people that he has been trying to defend are not worth it. Nevertheless, he does defend them. Corporal Pruitt in *From Here to Eternity* grows to loathe the peacetime Army and all that it stands for, but when Pearl Harbor occurs, he sacrifices himself for the cause. In *A Hatful of Rain*, however, it is not really an outside force that erodes the family; it is the hero's addiction, which he can neither resolve (he has already tried unsuccessfully to quit) nor face up to before his wife and father. All of the dramatic situations in the play follow from this one fault. The subtle morality of the hero's dilemma, however, was much less obvious to audiences than the sheriff's or Pruitt's had been in the earlier films. Also, with the wholesomeness came one other factor that served Zinnemann less well— intelligence. Murray, Franciosa, and Saint simply seem too smart, too aware a trio to have fallen into the dilemmas that the plot specifies. Saint in particular comes across as too doggedly intuitive and rationally observant to spend as much time as she does worrying about another woman. Murray's character seems too outgoing and bright not to have sought outside help for his problem long earlier. Zinnemann greatly admired his actors' instincts and improvisational abilities, but the alertness and agility that were a part of those performers' attributes did not help the film as it should have.

What did help was the location. New York portrayed at its bleakest permeates the film. The parks are nothing but gritty snow impaled upon grey wisps of grass. The streets bear a more obvious grime, an impersonal dirt that neatly continues the theme of institutional dullness permeating the cramped apartment and the metallic housing project hallways, not yet littered with 1960'a graffiti and all the more dingy for it. There is an almost ghostly shot of a policeman's horse late at night gently nudging the drunken Johnny down the street that neatly sums up the foreboding impersonality of the city.

Despite the problems mentioned above, Zinnemann obtains insightful performances from his cast. Franciosa's portrayal of the glib extrovert was so definitive that it typed him immediately as far as Hollywood was concerned.

Murray conveys the desperate sincerity of a man who has always counted upon being everyone's favorite and is as much afraid of losing their good opinion as he is of facing the illness. Finally, Nolan is wonderfully querulous and testy, an essentially unpleasant and unobservant man stripped to the bone by age and disappointment.

A Hatful of Rain still seems much less like a Zinnemann film and more like the sort of moral issue discussion that television was to attempt at about the same time in New York-based series such as *The Defenders* and *Naked City*. The film never tries to slip public service information into the dialogue as the television shows often did, but it does have the almost too careful look of something that is being done for the public good. Although we do not see needles and the rest of a drug addict's paraphernalia, the way that these things are hidden and the "it-is-not-his-fault" nature of the hero's addiction help suggest that the real core of the problem has not been approached. Instead, a compelling story with a realistic setting has been built around the problem in order to hook the audience better into considering it—even though the story itself is not very indicative of the subject matter. It is a practice that television drama with its lack of big budgets and location panoramas was then doing quite well. *A Hatful of Rain* was more honest and even more realistic than sponsor-oriented television could then be, but it stands today more as a sign of what films could do at that point in time than as a study of a desperately real and timeless problem.

Lewis Archibald

THE HAUNTING

Released: 1963
Production: Robert Wise for Metro-Goldwyn-Mayer
Direction: Robert Wise
Screenplay: Nelson Gidding; based on the novel *The Haunting of Hill House*
 by Shirley Ann Jackson
Cinematography: David Boulton
Editing: Ernest Walter
Running time: 112 minutes

Principal characters:
Eleanor Vance .... Julie Harris
Theodora .... Claire Bloom
Luke Sanderson .... Russ Tamblyn
Dr. John Markway .... Richard Johnson
Grace Markway .... Lois Maxwell

The movie version of Shirley Ann Jackson's novel, *The Haunting of Hill House* was as eagerly awaited by her fans as was the recent movie version of Stephen King's *The Shining* (1980). Both novels were considered modern classics of the haunted-house genre. *The Shining*, unfortunately, was a complete disappointment to the novel's admirers, but *The Haunting* faithfully followed the novel and successfully captured all its horror.

The Haunting is about a doctor's experiment in ESP and the supernatural. His laboratory is a large deserted house which he is able to rent for a few months only after lengthy negotiations with the wealthy old woman who owns it. She rents the house to Dr. Markway (Richard Johnson) with the stipulation that her worthless young nephew Luke (Russ Tamblyn) also be present. She persuades Luke to stay in Hill House for the experiment by threatening to cut off his allowance if he will not humor "Aunty," who has all her fortune willed to him, including Hill House.

Dr. Markway has mailed out more than one hundred invitations to psychics he has tested in his long and scientific delvings into the supernatural. One by one they decline his invitation to spend the two all-expenses-paid months at the mansion, however, and on the first day of his stay at Hill House only two women arrive. The first is thirty-two-year-old Eleanor Vance (Julie Harris). The only person in the world she hates, now that her mother is dead, is her sister, with whom she now lives. She has no friends, and she likes to blame this on the fact that she has spent eleven years caring for her invalid mother. When Dr. Markway's invitation arrived, she was at a turning point in her life and accepted the invitation over the protests of her sister, who refuses even to let her take the car, half of which is Eleanor's. Eleanor sneaks off with the car anyway, and is the first of the group to arrive at the locked gates of Hill

House. She demands that the caretaker let her in, and after warning her about local superstitions, he does so. His wife, the housekeeper, watches Eleanor drive up and stare with amazement at the huge quarried stone Victorian edifice.

Theodora (Claire Bloom) arrives next, and of course unsuspectedly bumps into Eleanor, causing mutual shock. Theodora is beautiful and very bright, and her character attracted considerable attention at the time of the film's release because of strong overtones of lesbianism. This element was added by the producer, for it was not in the novel, and although it does not really distract from the story it does add a twist to this tale of the supernatural. The two women become close immediately. They soon find themselves in the main hallway, which has countless doors which confuse them. Then a cold feeling causes them both to freeze in fear. Eleanor remarks that she feels as if the house were alive, and that they are tiny creatures devoured by it and trapped in its stomach. Theodora sees that Eleanor is being pulled into a spell and she madly tries more doors until she suddenly comes upon Dr. Markway and Luke in a study. Both women run to the doctor in fear and then jokingly announce that they immediately detect some presence here and that their stay should be interesting.

After the housekeeper shows the four around the huge house, she tells them that she leaves every night at 5:30 and that they should leave the dirty dishes on the table for her to clean up the following morning when she returns. The strangest part of Hill House is the many doors separating its many rooms. All the heavy oak doors have been hung so that they will close by themselves. Dr. Markway tells Luke, Theodora, and Eleanor that they must take pains to learn the floor plan of the huge place because it is easy to get lost in Hill House.

That night the two sleeping women suddenly sit bolt upright in bed and listen intensely as they hear giant footsteps clomping down the corridor outside their bedroom. When the footsteps stop, their bodies droop with relief, but again tense as they realize that the thing is outside their door, listening quietly, except for its heavy breathing. Fear causes Eleanor to whimper, and the creature knows for sure that they are there. It knocks, then bangs louder. The door is three inches thick and made of solid oak, yet the power of the phantom is so great that the wood bulges inward as if it were rubber. (This effect was so memorable and frightening that when Disneyland created an amusement ride called "The Haunted Mansion," they had rubber doors molded to look like wood which are pressed to achieve the same effect.) Again, the monster grows quiet, and the two women's fears subside momentarily until their eyes stare in disbelief as the ornate doorknob is slowly turned back and forth. Faster and harder the creature turns the locked door handle until it realizes it is thwarted, and stomps away.

Alerted by the noise, the professor is knocking at their door and asking if they are all right. When they let him in, he asks what has happened. Eleanor says, "Nothing in particular. Someone just knocked on the door with a cannon ball." Then the two girls look at each other and begin laughing hysterically. Dr. Markway and Luke tell the two women they heard nothing because they were outside chasing a ghostlike dog which ran down the hall and led them away. It is then that Eleanor knows that Hill House is trying to separate them, and her particularly.

The audience is made privy to Eleanor's thoughts by an impressive use of voice-over, and her mental disintegration is observed in her internal dialogues. The audience knows long before the other characters do that Eleanor is the House's prey and that she is cracking under the pressure. Eleanor's final push comes from her fanciful crush on Dr. Markway and the unexpected arrival of his wife (Lois Maxwell). The doctor begs his wife to leave, but the dutiful and practical Mrs. Markway insists that she stay and even sleep in the "heart" of the house. She jokingly badgers them to tell her which room is most haunted. They all assure her that there is no such spot, but Eleanor suddenly says "There's the nursery," and Mrs. Markway takes her luggage there over the protest of her husband. At the top of the stairs she stops, surveys the entrance hall, and sacrilegiously tells the frightened group, "The real fiend of Hill House is the interior decorator." That night, Mrs. Markway mysteriously disappears from her bed in the nursery, and while they search for her, Eleanor is pulled toward the library. The library is a round tower with an iron, circular staircase which twists up a hundred feet. Eleanor's climb upward is punctuated with close-ups of the iron bolts tearing loose from the masonry walls. The search party enters the room in time to see Eleanor standing atop the swaying, coiled staircase. Dr. Markway then rescues the dazed Eleanor in the tense scene which follows.

Dr. Markway decides that Eleanor must leave Hill House and forces her to drive off in her car. Eleanor's mind totally belongs to Hill House, however, and she smashes her car into one of the huge oaks that line the drive. The house has won another resident, and the group realizes that Eleanor will now walk the halls of Hill House.

If *The Haunting* is viewed on television, its effect is enhanced if one is alone. If it is viewed in a crowded theater, its effect can be harmed by just one heckler which frequently happens during the screening of popular horror films. This is why the film was not a commercial success, but has become a very popular television film and has risen to the status of "cult" film.

Larry Lee Holland

THE HEART IS A LONELY HUNTER

Released: 1968
Production: Thomas C. Ryan and Marc Merson for Warner Bros.
Direction: Robert Ellis Miller
Screenplay: Thomas C. Ryan; based on the novel of the same name by Carson McCullers
Cinematography: James Wong Howe
Editing: John F. Burnett
Running time: 123 minutes

Principal characters:
John Singer	Alan Arkin
Mick	Sondra Locke
Spiro Antonapoulos	Chuck McCann
Mr. Kelly	Biff McGuire
Mrs. Kelly	Laurinda Barrett
Blount	Stacy Keach
Portia	Cicely Tyson
Doctor Copeland	Percy Rodriguez
Willie	Johnny Popwell

In 1940, at the age of only twenty-two, Carson McCullers wrote *The Heart Is a Lonely Hunter*, her first novel and according to some critics her best. Almost thirty years after the novel's initial appearance, screenwriter Thomas C. Ryan updated the Depression setting of the novel to the present time and adapted it to film. Because the novel was a very difficult one to adapt, the film was not considered a total success. Whereas McCullers' writing is beautifully poetic, the film is unable to capture the true spirit of the original work. Also, some of the problems which existed in the Depression were not easily transformed to the late-1960's. Whatever the problems with the screenplay, however, the film did earn rave reviews for its star, Alan Arkin.

In the film, Arkin plays the story's main character, deaf-mute John Singer. Singer is a kind and gentle silver engraver living in a small Southern town. He is a lonely man, and his only real friend is a fat, bearlike, simple-minded Greek named Spiro Antonapoulos (Chuck McCann). Spiro is also a deaf-mute, and he and Singer gently communicate through dactylology (sign language), silently expressing themselves in words that can only be understood by the two men. Because Spiro, who is mentally retarded, becomes more and more disturbed, he must be sent to a mental institution. With his only companion gone, Singer decides to move to another town which is closer to the sanatorium where Spiro will be staying. In the new town, Singer finds a room with the Kelly family, who need money to offset the expenses of a recent hip injury suffered by Mr. Kelly (Biff McGuire). The Kellys' daughter Mick

(Sondra Locke) has to give up her own room to house the boarder, so she resents Singer at first, but he tries to win her friendship. Eventually he does, by encouraging her love of classical music, and they share some happy moments as Mick plays the piano and tries to explain to Singer what music is like. Mick is supposed to represent McCullers as a young girl, and her characterization by Locke is a very moving portrayal of a sensitive girl trying to find her own identity.

While he is staying with the Kellys, Singer also befriends Blount (Stacy Keach), who is a heavy drinker, and Dr. Copeland (Percy Rodriguez), a black physician. Dr. Copeland's character is the most changed from the original novel, possibly because the Back to Africa movement, which was well-known during the 1920's and 1930's, and of which the novel's Dr. Copeland was a part, meant little in 1968. What was a significant subplot in the book becomes rather weak and insignificant in the film, although Rodriguez tries his best in the part. Copeland is dying from cancer, but he is keeping his illness secret from his daughter Portia (Cicely Tyson), an educated woman who has become estranged from her father because of her father's objections to her husband Willie Hamilton (Johnny Popwell), a field hand.

In the course of the film, Singer goes to visit Spiro, who is now suffering from a kidney infection. They go for an outing, but when Spiro becomes almost wild in his behavior, Singer goes home very despondent. Not long after this, Portia becomes reconciled with her father when she learns, through Singer, that he is dying. This brings Singer one victory, but it is later offset by Mick's renewed animosity toward him. Depressed because of a bad first sexual experience, Mick refuses to accept Singer's friendship, and Singer again begins to feel lonely for his only friend Spiro. Shortly after this, however, when he goes to visit Spiro, he learns that the Greek died a few weeks before. After sadly visiting Spiro's grave and saying good-bye in sign language, Singer goes home and commits suicide, feeling that there is not one whom he can call a friend anymore.

Almost as an epilogue to the story, a few months after Singer's death, Mick goes to his grave with flowers and meets Dr. Copeland. There she tells him that it was really Singer who helped her to grow up and that his gentle strength will help her to face the future. Locke is very good in the role of Mick and received some of the film's better notices. After a career which consisted of small supporting roles in numerous films in the late 1960's and early 1970's, she finally came to prominence in a series of films with Clint Eastwood, most notably *The Gauntlet* (1977) and *Bronco Billy* (1980). Unfortunately, the subtleness which characterized her performance in *The Heart Is a Lonely Hunter* has been missing from her more successful ventures as Eastwood's leading lady, and her career seems to have reached a leveling-off point.

Arkin is the "be-all, the end-all and, whenever he is in sight, the cure-all of *The Heart Is a Lonely Hunter*," according to *Newsweek* critic Joseph Morgenstern, an opinion that pervaded most of the reviews of the film. An extremely versatile actor, Arkin, although not of the "superstar" ranks, has been a very successful leading man and character actor. He has taken on a very wide spectrum of roles, and throughout his career he has gone back and forth between leads and supporting parts with equally successful results. He has also been successful on the Broadway stage and earned a Tony award for his first starring role, *Enter Laughing*.

Others in the film who give good performances are McCann as Spiro and Tyson as Portia. Although their roles lack the depth of Arkin's, they at least make the best of their parts. It is unfortunate that a novel with the power of McCullers' did not have an adaptation which did more of what the original did. Some reviewers felt that it should not have been updated, and perhaps it might have been better produced as a period piece. Unlike McCullers' *The Member of the Wedding*, which had less of an attachment to a particular time period, *The Heart Is a Lonely Hunter* should have been left in the Depression in order to convey more of the feeling of a Southern town in a time when things were economically difficult for everyone.

The film was shot on location in Selma, Alabama, by veteran cinematographer James Wong Howe. This was his fiftieth film, and the beautiful scenes of rust-colored footage pay tribute to one of the great geniuses of the film medium. *The Heart Is a Lonely Hunter* did not do very well at the box office, probably because the rather melodramatic production was not the type of thing which readily appealed to a mass audience. It did win the Best Actor Award for Arkin with the New York Film Critics, and it also brought Arkin an Academy Award nomination for Best Actor and Locke a nomination for Best Supporting Actress.

Janet St. Clair

HEARTS OF THE WEST

Released: 1975
Production: Tony Bill for Metro-Goldwyn-Mayer
Direction: Howard Zieff
Screenplay: Robert E. Thompson
Cinematography: Mario Tosi
Editing: Edward Warschilka
Running time: 102 minutes

Principal characters:

Lewis Tater	Jeff Bridges
Howard Pike	Andy Griffith
Miss Trout	Blythe Danner
Kessler	Alan Arkin
A. J. Nietz	Donald Pleasance
Fat Man (Swindler)	Richard B. Schull
Thin Man (Swindler)	Anthony James
Pa Tater	Frank Cady

Hearts of the West is a favorite cult film which was financially unsuccessful upon its release, but which has gained a large number of devoted followers, who admire its subtle comedy and good-natured criticism of the film industry. The film's comic tone is established with its opening: the M-G-M trademark lion in black-and-white followed by a screen test, also in monochrome, of a bumbling actor identified as Lewis Tater (Jeff Bridges). Lewis completes his scene and turns to the camera, smiling for his close-up.

The balance of the film, in color, delightfully unfolds the picaresque odyssey of Lewis Tater, beginning with a scene in the bedroom of his Midwestern home. Here, circa 1930, Lewis writes florid Western prose, surrounded by the colorful pulp magazines that inspire him. His father (Frank Cady) and brothers, all practical farmers, scorn Lewis' ambitions. As an act of defiance, Lewis vows to attend a correspondence school of Western writing in person. Arriving in a one-horse Nevada town by train, Lewis discovers that the "school" consists only of eight post-office boxes. Bewildered, he ends up spending the night at a nearby hotel. The two swindlers (Richard B. Schull and Anthony James) who operate the bogus school learn of his presence, and one of them slips into Lewis' room during the night to rob him. Lewis awakes with a start and overpowers the intruder. After escaping in the swindlers' car, Lewis runs out of gas in the desert. Searching the car for provisions, he finds only a metal box containing a revolver and school stationery. Lewis sets out on foot in the desert, unaware that the swindlers are not far behind. Later, Lewis is almost trampled by cowboys on horseback. One of the cowboys, Howard Pike (Andy Griffith), gives Lewis a ride back to their camp. There

Lewis discovers he has stumbled onto the location of a low-budget Western movie. In awe, he observes the egotistical director Kessler (Alan Arkin) choreograph a fight scene. Then the aspiring writer meets the attractive Miss Trout (Blythe Danner), a script supervisor.

When Lewis gets a ride to Los Angeles with the stuntmen, Howard tells him what it is like to "ride up front" with the director and stars. After finding a room in a boarding house, Lewis works washing dishes at the Rio Café until Tumbleweeds Productions calls on him to be an extra. Several humorous episodes follow: Lewis ruins a scene, injures himself after volunteering to do a dangerous stunt, and narrowly escapes the swindlers, who trace him to the Rio Café. Back in his room, Lewis discovers thousands of dollars in cash underneath the gun and college stationery in the metal box, and he finally realizes why the swindlers still pursue him: he possesses the entire proceeds of their bogus school.

Even with the swindlers searching the local studios for him, fortune seems to be in Lewis' favor. Kessler offers him a chance to become the leading villain in his next production; Miss Trout, attracted by his charming innocence, romances him; and he completes his first novel, *Hearts of the West*. Trusting Howard's advice, Lewis gives him the manuscript to read. After Kessler fires him when they cannot agree on salary, Lewis takes his manuscript to producers around town, promising to contribute two thousand dollars toward the budget.

Lewis' good fortune turns sour as he delivers the money and a copy of the manuscript to publisher A. J. Nietz (Donald Pleasance). Nietz admits he likes the story, but that it is identical to another manuscript he has already bought, and introduces Lewis to the alleged author, Howard Pike. In the ensuing scuffle, Howard reveals that he was once the famous Western star Billy Pueblo, now out of money, and that he sold the script to pay alimony.

Lewis, turning to the only person he still trusts, goes to Trout's apartment. When he finds Kessler there in a drunken state, he leaves with the false impression that Kessler and Trout are romantically involved. Trout races to Lewis' apartment to find him. The swindlers, having found Lewis' address from Tumbleweeds, see the light on in his apartment and decide to follow Trout when she departs. Trout's next stop is the Rio Café, where she implores the surly Howard to help her. Finally one of the stuntmen tells her that Lewis is hiding in his apartment. Just as Trout arrives at the room, the swindlers burst in demanding their money, and when Lewis argues that the money was ill-gotten in the first place, one of the swindlers shoots him in the elbow. Howard, in full Western costume, bursts in with guns blazing, locking the thieves in a closet. Lewis admiringly tells Howard, "You looked just like Billy Pueblo." As the ambulance drives away, a bystander asks, "Who is that kid?" Howard replies, "Lewis Tater. He's a writer. Just sold his first novel."

In *Hearts of the West* Bridges exhibits a flair for comedy not seen in his earlier roles, making the exaggerated ingenuousness of Lewis Tater convincing. Standout scenes include his extemporaneous composition of melodramatic Western prose as he walks the desert; his ill-fated movie stunt; and his salary meeting with Kessler. Bridges handles the potentially difficult role with delicacy and makes his character affable enough to carry the story.

The other actors fit perfectly into the ensemble. Arkin, in a departure from previous parts, accurately conveys the egotistical fanaticism of the director Kessler. Danner is engaging as the pragmatic script supervisor with a weakness for Lewis' trusting soul. In the likable heel Howard Pike, Griffith creates his strongest characterization since Lonesome Rhodes in the Elia Kazan/Budd Schulburg film *A Face in the Crowd* (1957). Schull and James lend able support as the comic villains.

Hearts of the West is a film about filmmaking. Its light tone is similar to Stanley Donen and Gene Kelly's *Singin' in the Rain* (1952) and Peter Bogdanovich's *Nickelodeon* (1976). Thematically, however, it is unique because it is the only comedy to deal with the corruption in the business and with the ephemeral nature of fame and success, while at the same time affirming the power of idealism over egotism and corruption.

As the first solo production of Tony Bill since his highly successful co-production of *The Sting* (1973), *Hearts of the West* was not destined to enjoy the same box-office success. Director Howard Zieff's first film, *Slither* (1974), which was not financially successful either, is similar to *Hearts of the West* in its offbeat characters and in its theme of corruption involving the innocent. In both movies, Zieff displays a keen sense of character and of comic timing which has unfortunately been lost in his more recent films such as Barbra Streisand's *The Main Event* (1979) and Goldie Hawn's *Private Benjamin* (1980), both financially, if not critically, successful. With more personal projects, Zieff could possibly fulfill the promise of the earlier films, but *The Main Event* and *Private Benjamin* were pet projects of their respective stars.

Perhaps the box-office failure of *Hearts of the West* is due to the major weakness in its story: an unconvincing ending. Although writer Rob Thompson's original characters, comic situations, and natural dialogue ring true, the last-minute rescue by Howard Pike stretches credibility even in a comic context. In the preceding scene with Trout, Howard expresses disgust at her concern for Lewis. No dramatic foundation for his sudden change in attitude in the following scene is built. The renewed trust and respect between Howard and Lewis comes all too quickly and without development.

Even with its flawed denouement, *Hearts of the West* remains a rarity in recent films: a pure entertainment movie that, for the most part, realizes its purpose.

Stephen Myers

HEAVEN KNOWS, MR. ALLISON

Released: 1957
Production: Buddy Adler and Eugene Frenke for Twentieth Century-Fox
Direction: John Huston
Screenplay: John Lee Mahin and John Huston; based on the novel of the same name by Charles Shaw
Cinematography: Oswald Morris
Editing: Russell Lloyd
Sound: Basil Fenton-Smith
Music: Georges Auric
Running time: 106 minutes

Principal characters:
Sister Angela .... Deborah Kerr
Marine Corporal Allison .... Robert Mitchum

Heaven Knows, Mr. Allison strikes a responsive chord primarily because it is a film without apparent artifice. Its ability to reach out and touch audiences lies in its simplicity, which is one of the key aspects of its greatness. The story line is simple: a rough marine corporal and a young Irish nun are thrown together on a remote Pacific island during World War II. Their story is one of struggle, strength, and courage in the face of two formidable adversaries—the enemy Japanese and a growing and impossible love for each other.

In the opening sequence, a lone dinghy is swept toward shore over a vast stretch of rolling waves. From the first shot, director John Huston places the audience in dual roles as observers and participants. We too are carried over the crest of the sea to the unknown beach of a tropic paradise. An exhausted marine (Robert Mitchum) begins a cautious search of the seemingly deserted island. The audience moves with him through the lush rain forest in a series of tense tracking shots, with sunlight filtering in through the overhanging palms. Light comes up with sparkling brightness as the marine discovers some abandoned huts, and there is a quiet, tense pause as a rustling sound is heard inside the white church. In a golden glow, a nun (Deborah Kerr), dressed in the habit of her order, emerges, sweeping through the church doors. Being the only survivor on the island, at first Sister Angela regards the marine with fear, then happy recognition as he collapses from exhaustion in the interior of the semilit church.

The young and delightful Sister Angela makes every provision she can for the comfort of her new companion. In a series of idyllic scenes, we see the unlikely twosome collecting coconuts, happily exchanging stories, and preparing a makeshift vessel they hope will carry them to safety. Both are bound, it seems, by bonds of service, being dedicated to their respective paths—the Marines and the Catholic Church. This idea is reinforced as Sister Angela weaves palm fronds into a mainsail for the raft that is to carry them over the unstable waters of the wartorn Pacific. The hot sun shines brightly on the pair as they work industriously together. Allison regards her with reserve and respect while at the same time revealing to us, but not to her, a growing feeling of affection.

A rumble of bombers is heard in the distance, and Japanese planes are soon over the island blasting everything: buildings, trees, immaculate beaches, and the mainsail and boat. Allison throws himself upon the running Sister Angela, covering her with his body as the island is showered with bullets. Remarkably, they emerge alive and unhurt, but their hopes of leaving the island are as smashed as the little church, which is now a smoldering wreckage. Allison pokes through the debris and retrieves the charred altar crucifix for Sister Angela. It is interesting to consider that the crucifix holds no personal meaning to Allison, yet his gesture of salvaging it and giving it tenderly to Sister Angela shows his developing regard for her calling. There is an interesting counterpoint developed as well, for shortly after this moment, a Japanese destroyer rounds the island point, and its portent is ominous. The crucifix, therefore, is now more than merely a personal symbol. It becomes a universal object, signifying hope, faith, and transcendence in darkest hours.

As the Japanese invade the island, Mr. Allison and Sister Angela are forced to flee to a deserted cave, a natural hideaway. Together, they subsist there. She engages in prayer and meditation while the fascinated marine looks upon her with expressive adoration. He spends hours carving a comb for her which he places with bright red flowers below the crucifix on the cave rockshelf and ventures out under cover of night to spear fish for her. Unfortunately, the raw fish sickens her, and her hair is cut too short to require a comb. Clearly, Allison will need to develop faith to understand her.

By the time the Japanese leave the island the marine and the nun have become deeply attached to and dependent upon each other. Allison is clearly in love with her, but her feelings for him are those of friendship. They jubilantly celebrate, and the charming little song "Don't Sit Under the Apple Tree" is sung by Allison with more than casual gaiety. They do a jig under the moonlit sky and share a good supper of cooked rice and canned goods. Later Sister Angela finds a bottle of sake in a flour sack and Allison proceeds to get drunk, ruining what had been a happy occasion. With drunken bravado, Allison becomes physically aggressive and brutally truthful about their chances of survival. When he tries to embrace her, she rushes in fear and panic into the pelting downpour of a tropical storm.

This is the critical sequence for which Huston has carefully prepared. For Sister Angela, the intoxicated amorous marine is more menacing than the Japanese. His overture toward her prompts her to run from the dark side of her inner self, her suppressed feelings, and subdued sexuality. On the spiritual path to which she has dedicated her life and heart, she has had to renounce and possibly repress natural emotional and physical desires. Now she flees from her friend and protector in a hysterical panic of identity. Her flight through the storming rain forest, with Allison in delirious pursuit becomes our means of sharing the frustrations of both characters.

Allison forages through the jungle searching and calling for her. Finally, at dawn, he finds her lying shivering and delirious in a mud slick, her white habit saturated with rain and earth. Tenderly and apologetically, he grabs her to him, carries her back to the cave, and undresses her. Her condition is serious as she shakes with fever and delirium. He must get her warm clothing and food, but the Japanese have returned. In the suspenseful sequence which follows, he ventures into the Japanese encampment and succeeds in obtaining the necessary provisions, but in the process, he is discovered and forced to kill a Japanese soldier. When Sister Angela regains consciousness, her eyes fall on her dirty habit which hangs up drying, and she realizes that Allison has changed her clothes and cared for her during her illness. Her appreciation lends a new degree of understanding to their relationship, and she humbly assumes responsibility for the killing of the Japanese soldier, perceiving her effort to escape Allison's advances as the direct cause of the incident.

It is important to stress that Allison has consistently expressed the desire to look after Sister Angela, and it is important to remember that early in the film she mentions that she has not yet taken her final vows. The possibility exists, if they survive, that the regard she feels for him may develop into the romantic, that they could conceivably marry given time and circumstance. Huston never lets us forget, however, that first and foremost, the combination is unlikely, and that the first priority is service and survival.

In the action-packed and bittersweet conclusion, Allison is apparently divinely inspired to sabotage the enemy weapons, facilitating a relatively safe American landing, but under direct fire he sustains a serious shoulder wound. His courage and Sister Angela's supportive attitude are short-lived, however, as the Americans land on the island. The audience regards the American force with mixed feelings, for they, not the Japanese, are clearly going to separate the couple. Allison is carried downhill on a stretcher, with Sister Angela walking beside him and putting a cigarette between his lips, as the camera rests for a moment on the charred crucifix and comb she holds tightly. As they approach the beach and an awaiting ship, our perceptions of the meaning of this departure are displayed in a shower of tropical light. On a romantic level, we feel a deep and sad resignation that silently emanates from the principal characters. On a higher spiritual plateau, we experience a mood of hope, acceptance, and contentment. The words of Sister Angela echo in our minds. "Wherever I go, wherever I may be, you will always be in my heart, dear Mr. Allison, always." This suggests a transcendental love that will forever be sustained by thought, experience, and ultimately, memory. That this love will live in the hearts of both Sister Angela and Allison is reinforced by the eternal motion of the gently moving sea in the background. Although the sea is a vehicle used to unite and possibly separate the pair, Huston uses the device to leave ultimate interpretation to the audience. The component that makes this an affecting and successful picture is the consistent clarity of the storytelling with no trace of heavy-handedness. The muted romanticism is evoked by the film's controlled tempo. Huston deals with a theme that has fascinated him before and since, that of isolation as a microcosm (*The Treasure of the Sierra Madre*, 1947, *The African Queen*, 1951, and in one of his more successful later films, *The Man Who Would Be King*, 1975). He is at his best in handling twists in human relationships when people are forced away from the mainstream of society.

Heaven Knows, Mr. Allison is moving, exciting, and well made. Huston and John Lee Mahin complement each other brilliantly in their collaboration on the script. Basil Fenton-Smith also merits praise for contributing an unmuffled soundtrack, much of it recorded live against great obstacles on the island of Tobago. Under Huston's direction, Mitchum and Kerr create very human characters. Without the support of other players, they sustain rapt audience attention for the duration of the film with a dynamic chemistry which recalls and compares favorably with that of Humphrey Bogart and Katharine Hepburn in Huston's similarly styled *The African Queen*. Kerr received a deserved Oscar nomination, but Mitchum, an often neglected actor, was again overlooked.

Huston has always been regarded as a rugged individualist whose own flamboyance has overshadowed his *oeuvre*, but he has succeeded in demonstrating that his films are a rugged and colorful reflection of his own *persona*. This film shows the flash of genius that erratically surfaces in his finer work. *Heaven Knows, Mr. Allison* belongs with the best of the Huston canon.

Elizabeth McDermott

HELP!

Released: 1965
Production: Walter Shenson for United Artists
Direction: Richard Lester
Screenplay: Marc Behm and Charles Wood; based on an original screen story by Marc Behm
Cinematography: David Watkin
Editing: John Victor Smith
Running time: 90 minutes

Principal characters:
John Lennon	Himself
Paul McCartney	Himself
George Harrison	Himself
Ringo Starr	Himself
Clang	Leo McKern
Ahme	Eleanor Bron
Professor Foot	Victor Spinetti
Algernon	Roy Kinnear
Superintendent	Patrick Cargill

By 1965, the Beatles were a worldwide phenomenon. Their records were dominating the charts more than those of any artist since the heyday of Elvis Presley a decade earlier. Unlike Presley, however, the Beatles had something in addition to wealth and fame—they had intellectual respectability. This was due in large part to the reception of their first film. Critics expected their initial screen appearance to be a quickie exploitation film like *Don't Knock the Rock* (1957), *Rock Pretty Baby* (1956), and most of the films in the Presley canon: brief, largely plotless exercises which function primarily as an excuse for the stars of the day to sing a few quick songs and make a fortune. What they got instead was *A Hard Day's Night* (1964).

Directed by Richard Lester, *A Hard Day's Night* portrays the Beatles as musical Marx Brothers—four hip, witty young Englishmen with a healthy disrespect for authority and a refreshing sense of the absurd. *Help!* was Lester's and the Beatles' follow-up and an attempt to expand their cinematic horizons. In contrast to *A Hard Day's Night*, which was fairly realistic and had a world view that was a bit cockeyed but never totally implausible, *Help!* was frankly fantasy. It took the Beatles out of London and gave them the whole world as a playground. The black-and-white subtleties of *A Hard Day's Night* gave way to riotous color. If, in the end, all of this freedom proved a bit too much for the director and his stars—*A Hard Day's Night* is a more disciplined, and hence a more mature work—the final result is still more than worthwhile.

Help! opens in the midst of a bizarre religious rite. Clang (Leo McKern), a robed priest, is chanting prayers to the many-armed statue of the dread goddess Kaili. A pretty young girl, painted red for the occasion, is about to be sacrificed. Suddenly the priestess Ahme (Eleanor Bron) interrupts the proceedings. The girl is no longer wearing the sacrificial Ring, and the rite cannot be continued. It develops that the Ring is now on the finger of her favorite Beatle, Ringo Starr. Clang and his fellow cultists scowl and throw darts at a movie screen on which a black-and-white film clip of the Beatles singing "Help!" is being shown. The credits roll on amidst the rain of darts, and the cultists leave for England to recapture the Ring, or, failing that, to sacrifice Ringo. The film then becomes, in effect, one long chase sequence, punctuated by the Beatles' attempts to get on with recording their songs. The plot defies coherent summary, with puns—both visual and verbal, sophisti- cated and sophomoric—littering the film. *Help!* steadfastly refuses to take itself seriously, and therein lies its charm.

The cultists of *Help!* are a parody of the Thugees in George Stevens' 1939 adventure classic *Gunga Din.* Most, however, are completely Western in appearance; Clang, in particular, bears a marked resemblance to W. C. Fields. They make several distinctly improbable attempts to steal the Ring from Ringo's finger. One of these attempts occurs during a recording session as the Beatles sing "You're Gonna Lose That Girl." The recording engineers notice a persistent buzz on the tape which turns out to be from a chainsaw which is busily sawing a hole in the floor around Ringo's drums. As Ringo falls into the cellar, he is attacked by the cultists, only to be rescued by Ahme, who, it develops, has a crush on Paul. The plot has thickened.

It thickens again when, upon learning of the Ring's significance, Ringo attempts to give it back to Clang, only to discover that it is stuck on his finger. In desperation, he and his friends visit the mad Professor Foote (Victor Spinetti) and his bumbling assistant Algernon (Roy Kinnear). Foote's am- bition is to rule the world, and he would be a worthy rival to the villains of the James Bond films he is meant to parody if only his fiendishly clever equipment did not fail at strategic moments (owing to the inferior quality of the British components therein). Intoxicated by thoughts of the Ring's power (and by thoughts of the government grants that its possessor could surely command), Foote and Algernon join the chase.

More attempts on the Ring follow, with the cultists and the scientists suc- ceeding only in getting in one another's way. The Beatles even flee to the Alps in an attempt to elude their pursuers, but to no avail. Finally, the Beatles seek the help of Scotland Yard. The Yard's chief Superintendent (Patrick Cargill) is initially skeptical, but when a bizarre attempt on Ringo's life is made in his very office, protection is made available: in the shadow of Stone- henge in the middle of Salisbury Plain on a cold, blustery day, the Beatles record "I Need You" and "The Night Before," surrounded by the armed might of the British Army, tanks and all.

Nevertheless, the Kaili cultists launch a frontal attack with tanks and bazookas of their own. With the help of the faithful Ahme, the Beatles escape unscathed, but they begin to suspect that the protection of Scotland Yard is of little help against the power of their pursuers. This suspicion is borne out by an attack on Buckingham Palace itself, where the four have taken refuge. Foote and Algernon have slipped past the guards and into the Palace with something called a "Relativity Cadenza," which reduces everything in its path to slow motion. Fortunately, it proves to be too powerful for the Palace's power supply and blows a fuse, permitting the Beatles to make yet another narrow escape.

Disguised, the Beatles fly to the Bahamas—followed, of course, by their adversaries as well as by their protectors. The Beatles cavort briefly on the beach to the tune of "Another Girl," but their respite is short-lived. The cultists have transported their entire temple—Kaili and all—to the Bahamas for a last desperate assault on Ringo and the Ring.

Clang and Foote take turns capturing and losing the Ring, and the film ends in a wild, *Gunga Din*-like melee on the beach in which Ringo, captured one last time, gestures wildly, the Ring slips off his finger, and it is tossed around like a hot potato, since no one wants to end up a sacrifical victim.

If Lester made the Beatles into film stars in *A Hard Day's Night*, he risked undoing them in *Help!* The film's direction is not one of its strong suits. Individual scenes are hilarious, but too often Lester fails to meld them into a coherent whole; the picture comes perilously close to being an episodic jumble. In addition, the Beatles evidently provided him with more songs than he could successfully integrate into the film, and too often when the songs appear on the soundtrack, he interrupts the narrative and fills the screen with a montage of shots featuring the Beatles mugging for the camera and generally acting cute and cuddly, thus undercutting the sardonic wit in which they (and he) specialize.

Help!'s strength lies in its acting. Bron is merely adequate as Ahme, but the rest of the supporting cast is outstanding. McKern as the corrupt Clang ("Without the Ring, there will be no sacrifice, and without the sacrifice . . . no more *me*!") hams it up amiably; Spinetti as the hypertense Foote (he played a hypertense television director in *A Hard Day's Night* and Kinnear as his bovine assistant Algernon work hilariously well together; Cargill, as the Scotland Yard Superintendent who steadfastly refuses to be impressed by the eminence of the four musicians from Liverpool, is consistently amusing.

The film, however, begins and ends with John, Paul, George, and Ringo. *A Hard Day's Night* and a year's worth of almost constant media exposure has long since established their characters in the public mind, and all they had to do in *Help!* was be themselves. Their music and their personalities are more than enough to compensate for any rough edges in the film's construction. Lester and the Beatles made a marvelously engaging team. It is unfortunate that *Help!* was their final collaboration.

Robert Mitchell

HEMINGWAY'S ADVENTURES OF A YOUNG MAN

Released: 1962
Production: Jerry Wald for Twentieth Century-Fox
Direction: Martin Ritt
Screenplay: A. E. Hotchner; based on ten short stories by Ernest Hemingway
Cinematography: Lee Garmes
Editing: Hugh S. Fowler
Makeup: Ben Nye
Running time: 145 minutes

Principal characters:
Nick Adams .... Richard Beymer
Dr. Adams .... Arthur Kennedy
Mrs. Adams .... Jessica Tandy
Rosanna .... Susan Strasberg
Ad Francis .... Paul Newman
Bugs .... Juano Hernandez
Rosanna's father .... Tullio Carminati
Joe Boulton .... Simon Oakland

Films made from works by Nobel Prize-winning author Ernest Hemingway have usually pleased the public greatly, the critics less so, and Hemingway not at all. Hemingway had little or no control over the films made from his books in the 1940's and 1950's, but the film that was finally titled *Hemingway's Adventures of a Young Man* promised to overcome many of the faults the writer saw in such films as *The Sun Also Rises* (1957) and *A Farewell to Arms* (1957), neither of which he was able to watch all the way through. Hemingway sold the rights to ten of his short stories for a single film with the understanding that A. E. Hotchner would write the screenplay. Hotchner was the only adapter he would trust because Hotchner had satisfactorily dramatized several of Hemingway's stories for television. Hemingway also intended to exercise additional control, planning to read Hotchner's script as he wrote it, page by page. He reportedly told Hotchner, "You might get me a movie I can sit through."

Hemingway, however, became very ill and was not able to supervise the writing as much as he had planned; then, before production began, he committed suicide. In addition, the script by Hotchner was changed considerably, and—in the opinion of nearly every critic—the casting of Richard Beymer in the central role made it impossible for the film to convey the essence of the somewhat autobiographical stories upon which the script was based. Beymer had some success in roles in *The Diary of Anne Frank* (1959) and *West Side Story* (1961), but the unfavorable notices he received for the Hemingway film and several others released in 1962 and 1963 led him to abandon his career as an actor in Hollywood. Certainly he did not in 1962 have the ability and range as an actor to convey what was to be the theme of the film—a young man's experience of life maturing him and making him into a writer. *Hemingway's Adventures of a Young Man* presents the adventures often quite well, but fails in the admittedly difficult task of conveying their effect upon the young man.

In the process of converting ten individual stories into one episodic narrative, some stories were changed very little and others were changed or expanded greatly. In the latter category is "A Very Short Story," a two-page story about a wartime romance between a wounded man and a nurse that ends with the man returning to the United States and the woman writing him that "theirs had been only a boy and girl affair." In the film this becomes a major episode. Nick Adams (Richard Beymer) is wounded in the war and cared for by a nurse named Rosanna (Susan Strasberg). They fall in love and want to get married. While Nick is visiting Rosanna's father (Tullio Carminati) and getting his blessing for the marriage, Rosanna is seriously wounded in an air raid. When he finds Rosanna lying in a church that is being used as a temporary hospital, Nicks asks a priest to marry them. In the middle of the brief ceremony, however, Rosanna dies, and the grief-stricken Nick smashes the candles at the altar of the church.

The film, however, begins more than a year earlier in 1916, and shows Nick living at home with his kind and competent but somewhat servile father (Arthur Kennedy) and his domineering, insensitive mother (Jessica Tandy). Nick watches his father back down in an argument with a half-breed handyman from the Indian Camp, Joe Boulton (Simon Oakland). He is further disturbed and embarrassed to see his father fail to stand up to his mother when she is patronizing toward him about the event. He regains some respect for his father, however, when he sees him at work. His father is a doctor, and Nick is present when he skillfully and successfully performs an emergency caesarean section in a house at the Indian Camp.

Finally Nick can no longer endure his mother, who wants to regulate every aspect of his life, and his father, who will not assert himself or stand up for Nick. His father asks Nick to compromise in order to keep the peace, but Nick responds, "Aren't you a little tired of keeping the peace?" Shortly thereafter, Nick leaves home to make his way on his own.

Nick's main adventure before the wartime romance is his encounter, after he is thrown off a freight train, with a punch-drunk old fighter, Ad Francis (Paul Newman). Nick joins the fighter at his campfire and soon discovers that he travels with a soft-spoken black man, Bugs (Juano Hernandez). Bugs understands Francis and humors him at times and protects him when necessary. Nick listens to the ravings and self-confessed craziness of Francis with interest, and all three get along well until Bugs tells Nick not to give Francis a knife. Bugs is merely trying to protect the old fighter, but Francis does not understand and becomes very hostile to Nick. Finally, Bugs has to tell Nick to leave and is only able to calm Francis by hitting him with a blackjack.

This episode is based upon the story entitled "The Battler" and follows it fairly closely. Newman had played the role on television in 1955 and played it again in the film despite the conventional wisdom that a star should not take a small role. Francis, "The Battler", has been battered mentally and physically by his life in the ring, a career which scarred and distorted his face. The convincing makeup by Ben Nye makes Newman almost unrecognizable as the handsome star whose roles tended to emphasize his good looks in such films as *Sweet Bird of Youth* (1962). The fact that The Battler was Newman in a character part with grotesque makeup, however, tended to distract the viewer and thus reduce the effectiveness of the episode. The fine performance of Hernandez luckily suffers from no such distractions.

After he goes to Europe and after his tragic romance, Nick returns home. He is greeted as a hero at the train station, but while still there he finds that his father has committed suicide. His mother had written him about it, but he had not received the letter. After all these experiences Nick is unable to stay at home with his still domineering and insensitive mother. She treats him as she always has, but he tells her that after having a soldier blown to pieces next to him and a girl he was about to marry die in his arms he cannot become involved in dates for a square dance and asking his mother if he can use the car. He informs her that he is going to become a writer and write about the things that have happened to him. The film ends with Nick looking over the lake while the voice of the narrator says, "So for the last time you look at the lake beside the house where you were born. For tomorrow you will try again, but this time you're not running away; you're moving toward something."

Hemingway's Adventures of a Young Man has some moving and effective moments, some impressive location shooting in Italy and Michigan, and some reminders of the style and themes of Hemingway, but as a whole it was a disappointment to critics and to its adapter, A. E. Hotchner. At the box office it also fell far short of the level achieved by most previous films based upon works by Hemingway.

Sharon Wiseman

HENRY V

Released: 1944
Production: Laurence Olivier for Two Cities Films; released by United Artists
Direction: Laurence Olivier
Screenplay: Laurence Olivier, Dallas Bower, and Alan Dent; based on the
  play of the same name by William Shakespeare
Cinematography: Robert Krasker
Editing: Reginald Beck and Laurence Olivier
Costume design: Roger Furse
Music: William Walton
Running time: 153 minutes

Principal characters:

Chorus	Leslie Banks
King Henry V	Laurence Olivier
Archbishop of Canterbury	Felix Aylmer
Bishop of Ely	Robert Helpman
Lieutenant Bardolph	Roy Emerton
Ancient Pistol	Robert Newton
Captain MacMorris	Nial MacGinnis
Captain Gower	Michael Shepley
Captain Jamie	John Laurie
Fluellen	Esmond Knight
Sir John Falstaff	George Robey
The Dauphin	Max Adrian
Princess Katharine	Renee Asherson
King Charles VI of France	Harcourt Williams
Duke of Bourbon	Russell Thorndike

Laurence Olivier's *Henry V* blends history and romance within the context
of both theater and film. It was the first Shakespearean film to achieve popular
success and critical acclaim as an artistic work and was also the first Shakespearean film in color. Additionally, Olivier received a special Academy
Award in 1946 for his outstanding achievement as actor, producer, and director of the project.

Olivier cut out about half of William Shakespeare's text in order to simplify
the story and avoid Renaissance ideas of kingship unfamiliar to modern audiences. He made the focal point of action the Battle of Agincourt, in which
outnumbered English troops routed the French in 1415. The parallel with
wartorn Britain under the daily Nazi bombing of London was not lost on the
audience since the movie was filmed between June 9, 1943, and July 12, 1944,
in Eire and England. The world premiere was November 22, 1944, in London.

The play is framed by a realistic pan shot of Shakespeare's London (actually
a fifty-by-seventy inch model based on Visscher's seventeenth century map-

view of the city) which focuses on a play about to begin at the Globe Theatre. The camera moves down from the Chorus (Leslie Banks) to the balcony where a brief comic scene with the bishops of Ely (Robert Helpman) and Canterbury (Felix Aylmer) takes place. Then we glimpse the frantic backstage activities as actors in makeup prepare to go onstage where Henry (Laurence Olivier) listens to the bishops' arguments justifying his claim to France; he answers the insults of the Dauphin (Max Adrian) with a declaration of war. This "realistic" look at the Globe is often excerpted to show school children what an Elizabethan playhouse was probably like.

The film then begins a journey through different modes of reality. While the Chorus draws up a curtain on which is painted a stylized view of Southhampton Harbor, the camera dissolves out of the Globe and into a real harbor. The action then moves to France, where a more naturalistic style is employed, returning to the framework of the Globe only at the end of the film to view the wedding of Henry and the French princess Katharine (Renee Asherson).

Four production problems confronted Olivier in adapting the play to film, and his solutions to these problems provide some of the picture's most memorable touches. They have also influenced subsequent Shakespeare films. The first two problems were how to make Shakespearean language seem natural to a modern audience and how to treat Shakespeare's Chorus, which appears at the beginning of each act. The decision to have the Chorus resemble an Elizabethan actor suggested the framing device which opens and closes the film. The flamboyant language of the Chorus offers a contrast which makes the blank verse and prose which follow seem more natural.

The filming of long speeches was a third problem. Olivier's solution was to begin them with close-ups and then move the camera back. This constituted a major innovation in the filming of Shakespeare and a technique that Olivier would use again in *Hamlet* (1948) and *Richard III* (1956). Finally, the problem of an appropriate background and setting for a film that Olivier planned as "a 'painter's eye-view' of moving events" was solved by using painted backdrops based on medieval illustrations, primarily from a fifteenth century illuminated manuscript, the Duke of Berry's *Book of Hours*. On viewing the film, one is struck by the balanced, formal, almost stylized, yet poignant pictorial qualities of the characters—for example, those in the French court.

Olivier uses spatial relationships effectively throughout the film. When Henry walks through his camp on the eve of battle, the audience is presented with a subjective view of the English as the disguised King talks to and identifies with his men. In the rousing St. Crispin's Day speech sequence, Olivier has Henry rise from intimate conversation with a few friends to make a rallying speech before the entire army. The climactic build of the lines is staged with subtle changes in angle and levels of camera action. Henry begins on the ground, addressing a small group of nobles; as he warms to his subject, walking through the camp, more and more soldiers gather and Henry's voice rises in volume. In order to be visible to more of them, the King mounts a wagon and uses it as a speaker's platform. His delivery quite naturally expands from a conversational to an appropriately flamboyant oratorical style, and it is at this point that the camera, which began in close-up, draws back. When Henry reaches the climax of his speech ("Once more unto the breach, dear friends, once more";) we see a united English army ready to battle to the death for king and country.

The film then focuses on the battle preparations of the French, who drink wine and are lowered onto their horses by a crane (as opposed to Henry's vaulting onto his horse), then to the English lines where men sharpen stakes and test their bows, and where Henry rejects Montjoy's ransom offer. On the field of Agincourt one of the great battle scenes in film history occurs as rapid shots of the hardy English are contrasted with the more effeminate actions of the French and their senseless murder of young boys in the English camp. The English victory ends with a dissolve on the dead soldiers in the field as a "Te Deum" is sung. Then the film cuts to a comic interlude in which Fluellen (Esmond Knight) makes Pistol (Robert Newton) eat a leek and we learn of the death of Falstaff (George Robey). Henry woos Princess Katharine in the French palace, and a final scene returns the actors to the Globe where they bow to the audience's applause. The Chorus delivers the Epilogue; the flag flying over the Globe is lowered; and as the camera again pans London, a playbill with credits floats into the frame.

There are three visual styles evident throughout the film. The first, noted by critic Harry Geduld, is "antiillusionistic" (as in the framing scenes in the Globe); the second is "quasinaturalistic" (the style most prevalent in the film); and the third is "illusionistic-stylized." The latter concerns the artificial and stylized settings around which most of the controversy has focused. The realistic battlefield is *"Henry's* world where he confronts the French . . . ; the unreal palace is *Katharine's* world, and to woo and to win her on her ground Henry attempts what is unreal to him; the gallantries and flatteries of the courtly lover," according to Geduld. The docility and frivolity of the French court is suggested by the pastel colors of the costumes (mainly blue), as well as by the painted background against which the characters move. These colors reinforce the impression that the French are essentially out of touch with reality. The English, by contrast, dress in reds and browns and are less concerned with pageantry; neither decadent nor vain, the hardy English overcome an effeminate enemy.

Henry V did not win unanimous critical acclaim, although it was a popular film. Some critics felt that the textual cuts oversimplified Henry's character (which they do); some objected to the film's jingoism; while others felt uncomfortable with the attention given the comic characters. The film broke new ground in the use of Technicolor and music: almost all of the critics praised William Walton's powerful score, which was performed by the London

Symphony Orchestra under the direction of distinguished film conductor Muir Mathieson, and the coordination of music and images. Controversy, however, still focuses on the mixture of cinematic styles which Olivier managed to fuse into a classic film.

Andrew M. McLean

THE HIGH AND THE MIGHTY

Released: 1954
Production: A Wayne Fellows Production for Warner Bros.
Direction: William A. Wellman
Screenplay: Ernest K. Gann; based on his novel of the same name
Cinematography: Archie Stout
Editing: Ralph Dawson
Running time: 147 minutes

Principal characters:
Dan Roman	John Wayne
May Holst	Claire Trevor
Lydia Rice	Laraine Day
Sullivan	Robert Stack
Sally McKee	Jan Sterling
Ed Joseph	Phil Harris
Gustave Pardee	Robert Newton
Ken Childs	David Brian
Flaherty	Paul Kelly
Garfield	Regis Toomey
Jose Locola	John Qualen

The High and the Mighty is a unique film, outdated and perhaps doomed by its own success. Yet even today, it remains the standard by which its successors must be judged. Made in 1954 by William A. Wellman from the best-selling novel by Ernest K. Gann, it became the first slick modern disaster film and, in the process, established the basic formula for these films—one that would be followed for the next thirty years.

While it is true that earlier films, among them *Stagecoach* (1939) and *Lifeboat* (1944), had employed a similar theme of exploring relationships among a group of lost souls thrown together on a doomed journey, the elements of disaster were secondary and usually employed to advance development of character. *The High and the Mighty* elevated the element of disaster to the preeminent position among the concerns of its plot—a twist that would not go unnoticed by the host of imitators that followed. The series of Airport films (*Airport*, 1970, *Airport 1976*, and *Airport '77*) are the ones most obviously influenced by Wellman's film, but *Abandon Ship* (1957), *A Night to Remember* (1958), and *The Poseidon Adventure* (1972) also owe obvious debts to the formula set by *The High and the Mighty*.

It could be argued perhaps that Wellman and screenwriter Gann might, in fact, be obligated to Edmund Goulding's 1932 *Grand Hotel* for its collection of troubled characters and personal crises. Although Wellman admittedly does provide a cabinload of lost souls and examines to some degree their reactions to one another and to the imminent catastrophe in terms of their past experience, this is primarily padding inserted to delineate and to enhance the crisis. Through this means, Wellman is able to get lively footage out of his scenes of an airliner in distress.

As would obviously be expected in a film which contains multiple personal dramas enacted against a life-and-death background, the *Grand Hotel* type of embellishments suffer by comparison. Gann and Wellman, however, have introduced the assorted individual dramas with professional smoothness beginning with the moment that each passenger arrives to pick up his tickets at the Hawaiian airport's reservation counter for the flight to San Francisco. The travelers are then introduced to us by the reservations clerk, who shapes our initial impressions about their characters. To his credit, Gann in his script avoided most of the obvious clichéd situations that would be tempting to any writer dealing with a large number of characters in a situation such as this. No romance develops during the flight, for example, and when the plane door is opened to jettison the excess baggage, no one falls out or is in any danger of doing so.

As the passengers are seated on the plane, we learn more about them and quickly discover that each is burdened with a great deal of excess emotional baggage. The pilot, Sullivan (Robert Stack), is a nervous man harboring secret fears and is bordering on a nervous breakdown. His second-in-command, Dan Roman (John Wayne), although much calmer than his captain, harbors dark memories of losing his own captain's license because he was the pilot of a plane that crashed killing everyone on board except himself, including his wife and child.

Among the passengers, Lydia and Howard Rice (Laraine Day and John Howard) are returning home with the intention of getting a divorce. Gustave Pardee (Robert Newton) is a loud-mouthed theatrical producer, and Ken Childs (David Brian) is a cowardly playboy. Flaherty (Paul Kelly) is a demoralized atomic scientist who worries throughout the flight about political misuse of the force that he and others like him have unleashed in the world. Also, as might be expected, there is a woman of easy virtue, May Holst (Claire Trevor, repeating her *Stagecoach* role), who possesses the proverbial "heart of gold" with which such women are often imbued in films like this one. A number of other troubled characters, as well as Jose Locola (John Qualen), a sympathetic figure with no problems who only got on the plane to go to San Francisco, complete the passenger list.

As the plane flies out over the Pacific the individual dramas unfold. In the background, however, some disquieting things are happening. One of the stewardesses notes a recurring vibration that is so subtle at first that it does not do more than spill a few drops of coffee out of a cup. The passengers do not notice, however, because a jealous husband is wielding a gun and threatening to shoot Ken Childs for having an affair with his wife. He is soon calmed down by copilot Roman and returns to his seat.

The vibration now begins to alarm Roman, who starts searching the plane for the cause. Things start to go wrong in rapid succession. First, an engine catches fire and goes out of commission, ripping a hole in a gas tank in the process. The fuel leak severely limits the amount of fuel available to cover the 2,400-mile run and reach San Francisco. The specter of a night crash-landing on the ocean begins to loom larger. To lighten the load and ease the strain on the fuel supply, Roman opens one of the cabin doors and begins to jettison as much luggage as possible. In the midst of this crisis, Captain Sullivan finally goes to pieces under the stress but has some sense knocked into him by his copilot Roman, who has been through it all before.

It now becomes a race against the declining fuel supply for the plane and crew, with their flying efficiency diminished, to make San Francisco. With the plane in trouble, personal dramas are resolved. The plane's captain learns to conquer his fear; a pair of honeymooners develop confidence in their mutual ability to face life. The wealthy Lydia Rice makes up her mind to forget the divorce and go to the Alaska mining country and give her kept husband a chance to try to stand on his own two feet. There are equally suitable resolutions for the prostitute, the atomic scientist, the jealous husband with a pistol in his pocket, and a horde of others, although one is not fully confident regarding the permanence of these changes once the airliner lands.

The plane barely reaches San Francisco with its fuel tanks reading empty when it touches down. After all of the passengers depart to make good on their various "new starts," Roman stands under the plane contemplating all that has happened. He is approached by Garfield (Regis Toomey), who, after checking the plane, informs the copilot how little fuel was actually left. Suspecting that Roman's cool competence was a factor in the plane's survival, he tells him to come to his office tomorrow to discuss his reinstatement as a captain.

The High and the Mighty utilizes a sure-fire film situation: a group of people from diverse backgrounds with individual human problems faces and reacts to a common deadly crisis. Although most of the airplane's passengers and their problems might in retrospect seem bizarre and to some degree contrived, Trevor, through sheer acting ability, does create a certain credibility for the highly specialized plight of an erstwhile tarnished lady; but the other passengers are pretty much only along for the ride.

Wayne delivers his normal characterization as the rock-steady copilot who makes the right decision when the pilot cracks under stress. He maintains his cool composure but at the same time exhibits the courage to knock some clear sense into the Captain's muddled head. For his part, Stack as the captain gives a convincing performance of a highly neurotic man walking a tightrope between nervous sanity and a complete breakdown. *The High and the Mighty* marked a turning point in Stack's acting career. Prior to this film, he seemed relegated to playing light romantic roles and secondary leads. After his performance as the captain, however, he went on to star in *Written on the Wind* (1956), for which he received an Academy Award nomination, and to play the lead in the long-running television show, *The Untouchables*. Both of these roles were made possible by the new image that he established as a dramatic actor in *The High and the Mighty*. Both director Wellman and Gann have an excellent knowledge of the mechanics of flying and a relatively good idea of the psychology of the men who fly the planes. There are some occasional technical errors, but the only major one is the opening outward of a passenger door while the plane is in flight. The sets, instrument panels, and particularly the airports look businesslike and professional. The aerial cinematography is stunning and is enhanced by the use of color and CinemaScope.

When *The High and the Mighty* turns from the emotional problems and entanglements of its passengers, it is an absorbing drama of a race against time. There is no denying that the parts of the film dealing directly with the crippled plane's dilemma are tremendously effective. The film suffers in retrospect only because viewers seeing it today for the first time have been exposed to its many successors which have taken its stock characterizations and situations and rendered them trite. Although the airline disaster formula was formalized by Wellman and Gann, it has not been changed imaginatively or sufficiently by later directors. Thus a new viewer could be excused for thinking of it as *Airport 1954*—a victim of the style it created.

Stephen L. Hanson

HIGH ANXIETY

Released: 1977
Production: Mel Brooks for Twentieth Century-Fox
Direction: Mel Brooks
Screenplay: Mel Brooks, Ron Clark, Rudy De Luca, and Barry Levinson
Cinematography: Paul Lohmann
Editing: John C. Howard
Running time: 92 minutes

Principal characters:
Dr. Richard H. Thorndyke	Mel Brooks
Victoria Brisbane	Madeline Kahn
Nurse Diesel	Cloris Leachman
Dr. Charles Montague	Harvey Korman
Brophy	Ron Carey
Professor Lillolman	Howard Morris
Bellboy	Barry Levinson
Arthur Brisbane	Albert J. Whitlock
Braces	Rudy De Luca

Mel Brooks began his career as a nightclub and television comedian, achieving a great deal of success both as a performer and as a writer, particularly for his work on Sid Caesar's television shows. In 1968 he wrote and directed *The Producers* and two years later wrote, directed, and acted in *The Twelve Chairs.* Although he received an Oscar for his script of *The Producers*, both of these films were only moderately successful at the box office, attracting a relatively small but devoted group of followers. It was not until *Blazing Saddles* in 1974 that Brooks developed a recipe for reaching huge audiences: broad comedy combined with take-offs on popular types of film. *Blazing Saddles* parodies the Western, *Young Frankenstein* (1974) the horror film, and *Silent Movie* (1976) the slapstick silent comedy. In 1977 he turned to the works of director Alfred Hitchcock to produce, direct, write (with three others), and act in *High Anxiety*, which is intended to be a tribute to, as much as a parody of, the "master of suspense."

The resulting film consists of three interwoven elements: a suspenseful thriller plot, broad comedy, and continual references to the works of Hitchcock. It is a mixture that brought great numbers of people to the box office and gave Brooks his fourth film in four years to be one of the top money-making films of the year. Indeed, in *Variety*'s 1978 list of All-Time Film Rental Champs, all four of these films appeared in the top one hundred and fifteen. No other director has achieved that distinction.

The plot of *High Anxiety* is, to a great extent, a combination of the plots of a number of Hitchcock films, such as *Spellbound* (1945), *Vertigo* (1958), and *North by Northwest* (1959). Dr. Richard H. Thorndyke (Mel Brooks), a psychiatrist, Nobel Prize-winner, and former Harvard professor, arrives to assume his new post as director of the Psycho-Neurotic Institute for the Very, Very Nervous, the previous director having died under mysterious circumstances. He is met by Brophy (Ron Carey), who introduces himself as "your driver and sidekick." We soon learn that two members of the staff, the grotesque Nurse Diesel (Cloris Leachman) and Dr. Charles Montague (Harvey Korman), are involved in a plot to keep healthy "patients" in the Institute in order to continue receiving the twelve-thousand-dollar-per-month fee charged by the Institute. We also learn that Thorndyke himself suffers from a severe psychological disorder—an acute fear of heights called "high anxiety."

When he attends a convention of psychiatrists in San Francisco (where the main meeting room features giant pictures of the greats in the field—Rank, Sigmund Freud, Carl Jung, Alfred Adler, and Dr. Joyce Brothers), Thorndyke meets Victoria Brisbane (Madeline Kahn), who tells him that her father is being held against his will at the Institute.

When Nurse Diesel and Dr. Montague realize that Thorndyke is discovering their plot, they arrange to have a hired killer called Braces (Rudy De Luca) disguise himself as Thorndyke and kill a man in public so that Thorndyke cannot go to the police because they will arrest him for murder. In fact, a photograph of the deed appears on the front page of the newspapers.

Realizing that the picture must have been taken by Brophy, a compulsive shutterbug, Thorndyke, who is still in San Francisco, has Brophy, who has returned to the Institute, enlarge the negative to show that he, the real Thorndyke, is in the background of the picture and thus cannot be the man with the gun. (This sequence is a takeoff on a non-Hitchcock film, *Blow-Up*, 1966.) Diesel and Montague discover what Brophy has done and call Braces in San Francisco with orders to kill Thorndyke. The killer tries to strangle the doctor in a telephone booth while he is trying to talk to Victoria. She merely thinks it is an obscene caller, but Thorndyke escapes by impaling Braces on a shard of broken glass in the telephone booth.

Then Thorndyke and Victoria must quickly get to the Institute to save Victoria's father and Brophy. First they must escape detection by the police. Thorndyke's strategy, as he explains it to Victoria, is that they will get by the police, not by sneaking, but by being "loud and annoying." So they dress in Salvation Army clothes and stage a big scene in the airport. It attracts everyone's attention, but the two policemen on hand have no suspicion that this is the man for whom they are looking, and Victoria and Thorndyke board the airplane. Once at the Institute they find that Victoria's father, Arthur Brisbane (Albert J. Whitlock), is being taken to the top of the tower where he will be pushed to his death. Thorndyke has to overcome his high anxiety to climb up the stairs and save Brisbane, but halfway up a stair gives way and he is suddenly hanging in midair. It takes some hasty, on-the-spot psychoanalysis by Professor Lillolman (Howard Morris) from below to cure him so that he can pull himself back up and go on to rescue Brisbane. After he does so, Victoria says she will marry him and, with an out-of-focus shot for a transition, we see the happy couple in their wedding clothes in their honeymoon suite. As the camera begins pulling away we hear the men behind the camera shout a warning as the camera smashes back through the wall and continues receding. As the film ends the camera continues pulling back to show us the honeymoon cabin with a hole in the wall.

High Anxiety is packed with references to the films of Hitchcock, and Brooks claims to have gotten suggestions from Hitchcock himself. The ending is like the ending of *North by Northwest* in that it moves directly from a rescue to a honeymooning couple. Thorndyke is like the heroes of many Hitchcock films in that he is an innocent man who finds himself in the middle of a criminal plot. Indeed, the device of a newspaper photograph that purports to show the hero in the act of committing a murder is from *North by Northwest*. Kahn as Victoria Brisbane plays the cool blonde woman played by such actresses as Grace Kelly, Eva Marie Saint, and Tippi Hedren in Hitchcock films, although her own comic sense brings a brassiness to the role not characteristic of those women.

Besides these basic similarities, there are dozens of other scenes, situations, or phrases that recall the films of Hitchcock. In *Psycho* (1960), for example, one of Hitchcock's most famous and most terrifying scenes shows a woman being stabbed to death in a shower. The scene ends with a shot of blood running into the drain and then a shot of the dead woman's open eye. In *High Anxiety* the entire scene is duplicated almost exactly except that the person in the shower is a man (Thorndyke) and the assailant wields not a knife but a rolled up newspaper. He is a bellboy (Barry Levinson) angered at Thorndyke's repeated demands for a newspaper. The scene ends with *ink* running into the drain and with a shot of Thorndyke's eye. Thorndyke, however, is not dead. He merely remarks that the bellboy will get no tip. In a take-off on *The Birds* (1963), Thorndyke is sitting in a park when a flock of birds pursue him and splatter him with droppings. (In fact, Brooks used the same bird trainer that Hitchcock used.)

High Anxiety does not, however, depend entirely on its suspense plot and its references to Hitchcock for its appeal to audiences. The film is essentially a comedy and contains a great many funny scenes besides the Hitchcock parodies. Some of these scenes are connected to the plot and some are not. For example, Thorndyke is accosted in an airport by an official-looking man who turns out to be a homosexual flasher. Another time he is in a cocktail lounge with Victoria and is asked to sing. He responds with a professional rendition of a song called "High Anxiety" (written by Brooks himself). "Have you ever thought of singing professionally?" Victoria asks him. "No, the big bucks are in psychiatry," he replies. The underlying comic theme, indeed, is that psychiatrists are as crazy as their patients.

Once when he was asked to compare his films with those of Woody Allen, Brooks said, "My movies are basic, primitive, vulgar and direct." This perfectly describes the writing and directing style of Brooks and the acting of the cast of *High Anxiety*. The film is a broad comedy that has pleased most critics and millions of filmgoers.

Clifford Henry

THE HIRED HAND

Released: 1971
Production: William Hayward for Universal
Direction: Peter Fonda
Screenplay: Alan Sharp
Cinematography: Vilmos Zsigmond
Editing: Frank Mazzola
Running time: 93 minutes

Principal characters:
Harry Collings	Peter Fonda
Arch Harris	Warren Oates
Hannah Collings	Verna Bloom
Dan Griffen	Robert Pratt
McVey	Severn Darden
Janey Collings	Megan Denver

The Hired Hand is not a typical Western, although it shares the time, place, and basic good-guys-versus-bad-guys aspects of its genre. What separates it from the others is its highly stylized approach and its attempt to portray the significance and meaning behind the action. After his success in the role of Captain America in *Easy Rider* (1969), Peter Fonda offered this film as his directorial debut and added to the Western some of the mystical, surrealistic overtones that had characterized that more popular film. Like *Easy Rider*, *The Hired Hand* deals with basic American values; it differs significantly in that it affirms these values rather than questioning the contemporary cultural malaise.

The plot is not very complex. In the first sequence, Harry Collings (Peter Fonda) and Arch Harris (Warren Oates) avenge the death of their friend Dan Griffen (Robert Pratt), who has just been shot down by the sadistic McVey (Severn Darden). Instead of killing McVey, they shoot him in both feet—an example of the often oblique symbolism employed throughout the film. Tired of wandering, Collings returns to his wife and daughter whom he had deserted seven years before. Hannah (Verna Bloom) is understandably cool and suspicious, at first only accepting him as another of the hands she has hired, but eventually accepting his return as her husband. Harris, now a threat to her security, soon leaves. Later, a messenger from McVey gives proof that they have captured Harris. Collings must leave to meet McVey at once or they will cut off another finger for each day's delay, eventually taking his life. It is a hard decision to make, with the guilt of Hannah's past betrayal still weighing on him; but he must try to save his friend's life. Promising to return, he leaves, only to be killed in the ensuing showdown with McVey. Harris survives, however, and returns to the farm to take Collings' place as Hannah's hired hand.

On the surface the film portrays the values of the Old West: loyalty, courage, responsibility, hard work, and pain. Fonda and screenwriter Alan Sharp have blended a romanticized vision of these idealized attributes with a story whose characters live in a very real, harsh world. The result is a latter-day morality play. Each of the characters embodies certain qualities, and their interactions illustrate and emphasize the human values that reaffirm life. Collings, Hannah, and Harris form a triad whose lives illustrate the basic struggle of life on the frontier. Sin, guilt, and atonement can easily be read into the plot as Collings' return does not totally expiate his sin of having left Hannah. His return creates another moral conflict since he must end his association with Harris in order to stay with her. Only his death and Harris' return to Hannah restores order.

At the center of the triangle is Hannah Collings. Compared with other Western heroines, Hannah is refreshingly realistic. She looks as if she has spent many years working hard, and her face mirrors the struggles she has had to survive. Underneath, however, there is a softer, more feminine woman whom Bloom beautifully exhibits in shy and touching ways. When Collings is finally accepted back into the house, she dresses and primps like the young bride she once was, clearly trusting Collings and accepting her wifely role again. Although other hired hands have shared her bed, we sense that this one is different, more significant. Collings' actions at this point are also indicative of his inner feelings and his commitment to a new life. The entire sequence in which both go through a ritual cleansing and preparation establishes the import of their renewed relationship. Completing the triangle, Oates plays Harris as an interesting blend of strength and sensitivity. Like Collings, he is weary of traveling and is envious of the home Collings has rediscovered. In a beautifully played scene marking Harris' realization that he must leave, he and Hannah experience a natural attraction for each other. Both characters realize at once what is happening but both instinctively retreat. Collings is important to both of them, and neither wishes to upset the newly reestablished union.

On the surface, the main weakness of the film is the characterization of Collings. While trying to reduce the character to a simple, everyday cowboy, Fonda has left little substance to the man. Only his choices and decisions carry any significance, while his daily activity is something of a puzzle. Fonda, as Collings, delineates a character so painfully nonverbal and seemingly unemotional that it is difficult to understand fully his motive in returning to his wife or her attraction for him. Presumably, Collings' seven years' absence and his close association with Harris, who seems more likable, have taught him the meaning of the loyalty, responsibility, and love which he clearly lacked earlier. The key is that we are not supposed to read too much into the character's individual actions, but to appreciate the wider human implications of the drama. The people are simple and the dialogue sparse on purpose.

The visual effects support these mythical dimensions. The lingering dissolves, the slow motion, and the superimposed multiple images remove the action from reality. Technically, the audience is treated to a lushly beautiful picture of a harsh, rugged landscape, but many have agreed that this does not compensate for the film's slow pace. In fact, many critics have felt that the editing contributed to the film's failure. Many of the techniques used are now rather commonplace, however, and this might make their predominance in the film seem less intrusive to a more sophisticated audience. The fact that the film appeared immediately after the psychedelic fervor of the late 1960's may have hurt its reception, since many critics felt that its mystical overtones and solemn acting were pretentious; but time may blur some of those objections. Although it will probably never be widely acclaimed, over the years *The Hired Hand* has attracted a cult following whose members appreciate its beauty and uniquely simple charm.

Christine Gladish

THE HIRELING

Released: 1973
Production: Ben Arbeid for World Film Services and Champion Productions; released by Columbia
Direction: Alan Bridges
Screenplay: Wolf Mankowitz; based on the novel of the same name by L. P. Hartley
Cinematography: Michael Reed
Editing: Peter Weatherley
Running time: 108 minutes

Principal characters:
Lady Franklin .... Sarah Miles
Steven Ledbetter .... Robert Shaw
Cantrip .... Peter Egan
Lady Franklin's mother .... Elizabeth Sellars
Connie .... Caroline Mortimer

The Hireling received the Cannes Festival Grand Prize (sharing the honor with *Scarecrow*), but was neither a critical nor a popular success in the United States, where critics treated it as a failed attempt to film L. P. Hartley's novel of the delicate romance between an unstable titled lady and her chauffeur in post World War I England. The major themes are the relationship between classes and the landscape of madness.

Madness—the inability to cope with both one's self and the world at the same time—seems nearly an occupational hazard for women in a culture whose definitions of desirable feminine characteristics and unhealthy human characteristics include the same qualities: passivity, nonaggression, noncompetitiveness, lack of ego, denial of self, insecurity, and dependence. An equally important but often ignored corollary is that, just as acting in accordance with the established norms of feminine aspirations leads women to maddeningly inadequate lives, the "healthy" masculine character traits—aggressiveness, denial of emotion, selfishness, constant strength, and stability—may allow men more quantitative freedom in the world at the expense of qualitative freedom. The result for both sides is that personal relationships between men and women become destructive and, in a very real sense, impossible.

In *The Hireling*, a beautifully made, intensely involving film, a woman moves from madness in a traditional sense to "adjustment," but is probably even more disturbed as a result of the adjustment than she was at the beginning. Her "hireling" moves from normality according to society's standards to violence, frustration, and irrationality. The point at which they almost cross is an emotionally moving glimpse at the impossibility of their relationship in a rigidly structured class society, and perhaps in any society.

The film opens on the day Lady Franklin (Sarah Miles) is well enough to leave the hospital in which she has been confined following the death of her husband. Cold blue light illuminates her point-of-view shot of the world over the credits and remains a motif of alienation throughout the film, ending with the frustrated self-destructiveness of Steven Ledbetter (Robert Shaw) in the cold blue night. The other inmates of the hospital are each visually isolated in the cold light by windows, doors, or their own hats which hide their faces, expressive of their withdrawal from a world which cannot respond to them. In her last interview with her doctor, Lady Franklin tries to talk to him about her breakdown, but she is cut off and channeled into very specific, restrictive subjects and attitudes. The exchange is a copy of the ones with her mother to follow: she is allowed a very narrow range of response, and any attempt to overstep it is received with censure, uneasiness, and withdrawal of concern for her, betraying perhaps the narrow boundaries of emotional exchange in her aristocratic world.

Driving her home from the hospital, Steven Ledbetter, who is an ex-sergeant major in the army trying to build up his car-hiring business, creates a totally different environment for her which is as relaxing and comforting as the other had been stifling and threatening. He does not watch her, as do her mother and "friends"; instead, she watches him during the long, dreamlike ride to the home she dreads. He is outwardly supremely secure in his capacity as driver and even creates for her an equally stable, safe, private life for himself in response to her questions by inventing a mythical wife and two children. Because of their very strictly defined relationship in terms of their class and mistress/servant status in 1920, her insecurity and fragile grip on herself do not make him uneasy, and he treats her with respect, concern, and easy affection which comes first from his need of her patronage. In her world of barriers, the very firmly entrenched class barriers between them allow her to break down others, and she can ask him to lower the window between them, and later sit beside him in the front seat. He becomes her bulwark against the world which terrifies her. She is also strengthened by the lies he creates for her, such as his stable working-class family. She identifies with his wife, and he begins to identify her with a wife-figure, telling her, when she asks, that his wife looks like her. Through such questions, Lady Franklin gets closer to him and to her own feelings about being a wife. She asks what his wife would do if he died suddenly, and she takes his answer—"get on with it," with life, and perhaps find another husband—seriously.

During her first frightened encounter with her own kind of society—a boxing match at which she is to present the winner's cup—Steven is able to act as a kind of go-between. He is not part of high society, but because he coaches the boys he has a certain authority there. She asks him not to leave her alone, and with the world around them, they are more a real couple than in their previous dreamy isolation. He resisted any equality between them when they were alone, perhaps making a kind of union possible in a way nothing else could. At the boxing match they are in two-shot, huddled close together as he tells her about boxing and enjoys her enthusiasm. The scene is intercut with Cantrip (Peter Egan), her tardy escort for the evening, an insensitive aristocratic lout who will become her second husband, and his mistress, structurally disrupting the closeness between Lady Franklin and Steven. When Steven must leave his place beside her to referee, Cantrip takes it, having finally arrived. He is linked to her late husband through politics and begins that night to take over Steven's role. Lady Franklin is now confident enough to act within her own world without Steven's stable structures to support her.

She in fact begins to be supportive of Cantrip, encouraging his political plans and giving a dinner party for him to announce his candidacy to influential people. Her house, once lit with cold green light and devoid of articles of warmth, is now overflowing with fruit, flowers, and fires, symbolizing the renewed life in her. It is Steven who initiates this warmth metaphorically, when he goes with her into her basement to start the electrical generators which light her home. The candlelight of this sequence suggests the repressed sexual implications of their friendship, and it becomes suffocatingly intense as she watches him take off his shirt to work. The point-of-view shots of her watching him are quick, intense, and immediate, unlike the shots of him watching her in her house as he waits to drive her, which are long, brooding shots rimmed with mediating objects—windows, curtains, and the house itself.

Needing him no longer after the boxing match, she ceases to "hire" him, and he is forced into action that begins the process of breaking down those structures which made their friendship possible in the first place. First he breaks some of the rules of class behavior, forcing the unspoken bond between them by telling her he is in trouble now. Her offer to help with money serves a dual purpose. To him it seems an acknowledgment of their bond, but when she gives it, it is as though she were paying off the debt she owed him. Their feelings about each other are expressed visually as he follows her through the house. When he first drove her to her house, she was so insecure and fragile that he took over the ordering of the servants and seemed more in control there than she as mistress. This time, however, the roles are reversed. She is in total control and scarcely looks at him as he follows her in intense point-of-view tracking shots. He walks up to her at her desk, each in one-shots that isolate them from each other and gradually from the house as well, as the background goes out of focus behind him with the increasingly long focal length of the lens. This disturbing sequence visually reinforces her independence and his growing need for her. He asks for money, but he leaves with a deep sense of frustration and starts a fight with his partner, resulting in his partner's clothes catching on fire, symbolizing his repressed desire erupting.

In a last, desperate attempt to reach her, Steven tells her he has no family and that he loves her. Now that he has destroyed the structures which allowed their closeness but which denied their intimacy, she reconstructs them. She steps out of the car after his confession, then gets in the back seat, reinstating the very barrier she earlier removed. Once Steven has become totally vulnerable to her, he cannot go back to the stability of his role as "hireling" and the safety of his class-dictated "place." The film ends with images of frustration and unfulfillment: Lady Franklin on the sofa, isolated from Cantrip in a wide two-shot, and Steven destroying his car (his livelihood) as he crazily runs it back and forth into stone walls, singing at the top of his lungs. Her madness has been exchanged for his, leaving both alone, having passed each other dangerously closely in a culture which makes open relationships between men and women insurmountably difficult.

Janey Place

THE HOLLY AND THE IVY

Released: 1952
Production: Anatole de Grunwald for London Films
Direction: George More O'Ferrall
Screenplay: Anatole de Grunwald; based on the play of the same name by
Wynyard Browne
Cinematography: Edward Scaife
Editing: Bert Bates
Running time: 83 minutes

Principal characters:
Reverend Martin Gregory .... Ralph Richardson
Jenny Gregory .... Celia Johnson
Margaret Gregory .... Margaret Leighton
Michael "Mick" Gregory .... Denholm Elliott
David Patterson .... John Gregson
Aunt Lydia .... Margaret Halstan
Aunt Bridget .... Maureen Delany
Richard Wyndham .... Hugh Williams

The Holly and the Ivy, a 1952 film, based upon a successful London stage play written by Wynyard Browne, is a contradictory work and one which graphically illustrates the inherent problems in transferring a work from stage to screen. The film's leading actor, Ralph Richardson, summed up the difference between performing on the stage and on the screen by stating that if an actor does something wrong in the theater, it becomes immediately apparent. "The audience starts coughing! The art of acting consists in keeping people from coughing." In a film, however, the actors cannot hear the coughs.

In *The Holly and the Ivy*, it is the acting that overcomes the other flaws in the production and sustains the film, although, interestingly, it is Richardson's performance that is the weakest. Richardson's failure can be traced to a weakness in the script. Although the screenplay raises serious questions and in doing so brings the audience to serious attention, it cheats expectation by attempting to resolve the issues with platitudes. Yet under the masterful direction of George More O'Ferrall and the skillful performances by the distinguished cast, the charade of true feeling depicted in the script actually inspires genuine emotion in the audience.

The subject of the film is a family reunion which takes place at Christmas at the home of an aging country vicar, Reverend Martin Gregory (Ralph Richardson). The vicar's wife is recently deceased, and his daughter Jenny (Celia Johnson) has taken charge of the household. Jenny is one of those selfless daughters who is on the verge of renouncing her suitor, David Patterson (John Gregson), and her personal dreams in order to continue taking care of her father.

Among the relatives welcomed by the vicar and his daughter on Christmas Eve are the son, Mick (Denholm Elliott), a somewhat irresponsible youth serving in the army, and two elderly aunts, Lydia (Margaret Halstan) and Bridget (Maureen Delaney). A cousin, Richard Wyndham (Hugh Williams), arrives with the news that the younger daughter, Margaret (Margaret Leighton), a fashion designer in London, is ill and cannot attend. Margaret does arrive, however, on a later train and it soon becomes obvious that her illness is alcoholism which originates from her brooding over an unhappy past.

At this point, the rather talkative and overly stagey screenplay has gathered the group of people in one place to mull over their problems and their conflicts with one another. Jenny is in love with David, an engineer. She wants to marry him and be free to travel with him to South America or wherever the job takes him. She hopes that her sister Margaret will take over her role and stay home and care for their father. Yet Margaret finds the atmosphere of the vicarage rather oppressive. She has had a child out of wedlock who later died, and she cannot face the pretense of living with a man such as her father who cannot be told the truth. Burdened with guilt and self-pity, she goes out that night with Mick and gets drunk. In fact, although all of the guests are burning with their secret problems, none of them feels free to discuss them with the vicar since he is a parson and might presumably be shocked. "We're involved in a sort of perpetual pretense," states Mick.

The problem of communication is solved on Christmas Day when an argument erupts over Margaret's drinking. Mick becomes angry and speaks a few harsh truths. The vicar finally learns the truth and then sums up his realization of human weaknesses in a rather wordy monologue which indicates that he has arrived at a closer understanding of his children. The two daughters also resolve their problems to their mutual satisfaction. Jenny decides to marry David, and Margaret realizes that she can find genuine happiness in staying home with her father.

It is the crucial scene between the vicar and his prodigal daughter Margaret that causes much of the dissatisfaction with the film on the part of many critics. When she has at last found the courage to discuss her troubles with her father, he can offer no answers beyond some consoling but pious truisms. These statements offer scant evidence to support her sudden conversion to the belief that the vicar was a man of practical wisdom all along. Richardson, although convincing and even touching in other scenes, projects an image in this critical scene of a man who is still too pious to be confronted with sordid reality. The solutions are also too neatly worked out to convey a significant emotional resolution. It is unbelievable, for example, that a father, even one living in a dream world, could fail to notice that his daughter is in love and then, upon finding out after all those years, change his whole life in five minutes to accommodate her needs.

Although the answers to this host of problems gathered under one roof work out rather too easily, *The Holly and the Ivy* is fascinating from start to finish largely because of some first-rate acting. Johnson is the definitive example of domestic devotion and daughterly self-sacrifice right down to the subtle twitch of self-pity at the corner of her mouth. Elliott as Mike, the rebellious son, is splendid in his tantrums and vivid in his drunkenness. Richardson in many scenes is genuinely touching but in others a little too clever with his facial gestures and with his hands. The script by Anatole de Grunwald crackles with lively, bright dialogue and maintains a balance between a spirit of Christmas that is at times sentimental and at others realistic. The script, however, was adapted from the stage play and still looks stagey and confined with little done to open it up, a problem typical of many adaptations of successful plays.

As a drama of minor complication, *The Holly and the Ivy* is, on the whole, literate and deftly performed. It is an adult Christmas story, and if one overlooks its relatively minor flaws and concentrates on the fine acting, it will provide considerable pleasure.

Thomas A. Hanson

HOLLYWOOD BOULEVARD

Released: 1936
Production: William LeBaron for Paramount
Direction: Robert Florey
Screenplay: Marguerite Roberts; based on the story of the same name by Max Marcin and Faith Thomas
Cinematography: Karl Struss
Editing: William Shea
Running time: 83 minutes

Principal characters:

John Blakeford	John Halliday
Patricia Blakeford	Marsha Hunt
Jay Wallace	Robert Cummings
Jordan Winslow	C. Henry Gordon
Flora Moore	Esther Ralston
Alice Winslow	Frieda Inescort
Dr. Sanford	Albert Conti
Detective	Thomas Jackson

Hollywood Boulevard is by no stretch of the imagination a major motion picture, but it does typify the type of film directed by Robert Florey, a man of intelligence and craftsmanship who was responsible for some of the American cinema's best second features and later went on to direct many popular television series, including *The Loretta Young Show* and *Four Star Playhouse*. Born in Paris, France, in 1900, Florey came to the United States in 1921 as a correspondent for the French film magazine, *Cinemagazine*; he later became foreign publicity director for Douglas Fairbanks and Mary Pickford and handled Rudolph Valentino's tour of Europe in 1923. Florey graduated to directing from the position of assistant director, and in 1928 codirected with Slavko Vorkpapich one of the most important American avant-garde shorts, *The Life and Death of 9413—A Hollywood Extra*. Among Florey's more than sixty features are *The Coconuts* (1929, and the first Marx Bros. feature, codirected with Joseph Santley), *Murders in the Rue Morgue* (1932), *The House on 56th Street* (1933), *King of Alcatraz* (1938), *The Desert Song* (1943), *God Is My Co-Pilot* (1945), *The Beast with Five Fingers* (1946), and *Monsieur Verdoux* (1947, codirected with Charles Chaplin). Florey died in Los Angeles on May 16, 1979.

Hollywood Boulevard is unquestionably the best film ever made with a Hollywood filmmaking setting, far superior, for example, to *The Day of the Locust* (1975) or to Florey's earlier *The Preview Murder Mystery* (1935). It provides fascinating glimpses of Hollywood in the 1930's, of the Hollywood-land Sign, the Hollywood Brown Derby, Grauman's Chinese Theater, The

Trocadero, and Sardi's, as well as glimpses of filmmaking at Paramount, obviously staged but nevertheless realistic. More importantly, *Hollywood Boulevard* provides a useful social commentary on the Hollywood scene, its hypocrisy and its compromises.

After a montage of Hollywood landmarks seen under the credits, the film opens in the Brown Derby restaurant, where waiters are seen nailing a caricature of a new Hollywood star, Fred MacMurray, to the wall, and as they do the caricature of a fading star, one John Blakeford, falls to the floor. The two waiters discuss Blakeford, indicating that he is probably now walking Hollywood Boulevard, because "When they put the skids under you in this man's town, you're out," as one waiter succinctly puts it. The mood is set, and in the next scene we do indeed see John Blakeford (played in a suave and urbane manner by John Halliday) walking Hollywood Boulevard. He watches a new star put her footprints in the cement at Grauman's Chinese Theater and overhears a disparaging remark about himself from a child in the crowd. He purchases a newspaper after the newsboy has told him it contains a picture of himself, only to find that the photograph is next to a story about his being sued by his tailor.

When Blakeford visits The Trocadero, a popular Hollywood restaurant and night club of the period on the Sunset Strip, he learns the painful truth from the manager that he is heavily in debt to the establishment and his presence is no longer welcome there. It is also at The Trocadero—in the men's room— that he is approached by a wealthy publisher of scandal magazines, Jordan Winslow (C. Henry Gordon), and offered a considerable sum of money for his life story. Blakeford believes it is because he is a star, but Winslow is only interested in the scandalous love affairs in Blakeford's life. Winslow, unfortunately, is not aware that one of those scandalous love affairs was with his own wife, played in a typically cold and ladylike fashion by Frieda Inescort.

Hollywood Boulevard next moves up the coast from Hollywood to Santa Barbara, where the audience meets Patricia Blakeford's daughter, charmingly portrayed by Marsha Hunt—then new to the screen—who is first seen surrounded by flowers, a shot which accentuates her loveliness and innocent quality. Patricia meets a young writer, Jay Wallace, not too well acted by Robert Cummings, who appears to be giving an impersonation of James Stewart. Wallace gets assigned to a film starring temperamental star Flora Moore (Esther Ralston), another of Blakeford's ex-loves, and while the two are at a Hollywood nightspot, Wallace accidentally punches Blakeford—the punch was intended for a prying photographer—creating further publicity about the fading star and his love life.

Patricia visits her father and begs him for the sake of herself and her mother to end the magazine series. Blakeford has a contract with Winslow, however, which the publisher is unwilling to break, particularly now as he is also secretly financing a film starring Blakeford which will be successful thanks to the publicity from Blakeford's life story. Now Blakeford has met Mrs. Winslow and recognizes her. She goes to his house at night to beg him not to reveal her past, and when Blakeford tries to explain the predicament he is in, she shoots him. At this point, Winslow arrives and, learning the truth, agrees to cancel the series if Blakeford will say the shooting was accidental. No sooner have the Winslows left than Patricia arrives to apologize for her rudeness on her last visit. Unaware of her father's bullet wound, she rushes from the house to join Jay Wallace and drive to Arizona to be married.

She passes friends of Blakeford's as she departs, and when they find the wounded actor and call the police it is not long before Patricia is arrested on suspicion of trying to kill her father. Meanwhile Wallace has discovered that Blakeford had left the Dictaphone, on which he was recording his memoirs, still running while Mrs. Winslow visited him. Armed with the recording, Wallace visits the Winslows, and they and Patricia and the police all troupe to Blakeford's bedroom, where the wounded man announces his shooting was an accident.

If the plot sounds clichéd, the dialogue is even more so. At one point, Blakeford remarks, "Does it occur to any of you that we're acting like the characters in a play—and a very bad play?" Among the more interesting comments in the dialogue are "Only the young could be so bitter" and "Revenge is a pretty cheap emotion." The young writer, Jay Wallace, announces the title for the story he is writing about Hollywood will be "Too much too soon—too bad."

Interestingly, it was director Florey who provided the original story for *Hollywood Boulevard*, and, in fact, based the Cummings character on himself. When Cummings talks of writing a script for a monster movie, Florey is recalling his own first script for the original 1931 production of *Frankenstein*. Much of Florey's story and many of the Hollywood scenes that Florey shot were cut before the release of *Hollywood Boulevard*, as was a cameo by Harold Lloyd, leaving only one cameo appearance—by Gary Cooper—in the film.

What makes *Hollywood Boulevard* particularly fascinating is its use of silent stars, and there are more than twenty such players in the production, including Mae Marsh as Patricia's mother, Francis X. Bushman and Maurice Costello as directors, Charles Ray as an assistant director, Herbert Rawlinson as the manager of Grauman's Chinese Theater, Ruth Clifford as a nurse, and Betty Compson as a film star. No other film featured such an array of talent from the silent era, and the only regret is that too few of the stars receive adequate recognition on the screen. Only two, Creighton Hale (who was once Pearl White's leading man) and Jack Mulhall play themselves.

Hollywood Boulevard was well received by contemporary critics as a minor feature. *Variety* (September 23, 1936) thought it had "one of the best scripts ever possessed by a behind-the-scenes-in-Hollywood picture." Today, the film entertains and even enlightens as a social commentary. This is not a bad record for a "B"-picture of forty years ago.

Anthony Slide

HOME OF THE BRAVE

Released: 1949
Production: Stanley Kramer for United Artists
Direction: Mark Robson
Screenplay: Carl Foreman; based on the play of the same name by Arthur Laurents
Cinematography: Robert de Grasse
Editing: Harry Gerstad
Running time: 88 minutes

Principal characters:
Peter Moss	James Edwards
Major Robinson	Douglas Dick
T. J.	Steve Brodie
Doctor	Jeff Corey
Finch	Lloyd Bridges
Mingo	Frank Lovejoy
Colonel	Cliff Clark

For almost a century after Reconstruction the American black was consigned to the back of the bus, a third-class citizen in a society dominated by Jim Crow. Hollywood reflected and exaggerated this reality. Into the 1940's, most film parts for blacks were as servants or Pullman porter types, characters who seldom developed beyond the shuffling, one-dimensional "mammie/Uncle Tom" stereotypes.

After the Great Depression and World War II, white movie audiences were no longer solely content with the mindless, entertainment-oriented musicals and melodramas which dominated the prewar cinema. A market emerged for films which examined inadequacies in the American system, particularly in the areas of race relations and religious discrimination. With television encroaching upon and soon undermining the box office, the studios had no choice but to comply with the wishes of their public.

Crossfire and *Gentleman's Agreement*, both released in 1947, focused on anti-Semitism. Two years later, no less than four major productions, each of which was well made and critically acclaimed, indicted racial discrimination while preaching tolerance and communication. Each featured protagonists who were black and three-dimensional, each being as honest, as tormented, and as complex as their white counterparts. Each film focused on characters who existed in a society that was inherently racist and who suffered solely because they were born with sepia skins.

In *Lost Boundaries* a light-skinned doctor and his family pass for white and are hypocritically shunned by their neighbors when the truth about their race is discovered; *Intruder in the Dust* features a black man who is falsely accused of murder; in *Pinky* a light-skinned nurse, who has passed for white while living in the North, returns to the racist ambience of her Deep South roots; and, finally, there is *Home of the Brave*. The first to be released, the latter picture is based on a critically acclaimed 1946 Arthur Laurents Broadway play about a young Jewish soldier. A black private named Peter Moss (James Edwards) is substituted in the film, which chronicles his mental breakdown after he is ignored and maligned by some of his fellow GI's while patrolling a Japanese-held island during World War II.

The plot is revealed in flashback. As Moss is examined by an understanding psychiatrist captain (Jeff Corey) after returning from the mission in a state of shock and paralysis, he relates a series of incidents culminating in his illness. In particular, he is bothered by a brazen bigot called T. J. (Steve Brodie), who mercilessly harangues Moss because of the color of his skin. He eventually breaks down when he sees his one real friend, Finch (Lloyd Bridges), killed. It is clear, however, that Moss's troubles are caused as much by the racism to which he was exposed while growing up in America as by the abuse he suffers during the mission. By the age of ten, he tells the captain, he was used to being called a "dirty nigger." After all, "If you're colored, you stink." Yet he is ultimately just another man fighting for his country and should be accepted as such. The film concludes on an upbeat note: Moss, now fully recovered, plans to open a bar with Mingo (Frank Lovejoy), a sympathetic white soldier. The partnership will work because the men respect each other as equals.

Home of the Brave, produced by Stanley Kramer, is one of the producer/director's first "message" films. It is the ancestor of Kramer's *The Defiant Ones* (1958) and *Guess Who's Coming to Dinner* (1967), integrationist features stressing unity between the races. Kramer's contribution is more noteworthy than director Mark Robson's, who that year also directed the hard-hitting *Champion* (1949) for Kramer, and whose uneven filmography ranges from the touching *Bright Victory* (1951) and gritty *The Harder They Fall* (1956) to the dull *Return to Paradise* (1953) and the atrocious *Valley of the Dolls* (1967).

To ensure a maximum amount of publicity and profits and to avoid pre-production protests, *Home of the Brave* was shot in secret. The working title of the project was later used for a film which Kramer produced a few years later and which now is a classic Western—*High Noon* (1952). No "marketable" stars were featured: Douglas Dick, Cliff Clark, and Corey were the only other members of the cast in addition to Edwards, Lovejoy, Bridges, and Brodie.

Yet the historical impact of *Home of the Brave* is monumental. The film, hopelessly dated by today's standards, is intended for white audiences since it depicts blacks in relationship with whites instead of as themselves, and since it ends on a note of well-intentioned although superficial idealism. Although well acted, and adequately scripted by Carl Foreman, the production is far too stagy. The film was, however, the first to deal directly and bluntly with racial discrimination and was also the first in which such words and phrases as "nigger," "nigger lover," and "boogie" were uttered on screen. *Home of the Brave* was praised for its forthrightness and honesty in 1949, with Edwards' acting singled out for commendation. The production was named to the National Board of Review's list of ten best films of the year. While it was banned in South Africa, the response to the film in America was heartening. For example, prointegration protesters picketed a segregated theater in Austin, Texas, in which the film was being screened.

The production, release, and acclaim of *Home of the Brave* marks the turning point in the manner in which black Americans have been depicted by Hollywood. This reception allowed for the acceptability of filming screenplays which explored and condemned racial prejudice. Of the four "message" films, *Pinky* was by far the biggest hit. It was the second highest grossing feature of the year, taking in $4,200,000. *Home of the Brave*, which cost only $511,000 to produce, was ranked a respectable twenty-seventh for the year and earned a tidy profit: box-office receipts totaled $2,500,000. *Lost Boundaries* was forty-eighth, with $2,000,000, while *Intruder in the Dust* (curiously, the best of the lot due largely to Juano Hernandez' bravura performance) was not among the top ninety-two films listed in *Variety*; it garnered less than $1,500,000.

A year after *Home of the Brave* was released, a young actor named Sidney Poitier appeared in his first film, *No Way Out*. That drama focuses on a young black doctor whose budding career is almost ruined by a racist hoodlum who accuses him of murdering the gangster's brother when the pair are wounded and hospitalized after an attempted robbery. Poitier's looks and charm enabled him to become the first black actor to achieve full-fledged Hollywood stardom. That success eluded Edwards, although the appearance and demeanor of the *Home of the Brave* star was certainly acceptable to white audiences. In the same year that the film was released, Edwards gave a sparkling performance as a perceptive young prizefighter in *The Set-Up*; the actor was then a prime candidate to become the model of the integrationist black who was to emerge on screen during the next decade. During the early 1950's he was effective as a patriotic soldier fighting the Korean War in *The Steel Helmet* (1951), and as a sightless GI befriended by a blind, bigoted white man in *Bright Victory*. He refused, however, to testify concerning his politics before the House UnAmerican Activities Committee and, as a result, lost a prominent role to Poitier in *Red Ball Express* (1952). He appeared inauspiciously in features ranging from *The Member of the Wedding* in 1952 to *The Sandpiper* (1965). His last part was in 1970, a bit as George C. Scott's valet in *Patton*. He died that same year.

Rob Edelman

THE HOME TOWNERS

Released: 1928
Production: Warner Bros.
Direction: Bryan Foy
Screenplay: Addison Burkhart and Murray Roth; based on the play of the same name by George M. Cohan
Cinematography: Barney McGill
Editing: no listing
Running time: 94 minutes

Principal characters:

Vic Arnold	Richard Bennett
Beth Calhoun	Doris Kenyon
P. H. Bancroft	Robert McWade
Mr. Calhoun	Robert Edeson
Lottie Bancroft	Gladys Brockwell
Joe Roberts	John Miljan
Mrs. Calhoun	Vera Lewis
Wally Calhoun	Stanley Taylor

Late in October, 1928, Warner Bros. released a third all-talking feature, *The Home Towners*. The studio had learned from its two previous experiences, *The Lights of New York* (1928) and *The Terror* (1928), that if a picture is going to talk, the dialogue must be worth listening to. *The Home Towners* was adapted from a successful Broadway play by George M. Cohan, and all of its players had had years of experience in the theater. As the weekly *Variety* critic noted, *The Home Towners* is probably the first instance in the use of dialogue where tempo is achieved. Every reel of *The Home Towners* is entertaining, and the situations build to natural climaxes, which could hardly be said for either *The Lights of New York* or *The Terror*.

Performances benefited also because Robert McWade, playing P. H. Bancroft, was translating to the talking screen a role he had successfully created on the New York stage. Bancroft is a do-gooder who comes from South Bend, Indiana, all the way to the big city to serve as best man at his best friend's wedding. The friend is Vic Arnold (Richard Bennett), a man in his late forties, of considerable means, who is about to marry a woman only about half his age, Beth Calhoun (Doris Kenyon). Bancroft suspects the worst, that the woman has to be a fortune hunter. To his mind no young lady of her years would consider a man of Vic Arnold's maturity. Bancroft's genial wife, Lottie (Gladys Brockwell), tries to keep her husband from interfering in affairs that are not his, but Bancroft's mind is that of the suspicious small-towner who believes that women seeking husbands have got to have an ulterior motive: in this case, the groom's considerable wealth.

Bancroft is well-meaning, but he is not content until his suspicions color Vic Arnold's thinking, and Beth, in a cool rage, returns her engagement ring. Almost at once, Bancroft learns that Beth and her family are richer than Arnold has ever been. Contrite, Bancroft now tries to patch up the differences he has caused, creating new suspicions and aggravating his own wife to a point that she almost washes her hands of him. The situation is finally resolved, however, and the wedding takes place, with the principals reunited, contrite, and ready to let bygones be bygones.

Onstage it was a typical Cohan domestic comedy, with believable characters in a believable predicament, and lots of good, hearty, middle-class American humor. All this was transferred to the screen. One would never know that Bryan Foy, who directed this very lively and human comedy, had also been the director for *The Lights of New York*. This time he was successful because he had a good script and better than competent actors. He wisely created an almost literal transcription of the successful Cohan comedy; he had enough sense not to try and improve it, but simply to stage it for the camera much as it had been played in the theater.

McWade's performance of a small-town American, complete with all his faults and prejudices, distrustful of any "citified" sophistication, is neatly balanced by Richard Bennett as the city friend who for once trusts his heart and is nearly brought to disaster by loyalty to an oldtime friend who has not kept up with the changing times.

Brockwell's performance as Lottie Bancroft is highly commendable, and Brockwell, one of the best players in silent films, a star at one time in her own right on stage and screen, was bound for a new career in talking pictures, where her talents as a character actress could well have been utilized. Unfortunately, the very next year after *The Home Towners*, in 1929, she was killed in an automobile accident in Hollywood.

The Home Towners was a talkie debut for Kenyon, who had been a star in silent specials at First National with her husband, Milton Sills. Widowed, she filmed *The Home Towners* the year following her husband's tragic death. Any criticism her performance evoked, largely that her voice was pitched too high to be natural, was to be corrected when the Vitaphone process of recording was abandoned. Kenyon continued as an important film player until 1939, and then played television roles successfully during the 1950's.

One thing that *The Home Towners* did was to show film producers that there was a market for domestic situation comedy, and the next decade was to exploit that genre to the fullest. It also showed conclusively that the one-hundred-percent talking feature was here to stay. With only two previous ones at Warner Bros., both of which had more than their share of faults, the talking feature nearly came of age in *The Home Towners*. Critics complained that the players still walked about the sets only in order to reach a vase of flowers or some *objet d'art* masking the presence of a microphone, but the actors were professional and went about their business naturally. Only a carping critic of the medium would know where a microphone might be hidden.

With every production, the talking feature showed more finesse. When one considers that the silent medium was based entirely upon pantomime, it is all the more remarkable that actors and directors could adapt so quickly to the talking feature, which made entirely different demands upon a player. There was more than visual action and reaction; vocal skill was mandatory. The players from the theater who were imported to Hollywood and did not click, failed because they lacked that one thing the silent player had made a part of his performance: action and reaction and expressing thought with the eyes, so often called "the mirror of the soul." With the talking film, listening was now more important than it had ever been because it was coexistent with speech. During the next year, 1929, the new art of the talking film would really reach its first fine budding.

DeWitt Bodeen

HORSE FEATHERS

Released: 1932
Production: Paramount
Direction: Norman Z. McLeod
Screenplay: Bert Kalmar, Harry Ruby, and S. J. Perelman
Cinematography: Ray June
Editing: no listing
Music: Bert Kalmar and Harry Ruby
Running time: 69 minutes

Principal characters:
Professor Wagstaff .... Groucho Marx
Harpo .... Himself
Chico .... Himself
Zeppo .... Himself
Connie Barley .... Thelma Todd
Jennings .... David Landau

Considered by some critics as second only to their masterpiece *Duck Soup* (1933), *Horse Feathers* is one of several classic films in which the Marx Brothers starred. It was their fourth film, and it is a remarkably balanced vehicle designed to exploit the brothers' singular comic virtues while at the same time merging each distinctive *tour de force* into a championship team performance. On the surface are the personalities and comic elements that have been so well remembered by American audiences. Groucho, as Professor Wagstaff, brims with his familiar insults and idiosyncratic romancing as he engages in some of the best anarchic, nonsensical dialogue of his film career. Harpo, whose infamous pockets this time even provide him a hatchet with which to cut in half a deck of cards, storms through his obsessive girl-prodding, slapstick, and gags. Chico, a bootlegger, projects his personal brand of swindling and connivery, and Zeppo, the straight man, portrays a character of more dominance with more screen time than usual. As in all of the films written specifically for the Marx Brothers, the viewer can expect nothing to be considered sacred. Nonsense is the name of the game.

Although inconsistent (as was usual), the plot seems uniquely suited to the Marx Brothers' individual talents. The film opens with Professor Wagstaff assuming the presidency of Huxley College. He accepts the offer in order to save his son, Zeppo, from a helpless infatuation with Connie Bailey (Thelma Todd), a campus widow. Zeppo is not concerned with his affair, however, and worries that his father may not meet the challenge of his new position. There has been a different president at the school each year since 1888, when Huxley last won a football game. Zeppo suggests that only a winning football team can remedy the sagging, infirm college, so Wagstaff goes off to a speakeasy to recruit a couple of athletes with whom he might beef up his team for an upcoming game against Darwin, a rival school. Chico and Harpo, who distribute contraband alcohol, are speak-easy regulars, and Wagstaff mistakenly recruits them for his team; the two real athletes were already recruited by Jennings (David Landau), who works for the Darwin team.

The fast-paced story jockeys back and forth along the paths that the different characters pave, allowing ample time for gags and general nonsense. Groucho tries to straighten out Zeppo's lovelife by paying a visit to the vivacious Mrs. Barley, and promptly attempts to seduce her. "I tell you, you're ruining that boy. You're ruining him. Why can't you do as much for me?" he begs. It is the beginning of a scene that features all four brothers, playing a classic game of hide-and-seek and musical couch. The innocent Zeppo is made a cuckold; Groucho cuts up with puns and his unique doing-one-thing-and-blaming-another routines; Chico swoons in Italian; and Harpo seems to capture the nature of it all by scrambling in and out of the room with a huge block of ice, finally heaving it through an unopened window. The scene also includes Chico and Harpo at their respective instruments, the piano and harp. As always, these musical numbers serve as an interlude to the burlesque, but the effect is achieved with performances that stress style rather than any serious musical interest. Certainly, Zeppo and Groucho's opening number, "I'm Against It," is more original and appealing than the later numbers. Perhaps instinctively, Groucho acknowledges the problem by walking up to the camera and speaking to the audience, "Listen, I have to stay here, but why don't you folks go out for a smoke until this thing blows over?"

Unfortunately, when the brothers separate again the sequences begin to lag and, with the exception of Groucho and Mrs. Barley's "romantic" canoe ride, lose the energy of the earlier scenes. This was not entirely the fault of the Marx Brothers, however; it was a musical comedy convention of the time to tie the film into a tidy, anticlimactic conclusion. The attention in the latter episodes all too deliberately focuses on the subsequent football game, which involves the expected pratfalls that lead to the expected results. The film ends abruptly with a brief scene in which Mrs. Barley marries each of the victorious brothers.

Horse Feathers is a particularly successful film because Norman McLeod, also responsible for *Animal Crackers* (1930), affords the Marx Brothers a relatively free hand to display their special brand of comedy. It transfers onto the screen the best of the personalities that took years of vaudeville and theater to develop. At one end of the spectrum, the leader, Groucho, is a supreme punster and comedian with a mouthful of insults, and Harpo, at the other end, is the champion gag-man who perfected his brilliant stage pantomine methodology on the screen. Their collective personalities provide a unique brand of catharsis for the audience with no punches held back. If they are funny, it is because the barrages of lunacy are cartoonish and absolutely detached. Groucho and Chico's conversational virtuosity penetrates a lavishly nonsensical world, like that of Harpo's, and stays there. The Marx Brothers' "lickety-split" craziness disguises its meaningful commentary. The audience is properly distracted and relieved of the social and political implications that dominate other schools of humor. At the base of the brothers' free-for-all comedy, there is a recognizable idealism. A kind of heroism, in fact, is found in their subversion of authority and in their ability to put themselves in positions of power, where, of course, they can be most destructive to society. When the Marx Brothers are given the screen time to be funny for humor's sake, as they are most of the way through *Horse Feathers*, a memorable piece of comic film history results.

Ralph Angel

THE HORSE'S MOUTH

Released: 1958
Production: John Bryan for Knightsbridge/United Artists
Direction: Ronald Neame
Screenplay: Alec Guinness; based on the novel of the same name by Joyce Cary
Cinematography: Arthur Ibbetson
Editing: Anne V. Coates
Running time: 96 minutes

Principal characters:

Gulley Jimson	Alec Guinness
Coker	Kay Walsh
Sarah	Renee Houston
Nosey	Mike Morgan
Hickson	Ernest Thesiger

There are many things to praise about *The Horse's Mouth*. Foremost is the fact that it is as fresh now as it was upon its first release in 1958—and if possible, even more enjoyable. It also stands as a peak in the career of Alec Guinness, who not only starred in the film, but wrote the screenplay as well, based on the novel of the same name by Joyce Cary. The film has no "plot" as such, although it does tell a story: the forward movement comes from showing its hero, Gulley Jimson, in all of his phases. Jimson (Alec Guinness) is a painter, revered as a genius although he is never much more than flat broke.

He is introduced as he comes out of jail after a month's stay, having been imprisoned for threatening an elderly art collector named Hickson (Ernest Thesiger). Gulley is getting on in years himself, and his feud with Hickson goes back a long way—as do his feuds with everyone else. Within five minutes of being released he not only threatens Hickson a second time (by phone, using a chorus of mimicked voices), but also steals a bicycle from the admiring boy who came to welcome him (Mike Morgan). This boy, called "Nosey," considers himself the disciple of Gulley Jimson "the great artist," although neither this nor his patience with the theft makes him more likable to Gulley, who leaves the boy stranded all the same.

What follows is a blow-by-blow account of Gulley's ongoing struggle, harassing Hickson his old patron, Sarah his ex-wife (Renee Houston), Coker his present lady friend (Kay Walsh), and his indefatigable disciple Nosey, not to mention the sundry strangers he runs across, all for the purpose of keeping himself free to continue performing his art. It is the one thing more important to him than life itself, and the result is a comic vision of *The Agony and the Ecstasy*: the suffering artist as slapstick hero.

No matter how broad the comedy, the film never detracts from, or makes unnecessary light of, the profound truths it addresses. If anything, it deepens the view. Lying in the cabin of his ramshackle houseboat, Gulley foresees what will be the crowning achievement of his life's work, a triptych of religious oils: *The Garden of Eden*, *The Raising of Lazarus*, and *The Last Judgement*. *The Garden of Eden*, as it happens, is almost complete. (The paintings are, in actuality, by John Bratby.) Gulley's style as a painter is beautiful but hardwon—tortuous, vivid, alive, difficult—very much like himself.

Invited to a wealthy man's home to discuss "art," he sees a wall upon which he feels his Lazarus must be painted. He falls in love with the wall the way the hero of any other story would fall in love with another person: moonstruck, in love with the possibilities. Brought in reality to flatter the wife's watercolors, Jimson flatters the rich man's wall instead and offers to grace their apartment with his mural of Lazarus. The couple (who prefer the status of collecting artists to the more visceral demands of art) demur; they offer the excuse that they are going on a holiday. Jimson nods cryptically. The moment they are out the door he is scheming to let himself back in—which he does, pawning their furniture to buy materials, devastating their apartment when he invites a sculptor friend to join him, and completing his *Lazarus* one day in advance of their shocked return. He is dissatisfied with the results, however; the vision is always far more beautiful than the execution.

Returning home, he falls ill and is told upon his arrival that Hickson has died. Gulley feels his own death closing in. In his melancholy, he falls back into the pattern of harassing his mistress and his ex-wife. After a small misadventure in which his ex-wife is knocked unconscious in a tug-of-war over one of Gulley's early works that is worth a great deal now, but is of sentimental value to his wife, he jumps out the bedroom window emptyhanded and hides mournfully in the nave of an old cathedral. There he is aroused with fresh enthusiasm as he sees the wall upon which he will erect *The Last Judgement*. He has Nosey place an advertisement in the newspaper, announcing art lessons. The name Gulley Jimson, widely revered by now as a result of an exhibition of his paintings at the National Gallery, draws an immense crowd of young people, each of whom have to pay six shillings and are more than eager to carry out Gulley's instructions. The tuition goes to pay for materials. *The Last Judgement* is completed, and Gulley is pleased with his work for the first time. The cathedral, however, is condemned. In the climactic scene, the young people fight the wrecking crew in vain. The iron ball swings, and Gulley's great masterpiece collapses into dust. Strangely, Gulley is not overly ruffled by this disaster: he completed the work and put it into the world, whatever its fate. It is on this note of unprecedented resignation that he dashes from the scene of the wreck, hops aboard his houseboat, casts off, and sets sail downriver for the open sea to seek his further destiny. Nosey props himself on the rails of a bridge, calling out to Gulley that he was the equal of the greats: "Michelangelo, Rubens, Blake—you're one of them!" By this time, of course, Gulley is well out of earshot.

"You asked me," Guinness once told *The New York Times*, "to write you a synopsis of *The Horse's Mouth*, but I'm afraid I find it an impossible task." It is also difficult to discuss his screenplay. Another title for the film might have been "The Dream of an Artist," because that is both what it shows and, in the substance of its tale, from where it comes. It operates on a complex level, being at once a very realistic account of an extraordinary life, a surrealistic account of an average artist's life, and a fabulous and magical dream of what life is like, for everyone, at its core. Art is, in any case, the defining principle. It has a positively mystical value in the universe of Gulley Jimson, one that is harmonious with traditional religions, as witnessed by the subjects of his murals. Further, Guinness is himself a practicing Catholic, a fact which is both reflected in and goes a long way toward explaining this as his choice for a vehicle. That Gulley is using traditional forms to express himself freely embodies both a Christian mystery and an artistic paradox. The film, overall, has the quality of symbolic litany, like the stations of the cross, an effect heightened by the nature and chronological order of the three murals; the paintings are a metaphor for Gulley's inner and outer progress.

The dialogue is first-rate and relies heavily upon Cary's novel, from which it was adapted. Gulley's incessant mumblings, monologues, and dialogues have about them the novelistic quality of stream-of-consciousness. In addition to proving himself an able screenwriter, Guinness is a consummate actor, here, as elsewhere. A master of disguise, he had filled eight roles in *Kind Hearts and Coronets* (1949), playing an entire family of heirs to a dukedom. In this film he plays a white-haired septugenarian and later, in *Tunes of Glory* (1960), also directed by Ronald Neame, he plays a Scottish officer on the plateau of middle age.

Neame is a strong disciple of relentless dramatic structure. After directing *The Horse's Mouth*, he went on to do *Tunes of Glory*, *Gambit* (1966), and *The Prime of Miss Jean Brodie* (1969). Each of his films displays a compulsion to keep audience interest alive, to create the necessary momentum toward the climax. There is likewise a steady building of interest in *The Horse's Mouth*. The subtle foreshadowings of death that present themselves to Gulley and give this ending so much meaning are all in Guinness' reactions to the signs. In weeping at Hickson's death, for example, the understanding that his bitterest antagonist would also be his dearest friend is beautifully rendered in Gulley's face, in addition to providing the right impetus for him to confront his own death, both physical and artistic, and to bring about his catharsis in *The Last Judgement*.

If the film has any weakness, it may be that it is too episodic and that some degree of confusion keeps these separate elements from illuminating one another fully and thus producing their maximum effect. Yet the contribution of *The Horse's Mouth* to film history is prominent, if only because it manages, through its screenplay and Guinness' performance, to be the pure and personal expression of one of the cinema's great artists. Critical reaction upon the film's first release was positive, and it had a good box-office run, with the screenplay being nominated for an Oscar. It has had a long and fruitful life both on television and in rerun theaters because of its fresh ability to delight, decades after its first run. *The Horse's Mouth* does not date with age, it improves with it.

F. X. Feeney

HOT MILLIONS

Released: 1968
Production: Mildred Freed Alberg for Metro-Goldwyn-Mayer
Direction: Eric Till
Screenplay: Peter Ustinov and Ira Wallach
Cinematography: Kenneth Higgins
Editing: Richard Marden
Running time: 107 minutes

Principal characters:
Marcus Pendleton .... Peter Ustinov
Patty Terwilliger .... Maggie Smith
Carlton Klemper .... Karl Malden
Willard C. Gnatpole .... Bob Newhart
Caesar Smith .... Robert Morley

Hot Millions is a crime caper, but it should not be dismissed as a nonsensical bit of fluff. It is a cleverly wrought, cosmopolitan comedy in which two of Britain's most accomplished performers skillfully display the broad range of their talents. A distinguished actor and director, Peter Ustinov tapped his writing genius to collaborate with Ira Wallach in creating a character perfectly matching his comic screen *persona.* Ustinov plays Marcus Pendleton, who is about to be released from a term at Wormwood Scrubs prison once he completes the falsification of the warden's tax return. He is a liberal who has been serving time for embezzling from the Central Conservative Office. Although he was caught not by the police but by a computer, he resents computers not for their crime detection but because they have rendered obsolete embezzlers who require books to juggle.

Once he is a free man on the streets of London, Pendleton is faced with the exigencies of finding a job. Our faith in his reformed ways is inspired when he picks up several booklets outlining careers in data processing seemingly in preparation for learning an honest trade. He reads them only to catch the jargon, however; he then poses as a gentleman, wearing a new, bought-on-time pinstripe suit and bowler hat, and gains entry into an elite club to hobnob with the upper classes. At the club, Pendleton astoundingly gleans enough inside information on the hierarchies of computer-based corporations to plot his next move. Robert Morley portrays a renowned British authority on computers, Caesar Smith. As part of his scheme Marcus cunningly persuades Smith to leave for South America to pursue his passion, moths.

The plight of Patty Terwilliger is meanwhile unfolding. Maggie Smith, an actress capable of such deeply dramatic performances as the title role in *The Prime of Miss Jean Brodie* (1969) and well-known as the blasé sophisticate in the play *Private Lives*, here exhibits her versatility playing Patty, a dizzy

London woman with an outrageous Cockney twang. All legs and no brains, she takes a flat in the same seedy rooming house as Marcus but is barely able to support herself because of her inability to hold a job. The dimwitted redhead fails as a meter maid, a bus conductress, and even as an usherette.

Now passing himself off as the computer expert Caesar Smith, Marcus is hired by Carlton Klemper (Karl Malden), president of Ta Can Co, an American industrial conglomerate headquartered in London. The secretary hired for him is, alas, Patty. Nearly as inept as Patty, Marcus bluffs his way through some tight moments, many under the gaze of suspicious Willard Gnatpole (Bob Newhart), Klemper's officious and unctuous right-hand man. Fearful of smudging her dress while coping with the yards of ribbon the typewriter has mysteriously spewed out, Patty one morning greets Marcus in only her slip. When Gnatpole learns of the compromising situation in which she and Marcus have been discovered, his interest in her is immediately aroused. To discourage Gnatpole, she invites Marcus to dinner when Gnatpole can hear her. Her boss reluctantly agrees, although he prefers returning to the office late at night to continue his nefarious investigation of the elaborate hardware.

One night Pendleton is discovered investigating the computer's failsafe system and is delivered to the alarmed Klemper and Gnatpole. His nonchalant tale that he was testing the equipment's security system ingratiates him with Klemper but further alienates the contemptuous Gnatpole, his rival at the office and for the affections of Patty. Marcus perseveres and is finally rewarded with the secret of successfully putting the computer out of operation when he secretly witnesses the company's charwoman warming her tea on one of the computer's hot coils, thus temporarily putting the machine out of function. He is then able to use the computer to his own advantage by programming it to print sheets of checks made out to bogus corporations of which Marcus is the "director." He makes monthly trips to a Paris bar, a Roman barbershop, and a Frankfurt bakery, the locations of these "corporations," to retrieve and cash the checks.

Because they discover that they can play classical music together—Patty on the flute and Marcus on the piano—and because Patty needs a means of support, having been fired by the computer for frequent tardiness, Patty and Marcus tremulously permit the deck of cards to decide their future: the queen of hearts decrees marriage. A dutiful but dotty wife, Patty retrieves the large amounts of foreign currency she finds carelessly left in her husband's suits as she sends them to be dry cleaned. Fearing for Marcus' health, she asks Gnatpole to relieve him of the great deal of foreign traveling he has been doing for the business, unwittingly alerting Gnatpole to the malfeasance.

So that he can collect one last time the checks awaiting him in Europe, Marcus has Patty, now wise to his scheme, detain Gnatpole to delay his investigation of the foreign affairs. Marcus has meanwhile learned of his impending fatherhood and resolves to provide a safe haven for his family in

Rio de Janeiro. He and Patty arrive there soon after Gnatpole discovers elegantly lettered corporate titles on the doors of the bar, barbershop, and bakery. The real Caesar Smith, called back from his moth-hunting expedition to explain to the board the technicalities of Marcus' machinations, is delighted with the embezzler's genius at mastering the system.

The enraged Klemper and Gnatpole, however, cannot press charges against Marcus lest the bad publicity force Ta Can Co stock to nosedive. Unknown to Marcus, Patty invites the two to Brazil and suggests that her husband be forgiven in exchange for one half of the thousands of shares of stock in Ta Can Co's holdings that she has bought these last months with the money she has gleaned from Marcus' suits. She further suggests for him the post of treasurer of the company. His flabbergasted colleagues are only too happy to comply. With the fortune Patty has amassed, the two are able to pursue their dream: Marcus as a flailing conductor of a symphony orchestra and Patty as his first flutist.

Even the most jaundiced critic will succumb to the endearing nuttiness and dizzy logic of this pair. The ease and timing with which they deliver their comic lines and droll asides are astonishingly delightful. Ustinov's facial gymnastics are brilliant and varied, particularly when he is putting on airs. His takes, especially in response to Smith's idiocy, clinch scenes, and director Eric Till swiftly cuts to the consequent action. The smooth composition of the film permits full attention to be focused on the humor.

The screenplay wisely spares us undue preoccupation with the details and tedious techniques of the crime itself. It is through depth of characterization of Marcus Pendleton that criminality is revealed. A man capable of intense concentration and tenacity, he is also highly inventive in coping with either a computer program or an empty-headed woman. If his lack of malice does not redeem him, his love and practice of fine music should temper our judgment of him.

Originally entitled *Hot Millions: Or, a True Tale of Crime and Rascality*, this absurdly funny film is sophisticated enough in its presentation and dialogue to provoke adult laughter, from giggles to guffaws.

Nancy S. Kinney

HOUR OF THE GUN

Released: 1967
Production: John Sturges for United Artists
Direction: John Sturges
Screenplay: Edward Anhalt
Cinematography: Lucien Ballard
Editing: Ferris Webster
Running time: 101 minutes

Principal characters:

Wyatt Earp	James Garner
Doc Holliday	Jason Robards
Ike Clanton	Robert Ryan
Virgil Earp	Frank Converse
Morgan Earp	Sam Melville
Andy Warshaw	Steve Ihnat
Pete Spence	Michael Tolan
Frank Stilwell	Robert Phillips
Curly Bill Brocius	Jon Voight

In the annals of the Old West, there are few events more celebrated than the shootout between the Earps and the Clantons at the O. K. Corral in Tombstone, Arizona. Wyatt Earp had made a name for himself as a lawman in the rough cowtowns of Wichita and Dodge City; by the early 1880's, he and his brothers, Virgil, Morgan, and Warren, had gravitated to Arizona Territory, where they became embroiled in a dispute with Ike Clanton, a local patriarch. Matters came to a head on October 26, 1881, when the Earps and their friend Doc Holliday, a dentist turned gambler, drinker, and gunfighter, shot it out with the Clanton gang at the O. K. Corral.

It was a classic Western scenario, and one that has attracted a number of filmmakers. *Law and Order* (1932), *Frontier Marshall* (1939), and *Wichita* (1955) all retold various aspects of the Earp story, as did *The Life and Legend of Wyatt Earp*, a popular television show of the 1950's. The two most notable tellers of the Earp tale, however, were directors John Ford and John Sturges. Ford's version of the Earp/Holliday legend was his magnificent *My Darling Clementine* (1946). Although Ford took more liberties with the facts than did other directors, *My Darling Clementine*, featuring Henry Fonda as Wyatt Earp and Victor Mature as Doc Holliday, is surely one of the finest Westerns of all time.

In 1957, Sturges first addressed himself to the shootout with *Gunfight at the O. K. Corral*, with Burt Lancaster as Earp and Kirk Douglas as Holliday. Both Ford's film and this one, however, concentrated on the development of the relationship between Earp and Holliday (with Ford adding a little romance along the way). These films, like the other versions of Earp's career, ended, for all practical purposes, with the dramatic gunfight.

Ten years after *Gunfight at the O. K. Corral*, Sturges shot what might be considered a sequel to his earlier film. *Hour of the Gun* featured James Garner as Wyatt Earp and Jason Robards as Doc Holliday, and dealt with the aftermath of the gunfight, as the survivors continued their feud. *Hour of the Gun* begins with the gunfight. As the credits appear on the screen, we see two bands of men maneuvering around the Corral. There is no dialogue, although the music on the soundtrack heightens the tension. Guns blaze, and the men inside the Corral fall dead, although several of their allies leave the scene without a fight.

The dead men, of course, are members of the Clanton gang; Ike Clanton (Robert Ryan) is one of those who abandons the field. There is a brief verbal dispute between the victorious Earps and the Cochise County sheriff, Jimmy Ryan (Bill Fletcher), who is on Clanton's payroll, and who attempts to arrest the Earps and Holliday for murder. It soon becomes clear that, whatever the specific incident that led to the showdown, the real battle is for political control of Tombstone, where Virgil Earp (Frank Converse) is the town marshal.

Sturges introduces most of the principals in the film through their testimony at the Earps' murder trial. First to testify is Doc Holliday, who describes his transformation from dentist to gambler thus: "I discovered that there was more gold in people's pockets than in their mouths." Robards' Holliday is a charming rogue with an irreverent disdain for the niceties of society, but he is also intensely loyal to his comrade: "I'd go to hell and back on the word of Wyatt Earp," he says defiantly. Next to testify is Ike Clanton, who suavely describes his hired killers as accountants and stock breeders. Lurking beneath his bland public mask, however, is a man completely without scruples, who has sacrificed his son Billy to try to gain political and economic control of Tombstone, and who is capable of treating his employees with the same contempt with which he treats his enemies.

Wyatt Earp is the last witness to take the stand. He calmly acknowledges his family's grudge (the nature of which is never specified in the film) against the Clantons, but just as calmly—and convincingly—denies that his feelings about the Clantons led him to commit any crime at the O. K. Corral. He and his colleagues were forced to kill the Clanton gang in the line of duty. Indeed, the concepts of duty and respect for the law appear again and again in Earp's statements in the early part of the film, reinforcing his image as a just and dispassionate man. As the film progresses, Sturges reveals that Earp's public image, like Clanton's, masks a darker side of his character. At present, however, this side of Earp is hidden from the audience, and from Earp as well.

As the trial ends, the judge weighs the evidence and finds the Earps and Holliday innocent; but their acquittal only serves to set the stage for more violence. At first, all of the violence comes from the Clantons. Determined to eliminate his opposition, Ike Clanton orders the ambush first of Virgil and then of Morgan Earp (Sam Melville). Virgil survives, although he is crippled for life. Morgan is killed instantly. The two incidents snap something inside Wyatt, although outwardly he remains calm. He secures an appointment as federal marshal, with orders to hunt down Curly Bill Brocious (Jon Voight), Frank Stilwell (Robert Phillips), Pete Spence (Michael Tolan), and Andy Warshaw (Steve Ihnat), four of Clanton's hired gunmen who were identified as Morgan Earp's killers. In addition, there is a five-thousand-dollar reward for each man—if he is captured alive.

The film's perspective then begins to shift to that of Doc Holliday. Sturges leavens the hunt for the four killers with occasional bits of humor—Holliday's recruitment of a motley posse of two is priceless—but mainly we watch Holliday as he observes Wyatt Earp being eaten away by the desire for revenge, to the point that he abandons any attempt to bring the men in for trial. He simply catches up with them one by one and kills them. The problem, in Holliday's eyes, is not that Earp kills the men who murdered his brother, but that he refuses to acknowledge, to himself or to others, that he is killing for revenge rather than for justice. In each instance, he tricks or goads his captives into going for their guns, thus maintaining the pretense of shooting them in self-defense. The audience is gradually persuaded into thinking what Holliday knew all along: that Earp's actions are hypocritical.

Sturges introduces a subplot about Holliday's declining health—he is dying of tuberculosis complicated by alcoholism—that takes Holliday and Earp to a sanatorium in Denver. Watching his friend die slowly shakes Wyatt. He begins to examine his own life and concludes that Doc was right about his reasons for killing his brother's murderers: "I don't care about the rules anymore. I'm not that much of a hypocrite." Word reaches Denver that Ike Clanton has taken refuge in Nogales, Mexico. Earp determines to hunt him down, and Holliday, although he fears for Wyatt's sanity if he succumbs to the impulse to kill Clanton, nevertheless accompanies his friend.

They corner Clanton in Mexico, and in a tense scene, Sturges heightens the excitement with humor. Holliday: "You got some kind of plan?" Earp: "Yep." "You want to tell me about it?" "We take whoever gets in our way." "You call that a plan?" "You got a better one?" "Nope." Visually, the gun battle is reminiscent of the opening sequence at the O. K. Corral—there is no dialogue, and the tension is maintained by expert staging and editing. Inevitably, Earp shoots Clanton down. The film ends back in Denver. The two friends part, awkwardly at first, and then affectionately. Earp rides back towards Tombstone, there to pursue a career as a gambler. The dying Holliday watches silently from the balcony of the sanatorium as his friend departs.

Aside from the unusual plot premise—following the careers of Earp and Holliday *after* the O. K. Corral—*Hour of the Gun*'s principal charm lies in the performance of its cast. In truth, the acting in the film ranges from disappointing to outstanding. Garner, ordinarily a fine, relaxed actor, is surprisingly stiff as Wyatt Earp. In this film, Earp is a man whose sense of justice is confused by a stronger thirst for revenge—the type of role that John Wayne handled well in *Red River* (1948) and *The Searchers* (1956), for example—and Garner simply underplays the part. The result is that the geniality that Garner effortlessly breathes into less complicated characters such as Bret Maverick and Jim Rockford (his two popular television characterizations), is almost entirely missing in Wyatt Earp. Garner's performance is not bad, however; it merely pales next to that of Robards. Robards as Doc Holliday is the complete rascal. Writer Edward Ahnalt clearly saw Holliday as the film's most sympathetic character, a hard-eyed realist with a good heart and a sense of humor, and gave him the best lines. Robards obviously enjoyed the role and made the most of it. His performance is the highlight of the film.

Among the supporting cast, Fletcher as Sheriff Jimmy Ryan and a very young Voight as Curly Bill Brocious—both bad guys—stand out. Ryan is also fine in the role of Ike Clanton, the villain of the film. His Clanton was a truly contemptible man. He even hates his own employees. Ryan's best scene is at the Earp trial where his testimony is so palpably insincere that it is almost funny. Ryan made a career out of performances such as this.

Director Sturges' forte has always been the action film, as witnessed in his greatest successes—*The Magnificent Seven* (1960), *The Great Escape* (1963), and *Joe Kidd* (1972). *Hour of the Gun* is a typical Sturges film in this regard. Its best moments occur in the scenes in which explosive action or the threat/promise of such action occurs. The gunfight at the beginning of the film best exemplifies Sturges' skill. The sequence is filmed without dialogue because there is no need for it. The images on the screen are self-explanatory, and the staging and editing of the scene create a tension that renders words superfluous. It is in the intervals between the action sequences that *Hour of the Gun* occasionally bogs down. The presence of Doc Holliday, easily the film's most engaging character, remedies the situation in some scenes; but there are nevertheless undeniable lulls in the film.

Although imperfect, *Hour of the Gun* is in many respects a fascinating film. Sturges is to be commended for taking familiar characters and following them down unfamiliar paths. In addition to the exciting gunfights and the bravura performance by Robards, Sturges' film is a forerunner of the male bonding sagas that were to dominate American films in the 1970's. Sturges does not emphasize the relationship between Holliday and Earp in the same way that his successors would do eventually, but the dialogue between the two men before the final shootout could have served as the model for the entire script of George Roy Hill's *Butch Cassidy and the Sundance Kid*, produced two years later. Thus *Hour of the Gun* is eminently worth our attention.

Robert Mitchell

THE HOUSE ON 92ND STREET

Released: 1945
Production: Louis de Rochemont for Twentieth Century-Fox
Direction: Henry Hathaway
Screenplay: Barre Lyndon, Charles G. Booth, and John Monks, Jr.; based
   on the original story of the same name by Charles G. Booth (AA)
Cinematography: Norbert Brodine
Editing: Harmon Jones
Running time: 88 minutes

Principal characters:
Bill Dietrich	William Eythe
Agent George A. Briggs	Lloyd Nolan
Elsa Gebhardt	Signe Hasso
Colonel Hammersohn	Leo G. Carroll
Johanna Schmedt	Lydia St. Clair
Charles Ogden Roper	Gene Lockhart

The House on 92nd Street was the first of the Hollywood "pseudo-documentaries," a successful but brief film cycle that responded to a new interest in realism during the postwar era. The term "pseudo-documentary" relates to the manner in which these films re-create actual, documented events. *The House on 92nd Street* is based on a case history taken from the files of the Federal Bureau of Investigation. It also represents a move away from a studio-created product, and can be placed in the forefront of a trend toward location shooting. Earlier in 1945, Billy Wilder's *The Lost Weekend*, perhaps the most acclaimed film of the year, featured a scene in which Ray Milland walks up New York's Third Avenue trying to pawn his typewriter. Wilder used a hidden camera to film this harrowing scene on location, and critics of the day pointed to its effectiveness in giving the film a documentary feeling. In 1946, Roberto Rossellini's *Open City* was released in the United States, and the critical and financial success of this neorealist classic influenced the trend toward greater immediacy in the Hollywood fiction film. *The House on 92nd Street* also was a critical and financial success, as were subsequent pseudo-documentaries and the realistic, on-location films produced by Mark Hellinger at Universal, including *Brute Force* (1947) and *Naked City* (1948).

The motivating force behind the pseudo-documentary was producer Louis de Rochemont. De Rochemont began his career as a newsreel cameraman and then served as an editor with Pathé's newsreel division. He eventually became head of Time-Life's "March of Time" newsreels, and it was this series that exerted the greatest influence on *The House on 92nd Street*. The "March of Time" films used newsreel techniques to re-create important events of the day. Unlike newsreels as such, which filmed events as they happened, the

"March of Time" series perfected the art of staged documentary, adding a sense of drama to what had really happened. During the war, de Rochemont employed the methods of staged documentary to make several effective non-fiction films glorifying the American serviceman. Twentieth Century-Fox chief Daryl F. Zanuck had been impressed with de Rochemont's work. With studio production costs rising to an all-time high in 1945, Zanuck decided to try location shooting. To this end, he hired de Rochemont to head a production unit within Fox. De Rochemont was asked to apply the techniques of staged documentary to the fiction film. His first effort was *The House on 92nd Street*, followed by *13 Rue Madeleine* (1946) and *Call Northside 777* (1948). All three films were directed by Henry Hathaway. Another important pseudo-documentary produced by de Rochemont's unit was *Boomerang* (1947), directed by Elia Kazan. These films benefited from postwar perambulators which could achieve the same effects as heavier camera cranes, and fishpole microphone booms. This kind of equipment was light and mobile and made on-location filming practically error-free. Moreover, new techniques in film processing enabled studiolike lighting effects to be achieved in the laboratory.

The House on 92nd Street* set the tone for the pseudo-documentaries to follow. Its elements include an anonymous narrator whose voice-over not only imparts factual information, but also editorializes. *The House on 92nd Street* combines actual newsreel footage with footage devised by the film-makers to simulate newsreel footage (achieved by the use of grainy film stock). The film uses locations where actual events took place, including the FBI Headquarters in Washington, D.C., and a beauty parlor and bookstore in New York City. The use of little-known actors instead of stars in key roles adds to the sense of verisimilitude for which the film strives. The character-izations are purposely flat, and the dialogue is rendered in monotone. Later pseudo-documentaries, however, opted for proven box-office stars such as James Cagney in *13 Rue Madeleine*, James Stewart in *Call Northside 777*, and Dana Andrews in *Boomerang*.

The House on 92nd Street* interweaves two stories. One concerns the inner workings of the FBI during the war, specifically its attack on enemy spy rings based in the United States. It is this story that employs the majority of the actual documentary footage. At one point, for example, FBI Chief J. Edgar Hoover is seen in his office. The second story takes us "behind the scenes" of the first story, detailing the events involved in "The Christopher Case." This story uses simulated documentary footage, combining it with actual locations and studio sets to produce a conventional spy thriller containing elements of the detective story. The story concerns Bill Dietrich's infiltration of a Nazi spy ring in order to discover the identity of the mysterious "Mr. Christopher," the head of a Nazi spy ring. In typical detective-story fashion, the identity of "Mr. Christopher" is not revealed until the end of the film. The only clue to his identity is the pair of pointed shoes he wears; these are shown in close-up at several key moments in the film. Dietrich (William Eythe) must find out who "Mr. Christopher" is and destroy the spy ring before the Nazis can transmit information about the development of the atomic bomb back to Germany.

The second story is shot in fairly conventional fashion, much in the manner of *film noir* thrillers of the era. The waterfront café sequences, for example, are vaguely expressionistic in tone and impart an aura of menace and foreboding. The spy ring's hideout is filmed in a decidedly *film noir* style as well, notably in the use of heavy shadows which are cast on the walls by Venetian blinds. A hidden room and hints of perverse sexuality complete the melodramatic picture. (Hathaway went on to direct several *film noir* thrillers during the 1940's, notably *The Dark Corner* in 1946 and *Kiss of Death* in 1947.)

The two stories are combined to glorify the FBI, which is shown as an efficient organization totally dedicated to upholding American democracy. In the process, scientific methods of detection are also praised. The film shows us such things as two-way mirrors and devices used to break codes. Ultimately, *The House on 92nd Street* demonstrates how both efficient crime-fighters and ordinary Americans such as Dietrich worked to achieve a common goal—the defeat of the Nazi menace. In general, de Rochemont in these films was concerned with showing American institutions in a good light. In *13 Rue Madeleine*, the Office of Strategic Services is lauded; in *Call Northside 777* it is the news media; and in *Boomerang* it is the American judicial system. This tactic is one not to be found in the Mark Hellinger-produced realist films, which were highly sensationalized in the manner of the journalistic exposé (Hellinger had been a Chicago newspaper reporter during the 1920's).

The pseudo-documentary cycle died out by 1953, when the techniques of staged documentary were appropriated by television. Conversely, Hollywood began to draw upon television-style fictional realism to move in another direction of cinematic depiction. Films such as *Marty* (1955), *A Catered Affair* (1956), and *Bachelor Party* (1957) illustrate this new trend. They examine the lives of ordinary, simple people in much the same way as did the Italian neo-realist films, which by this time had successfully penetrated the American film market. De Rochemont grew weary of the increasing "Hollywoodization" of his films—the Zanuck-ordained move toward bigger star names and the distortion of the facts. He became an independent producer in the early 1950's, and while his modest films retained the documentary spirit of *The House on 92nd Street*, they never attained the same level of commercial success.

Audiences and critics of the day responded enthusiastically to the then-unique qualities of *The House on 92nd Street*. The film received an Academy Award for Best Original Story, and it appeared on the Ten Best Films lists of *The New York Times* and *Time*. It was also one of the top money-making films of 1945.

Although today's audiences are accustomed to location filming, hand-held cameras, and the use of factual material as the basis for filmed drama, *The House on 92nd Street* was a radical departure for its day. Its achievement lies in the way it demonstrates that Hollywood could move away from the studio to tell an exciting story (and the film is undeniably exciting, especially in its climactic rescue/raid sequence). Moreover, by using a minimum of glamor and stylization, the film merged documentary and fiction to satisfy a new public demand for realism.

Charles Albright, Jr.

HOW THE WEST WAS WON

Released: 1963
Production: Bernard Smith for Metro-Goldwyn-Mayer
Direction: Henry Hathaway, George Marshall, and John Ford
Screenplay: James R. Webb (AA)
Cinematography: William H. Daniels, Milton Krasner, Charles Lang, and
  Joseph LaShelle
Editing: Harold F. Kress
Sound: Franklin E. Milton (AA)
Music: Alfred Newman
Running time: 165 minutes

Principal characters:

Lillith Prescott	Debbie Reynolds
Eve Prescott	Carroll Baker
Linus Rawlings	James Stewart
Zeb Rawlings	George Peppard
Cleve Van Valen	Gregory Peck
Roger Morgan	Robert Preston
Jethro Stuart	Henry Fonda
General Sherman	John Wayne
General Grant	Harry Morgan
Charlie Gant	Eli Wallach
Zebulon Prescott	Karl Malden
Rebecca Prescott	Agnes Moorehead
Confederate solider	Russ Tamblyn
Rulie Rawlings	Carolyn Jones
Mike King	Richard Widmark

How the West Was Won is a film gigantic in length, cast, history, screen size, and ambition. It runs for two hours and forty-five minutes, and the list of more than twenty stars is breathtaking. It is one of the last films to have been shot in three-camera Cinerama, which requires a very wide screen and produces wiggly lines where the end frames meet the middle one. What the film ambitiously tries to do, in five loosely interwoven episodes, is depict the conquering of the American West.

The script, for which writer James R. Webb won an Oscar, is imaginative in that it spreads itself over several eras from the early 1800's to long after the Civil War. Its geographical span is most of the continental United States, yet the broad scope of the story still manages to give the audience characters to care about. Lillith Prescott (Debbie Reynolds) and her nephew Zeb Rawlings (George Peppard) are the threads connecting the film's five episodes. Lillith, Zeb, and their families help to open up the Middle Western regions, cross the plains to California and the promise of gold, fight the Civil War, complete the transcontinental railroad, and bring law and order to the new land. Reynolds' character progresses from an unmolded girl to a shrewd old woman. The actress' enthusiasm and indomitable presence buoy up the film; without her, it would have lacked the spirit and poetry a work of this magnitude needs to sustain itself.

Lillith, her sister Eve (Carroll Baker), and their parents (Karl Malden and Agnes Moorehead) move West of civilization to find better farmland. After a quiet ride on an Erie Canal barge, they build their own raft to travel further into the wilderness. The girls' parents are killed on an impressively filmed ride over the perilous rapids. Eve wins the heart of a rough-hewn, freedom-loving mountain man, Linus Rawlings (James Stewart), and the couple settles down to farming. Lillith appears in the next sequence, a few years later, as Lily, the world-weary dance-hall girl. The knowledge that an old admirer has left her a gold mine in California spurs her to join a wagon train headed for the far West. Her adventures along the way include an Indian ambush and proposals of marriage from a straightforward rancher named Roger Morgan (Robert Preston) and a romantic, handsome gambler, Cleve Van Valen (Gregory Peck). She ends up with Cleve and a played-out mine. Never daunted, they decide to try to establish a West coast shipping industry in San Francisco.

In the next sequence, the Civil War is calling young men to arms. Eve's oldest boy, Zeb, follows his father into battle, despite Eve's attempt to ship him off to "Aunt Lil's" in California. In a quick vignette with John Wayne as General Sherman and Harry Morgan as General Grant, Zeb saves the future President's life when a Confederate soldier (Russ Tamblyn) tries to shoot him. Zeb returns to his parents' homestead to find his mother's grave next to the memorial for his father's war death. Expressing the restlessness he has inherited from his father, he leaves the farm to his younger brother and heads West. There, as a scout for the ruthless railroad builders, he witnesses the systematic and merciless removal of Indians from their land. When he protests to the foreman, Mike King (Richard Widmark), he is fired and moves on. Finally, years later, after Marshal Zeb Rawlings vanquishes the enjoyably stereotyped bad guy Charlie Gant (Eli Wallach), he and his wife Julie (Carolyn Jones) and their children settle down with the irascible old Lillith among the dusty buttes and mesas of the Old West.

In addition to the Prescott-Rawlings lineage, there are two other links between the five chapters. One is the narration by Spencer Tracy which occurs at the opening of the movie and at the beginning of each of the five parts. This narration, which is something like a history lecture, is saved from banality only by the power of Tracy's esteemed voice; it is nevertheless an artificial link, which, however necessary to continuity, does not integrate the film as a whole. The other, more unifying connection is the score. The theme music is an upbeat, driving tune that punctuates the movie. Lillith's theme is "I'll

Build You a Home in the Meadow," sung to the melody of the ancient ballad "Greensleeves." With the chorus repeating the words "Come, come, there's a wondrous land, for the open heart, for the willing hand," she sings it as a teenager on the brink of a new life, as a hard-working show-boat trouper, and as an old woman, to her grandnephews. It is a song full of optimism, as performed by Reynolds, who ably embodies in Lillith the resilience of the pioneers. Her energetic rendition of "Raise a Ruckus Tonight" boosts the flagging morale of the wagon train in the hostile hinterland. Other touches, such as banjo music and male choruses singing "Shenandoah" and "Erie Canal," draw on the rich vein of native American music. The M-G-M sound department won an Oscar for its effort.

The film is filled with fine cinematic and dramatic moments. The stampede of buffalo through a rail workers' camp, instigated by angry Indians, and a harrowing train ride during which Zeb defeats his archenemy Gant show the techniques of Cinerama put to excellent use. The acting is, in general, very good. Stewart gives a wonderful, wry portrait of an uncivilized man who allows himself to be tamed by a determined woman. Of the rest, Wayne in a brief role as Sherman, Henry Fonda as a buffalo hunter, and Robert Preston as Lil's earnest suitor offer outstanding performances.

The film had three veteran Hollywood directors, each of whom directed different sections of the film. Henry Hathaway directed the portions dealing with the early move West, the wagon train-gold rush, and the outlaws; George Marshall, those dealing with the railroad; and John Ford, those covering the Civil War. Marshall and Hathaway's segments are competently handled. Although film historians consider Ford to have crystallized the components of the Western genre, his portion of this picture is the least satisfactory. It comes across as contrived, and after the climax of the scene, it simply stops with no denouement. The Civil War episode concerns Zeb's disillusionment in the aftermath of the bloody battle of Shiloh. A Yankee, he meets a deserting Confederate soldier who encourages his anger and frustration. The two happen to overhear Sherman and Grant talking alone, and the Confederate soldier tries to shoot Grant. Zeb instinctively bayonets the boy and prevents the murder. Unfortunately, this part of the film was shot all too obviously on a studio sound stage, a glaring fault in light of the authentic locations of the rest of the movie. Another problem is Peppard, who fails to capture the mood of a young boy tired of war. Ford fails to enhance the melodrama of his portion with the flavor of epic mythology that it needs.

Among the great number of Hollywood Westerns, *How the West Was Won* is an odd case. In spite of its scope, it does not have the power of, for example, Ford's *Stagecoach* (1939); although there is much of quality in it, it will be remembered instead for its quantity. The events it chooses to illustrate are typical, but not archetypal, of the history of the West. In the 1960's, a loss of faith in mythology caused ambivalent attitudes reflected in this film. In one part, for example, the Indians are typical Hollywood villains, while in the next they are the victims of railroad entrepreneurs; the final image is one of assimilation as represented by Zeb's wife, who is an Indian, although she dresses like a white woman. The scholarly, "this is history" tone of *How the West Was Won* prevents it from being one of the last great Western epics. The film was quite popular with the public, perhaps because of its large number of well-known stars; it was the fifth-highest box-office success of 1963. It has attracted a large audience in its television showings, although its considerable length has usually led to heavy editing. Unfortunately, the best aspects of the film—its scenery and sound—have much less of an impact when shown on the small screen.

Stephanie Kreps

THE HUMAN COMEDY

Released: 1943
Production: Clarence Brown for Metro-Goldwyn-Mayer
Direction: Clarence Brown
Screenplay: Howard Estabrook; based on the novel of the same name by
   William Saroyan (AA)
Cinematography: Harry Stradling, Jr.
Editing: Conrad A. Nervig
Music: Herbert Stothart
Running time: 118 minutes

Principal characters:
Homer Macauley .... Mickey Rooney
Tom Spangler .... James Craig
Willie Grogan .... Frank Morgan
Mrs. Macauley .... Fay Bainter
Diana Steed .... Marsha Hunt
Marcus Macauley .... Van Johnson
Bess Macauley .... Donna Reed
Tobey George .... John Craven
Ulysses Macauley .... Jackie "Butch" Jenkins

The prodigiously prolific William Saroyan made no pretense about being
a "literary" writer, but the innocent appeal of many of his stories certainly
stems from a poetic bent. He was unabashedly sentimental, with a penchant
to recall and wax sentimental about his childhood, which he depicted as a
time when everyone was good and there was no caste system. Saroyan was
born of Armenian heritage in Fresno, California, in 1908. His early life was
spent in an orphanage, and he worked at various jobs including one as a
messenger boy for a telegraph office as did the hero in *The Human Comedy*.
He began writing at an early age, and his message seemed to be one of
cockeyed optimism: all men are created good, and if we laughed and sang
a little more there would be fewer problems in the world. A man can hardly
be criticized for such sentiments, but many realists have done just that, and
The Human Comedy as both a film and a book has come in for its share of
that criticism.

Saroyan was introduced to M-G-M studio head Louis B. Mayer by musical
producer Arthur Freed. Mayer took an immediate liking to the ebullient
Saroyan and purchased the story, *The Human Comedy*, for sixty thousand
dollars, a sizable sum at that time. Mayer promised he would make Saroyan
into another Irving G. Thalberg (the legendary head-of-production at
M-G-M in the 1930's) and that he also would direct films. After closer scrutiny
of the rambling, episodic story, however, the production and direction were
entrusted to veteran Clarence Brown; all Saroyan was given to do was produce

and direct a short. Even so, Saroyan took advantage of his mini-mogul status and had a grand piano installed in his office and spent many hours each day in the M-G-M projection room—not viewing what he had shot, but catching up on old M-G-M movies he had missed. He and Mayer later parted company, but the screen version of *The Human Comedy* still remained one of Mayer's favorite films.

It is easy to see how Saroyan's wholesome view of American family life, and childhood especially, appealed to the overly sentimental Mayer, and why the project was given a first-class production with a large cast of capable players drawn from the large M-G-M stock company. The movie dealt with real "folks" and real happenings in their lives, and it touched on the death of young American soldiers with a poignancy extremely significant during those World War II days.

The title, which many intellectuals ridiculed for its pretentiousness, actually refers to the story of one family, the Macauleys, who are comfortably poor and very American. Homer Macauley (Mickey Rooney) is one of four children in the fatherless family in Ithaca, California; he represents any teenager in any town. Marcus (Van Johnson) is his older brother and a private in the Army who is engaged to Mary (Dorothy Morris), who lives next door to the Macauleys and is considered a member of the family already. Homer's sister Bess (Donna Reed) goes to college; five-year-old Ulysses (Jack "Butch" Jenkins) is just an average, cute, freckle-faced boy from anywhere; and Mrs. Macauley (Fay Bainter) is an idealized version of the American mother.

With Marcus in the Army, Homer becomes the man of the household, and with that responsibility comes the obligation to help with the family's finances. To do his share, Homer takes a job as a night messenger boy for the local telegraph office. The office is managed by goodlooking Tom Spangler (James Craig), who is in love with Diana Steed (Marsha Hunt), the daughter of one of the town's wealthiest families. Saroyan makes it clear that although she is rich, Diana is a likable girl. Homer works the nightshift with Willie Grogan (Frank Morgan), one of the oldest telegraphers in the business. Willie is a philosopher and a drinker, and when he has had a few too many, one of Homer's duties is to sober him up. In his job Homer meets people from all walks of life. He learns that, regardless of their station in life, they are all human beings and most are good people. Because it is wartime, the most difficult message for Homer to deliver is the one that reads: "The Department of War regrets to inform you that your son has been killed in action."

During his school days Tom Spangler had been a 220-yard hurdles champion, and Homer sets out to emulate him. He does well with the sport but on the day of the big race, his hopes are shattered when he and his major competitor are told they must stay after school and thus miss the race. The track coach intercedes for the other boy, whom he regards as his most valuable player, and when the teacher learns of this favoritism, she dismisses Homer, who goes on to win the race. Tom congratulates Homer and also tells him that he has met Diana's family, and that they have consented to his and Diana's marriage. Meanwhile, the Macauleys learn that Marcus is to be shipped overseas. Before he goes, he visits his family, bringing along his Army buddy, an orphan, Tobey George (John Craven). The Macauleys welcome Tobey warmly and have hopes that one day he and Bess will marry.

Homer and Bess go to the telegraph office one evening to find Willie slumped over the telegraph machine. Homer assumes Willie has been drinking again but after splashing water on his face with no response, he realizes Willie is dead. He sees a half-finished telegram in the machine and reads it. It is addressed to Mrs. Macauley and it states that Marcus has been killed. Tom arrives to find the boy in despair, and they go off for a walk and to play a few rounds of horseshoes. At the railroad station they see Tobey walking with a limp. Homer goes up to him, and together they walk to the Macauley home where the two enter the house arm in arm. Homer has found a new brother.

The sentimentality of the story cannot be denied, but the theme, for all its naïveté has a universal appeal. It certainly contained a message for America's wartime population, particularly for the mothers of the young boys who were being killed in action. Most critics responded with phrases such as "eloquent and deeply moving," "compassionate with sheer beauty," and "a combination of great charm and tenderness." That certainly was Saroyan's purpose, and the picture proved extremely popular, with Saroyan winning an Academy Award for his screenplay. *The Human Comedy* was also nominated for Best Actor (Mickey Rooney); Best Cinematography (Harry Stradling); Best Direction (Clarence Brown); and Best Picture.

Those critics who did not like the film called it "sentimental goo" and "banal" and said that Saroyan's speeches for many of the characters were not only unspeakable but also came off like sermons. Saroyan's idealism could be at once disarming and irritating, and, particularly in this film, more precise editing was needed to remove some of the preachiness and long-windedness. Such editing would have helped the film show what it meant to show: real people in the honest pursuit of living and sharing the everyday happiness and disappointment that life brings.

The acting in the film raises it far above the level of the usual wartime sentimental story. Members of the cast including Morgan and Bainter give realistic, low-keyed performances, and Rooney gives a remarkably appealing and restrained performance as Homer. It is one of his best, being representative of American boyhood, and not displaying the show-off mannerisms that had become a part of his lighter assignments. Jenkins was a delight—a nonactorish, guileless Ulysses who was adorable without being too adorable, as frequently is the case with child actors.

Ronald Bowers

HUSBANDS

Released: 1970
Production: Al Ruban for Columbia
Direction: John Cassavetes
Screenplay: John Cassavetes
Cinematography: Victor J. Kemper
Editing: Peter Tanner
Running time: 138 minutes

> *Principal characters:*
> Harry .... Ben Gazzara
> Archie ....Peter Falk
> Gus .... John Cassavetes

The director is often the focus of critical comment on film. In many cases, especially European films, the director is also the writer. Even when this is not true, the *auteur* theory (which asserts that in most cases the director is the primary artistic consciousness behind the film, the one who "orchestrates" the creative contributions of others as well as having primary creative responsibility for camera and actor direction) spotlights the director. John Cassavetes is definitely the focus of attention generated by any of his films, but for an additional reason. Cassavetes is first an actor, and besides writing and directing *Husbands*, he is one of the three stars in this film which subjugates everything to acting performance.

In 1968, *Faces*, Cassavetes' highly experimental very personal film, was an unexpected commercial success. It was praised for its superb acting, emotional honesty, and its powerful, direct impact. This success gave Cassavetes a nearly blank check for *Husbands*, which he shot in the same *cinéma-vérité* style. This remains the most interesting element of *Husbands*: the subject matter dates rapidly and the acting begins to look overindulgent, but the style was experimental for 1970, especially in a big-budget commerical film. The film received a great deal of attention when it was in production and after it opened, most of which was centered on Cassavetes and his actors. It was considered an important film, honest, painful, powerful, and direct. Many articles about *Husbands* never reviewed the film at all, but instead interviewed Cassavetes (often with Peter Falk and Ben Gazzara, his costars) or bestowed lavish praise on the spontaneous style and described the actors' technique. Even those reviewers who did not especially like the film had nothing but praise for its fresh, daring style.

Husbands can not really be considered total *cinéma-vérité*. This style was made possible by faster film stocks which made shooting in available light possible and by portable, light sound equipment which made syncronous sound possible even in difficult locations, as well as by the acceptance of the

16mm format which made it economically feasible to shoot a great deal of film. This is necessary when the camera follows the action rather than the action being staged for the camera, and is an essential part of the *cinéma-vérité* aesthetic. The basic goal in *cinéma-vérité* is nonintervention. Used primarily in documentary and news films to give a "you-are-there" feeling, *cinéma-vérité* made it possible to dispense with many of the artificialities of fiction film—studio lights, studio sets, huge bulkly camera, and sound which was created and mixed primarily in postproduction. *Cinéma-vérité* relies on long takes which can follow action in one continuous shot rather than breaking it up into an edited sequence of long shots, medium shots, and close-ups. The technique gives documentary film a veracity, an honesty that greatly increases its power to affect people. Further characteristics of this documentary aesthetic include unscripted situations, use of "real" people (rather than actors), and no extraneous interpretative devices such as mood music, voice-over, or explanatory narrators.

Many elements of this style were readily adaptable to fiction film, where they created the same feeling of honesty and directness. *Husbands* is a scripted film, and all the actors are professionals, but there is a great deal of improvisation which allows the actors to be spontaneous rather than tied to line readings. This method gives their interactions and each individual performance a level of intimacy rarely seen. Scenes are allowed to run as long as they require, and the camera uses both long follow shots and close-ups which are often hastily composed. The working aesthetic is to let the acting dominate by being completely unhampered by the requirements of the shooting, and the technical imperfections which result are easily accepted as a small price to pay for the spontaneity of performances which are created right before the camera. It takes a great deal of film to shoot this way, since many scenes will ultimately not "work," and critical compositions or lines may be missed and have to be retaken. There were regularly two hours of daily rushes on *Husbands*, rather than the usual twenty to thirty minutes. Even in the editing, performance is king, and shots (with a far greater than average percentage of long takes) are arranged to maintain the intensity of the acting.

Husbands is about three men, friends and neighbors in a suburb of New York, for whom the death of the fourth member of their group triggers for each what might be called a "midlife crisis." They go on a two-day binge following the funeral, leaving wives and children behind in a nearly hysterical attempt to demonstrate to themselves that they are alive, free, young, and loved. They tussle like teenagers in the streets, punching each other and laughing; they go to a gym to swim and bounce balls and to a bar to drink and sing in boozy camaraderie, proclaiming their love for one another and then recoiling in embarrassment. Finally they end up vomiting and sick in spirit in a toilet, each afraid of rejection by the others and unable to name their growing anxiety.

Harry (Ben Gazzara) seems the most unstable, accusing the others of putting him down while he nervously puts them down. His marriage is breaking up, and he exhibits more overt homosexual yearnings than the others. He fights violently with his wife when the men briefly return home, then begs the others to go to London with him. They first refuse, then, after finding that they cannot simply resume their normal lives at work, they agree. In London the three behave like loud, abrasive Americans and try to pick up women in an achingly painful series of scenes. They return to their hotel with three women and then crowd awkwardly into one room, clearly reluctant to leave their buddies in this erotically charged situation. Only when Harry begins to cry and the woman he is with takes him off to his own room do they separate. Gus (John Cassavetes) has a violent, sometimes playful, but very neurotic lovemaking session with his tall blonde, and Archie (Peter Falk) has a tender and sad scene with his Chinese girl, who will not talk to him until later, when she runs out into the rain babbling in Chinese. The men regroup; Harry tries to get them to stay with him and three more women, but Gus and Archie finally leave for home. The two part at their neighboring driveways, laden with bags of toys for their kids, wondering what Harry will do "without us." The camera follows Gus into his driveway, where he kneels to hug his daughter and is greeted by his son saying "Boy, are you in trouble!" Finally Gus walks away from the camera around the corner of his house where, presumably, his angry wife waits.

The failure of all three men to communicate or achieve intimacy with anyone, including one another, is painful and powerful, but there is so much self-pity in their attempts and so much self-indulgence in their performances that it is difficult to maintain sympathy for them. Women are routinely trashed in the film, from Gus's hysterical dental patient (shot at an unflattering and vulnerable angle); to Harry's wife (who torments him by declaring she does not love him, demonstrating her greater loyalty to her mother, who seems to live with them, and finally even threatening him with a knife); to the English women (who range from a weird, heavily made-up elderly lady who seems ready to rape Archie); to the generally unattractive and often ridiculous women they pick up. Much of the source of their fear is sexual, and had this fear been expressed in relation to equally physically attractive (all three men are Hollywood-actor handsome) and emotionally appealing women, the film could have achieved a depth and poignancy. The women we see in the film, however, are so clearly deserving of the contempt and hostility they receive that it is difficult to see much emotional honesty in the men's pain.

Husbands looks today like an overlong (138 minutes in which many sequences run on with unintelligible dialogue or none at all), precocious film. The characters seem like spoiled, self-deceptive adolescents insensitive to everything except their own pain. The film remains interesting historically and for its *cinéma-vérité* style, but lacks the emotional honesty for which it was praised when it was released in 1970.

Janey Place

I CONFESS

Released: 1953
Production: Alfred Hitchcock for Warner Bros.
Direction: Alfred Hitchcock
Screenplay: George Tabori and William Archibald; based on the play *Nos Deux Consciences* by Paul Anthelme
Cinematography: Robert Burks
Editing: Rudi Fehr
Running time: 95 minutes

Principal characters:

Father Michael Logan	Montgomery Clift
Ruth Grandfort	Anne Baxter
Inspector Larrue	Karl Malden
Willy Robertson	Brian Aherne
Otto Keller	O. E. Hasse
Pierre Grandfort	Roger Dann
Alma Keller	Dolly Haas

Alfred Hitchcock's *I Confess*, the film immediately following his masterpiece *Strangers on a Train* (1951), was considered to be something of a failure by its director himself. Finding the completed product lacking in humor, an important element in most of his films, he tended to dismiss its importance. Perhaps for this reason, the film is frequently ignored as an integral part of his *oeuvre*. The film is worth analysis, however, if only as a reflection of Hitchcock's own Catholicism. As an *auteur*, Hitchcock did not blatantly illuminate his films with religious symbolism, as was frequently the case with John Ford in his films. In many ways, however, Hitchcock's films do have a religious or at least moral undercurrent. In *I Confess*, one of the major themes of the mystery centers on a priest's moral dilemmas, one of which has a direct bearing on his role as a priest.

The film begins during an attempted robbery when Otto Keller (O. E. Hasse), a caretaker for a local Catholic church, murders a second-rate Quebec lawyer named Vilette. Returning to the church, he confesses his recent crime to Father Michael Logan (Montgomery Clift), who, because of Church law, is unable to divulge information received during confession. Once this fact sinks into the warped mind of Otto, he forgets any thought of going to the police and giving himself up, feeling sure that no one else besides Father Michael will ever know of his crime.

The situation becomes more complex when the local police begin to suspect Father Michael himself of being the murderer. Witnesses in the form of two young schoolgirls testify that they saw a man dressed as a priest leave the murdered man's house on the night of the crime, and Father Michael was also seen at the lawyer's house the next day as the police were beginning their investigation. Other evidence reveals that he had also diverted Ruth (Anne Baxter), the wife of an elected official, away from the scene. With all the circumstantial evidence pointing against him, coupled with his own mysterious silence, the police move to arrest Father Michael for the crime.

In a courageous move, Ruth confesses to the police that she was being blackmailed by the dead lawyer. She reveals that years ago she and Michael were engaged to be married, but World War II began and altered their plans. A lonely Ruth turned to her boss, Pierre Grandfort (Roger Dann), for comfort, eventually marrying him, but never truly forgetting Michael. When he returns home after the war Ruth is there to greet him. She spends the day with him, but conveniently fails to tell him of her subsequent marriage. She is hurt and humiliated when he tells her that he wants to be a priest. They are caught in a sudden rainstorm and forced to spend the night in the garden of a deserted house. Although they were innocent of any adultery, in the morning the owner, a lawyer named Vilette spots the couple and begins to make a scene. Vilette recognizes Ruth as Grandfort's wife, and dismisses the incident as a simple misunderstanding. A short time later, however, Ruth is confronted by Vilette, who asks for money and political influence. If she refuses, the unscrupulous lawyer threatens to tell her husband of his interpretation of the incident in the garden. This blackmail continues until the morning when she meets Michael in front of Vilette's house.

This confession does little more than provide a motive for Father Michael to have murdered the lawyer. He goes to trial, but is acquitted because of lack of evidence. He is branded as a murderer and a poor excuse for a priest by the citizens of Quebec, however, and as he leaves the courthouse he is mobbed by the crowd which has gathered to hear the verdict. Otto's wife, Alma (Dolly Haas), unable to bear the burden of his guilt while the priest suffers silently for a crime he never committed, struggles through the crowd to ask his forgiveness. Otto overreacts to this and shoots his wife while trying to kill Father Michael. He is chased into a hotel and eventually shot by the police in an empty ballroom, where Father Michael goes to him, hears his last confession, and performs the religious rite of *extreme unction* before Otto's death.

I Confess is unlike any other Hitchcock film, with none of the usual fast-paced adventure or suspense associated with the director's more famous films. The audience is aware who the murderer is from the very beginning, so the story's tension must come from watching a man bound by a holy oath, "the seal of the confessional," persecuted for a crime he did not commit. During the late 1940's and early 1950's, Hitchcock was experimenting with the form of film. In *Rope* (1948), produced a few years earlier, he had explored the possibility of shooting a film which gave the illusion of one continuous camera take; in *Strangers on a Train* he experimented with characterization; *I Confess* was an experiment in philosophy.

A large portion of the audience for *I Confess* was not able to understand the religious conviction which allowed a man to be tried for a crime he never committed when he knows who is really guilty. In a real sense *I Confess* becomes an obvious analogy, with Clift's Father Michael taking on a Christlike dimension. The juxtaposition of Clift walking past a sculpture showing Christ dragging his cross to Mount Calvary and the overly sentimental flashback which accompanies Ruth's confession show Hitchcock's predilection for obvious symbolism.

There is a brooding quality to Clift's performance in *I Confess* that can almost be interpreted as an unusual disinterest in the events that affect Father Michael's life. Clift tailored his performance to an emotional level, and in much of the film he is silent, allowing his feelings to be conveyed through expression. The other characters approach their roles less intensely. Karl Malden as police inspector Larrue is effective in his stubbornness to prove the priest's guilt. Baxter is uninspired in her breathy portrayal of Ruth, with the flashback sequence, presented with overdubbed narration, allowing her the most freedom in her otherwise bland characterization.

It is apparent that *I Confess* was adapted from a stage play, since the construction of the dialogue is highly theatrical. Only in a few scenes does Hitchcock manage to break away from the static conversational development of the plot and concentrate on visual aspects of the film. The opening scene, for example, in which Otto murders Vilette and makes his way down the deserted streets of Quebec, is totally expressionistic. Low camera angles, which dominate much of the film, also give a sense of expression to the cinematic quality of the film. Another scene, shot in an actual cloudburst, showing the two former lovers confronting each other in a garden setting, beautifully prefigures the violence which will later cause the final break. The physical action which erupts at the end of the film provides Hitchcock with an opportunity to use the Quebec location cinematography to his advantage. There is an "old world" flavor to *I Confess*, with the atmospheric flavor of Quebec, the religious bias, and the naïve sexual blackmail all seeming out of place in an environment of films desensitized to simple emotions.

I Confess is a controversial film among critics. It is easy to dismiss it as a dull and overblown project directed by an acknowledged master filmmaker, but on the other hand, it also presents a mature Hitchcockian outlook to his much-discussed "wrong-man" theme. This film is one of the few cases in which Hitchcock was willing to allow the material to overshadow the filmmaking. There is a disquieting feeling which accompanies *I Confess*; the film is captivating and involving. Its brilliance rests in its ability to make the Christlike analogy work within the context of a contemporary melodrama.

Carl F. Macek

I COVER THE WATERFRONT

Released: 1933
Production: United Artists
Direction: James Cruze
Screenplay: Wells Root; based on the novel of the same name by Max Miller
Cinematography: Ray June
Editing: Grant Whytock
Running time: 70 minutes

Principal characters:
Julie Kirk	Claudette Colbert
Joe Miller	Ben Lyon
Eli Kirk	Ernest Torrence
McCoy	Hobart Cavanaugh
John Phelps	Purnell Pratt
Old Chris	Harry Beresford

I Cover the Waterfront is an unjustly neglected film that skillfully combines three popular types of cinema: the crime story, the newspaper story, and the romance. It is very loosely based upon elements in the novel of the same name, a collection of sketches about life and newspaper reporting on the waterfront in San Diego, California. The film chronicles the story of a newsman covering the waterfront, but it focuses on only one story he covers, one in which he becomes personally involved.

The opening credits are imaginative, especially in view of the fact that in 1933 most credits were simple white words on a black background. *I Cover the Waterfront*, however, immediately establishes its milieu by showing most of the credits as if they were printed in a newspaper. The three opening scenes then quickly and economically establish all the elements of the narrative. First, Joe Miller (Ben Lyon) arrives at his rundown waterfront room to find a strange man sleeping in his bed. Joe finds that the intruder, McCoy (Hobart Cavanaugh), is an out-of-work journalist who knows one of Joe's old classmates in Chicago. A very short conversation between McCoy and Joe establishes that Joe is discontented with the waterfront, with his job, and with the West Coast, and that he is writing a novel.

Just as Joe is about to go to sleep, he gets a telephone call that shows us why he does not like his job. Having been up all night working on a story, Joe is now ordered by his editor to investigate a report that a woman has been seen swimming nude in a remote cove. Not at all graciously, Joe obeys the order; he discovers that the report is indeed true. He waits on the shore with the young woman's bathing suit until she comes in and then conducts his "interview" with her while she stands behind a convenient shoulder-high rock waiting for him to give her suit to her. He finds that she is Julie Kirk

(Claudette Colbert), the daughter of a man he knows on the waterfront. When Joe reports the story to his editor John Phelps (Purnell Pratt), he lets Phelps (whom he calls a "mental midget") know that he considers it a silly item and that he believes the real story is Julie's father, Eli (Ernest Torrence), whom Joe suspects is smuggling Chinese into the harbor. The editor agrees to let Joe pursue the smuggling story, and the plot of the film is under way: Joe pursues Eli Kirk while falling in love with his daughter, Julie.

We soon see that Joe's suspicions of the old man are well founded. Eli pretends to be a fisherman, but the main cargo his ship carries when it returns to port is human—illegal Chinese immigrants. Joe gets the Coast Guard to stop and search Eli's boat, but Eli has the Chinese man on board bound, gagged, weighted down with chains, and dropped overboard when he sees the Coast Guard boat coming. Later, Joe is talking with Old Chris (Harry Beresford), an old man who drags the harbor bottom for what salvage he can find, when he finds the body of the unfortunate Chinese man. Convinced that this proves Eli's guilt, Joe takes the body (wrapped in canvas) to the editor and wants to print the story, but even though Joe finds that the chain on the body matches the chain on Eli's boat, Phelps is afraid to publish the story until there is more definite evidence.

Meanwhile, we see that Julie is devoted to her father and ignorant of his smuggling activities. Not even the Chinese coat he gives her arouses her suspicions. She does not, however, think her father is flawless. When he is gone one night, she knows exactly where to find him—at a brothel. The filmmakers, incidentally, do nothing to conceal the fact that the establishment is a brothel except to have it referred to as a speakeasy and a boarding house. At the brothel she again meets Joe, who has gone there to see Eli also, hoping to find him drunk and talkative. Although he does not get any information from Eli, Joe does begin a romance with Julie, which is another method he has planned to find out about the smuggling. After they take her drunken father home, Joe and Julie sit and talk in the moonlight. She tells of her love of the waterfront and he of his aversion to it and to the writing he does for the newspaper. He also tells her that he has been trying for five years to write a novel. When he notices that she is wearing a Chinese coat, he adds that item to his store of information on the smuggling case.

McCoy, who has by now become Joe's confidant and sidekick, thinks Joe's interest in Julie is more romantic than professional. He deduces this from the fact that the love scenes in the novel Joe is writing are becoming more believable. Joe, of course, denies this, but we can see his feelings for Julie developing throughout the film.

Also developing is Joe's unraveling of the smuggling story. He finds out from Julie that Eli is going to land at the harbor's Chinese settlement one night, and he alerts the Coast Guard. An officer boards the ship when it lands, but can find nothing illegal until Joe discovers that there is a Chinese inside the body of each of the huge sharks on board. Although Eli is seriously wounded by a Coast Guardsman, he escapes. Joe, however, does get his story, a raise, and a bonus. The headline reads "Chinese Smugglers Exposed—New Version of Jonah and the Whale Uncovered."

Now the feelings of Joe and Julie for each other are reversed. Joe has come to realize that he truly loves Julie but she has found out that she has been used and orders him away when he comes to see her. Then Eli sees Joe and shoots him, and Julie finds that she cannot leave him to die. Since Eli and Julie are ready to leave for the Mexican border in a small boat, they take Joe along. Then Eli, who is still losing strength from his own wound, realizes that Joe must have a doctor and returns to the harbor. "If you love him, he's worth it," Eli tells his daughter just before he dies of the wounds he received earlier. "That's more than I ever was."

We next see Joe returning home from his recuperation in the hospital. He finds the place completely redecorated—cozy and comfortable with clean windows, curtains, and even a fireplace. Then Julie comes in, and he realizes that she has done it all. Joe announces that he has thought of the ending for his novel: the hero marries the girl. "That's a swell finish," Julie says as the film ends.

The two principal interwoven elements of the plot, the newspaper story and the romance, are well handled by the filmmakers. Joe's dedication to doing a meaningful story despite the objections of his editor and his slipping into unethical means (pretending to love Julie) in his obsession with the story are made believable. Equally fascinating is the romance between Joe and Julie, especially as it alternates between flippancy and deeper emotion and as the underlying feelings of the two change, with Joe falling in love despite himself and then Julie finding herself unable to deny her love once she finds out what Joe has done. In the end Julie and Eli both seem to accept Joe's reasoning for what he has done to Eli: "That's my job, and he had it coming to him."

Lyon as Joe and Cavanaugh as McCoy are good, but the outstanding performances in *I Cover the Waterfront* are given by Colbert and Torrence. Indeed, some critics consider Colbert's performance one of the best of her thirty-year career. She is able to display her talent for sophisticated comedy that earned her an Academy Award the next year for *It Happened One Night*, but she also conveys the deeper emotions of a daughter's love for a father who does not deserve it. Torrence's portrayal of the father brings out his greed and cruelty without making him seem a purely evil character.

Also quite important to the overall effect of the film is the nearly documentary style of director James Cruze, which emphasizes darkness and glamorizes almost nothing.

Marilynn Wilson

I NEVER SANG FOR MY FATHER

Released: 1969
Production: Gilbert Cates for Columbia
Direction: Gilbert Cates
Screenplay: Robert Anderson; based on his play of the same name
Cinematography: Morris Hartzband
Editing: Angie Ross
Running time: 93 minutes

Principal characters:
Tom ....Melvyn Douglas
Margaret .... Dorothy Stickney
Gene .... Gene Hackman
Alice .... Estelle Parsons
Peggy .... Elizabeth Hubbard
Norma .... Lovelady Powell

I Never Sang for My Father is a disturbing film about the vicissitudes of growing old and about the pain and sense of loss elderly people experience. It also concerns the problems their children experience in trying to help them adjust to roles that are almost reversed: the older person is dependent, while the younger ones have the choices.

Except for a recent trip to California where he met the woman he plans to marry, Gene Garrison (Gene Hackman) has always lived near his parents. When they return from a trip to Florida, he takes up his former relationship with them, visiting them often in the suburbs. His father, Tom (Melvyn Douglas), is forgetful, repetitive, and irascible; his mother, Margaret (Dorothy Stickney), who has had a heart attack, is sweet and patient. When Margaret dies, Tom is left alone, and Gene's sister, Alice (Estelle Parsons), who was banished from the family circle for marrying a Jew, comes East for the funeral. Alice has the courage Gene lacks. Gene always seeks *rapprochement* with his father, whereas Alice knows that this is impossible and warns Gene that he must not sacrifice his life for his father. After a quarrel, Gene leaves his father's house, never to return. His voice on the sound track says that he went to California and that Tom entered a hospital where he died alone. "Death ends a life," Gene says, "but it does not end a relationship which struggles on in the survivor's mind toward some resolution which it may never find."

I Never Sang for My Father is full of pain and regret, of the impossibility of getting close to people and understanding them, and of the gallant effort Gene makes to reach his father. The film is completely verbal, and since the subject matter is so touchy, it is a difficult film to watch; it constantly presents disturbing parallels with one's own life.

The last, extended scene between the two men encapsulates everything scriptwriter Robert Anderson had to relate about his characters. Tom and Gene are in Tom's bedroom, and Tom is looking through old papers and photos and telling Gene the oft-repeated tales of his youth. His father was a drunk who deserted the family, leaving Tom to care for a younger brother and sister. It is understood that the rift between Tom and his father is recapitulated in the relationship between Gene and Tom. Tom reiterates the old litany: how hard his youth was, how, as he says, "I was only tolerated in this house because I paid the bills," and how he worked his fingers to the bone. Tom is a man as full of yearning and sadness as Gene, and it is their tragedy that they never once are able to bridge the emotional chasm that separates them—even on this night when their feelings are exposed as never before. When Gene says that he wanted to love Tom, that he hoped to draw nearer to him, there is such remorse and such understated agony at the missed opportunity that the audience can feel clearly Gene's frustration and thwarted expectations.

Still, there is some evidence of closeness; Tom and Gene embrace when they meet, an act as rare on screen as it is in real life. Gene loves his mother and feels an emotional rapport with her. Tom recalls hearing Gene singing with Margaret—Gene always seemed to be finishing as Tom came into the room. Tom says he wanted to hear Gene sing "When I Grow Too Old to Dream," but he never did. Of course, this is the origin of the title and a perfect metaphor for the relationship between the two men, who are continually on different wave lengths, talking past each other, screaming without being heard.

If Tom has failed in one way with Gene, he has alienated his daughter completely, literally driving her away. Alice sees their relationship clearly and knows that the guilt Gene feels will trap him into staying with Tom instead of marrying Peggy (Elizabeth Hubbard) and living his own life. He cannot face the fact that their relationship is unworkable. Alice is as damaged in her way as Gene is in his. She is bitter, resentful, cut off from her parents, saying she appreciates the lesson Tom taught her—that one has to be tough and accept the fact that one is alone in the world. She is whistling in the dark however, for underneath her bravado she is a frightened child who would very much like to feel close to her father.

The performances are virtually perfect. Douglas had the professional courage to play an unlikable character. Tom is bossy, garrulous, crotchety, and often wrong-headed, but he is also sympathetic and understandable, a real person with mortal dimensions. Douglas plays him on a human scale, not larger than life, but as a man who could be the old "geezer" next door, shouting in frustration when he cannot get his own way. It is a long way from the suave boulevardier he played in *Ninotchka* (1940), but Douglas managed the transition with grace, becoming an elderly character actor of undiminished talent who has won two Oscars since the age of sixty.

In 1970, Hackman was at the peak of his stardom. He had done solid work in *Bonnie and Clyde* (1967) and *Downhill Racer* (1969), and he would soon win an Academy Award for *The French Connection* (1971). Hackman unfortunately burnt his career out through overexposure. He appeared too frequently, sometimes in worthwhile films, but too often in inferior ones. Here he is at his best; his ordinary looks are just right for Gene, and his underplaying (sometimes Hackman can be overly melodramatic) is what is needed for this role. He is expresssive in his frustration at being treated like a child, folding up inside when he cannot make contact with Tom, although the role is not an expressive one. Hackman makes Gene something more than what is written; his naturalism transcends the lapses in Anderson's screenplay, and he gives us a Gene more fully rounded and more thought-out than the one in the script.

Parsons, who played Hackman's wife in *Bonnie and Clyde*, here plays his sister. Parsons is a plain woman, and in *I Never Sang for My Father* she is an aggressive complainer and something of a know-it-all, but she is not on the screen long enough to become annoying. She too feels the ache of estrangement, but she has erected such a protective barrier around her damaged feelings that she is scarcely able to acknowledge the extent of her unhappiness. Parsons gives an even-tempered performance, neither strident nor long-suffering. As a performer she can fall into Method-type acting mannerisms, but here she is sweetly restrained.

If there is any thematic unity to director Gilbert Cates's work, it has to do with the problems of people reaching middle age, as demonstrated in *Summer Wishes, Winter Dreams* (1973), which presented Joanne Woodward as a discontented woman unable to focus on the reasons for her anxiety. Of course, *I Never Sang for My Father* shares *its* subject with an American classic, Eugene O'Neil's *Long Day's Journey into Night*, a play conceived on a far larger scale than Anderson's, and one that by the very nature of its greatness is perhaps less forceful than Anderson's small, intimate drama.

Cates's direction is crude, the lighting is poor, and there is no discernible visual style; yet the film is affecting. It refuses to show a way out of these individuals' dilemmas, to indulge in false reassurances, or even to say that these troubled people can ever hope to find peace. It simply presents them in a realistic, identifiable manner.

Judith M. Kass

I REMEMBER MAMA

Released: 1948
Production: George Stevens and Harriet Parsons for RKO/Radio
Direction: George Stevens
Screenplay: DeWitt Bodeen; based on the play of the same name by John
   Van Druten and on the book *Mama's Bank Account* by Kathryn Forbes
Cinematography: Nicholas Musuraca
Editing: Robert Swink
Running time: 119 minutes

Principal characters:
Mama	Irene Dunne
Katrin	Barbara Bel Geddes
Uncle Chris	Oscar Homolka
Papa	Philip Dorn
Mr. Hyde	Sir Cedric Hardwicke
Mr. Thorkelson	Edgar Bergen
Aunt Trina	Ellen Corby
Doctor Johnson	Rudy Vallee
Florence Dana Moorhead	Florence Bates
Jessie Brown	Barbara O'Neil

RKO producer Harriet Parsons was so enchanted with *Mama's Bank Account*, Kathryn Forbes's book of stories about a Norwegian family living in San Francisco around 1910, that when she learned her studio had bought the film rights, she immediately asked studio executives to assign the production to her, which they did.

When a treatment was approved and the screenplay written, preproduction plans began, but were brought to a sudden halt when composers Richard Rodgers and Oscar Hammerstein bought the dramatic rights to *Mama's Bank Account* from RKO and signed John Van Druten to dramatize and direct it for the theater. Wisely, the studio retained the rights of first refusal on buying back the film rights after the play's premiere, and the new version was to be called *I Remember Mama*. When the play which Van Druten fashioned opened on Broadway under the auspices of Rodgers and Hammerstein and was an immediate success, RKO eventually acquired the film rights to the property again. This new success of the story made many producers interested in it, but Parsons remained firm in her desire to produce the new film herself, and eventually studio executives acquiesced and assigned her to the project again.

The film was to be a big-budgeted special with a long shooting schedule. There were certain problems in adapting the play to the screen which had not existed when the story basis had been a series of short stories. First, much of the action had to move from inside the house onto the streets of San

Francisco, where the company was to go for exterior location shots. There were, furthermore, two censorship problems in the story, not censorable in the theater, but definitely so on the screen: in the hospital sequence in which Arne, the little nephew, has had surgery for a malformed leg, Uncle Chris could not teach the boy to say "Damn!" when the pain became bad and "God damn!" when it became very bad; and Uncle Chris's longtime mistress, Jessie Brown, had at some point to become his legal wife or be separated from him. These matters were taken care of satisfactorily, with Uncle Chris teaching Arne to say something harmless in Norwegian; and before Uncle Chris dies, he confesses to Mama that years ago Jessie and he were married, but he never wanted the aunts to know because they had been so mean to her.

Irene Dunne, who was a youthful-looking fifty at the time, was the favorite for the role of Mama, but, although she loved the role, she realized that playing a mother of four growing children and changing her physical appearance to conform to character might keep her from that point on in character roles. She had director approval, however, and finally agreed to accept the part of Mama if one of five directors whose names she proposed was given the assignment. George Stevens, back in Hollywood after a longterm service in the Army overseas, was one of the directors listed, and he accepted the assignment as his first after his discharge. He wanted certain changes in the screenplay, so an entirely new version was written to his specifications.

I Remember Mama is more than a mother-love narrative; it is a simple family story with Mama an understanding matriarch, the ever-present lead. The focal character, however, is the "I" of the title; she is the oldest daughter, Katrin (Barbara Bel Geddes), who wants to be a writer. The picture fades in on her in her attic studio (her "boudoir," as she calls it) where she is writing the story of her family, and her voice over the scene narrates the action that opens the story outside the frame. Although Papa (Philip Dorn) is a hard-working carpenter, providing the means of support, it is first and foremost Mama who runs the family, who is its heart and its very life. Every Saturday night when Papa brings home his salary for the week, the family, father, mother, three daughters, and a son, all gather around the kitchen table, and as the weekly expenses are itemized, Mama counts out the sums in cash for which the money is to be spent—even the little things, such as ten cents for a new notebook. The children hover anxiously, watching Mama as she adds the items and then smiles in satisfaction, saying, "Is good. We do not have to go to the bank."

When Lars, the oldest child and the only son, confesses that he would like to go on to high school, each member of the family commits proudly to sacrifices so that he may go. Christine and Dagmar, the youngest sisters, promise to take on new chores that will bring in pennies; so does Katrin; Lars himself will take on an early paper route; Papa will give up tobacco for his pipe; and Mama will do without a new coat for the winter. Thus Lars's going on to high school becomes more than a possibility; it will be a fact. The family stays together because they help one another, which was once the way of the American family.

Mama has three sisters, and the aunts are frequent visitors. Mama also has an older brother known as Uncle Chris (Oscar Homolka), a rough-going character who runs a ranch in Ukiah, and who sometimes arrives without warning in his automobile, bringing boxes of oranges and good fresh food. He also brings with him Jessie Brown (Barbara O'Neil), known to the aunts as "that woman," who sits quietly in the car and waits while Uncle Chris concludes his cyclonic visit inside with Mama. On one occasion it is he who bundles up Mama, carrying little Dagmar, who is very ill with a mastoid, and drives them to the hospital for surgery.

The hospital sequence evokes both tears and laughter, bordering on sentiment that does not spill over into sentimentality. Mama, denied entry to the ward where Dagmar lies in postoperative recovery, contrives a scheme for entering the ward. She takes over for a scrubwoman, and, scrubbing her way past the watchful nurses on duty, gets into the forbidden ward, assures Dagmar that there is nothing to fear, and softly sings an old Norwegian lullaby so that not only her child but also all the children in the ward go peacefully to sleep.

I Remember Mama is a story of little things which, in time, become the most important, the best-remembered events in a family's life. In the end it is Mama who gets Katrin's manuscripts to a visiting authoress at the Fairmont Hotel in San Francisco and makes a deal with the lady so that Katrin eventually is represented by an agent. When the word comes that Katrin's story has been accepted and a check is enclosed, Katrin turns the check over to Mama and asks her to put it in the bank. With honest embarrassment, Mama confesses that she has never been inside a bank; there is no bank account; it had been a myth so that the children would not feel afraid and be insecure. By Scandinavian thrift the family has survived over adversity, and if Mama has been forced into deception to give her family a feeling of security, it is a kindly lie that can be forgiven, for the family has come of age, and they possess the one security that money will never buy—lasting love.

At a time when audiences were surfeited with big films on big postwar subjects, the simplicity and nostalgic charm of *I Remember Mama* also captured their fancy. It had its premiere, along with a big Easter stage show at Radio City Music Hall in New York City, where it ran for more than a month, earning excellent notices and public approval. When Academy Award time came, cinematographer Nick Musuraca and four of the cast members garnered nominations. Dunne received her fifth and last nomination as Best Actress, and she has stated that *I Remember Mama* and *Love Affair* (1937) are her two favorite roles. *I Remember Mama* is still shown in retrospectives. A true period piece, it has never dated, and audiences have never tired of laughing and crying, of living and remembering with Mama.

DeWitt Bodeen

I WALKED WITH A ZOMBIE

Released: 1943
Production: Val Lewton for RKO/Radio
Direction: Jacques Tourneur
Screenplay: Curt Siodmak and Ardel Wray; based on an original story by
  Inez Wallace and the novel *Jane Eyre* by Charlotte Brontë
Cinematography: J. Roy Hunt
Editing: Mark Robson
Art direction: Albert S. D'Agostino and Walter E. Keller
Sound: John C. Grubb
Music: Roy Webb
Running time: 68 minutes

Principal characters:
Wesley Rand .... James Ellison
Betsy Connell .... Frances Dee
Paul Holland .... Tom Conway
Mrs. Holland .... Edith Barrett
Dr. Maxwell .... James Bell
Jessica .... Christine Gordon
Alma .... Teresa Harris
Calypso singer .... Sir Lancelot
Carrefour .... Darby Jones

In *The Bad and the Beautiful* (1952), Hollywood producer Jonathan Shields (Kirk Douglas), the film's fictional protagonist, comes into his own with a little sleeper called *The Curse of the Cat Men*, in which horror is suggested rather than shown. Anxious to move on to bigger things, he is openly scornful of his next assignment, *The Son of the Cat Men*. The real Val Lewton, whose own success with *Cat People* (1942) inspired that section of the later film, was in actuality the temperamental opposite of Shields. He might not have wanted his next film to be called *I Walked with a Zombie*, but the title was his only compromise. He was happy to make modestly budgeted films, created with loyal and valued collaborators of his choosing under conditions of maximum freedom. Although another of his subsequent productions was christened *The Curse of the Cat People* (1944) by the studio, it involves neither curses *nor* cat people, being a work, much admired by child psychologists, about a lonely child and her imaginary playmate. Lewton's central preoccupation was the relationship between death and life, and he used the horror genre to approach this subject with resolute seriousness. If his first three films, *Cat People*, *The Body Snatcher* (1945), and this film, remain his best, this may be attributed to the presence of director Jacques Tourneur, who realized Lewton'a ideas with uncommon visual acuity and poetic suggestiveness, humbly contributing a few ideas of his own.

Tourneur's expressiveness is best displayed in *I Walked with a Zombie*, an enchanting film possessed of a subtlety at odds with the conventions of its genre and a beauty which might be described as otherworldly. Tourneur believed in the supernatural, and while the narrative action often seems susceptible to rational explanation, ultimately it escapes the rational and demands of us that we scorn reason, embracing elusive truths which initially seem fanciful. The opening image and voice-over narration beautifully establish the work's mood and are immediately evocative of how the film elicits an openness of response. The distant figures of two women, later to be identified as Betsy (Frances Dee) and Jessica (Christine Gordon), are seen walking in long-shot along a beach beneath a tranquil sky barely disturbed by drifting white clouds. Betsy speaks her narration quietly and sensibly. "I walked with a zombie. It sounds funny, I know. A year ago I didn't even know what a zombie was. . . ."

That image, seemingly a fragment of Betsy's consciousness as she recalls the events of the story, never appears again. Her voice assures us that the story will be subjectively related, but the image objectifies her. The heroine, whole and alive, she is at the same time identified as the companion of Jessica, a zombie, dead within a continuing physical existence. In this manner, death and life walk hand in hand throughout the film, metaphorically coexisting as determining factors of the destinies of the characters. Further, Betsy's control of the narrative proves to be illusory. Midway through the film, the voice-over narration stops, following Betsy's conscious recognition that she has fallen in love. Verging on the mysterious and unexplainable, the film must finally reject Betsy as a reasonable observer and absorb her into its ambiguous texture, pointedly at the moment when her emotions conquer her cultivated good sense.

Betsy is a Canadian nurse, sent to the island of St. Sebastian in the West Indies to take employment in the home of the owner of a sugar cane plantation, Paul Holland (Tom Conway). Paul's wife, Jessica exists in a state of what her doctor (James Bell) explains as a form of paralysis which has left her mind empty of thought and emotion, although her physical movements are unrestricted. The cause of her condition is mysterious, although several explanations are ultimately offered. It develops that Paul's half-brother Wesley Rand (James Ellison), now a hard-drinking wastrel, had been in love with Jessica, and the two had planned to run away together. That night, an encounter between husband, wife, and lover had resulted in Jessica's helpless state. Paul and Wesley's mother (Edith Barrett) later admits that she feels some of the responsibility for what happened, and her two sons each share her guilt. Betsy attempts to be dispassionate in her dealings with the family, but Paul's kindness and sensitivity arouse her sympathy, and, ultimately, her love. At this point, she resolves to do everything possible to cure Jessica, and her efforts include a nocturnal visit to a voodoo ceremony. Jessica remains a zombie, and Betsy is certain that Paul, although he shares her love, will never be free. Voodoo intervenes, and Wesley, in a trance, kills Jessica and carries her body, now as lifeless as her mind, into the ocean, dying himself. Paul and Betsy are united, and a chant spoken by the islanders warns that life should be spent with the living, while the dead should be left with the dead.

The thrust of the work is to affirm that people who have the capacity for living (Paul and Betsy) should not linger on the spectre of death, however morally conscientious their motives might be, and that a man like Wesley, seeking oblivion through drink and without the will to resume his life positively once Jessica is lost to him, belongs to the world of death and rightfully gives himself to it. Wesley, however, is no less sympathetic than the other characters, and Jessica, a haunting presence throughout the story, is treated as being deserving of compassion in spite of the seeming meaninglessness of her continued existence. The resolution in death of this couple's love occurs in the same sea upon which Betsy had gazed as her love for Paul was born, and this connection is symptomatic of the disturbing complexity with which the concept of death is imbued throughout the film. In the garden of the Holland home is a statue of St. Sebastian which the blacks call T-Misery. It had formerly been the figurehead of a slave ship, and it is the legacy of both the white and black characters who inhabit the island to remember that slavery somberly colors the island's history. For this reason, the blacks still rejoice when someone dies and weep when a baby is born. The telling effect of historical memory on the lives of the characters is thematically linked to the family history and to the "death" of Jessica.

This detailed context for an intimate story permeates the texture of the work, providing substance for its pervasive tone of melancholy and its twilight atmosphere. It is characteristic of the Tourneur-Lewton films (although not those Lewton made with others) for tragic episodes of historical oppression to be woven into events of the present. Similar motifs, the source of superstition and fantasy from which outsiders such as Betsy initially disengage themselves, are vital to *Cat People* and to the final collaboration, *The Leopard Man* (1943). *I Walked with a Zombie*, however, most thoroughly assimilates these past associations into its narrative. Slavery is implicitly linked to the state of living death embodied by Jessica. The imposing figure of Carrefour (Darby Jones), the black guardian of the crossroads, is also a zombie, and it is he who implacably follows Wesley to the sea in the climactic sequence and carries Jessica's body back to the house. Another black character, the calypso singer (Sir Lancelot), provides a narrative voice as authoritative as Betsy's. His song relates to her the history of the Rand-Holland family. The character's wry sense of humor and the song's gay and lilting melody contrast affectingly with the gentle resignation of the characters and the plaintiveness which typify Tourneur's rendering of the story.

Experience of the film reveals it to be very elaborate, but its story is quite simple. Nuance and detail, superficially incidental but essential to the film's philosophical tendencies, endow the narrative flow with a richness at once complementary to the lucidity with which it develops characters and describes events and unexpected in a film running only sixty-eight minutes. The intricacy of lighting, gracefulness of camera movement, and care taken in the art direction and editing testify to the flair of Lewton, Tourneur, and their colleagues for utilizing careful preparation and ready imagination to the best advantage. The artistry achieved in the film on a brief shooting schedule deserves to be envied by the makers of countless films not suffering from restraints of time and budget. The nonstar cast also contributes to this impression, especially the lovely Dee, a sadly underrated actress, as the idealistic but naïve Betsy, and Teresa Harris as Alma, a black servant who persuasively argues the superiority of voodoo over Christian medicine. Tourneur's contribution to the playing of his films is a very distinctive one. He encourages his actors and actresses to speak very quietly and to be dramatically restrained so that our attention to them becomes keener. While eerie and unsettling, sequences rooted in fear and the inexplicable are not handled for shock effect, making it difficult to relate *I Walked with a Zombie* to what is commonly thought of today as the horror genre. Its screenplay owes as much to romantic novels, especially Charlotte Brontë's *Jane Eyre*, which suggested the outline of the story. Critic Robin Wood, an ardent and insightful admirer of the film, was quite perceptive when he chose to describe it as a poetic fantasy.

Tourneur's style disdains scare tactics at the same time that it demonstrates an imposing respect for the supernatural. This stylistic individuality is discernible throughout the film, as Tourneur characteristically approaches every scene by seeking its overall mood rather than attempting to isolate and emphasize specific dramatic elements. He is most comfortable with long shots and camera movements which minimize the significance of particular actions and maximize the relationship of those actions to connected actions. This directorial attitude is of crucial importance in sequences that are primarily visual, most impressively that of the journey through the cane fields to the voodoo ceremony. This sequence introduces a new setting to the film, a world traveled at night which is strange and foreboding. Alternations of black and white, which extend from the costumes of the two women to the contrast of their pale faces with that of the silent Carrefour who materializes with disquieting suddenness in their path, provide an evocative link to unstated themes of the island's tragic racial history and the life-death symbiosis which governs the lives of all the central characters. The series of swift and graceful tracking shots which follow as Betsy resolutely leads Jessica through the rows of discreetly rustling cane vividly enhances the impression that the heroine is bravely venturing forth into a perilous unknown. Like her own emotional needs of which she is only semiconscious, the voodoo ceremony into which she and Jessica emerge is a half-comprehensible and half-frightening alien world. It is the strategy of the sequence to encourage the ambiguity of these impressions. Calm and assured, Tourneur invites tentative acceptance of the mysterious truths of the world he evokes, not oppressively but with a gentle magic.

Blake Lucas

I WAS A MALE WAR BRIDE

Released: 1949
Production: Sol C. Siegel for Twentieth Century-Fox
Direction: Howard Hawks
Screenplay: Charles Lederer, Leonard Spigelgass, and Hagar Wilde; based on a story of the same name by Henri Rochard
Cinematography: Norbert Brodine
Editing: James B. Clark
Running time: 105 minutes

> *Principal characters:*
> Captain Henri Rochard .... Cary Grant
> Lieutenant Catherine Gates .... Ann Sheridan
> WACS .... Marion Marshall and Randy Stuart
> Tony Jowitt .... Eugene Gericke
> Innkeeper's Assistant .... Ruben Wendorf
> Seaman .... Kenneth Tobey
> Lieutenant .... Robert Stevenson

Howard Hawks, one of cinema's universally acknowledged masters, made a number of comedies based on the battle of the sexes, and, more often than many of his colleagues, Hawks saw to it that his female characters gave as good as they got. Like *I Was a Male War Bride*, Hawks's *Bringing Up Baby* (1938), *His Girl Friday* (1940), and *Monkey Business* (1952) each featured Cary Grant versus a wily yet feminine antagonist. In *I Was a Male War Bride* more than any of the other films, Grant's character is completely put to rout— perhaps because his opponent, Ann Sheridan, has an accomplice that no other Hawksian heroine had: the American and French military bureaucracies.

I Was a Male War Bride falls neatly into two parts: Sheridan's pursuit of and ultimate capture of Grant; and, this capture having been effectuated, Grant's efforts to consummate his marriage on a wedding night and honeymoon during which all events appear to be conspiring to deny the couple any privacy.

As the film opens, Captain Henri Rochard of the French Army (Cary Grant) finds himself lost in Occupied Germany shortly after the close of hostilities in World War II. His driver, also French, asks a German citizen for directions to Heidelberg, and the two launch into a comical argument in French and German. Exasperated, Rochard stops a passing American GI, who gives him clear, concise directions to his destination. The scene is funny, and it also serves a purpose. Hawks uses this simple encounter to lay the groundwork for much of the action in the second half of the film. At this point, American efficiency serves Rochard well. Before long, however, he will be exposed to the opposite side of the same coin: a maze of perfectly logical bureaucratic regulations that will frustrate and ultimately unman him.

Henri Rochard has two missions in Heidelberg: to locate a German citizen named Schindler and to return some undergarments to Lieutenant Catherine Gates (Ann Sheridan), an American WAC with whom he has had an earlier run-in. The Lieutenant's underwear came into Rochard's possession through a mistaken laundry delivery, but the Captain makes the most of his opportunity to embarrass her—returning the garments in public, with a few appropriately suggestive remarks. When Catherine insists that he retract any intimation of a romantic connection between the two of them, he neatly turns her demand to his rhetorical advantage. "I'd be glad to explain that *any* connection between you and me is revolting." For the first and last time in the film, Rochard has the last word.

Rochard is dismayed to discover that Catherine, the object of his unofficial mission, is about to join him on his official mission; she has been assigned by the American forces to help him locate Herr Schindler. Rochard's sputtering protests are to no avail. "She's your man, all right," says the WAC major, ending the argument. A line like that could have been the focus of the whole scene, but Hawks tosses it out casually. He and his writers, Charles Lederer, Leonard Spiegelgass, and Hagar Wilde, have loaded the script with marvelously witty lines, and Hawks has the sense not to sledgehammer them into the viewer's consciousness. They are, rather, a part of the film's flow. This particular line, of course, will reverberate ironically later in the film, when Catherine, by then Mrs. Rochard, becomes a female war groom.

Hawks's next bit of business is to illuminate the origins of the tiff between Catherine and Rochard—a shaggy dog story which culminates in Gates's having pushed Rochard into a vat of blue dye. "I thought it was water," she giggles innocently. "He's a lot of fun to fight with," she confides to one of her friends after Rochard leaves; and thus we get our first inkling that the feud may have a romantic ending.

Meanwhile, Captain Rochard's struggles with the American military bureaucracy are just beginning. Their mission requires them to go to Bad Neuheim. The only transportation available is a motorcycle, which regulations say must be driven by an American—Catherine Gates. Rochard's misery at being driven by a woman is compounded when the cycle's side car, in which he is to ride, comes uncoupled when Catherine starts up, and she rides off leaving him behind (a scene which Hawks will repeat, with a variation, later in the film).

They arrive at Bad Neuheim and check into an inn—two rooms, of course. Hawks reveals a bit of Catherine's more feminine side in the scene that ensues. Stiff from the long motorcycle ride, Catherine nevertheless spurns Henri's offer of a back rub. Her cockiness vanishes, and she seems genuinely vulnerable and alarmed at the prospect of being alone in a bedroom with Rochard. He quiets her fears, however, and promising to leave the room as soon as she falls asleep, begins to massage her back—through her pajama top.

The funniest sustained sequence in the film comes as Catherine drifts off to sleep, and the honorable Rochard, trying to return to his own room, cannot get out of hers when the doorknob comes off in his hand. "She'll never believe me," mutters Rochard, looking for a way out of his dilemma. His egress from the room blocked, he begins to search for a way to spend the night in comfort; but no matter how he contorts himself in various chairs, sleep eludes him. Finally he gives up, and, fully clothed, lies down (on top of the covers) next to Catherine and goes to sleep.

"You unspeakable weasel," Catherine cries when she awakens to find him in (or rather, on) her bed. He tells her about the doorknob; naturally, when she tries it, it works perfectly. After much hilarity, the matter is finally straightened out. Once again, Hawks has constructed a scene that is both funny and useful. The back rub is the closest Rochard will come to consummating his relationship with Catherine, and the whole incident foreshadows his later problems in finding a suitable place to sleep—with or without Catherine. To compound Rochard's embarrassment, Catherine beats him to Herr Schindler. Now professionally as well as socially humiliated, he says that he never wants to see her again. Catherine is shocked. "After all we've done together. After all we *haven't* done together."

On their way back to Heidelberg in the motorcycle, however, Rochard softens. They talk, and Catherine parks the cycle for a bit and gets out. When the cycle begins moving again, he resumes the conversation. "I like you very much," he admits. "I'd miss you if you weren't here." He is so wrapped up in his confession of love for Catherine that he fails to notice that she *is not* there—that, in fact, the cycle had begun rolling without her, and was at that very moment plunging headlong towards a haystack. After the crash, Henri discovers that he has been "fooled" again, and is momentarily furious, but Catherine calms him down with a kiss.

The next scene occurs at WAC headquarters in Heidelberg. Catherine's announcement to her superior that she and Rochard want to get married signals the beginning of the second half of the film. Having succumbed to Catherine, Henri proceeds to take on, and lose to, the American military bureaucracy. If the second half of the film is a bit less interesting than the first half, it is because Catherine Gates makes a much more delightful antogonist for Rochard than does a bureaucracy.

Struggling against red tape, the pair are married (the ceremony is conducted three times, in three different languages, before everyone is satisfied). Their troubles, however, are just beginning. The wedding night is interrupted when Catherine is ordered to return to her quarters immediately. She is being sent home to the United States. Nevertheless, Catherine is more fortunate than her husband. She has a bed. In England, *I Was a Male War Bride* was released as *You Can't Sleep Here*; this is the litany that Captain Rochard hears over and over again as he seeks a place to sleep—first with his wife, but finally just to sleep, period. They are up against a Catch-22 in the immigration regulations, which provide for the immigration of an American officer's spouse—but the spouse is always assumed to be a woman.

Finally, a desperate Henri bows to the inevitable. If he must become a woman to be with his wife, he will do so. Donning a WAC's uniform and a wig fashioned out of a horse's tail, Rochard is finally granted admission on the ship sailing for America. His humiliation is complete. The ruse does not remain undetected for long, of course, and Rochard is soon arrested. Even after the ship's Captain frees him, he elects to remain in the brig, since he is not allowed to see his wife. When at long last Catherine is permitted to visit him, he ecstatically locks the door behind her and throws the key out the porthole. She asks him how they will get out, and he replies grandly "I'm not going to worry about that until the Statue of Liberty goes by that porthole." As Rochard speaks, Hawks inflicts one last defeat on the poor Captain. He cuts to the porthole, through which we see Miss Liberty in the harbor. The ship has arrived, and Rochard's marriage will have to wait a bit longer to be consummated.

Although Hawks has named *I Was a Male War Bride* as one of his favorite films, critics have generally neglected it in favor of his other comedies, particularly *His Girl Friday* and *Bringing Up Baby*. Certainly the film is not helped much by its title, which suggests a movie far less sophisticated than the film Hawks actually turned out. In addition, *I Was a Male War Bride* is, in visual terms, easily the starkest of Hawks's comedies. The lighting is subdued, and many scenes take place at night and/or indoors. Most of the interiors are furnished sparely, and most of the characters in the film wear military uniforms. But the superficial drabness of the film is also, in a sense, a strength. The spartan decor not only helps to lend a sense of realism to the film; but against this grayness, the sparkle of the dialogue also takes on added luster.

Of course, the brightest dialogue would be of little use without talented actors to deliver it; and Grant and Sheridan fill the bill nicely. Catherine Gates is, in many ways, the least feminine of the female leads in Hawks's comedies, and Sheridan is careful to add the touches of girlishness—an occasional giggle, her convincing alarm at being alone with Rochard in her room at the inn—that keep the part sympathetic. Just as Catherine Gates is a match for Henri Rochard, Sheridan is a worthy "opponent" for Grant.

Grant, of course, is a past master at this sort of comedy. His wit and charm shine through the part; he is lovable even when he is irritable. Grant also excels at reaction comedy—he is as effective as the victim of a joke as he is as the perpetrator—and Hawks and his writers gave Grant plenty to react against in *I Was a Male War Bride*.

While it would be exaggerating things to call *I Was a Male War Bride* a classic screen comedy, it is nevertheless a rewarding film. Grant and Sheridan turn in memorable performances, and Hawks shows his inimitable style. He wastes nothing; the film is a study in economy. Scenes that are funny in and of themselves are used to set up and foreshadow even funnier scenes later on. Clearly, *I Was a Male War Bride* is the work of a master craftsman.

James P. Girard

IF. . . .

Released: 1968
Production: Lindsay Anderson and Michael Medwin (Memorial Enterprises) for Paramount
Direction: Lindsay Anderson
Screenplay: David Sherwin; based on the original screenplay "Crusaders" by David Sherwin and John Howlett
Cinematography: Miroslav Ondricek
Editing: David Gladwell
Production design: Jocelyn Herbert
Music: Marc Wilkinson
Running time: 111 minutes

Principal characters:
Mick Travers	Malcolm McDowell
Johnny	David Wood
Wallace	Richard Warwick
The Girl	Christine Noonan
Rowntree	Robert Swann
The Headmaster	Peter Jeffrey
Mr. Kemp	Arthur Lowe
Bobby Philips	Rupert Webster

If. . . . takes its title from a Rudyard Kipling ballad and, like Kipling's work, it concerns itself with the stuff from which the British Empire was forged. Unlike Kipling, however, it is devoted to the belief that the Empire was more likely lost than won on the playing fields of Eton. Its theme of student revolt made it particularly timely, since shooting began in March, 1968, two months before the May, 1968, student riots in Paris; and timeliness briefly gave it the reputation of being more revolutionary than it in fact was. *If.* . . . also acquired a different kind of notoriety, since it contained both male and female full frontal nudity. Interestingly, this did not appear to concern the National Catholic Office for Motion Pictures, which passed it A-4 (morally unobjectionable for adults, with reservations), on the grounds that the exhibition of genitalia was not, in itself, reason for condemning a film. The MPAA, on the other hand, still in the first year of its ratings system, decided it needed to rely on what it called "objective" criteria rather than interpretation, and these criteria had a very simple message: genitalia warrant an X-rating. An appeal by Paramount in March, 1969, did not alter the situation. Finally, to gain an R-rating, the offending frames were removed, and *If.* . . . was shown in the United States at a running time one minute shorter than the British release version.

Given the film's consummate skill, it seems strange to realize that *If.* . . .

is only Lindsay Anderson's second feature as a director. He had previously made *This Sporting Life* (1963), as well as a number of highly praised shorts, dating back to his days as one of the founders of the British Free Cinema movement (along with Karel Reisz and Tony Richardson) in the 1950's. Anderson's chief area of activity was (and is) the theater, and many of the people he brought with him to work on *If.* . . . came from a theater background. Two of the three leads, David Wood and Richard Warwick, were new to films; the music was composed by the musical director of the British National Theatre; and the production was designed by a stage designer, Jocelyn Herbert, who had previously worked with Tony Richardson on *Tom Jones* (1963).

The screenplay belongs in one of the stranger backwaters of British juvenilia: the public school novel. British public schools are, in fact, private and fee-paying: they are the expensive preserve of the aristocracy and the upper-middle class, accounting for only five out of every two hundred schoolboys, but providing, at the time of the film's release, one in every three entrants to the Universities of Oxford and Cambridge. They are, in short, the roots of the British class system, the source of the "old boy network," and the breeding ground for the values and privileges of the British Establishment. David Sherwin and John Howlett had written the first draft of *If.* . . . (under the title "Crusaders") shortly after leaving a public school for Oxford. Like most such works, it exposed the pomposity, brutality, and generally Dickensian behavior of British public school life. The film itself, for which Sherwin alone wrote the screenplay, was shot on location at a public school, Cheltenham College, in Gloucestershire.

If. . . . is the story of three senior students at College House—Mick (Malcolm McDowell), Johnny (David Wood), and Wallace (Richard Warwick)— who rebel against the authority of the house prefects ("Whips"), at first tacitly, through insubordination, for which they are flogged by the head Whip, Rowntree (Robert Swann); next through a brief forbidden jaunt into town where they steal a motorcycle; then, more fundamentally, by bayoneting the school chaplain during a cadet training field exercise. The headmaster (Peter Jeffrey) offers them a chance to redeem themselves by clearing out the junk from beneath the stage of the school hall, where they happen across some arms and ammunition. When Speech Day arrives and the hall is filled with parents and guests listening to the jingoistic sentiments of a general, the three boys, accompanied by a younger boy (Rupert Webster) and a girl from the town (Christine Noonan), climb onto the chapel roof and open fire. The headmaster is shot between the eyes. As the film ends, the boys are still up on the roof, firing on a counterattack led by the general.

If. . . . has one clear cinematic predecessor: Jean Vigo's 1933 French masterpiece, *Zéro de Conduite*, which also concerned a school revolt and which is more or less openly acknowledged in the final sequences on the chapel roof. In Vigo's film, the dividing line between fantasy and reality is consciously blurred by the device of presenting the entire story from the boys' point of view. In *If. . . .*, the point of view remains constantly external (or directorial), and the question of what is or is not fantasy seems to have greatly perplexed critics at the time of the film's release. Does the housemaster's wife really wander naked through the deserted dormitories, touching articles of the boys' clothing? Is the chaplain really pulled from a drawer in the headmaster's study? Do Mick and the girl really end up naked on the floor of a cafe? Finally, do the boys really open up on the authorities with machine guns at the end?

The questions are probably unanswerable, but, more importantly, the film's literal (rather than literary) title encourages the viewer to deal with a realistic portrayal of a hypothesis: this is what would happen if. . . . The hypothesis is not a particularly attractive one. Mick, Johnny, and Wallace are, for all their revolt, very much products of the public school system. They lurk in their rooms, staring at their faces in the mirror for signs of age, and endlessly playing the primitive chants of the Congolese "Missa Luba" (for which the film created something of a cult in Britain). More importantly, they are, like all public school boys, given extensive military training (on the assumption that discipline is a key factor in a gentleman's education, and that learning to kill people is also useful). In the end, they learn the lessons. They turn the establishment's weapons back on itself. Their revolt is contained within the system against which they are rebelling, and, lacking any theoretical framework, their revolt is bound to fail. Only a fade-out can save them, and life has no fade-outs.

Anderson's approach to the telling of this bizarre story is essentially straightforward. He avoids fancy camera angles and all the other progressive filmmaking techniques prevalent in the late 1960's. His one apparent deviation from the norm—the use of occasional black-and-white footage—appears to have been dictated by financial or technical considerations (lack of money or light), rather than any desire to add a symbolic dimension. If there is one fashionable adjective that might justly be applied to *If. . . .*, it is "Brechtian," not because of any obvious alienating devices (although the film is divided up into labeled chapters), but because Anderson maintains an equal distance from *all* his characters. Mick, Johnny, and Wallace are attractive because they rebel against a patently unjust and absurd system; but they are not particularly attractive characters in their own right. On the other hand, some of the figures of authority, although clearly part of an oppressive regime, have definite human characteristics.

If. . . . was a brave follow-up, on the part of Albert Finney and Michael Medwin's Memorial Enterprises, to their equally brave debut with *Charlie Bubbles* the previous year. Miroslav Ondricek's cinematography is very fine, and the general level of performance by a host of British character actors

(Peter Jeffrey, Arthur Lowe, Mona Washbourne, Geoffrey Chater, Graham Crowden, and Charles Lloyd Pack) is exceptional. The three newcomers in the starring roles give excellent performances (McDowell has, of course, since gone on to major stardom), and there is also a sensitive portrayal by Rupert Webster of a pretty young boy who becomes the focus of the homosexual affections of one of the Whips, and who ends up joining Johnny, Mick, and Wallace in their revolt. Although the film may have certain weaknesses—the second half, in particular, lacks the crisp cumulative effect of the opening scenes, especially that of the boys' return to College House at the start—it nevertheless remains one of the truly memorable British movies of a decade in which the British cinema seemed, for a while, as though it was due for a major renaissance.

Nick Roddick

IF I WERE KING

Released: 1938
Production: Frank Lloyd for Paramount
Direction: Frank Lloyd
Assistant direction: William Tummell and Harry Scott
Screenplay: Preston Sturges; based on the novel and the play of the same name by Justin Huntley McCarthy
Cinematography: Theodore Sparkuhl
Editing: Hugh Bennett
Special effects: Gordon Jennings
Running time: 100 minutes

Principal characters:

François Villon	Ronald Colman
Louis XI	Basil Rathbone
Katherine de Vaucelles	Frances Dee
Huguette	Ellen Drew
Captain of the Watch	Henry Wilcoxon
Father Villon	C. V. France
The Queen	Heather Thatcher
René de Montigny	Stanley Ridges
Oliver le Dain	Ralph Forbes
Thibaut d'Aussigny	John Miljan
Tristan l'Hermite	Walter Kingsford
Robin Turgis	Sidney Toler
General Barbezier	William Farnum
General Dudon	Montagu Love
General Salier	Lester Matthews

François Villon (1431-1463?), the greatest poet of medieval France, had a master's degree from the Sorbonne, but he was also a vagabond and rogue who killed a man and became a member of the *coquillards*, a band of thieves which flourished at the end of the Hundred Years' War. Born François de Montcorbier, Villon took his name from a priest who reared him. His poetry, some of it in thieves' jargon, consists of *The Little Testament* and *The Grand Testament*, works that in their picture of the underworld, criminals, and prostitutes, and in their obsession with death, rebelliousness, bawdry, gallows humor, pathos, repentance, and intense self-analysis, have appealed to such modern poets as Ezra Pound and T. S. Eliot.

After the Renaissance, Villon's life and works were largely forgotten until the nineteenth century, when Théophile Gautier revived his writings in France, and the English pre-Raphaelites Dante Gabriel Rossetti and Algernon Charles Swinburne translated some of his best works and presented him as a fellow Bohemian rebelling against Victorian restraints. Suddenly Villon came into vogue among the Victorians; other poets translated all of his work, and Robert Louis Stevenson wrote a story about him entitled "A Lodging for the Night" (1877). For the most part, the Victorians portrayed Villon as an engaging but scurvy rogue; but in 1901, Justin Huntly McCarthy, a member of the British parliament from 1884 to 1892, transformed him into a noble romantic hero in the novel and play *If I Were King*. The novel, with three sets corresponding to the acts of a play, is a stagy affair full of what W. S. Gilbert called "platitudes in stained-glass attitudes." It nevertheless appealed to audiences in an era when historical romances flourished as best-sellers. In 1925, Rudolph Friml turned the story into the popular operetta *The Vagabond King*.

Eventually the story of Villon was picked up by Hollywood. Dustin Farnum starred in a 1920 film version of *If I Were King*, and in 1926 John Barrymore played Villon in *The Beloved Rogue*, with Conrad Veidt as King Louis XI. One of the first sound musicals was *The Vagabond King* (1930), starring Dennis King and Jeannette MacDonald.

The fourth and best film version of Villon is *If I Were King* (1938), starring Ronald Colman as Villon and Basil Rathbone as Louis XI. At that time, Colman rivaled Errol Flynn as the chief swashbuckler in films. Although Colman also did drawing-room comedy, serious modern drama such as *Arrowsmith* (1931), and classics such as *A Tale of Two Cities* (1935), he had swashbuckled spectacularly in such silent films as *The Night of Love* (1927), *The Magic Flame* (1928), and *Two Lovers* (1929) and had recently been the dashing hero of *Clive of India* (1935) and *Under Two Flags* (1936). His latest hit, and one of the most popular films of 1937, was *The Prisoner of Zenda*, in which he played an Englishman who impersonates the abducted King Rudolph of Ruritania and saves the king by a spectacular duel in Zenda castle. *If I Were King* seemed a suitable successor; its very title recalled the plot of *The Prisoner of Zenda*. Furthermore, Colman's mellifluous voice seemed ideal for Villon's verse.

Fortunately, Preston Sturges was selected to write the screenplay. Although he retained McCarthy's basic plot, Sturges threw out the melodramatic and stilted dialogue and replaced it with a witty script full of amusing repartee, especially between Villon and the king. Accordingly, *If I Were King* is as much a sophisticated romantic comedy as it is a swashbuckler.

The film opens with a panorama of medieval Paris at night. After the credits, shown on various peaked rooftops, the story begins when Villon and his band rob one of the king's storehouses. One of his men, René de Montigny (Stanley Ridges), wants to cut the throat of the watchman, but Villon stops him, saying that he is sure the watchman will forget them and that in any case they are not murderers. Their activities interrupted by the watch, most of the band escape by boat. Villon, guarding their rear, flees on foot with the watch at his heels. After a lively chase, he takes refuge in the parsonage of his foster-father, a priest. Father Villon (C. V. France) berates him for his roguery but shelters him and offers him his own breakfast. At that point, the watch arrive, and the captain (Henry Wilcoxon) demands to know Villon's whereabouts. The priest replies, truthfully, that he did not see anyone climb over his wall; he fails to tell them that Villon is hiding upstairs. The watch nevertheless search upstairs and find knotted sheets hanging from the bedroom window. After they climb down and go off into the night, Villon emerges laughing from a wardrobe.

He wishes to finish his breakfast, but instead, the priest hauls him off to church to repent his wicked ways. While kneeling, supposedly at his prayers, Villon is struck by the beauty of a courtly lady praying at a side altar. When she leaves, he hobbles on his knees to the door and follows her. Fortunately for him, her carriage has been delayed because the postillions are gambling. When her chaperone goes to fetch them, Villon accosts the lady, rhapsodizes over her beauty, and recites to her the poem "If I Were King." He is interrupted by the watch, but the storehouse watchman, whose life Villon had saved, swears he never saw the poet, and the lady tells the watch that Villon was in church with her. He roars with laughter as the watch reluctantly let him go.

We then follow the lady, Katherine de Vaucelles (Frances Dee) to the royal palace. There we learn that Paris is surrounded by a Burgundian army and that Louis XI has been unable to get his generals and their soldiers to fight. The prospect looks like slow starvation for the court and quick starvation for the already famished populace. Louis, however, discovers that there is a spy in his court. An arrow containing a message intended for the spy was shot over the wall, and the man who picked it up was apprehended. Going to the torture chamber, the king learns from the prisoner only that there was to be a rendezvous at the Fircone tavern. Although the tavern is in the Court of Miracles, Paris's den of thieves, Louis determines to go there in disguise, accompanied by his chief of intelligence, Tristan l'Hermite (Walter Kingsford).

There, they are accosted by two wenches who sit in their laps, fondle them, and ask for drinks. Louis is enjoying himself, but the sport is interrupted by the arrival of Villon and his band with the spoils of the storehouse. Immediately a feast is set in progress among the hungry thieves and beggars. Hailed and embraced by Huguette (Ellen Drew), one of the wenches who both loves him and is infuriated with his errant ways, Villon engages in conversation with the disguised king, whom he insults as a dried-up husk. He also protests Louis XI's do-nothing policy with the Burgundians, and when challenged to provide a better plan, boasts of how he would rule better, hang the court's knaves, beginning with Tristan l'Hermite, and trounce the army besieging the city. Louis is both amused and outraged by such braggadocio.

Their dialogue is interrupted by the watch, still in pursuit of Villon, but this time headed by the Grand Constable himself. As his password to the tavern, Louis had produced the spy's arrow and given it to the landlord. Now the landlord turns it over to the Grand Constable, indicating that he was the spy at court. Louis notes this, while the captain of the watch attempts to arrest Villon. The poet whips out his sword, and instantly a great brawl erupts, during which Villon kills the Grand Constable. The watch finally restore order, and the captain orders Villon's hanging, when the king reveals himself and orders the rioters taken to the royal dungeons.

There Villon composes and recites "The Ballade of the Hanged." Instead of being hanged, however, he is summoned alone to the king, who feels compelled to punish him for robbery and murder but to reward him for executing the spy. In a moment of perverse whimsy, Louis makes Villon Grand Constable, with the title Count of Montcorbier, to replace the man he killed.

Bathed, his beard shaved off, and dressed in courtly attire, the new Grand Constable summons the Fircone rioters before him for trial. Hidden behind a massive book, he enjoys playing cat and mouse with them but pardons them all as the first step of what he calls the king's new policy of mercy. Louis has observed this scene from a balcony and is more amused than outraged. He and the entire court are impressed when Villon gives a ringing speech of defiance to the insolent Burgundian herald who has come to demand the city's surrender. Villon learns, however, that it is easier to speak bold words than to get the French generals to fight. He is more successful in wooing the lady Katherine, who does not realize that the new Grand Constable was the ragged poet Villon. Villon gives Louis good advice on how to govern through mercy rather than terror and how to replace despair with hope by helping the people rather than by oppressing them, but Louis does not learn. When Villon asks for more time in which to defeat the Burgundians, Louis informs him with a sinister cackle that he is Grand Constable for only a week, at the end of which time he will be hanged. Meanwhile, he is under guard.

Assuming that if they are as starved as the populace, the court will have to fight, Villon takes the guard with him and opens all the royal warehouses to the starving vagabonds of Paris. Still the army will not fight, however, and the week runs out. On the last night, Villon confesses his true identity to Katherine, who is momentarily crushed by the deception. At that moment, Father Villon arrives with news for the Grand Constable that the Burgundian army has broken through the west gate of the city and that René de Montigny has gathered an army of vagabonds to loot Paris during the battle. He urges François to stop them.

Villon makes a daring escape from the palace and rides to the Court of Miracles, where he puts down Montigny and recruits the vagabonds to fight for the city and against the Burgundians, whom he calls rival thieves poaching on their preserve. Accordingly, troops armed with pitchforks, scythes, and any weapons at hand roar out of the Court of Miracles and attack the Burgundians from the rear. The invaders are defeated, but in the fight, Huguette is killed. Villon is arrested; but when the king learns that it was he and not the army who saved the city, he commutes the sentence to banishment from Paris. Villon leaves without seeing the Lady Katherine, but she learns his route and follows after him, waiting until he becomes very tired of walking before she comes up with her carriage, because "He is a very obstinate man."

The plot of *If I Were King* is contrived, and of course it grossly violates history. Charles the Bold of Burgundy did rebel against Louis XI, but he never actually besieged Paris, nor did Villon and his vagabonds defeat him. Villon never became Grand Constable of France. He was tortured by Thibault d'Aussigny (who was actually Bishop of Orleans), was exiled from Paris, and vanished from history not long after his thirtieth year. His heroics are entirely fictitious. Katherine de Vaucelles was actually a coquette whom Villon called his "lady of the crooked nose," and Huguette was really the Abbess of Port Royal, a disgraced nun notorious for her sexual activities. Villon was not made Count of Montcorbier; de Montcorbier was in fact his real name. Furthermore, it is ironic that the title poem, probably thought to be the best-known poem of Villon (Douglas Fairbanks, Jr., once recited it on television as a poem by Villon) was not written by Villon at all but by McCarthy.

Such inaccuracies do not really matter, however; the Robin Hood and Man in the Iron Mask stories certainly violate history at least as much. What does count is Sturges' clever repartee, Frank Lloyd's energetic direction, the spectacular sets and good production values, and the bravura performances by Colman and Rathbone. As a swashbuckler, Colman is gentler, more debonaire, and less athletic than Flynn, but he portrays Villon with an enormously engaging panache and contagious high spirits. Rathbone, usually a suave and sneering villain when he was not playing Sherlock Holmes in the long-running series of films, has one of his few chances to do some character acting. As Louis XI, his aquiline features are almost unrecognizable. He is bent over and shriveled and speaks with a shrill cackle which belies his own marvelous speaking voice. For his performance, Rathbone was nominated for an Academy Award as Best Supporting Actor. Although Colman usually gets the last word, the king is clever too, and the battle of wits between them is a *tour de force*. Colman handles the poetry with a fine flair and gets to deliver two authentic Villon poems—"The Ballade of the Hanged" and part of "The Ballade of Dead Ladies"—as well as McCarthy's spurious "If I Were King."

Practically all of the film—even the opening credits—takes place either at night or indoors, creating a sense of the underworld, of confinement and imprisonment that matches the mood and plot. The only daylight scenes are a brief one outside the church when Villon first speaks to the lady Katherine, the one in which he opens the warehouses to the people, and the ending when he is hiking out of Paris into the open countryside. All of these are scenes of liberation.

The first half of the film is the best; the vagabond sequences have a raffish quality that dissipates somewhat when Villon is transformed into an elegant courtier. The plot, too, falls off in the second half; Villon's repeated and unsuccessful exhortations to the generals become a bit tiresome. The ending, however, with Villon recruiting the vagabonds and the vigorous battle, picks up again, so that when the film was briefly revived in Los Angeles in 1975, it received an ovation from the audience.

Villon was portrayed on screen one final time in a disastrous 1956 version of *The Vagabond King*, starring opera singer Oreste and Kathryn Grayson, with Sir Cedric Hardwicke as the king. Louis XI was portrayed again on screen in 1939 in *The Hunchback of Notre Dame*, in which Harry Davenport plays him as a benevolent grandfatherly type, and in *Quentin Durward* (1956), in which the corpulent English actor Robert Morley is grossly miscast as the cadaverous monarch. As for Colman, he again played Villon on the radio, both in a broadcast of *If I Were King* and in Stevenson's "A Lodging for the Night." It is one of the roles for which he is best remembered.

Robert E. Morsberger

IF IT'S TUESDAY, THIS MUST BE BELGIUM

Released: 1969
Production: Stan Margulies for David L. Wolper; released by United Artists
Direction: Mel Stuart
Screenplay: David Shaw
Cinematography: Vilis Lapenieks
Editing: David Saxon
Running time: 98 minutes

Principal characters:

Samantha	Suzanne Pleshette
Charlie	Ian McShane
Jenny Grant	Mildred Natwick
Fred Ferguson	Murray Hamilton
Jack Harmon	Michael Constantine
John Marino	Sandy Baron
Harve Blakely	Norman Fell
Edna Ferguson	Peggy Cass
Bert Greenfield	Marty Ingels
Freda	Pamela Britton
Harry Dix	Aubrey Morris
Irma Blakely	Reva Rose
Giuseppi	Mario Carotenuto

If It's Tuesday, This Must Be Belgium is a bit of fluff slickly produced in 1969 to capitalize on the American passion for travel in Europe, which reached its peak around that time. It is not a great film, but because it contains elements of "travel humor" which are meaningful to anyone who has ever taken a European tour, it has become something of a middle-aged, middle-class cult favorite on television. In fact, the title of the film has since become synonymous with the type of "five-countries-in-five-days" travel arrangements which are still popular. Although it is not a critical masterpiece, there are some very funny moments in the film, some charming performances, and an early example of the voyage genre. In a comic way, *If It's Tuesday, This Must Be Belgium* was the first of the so-called "disaster" films of the 1970's, preceding *Airport* by one year. In this case, however, rather than one serious disaster loosely linking individual stories, a number of small, funny disasters are linked together by the trip. In *If It's Tuesday, This Must Be Belgium*, the bus does not explode, however—the occupants do.

The tone of the agonies and expectations of the trip begin with the opening credits. A montage of several people discussing and preparing for a two-week European tour with a company based in London shows vaccinations, apprehensions, and various other typically travel-oriented activities. Much background information about the characters is given succinctly as each one approaches his trip in a different way. One family wants to take their boy-crazy daughter away for a while; one man wants to return to the location of the highlight of his life, Europe in World War II; another man wants to visit his family in Italy; and so on. Some are enthusiastic, some are frightened, and some are cynical about the whole enterprise. It is not an exaggeration to say that almost every stereotype that one might encounter on such a trip is represented in this film.

The first "disaster" occurs when the tourists arrive at Heathrow Airport and are not met on time by the company's guide, Charlie (Ian McShane), who has overslept because of his amorous adventures with an attractive girl. This mistake starts the trip off badly, but the fledgling travelers go forward to see London. The film has many montages as various members of the group discuss what they see, what they miss, their cameras, and their tired feet. Also, the montages enable the audience to get the feeling of a whirlwind trip. Each morning the hallway outside the group's rooms is seen vacant; then the film speeds up to show the various suitcases appearing in rapid-fire succession, all ready to board the bus at eight o'clock.

At first, most of the tourists are enthusiastic, but as the trip goes faster and faster, they become tired, disgusted, and anxious. Much of the action takes place in subplots concerning the various tourists, none of which seems to dominate the others except for the one concerning Charlie and Samantha (Suzanne Pleshette), one of the tourists who has taken the trip to think over her relationship with her rather staid fiancé back home. Although he is per-petually chasing women, Charlie begins to fall in love with Samantha. She at first rebuffs his attentions, thinking that he is an opportunist, but she later becomes infatuated with him after a romantic evening spent at the trip's "Complimentary Fondue Fun" evening in Switzerland.

Two or three vignettes are the highlights of the film. Chronologically, the first concerns a husband and wife, Harve and Irma Blakely (Norman Fell and Reva Rose), who become separated when Irma falls asleep in the wrong tour bus after she becomes sick at a cheese-tasting festival in Holland. In a sea of large tour buses, the nauseated woman accidentally boards a bus intended for a Japanese tour group, and she winds up taking the rest of the trip with them. The Japanese tour crosses paths with Charlie's tour at several points, and we see the anxious husband waving at his wife (who is now dressed in a kimono) as they go in opposite directions. The most clever incident occurs when they have scheduled to meet after their Rhine River cruises, but realize as their ships pass on the river that their respective tours are going in opposite directions.

The next important incident occurs at the monument to the Battle of the Bulge in Belgium. Jack Harmon (Michael Constantine) considers this the highpoint of the trip. As it turns out, he has taken this particular tour only because it follows the same route that he took as a GI in World War II. When he approaches the monument, he explains to fellow passenger Freda (Pamela Britton) the way the Americans fought against the Germans, complete with arm motions and rat-a-tat-tat mock machine-gun sounds. The camera then goes back for a long shot, and the audience sees another man telling his wife the story of the Battle of the Bulge, only this time in German. As the German man makes almost the same motions and sounds as the American, the two couples pass, each one impervious to the presence of the other.

Perhaps the single funniest scene in the film occurs when John Marino (Sandy Baron) goes to visit some relative in Venice. At first the house of his relatives seems dark and foreboding, but once his cousin Giuseppi (Mario Carotenuto) realizes who he his, the Italian pulls him into the house, and almost immediately, dozens of loud, boisterous Italians surround him. Poor John does not understand a word they are saying, but senses (correctly) that they want him to marry their rather heavy daughter. In the middle of the loud talk, food, and frenzied activities of the family, John sees the bathroom as his only means of escape. He locks himself in, then escapes through the open window and jumps into the canal. Later, when the tour is in Rome, he deftly avoids meeting another cousin, who constantly calls at his hotel, only to discover as the tour is leaving that his Roman cousin is a beautiful woman, played in a cameo part by Italian actress Virna Lisi.

All of the stories eventually come to a close in Rome, the tour's last stopping point. The tourists, who have now all come to love traveling, are starting to plan their next trips. The only sad note is that Charlie, heretofore a thoughtless womanizer, is left by Samantha, who wants to return home to her more real-life existence. In the final scenes, Charlie is seen on another bus with a new, green group of tourists, starting another tour. This time, however, he seems to have softened and promises them "romance," which he says has often happened in Europe, even on that very bus.

The two stars of the film, McShane and Pleshette, are good in their roles, but as the only two "straight" characters in the film, their story is rather forgettable next to the pratfalls of the other members of the tour. Especially good are Baron as the Italian-American, Marty Ingels as the unsuccessful woman chaser who sends photographs of beautiful women back to his buddies at home, Constantine as the ex-GI who still uses military time, and Murray Hamilton as the anxious father who is dragged on the trip but winds up having a wonderful time. In addition to the character actors, there are several cameos in the film which are noteworthy, among them those by John Cassavetes, Virna Lisi, and Vittorio De Sica. De Sica is particularly good as a shoe salesman who impresses Fred Ferguson (Murray Hamilton) with his crafts-manship and honesty, immediately afterwards wrapping up a pair of prefab-ricated but purportedly handmade shoes to be sent to Hamilton back home in the United States. The increasingly loud talking and sign language used between two men, neither of whom understands the other's language, is a classic tourist encounter. It seems to follow the traveler's adage that if a foreigner does not understand what you are saying, simply say it louder and he will.

The sleeper performance of the film is given by Aubrey Morris as Harry Dix, a mild-mannered, soft-spoken single man who takes advantage of every premium the tour package has to offer and matter of factly steals every possible souvenir he can, from ashtrays to telephones. At the end of the film, his by-now lead weight suitcase drops, and all of the precious reminders of the trip fall out. Anyone who has ever stolen a hotel ashtray or thought of stealing one can appreciate Mr. Dix, who, in the final shot of a sign reading "The End," steals the sign.

If It's Tuesday, This Must Be Belgium did not win any major awards, but it did do reasonably well at the box office. Its main assets are the character performances by many familiar supporting players, beautiful location cinematography, and a funny script. As an ironic sidelight to the film, the travel agency which supplied the buses for the cinematic tour did not like the final product. Before the film's production, many tour companies had competed for the honor of supplying the name to be used, but when the film was released and people laughed so much at the mishaps on the tour, the "honor" backfired, and the agency lost considerable business.

Roberta LeFeuvre

I'LL CRY TOMORROW

Released: 1955
Production: Lawrence Weingarten for Metro-Goldwyn-Mayer
Direction: Daniel Mann
Screenplay: Helen Deutsch and Jay Richard Kennedy; based on the book of
  the same name by Lillian Roth, Mike Connolly, and Gerold Frank
Cinematography: Arthur E. Arling
Editing: Harold F. Kress
Costume design: Helen Rose (AA)
Music: Alex North
Running time: 117 minutes

Principal characters:

Lillian Roth	Susan Hayward
Tony Bardeman	Richard Conte
Burt McGuire	Eddie Albert
Katie Roth	Jo Van Fleet
Wallie	Don Taylor
David Tredman	Ray Danton
Selma	Margo
Ellen	Virginia Gregg
Jerry	Don Barry
Lillian (younger)	Carole Ann Campbell

If for no other reason, *I'll Cry Tomorrow* is an important motion picture because it contains the performance for which Susan Hayward should have won the Academy Award. It was the third of Hayward's four nominations for Best Actress, which included *Smash Up—The Story of a Woman* (1947), *With a Song in My Heart* (1952), *I'll Cry Tomorrow* (1955), and *I Want to Live!* (1958), but she lost the Oscar that year to Anna Magnani for *The Rose Tattoo*, later going on to win in 1958 for *I Want to Live!*.

I'll Cry Tomorrow is also important for several other reasons. Hollywood's most significant and realistic portrait of an alcoholic had been Ray Milland's Oscar-winning impersonation of Don Birnam in Billy Wilder's *The Lost Weekend* (1945), which had been based on Charles Jackson's harrowing account of five days in the life of a dipsomaniac. It is a landmark film, an example of the post-World War II neorealism of Hollywood films and a mature study of a serious social problem. Two years later, in 1947, Hayward earned her first Oscar nomination playing an alcoholic nightclub singer in another realistic account of the life of an alcoholic.

When Lillian Roth published her frank, no-holds-barred autobiography *I'll Cry Tomorrow* (1954, coauthored by Mike Connolly of *The Hollywood Reporter* and Gerold Frank), it became a landmark for its honesty and courage in exposing the life of a well-known show-business personality who had been an alcoholic. The days of the proliferation of celebrity "tell-all" autobiographies was still two decades away, and *I'll Cry Tomorrow*, along with Mary Astor's *My Story* five years later in 1959, remain two of the most honest and dignified of that kind of personal exposé.

Roth was born Lillian Rutstein in Boston in 1910. By 1916, she and her sister Ann were "baby stars" for Educational Pictures in New York City. In 1918, she was dubbed Broadway's youngest star in *Shavings* and went on to appear in Earl Carroll's *Vanities of 1928* and Florenz Ziegfeld's *Midnight Follies*. She pursued an acting career in motion pictures in such films as *The Love Parade* (1929)with Maurice Chevalier, *The Vagabond King* (1930) with Jeanette MacDonald, *Animal Crackers* (1930) with the Marx Brothers, Cecil B. De Mille's *Madam Satan* (1930), and *Honey* (1930) with Nancy Carroll, in which she sang a wonderful rendition of "Sing, You Sinners." Her life then disintegrated into a series of personal tragedies including five marriages, sixteen years of alcoholism, and a serious battle with mental illness. Finally she pulled her life together with the help of Alcoholics Anonymous and came back to appear in clubs, on Broadway in *I Can Get It for You Wholesale*, with the national company of *Funny Girl*, and in a final film in 1979, *Boardwalk*. She died following a stroke on May 12, 1980.

When Hayward read *I'll Cry Tomorrow*, she immediately began a campaign with her new studio boss, Twentieth Century-Fox's Buddy Adler, to help her in obtaining the role which was to be filmed by M-G-M. Roth had agreed to sell the book to M-G-M, and she also had requested they cast Hayward in the part. With Roth's encouragement and Hayward's own ability to convince M-G-M head Dore Schary that she was right for the role, Fox and M-G-M worked out a loan which had Spencer Tracy go to Fox to star in *Broken Lance* (1954).

In preparation for the part, Hayward met with Roth several times, and, as Roth later recalled, Hayward asked dozens of questions and studied Roth's mannerisms until "I don't know whether she was imitating me or I was emulating her." At first reports it was assumed that Hayward would lip-synch the songs to Roth's own still very capable singing voice, but the M-G-M musical supervisor was convinced Hayward could sing the songs herself. After recording several songs, the studio executives agreed that Hayward's throaty contralto was more than satisfactory for the musical drama. The decision was a blow to Roth, but as she said, "When Susan Hayward made up her mind, it was made up," and they still managed to remain friends.

The plot of *I'll Cry Tomorrow*, as adapted from the book by Helen Deutsch and Jay Richard Kennedy, opens in the days of Roth's childhood (in these scenes the young Lillian is portrayed by Carole Ann Campbell), with Lillian's stagestruck, impoverished mother Katie Roth (Jo Van Fleet) pushing the young child toward a stage career. It was Katie Roth's obsession to use her daughter's talents to get them out of their West 43rd Street tenement life, and by doing so the mother drove the child into a career, never allowing her time to be a child or make lasting childhood friends. Whenever little Lillian would cry as a result of her mother's unending determination, Katie Roth would reply, "Cry tomorrow. You'll have the whole day to cry tomorrow."

Lillian does become a star, and, now portrayed by Susan Hayward, she resumes a friendship with a rare former childhood friend named David Tredman (Ray Danton). They fall in love, but their romance is overshadowed by Katie's objections that love will interfere with Lillian's career and by the fact that David is ill. They become engaged over Katie's objections, but one evening just as Lillian goes on stage, Katie receives a telephone call backstage informing her that David is dead. Lillian rushes to the hospital in despair, finds the body already gone, has a serious quarrel with her mother, and is consoled by a friend, a nurse named Ellen (Virginia Gregg), who gives her a drink to help her sleep. The nightly drinking becomes a habit at bedtime, then prior to going on stage, then anytime Lillian needs her confidence bolstered.

Lillian goes out on the town with an aviation cadet (Don Taylor) and wakes up in a hotel room the next morning married to him. Their marriage is based on partying and drinking rather than love, and they divorce in a matter of months. Now at the peak of her career, Lillian continues to party and drink until she meets Tony Bardeman (Richard Conte), a sadistic schemer who lives off her and keeps her drunk until she is penniless. Lillian finally manages to shed Bardeman, but her career is now in ruins, and she begins to pawn her possessions to pay for liquor. Her life disintegrates into one of degradation in second-rate bars and finally Los Angeles' Skid Row. Now a hopeless alcoholic, emotionally paralyzed and unable to help herself, she turns to her heartbroken mother for help, but Katie herself is now penniless. Lillian attempts suicide by jumping out of a window but is so weak from drinking that she faints. She eventually seeks out Alcoholics Anonymous for aid.

There she meets AA members Selma (Margo), Jerry (Don Barry), and the crippled Burt McGuire (Eddie Albert). In undergoing treatment she suffers delirium tremens, but her new friends pull her through. Her life now for the first time encompasses hope. The film ends with Lillian and Burt married, and Lillian about to appear on television's *This Is Your Life* program in the hope that by telling her story publicly, it will help others.

This film takes certain liberties in presenting the "facts" of Roth's life; there are several gaps in the plot, and some of the characters are sketchily drawn. It is a hard-hitting, emotionally moving film, however, solidly held together by Hayward's finest performance. Here she sheds the mannerisms for which some critics had frequently criticized her and turns in a performance of depth and maturity. Her singing of the film's four songs—"Sing You Winners," "Happiness Is a Thing Called Joe," "When the Red, Red Robin Comes Bob,

Bob, Bobbin' Along," and "The Vagabond King Waltz"—was very professional, and her delirium tremens scene was incredibly realistic. As the ads claimed, the picture is "Filmed on location . . . inside a woman's soul." Hayward lost the Oscar, but was named Best Actress by *Look* magazine and at the Cannes Film Festival (1956). The film was also nominated for Academy Awards for Art Direction and Cinematography, and Helen Rose won an Oscar for her costumes. *I'll Cry Tomorrow* is a poignant film and contains Hayward's finest performance.

Ronald Bowers

I'LL NEVER FORGET WHATSHISNAME

Released: 1967
Production: Michael Winner for Universal-Scimitar
Direction: Michael Winner
Screenplay: Peter Draper
Cinematography: Otto Heller
Editing: Bernard Gribble
Music: Francis Lai
Running time: 99 minutes

Principal characters:
Andrew Quint	Oliver Reed
Jonathan Lute	Orson Welles
Georgina	Carol White
Nicholas	Norman Rodway
Louise Quint	Wendy Craig
Gerald Sater	Harry Andrews

The flippant title of the tragicomic film *I'll Never Forget Whatshisname* belies its serious subject. Indeed, the farcical handling of the entire story lightens the potentially downbeat theme of the futility of striving for personal integrity amid rampant corruption. The line of dialogue from which the title is taken occurs in the middle of the story during a faculty-student reunion at a prep school outside London to which Andrew Quint (Oliver Reed) has returned in his quest for the untainted simplicity of his youth. Tuxedoed schoolmasters and their former pupils profess great friendship and admiration for one another, yet cannot recall one another's names. For Quint, the fondly remembered place and people of his boyhood are rife with superficiality and hypocrisy.

Disillusioned with his life as a successful producer of television commercials which hype crass products, Quint begins his search to regain the zeal and idealism of his school days by ceremoniously quitting his job. He violently axes his office desk to pieces while his boss, Jonathan Lute (Orson Welles) cooly looks on. Quint exclaims to Lute that he is off to find an honest job. Snidely replying that none exists, the villainous chief executive mocks Quint's newfound morality. In a further step toward recovering personal decency, Quint abandons the trappings of many years of fraudulently won prosperity. This means disentangling himself from two mistresses, a wife, and a young daughter; but they too do not take him seriously. Freed of these trappings, he returns to his old job as associate editor of *Gadfly*, a left-wing, esoteric literary magazine edited by his long-time friend and hero, Nicholas (Norman Rodway).

Ruggedly handsome Reed is instantly credible as the slick, status-conscious, ad-agency type, yet he is not so sophisticated that his search for morality becomes unbelievable. He is right for the scenes of polished academia and a natural as the hip, creative director of a film crew on location. Insidious Jonathan Lute is wisely underplayed by Welles. A character of exaggerated evil, he might easily have been reduced to caricature. Lute is the ever-present cynic, taunting Quint and voicing Quint's deepest fears about what he has become. Lute epitomizes what Quint hates in himself; Nicholas represents what he will recover.

At the *Gadfly* office Quint meets Georgina (Carol White), whose guileless nature he finds an irresistible contrast to the world and women from which he has fled. White is too voluptuous to convince the audience that she appeals only to Quint's spiritual tastes. He nevertheless views her as a virtuous innocent, an image she encourages by donning overalls, wearing a girlish hairdo, and talking about her virginity. Their feelings for each other are nevertheless genuine.

Quint flouts convention by escorting Georgina to the all-male school reunion of nameless alumni. Instead of discovering where and why life started to go wrong for him, Quint witnesses a terrifying reenactment of adolescent bullying. The favored prey is once again senselessly pursued across distant school grounds by a pack of latent vandals in formal dress. Quint's attempt to save and defend the stampeded fellow earns him a decking from the leader of the gang, his arch rival from school days, Maccabbee (James Fox). In this campus microcosm of a world everyone is predator or prey, despite the veneer of education and socialization; Quint's position is ambiguous. The illuminating flashbacks to his boyhood, in which he shrinks from competition and is humiliated by Maccabbee, type him as a victim; yet his wealth and power in the advertising business and his control of several women qualify him as a predator.

In addition to seeking the inspiration of his "golden years" at Cambridge, Quint solicits a paper for *Gadfly* from Professor Gerald Sater (Harry Andrews). For Quint, Sater represents the essence of probity until he reveals that his manuscripts are available only to the highest-paying editor and that his taste runs to pornographic pictures. A tension is set up early in the story between Quint's belief in the rightness of his actions and the viewer's knowledge of his wrongheadedness. The viewer also perceives frailty in hero Nicholas, who hungrily eyes the ladies, bolsters the *Gadfly*'s circulation by running sex articles, and questions Quint on the cost of his flashy car. Quint is surprised to learn upon his return to the office that Nicholas has sold the journal to the highest bidder. His rationale for selling out is his wife's insistence upon leading the good life—the very life Quint rejects; in this case Nicholas deals in half-truths. Ironically, it is Lute who has acquired the obscure magazine. He intends to enhance his otherwise tarnished image, as his acquisition of valuable paintings and *objets d'art* is also meant to do. More important, he is bent on showing Quint that even Nicholas has his price. Quint finds himself again helplessly working for Lute.

In a suspiciously magnanimous gesture, Lute offers his new employee a chance to direct one last television commercial in complete artistic and technical freedom. Quint accepts, seeming at once to give in to Lute, yet triumphant in his independence. His lengthy, expensive masterwork is not, however, a clever paean to the product, a Japanese movie camera. It is a montage of grotesque and violent images of destruction intercut with scenes from his own ruined life, seemingly in demonstration of what one can photograph with the camera. Since the ad depicts the camera as rapidly outdated and destined for the trash heap, Quint may be commenting on the innate destructive nature of existence on this earth and man's "planned obsolescence." Quint's bitter, self-indictment on film wins the envied prize of the advertising industry, but the final brutal irony rests with Lute; he bribed the jury to award the prize.

For Quint, Georgina remains the only oasis of goodness and his means for self-redemption. While riding with a reckless Nicholas in his chic new car, however, she is killed in a fiery crash from which her boss escapes unharmed. In resignation, Quint forsakes his odyssey and accepts the lucrative offer of the advertising firm across the street, Lute's foremost competitor. He also returns to his wife.

Overall, *I'll Never Forget Whatshisname* is an unsatisfying film. Its production values betray budget constraints; lighting is harsh and especially unflattering to the actors. The color process fades complexions but brings out garish, disharmonious colors in the background. The music of Francis Lai, meant to convey modern, flashy London, is tinny and strident. Finally, Michael Winner's direction is jumpy. He wisely uses the device of quick cutting from an important question just posed, leaving the viewer to struggle with a solution, but the overall effect of the rapid-fire progression of the story is not stimulation but the discomfort of a bumpy ride.

As for characterization, Quint comes off as a self-indulgent dilettante. For all his laudable motives, he continues to see one of his mistresses; he expects his wife to be sexually compliant at all times; and he shows no responsibility toward or fondness for his child. Perhaps these lapses in rectitude portray him as only human and thus more sympathetic, but they also render his pontifications on integrity rather ludicrous. Quint does not relinquish everything in preparation to search for self-worth. His reserves, in the form of cars, women, and bank accounts, are placed in no jeopardy. He has nothing to lose; so little is at stake that his plight deserves no serious consideration.

Nancy S. Kinney

I'M ALL RIGHT, JACK

Released: 1960
Production: Roy Boulting with Boulting Brothers Production for British Lion
  Films; released by Columbia
Direction: John Boulting
Screenplay: Frank Harvey, John Boulting, and Alan Hackney; based on the
  novel *Private Life* by Alan Hackney
Cinematography: Max Greene
Editing: Anthony Harvey
Running time: 105 minutes

Principal characters:
Stanley Windrush .... Ian Carmichael
Fred Kite .... Peter Sellers
Major Hitchcock .... Terry-Thomas
Sidney de Vere Cox .... Richard Attenborough
Bertram Tracepurcel .... Dennis Price
Aunt Dolly .... Margaret Rutherford
Mrs. Kite .... Irene Handl
Cynthia Kite .... Liz Fraser

Considered the wittiest satire of twins Roy and John Boulting's numerous
comedies, *I'm All Right, Jack* focuses on the excesses of modern British
industry, sparing neither labor nor management in its scrutiny. Although this
film takes a biting stance towards management's illegal practices, it differs
from other satires on industry in that it also casts an equally discerning eye
upon labor, the first time that any film spotlighted labor faults to any extent.
This Boulting Brothers film was not only widely praised as funny and irreverent, but critics also publicized an already widespread rumor that this film's
release in 1959 lampooning nonproductive labor practices caused a landslide
conservative victory in the British parliamentary elections that same year.
The title is a reference to an old army phrase, "Blow you, Jack—I'm all
right," tidily summarizing the every-man-for-himself philosophy that is satirized in this film.

Stanley Windrush (Ian Carmichael), an amiable but naïve upper-class
youth, has been discharged from the service following World War II and is
now searching for employment, preferably as an executive in an industry
which allows him to have one afternoon a week off. His alma mater, Oxford
University, sets up job interviews for him: one with a company called Detto
Detergents and the other with Num Yum Blocks, a candy manufacturer. This
sequence of interviews is humorous from the start, as a shot of each manufacturer's billboard and television jingle prefaces Stanley's interviews. He
finds at Detto Detergent that, unknown to the public, they also manufacture

Detto's leading "competitor," Frisko Detergent, aiming their sales of the identical detergent in different labels to diverse segments of the population. When Stanley points out the exorbitant profit they must be making with these unscrupulous marketing practices, he is unceremoniously thrown out of the interview. He fares no better at the Num Yum Blocks factory, which again has its own billboard and banal television ditty. Stanley tours the factory with the head chemist, who urges him to sample Num Yum Blocks at each stage of manufacture. The huge, noisy machines which grace the candy assembly line have facial features—bulbs which light up for eyes, a protruding fixture for a nose, and an enormous mouthlike chute from which batter spills out periodically. Surrounded by these mechanical faces spewing out candy batter and ill himself from sampling too many sweets, Stanley turns pale and rushes to the nearest receptacle to vomit, ruining a huge vat of freshly made candy batter.

After this escapade, Oxford refuses to arrange any further interviews for Stanley, who, in desperation, visits his Uncle Bertram (Dennis Price) and Aunt Dolly (Margaret Rutherford) for ideas. Uncle Bertram and his friend Sidney de Vere Cox (Richard Attenborough) convince him that if he accepts an unskilled labor position in his uncle's factory, he will quickly work himself up to a high executive position. Unknown to Stanley, however, his uncle and Sidney hope that his enthusiasm for work will antagonize the other workers and induce a strike. Then a Middle Eastern country's missile contract will be forced to be transferred to Sidney's factory at a higher-priced contract, and Sidney, Bertram, and an Arab diplomat negotiating the contract will split the sizable difference between contract bids.

Stanley begins work at Missiles, Ltd. and is immediately mistaken for a motion-study expert. He is reported to the union steward, Fred Kite (Peter Sellers), who with his work committee visits Major Hitchcock (Terry-Thomas), the personnel manager, to complain about Stanley's inexperience and incompetence at his job. Since Hitchcock knew nothing about Stanley's being hired, he feels no compulsion to protect him and therefore readily agrees with Kite that he should be terminated. This quick agreement catches Kite off-balance, and he immediately fights to reinstate Stanley on the grounds that "incompetence is not just cause for dismissal." Hitchcock, although puzzled at this about-face, agrees only to prevent conflict, and Stanley is reinstated. Kite immediately bullies Stanley into joining the union and later offers him a room to rent in his home. Stanley is unconvinced that he wants to live this closely with the union leader until he meets Kite's daughter Cynthia (Liz Fraser), an extremely pretty young lady who is attracted to him. Stanley moves into the Kite home, charming Mrs. Kite (Irene Handl) as well as her daughter. Although Kite offers Stanley "light reading" from union theory to Marx and Lenin, Stanley prefers to amuse himself with Cynthia in his bubble-shaped car.

Uncle Bertram continues his plan to cause trouble among the workers when he hires a motion-study expert who studies Stanley without his knowledge. The motion-study expert turns in his report and based on the data contained there, Uncle Bertram has Hitchcock issue new, accelerated work schedules. Kite leads the workers out on strike—all except Stanley, who breaks through the picket line and continues to work, eventually becoming a hero to the British public who are tired of work stoppages and the exorbitant demands of unions. Kite throws Stanley out of his house and angers Cynthia and Mrs. Kite, who call a household strike until Kite himself returns to work.

Meanwhile, Uncle Bertram's plan fails because the workers in Sidney's factory go out on a sympathy strike with the workers at Missiles, Ltd. Soon all of Great Britain's industries are striking, and the unions are viewed as the villains. Both Management and Labor want to end the strike quickly, and Uncle Bertram sends Hitchcock to Kite's home to ask for terms. Kite demands that Stanley be fired, and both agree that he has been the root of the problem. Uncle Bertram offers to allow Stanley to resign because of overwork, but Stanley refuses. The individuals involved in this controversy are invited to air their views on television, and Sidney attempts to bribe Stanley to admit that he was wrong and resign. Stanley is furious with such dishonesty and reveals on television the whole plot to swindle the Arab country, angrily scattering thousands of British pounds of bribe money in the studio. He inadvertantly causes a riot as the studio audience claws at one another to grab the cash, and he is arrested and reprimanded for "disturbing the peace." Stanley, now thoroughly disillusioned with industry, resigns from Missiles, Ltd. and joins his father, who has been residing in a nudist camp to escape the greedy, grubby working world.

The tongue-in-cheek tone of the film is established from the opening credits when the theme song accompanies cartoon drawings of industry, the most humorous one being that of a motion-study expert studying a tortoise's movements. The film's narrator calmly expounds on "brotherhood and comradeship" among workers as we see the laborers shoving and fighting one another to punch the timeclock when the whistle blows before they are docked for tardiness. The screenplay won the British Film Academy's Best British Screenplay Award for 1959, and, combined with Boulting's fine direction, the film offers numerous comic gems. The strong supporting cast includes Rutherford as Aunt Dolly, who fears Stanley's exposure to dirt and sweat in the factory, and Terry-Thomas as the blasé personnel manager. Carmichael, who has appeared in many Boulting Brothers productions, plays well the innocent Stanley squeezed between two industrial giants, labor and management. The entire cast works well to create a splendid satire which needles and amuses.

The strongest performance in the film is by Sellers, who deservedly won the British Film Academy's Best British Actor Award for 1959 for his role as Fred Kite. He had first caught the public's attention when he played three zany roles in *The Mouse That Roared* (1959), but his role in *I'm All Right, Jack* firmly established his reputation internationally as an excellent actor and versatile comedian. His work in this film was universally praised as an incisive character study, precise in every detail including his stiff-legged mechanical walk and educated Cockney accent. In an interview after the film was released in the United States, Sellers revealed that he prepared for a part by creating the voice first and then filling out the rest of the character. His talent for mimicry enabled him to increase his ever-expanding repertoire of dialects ranging from a farmer from Cornwall to a well-bred BBC announcer. *I'm All Right, Jack* would be a funny film even without Sellers, but today it is viewed primarily as a good example of Sellers' early work, attracting a sizable audience of Sellers fans wherever it is shown, a fitting tribute to an exceptional actor who was enormously successful until his death in 1980.

Ruth L. Hirayama

IMITATION OF LIFE

Released: 1934
Production: Carl Laemmle for Universal
Direction: John M. Stahl
Screenplay: William Hurlbut; based on the novel of the same name by Fannie Hurst
Cinematography: Merritt B. Gerstad
Editing: Philip Cahn and Maurice Wright
Running time: 106 minutes

Principal characters:
Bea Pullman	Claudette Colbert
Stephen Archer	Warren William
Elmer	Ned Sparks
Aunt Delilah	Louise Beavers
Jessie Pullman (age three)	Baby Jane
Jessie Pullman (age eighteen)	Rochelle Hudson
Peola Johnson (age four)	Sebie Hendricks
Peola Johnson (age nine)	Dorothy Black
Peola Johnson (age nineteen)	Fredi Washington

Imitation of Life is a splendid example of what could be accomplished within the genre usually known as "the woman's picture" or the soap opera. Films in this genre, which flourished from the 1930's through the 1950's, focus on the concerns of a woman, usually contain melodramatic elements and stress choices involving romance, children, and careers. Although often disparaged, the genre produced its share of well-crafted, entertaining, and reasonably authentic films. *Imitation of Life*, based upon the best-selling novel by Fannie Hurst, boasts fine acting by Claudette Colbert and Louise Beavers, disciplined direction from John M. Stahl, and a script by William Hurlbut that effectively regulates the melodramatic elements of the story.

The first image in the film—that of a child's toy duck—is deceptively calm, for we soon see that Bea Pullman (Claudette Colbert) is engaged in a hectic morning ritual. She must bathe and dress her three-year-old daughter Jessie (Baby Jane), cook breakfast, and handle business calls on the telephone all at the same time. Since her husband has died, she must take her child to a day nursery so that she can continue his business of selling maple syrup to businesses in the area. The entire situation is thus established naturally and efficiently.

Then, while Bea is still trying to cope with three tasks at once, there appears at her door a black woman, Delilah Johnson (Louise Beavers), who has come to apply for a job as cook and housekeeper that was advertised in the newspaper. Bea points out that the advertised job is on Astor *Avenue* not Astor

Street and helpfully tells her how to get to the proper address. Delilah, however, talks Bea into hiring her. Bea's need for help is obvious, and Delilah asks only room and board for herself and her four-year-old daughter, Peola (Sebie Hendricks). Jobs in which she will not be separated from her daughter, she tells Bea, are very hard to find. Although Delilah is quite dark, Peola's skin color is very light.

Thus virtually all the themes and motivations for the entire film are established in the first five or ten minutes: the two mothers' love for their daughters, Bea's need to make money, and Peola's ability to pass for white. These will provide nearly all the troubles and happiness for Bea and Delilah until late in the film when Bea finally allows some romance into her life. That romance, however, will conflict with both her business and her love for her daughter.

Continuing with the story, Delilah and Peola immediately become almost part of Bea's family. Delilah is a good housekeeper, but it is her cooking that proves to be the most valuable. One day she makes some pancakes according to her grandmother's secret recipe, and Bea declares that she has "never tasted anything so good" in her life. Soon afterwards, when Bea sees an empty store, she thinks of an idea to make a better living: she will open a pancake shop. Without wasting a moment, she approaches the owner of the store about renting it. Since she has virtually no money, she has to persuade the man to give her two months free rent because she will be refurbishing the place. Then she talks a painter into painting the shop and waiting thirty days for his payment. The furniture and fixtures she gets with no down payment and fifty-dollar monthly payments. Her persuasion of these men is a virtuoso performance in which she never reveals how little money she has or how newly developed the idea is. She gets nearly everything she wants by making the men think she is compromising with them. For example, the owner of the shop expects to rent it as it is with payment in advance, but Bea asks for three months free rent and settles for two.

In the next sequence, it is five years later, the pancake shop is a success, and Bea has paid all her bills. Many men show obvious interest in her, but she ignores them to devote her attention to her daughter and her business. The only trouble comes from Peola (now played by Dorothy Black). She does not want to be black, and—unknown to Delilah—passes as white at school. When Delilah brings a raincoat to her at school one day, Peola is mortified and angered when Delilah identifies her as her daughter. "I hate you," she tells her mother, and promises never to return to that school.

One day at the pancake shop, a penniless man named Elmer (Ned Sparks) coaxes some free pancakes out of Bea. When he discovers how delicious they are, he offers to tell her two words that will make her rich if she will give him more pancakes. His advice is "box it." Bea considers a moment, then says that he can have all the pancakes he can eat and a job besides. Although Elmer is less than enthusiastic about the job, Aunt Delilah's Pancake Flour is soon being boxed, and Elmer is helping Bea manage the business, which is immediately successful. When Bea tells Delilah that they are making so much money that she can have her own house, Delilah replies that she does not want to move away from Bea and is content with things as they are.

A neon sign with a likeness of Delilah on it then announces that thirty-two million boxes of pancake flour have been sold. This leads into the party Bea gives to celebrate her tenth anniversary in the pancake business. She is now wealthy and lives and dresses well. One guest who does not know who she is begins telling Bea that he does not like businesswomen because they are so efficient and competent. He steadfastly maintains that he does not want to meet this "pancake queen" until Elmer sees him and introduces him to Bea.

That moment of embarrassment is over soon, however, and Bea and the man, Stephen Archer (Warren William), embark on a whirlwind courtship. Elmer complains that Stephen is keeping Bea away from her work too much, but Bea is enjoying fully the first extracurricular pleasure she has allowed herself. Stephen, it turns out, is an independently wealthy ichthyologist. He studies fish not only in his private aquarium but also on voyages to tropical seas, which he describes to Bea in poetic terms. Bea agrees to marry him, but asks him to keep their engagement a secret until her daughter Jessie returns to school after her upcoming vacation.

Things become complicated, however, when Jessie (now played by Rochelle Hudson) comes home from school and is immediately fascinated with Stephen. Then Delilah receives a letter that Peola has left the black college she was attending; so Delilah and Bea set off to find Peola, and Bea asks Stephen to entertain Jessie while she is gone. Delilah and Bea find Peola (now played by Fredi Washington) working as a cashier in a restaurant, but when Delilah speaks to her, Peola pretends that she does not know her. "I never saw you before in my life," she says. She finally does come to Delilah and apologizes, but then she announces that she is going to break all connections with her mother and go away and be white, not black. This, of course, devastates Delilah, who soon becomes seriously ill.

Discussing this situation with Jessie, Bea says, "If anything should ever come between us, it would kill me." Soon she discovers that Jessie has fallen in love with Stephen while she was gone, although neither Stephen nor Bea thought that Jessie would interpret Stephen's entertaining her during her mother's absence as evidence of a romantic interest. Only after Delilah weakens and dies does Peola reappear. She rushes to the casket and begs forgiveness for killing her own mother, who worked and slaved for her. Bea then puts her relationship with her daughter before everything else; she refuses to marry Stephen because if she did Jessie would always feel that Bea had come between her and her happiness. She tells Stephen that she will come to him only when Jessie forgets him; the film ends with Bea reminiscing with

Jessie about the day Delilah first appeared at their house, the first day shown in the film.

Although some contemporary reviewers dismissed *Imitation of Life* as a "tearjerker," others have recognized that it is not the melodramatic elements near the end that define the film. It is the fine acting and careful directing to establish and delineate the details that give the film its special qualities that elevate it above the ordinary. Colbert gives a well-rounded performance that conveys the various facets of Bea Pullman—maternal, entrepreneurial, and romantic. Only when the script calls for her to renounce her fiancé is she less than convincing. Beavers is also excellent, although her part is more limited and is often too stereotyped; it would be more than three decades, however, before Hollywood moved much beyond that stereotype.

In short, *Imitation of Life* has elements that are easy to criticize, but taken as a whole it is a well-made film with many rewards for the viewer. It was remade in 1959 by director Douglas Sirk. The later version, which starred Lana Turner and Juanita Hall as the two women, retained the same basic plot although the stage rather than the pancake business was Bea's work. That film was financially successful and, in retrospect, critically well-received, especially by devotees of the work of Sirk.

Timothy W. Johnson

IMITATION OF LIFE

Released: 1959
Production: Ross Hunter for Universal
Direction: Douglas Sirk
Screenplay: Eleanore Griffin and Allan Scott; based on the novel of the same name by Fannie Hurst
Cinematography: Russell Metty
Editing: Milton Carruth
Running time: 124 minutes

Principal characters:
Lora Meredith .... Lana Turner
Steve Archer .... John Gavin
Allen Loomis .... Robert Alda
Susie (older) .... Sandra Dee
Sara Jane (older) .... Susan Kohner
Annie Johnson .... Juanita Moore
Susie (younger) .... Terry Burhan
Sara Jane (younger) .... Karen Dicker
Frankie .... Troy Donahue

Imitation of Life, based on Fannie Hurst's novel of the same name, was a huge financial success for Universal in 1959. The last of director Douglas Sirk's collaborations with producer Ross Hunter (also responsible for the superb *Written on the Wind*, 1957), *Imitation of Life* is a final statement from Sirk; in spite of its great success, it is the last commercial film he made.

Sirk's pictures, even though most are set in the much-maligned "woman's-picture" genre, "disturb the mind" as the director hoped they would do. Melodrama is a genre in which the values of the woman's role in bourgeois life are affirmed. The sacrificing mother and the neglected wife are sanctified victims on the altar of success. Melodrama expresses some of the bewildered pain of the casualties of the feminine mystique, but its end result is to derail real understanding and criticism of the housewife's plight, which Simone de Beauvoir describes as a "gilded mediocrity," a phrase that perfectly describes the environment Sirk portrays. By abstracting conflicts to a realm (tragedy or transcendent love) in which they can be artifically resolved, melodrama removes any social-criticism aspect from its examination of women's lives. In *Imitation of Life*, exactly the opposite occurs: Sirk's characters realistically choose to refuse love for socially dictated goals of success. More important, their failure to love one another is shown to be a necessary part of the process of success, not their incorrect choice.

Hurst's best-selling novel was first published in 1933, and John Stahl's successful film (which was very close to the book) was released in 1934. The 1959 remake has many important changes which mark Sirk's very different approach. Bea Pullman, the heroine of the novel, becomes a businesswoman out of lucky accident and absolute necessity when her husband (almost a stranger to her) is killed, leaving her with a crippled father and infant daughter. Through back-breaking hard work, she becomes a rich restaurant owner, never noticing that life (which means love in the form of a man and children for a woman of 1933) has passed her by until it is too late. She gives her daughter "everything" by sending her to boarding schools, and when finally Bea slows down, falls in love with her young right-hand man, and brings her daughter home, the two of them fall in love. The novel finds this very tragic, of course, but "so right," because Bea is, after all, in her middle thirties, and her figure is beginning to go. Just beneath the surface of the narrative is the iron theme: a successful woman gives up her birthright to love and happiness by competing (and, worse, *winning*) in a man's world. Hurst is, of course, totally sympathetic to her heroine. Bea is forced into her unnatural life by dire financial straits, yet there is the cruel judgment that this final humiliation is her fault. The novel affirms that the only happy life for a woman is stay-at-home motherhood, and that women who walk any other path, for whatever reason, are doomed to hardship and sorrow.

In Sirk's film, the theater becomes the metaphor for Lora's (Bea in the novel) "imitation of life." Lora (Lana Turner) is an actress whose husband's death both requires and gives her the opportunity to pursue her chosen career. Her success takes her away from her daughter and Steve (John Gavin), who continues to love her, but the crucial difference between this film and the book is that her success brings her personal satisfaction and fame as well as material wealth. Lora's life is an "imitation of life" in the same way a successful man's is; she must neglect her daughter and lover to achieve success, and sees only too late that success is lonely. Unlike Bea Pullman, she is not rendered sexless or unnatural by her success.

Sirk shows Lora's dilemma graphically: when Steve insists she choose between him and an acting job, he is suddenly overbearing and dominating. The corridor seems to close in around Lora as Steve grasps her in a possessing, not loving, embrace. Her career, especially once it becomes successful, is equally oppressive. The big house Lora buys emphasizes the coldness and distance between the people who live in it in contrast to the crowded, cozy little apartment in which Lora and her daughter lived with Annie and Sara Jane. Indeed, Sirk's own decision to leave Hollywood (the dream factory—certainly an "imitation of life") at the height of *his* success is testament to the all-important change in theme from the book to the film: that the pitfalls of material success are the same for men and women. This is a more radical concept than it might first appear to be, because implicit in it is a criticism of the society which places material success so high, rather than being a lesson for women who might step outside their proscribed role. Sirk criticizes the culture whose highest goals are alienating and unfulfilling, not the individual who achieves success and finds it wanting.

Like *Written on the Wind*, *Imitation of Life* has secondary characters who are in many ways more interesting than the primary ones. Annie (Juanita Moore) is a black mother who comes to work for Lora and take care of both their daughters when Lora is just beginning her struggle to support herself. She is the heart of the film, and her daughter Sara Jane (Karen Dicker) is its most moving character. Just as Lora turns her back on her family for her "imitation of life," Sara Jane will do anything to pass for white. She "passes" in school, and is destroyed one rainy day when Annie brings her goloshes and identifies herself as Sara Jane's mother. Later Sara Jane (Susan Kohner) has a blond boyfriend named Frankie (Troy Donahue) who hits her and throws her in the mud, staining her white dress (a shocking and moving image) when he learns the truth about her. She takes a glittering array of jobs in nightclubs, performing mechanically in a chorus line. Sirk's images show her to be horribly trapped in her "freedom" from her blackness. Sandra Dee is magnificently cast as Susie, Lora's daughter. She is what Sara Jane longs to be, but we see her as the pale, vapid creature Sirk intends her to be in her blond, squeaky-voiced whiteness. Finally, when Annie knows she is dying, she finds Sara Jane in the dressing room of a strip joint. Because another girl is watching, Sara Jane denies her mother to maintain her lie. Annie accepts this final humiliation, pretending to be Sara Jane's "mammy," and asks to hold her baby one last time. With tears of anguish for the pain she is causing, Sara Jane lets her mother touch her for what will be the last time.

Annie's funeral is the climax and the last scene of the film. It is a brilliantly mounted production, magnificently elaborate, lush, and stately: even famed black gospel singer Mahalia Jackson is present to sing. In the sheer beauty and majesty of the funeral, the final gift of the unappreciated Annie to herself and to the world, the characters are given a glimpse of truth and love. Sara Jane bursts through the crowd to clutch at her mother's coffin, finally acknowledging publicly her blackness and her mother, and Lora holds her in the coach. For the first time in the film, the characters are united in their understanding of what is important. Sirk offers no guarantee or even hope that this experience will cure their blindness; it is his and Annie's magnificent farewell to America, a glimpse of enrichment that comes from something other than material success.

Janey Place

IN A LONELY PLACE

Released: 1950
Production: Robert Lord for Columbia
Direction: Nicholas Ray
Screenplay: Andrew Solt; based on the novel of the same name by Dorothy B. Hughes
Cinematography: Burnett Guffey
Editing: Viola Lawrence
Running time: 94 minutes

Principal characters:

Dixon Steele	Humphrey Bogart
Laurel Gray	Gloria Grahame
Brub Nicolai	Frank Lovejoy
Mel Lippman	Art Smith
Captain Lochner	Carl Benton Reid
Sylvia Nicolai	Jeff Donnell
Mildred Atkinson	Martha Stewart
Paul	Steven Geray
Charlie Waterman	Robert Warwick

Like his contemporary Don Siegel, Nicholas Ray's most successful film work has tended to be with low- to middle-budget genre films. Respected as a craftsman, it took years before he was discovered by the young French critics and hailed as a major *auteur* director. By then he had graduated briefly to large-scale epics; then he lapsed into silence before his death in 1979. Also like Siegel, Ray's films are populated with protagonists who are confused and tortured men, often at odds with the society around them. One such "hero" emerges in his 1950 film, *In a Lonely Place*.

Dixon Steele (Humphrey Bogart), a cynical screenwriter, is handed an assignment to adapt a trashy romantic novel. Unable to force himself to read it, he pays Mildred Atkinson (Martha Stewart), a garrulous hat-check girl at one of his favorite restaurants, to come back to his apartment and tell him the story. Hours after Mildred has left, Steele is aroused by a knock on the door. It is Brub Nicolai (Frank Lovejoy), an old army buddy who has joined the police force. Mildred Atkinson has been found strangled after being dumped from a speeding car, and Brub has been sent to bring Dix in for questioning.

From the film's initial scene of a near fist-fight with an irate motorist, we are aware that Dix Steele is a man with an often uncontrollable temper. This is reaffirmed by Captain Lochner (Carl Benton Reid) of the homicide division, who, in interrogating Steele, brings up the violent incidents in his past which have made him virtually unemployable in Hollywood until his agent and friend

Mel Lippman (Art Smith) managed to get him the assignment to adapt the novel.

Also called in for questioning is the girl in the apartment across from Dix's, Laurel Gray (Gloria Grahame). Laurel and Dix are immediately attracted to each other, and she impulsively supplies him with the alibi he needs, claiming that she saw Mildred leave Steele's apartment alone. Dix is released, but Lochner, over the protest of Brub, who blindly admires Dix, declares his intention to continue considering Steele a chief suspect in the case.

Dix and Laurel soon become lovers. She is a would-be actress who has just disentangled herself from a wealthy man who wanted to marry her. To Steele she is the woman he had despaired of ever finding, and when he is with her, his outbursts seem to disappear. He finds himself beginning to work on the script with a renewed vitality and enthusiasm that has been lacking in his writing since the war. The pressure of the investigation, however, begins to take its toll. Mildred's boyfriend, whom she stood up in order to read the novel to Dix, has his own alibi for the time of the murder and is cleared, making Dix the chief suspect once more. Gradually, under the growing strain, Dix begins to exhibit characteristics that convince not only Lochner, but Brub, his wife Sylvia (Jeff Donnell), and even Laurel and Mel, that he may indeed be capable of murder. This is most effectively shown in the scene in which Dix demonstrates, using Brub and Sylvia as stand-ins for the murderer and his victim, just exactly how Mildred Atkinson was probably killed.

Dix's writing continues to go well, and as his self-esteem returns he asks Laurel to marry him. She agrees, but the nagging doubts are beginning to make her afraid that the man she loves is indeed a psychopathic killer. Dix, learning that Brub has been assigned by Lochner to keep an eye on him, erupts. In a wild drive he almost collides with a young man in a jalopy and then leaps out, beating the driver senseless. Laurel is terrified. All she can think of is escape. She explains her feelings of panic to Mel, and he suggests that she not leave Dix until the screenplay is finished. She tells him that it is and gives it to him to show the studio bosses. It is the best work that Dix has done in years, and Mel and Laurel are hopeful that his renewed success will soften the blow of losing her.

Dix and Laurel go to Paul's, their favorite restaurant. Dix is excited and wants to elope with Laurel that very night, but underneath his seeming euphoria seethes the by-now out of control paranoia brought on by the pressure of the investigation. When he learns that the studio heads have read his script without his knowledge, he hits the faithful Mel. Laurel flees the restaurant, convinced at last that Dix really did kill Mildred. Dix follows her back to her apartment, and when he bursts in he finds Laurel packed and ready to run. In a rage he begins to strangle her, but the incessant ringing of her telephone manages to break the spell of violence, and Dix shakily answers it.

It is Brub telling Dix that Mildred's fiancée has turned out to be the killer all along. He expresses relief that the ordeal is over for Dix and Laurel, unaware that Dix's nominal innocence has been rendered meaningless and that what he had with Laurel has been destroyed. Lochner asks to apologize to Laurel, and Dix hands her the phone before walking out of the apartment. He is now a haunted, deeply troubled man who may or may not be able to come to grips with and overcome the blind rages which have brought him to the edge of murder. As she watches him go, Laurel repeats lines from the script which was born out of their brief affair: "I was born when I met you. I died when I lost you. I lived for a little while when I was with you."

Bogart and Grahame (who was married to director Ray at this time) are provided excellent support by Lovejoy and Donnell as the down-to-earth Nicolais, their steady relationship serving as a counterpoint to the stormy romance of Dix and Laurel. Smith, Steven Geray, and Robert Warwick are first-rate as the writers' friends. It is their loyalty and belief in Steele as much as Laurel's love which make the viewer want to believe him innocent. The relationship between Steel and Warwick's character, a washed-up Shakespearean actor with a fondness for drink, is particularly touching.

In a Lonely Place captures the mood of Hollywood at a particularly troubled time when the blacklist had settled like a cloud of fear over the entire film community. Through the device of the murder investigation, Ray perfectly captures the aura of suspicion and anxiety which prevailed. Telling the story of a love affair born out of a violent death and destroyed by rumor and suspicion, this film, in its dark way, is a highly romantic and moving work.

Michael Shepler

IN COLD BLOOD

Released: 1967
Production: Richard Brooks for Columbia
Direction: Richard Brooks
Screenplay: Richard Brooks; based on the novel of the same name by Truman
   Capote
Cinematography: Conrad Hall
Editing: Peter Zinner
Music: Quincy Jones
Running time: 133 minutes

Principal characters:
Perry Smith	Robert Blake
Dick Hickock	Scott Wilson
Alvin Dewey	John Forsythe
Reporter (Jenson)	Paul Stewart
Mr. Hickock	Jeff Corey
Mr. Smith	Charles McGraw
Mrs. Smith	Sammy Thurman
Prosecutor	Will Geer
Herbert Clutter	John McLiam
Bonnie Clutter	Ruth Storey
Nancy Clutter	Brenda C. Currin
Kenyon Clutter	Paul Hough
Mrs. Sadie Truitt	Herself
Myrtle Clare	Herself

A crime that rocked the nation took place in a small farm house in Holcomb, Kansas, on the night of November 15, 1959. Herbert Clutter, his ailing wife Bonnie, his teenage daughter Nancy, and his son Kenyon were murdered in cold blood by two ruthless killers who escaped with forty-three dollars in cash, a pair of binoculars, and a portable radio. Truman Capote attempted to explain what happened that night and why in his book *In Cold Blood* (1966), a nonfiction novel about the Clutter murders. In his search for the truth, he plumbed the backgrounds of the principals in this bizarre killing with the relentlessness of a newsman. His novel unfolds the facts of the case with the stark realism of a newsreel.

Richard Brooks, in his film adaptation of Capote's exhaustively researched and thoughtful book, picked up the search for truth where Capote stopped. He began at the Menninger Foundation in Topeka, Kansas, for it was here that the results of a study had been published several months before the Clutter murders predicting that inadequate methods for detecting and treating mentally ill prisoners would inevitably result in murders which could have been prevented. The Clutter murders were such an instance of preventable murder, thought Brooks. Unlike Capote, who maintained a cold objectivity, however, the director became personally involved. While remaining staunchly true in his portrayal of the facts, his attitudes and opinions are quite apparent.

Brooks's obsession with realism, his trademark in such films as *The Blackboard Jungle* (1955) and *Elmer Gantry* (1958), took him into the heart of Kansas and inside the four walls of the Clutter home where the crimes were actually committed. He further added to the authenticity by using many of the Clutters' neighbors as extras in the movie. In a *tour de force* of typecasting, Brooks tapped two relative unknowns for the major roles. Although Robert Blake and Scott Wilson both had acting experience before their starring roles as Perry Smith and Dick Hickock, they were not known to a wide audience. Their striking resemblance to the now-dead Kansas murderers closed the gap between live news coverage and film realism to a chilling degree.

Brooks begins the story slowly, establishing the separate strands that will soon be knit into a web of horror. Perry Smith receives a note from his former cellmate, Dick Hickock, outlining a job that will net them both a tidy sum of money. Smith subsequently violates his parole and returns to the state of Kansas, where he is joined at the bus depot by Hickock on the fateful morning of November 15. Their destination is a farm owned by the Clutter family where, according to Hickock's most recent cellmate, a wall safe contains over ten thousand dollars in cash.

The movie is filmed in black and white with extensive use of lightweight, hand-held camera equipment to contribute to the documentary atmosphere and stark reality of the story. Cinematographer Conrad Hall, in an attempt to remain faithful to the literary style of the novel, employs a film technique known as the "match-cut." For example, a phone call received by Nancy Clutter becomes an unrelated phone call placed to the state penitentiary by Perry Smith; Mr. Clutter, shaving, becomes Smith shaving. This technique is instrumental in establishing the pace of the movie. The score by Quincy Jones complements the cinematography. It is sparse and clean and reflects and enhances the visual momentum of the film but never intrudes as a separate entity.

As Smith and Hickock relentlessly cross miles of flat, monotonous Kansas landscape, drawing ever closer to their destination, the lights in the Clutter house go out one by one. The family sleeps peacefully, unaware of the madness and mayhem that will engulf them before this night draws to a shuddering close. True to the order of events in the novel, Brooks brings the audience up to the threshold of the Clutter home and then cuts away to the next morning's discovery of the dead bodies and the flight of Smith and Hickock.

Blake is excellent as the fantasy-ridden Perry Smith, portraying him with a latent violence lurking, barely concealed, beneath a hesitant, almost pathetic desire for respect and friendliness. He is a time bomb with the tragic events of his youth ticking away, needing only a trigger to release all of the pent-up rage and hostility that has been building inside him for so many years. Dick Hickock is that trigger. He is a born leader, hardened, holding a grudge against the world but possessing a quick intelligence and remarkable insight into human nature, an insight he uses to manipulate Perry into doing his bidding.

Cinematographer Hall employs a flashback to chronicle the tragic events of Smith's youth. For example, an incident in the fleabitten Mexican hotel where they are hiding out becomes a scene from Smith's past. As Hickock indulges himself with a prostitute, Smith remembers his mother, whom he had idolized. A proud, vibrant woman who had once been an outstanding rodeo star, she had degenerated into a whore and an alcoholic. Smith's memories of his father are even more bitter. His father was a prospector, a lone wolf, a man whose dreams Perry had shared and believed in. He was also a man who had turned a gun on his own son and pulled the trigger. The gun was unloaded, but it destroyed something in the soul of Perry Smith.

The men attempt to leave all of their possessions in Mexico, but Smith can no more release his personal possessions, containing the only physical evidence linking him to the scene of the crime, than he can release the torment of a youth that continues to haunt him. He instead ships his array of memorabilia to Las Vegas, their next destination, and he and Hickock then take a Greyhound bus back across the United States border unaware that a dragnet of detectives and police are relentlessly closing in. The detective in charge of investigating the crime (John Forsythe) and an interested reporter (Paul Stewart), with no witnesses and no clue beyond a bloody shoe print, patiently fit together the pieces of this gory puzzle.

Having exhausted their financial resources, Smith and Hickock steal a car in order to continue their journey toward Las Vegas. The scene that follows is a summation of the futility that permeates their lives. As they drive slowly along the desert road, they find a treasure. It is not what they had dreamed of, but merely a trash container filled with picnickers' garbage and enough empty soda pop containers to trade in at the next town for gas and a meal. As the two reach Las Vegas and boldly pick up the personal belongings that Smith had shipped ahead, the net closes around them and they are arrested.

Following the arrest, the police car with its two suspects speeds back toward Kansas. Again, the signpost for the Clutter farm comes into view. Through a flashback narrated by Smith, the horrors of that fateful night are finally revealed. We, the audience, are no longer just bystanders, for we have seen the fruitless struggle of these two flawed individuals in their inadequate attempt to cope with our complex social structure. We feel somehow responsible, for we now realize that neither man would have committed the Clutter murders alone. The main point of the film then becomes a question: Why did psychologists not pick up the murderers' early signals of distress, their cries for help? Why were they released on an unsuspecting society?

The final twenty-three minutes of the film deal with the trial and with the killers' five-year imprisonment on death row. Finally, they are hanged in a realistic, blood-curdling ritual. No better statement against capital punishment has ever been filmed than the final frame of the executed Smith, with the sound of a beating heart slowing. Finally, only blank film is left. Blake's performance in this final scene is reminiscent of the magnificent performance of Susan Hayward in the execution scene depicted in *I Want to Live!* (1958). His sensitive portrayal in this highly demanding role gained him recognition as a serious dramatic actor by both critics and filmmakers. Subsequently, in addition to a number of films, including *Tell Them Willie Boy Is Here* (1969), Blake was awarded his own television series in which he played the tough, streetwise detective, Baretta, a role which earned him the 1975 Emmy award as best male lead in a dramatic television series.

In Cold Blood received four Academy Award nominations: Brooks for Best Director and Best Screenplay; Hall for his innovative cinematography; and Jones for Best Original Music Score. The true impact and enduring value of the film, however, lies in its approach to the serious and controversial issue of capital punishment. Brooks's no-holds-barred treatment of this sensitive issue is an example of the responsible and socially conscious use of a powerful communications medium.

D. Gail Huskins

IN OLD ARIZONA

Released: 1929
Production: Twentieth Century-Fox
Direction: Raoul Walsh and Irving Cummings
Screenplay: Tom Barry; based on O. Henry's fictional characer, the Cisco Kid
Cinematography: Arthur Edeson
Editing: Louis R. Loeffler
Sound: Edmund H. Hansen
Running time: 95 minutes

Principal characters:
Sergeant Mickey Dunn	Edmund Lowe
Tonia Maria	Dorothy Burgess
The Cisco Kid	Warner Baxter (AA)
Tad	J. Farrell MacDonald
Russian Immigrant	Ivan Linow

In Old Arizona (1929) is not a classic Western of the calibre of *Stagecoach* (1939), *My Darling Clementine* (1946), or *The Wild Bunch* (1969); nevertheless, it is a landmark film. It was the first all-talking feature filmed outdoors, on location, and away from the sound studio, and it singlehandedly revitalized the Western genre. It introduced music to the Western, and also the character of the Cisco Kid, a quixotic caballero created by O. Henry who robbed stagecoaches, murdered on whim, and seduced beautiful women. It also won for Warner Baxter the second Best Actor Academy Award.

The time period for the film is the late 1890's, and the beautiful half-caste Tonia Maria (Dorothy Burgess), a temperamental flirt, lives in a little adobe house in a Mexican settlement near Wolf Crossing, a town close to the Grand Canyon. She is adored by the notorious Cisco Kid (Warner Baxter), a charming, daring, and often eccentric bandit. He is a murderer, but also a lover, and he has a five-thousand-dollar reward on his head. The Cisco Kid has such a reputation that in order to obtain a Wells Fargo strongbox, all he does is fire two warning shots, and the stagecoach drivers readily hand it over.

Sergeant Mickey Dunn (Edmund Lowe), an Irishman from Brooklyn who is attached to the 17th Cavalry, is dispatched to capture the Cisco Kid. Dunn is no less a ladies' man than the Kid, and he too is seduced by Tonia Maria. She also falls in love with him and is unfaithful to her outlaw lover. Dunn offers Tonia Maria the cash reward for her betrayal of the Kid and then waits in her home to take in the outlaw.

The Cisco Kid, meanwhile, has been involved with cattle rustlers in Guadalupe. When he returns to Wolf Crossing, he finds Tonia Maria in the arms of Dunn. The Kid then sings a song, which begins: "Don't you monkey with my lulu girl, or I'll tell you what I'll do. . . ." He soon overhears the two plotting to kill him and determines to settle matters with his faithless lover and the man who stole her from him. Tonia Maria sends Dunn a note asking him to go to her shack; the Kid gets hold of it and forges the writing, adding that the outlaw will be there dressed as a woman. Dunn arrives and accidently kills Tonia Maria. The Kid then escapes; unlike most cinematic law-breakers, he is neither caught nor killed at the finale.

In Old Arizona is a badly dated film with a clichéd love-triangle plot. It is certainly enjoyable, however, and it has the distinction of being the first film shot in Fox Movietone, Fox Studio's sound equivalent to Warner Bros.' Vitaphone. It was also filmed in its entirety away from Hollywood, not in Arizona but on location in the picturesque Zion National Park and Bryce Canyon in Utah, on the Mohave Desert at Victorville, California, at the old missions of San Juan Capistrano and San Fernando in California, and at other locations in the Southwest. Arthur Edeson's camera effectively captures the spaciousness and grandeur of the settings.

The film was the first to feature a "singing cowboy." "My Tonia," by B. G. De Dylva, Lew Brown, and Ray Henderson, is performed by Baxter, and singer Nick Lucas' recording of the tune became one of the hits of 1929. The sound track of *In Old Arizona* is remarkably unmechanical for its time, with background sounds—clanging bells, ticking clocks, frying bacon—nicely and naturally blended in with the dialogue. The film was billed as a "100 Per Cent Talking Fox Movietone Feature." The sound of horse hoofs growing dimmer and dimmer as the animals gallop away from the scene, for example, was no minor technical achievement in 1929.

In Old Arizona is codirected by Raoul Walsh and Irving Cummings. Walsh, who had directed Edmund Lowe in his best-remembered role, Sergeant Quirt (to Victor McLaglen's Captain Flagg), in *What Price Glory?* (1926), was originally set to play the Cisco Kid. The film was supposed to be a two-reeler; after viewing the first two days' rushes, however, Fox's Winfield Sheehan ordered that the film be expanded to five reels. Walsh filmed several chase sequences. While driving to Cedar City, Utah, however, he lost his right eye in a car crash, and had to be replaced by Irving Cummings. Baxter was chosen as star, and a new script was written by Tom Barry. Although Cummings is responsible for the bulk of the film, long shots done by Walsh remain in the final print.

Baxter had already appeared in the silents *Mannequin* (1926), *The Runaway* (1926), *Aloma of the South Seas* (1926), *The Great Gatsby* (1926, as Jay Gatsby) and *Ramona* (1928). Before entering films he had played stock, and his rich speaking voice enabled him to make the transition to sound effortlessly. His capable performance in this film beat George Bancroft (*Thunderbolt*), Chester Morris (*Alibi*), Paul Muni (*The Valiant*), and Lewis Stone (*The Patriot*) for the Oscar that year. Baxter was a popular, competent leading man of the 1930's, one of the highest-paid film stars of the decade. He starred in the classic musical *42nd Street* (1932), as well as *Broadway Bill* (1933), *Stand Up and Cheer* (1934), *The Road to Glory* (1936), and *Kidnapped* (1938). After his popularity waned, he became the lead in Columbia's "Crime Doctor" series during the mid-1940's.

Burgess made her screen debut in *In Old Arizona*. In 1929, Hollywood studios were raiding legitimate theaters and signing actors with stage experience, actors who knew how to speak. Burgess came into the film direct from an ingenue part in a Los Angeles stage production of *The Squall*. Her career lasted into the 1940's. Lowe, a romantic lead in silents who had acted in stock and on Broadway and was cast against type in *What Price Glory?*, appeared in dozens of "B" films well into the 1960's.

In Old Arizona received fine reviews, with critics foreseeing a great future for the sound Western. It was also a popular box-office hit, taking in $1,300,000, a handsome sum for the year in which the stock market crashed. In addition to Baxter's Oscar, it received four other nominations: Best Picture (the winner was *The Broadway Melody*); Director (only Cummings was nominated, and he lost to Frank Lloyd for *The Divine Lady, Weary River*, and *Drag*); Writing (Barry was beaten by Hans Kraly's *The Patriot*); and Cinematography (Edeson lost to Clyde De Vinna for *White Shadows in the South Seas*).

Baxter and Lowe starred in a Cummings-directed sequel, *The Cisco Kid* (1931), and Baxter alone appeared in *The Return of the Cisco Kid* (1939). The Kid was also portrayed by Cesar Romero beginning in 1939 (Romero played a character named Lopez in *The Return of the Cisco Kid*, released in April; nine months later, he had the title role in *The Cisco Kid and the Lady*), and Duncan Renaldo, starting in 1945. Two years earlier, the character was featured in a radio series with Jackson Beck and, later, Jack Mather. In 1949, the Kid became the popular hero of a long-running color syndicated television series starring Renaldo, who died in 1980. Pancho (Leo Carrillo) was his comic sidekick. By this time, the Kid had long been transformed into a one-dimensional good guy. In the television series, the Cisco Kid *never* kills anyone himself but tricks the bandits into killing each other. He and Pancho solve counterfeiting cases and stagecoach hold-ups. In 1959, the Cisco Kid celebrated his tenth anniversary on television, chalking up a domestic gross of nearly $11,000,000—the highest for a syndicated series to that date. It was recently announced that Metro-Goldwyn-Mayer is planning to star television star Erik Estrada in another film version of *The Cisco Kid*. Baxter in *In Old Arizona*, however, remains the best and most vivid of all Cisco Kids.

Rob Edelman

IN THE GOOD OLD SUMMERTIME

Released: 1949
Production: Joe Pasternak for Metro-Goldwyn-Mayer
Direction: Robert Z. Leonard
Screenplay: Albert Hackett, Frances Goodrich, and Ivan Tors; based on the screenplay by Samson Raphaelson and on the play *The Shop Around the Corner* by Miklos Laszlo
Cinematography: Harry Stradling
Editing: Adrienne Fazan
Running time: 102 minutes

Principal characters:
Veronica Fisher .... Judy Garland
Andrew Larkin .... Van Johnson
Otto Oberkugen .... S. Z. Sakall
Nellie Burke .... Spring Byington
Rudy Hansen .... Clinton Sundberg
Hickey .... Buster Keaton
Louise Parkson .... Marcia Van Dyke

In the Good Old Summertime was M-G-M's second treatment of *The Shop Around the Corner*, a play by Miklos Laszlo. In 1940 it had been presented under its original title in a successful film adaptation written by Samson Raphaelson that starred Margaret Sullavan and James Stewart. For the 1949 version the setting was changed from modern-day Hungary to turn-of-the-century Chicago, and the shop in question became a music store to provide an occasion for a number of songs. The result was one of the most popular films of 1949.

The opening sequence establishes a nostalgic atmosphere with the off-screen voice of Andrew Larkin (Van Johnson) fondly remembering the Chicago of his day—before the crowds and the skyscrapers. Then we go back to that time and see Larkin as a young man enjoying a picnic in the park with a band playing "In the Good Old Summertime" while the onlookers sing along.

The next day, on his way to work, Larkin stops to pick up a letter from his post-office box. He is so intent on reading the letter on his way out that he does not see Veronica Fisher (Judy Garland) coming in, and a collision ensues that knocks her down. Larkin's embarrassed attempts to restore Veronica to her feet and give her back her hat, parasol, and bag that she lost in the collision only make the situation worse. He then offers to pay for any damage, gives her the address of the shop where he works, and rides off on his bicycle—tearing off her skirt in the process.

Larkin works in a shop that sells musical instruments and sheet music. It is run by Otto Oberkugen (S. Z. Sakall) and also employs Nellie Burke (Spring Byington), Rudy Hansen (Clinton Sundberg), and Hickey (Buster Keaton). Oberkugen is an older man who is basically kindly but inclined to be a bit stubborn and dictatorial in running his shop. He and Nellie are in love, but their twenty-year romance has never reached the point of marriage. Hansen is a rather colorless clerk, and Hickey is a slow-witted and hapless person who is employed only because he is Oberkugen's nephew and because he alone pretends to like his uncle's violin-playing. When things go wrong, Oberkugen takes out his valuable Stradivarius and plays atrociously to soothe himself.

Veronica comes to the shop, but instead of wanting Larkin to pay for her ruined garments, she asks for a job. Larkin dislikes her and her manner and tells her that there are no jobs, but Veronica demands to see the owner; she shows him her selling ability by playing a harp and singing "Meet Me Tonight in Dreamland" to convince a reluctant customer to buy a harp. Oberkugen hires her over Larkin's objections, and a relationship of daily antagonism at the shop begins between Veronica and Larkin. Although they do not suspect it, however, they also have a quite different relationship with each other. Each has been carrying on an intense correspondence with an anonymous soulmate. They want to keep their letters on an "intellectual plane" above such matters as names and other mundane details. We soon learn what neither suspects: they are writing to each other.

There are four stages in their strange situation of antagonism in person and love in letters. When they first run into each other outside the post office, neither the audience nor the characters realize what the situation is; then the audience learns the truth while both characters remain ignorant. Next Larkin learns that Veronica is his correspondent, but he does not reveal to her that he is the "Dear Friend" to whom she is writing. Finally, his revelation that he is "Box 237" brings about the happy ending. This plot device is, fortunately, more than cleverness; it provides both comedy and commentary on misplaced idealism.

In a crucial sequence the two letter-writers arrange to meet in person at a restaurant one evening, but that same day Oberkugen—because of a spat with Nellie—demands that the entire staff stay late to take an inventory. The tension is high as both Mr. Larkin and Miss Fisher (as they call each other at work) worry about missing their engagements, each sure the other cannot understand the importance of finishing as soon as possible. They do, however, get away from work in time, but Veronica arrives at the restaurant first and Larkin—somewhat dubious about meeting in person his idealized friend—has Hansen peer into the restaurant for him to find out what she looks like. When he finds that his "Dear Friend" is the obnoxious Miss Fisher, he removes from his buttonhole the flower that is to identify him and goes in to taunt her about her friend not showing up.

The next day Miss Fisher does not come to work because of her "psychological" state—she is most upset because she believes that her correspondent came to the restaurant but left when he saw her with Larkin. Larkin, however, goes to visit her and begins to see her more as a person and less as just an antagonistic coworker. By Christmas Eve he has come to love her and she him, although neither has told the other and she still does not know that he is the writer of the letters she cherishes. He has a last bit of fun with her by telling her that he has found that her correspondent is a fat, bald man named Newspickle. Then he reveals that he is "Box 237." "Psychologically I'm very confused," she replies, "but personally I feel just wonderful." The camera then tilts up and when it tilts back down we see the happy young couple in summertime walking with their young daughter while we hear the title tune on the sound track. The daughter is played by two-year-old Liza Minnelli, Garland's real-life daughter.

Between the restaurant scene and the end are numerous complications involving a beautiful young violinist, Louise Parkson (Marcia Van Dyke), who has fallen in love with Larkin. Larkin lets her play Oberkugen's beloved Stradivarius violin, and for a time it seems that Larkin will lose both his job and Veronica, but when Oberkugen hears Louise play the instrument, he realizes that she can play it "as it should be played," and he cannot. Having already announced his engagement to Nellie, he gives the violin to Louise and everyone is happy.

Although Garland does sing several songs in the film, *In the Good Old Summertime* is not a musical. The songs do not express the emotions of the character she plays, and their content is not related to the plot. Veronica Fisher is a singer and sings two or three songs at the shop in order to demonstrate an instrument or a piece of sheet music and sings two more, most notably "I Don't Care," to entertain the guests at the engagement party for Nellie and Oberkugen. The songs are both good and well-performed, but they do not have the close interrelationship with the plot and characters that is present in a true musical. This does not mean that the film is inferior to a musical, only that it is another type—a romantic comedy with songs.

Overall, Garland and Johnson, with truly excellent support from Sakall as Oberkugen and Byington as Nellie, sustain our interest in the characters and the situations and keep us from noticing the manufactured elements of the story near the end. Director Robert Z. Leonard should also receive some of the credit for the film's success, although some of the blame for overdoing the slapstick comedy in a few scenes and for allowing the pace occasionally to become too slow is also his. It also must be noted that it is sad to see Keaton, one of the two or three best comedians of silent film, reduced to a role in which he does little more than say "Thanks, Uncle Otto."

Marilynn Wilson

INHERIT THE WIND

Released: 1960
Production: Stanley Kramer for United Artists
Direction: Stanley Kramer
Screenplay: Nathan E. Douglas and Harold Jacob Smith; based on the play
   of the same name by Jerome Lawrence and Robert E. Lee
Cinematography: Ernest Laszlo
Editing: Frederic Knudtson
Music: Ernest Gold
Running time: 127 minutes

> *Principal characters:*
> Henry Drummond .... Spencer Tracy
> Matthew Harrison Brady .... Fredric March
> E. K. Hornbeck .... Gene Kelly
> Sarah Brady .... Florence Eldridge
> Bertram T. Cates .... Dick York
> Rachel Brown .... Donna Anderson
> Reverend Jeremiah Brown .... Claude Akins
> Judge .... Harry Morgan

Inherit the Wind begins with a lone voice singing the gospel song "That Old Time Religion" while the camera pans past a statue of Blind Justice. The implications are clear, and the courtroom melodrama which follows is one of the most rousing of its decade. Both the film and the play on which it is based are really thinly disguised dramatizations of the infamous "Monkey Trial" of 1925 wherein Clarence Darrow for the defense and William Jennings Bryan for the prosecution clashed in the hill town of Dayton, Tennessee, over the right of John T. Scopes, a twenty-four-year-old schoolteacher, to propound Charles Darwin's theory of evolution to his high-school class. In actuality, Scopes volunteered to be the test case challenging a state statute which deemed it unlawful for anyone to "teach any theory that denies the story of divine creation of man as taught by the Bible." The real-life prototypes are given fictional names in the script: For example, the Darrow character is called Henry Drummond; Bryan becomes Matthew Harrison Brady; Scopes is called Bertram T. Cates; and H. L. Mencken, then a reporter for the *Baltimore Herald* and chief agent behind the trial's worldwide publicity, becomes E. K. Hornbeck. The town of Dayton is renamed "Heavenly" Hillsboro.

   Soon after it is announced that Matthew Harrison Brady (Fredric March), a longtime champion of fundamentalist belief, has volunteered his services for the prosecution, E. K. Hornbeck (Gene Kelly) arrives in Hillsboro with the news that his paper has procured Henry Drummond (Spencer Tracy) to defend the schoolteacher, Cates (Dick York). At the prospect of the great Chautauqua orator and former presidential candidate Brady waging holy war against Drummond, the champion of agnostic libertarianism, the whole town is thrown into a carnival spirit. When throngs of enthusiastic supporters greet Brady and his wife, Sarah (Florence Eldridge), at the depot, while Drummond slips unnoticed into town, it is obvious that the trial cannot be an impartial one.

Since *Inherit the Wind* is primarily a film of ideas with most of its action limited to a single courtroom set, much is gained from director Stanley Kramer's orchestration of the antagonists' lengthy speeches, Ernest Laszlo's prowling camera, and Frederic Knudtson's unobtrusive editing. Each performance is allowed to build smoothly to its climax, with the result that the audience soon forgets the claustrophobic setting.

From the start, Drummond's task is not easy: he must contend with biased jurors, Brady's honorary appointment as "Colonel" in the state militia, a sign above the courthouse door exhorting all who enter to "Read your Bible," and the announcement by the judge (Harry Morgan) of a prayer meeting on the first day of the trial. It is at this meeting that the film gains its title: when the Reverend Jeremiah Brown (Claude Akins) asks God's damnation for Cates and all who support him, including his own daughter, Rachel (Donna Anderson), even the fervent Brady is taken aback and must remind the Reverend of Solomon's wisdom in the Book of Proverbs: "He that troubleth his own house; Shall inherit the wind."

Drummond is repeatedly stymied in his attempt to build a case for the defense until he resolves to fight Brady on his own turf. In a highly unorthodox move, he calls Brady to the stand as a witness for the defense, based on Brady's self-proclaimed biblical expertise. Through a series of ingenious and humorous questions pertaining to textual inconsistencies in the Bible, Drummond begins to expose the seams in Brady's rhetoric, and in so doing, ever so slightly shakes the townpeople's faith in their prophet.

One of the most moving confrontations in the entire film occurs when Rachel goes to Brady's apartment to vent her rage at him for betraying her confidence in court. She is met at the door by a protective Sarah Brady, who, in illustrating the meaning of conjugal devotion, provides the final catalyst for Rachel's break with her father to join Cates. After Rachel's departure, Sarah comforts her rapidly disintegrating husband, who is all too aware of his waning popularity.

On the final day of the trial, the jury brings in a "quilty" verdict, but the judge, fearing political retribution, orders Cates to pay a token fine of only one hundred dollars. Brady protests the court's leniency, while Drummond insists that no fine, however small, will be paid by his client. The date for an appeal is set, court is officially adjourned, and Brady launches into a religious tirade that is ignored by most of the bustling throng in the courtroom. Frustrated in his attempted speech and exhausted by the heat, Brady is stricken and dies.

Left alone in the courtroom, Drummond weighs Darwin's book in one hand and the Bible in the other; finally, he jams both books into his valise while an a cappella voice sings "The Battle Hymn of the Republic" over his exit. There are no end credits.

Inherit the Wind was one of many social dramas directed and/or produced by Kramer throughout the 1950's and 1960's. Films such as *The Men* (1950), *The Defiant Ones* (1958), *On the Beach* (1959), *Judgment at Nuremberg* (1961), and *Ship of Fools* (1965) are all infused with Kramer's liberal sensibility, the same sensibility which informs and enhances the themes of *Inherit the Wind*. The play, following close on the heels of the McCarthy era, was very much an allegory of its time, and this dimension is fully exploited by Kramer and his screenwriters. Indeed, if the film can be faulted at all, it is on this level: the townspeople seem a trifle too bigoted, while Drummond's unrelenting altruism is equally suspect.

Many critics felt that both Tracy and March gave the performances of their respective careers in this film. Certainly, Tracy's idiosyncratic, even folksy screen presence is perfect for the Drummond role, while March's highly stylized, theatrical performance is equally suited to Brady. Their explosive confrontations speak volumes on acting style.

Two other performances are worth noting. Eldridge (Mrs. Fredric March in real life), primarily known as a stage actress, brings uncommon warmth and dignity to her portrayal of Sarah Brady. Her scenes with Tracy and particularly with Anderson are crucial to a total understanding of Brady's motives. Kelly, in one of his few straight dramatic roles, brings just the right degree of cynical detachment to the pivotal role of E. K. Hornbeck without once sacrificing the empathy of the audience.

Although *Inherit the Wind* was nominated for four Academy Awards in 1960 (Best Actor, Best Screenplay from Another Medium, Best Black and White Cinematography, and Best Editing) it lost in every category.

Karl W. Weimer, Jr.

THE INNOCENTS

Released: 1961
Production: Jack Clayton for Twentieth Century-Fox
Direction: Jack Clayton
Screenplay: William Archibald and Truman Capote; based on William Archibald's play of the same name and adapted from the short story *The Turn of the Screw* by Henry James
Cinematography: Freddie Francis
Editing: James Clark
Running time: 99 minutes

Principal characters:

Miss Giddens	Deborah Kerr
The Uncle	Michael Redgrave
Mrs. Grose	Megs Jenkins
Miles	Martin Stephens
Flora	Pamela Franklin
Peter Quint	Peter Wyngarde
Anna	Isla Cameron
Miss Jessel	Clytie Jessop
The Coachman	Eric Woodburn

The Innocents is based on Henry James's famous ghost tale, *The Turn of the Screw*. The best-known if somewhat apocryphal anecdote attached to the original story is that James purposely set out to write the most frightening story imaginable purely as an exercise in terrifying his readers. Having done so, he underscored his triumph both in choosing his title and in adding a prologue in which guests at a country home compete with each other for the best horror story. How well James succeeded is still a matter of literary debate. Whether or not one agrees with the opinion of James's narrator about his tale, however, that "it's beyond everything. Nothing at all that I know touches it," *The Turn of the Screw* is incontestably suspenseful and subtly unnerving. It is also one of the most widely read and respected novellas in the supernatural genre. Almost as famous as the work itself, published in 1898, was an alternate psychological interpretation which came into vogue among critics several decades later. This reading of James's plot was Freudian in nature and generally asserted that the ghosts which plagued his central character were not at all unworldly but merely symbols of libidinous desires conjured up by a troubled psyche.

James wrote the actual narrative of the young governess, Miss Giddens, in the first person as part of his conceit of a "discovered manuscript." That conceit itself was fairly common in the genre, but James's use of it in *The Turn of the Screw* is quite uncommon. Although technically this first-person format prevents the reader from receiving any information or from perceiving situations except through Miss Giddens' eyes, James employed elaborate and enigmatic prose to render the narrative less subjective. Given these significant contradictions, the challenge confronting the filmmakers who adapted James's writing was monumental. Because they were dealing with an accepted classic, faithfulness to the original work would be the prime criterion for many viewers. Which interpretation should they be faithful to, however—the one which accepted the ghosts as real or the other which considered them to be merely hallucinations? If the adapters chose an enigmatic treatment, what devices should be used to translate James's convoluted writing style to the screen? Even if the supernatural quality could be approximated by restricting the audience's perspective to an equivalent of the heroine's, how could the filmed image of a ghost, which must have a graphic and tangible screen presence, be rendered enigmatic?

The plot of *The Innocents*, as taken from James, is not complex. Miss Giddens (Deborah Kerr), a cultivated woman of modest means, is recommended to a wealthy gentleman as a suitable governess for his wards, an orphaned niece and nephew. Despite the fact that Giddens has not held such a position before, the unnamed Uncle (Michael Redgrave) is more concerned with whether she "has imagination" than he is in her background and references. Although uneasy about the amount of responsibility she will assume, Miss Giddens agrees to accept the job. From this first scene the filmmakers attempt to overcome the paradoxes of James's novella. The film, of course, must rely more heavily on its performances and its visual style for any degree of success. Two brief cuts actually open the film: a shot of a pair of hands being wrung, followed by a shot of Miss Giddens crying in distress. These constitute an informal prologue. After this markedly melodramatic beginning, the film dissolves back to a close-up of Kerr, smiling and self-possessed, at her job interview. Kerr's interpretation of the role immediately suggests that, despite her age, Miss Giddens has lived a sheltered life devoid of much worldly experience. On the other hand, Redgrave, as her prospective employer, epitomizes the suave, manipulative gentleman. He paces the room before her, explaining his discomfiture because of the death of his last governess and stresses his need for a reliable replacement; but he never interrogates Giddens on her qualifications. While the young woman may be apprehensive about taking over the sole responsibility for two children, she cannot resist the Uncle's charm. When he takes her hand and asks for her decision, she is, in effect, seduced into acquiescence.

The staging of this introductory sequence, juxtaposed with the disconnected impact of the first two shots, implies that Giddens' apprehension may prove to be well-founded. Even a viewer not familiar with the supernatural overtones of the source material can appreciate from Kerr's portrayal that Giddens' frame of mind as she starts her new career is one of more than slight naïveté and is susceptible to outside influences. Giddens arrives at the country house where she is to work still unaware of all the reasons for her employer's concern over his wards. Mrs. Grose (Megs Jenkins), the housekeeper, gives her no indication that there is anything extraordinary about the children whom she is to supervise. Giddens is charmed by Flora (Pamela Franklin), her youngest charge, and her older brother Miles. Although she is concerned when Miles (Martin Stevens) is discharged from boarding school for being a bad influence on his fellows, Giddens quickly reassures herself that Miles's intelligence and inquisitiveness must have been misunderstood by his schoolmasters.

The chain of occurrences which follows Miles's return are not conveyed through a literal exposition but filtered through Giddens' point of view. The childrens' behavior and the manner in which the film presents her perception of these occurrences sustain the ambivalent quality which was central to James's narrative. Giddens is gradually convinced that the children are being possessed by the ghosts of Miss Jessel (Clytie Jessop), their former governess, and Peter Quint (Peter Wyngarde), who was the estate's evil horsemaster. She sees apparitions of both Quint and Jessel and believes that they are somehow conspiring to harm the children. After several inconclusive attempts to compel the children to admit their relationships with the ghosts, Giddens sends Flora away with Mrs. Grose and girds for a final confrontation with Miles and the spectral Peter Quint.

The Innocents, like *The Turn of the Screw*, never resolves the issues of Peter Quint's actions in the final scene or of the nature of the ghostly presences. Clearly, there is some supernatural link between Miles and Flora. The first hint that Giddens receives that there is something unusual about the children is when Flora becomes excited at the prospect of Miles's coming home well before the letter arrives announcing his expulsion from school. The truth of the school's accusations against Miles is never verified, but his subsequent behavior, which vacillates between being childish and being surprisingly adult, makes Giddens uneasy. Her own immaturity is also implicit in the first scene when she is so quickly captivated by the Uncle's worldliness and self-assurance. She is also charmed by the handsome, adolescent Miles but disturbed and possibly sexually attracted to the adult *persona* which Miles consciously projects. Miles is aware of this effect on Giddens and revels in it, as when he asks for a goodnight kiss and suddenly covers her mouth with his, causing her to recoil in horror.

Giddens' horror of the ghosts is closely tied to her fears for Miles's and Flora's safety, but it is also related to a possible threat presented by Miles's sexual precocity. In fact, she is as shocked by what she considers his carnal behavior as she is by Mrs. Grose's tale of the perverse liaison between Jessel and Quint. These circumstances add credibility to the view that Quint is merely a product of Giddens' confusion and inexperience in dealing with either responsibility or sexuality. The staging of the final confrontation also supports this theory. Giddens peers out into the darkness surrounding the house but sees only the statues on the silent lawn. She turns, shakes Miles violently, and screams at him to confess that Quint is out there. Low-angle lighting makes her expression appear frantic, almost crazed. When she looks out again, a point-of-view shot pans across the lawn and stops on Quint, who now stands where a statue had been. When Quint enters the house, Miles and Giddens always share the frame, as if he could not be present without them. Even amid the chaos of this climactic moment, visual usage continues to undercut the reality of Quint's specter. Is he merely a statue animated by Giddens' terror? Is he actually in the room or only a manifestation of the emotional conflict between Giddens and Miles? Even after Miles has died and Giddens bends to kiss him and cry, "You're safe," the images do not hold on them to confirm or deny what has happened. They only suggest simultaneously the destruction of Miles's life and Giddens' obsession.

Alain J. Silver

AN INSPECTOR CALLS

Released: 1954
Production: A. D. Peters for Watergate; released by Associated Artists
Direction: Guy Hamilton
Screenplay: Desmond Davis; based on the play of the same name by J. B. Priestley
Cinematography: Edward Scaife
Editing: Alan Osbitson
Running time: 79 minutes

Principal characters:
Inspector Poole .... Alastair Sim
Arthur Birling .... Arthur Young
Sybil Birling .... Olga Lindo
Sheila Birling .... Eileen Moore
Eric Birling .... Bryan Forbes
Gerald Croft .... Brian Worth
Eva Smith .... Jane Wenham

Seen occasionally in the United States in retrospectives of British films or on the late show on television, *An Inspector Calls* was not an enormous box-office success at the time of its release. It received mixed reviews from the critics, who thought the script, based on the play by J. B. Priestley, ingenious and well-conceived, but the film nothing more than a mild diversion. The movie was filmed in 1954 by Guy Hamilton, who was later to direct a number of James Bond movies as well as *The Devil's Disciple* (1958), and who had been the assistant to noted British director Sir Carol Reed on several pictures, including *The Third Man* (1949).

An Inspector Calls is noteworthy for its rather unique and moralistic theme and approach; for the clever convolutions of its script; for its outstanding production values; and for the presence of Alastair Sim, a Scottish actor highly touted in Britain for his adroitness in comic as well as dramatic roles. In *An Inspector Calls*, Sim portrays the somewhat eerie, highly intuitive inspector of the title. Although not given much of a character with which to work, he still manages to exude a rather ominous, authoritative presence, veiled beneath an acceptably polite exterior. This presence is revealed primarily in the directness and haunting quality of Sim's gaze, which is required to make the other characters divulge their inner secrets.

An Inspector Calls is a film about social ills among the upper middle class, conscience, responsibility for one's actions, and responsibility to others, as illustrated by the story of the Birling family. Set around 1912 at the dawn of a new era of optimism and technical advancement and the possible threat of war, the film opens with the family gathered around the dinner table, glasses of port in hand, to celebrate the engagement of the daughter, Sheila (Eileen Moore), to young Gerald Croft (Brian Worth) of Crofts Limited. Into this harmonious setting steps the mysterious Inspector Poole with the distressing news of a young working woman's suicide. The family, understandably aghast, is rather puzzled as well, since they wonder how the news relates to them. The Inspector begins a rather intense, insightful probe which reveals the weaknesses, foibles, and all-too-few virtues of the Birlings and Gerald, beginning with the father, Arthur Birling (Arthur Young). As the Inspector explains, each one of them may have had something to do with the girl, and while not directly responsible for her suicide, may have started a chain of events which ultimately resulted in her death.

The father is apparently the one who started this chain of events when he fired the young woman, Eva Smith (Jane Wenham), from his factory for being the ringleader of a strike and asking for higher wages. Arthur Birling is revealed as a rather ambitious, bigoted, and insensitive man, concerned primarily with business and the acquisition of a knighthood. When confronted by his actions, he refuses to acknowledge that he has done anything amiss. The Inspector next interrogates Sheila, who admits to being responsible, in a fit of anger and jealousy, for having the young woman fired from her next position in a fashionable hat shop. Possessing somewhat more of a conscience than her father, Sheila is truly affected by her part in the affair, and listens remorsefully to the others and their gradual admissions of guilt. Gerald Croft, the next to be questioned, fares perhaps the best. Admitting to an affair with the young woman, who went by the pseudonym Daisy Renton at the time, he has, at least, acted out of compassion for her position and out of a definite feeling of affection. The breakup of the affair, the best episode so far in Daisy's life, was a severe blow to her. Back on the streets, again, she encountered Eric Birling, the wastrel son of the Birling family. (Eric is played by Bryan Forbes, who later went on to become the noted director of such films as *Séance on a Wet Afternoon*, 1964, and *The Whisperers*, 1966).

After a brief liaison, the young woman became pregnant. When she discovered that Eric's desperate efforts to aid her had resulted in the embezzlement of funds from his father's office, she broke off the affair. She sought charitable aid from a foundation chaired by Sybil Birling (Olga Lindo), Eric's mother. Insensitive and bigoted like her husband and pompous as well, Sybil Birling refused aid on the grounds that the girl was impertinent, irresponsible, and degenerate, and therefore undeserving of the financial support of the organization. Mrs. Birling disclaims any part of the blame for Eva Smith's suicide, stating that all the blame lies with the young man who got her pregnant—not realizing that the young man is in fact her own son.

The investigation leaves all members of the family shaken and their relations strained. Gradually, it becomes apparent that their mysterious interrogator is not actually on the police force. His identity is left for the Birlings and the audience to surmise. The realization that the family is no longer involved in a legal tangle has different effects on each member of the family. Mr. and Mrs. Birling, freed of any social embarrassment or impediment to his achievement of a knighthood, are immensely relieved and ready to return to their old lives as though nothing had happened. Gerald Croft, following in the footsteps of the old tradition, is somewhat of the same mind, although rather less so. Sheila and Eric, however, have been deeply and profoundly affected by the ordeal and are morally incapable of forgetting what is past. After all of the family's quarreling over the importance of the bogus Inspector's interrogation, the phone rings. Ironically, the phone call reveals that a young woman has just been reported dead by suicide and that a real inspector will be visiting the Birling family immediately. The film ends on this provocative note, leaving the audience to wonder at the outcome along with the characters in the drama.

Undoubtedly, the strongest aspect of the film is its script. With the plot unfolding in a compelling manner, and with the clever handling of the coincidental turns in the family's relationship with Eva Smith, the script also yields an elegance of language which lends a sense of old-fashioned style, wit, and polish to the film. Sim's Inspector becomes the physical embodiment, in the end, of a higher level of conscience. One minor note of interest is the change of the Inspector's name from the highly suggestive Goole of the play to the more pedestrian Poole. Once the Inspector arrives on the scene, the film alternates between the line of interrogation and a series of flashbacks, as each guilty member of the family traces his or her involvement with the late Eva Smith. While the use of flashbacks allows for an opening up of the script and an insight into the workingman's environment, as opposed to the comfortably wealthy one of the Birling's, it does give perhaps too much credibility to the actuality of the character of Eva Smith, which renders superfluous later doubts as to whether she is indeed one girl or a composite of several.

The production values of *An Inspector Calls* are excellent throughout. Interiors reflect the solid comfort of the upper middle class, which somehow lacks any homelike quality, while exteriors depict accurately the grime and degeneracy of the streets to which the lower classes are relegated. A somber, ominous mood pervades the film and is aided by the exceptional work of the cinematographer. Period costumes and settings add to the almost documentarylike level of reality attained.

The cast is likewise excellent. The performances of Sims and Forbes are especially noteworthy. Equally effective are the performances of Young and Lindo as the socially conscious, morally unconscious parents; Worth as the well-meaning young heir to Crofts Limited, destined to follow the prescribed social views of his elders; and Moore as the spoiled, impulsive, but good-hearted Sheila. As the poor girl driven to suicide, Wenham conveys a sweet, innocent quality and a sense of decency. The acting, production values, and script of *An Inspector Calls* combine to produce a film of style, intrigue, and depth.

Grace Anne Morsberger

INTERMEZZO

Released: 1939
Production: David O. Selznick for Selznick International and United Artists
Direction: Gregory Ratoff
Screenplay: George O'Neil; based on the screenplay of the same name by Gosta Stevens and Gustav Molander
Cinematography: Gregg Toland
Editing: Hal C. Kern
Musical direction: Lou Forbes; principal theme by Heinz Provost
Running time: 73 minutes

Principal characters:
Holger Brandt	Leslie Howard
Anita Hoffman	Ingrid Bergman
Margit Brandt	Edna Best
Thomas Stenborg	John Halliday
Ann Marie Brandt	Ann Todd

In 1939 producer David O. Selznick bought the rights from Svenskfilmindustrie to remake a popular Swedish film of 1936, *Intermezzo*. The practice of remaking foreign films flourished in Hollywood for a while during the 1930's. This was justified by Selznick on the grounds of economy—a scene-by-scene duplication of the original film would save time and creative energy. Selznick's American version of *Intermezzo* is interesting today, however, primarily because the producer had also acquired one of the film's original stars, the young Swedish actress Ingrid Bergman. Bergman was brought to Hollywood by Selznick to re-create her role of the pianist Anita Hoffman.

Subtitled "A Love Story," *Intermezzo* tells a thoroughly romantic tale of modest scope. Holger Brandt (Leslie Howard), a world-famous concert violinist, returns from a concert tour to his home in Sweden and is welcomed by his wife Margit (Edna Best), and eight-year-old daughter Ann Marie (Ann Todd). Soon he meets Anita Hoffman, who is Ann Marie's piano teacher. When Holger hears Anita play at Ann Marie's birthday party, he begins to fall in love with her. His feelings are reciprocated, and the two continue to meet surreptitiously. Although he loves his wife and child, Holger finally decides to leave Margit and Ann Marie. He sets off on an extended concert tour with Anita as his accompanist—both musical and romantic. Holger eventually misses his home and daughter, however, and Anita, realizing that she stands in the way of his true happiness, decides to accept a scholarship to study in Paris, and they part. Holger returns to Sweden. As Ann Marie rushes across the street to greet him, she is run over by a car. Holger is overwhelmed with grief, but the doctor reassures him that the child will, in time, recover.

Begging forgiveness for his "tragically human" faults, he is finally reconciled with his patient wife Margit.

Clearly, the screenplay does not seem very original to modern audiences, as much of it has become overly familiar and cliché-ridden. At one point Bergman actually delivers the line, "I hate meeting like this—in out-of-the-way-places and dark corners." The moralistic ending, in which Holger, through his daughter's accident, is punished for his transgressions, is melodramatic in the extreme. In fact, for about five minutes the screenplay gives the distinct but erroneous impression that the little girl has died as a result of the automobile accident—an inexcusable manipulation of the emotions of the audience. Moreover, the relationship between the romantic couple, Holger and Anita, will not find such tearful acceptance among modern audiences as it did in 1939. Anita readily subordinates her ambitions to Holger's, and in the end she willingly sacrifices her happiness for his ultimate well-being—actions which seem incompatible with today's more enlightened and liberated attitudes toward sex roles.

In spite of such dated devices in the screenplay, however, the film still retains much of its original appeal. That it does is largely due to the restrained and unsensational style of director Gregory Ratoff and the competence of the cast. Howard, whose work in *Intermezzo* was performed simultaneously with his acting assignment in Selznick's *Gone with the Wind* (1939), gives a controlled, understated performance as the violinist Holger Brandt. He manages to overcome some of the difficulties inherent in the role and makes the character of a weak middle-aged man who has a romantic fling (an "intermezzo," according to the script) with a younger woman fairly sympathetic. It is Bergman's performance as the beautiful young pianist, however, that remains the most rewarding aspect of this film. In this, her American motion picture debut, she plays her role with such intense warmth and charm that the violinist's desertion of wife and child seems quite believable, almost laudable. John Halliday also gives a good, grandfatherly performance as Thomas Stenborg, a mutual friend of Holger and Anita who is occasionally called upon to offer wise counsel to the lovers.

In most motion pictures about musicians, the simulated instrumental technique of the actors is usually rather primitive. *Intermezzo*, however, avoids this pitfall almost entirely. Bergman, who actually plays the piano, displays a remarkably convincing keyboard technique. Therefore, when she sits down to play, the camera is allowed considerably more freedom than the usual front view of the actor-pianist swaying at the keyboard, hands discreetly masked from view by the piano. Similarly, close-ups of Howard playing the violin are very credible. (There is some evidence, however, that in these close-up shots the actual fingering and bowing of the instrument were done by the hands of trained violinists standing next to the actor.)

As would be expected, music plays an important part in this film. The

"Intermezzo" of the title refers not only to the romantic episode in the lives of the main characters, but also to a musical composition written by violinist Holger. He plays this piece on several occasions during the course of the story, and it becomes a leitmotif associated both with his love for Anita and with his affection for home and daughter as well. This haunting theme melody was composed by Heinz Provost for the original Swedish production. It became tremendously popular, was frequently recorded, and has attained the status of a classic motion picture theme. The sound track assembled by music director Lou Forbes is lengthy and includes liberal excerpts from the compositions of the Norwegian composer Edvard Grieg. The musical numbers performed on screen as part of the story frequently merge without pause into the almost nonstop background music. More silence on the music track would, perhaps, have given these important musical moments greater prominence in the film.

The cinematography by Gregg Toland underscores the light romantic flavor of the film. Although more conventional than his innovative and impressive work in such films as *The Grapes of Wrath* (1939) and *Citizen Kane* (1941), Toland's work in *Intermezzo* is solid and does contain some imaginative touches. An early scene in which Anita temporarily takes leave of Holger is shot entirely as it is reflected in a store window before which the two have been window-shopping. Toland's shots of the leading lady have obviously been done with considerable care. Indeed, he has contributed through his work the single most memorable visual detail of the film, Bergman's luminous smile.

Warmly received by American audiences in 1939, *Intermezzo* successfully launched Bergman's Hollywood career. Discovered in Sweden by motion picture talent scouts searching for a "new Garbo," Bergman was able to resist the comparison to the other actress and went on to develop a long international career as a talented actress in her own right. In 1981 the thrice-Oscar-awarded actress said that her film career was over. Her voluntary retirement from films ironically began after her successful return to Swedish films in director Ingmar Bergman's *Autumn Sonata* (1979). In this film she played a concert pianist who comes into conflict with her grown daughter, played by Liv Ullman. Bergman was nominated for Best Actress of the year by the Motion Picture Academy for this film which seemed to be a fitting end to her cinematic career. Fortunately for her millions of admirers throughout the world, Bergman's retirement plans were changed and she was announced as the actress who would play Israeli Prime Minister Golda Meir in a film due for release in 1982.

David Bahnemann

INTERRUPTED MELODY

Released: 1955
Production: Jack Cummings for Metro-Goldwyn-Mayer
Direction: Curtis Bernhardt
Screenplay: William Ludwig and Sonya Levien (AA); based on the auto-
biography of the same name by Marjorie Lawrence
Cinematography: Joseph Ruttenberg and Paul C. Vogel
Editing: John D. Dunning
Music direction: Saul Chaplin; operatic recordings directed and conducted by
Walter Du Cloux
Costume design: Helen Rose
Running time: 106 minutes

> *Principal characters:*
> Dr. Thomas King .... Glenn Ford
> Marjorie Lawrence .... Eleanor Parker
> Cyril Lawrence .... Roger Moore
> Bill Lawrence .... Cecil Kellaway
> Vocal student .... Eileen Farrell

Opera on screen, no matter how competently it may be depicted, has never been popular fare to the filmgoing public. It remains a specialized art form for a specialized audience. The most popular examples of opera on film have been those special guest appearances by an opera star who dazzles briefly with an aria or two, such as Rise Stevens in *Going My Way* (1945). *Interrupted Melody* is a hybrid example of opera on screen, for it is the personal, warm-hearted, tragic, and inspiring story of Australian opera singer Marjorie Lawrence, whose successful singing career was interrupted when she contracted polio. The film is based upon Lawrence's autobiographical book of the same name and is a moving account of the struggle by a beautiful and creative individual to overcome the despair incurred by her personal tragedy.

The story has all the ingredients for a motion picture love story of the most uplifting kind. Just three years earlier, Susan Hayward had triumphed in a similar musical story when she impersonated popular singer Jane Froman in *With a Song in My Heart*. Froman's successful career had been tragically interrupted by a plane crash which left her crippled, and the film movingly depicted her fight to walk and sing again professionally. No doubt the success of that film with the public encouraged Metro-Goldwyn-Mayer to produce *Interrupted Melody* in Cinemascope and Eastman color with lavish operatic sequences. The role of Lawrence had originally been intended for M-G-M's first lady, Greer Garson, but it eventually went to beautiful, talented, and underrated Eleanor Parker, who, new to the M-G-M stable, had earned her considerable reputation at Warner Bros.

Interrupted Melody, with its emotionally charged leading role, is the kind of motion picture which depends almost solely on the casting of the lead role. In this case, since the lead character is an opera singer, the role requires an actress with "class." Garson possesses this quality and would most certainly have turned in a creditable performance; however, Parker likewise possesses that quality and was an excellent choice for the role. Still, some people were surprised at the casting, since Parker had for years been considered a beautiful and extremely talented woman but an actress who simply had never achieved top stardom precisely because she did not have "class" and refused to "play the publicity game." With just a small amount of stage experience, Parker had been signed to a Warner Bros. contract on her nineteenth birthday. She was schooled in the art of film acting there but only occasionally was she cast to good advantage. The studio did not seem to know quite what to do with her, and the showy roles always went to the high-powered stars: Bette Davis, Olivia de Havilland, and Ida Lupino.

Parker first attracted attention as the daughter of Ambassador Davies (Walter Huston) in *Mission to Moscow* (1943) and was shown to good advantage in *The Pride of the Marines* (1945), *The Voice of the Turtle* (1947), and *Caged* (1950), probably her best screen performance and the part that earned the first of her three Academy Award nominations. She left Warner Bros., starred in Paramount's *Detective Story* (1951), and picked up a second Academy Award nomination, after which she was signed by M-G-M and cast in *Interrupted Melody*.

It was obvious that Parker would not be singing the operatic arias herself, and that minor problem was solved by using the expert voice of opera star Eileen Farrell (who also plays a small part in the film) to which Parker ably lip-synchs. To provide the audience with the most accessible of opera music, certain licenses were taken with the repertory, making room for arias from such operas as *La Bohème* and *Carmen* rather than some of the heavier items that Lawrence actually sang. The music also included "O don fatale," Act I from *Il Trovatore*, "Un bel dì vedremo," *Samson and Delilah*, the Immolation Scene from *Götterdämmerung*, excerpts from Act 3 of *Tristan und Isolde*, "Annie Laurie," "Over the Rainbow," and "Waltzing Matilda," creating a rare feast for moviegoing music lovers.

The highly entertaining film begins by showing the tranquil farm life of the Lawrence family near Winchelsea, Australia. The young Marjorie is preparing to participate in a local singing contest which eventually takes her to Paris to study. She becomes an opera star after much hard work, and her career is managed by her brother, Cyril (Roger Moore). On the night of her first singing triumph, Marjorie meets a young American doctor, Thomas King (Glenn Ford), who is about to return home to the United States. They fall in love at once, but a number of years go by before he returns to Paris where they continue their courtship and soon marry over the protestation of brother

Cyril, who feels that marriage will interfere with Marjorie's career. It does in a way, for Marjorie decides that she will accept singing engagements only in New York City where her husband's medical practice is located because he has made it clear that he will not give up his practice to follow her around the world as a useless left arm. Her brother continues to object, and Marjorie realizes that she should be singing more and learning more, so she accepts a singing tour of Latin America.

Up to this point, the film has been a touching love story with beautifully mounted opera production numbers. Then, on the Latin American tour, Marjorie contracts polio; she is paralyzed and her career is shattered. King gives up his practice to take her to the top specialists available, and they finally move to Florida where King devotes his time to her agonizing recuperation. Their lives are overwhelmed by her disease and by her severe depression over the hopelessness of ever being a useful and productive human being again. King remains stoically determined to help her, while she just as intensely feels there is no hope. When she learns that their savings have been depleted, she realizes what a burden she has placed on her husband and his career and attempts suicide.

King perseveres. She becomes able to sit in a wheelchair, and finally, to help with their financial problems, she agrees to sing with the Miami Civic Symphony. Just as she is to go on in her wheelchair, however, she panics, loses her courage, and rushes home. The incident makes her see that her husband must return to New York to his medical practice and that she must seek her own solution to her problem independent of him. He returns to New York, therefore, and she once again agrees to sing, this time for the wounded soldiers in an Army veterans' hospital. In a lovely scene, she, disabled herself, sings "Over the Rainbow" for the wounded soldiers and is moved and encouraged to endeavor to resume her career.

Lawrence sets out on a tour of the battlefields in Europe and the Pacific with her husband's consent, and upon returning, she is invited to sing at the Metropolitan Opera in a special performance of *Tristan und Isolde*. Again, just as she is about to go on stage, she panics, but this time King ignores her pleas to help her leave the auditorium, and as the curtain rises she is able to go on and stands for the first time at the end of the scene.

The production values are first-rate, and Curtis Bernhardt's direction is well handled. The story and screenplay by William Ludwig and Sonya Levien won the Academy Award; their script indeed presents the human interest side of the story without overemphasizing the obvious sentimental aspects of Lawrence's illness. Helen Rose's costumes also received an Oscar nomination.

Ford turns in a quietly restrained performance as the ever-hopeful husband. Parker justly received a nomination as Best Actress for her brilliant and courageous interpretation. In the early musical sequences of the film she was able to reveal a versatility and a variety of looks as the opera heroines, particularly as the beautiful, dark-haired, and fiery Carmen. Competing with her that year for Best Actress were Susan Hayward for *I'll Cry Tomorrow*; Katharine Hepburn for *Summertime*; Jennifer Jones for *Love Is a Many-Splendored Thing*; and Anna Magnani, who won the award, for *The Rose Tattoo*.

Ronald Bowers

INTRUDER IN THE DUST

Released: 1949
Production: Clarence Brown for Metro-Goldwyn-Mayer
Direction: Clarence Brown
Screenplay: Ben Maddow; based on the novel of the same name by William Faulkner
Cinematography: Robert Surtees
Editing: Robert J. Kern
Running time: 86 minutes

Principal characters:

Lucas Beauchamp	Juano Hernandez
Chick Mallison	Claude Jarman, Jr.
John Gavin Stevens	David Brian
Miss Habersham	Elizabeth Patterson
Sheriff Hampton	Will Geer
Nub Gowrie	Porter Hall
Aleck	Elzie Emanuel

The years following World War II gave rise to a genre in American cinema known as the "problem" film. Dealing with a variety of subjects ranging from alcoholism (*The Lost Weekend*, 1945) to anti-Semitism (*Gentleman's Agreement*, 1947), one of the most common problems on which filmmakers turned their cameras was racism in America. Although directed by white directors and using mostly white casts, these films tried to get away from the unflattering stereotypes of blacks so often employed in American films of the past. *Pinky*, *Home of the Brave*, and *Lost Boundaries* all came out in 1949, as did *Intruder in the Dust*, the best of the group. Directed by Clarence Brown, *Intruder in the Dust* was adapted for the screen by Ben Maddow from William Faulkner's well-known novel. Like the book, the film deals with the efforts of a small community in Mississippi to come to terms with a black man who will not play "the nigger."

Beautifully portrayed by Juano Hernandez, Lucas Beauchamp is a proud black who owns his own land and maintains an eloquent sense of isolation from the whites in the town. When he is accused of murder, he seems to refuse to help himself. How Lucas' firm and proud moral stance affects the lives of the people in the small Mississippi town is the theme of the film. Brown directs in a deliberate, slow, and rather mannered fashion, leaving in much of Faulkner's florid prose. He cast Claude Jarman, Jr., as Chick, the boy who eventually helps to save Lucas' life. Discovered by Brown for *The Yearling* (1947), Jarman's performance as a young boy who rapidly matures by trying to bring about change is a marvel to behold. Chick cannot understand a man like Lucas—everything in his background prevents it. Yet, perhaps because of his youth, he grows to see Lucas as a human being rather than an object and risks much for him.

The film was photographed by Robert Surtees in Faulkner's home town of Oxford, Mississippi, which had a population of 3,500 in 1949. There is an aura of an old-time Southern town in the film, especially in the first few shots. It opens on a dusty, small-town street with a barber shop, a church, a jail house, and frame houses with large front porches. It is very gradually that the viewer realizes that the residents of this town, who seem like good, simple folk, have dressed up in their Sunday best to witness the lynching of a black man. At the anticipated lynching, the camera pans slowly across their faces and shows the joyous expectancy of the event. It then becomes clear exactly what Faulkner is dealing with and why he says that the black man was not in trouble—the town was. The film pulls no punches and is an unusual one to have been made by M-G-M, which was not known as a social-consciousness studio. No better film about race and people's attitudes in the South has come out of Hollywood.

The film centers around Chick Mallison (Claude Jarman, Jr.), the young nephew of the town's most liberal lawyer, John Gavin Stevens (David Bryan). Chick has been taught to respect every human being, but has never met blacks on an equal level. When he falls into an icy creek one winter, Lucas Beauchamp (Juano Hernandez), a black man who owns a farm near the creek, fishes him out and gives him some supper while his clothes dry. Chick offers Lucas payment, but he refuses to take it. Chick is puzzled by this and throws some money on the floor before leaving Lucas' house. Miserably, he later speaks of this episode to his uncle and realizes that Lucas knew what he did not, that Chick was a guest in his home. Several years pass after this event with Lucas becoming more and more of an enigma to the whites in the town, for he does not behave according to their preconceived notions of how a black should act. Then a white man is brutally murdered, and Lucas is accused of the killing. Chick half believes that Lucas is guilty, but still helps to persuade his uncle to defend him. Lucas will not tell either his attorney or the sheriff the truth because he feels it will do no good as they will not believe anything he says. They are too hardened in their prejudice. He does tell sixteen-year-old Chick that if he can dig up the body of the dead man, it can be proven that he was killed by a rifle bullet rather than one from Lucas' revolver.

Chick tries to get his uncle to authorize such an act, but is not successful, so he, Miss Habersham (Elizabeth Patterson), a woman of eighty, and Aleck (Elzie Emanuel), a young black boy, undertake the grisly business of exhuming the body themselves. Chick finds that Lucas was correct; the bullet implanted in the dead man's rib is indeed a rifle bullet. The boy is now determined to get his uncle to listen to him and to set Lucas free. In the meantime, lynching fever takes over the town, and the dead man's brother threatens to attack the jail and to take the law into his own hands. Miss

Habersham takes a position on the porch of the jailhouse, and for two days, calmly sits alone in front of the jail knitting. She tells the angry crowd that has gathered that they must get her first if they want Lucas. With the help of Stevens and the town's level-headed sheriff (Will Geer), the real killer, a white, is apprehended. Feeling cheated, the mob moves away—they must wait for their sport until another day. In a touching climax, Lucas comes to pay John Gavin Stevens his fee for defending him. They agree on a price, and the black man strides proudly out of Stevens' office. The lawyer remarks to Chick that Lucas is still "insufferable," but that is all right because he is their conscience.

Brown gets astonishing performances out of all of his principals. Besides Jarman, Hernandez, a Puerto Rican actor, is unforgettable as Lucas and won two European film awards. Patterson plays the heroic Miss Habersham with much spirit, and Brian plays the lawyer who slowly begins to realize how hard it is to act according to one's often-mouthed principles. The film was well received in Europe and reminded some critics of a neorealist film. Pauline Kael has compared Lucas Beauchamp to the old man in Vittorio De Sica's great *Umberto D* (1955), for both men insist on their rights and dignity, which alienates them from the community that did not want to be reminded of their existence. Unfortunately, the unavailability of prints of *Intruder in the Dust* makes it difficult for the film to be revived or even shown on television. No other American film speaks so eloquently about the nature of black-white relations in the South, and deserves to be seen, for it is a film of great power and sensitivity. It was one of Brown's last directorial efforts in his distinguished career, and it was certainly one of his best, the only film with a clear-cut social message. His other films were mostly romances or light comedy/dramas such as *Ah, Wilderness!* (1935) and *National Velvet* (1945).

Joan Cohen

THE INVISIBLE MAN

Released: 1933
Production: Universal
Direction: James Whale
Screenplay: R. C. Sherriff and Philip Wylie; based on the novel of the same name by H. G. Wells
Cinematography: Arthur Edeson
Editing: no listing
Special effects: John P. Fulton
Running time: 71 minutes

Principal characters:
Jack Griffin	Claude Rains
Flora Kemp	Gloria Stuart
Doctor Kemp	William Harrigan
Doctor Cranley	Henry Travers
Mr. Hall	Forrester Harvey
Mrs. Hall	Una O'Connor
Chief of Police	Holmes Herbert

The technical qualities that made *The Invisible Man* a milestone in American cinema trace their origins back to France at the turn of the century. In 1896, Georges Melies, a French stage magician of some repute, discovered that the movie camera was potentially a Pandora's box containing innumerable marvels and horrors waiting to be unleashed on an unsuspecting world. In the Paris suburb of Montreuil, he built the first film studio in the world, with walls and ceilings made of glass and stages honeycombed with trapdoors and trick curtains. In order to utilize his creation fully, he began to write complex scripts and direct the action before the camera, and in so doing, he became the first real film director.

The camera, in Melies' mind, was a machine with which to record the worlds of the imagination, dreams, and the supernatural. Thus, it was only a matter of time before he created his first special effect. He achieved it later that year by making a woman disappear under the watchful eye of the camera. He simply stopped the camera while the woman slipped out of sight and then resumed filming. In 1897, for a film called *Battleship Maine*, he became more ambitious, achieving an underwater effect by shooting through a large fish tank placed in front of a prop representing the submerged hull of the *Maine* while actors cavorted in diving suits in the foreground. In 1898 in *The Haunted Cave*, he discovered double exposure, and in 1900 he expanded on the concept in *The One Man Band*, in which he managed to appear simultaneously in seven roles through a multiple exposure process. From that point, he went on to experiment with running the film backward, fast motion, slow-and-stop motion, and two techniques that have become a staple of all subsequent films: the fade (the gradual appearance or disappearance of an image) and the dissolve (the slow transition from one image to another). In 1902, he put it all together with *A Trip to the Moon*, one of the outstanding achievements of the first decade of film.

A Trip to the Moon was also the first science-fiction film, a genre that perhaps reached its zenith with the special effects-laden extravaganzas of *Star Wars* (1977), *The Empire Strikes Back* (1980), and *Superman II* (1981). An important offshoot of science fiction, however, and one that developed and refined the special effects invented by Melies, was the horror genre, which was for all practical purposes born in 1908 when Thomas Edison produced a film version of Mary Wollstonecraft Shelley's *Frankenstein*. The horror film reached what most *aficionados* consider to be the peak with the 1930's Hollywood productions of Tod Browning and James Whale. Both of these directors could trace their influences to the German "cinema of the macabre," particularly to the work of Paul Wegner (*The Golem*, 1920), Robert Weine (*The Cabinet of Dr. Caligari*, 1919), and F. W. Murnau (*Nosferatu*, 1922). In the hands of Browning and Whale, the horror film developed into a singularly American institution and became a staple of the motion picture industry.

Browning got a head start on Whale by coming to the genre much earlier and by dominating it through the 1920's. He was aided considerably by his judicious selection of a stage actor named Lon Chaney to star in a number of his major efforts. In 1931, he discovered Bela Lugosi and introduced him to filmgoers in *Dracula*. By the mid-1930's, Browning was considered the "Edgar Allan Poe of the cinema," and his work was beginning to influence a new school of surrealistic filmmakers.

Whale, who would employ special effects beyond Georges Melies' wildest dreams in *The Invisible Man*, came to the horror genre by a circuitous route but became only a little less prominent than Browning during the 1930's. Originally a cartoonist, stage designer, and dialogue director, Whale came to Hollywood from England to work on film dialogue. He directed his first film, *Journey's End*, in 1930. Since he had first directed it on the stage in England, the transition to films was a fairly easy one. His second film, *Waterloo Bridge*, produced the same year, made very little impact on the public, but his third film, *Frankenstein* (1931), established him as a major competitor to Browning. It was also the first indication of Whale's unusual flair for casting, a knack that would eventually introduce Claude Rains in *The Invisible Man*—a major reason for its success. *Frankenstein* made a star of William Henry Pratt, a British actor whom Whale had noticed in a film called *Graft* (1931). He became famous under the name of Boris Karloff.

By 1933, Whale was hitting his stride as a director and was ready to attempt a creative departure from the usual monster film. He wanted to explore the potential of the kind of special effects that had earlier interested Melies, but with more sophistication. Accordingly, when Universal bought for him the rights to H. G. Wells's fantasy novel *The Invisible Man*, Whale hired John P. Fulton, a wizard of special effects, to develop the illusions suggested by the story. Fulton's work on *The Invisible Man* was, in fact, the embodiment of an important early justification for regarding the cinema as a separate and distinct art form unto itself. The screen, unlike the stage, was well suited to the staging of what film scholars term the "invisible romance" or the achievement of visual effects pertaining to totally imaginary situations. Thus, the entire realm of folklore, fairy tales, and magic legends which could not be made real on the stage could be realistically visualized through expert tricks of cinematography. *Fantasia* (1940), *Star Wars*, and *Superman II* reflect the high points of this photographic form. Yet without the pioneering work of such geniuses as Melies and Fulton, that extra dimension that makes the cinema a creative art of the highest order might not exist.

Because of the special effects of *The Invisible Man*, Rains made his screen debut under more peculiar circumstances than ever confronted any other actor in his first role: he became a star although his face was seen by the audience for less than half a minute throughout the entire film. During the remainder of the time, the film features him either invisible or with his head completely covered with bandages. His voice, however, is heard to good advantage.

Rains portrays a young chemist named Jack Griffin who is in love with a colleague, Flora Kemp (Gloria Stuart), but is even more obsessed with the desire to discover the secret of invisibility. One day he disappears from London, and on the same day a mysterious stranger arrives in the village of Ipping, wearing dark glasses over a face wrapped in bandages. On his hands are gloves. He rents a room at the local inn and begins to work frantically in search of a mysterious chemical. He behaves toward the innkeeper (Forrester Harvey) and his wife (Una O'Connor) with such a tyrannical demeanor that they decide to evict him. They imagine him to be an escaped criminal in hiding, or possibly someone who has suffered hideous injuries in an automobile accident. The other villagers share their uneasiness and summon the town constable to confront the enigmatic stranger. The crowd barges into the newcomer's rooms, whereupon he unwinds the bandages from around an invisible head, discards his clothing, and completely vanishes right before the eyes of the horrified intruders.

Meanwhile, Flora Kemp, her brother, Dr. Kemp (William Harrigan), and Griffin's other colleague, Dr. Cranley (Henry Travers), are baffled by their friend's disappearance. It is now obvious that Griffin is, indeed, the invisible man. On the run from the villagers of Ipping, he returns to the city and seeks shelter at Kemp's lodgings. Kemp is, of course, understandably uneasy at receiving his invisible visitor, but Griffin tells him the story, explaining that while experimenting with an Indian drug called monocaine, he discovered that it had the power to render human flesh invisible when injected under the skin. At this point, however, Griffin is unaware that his use of the drug is driving him to madness. Overcome by megalomania, Griffin expresses his plans to take over the world through a campaign of terror. "We'll start with a few murders—big men, little men—just to show we make no distinction." A shaken Kemp summons Dr. Cranley and Flora. Flora becomes terrified at the condition of the man she loved. As his sickness becomes more advanced, he raves at her: "Power! To make the world grovel at my feet, to walk into the gold vaults of nations, the chambers of kings, into the holy of holies. Even the moon is frightened of me, frightened to death. The whole world is frightened to death."

Faced with such chilling polemic, Kemp calls the police, but once again Griffin escapes and then embarks on a reign of terror by robbing a bank, derailing a train, and committing senseless murders. He does not neglect Kemp either. In spite of some police protection, Kemp soon pays for his betrayal with his life when Griffin places him in a car and drives it over a cliff, leaving him to die in the wreckage. Finally, an alarmed Scotland Yard pursues Griffin in force but is totally unsuccessful until a snowstorm forces the fugitive into a barn where he falls asleep in a haystack. The sound of his heavy breathing arouses the suspicions of a farmer, who notifies the police. The police surround the barn and set fire to it in a scene reminiscent of the end of *Frankenstein*. As footprints appear on the snow, the police open fire. Griffin is mortally wounded and is taken to a hospital, where he dies. In death, he becomes once again visible as the effect of the drug dies with him.

The Invisible Man demonstrates in a remarkable manner many of the techniques that its director Whale learned in his precinema career. The film's dialogue, for example, is quite erudite for a horror film and often reveals flashes of the offbeat humor that Whale loved. The scene in which Griffin enumerates the drawbacks of his condition—such as staying out of sight for an hour after meals, avoiding rain ("It would make me shine like a bubble"), and keeping rigorously clean in order to prevent appearing as a dark outline—reveals a somewhat less menacing and more practical private aspect of Whale's monsters.

Another technique, one that Whale learned from his experience as a set designer, was the importance of creating the proper setting to enhance the believability of his story. In *The Invisible Man*, he has taken great pains to dramatize the setting—an aspect that is usually ignored by directors attempting to portray the far-fetched hypotheses of science that form the premise of most horror films. In most of these stories the viewer is plunged suddenly and without warning into a strange and violent world without being given sufficient time to adjust his logic to one that is so radically different from the one that confronts him in his daily life. This usually results in varying degrees of skepticism on the part of the viewer, who cannot suspend his disbelief.

Whale, on the other hand, reminds us first of the commonplace in order to make us accept the unusual. He begins *The Invisible Man*, for example, with a carefully documented setting of a small country inn in England. The furnishings, the atmosphere, and the occupants are instantly recognizable to us and yet they are at the same time highly individual as befits the story. The framework is solidly filled out so that the viewer can have no doubt as to the reality of the people or the places that he is watching. Everything is ready for the invisible man to enter.

The invisible man himself is ideally suited only to the talking screen since he consists of only a voice and no body. The visual effects, as interesting as they are, like the words upon Wells's printed page before them, cannot be so disturbingly eerie or as haunting as the sound of Rains's voice projecting from empty chairs and unoccupied rooms. Rains's richly suggestive voice was, in fact, no less responsible than Whale's direction for the unique quality of the film. Its almost supernatural blending of heroic merriment and tragic desolation lends a serious, moody tone that would otherwise be lacking. As a vehicle for Whale's ideas, Rains's voice made the most of opportunities for humor, pathos, and sheer metaphysical horror that were inherent in the premise of the sound camera. This technique heightens the film's qualities of suspense and, ultimately, the impact of the final revelation of the mad scientist's features in the last few feet of film.

The visual special effects, as indicated earlier, are not to be taken lightly. Through Fulton's work, the invisible man is able to signal his entrance into a room by having books jump from a table and move through the air to the windowsill. In other scenes, chairs topple over and pajamas walk around with nobody visible wearing them. Many of these effects are more sophisticated versions of Melies' earlier magician's tricks which employed wires and dark curtains. Yet the quality that heightens Fulton's illusions, as it does all other aspects of the film, is the dark humor of director Whale. Indeed, in one episode, Griffin steals a policeman's trousers which are later revealed through one of Fulton's illusions to be skipping down a country lane as if by themselves. At another point when some policemen join hands to surround a building, the invisible Griffin moves among them, slapping their faces and kicking them in their rears. These instances show that Whale was more than a mere purveyor of horror. The mordant humor that he exhibited in *The Invisible Man* would later be lightened and broadened for musicals such as *Show Boat* (1936) and full-fledged comedies such as *Wives Under Suspicion* (1938).

The Invisible Man is a notable achievement for its superb special effects (including Rains's voice) and its humor, which verges on slapstick but also carries an interesting message. The invisible man admits before his death that, like Robert Louis Stevenson's Dr. Jekyll, he has tampered with things man should never touch. Part of the nature of evil, as depicted in this film, is the desire to penetrate beyond the limits which God and nature have imposed upon man. This theme has formed the basis of almost all succeeding horror films that have become successful. In this respect and others, Whale's best work exerts tremendous influence on modern filmmakers, and his films remain today consistently fresh and lively.

Stephen L. Hanson

THE IPCRESS FILE

Released: 1965
Production: Harry Saltzman for Universal
Direction: Sidney J. Furie
Screenplay: Bill Canaway and James Doran; based on the novel of the same name by Len Deighton
Cinematography: Otto Heller
Editing: Peter Hunt
Running time: 107 minutes

Principal characters:
Harry Palmer	Michael Caine
Dalby	Nigel Green
Ross	Guy Doleman
Jean	Sue Lloyd
Carswell	Gordon Jackson
Radcliffe	Aubrey Richards
Bluejay	Frank Gatliff
Barney	Thomas Baptiste

The Ipcress File was made in the wake of the highly successful James Bond films. While cashing in on the general popularity of the spy film genre, producer Harry Saltzman, who coproduced a number of the original Bond films, was successful in creating a totally different type of spy film. A more sophisticated plot coupled with Sidney J. Furie's stylish direction contributed to the unique quality of the film which earned the Best Picture Award from the British Film Academy. Billed as "the thinking man's *Goldfinger*," *The Ipcress File* contains no bevy of blonds in bikinis or any of the elaborate superspy gadgetry so often evident in the Bond films. Instead, the film has a dark, sinister quality created by atmospheric lighting and natural locations shot in an innovative manner. The contributions of production designer Ken Adams (also from the Bond films) and cinematographer Otto Heller were also honored by awards from the British Film Academy.

The hero of the film, Harry Palmer (Michael Caine), represents another major departure from the spy-as-super-hero image. Unlike the one-dimensional, chic Bond, Harry Palmer is a wise-guy cockney who listens to Mozart and enjoys the finer things of life, including exotic food which he cooks and serves himself. Palmer, as played deftly by Caine in his first starring role, is the perfect anti-hero. The problems of a working-class hero trapped in the bureaucratic maze of the British secret service provides an ironic theme which quickly sets up Palmer's character and helps the audience to identify with him. Caine is at his best making smart rejoinders to his superiors, and his life seems more accurate in portraying the daily aspects of ordinary spying.

Virtually blackmailed into being an agent, Palmer is the most reluctant of spies. While stationed in Berlin, he was caught illegally acquiring money from the German army. Ross (Guy Doleman), as head of Army Intelligence, intervened to keep him out of jail and at the disposal of Her Majesty's intelligence forces. Despite his cocky attitude, Palmer's talents are useful in the spy business, and as the film opens, he is being transferred to Civilian Intelligence and is pleased to get away from Ross, whom he despises. His new boss is Dalby (Nigel Green), a bristly and efficient fellow who puts Palmer to work finding "Raven," the code name for a scientist kidnaped by enemy agents and possibly taken to Eastern Europe. Palmer is pleased to be back in civilian life and even more pleased when he gets to know his co-worker Jean (Sue Lloyd).

Palmer, in typical maverick style, ignores the normal plodding, operational procedures and forms and quickly makes use of his personal sources in the intelligence community. His search leads fairly easily to Bluejay (Frank Gatliff), who wants twenty-five thousand pounds in exchange for Raven. Palmer becomes suspicious, and, on a hunch, orders an unauthorized raid on a warehouse he believes to be the kidnapers' headquarters. The raid turns up nothing but a tape of jumbled noise labeled "Ipcress," and Palmer is shielded from official discipline by Dalby.

In subsequent action, the planned exchange occurs, but Palmer gets into more trouble by accidentally shooting a CIA agent at the scene. Meanwhile, another British agent, Carswell (Gordon Jackson), has noticed a pattern in the kidnaping of scientists and, believing the tape to be important, combines his information into the "Ipcress" file. He has noted that Raven, like previous victims, has lost his scientific memory, but Carswell is shot before he can talk to Raven further about the matter. At first Palmer is worried that the bullet was meant for him, but when he returns home and finds the body of another CIA agent he realizes that he is being framed. He suspects that Ross is a double agent and tells Dalby all of his suspicions. Dalby agrees to aid him again and promises to tell no one that he has talked to Palmer.

Against Jean's advice Palmer tries to escape, but as the train pulls slowly out of Victoria Station two men seize and drug him. He awakens in what appears to be an East European prison, where he undergoes a highly concentrated form of brain washing which uses the Ipcress tape sound as part of its psychedelic method. Recognizing the sound, Palmer is able to realize what is happening and uses pain to keep his mind clear. It is obvious that his strong sense of self-identity is what again saves him. Eventually, however, his captors succeed in eliminating the Ipcress file from his mind.

After his release, Palmer recognizes London and quickly realizes that his prison was the warehouse raided earlier. Calling Dalby, he is told to contact Ross as well. When the three meet at the warehouse, Palmer is confused, not quite sure which of these men is really the double agent. Looking out across

Palmer's gun barrel we look first at Ross and then at Dalby. As Dalby reaches for his pocket Palmer makes an almost instinctive decision and fires. True to his nature, Ross walks off and says to the distraught Palmer, "That's what you're paid for."

The plot by itself is fairly routine with the usual number of twists and surprises. Like most 1960's spy thrillers, the lead character is a crucial element. Palmer's offbeat, lower-class epicureanism was highlighted by critics as an enjoyable spoof of the Cambridge-educated James Bond, and his popularity with the public led to two sequel Harry Palmer films: *Funeral in Berlin* (1966) and *The Billion Dollar Brain* (1967).

The technical elements of the film must ultimately be credited for the film's success. Furie and Heller's teamwork perfectly matches the visuals to the story. The highly angled perspectives and obscure views through windows and fences and from rooftops and telephone booths conveys the mystery of the action to the audience. Like Palmer, we cannot see the details clearly enough to solve the puzzle. Using noise for effect and closely cropped and framed visuals, as in the train sequence and the park band performance, the information given to the audience is critically controlled to build suspense and excitement. The choice of real street locations rather than sets, coupled with heavy blue shading and murky shadow shots, also helps to create the special ambience of mystery which permeates the film. At a critical stage, the gloom is broken by the psychedelic madness during Palmer's torture, and his blood glows as it drops to the floor. Such care taken with artistic direction is reminiscent of Alfred Hitchcock's subtle work and makes *The Ipcress File* a fine example of the British suspense genre.

Christine Gladish

IRMA LA DOUCE

Released: 1963
Production: Billy Wilder for United Artists
Direction: Billy Wilder
Screenplay: I. A. L. Diamond and Billy Wilder; based on the play of the same name by Alexandre Breffort
Cinematography: Joseph LaShelle
Editing: Daniel Mandell
Running time: 147 minutes

> *Principal characters:*
> Nester Patou/Lord X ....Jack Lemmon
> Irma La Douce .... Shirley MacLaine
> Hippolyte .... Bruce Yarnell
> Moustache ....Lou Jacobi
> Inspector Lefevre .... Hershel Bernardi

In *Irma La Douce*, a successful comedy, director Billy Wilder cast Shirley MacLaine, an actress who, at the time, had a screen identity almost synonymous with the "hooker with a heart of gold." The resulting comedy is not simply a study of prostitution, but a look at the attitudes of films toward good-hearted prostitutes. Wilder, always interested in the humor of sexual role-playing, finds a wide field for play in this offbeat romance. The opening scenes, interspersed with the titles, make it clear that this film is no apology for the morals of hookers; on the other hand, all indications of moral corruption are shown to reside in the hypocrisy of the hookers' clients. Customer after customer, pulling on his pants, quizzes Irma (Shirley MacLaine) about her motives in becoming a hooker. Answering one, Irma spins a yarn about a promising career as a concert pianist which was ruined when the lid of the baby grand fell on her hand. "After that, I didn't care what happened to me," she says. The next man hears about her unspeakable childhood in the Belgian Congo with missionary parents and a current need to buy blood for a sister in the hospital. Each story results in more money from the solicitous customer. With these opening vignettes, the comedy directs attention not to the hooker's motives, but to the motives and morals of her clients.

The man who makes all of the discrepencies in client's attitudes toward hookers clear is policeman Nestor Patou (Jack Lemmon). During the course of the film, Nestor plays several roles which are dependent upon prostitution for their definition. He moves from righteous protector of decency to protective pimp to possessive client, all in the best interests of Irma La Douce. Nestor's ribald education begins when he is transferred to a new beat. It slowly dawns on the very green cop that the street he patrols is lined with women selling themselves. He does not really know what to make of the prostitutes, but he knows where his duty lies. He raids the Hotel Casanova, where the women work, and hauls a patrol wagon full of half-dressed hookers off to jail. The women are hardly put out by the disturbance, enlisting Nestor to help them dress in the patrol wagon. Nestor, trapped between stockings, makeup mirrors, and outstretched legs, is overwhelmed by the signs of vice around him. The man most put out by the raid, however, is Nestor's boss at the police station. It seems he was in the Hotel Casanova when the place was raided, and he did not appreciate the interruption. Nestor, therefore, is suddenly out of a job.

By nightfall Nestor is back at the bar across from the Hotel Casanova. The bartender there tries to explain to Nestor the facts of life about police, prostitutes, and pimps. One of the women arrested in the raid, Irma La Douce, comes in off the street, and Nestor buys her a drink. Their conversation is rudely interrupted by Irma's pimp, however; Hippolyte (Bruce Yarnell) is a big bruiser who bullies all the other pimps as well as Irma and orders her back onto the street. When Nestor notices the weariness with which Irma heads for the door, he gallantly comes to Irma's aid and is instantly hurled across the room by Hippolyte. In the ensuing brawl Wilder has fun with visual puns. Nestor first stuffs a billiard ball in the bruiser's mouth, then bangs him a few times with some spherical lamps, and finally knocks him out by smashing him into a pinball machine. Nestor has figuratively displayed "bigger balls" than Irma's pimp.

Not only has Nestor come to the lady's aid, but he has also acquired the lady. As Irma's new protector, he is taken home to her modest garret. Nestor, whose idea of protection is impractically steeped in the traditional behavior of a gentleman, takes care to cover all the windows of Irma's apartment with newspaper. Once their privacy is established for decency's sake, he goes to bed with her.

The problem of establishing respectability with a prostitute lover continues to plague Nestor throughout the film. Irma refuses to give up her profession— she is good at it. What is more, she is anxious that Nestor not disgrace her by failing in his role as a respectable pimp. Now their love affair becomes a problem of social status. Irma, the breadwinner, has a status to maintain among her coworkers and is determined for Nestor to keep up appearances as her pimp. Nestor becomes a kept man, instructed in the etiquette of bar-lounging and pool-playing. He is dressed with careful attention by Irma to be as well-turned-out as any of the other pimps. The irony of Nestor's role as a pimp hinges on the idea of respectability. As a policeman, Nestor was once concerned with the respectability of a neighborhood with prostitutes on a street, since prostitutes were clearly not respectable. Now he maintains a hooker's respectability within her working world by observing the decorum of a proper pimp. Nestor, like many a diplomat's wife, is responsible for exhibiting the social respectability of a "spouse."

Nestor could manage the business, but he cannot contain his jealousy within a proprietory interest. He does not want Irma to sleep with other men. When Irma casually mentions a former client who paid her enough money to enable her to refuse other customers, Nestor has an inspiration. Obviously the only way to keep Irma to himself is to pay for it. If he were to pay Irma as her pimp, however, she would lose her status as a self-respecting hooker, so Nestor adopts a disguise. He poses as "Lord X," who pays Irma enough to keep her away from other clients. Not only that, but "Lord X" is also impotent, so he requires only platonic chitchat from Irma twice a week.

At first Nestor finances Irma's fidelity by borrowing money from the friendly bartender, but soon he is forced to take a backbreaking night job at the local marketplace. This means, of course, that he is too tired to pay attention to Irma. Thus the real comedy of fidelity begins. Nestor is breaking his back to pay for the fidelity of a woman with whom he cannot spend time because he is too exhausted from paying the fee she charges. Irma becomes suspicious when Nestor stops paying attention to her, assuming that he has another woman. One night Irma gives "Lord X" a friendly kiss. Nestor neglects to wipe the lipstick off and returns to Irma in his real identity with a tell-tale smudge, causing Irma to become suspicious of another woman, who is, of course, herself. When she awakens one night after Nestor has slipped away to his night job, she sees the empty bed and is convinced that Nestor is cheating on her. Of course, the only thing on which he is cheating is the business arrangement of a hooker and her pimp, but Irma kicks him out of her apartment. Now Nestor can visit Irma only as "Lord X." When she next sees her client, she asks to move to England with him. "Lord X" says that that is impossible: after all, he is impotent. Then he allows Irma to cure him of his impotency, and the question becomes, who is cheating on whom?

With all his roles badly mixed up, Nestor decides to end the disguise. To be rid of his "Lord X" identity completely, he takes his "Lord X" clothes down to the river and throws them in. Hippolyte, seeing the clothes in the water and Nestor at the river's edge, accuses Nestor of murder. Nestor is unable to prove that he did not kill a man who never was, and he is sent to prison. Finally, all the identities Nestor has assumed are resolved by Irma's pregnancy. When Nestor learns that Irma is pregnant, he escapes from prison to marry her. Irma at first refuses, thinking that the baby is "Lord X's," but Nestor nobly says that he does not care who the father is. They are married; Irma collapses and gives birth. Now, as a mother, Irma is determined to give up prostitution. That makes it possible for Nestor, who has proven his innocence in the murder, to go back to work for the police and provide for his wife. Thus the problems encountered by Nestor in his struggle to support a prostitute are finally resolved by a change in status for Irma to that of an honest woman. With that ending, the film allows the questions of customers' relationships to prostitutes to stand. The business of prostitution requires some double standards for the clients who support it. One of the problems is that the idea of the hooker with a heart of gold as a woman who must be protected is contradicted by her status as an entrepreneur.

The film did very well at the box office and although it failed to win any major awards, it received favorable notices, with MacLaine and particularly Lemmon cited for their excellent work.

Leslie Donaldson

ISADORA

Released: 1968
Production: Robert Hakim for Universal
Direction: Karel Reisz
Screenplay: Melvyn Bragg and Clive Exton; based on the books *My Life* by
Isadora Duncan and *Isadora Duncan: An Intimate Portrait* by Sewell Stokes
Cinematography: Larry Pizer
Editing: Tom Priestley
Music: Maurice Jarre
Running time: 131 minutes

Principal characters:
Isadora Duncan	Vanessa Redgrave
Roger	John Fraser
Gordon Craig	James Fox
Paris Singer	Jason Robards
Sergei Essenin	Ivan Tchenko
Mrs. Duncan	Bessie Love

Dancer Isadora Duncan once remarked: "There are a few inspired moments in life, and the rest is nonsense," and that description could also be applied to director Karel Reisz's film interpretation of this extraordinary woman's life. *Isadora* is a lavish but extremely fragmented film biography which never quite comes to grips with the motives behind Duncan's romantic, bohemian approach to life. She seemed to be railing against the hypocrisies of her time and at the same time running from some demon inside her which she chose not to face. This film, however, scripted by Melvyn Bragg and Clive Exton and based upon Duncan's own memoirs, *My Life*, and upon *Isador Duncan: An Intimate Portrait* by Sewell Stokes, never offers insights into what really drove her. What the film does present unequivocally is a transcendent performance by the brilliant Vanessa Redgrave, possibly the best ever by this outstanding actress.

In its original form the film was simply titled *Isadora* (that title still remains on the screen credits) and ran for 177 minutes. It was screened in Los Angeles on December 18, 1968, to qualify for the Academy Awards, and the reviews were so negative that Universal canceled its special reserved seat presentation, cut and reedited it twice, and finally released it in its current 131-minute form with its new title, *The Loves of Isadora*, in 1969. In this truncated version, the film begins in 1927 (the year Isadora died at age forty-five) in a small hotel on the French Riviera where an aging, flighty, alcoholic Isadora is dictating her memoirs to her steadfast companion, Roger (John Fraser). The story flashes back to show a young Isadora in her native San Francisco, burning her parents' marriage license to declare her belief in free love and the pursuit of art and beauty.

As Isadora matures we see her performing in a music hall under the name "Peppy Dora" and where she coerces the theater manager into paying her three hundred dollars, which she uses to take her family, including her mother (Bessie Love) and her artist brother Raymond (Tony Vogel), to London. In London she and Raymond visit the British Museum, where Isadora is overcome and inspired by the classical Greek sculpture. She molds her dancing style on these free-form statues and soon makes a name for herself in London and on the Continent. In Berlin she meets a "twin soul" in stage designer Gordon Craig (James Fox). Craig was the son of famed actress Ellen Terry and earned a brilliant reputation for his abstract stage sets which greatly influenced modern stage design as we know it. He was six years older than Isadora and died in 1966. Theirs is an immediate and passionate love affair which leaves Isadora pregnant. She refuses to marry Craig, however, saying, "I'm an artist," and he goes off to Moscow, where he creates his famous stage designs for *Hamlet*. Isadora joins her mother at a seaside town and gives birth to a daughter named Dierdre.

We next find Isadora in Paris where she is courted by Singer sewing-machine heir, Paris Singer (Jason Robards), who lavishes her with expensive gifts. When she sells an expensive diamond necklace which Singer had given her, she explains she did so to raise the money to establish her own dance school. "To dance is to live and that's what I want—a school for life." The beguiled Singer purchases a beautiful chateau near Paris in which Isadora opens her school. Isadora, although still openly opposed to marriage, asks Paris, "Shall we have a child? I want to have all my children by beautiful men." A son, Patrick, is born and the entourage moves to Singer's England estate. The sedate British life bores Isadora, and to humor her Singer hires a pianist, Armand (Christian Duvaleix), to accompany her dancing. At first she is repulsed by this ugly man whom she says looks like a frog and even hides him behind a screen while she dances. Armand, however, is enamored of this free spirit, and when he pounces on her for a passionate kiss, the impulsive Isadora enters into an affair with him to spite Paris.

Isadora's unconventional life style is shattered when her two children drown in an accident in her chauffered car when it coasts backwards off a bridge into the Seine River in Paris. The tragedy causes Isadora to leave Singer and "fly from the horror of it," and she spends the next several years wandering through Europe.

In 1921, she is invited by Russia to open a school in Moscow. She accepts and is horrified by the poverty she finds, yet fascinated and drawn to the Russian peasants. She also enters into her most tempestuous love affair with Russian poet Sergei Essenin (Ivan Tchenko). Essenin was born into a peasant family in 1895, and by the time Isadora meets him, he has gained a reputation as a poet. They enjoy a free-wheeling love which results in her marrying him to facilitate his gaining a visa to the United States. They plan to present programs of poetry and dance, but Essenin's outrageous behavior against anti-Bolshevik sentiments and Isadora's infamous baring of her breasts on stage cause them to be reviled and their marriage to disintegrate. (In 1925, without ever having divorced Isadora, Essenin married Leo Tolstoy's grand-daughter, and less than four months afterward committed suicide by hanging himself.)

Isadora attempts to pull her life together by reopening her Paris school, and she sells all her possessions to do so. At a café in Nice where she has gone to rest and work on her memoirs, she meets a handsome Italian, Brugatti (Vladimir Leskovar), performs a sensuous tango with him, and then speeds off in his open sports car. Isadora's long, flowing scarf (in actuality a shawl) becomes snarled in the spokes of one of the wheels and her head is snapped back and her neck broken; she dies instantly.

Critical reaction to this film was considerably mixed, with many reviewers stating that Reisz's original version should have been allowed to remain. Reisz had earlier earned critical acclaim for *Saturday Night and Sunday Morning* (1960) and *Morgan!* (1966) also with Vanessa Redgrave, but here, despite the amount of editing, he does not seem to be in control of his subject. It is unclear what he really is trying to tell us about Duncan. The film is so frag- mented, so assembled, that we never glimpse the soul behind the flamboyant exploits of this truly revolutionary American woman. Instead we are served up a variety of colorful, sometimes humorous, sometimes outrageous sequences in Isadora's life with very little sense of purpose—and the real Duncan did have a sense of purpose.

The casting and acting in general are more than adequate, with only Fox failing to capture the fire and genius of Gordon Craig. Redgrave is positively luminescent in the title role. The only objection critics voiced was over her lack of dance experience, but disregarding that shortcoming, her peformance was highly praised, with many firmly agreeing that she should have received the Academy Award which she lost—in a tie—to Katharine Hepburn for *The Lion in Winter* and Barbra Streisand for *Funny Girl*.

Isadora is indeed an interesting failure which offers many exceptional ingredients, not the least of which is Redgrave; but the film is never able to combine these ingredients into a credible whole. Perhaps Stanley Kauffmann expressed it best in the *New Republic* when he said there is indeed a film to be made about Duncan, but this film is not it.

Ronald Bowers

ISLAND OF LOST SOULS

Released: 1933
Production: Paramount
Direction: Erle C. Kenton
Screenplay: Waldemar Young and Philip Wylie; based on the novel *The Island of Dr. Moreau* by H. G. Wells
Cinematography: Karl Struss
Editing: no listing
Running time: 74 minutes

Principal characters:
Dr. Moreau	Charles Laughton
Edward Parker	Richard Arlen
Ruth Thomas	Leila Hyams
Lota the Panther Woman	Kathleen Burke
Montgomery	Arthur Hohl
Captain of the *Covena*	Stanley Fields
Captain Donahue	Paul Hurst
Ouran	Hans Steinke
Sayer of the Law	Bela Lugosi

In the 1930's, British film censors banned a number of horror films because they allegedly had no qualities to redeem the violence and suggested eroticism which characterized them. Among the proscribed films was *Island of Lost Souls*, the first cinematic treatment of H. G. Wells's novel, *The Island of Dr. Moreau* (1896). The censor's decision to ban this film seems particularly myopic since it explores several significant issues and does so artfully.

Wells, the most important science-fiction writer in Victorian England, used his novel about a mad scientist on an isolated island in the South Pacific as a vehicle for his pessimistic ideas about God, science, and human nature. On one level, the book is an allegorical indictment of a creator-God who fails to equip His creatures suitably for their environment and then attempts to correct His oversight by imposing arbitrary decrees which stifle their natural impulses. On another level, the novel develops a criticism of an experimental science which does not foresee or take responsibility for its consequences. Finally, the book presents a bleak view of human nature in which the beast and rational being are at constant odds. Although *Island of Lost Souls* does not follow the letter of Wells's novel in terms of plot, it preserves the book's thematic thrust on at least two of the levels.

The film opens as Edward Parker (Richard Arlen), adrift on a raft from the foundered ship *Lady Vain*, is rescued in the midst of the Pacific Ocean by the *Covena*. The ship's first "port of call" is an uncharted island—said by the *Covena*'s captain (Stanley Fields) to "stink all over the whole South

Seas"—where it is to leave Montgomery (Arthur Hohl), agent of Dr. Moreau (Charles Laughton), and his cargo of wild animals. Because Parker offends the drunken captain, he too is put ashore. There he discovers Dr. Moreau living in a tropical paradise among filthy, loutish, and tomentose "natives." These, Parker learns, are the results of Dr. Moreau's experiments. The doctor has taken animals and through painful ordeals of plastic surgery, blood transfusions, and gland extracts attempted to transform them into humans. Meanwhile, at Apia, Parker's original destination, his fiancée Ruth Thomas (Leila Hyams) discovers what has become of him. Accompanied by Captain Donahue (Paul Hurst), she sets out for Dr. Moreau's island. There she finds Parker, and with Montgomery's aid they escape, leaving the mad scientist in the clutches of the mutant creatures whom he has tortuously metamorphosed.

One theme that the film adopts from Wells's novel is the distrust of the amoral scientist who is willing to let nothing stand in the way of his work. Although the film's Moreau is not al'egorically equated with God as he is in the novel, he is clearly portrayed as playing at being God. Instead of indicting God as the novel does, the film indicts the egomaniacal scientist whose cold intellect allows no compassion for the beings he creates and manipulates. As he explains his work to Parker, Moreau emphasizes that he is speeding up the process of evolution—taking nature into his own hands. In a question that could have come from the lips of Dr. Victor Frankenstein, Moreau asks Parker, "Do you know what it means to feel like God?" Yet Dr. Moreau does not concern himself with the effects of his work on his subjects. He realizes that the creatures which result from his "bioanthropological research" tend to revert to their bestial form and nature. Instead of attempting to assist their adjustment to the profound changes they undergo, Dr. Moreau's only response is to subdue them and prevent their interference with his continuing work. This he does, wielding a whip and pistol. He also uses the threat of a return to the House of Pain, the laboratory where his vivisections are carried out. Moreover, he has decreed a set of laws which the beast-people chant in a litany led by the Sayer of the Law (Bela Lugosi). The litany emphasizes that activities such as eating meat, going on all fours, spilling blood, and gnawing the bark off trees must be avoided, for, as the beast-people chant, "Are we not men?" Dr. Moreau's imposition of these laws is not an attempt to socialize his creatures, but to dominate them and to prevent them from inconveniently disturbing his work.

The most significant example of Dr. Moreau's amorality is his attempt to manipulate Parker into testing the success of the mad scientist's masterwork, Lota the Panther Woman (Kathleen Burke). A beautiful creature, Lota lacks the obvious physical hints of bestiality present in all of Moreau's other subjects. He hopes to determine if the bestial has also disappeared from her nature by promoting a romantic involvement with Parker. Such an involvement would be impossible with Moreau himself or with Montgomery because

Lota associates both with the agonies endured in the House of Pain. Parker is almost seduced by Lota's sensuality until her talonlike fingernails, a manifestation of her reversion to the "stubborn beast-flesh," reveal her as one of the vivisectionist's creations.

The "stubborn beast-flesh" relates to a second theme in the film also present in Wells's novel. Not only do Dr. Moreau's creatures retain something subhuman, but also most of the fully human characters in the film demonstrate that they are capable of base inhumanity. Most obvious is the behavior of Dr. Moreau himself, who lacks compassion and understanding and is so obsessed with his own work as to be inhumanly blind to the needs of others. The captain of the *Covena* also demonstrates a reversion to the "beast-flesh" in his perpetual state of drunken rage which leads him to abandon Parker to the mercies of Dr. Moreau, whom the captain calls a "grave-robbing ghoul." Captain Donahue, responsible for Ruth Thomas' safety on her rescue mission, also allows the "beast-flesh" to surface. His drinking makes him a useless escort and, in fact, causes his own death at the hands of Ouran (Hans Steinke), one of Moreau's creatures. Even Parker exhibits some reversion to the beast state by allowing his lust to go unchecked. He passionately kisses the alluring Lota despite having a fiancée waiting for him in Apia. Perhaps the only characters who emerge from the action of the film without succumbing to bestial reversion are Montgomery, who abandons amoral science to help his fellow humans escape from Dr. Moreau's island, and Ruth Thomas, who selflessly faces unknown peril to rescue her beloved. The film adheres to the novel by pointing out that centuries of civilization are but a thin veneer over man's bestial nature and that rarely does true humanity triumph over animal passion.

Two performances stand out in the film. Laughton, who had portrayed the Roman emperor Nero in *The Sign of the Cross* the same year, is convincing as the demented vivisectionist. With spotless white suit and impeccably oiled goatee and mustache, he exudes effete amorality as he oversees his estate and its fearful inhabitants. Lugosi, in the small part of the Sayer of the Law, is also memorable, conveying the deep horror of the beasts who attempt to chant their way to humanity. Although heavy makeup disguises his features, Lugosi's unforgettable voice lends a special sonority to the litany of the law. Lugosi took this slight part in *Island of Lost Souls* as well as minor roles in other films of the early 1930's to support the extravagant life-style which, after his success as the star of *Dracula* (1931), he had adopted.

The film is also enhanced by Karl Struss's cinematography, which makes effective use of the two major settings on the island. One, the village of the beast-people, is shot almost totally from above, the perspective Dr. Moreau takes when he oversees his creatures. The beast-people are seen against the light of their bonfires as they cringe at Moreau's feet. At Moreau's compound, the other important island setting, Struss manipulates shadows not only to enhance the eeriness of places such as the House of Pain but also to lend an atmosphere of malignancy to the living quarters. Probably the most effective scene in the film occurs when Moreau is finally trapped by the beast-people. Once again he is positioned above them, but their grasping talons tearing at his clothing and flesh reveal that his position is no longer one of dominance.

Island of Lost Souls deserves its reputation as a horror classic. Its themes are clearly articulated, and the performances are of high quality. Perhaps the only major flaw is Hurst's characterization of Captain Donahue, who appears as the stock figure of the comic drunk. As a translation of Wells's novel, however, *Island of Lost Souls* is far superior to the more recent attempt, *The Island of Dr. Moreau* (1977).

Frances M. Malpezzi
William M. Clements

ISLANDS IN THE STREAM

Released: 1977
Production: Peter Bart and Max Palevsky for Paramount
Direction: Franklin J. Schaffner
Screenplay: Denne Bart Peticlerc; based on the novel of the same name by
    Ernest Hemingway
Cinematography: Fred Koenekamp
Editing: Robert Swink
Running time: 105 minutes

Principal characters:
Thomas Hudson	George C. Scott
Eddy	David Hemmings
Captain Ralph	Gilbert Roland
David	Michael-James Wixted
Audrey	Claire Bloom
Tom	Hart Bochner
Andrew	Brad Savage

There is a highly individual, always fragile communion which occurs when a great writer in his solitude and an engrossed reader in his solitude share an insight upon a written page. This experience is frequently distorted and often destroyed when the written word is transferred to the medium of film. The true significance of a written passage or a subtle quality of style that is the author's personalized signature never quite survives translation to the cinema. This is not unusual; in fact, it is the norm. Classics as diverse as *Moby Dick*, *The Scarlet Letter*, *By Love Possessed*, and *War and Peace* have suffered varying amounts of degradation in their evolution from novels into films. One author in particular, Ernest Hemingway, has always presented film adapters with a special challenge. Yet it was by no means an unreciprocated feeling since the author disliked filmmakers and could rarely endure sitting through the filmed or televised versions of his own works. He once remarked that the best way for a writer to negotiate with Hollywood was to arrange a meeting with the filmmakers at the California state line. Then, "you throw them your book, they throw you the money, then you jump in your car and drive like hell back the way you came."

Beginning with Frank Borzage's *A Farewell to Arms* in 1932, a number of directors have tested their skills at interpreting Hemingway. Among them were Sam Wood (*For Whom the Bell Tolls*, 1943), Howard Hawks (*To Have and Have Not*, 1944), Zoltan Korda (*The Macomber Affair*, 1947), and John Sturges (*The Old Man and the Sea*, 1958). These directors had at their disposal the skills of major scriptwriters, including author William Faulkner, writer-director John Huston, and screenwriter Dudley Nichols. The results of all of these efforts, however, met with only limited degrees of success. For some reason, moviemakers have always tended to exaggerate and emphasize Hemingway's most glaring strains of mawkish romanticism (*A Farewell to Arms*), his pseudomacho heroics (*For Whom the Bell Tolls*), and his mixtures of exotic drinks, athletics, and anxiety (*The Sun Also Rises*, 1957).

Although *The Macomber Affair*, based on a short story, and *The Old Man and the Sea*, adapted from a novella, are interesting character studies and were moderately successful in their own time, the Hemingway adaptation with the most zest left in it today is *To Have and Have Not*. Director Hawks discarded most of the original novel and shaped what remained into a racy adventure yarn constructed around Humphrey Bogart and Lauren Bacall. It was Bacall's introduction both to Bogart (whom she later married) and to movie audiences, who quickly succumbed to her considerable charms. She delivered such lines as: "If you need anything, just whistle. You know how to whistle, don't you, Steve? Just put your lips together and blow!," combining her sultry looks with inviting tones.

Islands in the Stream, the latest attempt to bring a Hemingway work to the screen, is significant because it evidences a reversal of the normal process of diminution that occurs when a work of literature is filmed. The motion picture is, in this case, superior to its source, a highly personal but badly flawed novel. The novel was based upon material accumulated by the author as a war correspondent for *Collier's* magazine during World War II. The projected story was intended to devote separate volumes to the war on sea, on land, and in the air. The initial volume, *The Sea*, was to be set during the early days of the war and would be further subdivided into three sections: "The Sea When Young," "The Sea When Absent," and "The Sea in Being." By 1947, a rough draft of the first subsection of the sea novel was completed, but Hemingway changed the name of that selection from "The Sea When Young" to "The Island and the Stream." Four years later, he finished the second segment, "The Sea When Absent," and then inserted a brand new third portion entitled "The Sea Chase." Although not part of his original concept, he found a place for it preceding the last selection, "The Sea in Being." The first three sections, including the new addition, are unified through the central character, Thomas Hudson, an American artist living in Cuba at the outbreak of World War II who is nothing more than a thinly disguised personification of the author himself.

The fourth section of the sea novel, "The Sea in Being," was completed early in 1951. Although thematically this part merges easily with the three preceding episodes centering on Thomas Hudson, it does not deal with the artist at all but with an aging Cuban fisherman named Santiago who fully embodies the idea of the Hemingway code hero and symbolizes the very characteristics to which Hudson obviously aspires. Hemingway, however, never felt satisfied with the first three parts and withheld them from publication pending some needed polishing and the addition of some transitional material. The fourth part was of extremely high quality, and the author decided that it could easily stand alone. It was published in 1952 as *The Old Man and the Sea* and won the Pulitzer Prize in 1953, clinching the Nobel Prize for Hemingway one year later. It was ultimately made into a film in 1958 with Spencer Tracy in the title role.

Hemingway maintained the right of final script approval for that film and became involved in other aspects of the production as well. He even went to the extent of personally fishing for forty-two straight days off the coast of Peru to catch a Marlin large enough (one thousand pounds) to use as a prop portraying the fish caught by the old man in the film. He did not catch one of sufficient size and was heartbroken when the decision was subsequently made by the producers to use a foam-rubber fish in a studio tank. The picture was plagued by other problems as well, not the least of which was the author's objection to the choice of his friend Tracy to play the role of Santiago, the fisherman. When the film was completed, Hemingway criticized Tracy's performance as being that of a "fat, very rich actor playing a fisherman." Although Tracy was nominated for an Academy Award for his performance, he was hampered by the wavering, nondescript accent with which he pronounced Santiago's lines and by an obvious girth which further handicapped him in giving a convincing portrayal of an old Cuban fisherman. The film also did not prove to be the financial success that Hemingway had hoped for although it did attract respectable audiences in later years. This was, on the whole, a final crushing blow to an author who felt that he had sincerely tried to write a meaningful story about a real old man, an actual sea, and a real fish.

Despite his antipathy toward Hollywood, Hemingway always seemed to hope that a viable film could be made from one of his novels. In his mind, that novel would be the Thomas Hudson episodes. "I got one piece, a long book that would make a pretty good movie," he confided while advising on production of *The Old Man and the Sea*. Yet he felt that it would have to be significantly revised before it was ready for publication, much less for filming. The revision was never completed because, according to some critics, it was so heavily autobiographical that the task proved increasingly delicate and difficult to manage. Hemingway had also vowed never again to "interrupt the work" that he was "born and trained to do" to participate in a film project. Thus, the odds were against his last novel ever appearing on the screen. In 1970, however, in what was treated by the literary world as a long-awaited publishing event, Hemingway's widow released the Thomas Hudson saga under the collective title of *Islands in the Stream*. She, with her husband's editors, attempted to revise and polish the rough work, but the changes that resulted were far short of those that the author intended and would obviously have effected had he lived. The unwieldy work became a best-seller, however, and thus an obvious choice in many minds for a film. The film was made in 1977, two years after *Jaws*, a film featuring a rubber fish, broke every box-office record in film history.

As a film, *Islands in the Stream*, based upon the final published version of the posthumous novel, is a serious attempt to capture the fragile, personal notes of tenderness and benevolence that enlightened Hemingway's passages when he stopped swaggering and let his guard down. The novel the film attempts to interpret is noteworthy for its deeply moving effort to create an image of a virtuous man trying to be strong both in his art and in his human relationships. Hemingway believed strongly in the heroism of the artist. Yet he also knew that this heroism made the artist an inward-looking, self-centered eccentric who increasingly sacrificed the happiness and well-being of other human beings, usually his wives, lovers, or children. The painter Thomas Hudson is Hemingway, himself attempting a rapprochement with everything that he loved: his art, his children, his wives, and even his whores and his gin.

The director of the film version, Franklin Schaffner, is successful in catching something of the idyllic melancholy nagging at Hudson, particularly in his portrayal of the artist's relationship with his children. Also, screenwriter Denne Bart Petitclerc has reduced and compressed the somewhat disjointed novel to two or three episodes that are both comprehensible and yet fully compatible with Hemingway's original intent, retaining, in the process, much of the author's blunt dialogue. Petitclerc has also trimmed away the reams of embarrassing "hairy-chested" passages and long, drink-induced conversations that mar the novel.

The film is set at the outbreak of World War II when German submarines are prowling the Caribbean and small boatloads of Jewish refugees are escaping to the Bahama Islands en route to freedom in Cuba. In this atmosphere, Thomas Hudson (George C. Scott), a prominent sculptor who is twice divorced and living in the Bahamas, is visited by his three sons (Hart Bochner, Michael-James Wixted, and Brad Savage). It is the first reunion between the artist and his sons in four years. They spend a good summer together, primarily fishing while Hudson slowly, painfully reaches toward his sons across a canyon of isolation and pride (both his own and sometimes his sons'). At the end of the summer when the boys are leaving, the oldest, Thomas (Hart Bochner), announces that he is going to join the RAF.

An indeterminate time later, after the boys have left, the sculptor's first wife Audrey (Claire Bloom) suddenly arrives for a visit. It is a bittersweet interlude; she is the one woman that Hudson has really loved. He soon discovers that she has come to tell him that their son Tom was killed in the war. After she leaves, the dejected sculptor decides to leave the island. Making his way to Florida, he encounters sudden responsibility when he comes across a refugee runner's boat that is in trouble. Hudson picks up the refugees and their captain (Gilbert Roland) and runs them to Cuba, but in the process he is shot and killed by the Cuban Coast Guard.

The film is divided structurally, like the book, into three parts. At the center of the first segment, "The Boys," is the attempt of David (Michael-James Wixted) to land a hammerhead swordfish, an episode that might be labeled "The Young Man and the Sea," since it parallels Santiago's bout with the marlin in the earlier film. In this segment Hudson serves the function of code hero in that he tries to use the encounter to help David and his brothers learn about life from the experience. Although David loses the hammerhead, Hudson explains to the boys that David has been toughened by manfully confronting the challenge in a manner that will help him surmount other demanding challenges later in his life.

The pivotal visit of Audrey, whom Hudson still loves, comprises the middle section of the film, "The Woman." It reaches a climax with the revelation that their son, Tom, Jr., has been killed in the war and ends with the sculptor's realization, after she departs, that he has lost not only a beloved son but, with his death, the boy's mother as well. With the son's demise, the final link between Hudson and Audrey has been severed, dashing any hope of reconciliation.

In the final portion of the film, "The Journey," Hudson, overcome with grief, attempts to distract himself by recklessly helping to smuggle Jewish refugees into Cuba. The film's fast-paced finale ends with Hudson's death on the deck of his fishing boat from multiple bullet wounds. The sculptor has learned in his final meeting with his family and also through his buddy, Eddy (David Hemmings), that no man can remain an island once he learns to love those who love him. The artist must make his peace with the world. For Thomas Hudson, however, the insight comes too late.

In the book, there is little connection between these three episodes beyond a thematic one. The filmmakers, however, have made additional efforts to solidify the relationships. One of these devices is the planting of portents in the earlier stages of the film concerning incidents that will occur later. A striking example of this process is the discovery of the corpse of a German sailor on the beach near the Hudson home which foreshadows the ultimate involvement of both Hudson and his son in the conflict that will cost them their lives. The plot of the film is thus more cohesive than that of the written work upon which it is based because of these foreshadowings and other cross-references between various events in the screenplay.

Significant additional strength is also generated through the technique of borrowing speeches and bits of dialogue from other Hemingway works—a practice that the author himself obviously could not do. Thomas Hudson's dying reflections lying upon the deck of his fishing boat were actually composed by Hemingway for the character of Robert Jordan at the conclusion of *For Whom the Bell Tolls*: "I've had a lot of luck to have had such a good life. I wish there was some way to pass on what I've learned. I was learning fast there at the end." This remark was true of Jordan but certainly no less true of Hudson.

The final means by which the filmmakers are able to improve Hemingway's original written work is by the selection of Scott to bring the character of Thomas Hudson to life. Although the cameras cannot always create equivalents of many of the author's descriptive sentences, it does marvelously well at capturing his characters. Scott makes an admirable Hudson, particularly when one considers the difficulty of portraying the character who is based on Hemingway. To effect fully the resemblance between the personality and history of Hemingway and those of Thomas Hudson, Scott was costumed and made up to look like Hemingway at fifty or sixty, complete with a salt-and-pepper beard. His performance projects the Hemingway beneath the mask of macho; he is harsh yet affectionate, exacting yet forgiving. Hudson is a quiet, sure, taciturn man and an admirable father but one who has great difficulty in manifesting his affection for his sons. He is able to be loved although at times unable to understand why.

Scott receives strong support from Hemmings in the role of Eddy. Hemmings, who played the hip photographer of Michelangelo Antonioni's *Blow-Up* (1966), turns in an expressive portrayal of a local inhabitant who is equally devoted to Hudson and to rum. Roland is solid as a refugee-running boat captain, a role for which he has had much training in decades of action-on-the-high-seas melodrama, although his star billing for such a small role is somewhat mysterious.

Islands in the Stream, then, reverses the normal process that occurs when a novel is put on film by actually improving upon the written work. Whether or not Hemingway would have approved is conjectural, but he undoubtedly would have liked Scott's performance, and, had he lived, he might have provided a better vehicle upon which to build a character or construct a film. Unlike Thomas Hudson, however, the author did not perish at the hands of others trapped inside a situation beyond his control. His destiny was fulfilled when he took his own life three weeks before his sixty-second birthday—a solitary, misunderstood island in the stream of humanity.

Stephen L. Hanson

IT'S A GIFT

Released: 1934
Production: William LeBaron for Paramount
Direction: Norman Z. McLeod
Screenplay: Jack Cunningham; based on an original story by Charles Bogle
(W. C. Fields) and adapted from the play *The Comic Supplement* by
J. P.McEvoy
Cinematography: Henry Sharp
Editing: no listing
Running time: 73 minutes

Principal characters:
Harold Bissonette .... W. C. Fields
Mrs. Amelia Bissonette .... Kathleen Howard
Mildred Bissonette .... Jean Rouverol
John Durston (Mildred's fiancé) .... Julian Madison
Norman Bissonette .... Tom Bupp
Everett Ricks
(Mr. Bissonette's assistant) .... Tammany Young
Mrs. Dunk .... Josephine Whittell

Given W. C. Field's reputation as a master of verbal acidity, it is a bit
surprising to discover that he not only began as a silent film star, but also that
his film career actually suffered a decline during the early years of the talkies.
While the Marx Brothers were running riot in five films they made under the
Paramount banner, Fields, under contract to the same studio, was often relegated to secondary roles in otherwise fairly ordinary comedies. Perhaps it
is only coincidental, but Paramount did not really begin to provide Fields
with good star vehicles until 1934, the year following *Duck Soup*, the final
Marx Brothers film for the studio. During that year, he appeared in no less
than five Paramount releases. Typically, he stole the films in which his screen
time was limited to only a few scenes (*Six of a Kind* and *Mrs. Wiggs of the
Cabbage Patch*), but it was in the other three features (*You're Telling Me*,
The Old-Fashioned Way, and *It's a Gift* that his comic genius was finally
allowed full expression. The last of this trio is the best, and has often been
called Field's finest film.

The story involves a small-town storekeeper and family man, Harold Bissonette (W. C. Fields), whose overriding ambition is to own an "orange
ranch" in California, a dream which is constantly ridiculed by his shrewish
wife Amelia (Kathleen Howard) and his selfish children. With a fortitude
born of long and weary experience, he copes with the day-to-day headaches
provided by his family and an assortment of impossibly annoying customers
and neighbors. When he receives an inheritance from a deceased relative, he

sells out (over the loud objections of his family) and purchases his cherished orange grove—by mail. The family sets out for California in an old jalopy, but upon arriving, they discover that the unseen property is apparently worthless. Before long, however, Bissonette negotiates the highly profitable sale of the land to a promoter who wants to build a racetrack on the site. He gets his orange grove and presumably lives a life of ease ever after.

This flimsy narrative serves as the thread to connect four major comedy sequences, any of which could have provided enough material for an excellent short subject. Indeed, the first two sequences taken together can be seen as an expanded and more purposeful variation on Fields's short comedies *The Pharmacist* and *The Barber Shop*, made for Mack Sennett the year before. In both, he plays an irascible merchant or tradesman, bedeviled by his eccentric customers on one side and his family on the other. The difference in *It's a Gift* is that he is provided with an avenue of escape from this dreary life, his dream of a California paradise.

Counter to the somewhat misanthropic image we have of Fields today, his Harold Bissonette is surprisingly sedate, a simple, long-suffering man who calmly tries to keep a cheerful front in the face of the daily indignities he must endure. While not exactly mild-mannered, he does keep his grumbling largely to himself, never lashing back at his tormentors strongly enough to throw his character off balance or to endanger the audience's sympathy for his position. The net result of this is that his final triumph is all the more satisfying.

The first portion of the film establishes his lowly position in his own household and his various ways of coping with it—or ignoring it. In the second segment, we see him at work in his grocery store, faring badly in his attempts to hold his own amidst the chaos caused by his dimwitted assistant and exasperating customers (including a cantankerous blind man who regularly smashes through the plate glass in his front doors if Fields fails to see him approaching in time to open them).

The third and funniest major sequence is the hilarious "sleeping-porch" scene. Driven out of his own bedroom by one of his nagging wife's endless tirades, Bissonette retreats to a hammock on the porch outside his apartment, where he is kept awake by a series of neighbors, strangers, and "inanimate" objects. A coconut left by the milkman for the tenants on the top floor bumps down the stairs, pausing in middescent to rattle around in an overturned garbage can. An insurance salesman shows up looking for a "Karl LaFong, Capital K, small a, small r, small l. Capital L, small a, capital F, small o, small n, small g"; unperturbed at not finding Mr. LaFong, he climbs the stairs and unloads his sales pitch on Bissonette. At dawn, the upstairs neighbor Mrs. Dunk (Josephine Whittell) sends her not-too-bright daughter out on an errand. An inane and absurdly loud conversation between the two after the girl has reached the street occasions a muttered comment from Bissonette, which causes the strong-lunged Mrs. Dunk to yell, "I can't hear you! There's someone shouting on the floor below!" The construction of this lengthy sequence, one of the finest moments in any American comedy, is impeccable.

After such an excellent beginning and middle, there might have been some danger of the film losing momentum, but wisely, the remaining portion of the story—the trip to California and the subsequent events with the orange grove—is kept relatively short. It is also helped by the hilarious climax, which has Bissonette holding out for an astronomical sum for his property while his wife, completely unaware of its true value, to which Bissonette has been tipped off, frets and fumes as he turns down offer after offer, finally fainting dead away when he gets his price. "You're crazy!" responds Bissonette to one of the promoter's lower offers. The promoter comes back with "And you're drunk!," occasioning one of Fields's most celebrated wisecracks: "Yeah, but I'll be sober tomorrow and you'll be crazy for the rest of your life!"

The very end of the film is a satisfying picture of the classic California dream come true. Bissonette, seated on the porch of his house, reaches up to pluck an orange effortlessly from a tree; he squeezes a small amount of juice into a glass, adds a generous shot of liquor, and settles back contentedly.

At least partially written by Fields himself (under the *nom de plume* of "Charles Bogle"), *It's a Gift* reveals his penchant for verbal humor and telling observation of human behavior. Merely the diversity of the character names—Mr. Muckle, Bissonette (pronounced "Bis-son-ay" by Fields in a laughable attempt at dignity). Jasper Fitchmueller (who comes into Fields's store and demands "kumquats"), the unseen Karl LaFong, and the Dunk family (including Baby Dunk, played by Fields's celebrated screen nemesis, Baby LeRoy)—are indicative of the delight which he got from odd-sounding words and names. The characters who go with these names, however, are just as memorable, and all the funnier because they are recognizable, everyday types.

It's a Gift, despite its comic brilliance, was not considered exceptional by most contemporary critics. It is true that Norman McLeod's direction is undistinguished and that the production values of the film were not particularly high, but these things do not matter much in the final analysis. What is important is that Fields was finally being allowed to dominate films that deserved him and that were tailored to his peculiar talents. For audiences, this is more than enough, and *It's a Gift* is assured of its high place among American comedy classics.

Howard H. Prouty

IT'S IN THE BAG

Released: 1945
Production: Jack H. Skirball for Manhattan Productions; released by United Artists
Direction: Richard Wallace
Screenplay: Jay Dratler and Alma Reville; based on an original story by Lewis R. Foster and Fred Allen
Cinematography: Russell Metty
Editing: William Morgan
Running time: 86 minutes

    Principal characters:

Fred Floogle	Fred Allen
Jack Benny	Himself
William Bendix	Himself
Eve Floogle	Binnie Barnes
Parker	Robert Benchley
Psychiatrist	Jerry Colonna
Pike	John Carradine
Marion	Gloria Pope
Perry	William Terry
Mrs. Nussbaum	Minerva Pious
Homer	Dickie Tyler
Detective Sully	Sidney Toler
John Miljan	Himself
Singers	Don Ameche
	Rudy Vallee
	Victor Moore

Fred Allen (1894-1956) was a vaudeville performer who developed into one of the most popular, and certainly one of the most intelligent, radio entertainers of the 1930's and 1940's. Unlike many of his contemporaries, he generally wrote his own material, and, against the advice of almost everyone, he was continually critical of radio and its commercial and sponsorship ties both on and off the air. Herman Wouk, in a foreword to a collection of Allen's letters, described the comedian as "a classic humorist, one of those rare spirits who see the world as it is, and who laugh in order not to weep." In addition to work in vaudeville and radio, Allen was an accomplished writer, as his two autobiographies, *Treadmill to Oblivion* and *Much Ado About Me*, indicate. As a film performer, however, he proved a little less accomplished. *Love Thy Neighbour*, a 1940 Paramount production which was based on the long-running radio feud between Allen and Jack Benny, was far from successful. Four years later, however, Allen returned to films with *It's in the Bag*, a truly classic film comedy, about which the comedian had continuing doubts both before, during, and after production. "Every time I get to California some disaster befalls me," he told one reporter. "Last time it was *Love Thy Neighbour*, which I made at Paramount. We're right across the street from Paramount this time, which is as close as we can get since *Love Thy Neighbour*."

It's in the Bag is somewhat reminiscent of Ole Olsen and Chic Johnson's *Hellzapoppin* (1942). As in that production, characters will sometimes address themselves directly to the audience, but *It's in the Bag* is a far more formalized production, albeit with a far-fetched plot. The basis of the film, although not indicated by the credits, is a Russian novel of the 1920's written by Ilya Arnoldovich Ilf and Evgeni Petrov, translated into English as *12 Chairs*. The Ilf and Petrov novel has been the basis for at least eight feature films, including a popular George Formby British film of 1936, *Keep Your Seats Please*, and a 1970 Mel Brooks comedy, *The Twelve Chairs*, starring Ron Moody, Frank Langella, and Dom DeLuise. In the interests of brevity, Allen cut down the number of chairs in his production to five.

The film opens, as do most films, with the credits, but in this particular case, Allen also opens the film, commenting on the credits and belittling everyone for their participation in such a production. He explains that Jack Skirball gets his name up twice because he is the producer, that director Richard Wallace got the job because he is Mr. Skirball's father-in-law, that everyone else is related to the producer, and throws in the classic description of an associate producer, "the only person in Hollywood who would associate with the producer." The delivery of the credits sets the mood for the film and serves as an excellent introduction to the eccentric world of the characters of *It's in the Bag*, characters who might have been at home in a Preston Sturges production, but nowhere else.

Allen plays Fred Floogle, proprietor of Floogle's Flea Circus, a man of limited means, possessing a bespectacled, overintelligent son named Homer (Dickie Tyler), a nondescript wife (Binnie Barnes), and a daughter, Marion (Gloria Pope), who is in love with the son (William Terry) of a man named Parker (Robert Benchley) who believes himself on a higher social level than Floogle, but who is in reality a vermin exterminator. (Benchley, perhaps remembering the old maxim, has developed a better mousetrap, on the merits of which he delivers one of the classic Benchley lectures.) Floogle learns he has inherited a fortune from his long-lost uncle, but the fortune turns out to be five chairs, in one of which the uncle has hidden $300,000 in cash and the names of the villains who have robbed him of his fortune. Unfortunately, Floogle sells the chairs before learning of the contents of one of them, and the rest of the film is taken up with the comedian's efforts to track down the chairs.

The first chair has been bought by one of the most popular members of Allen's radio repertory company, Mrs. Nussbaum, played by Minerva Pious, who explains in very great detail the reason for her purchasing the chair and for her selling it to Allen's old radio nemesis, Jack Benny. The scenes between Allen and Benny are perhaps the funniest in the film, as the latter sets out to prove himself to be the meanest man in the world, in the words of Allen, a "guy who wouldn't give you the parsley off his fish." Benny's apartment contains a clothes closet complete with hat-check girl who charges guests twenty-five cents to leave their coats, a cigarette vending machine for guests wishing to smoke, and a price tag on every item in the place, even down to Benny's tie, which he happily sells to Floogle. Floogle poses as the president of the Jack Benny Fan Club of Nutley, New Jersey, anxious to have a memento of the comedian to help increase membership in the Club. Benny is loath to loan the chair to Floogle, but eventually succumbs when a rental fee of ten dollars a day is suggested.

Outside the apartment, Floogle is almost killed by a car whose occupants seize the chair, and he renews acquaintance with his uncle's lawyer Pike, one of the trio who stole the relative's fortune, brilliantly played by John Carradine, looking like a reject from the *Batman* television series. Pike explains that he is still trying to collect for the doctor who brought Benny into the world seventy years ago.

Floogle's son is the only member of the family who knows the names and addresses of the five new owners of the chairs, but, in a deliberately set fire which destroyed the furniture store to which the chairs were sold, his memory has become a blank. He is taken to a psychiatrist, played by Jerry Colonna, who keeps slapping imaginary tsetse flies on his cheek. Leaving their son in Colonna's care, Floogle and his wife decide to while away a few hours at a cinema, learning from the doorman outside that there is "immediate seating." In a brilliant parody of cinema-going, the two desperately seek seats in the jammed auditorium, constantly being told by ushers to move to the next aisle on the right, visiting floor after floor until they find themselves so high up, with the screen a distant tiny square, that Mrs. Floogle is about to faint from lack of air. In anger, Floogle visits the manager, who provides him with a chair—one of the missing five chairs, but not the one with the money.

The next visit is to a nightclub where two of the chairs are in use, and where the singing waiters are Don Ameche, Rudy Vallee, and Victor Moore, whom Allen joins for a chorus and verse of "You Made Me What I Am Today." Ameche explains he is reduced to singing in a nightclub because he has run out of things to invent in the movies, referring to his famous film role as Alexander Graham Bell. Vallee, who was on radio before Ameche invented it, explains he has run out of megaphones, while one-time romantic stage actor Moore, who used to chase chorus girls, explains he has run out of breath. After a brawl in the nightclub, during which villain John Miljan kills a patron, Floogle finds himself in jail, but he is released in time to follow up a clue to another of the five chairs, now owned by gangster William Bendix.

Breaking into the gangster's house, Floogle is forced to hide under the desk when the gang enters, and he overhears their plan to murder Bendix, a vitamin-eating, scared-of-noises gangster who only took over the gang because he inherited it from his mother. Floogle discovers the money and the name of his uncle's thieving colleagues in Bendix's chair, and the latter, who was thought killed by gunshots but is saved by his bullet-proof vest, helps torture Pike and Miljan into confessing to their crimes. Floogle returns home to his daughter's wedding, where all is noise and pandemonium. "All we need now is a brass band," comments Allen, and, sure enough, the doors open and a brass band enters.

Chief credit for the appeal of *It's in the Bag* lies with Allen and also, apparently, with writer Morrie Ryskind (associated for many years on stage and film with the Marx Brothers), who provided many of the ideas for the script. Most critics recognized the skills of these two gentlemen and were prompt with their praise. Howard Barnes in the *New York Herald Tribune* (June 11, 1945) wrote, "The show is as nutty as a fruit cake, but the star gives it considerable spice." *Time* (April 23, 1945) commented, "It is not in the same class with the funniest movies ever made—they stopped making them that funny about the time Hollywood learned to talk. But it is funny enough to do very well until a better one comes along, which is likely to be quite a while."

Allen made *It's in the Bag* because his doctors told him to take a break from radio because of his high blood pressure—perhaps brought on by fighting with censors and sponsors—and have a long vacation. Filmgoers then and now can take delight in Allen's enforced vacation.

Anthony Slide

IVANHOE

Released: 1952
Production: Pandro S. Berman for Metro-Goldwyn-Mayer
Direction: Richard Thorpe
Screenplay: Noel Langley; based on Aeneas MacKenzie's adaptation of the novel of the same name by Sir Walter Scott
Cinematography: Freddie A. Young
Editing: Frank Clarke
Art direction: Alfred Junge
Sound: A. W. Watkins
Music: Miklos Rozsa
Running time: 106 minutes

Principal characters:
Ivanhoe .... Robert Taylor
Rebecca .... Elizabeth Taylor
Rowena .... Joan Fontaine
De Bois-Guilbert .... George Sanders
Wamba (Ivanhoe's squire) .... Emlyn Williams
Sir Hugh De Bracey .... Robert Douglas
Prince John .... Guy Rolfe
Cedric ....Finlay Currie
Isaac ....Felix Aylmer
Locksley ....Harold Warrender
King Richard the Lionhearted ......Norman Wooland

Ivanhoe is set in England's age of chivalry in the early thirteenth century, and the story tells of knights, fair ladies, and kings. Richard the Lionhearted (Norman Wooland) has been taken prisoner during the Crusades and is being held for ransom, while his brother John (Guy Rolfe) has taken over the throne. A Saxon knight, Sir Wilfred of Ivanhoe (Robert Taylor), the bravest and most loyal of Richard's followers, makes an effort to raise the ransom, although he must be a stranger to his own house because his father, Cedric (Finlay Currie), has disowned him for riding to the Crusades. Isaac (Felix Aylmer), a Jew, and his daughter Rebecca (Elizabeth Taylor) help Ivanhoe avoid capture by the Normans, led by De Bois-Guilbert (George Sanders) and De Bracey (Robert Douglas). Rebecca falls in love with Ivanhoe, although he is betrothed to the Saxon Rowena (Joan Fontaine). Isaac helps Ivanhoe to raise the ransom, affirming that his people are loyal to Richard, who, although guilty of certain injustices, had been far more benevolent as king than the power-mad John would be. Ivanhoe is reconciled with his father, but they are taken prisoner along with Rowena, and Isaac and Rebecca are taken also. De Bois-Guilbert, although he must act as her enemy, reveals that he is deeply in love with Rebecca. Locksley (Harold Warrender) and his men, loyal supporters of Richard, surround the castle where De Bois-Guilbert and De Bracey are holding Ivanhoe and the others, and after a long siege, the Saxons prevail. Rebecca, however, is in the hands of De Bois-Guilbert, who takes her to John. When she is sentenced to burn at the stake as a witch, Ivanhoe steps forward as her champion. De Bois-Guilbert, chosen to act as the king's champion, offers to disgrace himself as a knight and refuse to fight if she will be his, but Rebecca refuses, and the two knights must fight to the death. Ivanhoe wins just as Richard returns to reclaim the throne.

If Sir Walter Scott's great story, of which the foregoing is as brief a description as possible, has a timeless appeal, it is because it shows a complex attitude toward chivalry, and that attitude is maintained in this film adaptation, a very handsome production which succeeds in compressing the narrative into a running time of less than two hours without compromising it. Against a vivid historical background, the film illuminates the major characters and their relationships with considerable insight. The chivalric code is a given, and each of the characters is defined in relation to it. Ivanhoe has a certain purity, manifested in his unswerving devotion to Richard and also in his heroic and wholly virtuous defense of Rebecca, whose love he does not return. Although Rebecca is easily as beautiful as Rowena (particularly in her screen personification by Elizabeth Taylor) and more sympathetic by virtue of her loneliness, Ivanhoe is not one to be frivolous about his affections. He considers his love for Rowena to be immutable, something which helps to define him as a good Saxon knight.

The direct opposite of Ivanhoe is the villain, De Bois-Guilbert. Unlike Ivanhoe, he follows his heart rather than the code, and a lack of purity distinguishes his actions. Valuing his love for Rebecca over all loyalties, he is ultimately placed in a tragic position of having to kill Ivanhoe and see Rebecca die as a result or be killed himself. The film implies that although De Bois-Guilbert is almost victorious, fighting fiercely and having the advantage over Ivanhoe until the last moment, he is glad to lose. In death, he is able to reaffirm tenderly his love for Rebecca as Ivanhoe is reunited with Rowena. Although the narrative supports the popularized moral and historical view which affirms the preservation of a just state ruled by Richard as the highest good, De Bois-Guilbert is the most sympathetic character. In him, romantic impulses are affectingly human. When the throne is restored to Richard in the last scene, we are grateful for the virtues of the hero, Ivanhoe, which have made this possible, but our sympathies are not with him. It is the antagonist slain by Ivanhoe who has won our hearts.

The two women also are perceived in relation to the chivalric code. Rowena shows some jealousy over Ivanhoe's bond with Rebecca, but ultimately she is able to accept the fact that this bond does not threaten her. She supports all of his actions, in the tradition of all fair ladies. Rebecca also accepts her role, although with a certain melancholy, never overtly seeking Ivanhoe's love even in the face of death. She wins sympathy by virtue of Ivanhoe's unwillingness to return any measure of her love, but she seems strangely coldhearted in feeling nothing for De Bois-Guilbert until he is at the point of death. Although his feelings for her are identical to hers for Ivanhoe, she remains insensitive toward him.

Film adaptations of classics are often guilty of a lamentable superficiality which provoke feelings of regret on the part of the reader that the treasured book was not left alone. *Ivanhoe* is not altogether free of this superficiality but it does successfully evoke the story and characters if even in an abbreviated form. Although Sanders is the inevitable standout as De Bois-Guilbert, all of the actors are perfectly cast. They read the stylized lines with total conviction and have the true bearing of knights and ladies—no small accomplishment, especially if one tries to imagine more contemporary actors and actresses struggling to be credible in these roles. The film everywhere reflects an admirable attention to detail. The art direction and Technicolor cinematography bring the historical period vividly to life, and the exteriors were shot in carefully chosen locations in England. The action sequences are exciting and well-sustained. The siege of the castle is very elaborate and well-staged, while the final duel between Ivanhoe and De Bois-Guilbert shows special imagination in its use of sound. As Ivanhoe swings his axe at his opponent, who strikes back with mace and chain, no music is heard, only the sound of the weapons clanging against the men's shields and the steady beating of a drum in the background. This use of sound heightens the tension of the merciless struggle and contrasts nicely with the greater part of the sound track, which is filled with Miklos Rozsa's sweeping score, itself one of the most distinguished aspects of the film.

As for director Richard Thorpe, his name is not a celebrated one, and most of his other films are forgettable, but it would be a mistake to deny him credit for the artistic success of *Ivanhoe*. Although all of the participants in the production contributed strongly, he is responsible for the film's cohesiveness. There are times when one wishes that he had shown more imagination in adding to the scenes rather that letting them play in a straightforward manner, but his belief in the material never falters. His other films in the genre of historical adventure, such as *Knights of the Round Table* (1954), confirm that his relatively limited talent flowers when faced with this blend of spectacle and romance. His staging of all the scenes is direct and authoritative, and when the conflicts in the story have been resolved, he gracefully tracks back for the knights and ladies bowing before King Richard in the final shot, a camera movement quite striking because Thorpe has chosen it for this moment alone.

Blake Lucas

JAILHOUSE ROCK

Released: 1957
Production: Pandro S. Berman for Metro-Goldwyn-Mayer
Direction: Richard Thorpe
Screenplay: Guy Trosper; based on an unpublished story of the same name by Ned Young
Cinematography: Robert Bronner
Editing: Ralph E. Winters
Running time: 96 minutes

Principal characters:
Vince Everett	Elvis Presley
Peggy Van Alden	Judy Tyler
Hunk Houghton	Mickey Shaughnessy
Prison Warden	Hugh Sanders
Mickey Alba	Don Burnet

Elvis Presley films are usually considered a genre unto themselves; and, like beach party movies and kung fu epics, not a particularly distinguished genre at that. On the whole, this is an accurate appraisal. Certainly the formulaic efforts that characterized the later part of his cinematic career do nothing to dispel this notion. Nevertheless, a few of Presley's films—*Jailhouse Rock*, *King Creole* (1958), and *Flaming Star* (1960)—transcend the "Elvis movie" formula and manage to make an artistic as well as financial statement on behalf of their star.

Jailhouse Rock was made at the height of Presley's pre-Army popularity, and Vince Everett, the character he portrays in the film, stands squarely alongside such 1950's rebel heroes as Marlon Brando in *The Wild One* (1954), James Dean in *Rebel Without a Cause* (1955), and the real-life Presley. Unlike his rebellious cinematic predecessors, however, Vince Everett takes on the world and wins. Sustained by the love of a good woman (no Elvis movie is entirely free of clichés), Everett triumphs over adversity and revolutionizes the popular-music industry in the process.

Vince Everett is a good-hearted, if impetuous, young Southerner with a fiery temper. As the film opens, he finds himself in the state penitentiary, where he is serving time for manslaughter because he accidentally killed a man in a bar room brawl. Everett is befriended by Hunk Houghton (Mickey Shaughnessy), a jailwise convict who had a promising career in country music before he was sent to prison. Despite Hunk's patronage, prison life is harsh for Vince. His hot temper and sarcastic wit keep him in constant trouble with the authorities. His insolence culminates in a brutal beating at the hands of the prison guards. The only thing that keeps him going is music. Vince's voice is raw and untrained, and his guitar playing is ludicrous, but Hunk realizes that his potential is unlimited. With Hunk as his mentor, Vince is rewarded with a brief spot on a television show featuring prison talent.

Vince's performance of "I Want to Be Free" is the hit of the show, drawing great quantities of fan mail—mail that Hunk and the warden (Hugh Sanders) never permit Vince to see until he is paroled. Vince leaves the penitentiary with a large chip on his shoulder ("You've been just like a father to me, Warden," he sneers on his way out), and he heads for a bar where Hunk has told him he might find work. Vince wants to be a singer; the owner of the bar needs a busboy. As usual, Vince's temper gets the better of him, and he stalks out, but not before making the acquaintance of Peggy Van Alden (Judy Tyler), a publicist for Geneva Records, and its star, Mickey Alba (Don Burnett), a popular crooner. Peggy spots a genuine talent behind his brashness and arranges a demonstration recording session for him.

The scene at the recording session is one of the best in Presley's screen career. In many ways it mirrors Presley's own experiences at Sun Records in 1954. Tapes of that recording session show Elvis and his band searching for the missing link that will turn an ordinary country song into something the world had never seen before—rock-and-roll. In *Jailhouse Rock*, much the same thing happens. Vince Everett runs through "Don't Leave Me Now." It is a pleasant enough song, but as Vince himself concedes, his performance is undistinguished. "Put your emotions into the song," Peggy urges. Vince does, and the result is enough to wake up even the jaded studio musicians. He has hit upon a new and vital musical style. No one who cares about rock-and-roll can remain unmoved by this scene.

As happened to many of Presley's contemporaries (although not to Elvis himself), however, Vince Everett's style is immediately stolen by a member of the music establishment: Mickey Alba records "Don't Leave Me Now" using Vince's arrangement, and Vince's own record is buried. Undeterred, Vince determines to bypass the recording establishment by setting up his own company. He and Peggy form Laurel Records, and Vince's "Treat Me Nice" is the label's first hit.

As it inevitably must in any Elvis movie, romantic complications arise. Peggy falls for Vince, who is still sufficiently mad at the world to be unable to reciprocate—or even notice—her feelings. In a particularly well-handled scene, Peggy takes Vince to a dinner party hosted by her parents. Vince feels out of place immediately, and his alienation deepens as the evening wears on. The talk turns to music, and when a matronly type patronizingly asks Vince what he thinks about modern jazz, he angrily replies "Lady, I don't know what the hell you're talking about," and stalks out of the house. Peggy and Vince spend most of the rest of the film sparring with each other. Peggy resents Vince's coldness, and Vince, although he needs Peggy's approval and affection, cannot bring himself to admit it. He is still too selfish and headstrong to place anyone's feelings above his own.

Meanwhile, on the eve of Vince's next big break—a network television special of his own—Hunk Houghton reenters Vince's life. Paroled from prison, Hunk hopes to resume his career in show business on Vince's coattails. Vince reluctantly agrees to let Hunk sing one song on the show—their roles are now precisely reversed from those of their prison days—but the producer axes Hunk's number at the last minute. Vince himself, however, is a smash hit. He admits his past legal difficulties on the show, and even turns them to his advantage by using them as a pretext for introducing his new record, "Jailhouse Rock," a number brilliantly choreographed by Presley himself. Vince and his fellow prisoners in the skit sing and act out the prison break described in the song without missing a beat.

As immature in success as he was as a struggling artist, Vince continues to treat Hunk and Peggy badly. He moves to Hollywood to break into motion pictures and flaunts his starlet-girl friends in Peggy's face. He gives his old buddy Hunk a job as a flunky whose primary task is to walk Vince's two basset hounds. Things come to a head when Vince unilaterally decides to sell Laurel Records. He is in the process of trying to explain this decision to a hurt and angry Peggy when Hunk walks in with the dogs in tow. Hunk, who is more than a little drunk, gives Vince a well-deserved tongue-lashing and then begins swinging his fists. One punch hits Vince in the throat, and he collapses, gasping for breath.

Vince recovers from the blow and makes his peace with Hunk and Peggy. He finally realizes that people care about him, and this realization seems to free him to care about them in return. He is, however, deathly afraid that the blow to his throat has permanently ruined his singing voice. After several false starts, he puts his fears to rest in a scene that is simultaneously corny and oddly affecting. Alone with Peggy (and a pianist for musical accompaniment), Vince begins to sing "Young and Beautiful." The film closes as Vince, his voice growing stronger and more confident with each note, finishes the song.

Presley possibly never surpassed his performance in *Jailhouse Rock*, and it is interesting to speculate why. His supporting cast was adequate but unexceptional. Peggy, as played by Tyler in her last film before her death in July of 1957, and Shaughnessy as Hunk are stock Elvis movie characters that could as easily have populated films such as *Fun in Acapulco* (1963) or *Girl Happy* (1965). The film's score, especially the title song, "Treat Me Nice," "Baby I Don't Care," and "I Want to Be Free," by Jerry Lieber and Mike Stoller, arguably the greatest songwriting team in rock history, is outstanding, but great Elvis songs do not, of necessity, make a great Elvis film, as witnessed by *Jailhouse Rock*'s immediate predecessor, *Loving You* (1957).

The lion's share of the credit for *Jailhouse Rock*'s success would seem to be due to the three men whose combined artistic vision formed the film's core. Writer Guy Trosper (who based his script on a story by Ned Young) deserves credit for making Vince Everett a young man with his share of flaws. Indeed, Vince is, in many respects, the least appealing of the film's major characters. The concept of the flawed protagonist all but disappeared from Presley's later films, as the Elvis movies got blander and blander. Not a little of the film's dramatic success rests on its steadfast refusal to sugarcoat the character of Vince Everett.

Richard Thorpe turns in the most subtle direction ever seen in a Presley vehicle. The musical numbers are integrated smoothly into the story, and the film's highlights, both comic and dramatic, are emphasized without being sledgehammered. Thorpe deserves credit first for recognizing that, for this film at least, his young star had suddenly blossomed into a genuine actor and second for being able to get that transformation across on the screen.

The third person responsible for the artistic success of *Jailhouse Rock* is, of course, Presley himself. While one should not overemphasize the parallels between Elvis and Vince Everett, one must also not ignore them. Presley and the character he portrays shared the same lower-class background, the same impetuosity, the same ambition, and the same volcanic talent: *Jailhouse Rock* is metaphorically, although certainly not literally, autobiographical. Given a character and a plot with which he could identify, Presley responded as he never had before and as he rarely did thereafter. The result is a stunning performance. Presley conveys all of Vince's warmth and petulance, all of his immaturity and genius, with never a false step. The result is *Jailhouse Rock*, one Elvis movie that lives up to the power and the glory of Elvis' music.

Robert Mitchell

JEREMIAH JOHNSON

Released: 1972
Production: Joe Wizener for Warner Bros.
Direction: Sydney Pollack
Screenplay: John Milius and Edward Anhalt; based on the novel *Crow Killer* by Raymond W. Thorpe and Robert Bunker, and the novel *Mountain Man* by Vardis Fisher
Cinematography: Andrew Callaghan
Editing: Thomas Stanford
Running time: 108 minutes

Principal characters:
Jeremiah Johnson	Robert Redford
Bear Claw	Will Geer
Del Gue	Stefan Gierasch
Mad Woman	Allyn McLerie
Caleb	Josh Albee
Swan	Delle Bolton
Paints His Shirt Red	Joaquin Martinez

Like the buttes of Monument Valley in John Ford's Westerns, the Rocky Mountains play a vital role in Sydney Pollack's *Jeremiah Johnson*. Not only do they provide a picturesque setting handsomely photographed by cinematographer Andrew (Duke) Callaghan, but they also represent the goal of the quest which engages the film's central character. That character, mountain man Jeremiah Johnson (Robert Redford), is a composite figure drawn from an actual frontiersman whose exploits survived in oral tradition and from a fictional character in a novel by Vardis Fisher. Yet the film's Jeremiah, although based on individualized characterizations, is flat, a symbol of the back-to-nature romanticism that has frequently appeared in American film and literature. Jeremiah's goal is to escape the constraints of civilization in the supposed freedom of the wilderness.

The film begins as Jeremiah disembarks at Robidoux's Trading Post, the threshold to the mountains. Although nothing specific concerning his background is revealed, the opening scene suggests that escape is one motive for his attraction to the wilderness. As he makes his preparations to go into the mountains to trap fur-bearing animals, the voices of a narrator and a ballad-singer indicate that he is a man who has known trouble and has become disillusioned because things are not what they should be. His garb, a pair of military trousers, further implies the source of his dissatisfaction—perhaps involvement in the Mexican War, an event contemporary with the film's setting. Turning his back on the Trading Post, the last outpost of civilization, Jeremiah heads West.

His unsuitability for survival in the wilderness is immediately apparent, for he lacks the skills requisite for a mountain man. For example, he unsuccessfully forages for food. In one telling scene, the raggedly clothed Jeremiah flounders in an icy stream vainly trying to capture a fish for his supper. He notices that he is being observed; "Paints His Shirt Red" (Joaquin Martinez), a Crow warrior, silently watches, a full string of fish at his side. Moreover, Jeremiah's lack of mountain sense has left him vulnerable; his rifle lies uselessly on the riverbank. Before he perishes in the cold of a mountain winter, Jeremiah fortunately meets Bear Claw (Will Geer), a veteran of the wilderness who teaches him basic survival techniques. In order to assert his independence from civilization, Jeremiah must become an apprentice, dependent on the older man's tutelage. He learns to hunt, trap, fish, and forage, and by winter's end he is ready to set out on his own. His first step in progressing from civilization to wilderness is complete.

Jeremiah's independence, however, is short-lived. He comes upon a woman (Allyn McLerie) and her son (Josh Albee), whose family has been massacred by Indians. After a burial scene involving rituals of the society Jeremiah has abandoned, the woman, driven mad by her experiences in the wilderness, insists that the mountain man take responsibility for the boy Caleb. Having thus acquired a son, Jeremiah next takes a wife. Accompanied by Del Gue (Stefan Gierasch), another mountain veteran, he blunders into a marriage arrangement with Swan (Delle Bolton), the daughter of a Flathead chief. Jeremiah, Swan, and Caleb set up housekeeping in a log cabin; the attempt to escape from civilization and become independent has backfired since Jeremiah is now head of a family, the basic institution of the civilization he flees. He is domesticated rather than liberated from social responsibility.

This bent toward social responsibility becomes more pronounced when Jeremiah responds to a military search party by agreeing to help them find a group of settlers stranded in the heavy snows across the mountains. In order to reach them quickly, he consents to trespass on a burial ground sacred to the Crow. This violation of a taboo imposed by the wilderness' native inhabitants proves Jeremiah an ally of the civilization he has supposedly repudiated. The dissonant images of deteriorating bodies in the burial ground contrast sharply with the rugged beauty of the landscape seen throughout most of the film and reflect Jeremiah's disharmony with the wilderness. When he returns from guiding the search party, he finds that the Crow have exacted vengeance for his sacrilegious act. Swan and Caleb have been killed, and the log cabin is in shambles. Ironically, Jeremiah's sacrifice of his family and of his wilderness ideals may have been pointless, for he left the search party before they reached the stranded settlers. The film does not reveal whether the rescue was effected.

The death of his family and his perception of his responsibility for their destruction stem Jeremiah's regression toward the values of society. Like a wilderness savage, he seeks out the killers, engaging in ruthless retaliation. In one especially revealing scene, he bursts into a hunting party's encampment, kills all but one of the hunters, and lies to rest among the corpses, sated with revenge for the moment. Isolating himself more and more from his fellow humans, Jeremiah expiates his guilt and obliterates his sense of society in the blood of the Indians. Moreover, his pursuit of them converts him into a fugitive himself. The Crow deem it a major accomplishment to slay their nemesis and have surrounded a grave they have prepared for him with ritual paraphernalia.

As the film concludes, Jeremiah again meets Bear Claw. Now they are virtual peers, for his destruction of the Indians in many ways recalls the older man's ongoing battle with the grizzlies from whom he has taken his sobriquet. Interestingly, these mountain men are depleting the wilderness of two of its natural resources, Indians and bear. Yet Jeremiah's participation in that depletion ceases when he encounters Paints His Shirt Red, the Crow who had witnessed his bumbling initiation. Now the two salute each other; they recognize each other as equally adept in the ways of the wilderness. The film ends as it began with Jeremiah at the beginning of another journey. Now, however, he is at peace with himself, heading deeper into the wilderness that is his home.

Critical response to *Jeremiah Johnson* was mixed. Some critics objected to the casting of Redford in the title role, implying that his acting lacked sufficient variety and depth. Others, however, praised the involvement of the landscape in the development of plot and theme. Some reviewers also suggested that the film broke new ground in portraying a character unlike those in most Westerns. Jeremiah represents a relatively conventional figure in American popular culture, however, through his desire to escape from confining civilization and through his status as initiate. A film which depicted a fully developed mountain man such as Bear Claw, Del Gue, or the mature Jeremiah as its protagonist would have more claim to being innovative. Despite its conventionality, *Jeremiah Johnson* possesses several positive qualities: the effective presentation of the landscape, the complexity of the protagonist's development, and the generally sympathetic portrayal of the Indians. A more innovative film, however, would be the sequel to this one, which might depict Jeremiah as a completely mature mountain man.

Frances M. Malpezzi
William M. Clements

JESSE JAMES

Released: 1939
Production: Darryl F. Zanuck for Twentieth Century-Fox
Direction: Henry King
Screenplay: Nunnally Johnson
Cinematography: George Barnes
Editing: Barbara McLean
Running time: 105 minutes

Principal characters:
Jesse James	Tyrone Power
Frank James	Henry Fonda
Zerelda "Zee" Cobb	Nancy Kelly
Marshall Will Wright	Randolph Scott
Major Rufus Cobb	Henry Hull
Runyon	J. Edward Bromberg
Barshee	Brian Donlevy
Bob Ford	John Carradine
McCoy	Donald Meek
Mrs. Samuels	Jane Darwell

When, in 1967, *Bonnie and Clyde* became a cinema sensation, many critics moralized that Hollywood had reached a new low by glamorizing murdering misfits. Of course, Hollywood had been doing so for decades (if not quite so wantonly), particularly in the genre of the Western in which such ruthless outlaws as Billy the Kid, the Dalton Brothers, and Butch Cassidy had been metamorphosed into glamorous heroes by studio script departments and matinee idols such as Robert Taylor. No desperado has been so frequently cosmeticized as Jesse Woodson James, who had joined Will Quantrell's infamous Civil War guerrilla gang at age fifteen, formed his own marauders at twenty, and terrorized the railroads and banks of five states until he died from an assassin's bullet at thirty-five. Yet only one film saga of his life has attained classic status, Twentieth Century-Fox's *Jesse James*, an exciting Technicolor melodrama that became the studio's top box-office hit of 1939 and is vividly remembered as one of the screen's greatest Westerns.

Darryl F. Zanuck initially opposed a production about Jesse James, believing it would only contain regional appeal in the South. Henry King, who had directed such Fox triumphs as *Lloyds of London* (1936), *In Old Chicago* (1938), and *Alexander's Ragtime Band* (1938), convinced him otherwise, however, and Zanuck insured the project's success with a budget of two million dollars, a large amount for 1939. The producer approved location shooting in the Ozarks, where King flew his plane over miles of countryside to find a proper locale after it was ascertained that Liberty, the James brothers' hometown, had become "too civilized" over the years. King chose Pineville, Missouri, where false fronts covered the modern stores, dirt covered the concrete streets, and townspeople were recruited as extras. It was there that the company, including the studio's top male star, Tyrone Power, in the title spot, assembled, lodging in houses rented by the studio. With a script by Nunnally Johnson which took great pains to build sympathy for Jesse, shooting began in Pineville in the summer of 1938.

Jesse James opens brutally. The real villain of the film is the St. Louis Midland Railroad, as represented by evil agent Barshee (Brian Donlevy). Out to snare the farmers' land for the railroad at the cutthroat price of one dollar per acre, Barshee gleefully bullies the farmers. We see him punch a teenage boy and then turn him over to his men for further punishment in order to accelerate the boy's hysterical mother into signing over her farm. Things are less simple at the James farm. The James boys' mother, Mrs. Samuels (Jane Darwell), refuses to sign; Frank James (Henry Fonda) punches Barshee; Barshee tries to decapitate Frank with a sickle, and Jesse (Tyrone Power) shoots Barshee in the hand. That evening, after the James boys take refuge in a cave, Barshee returns to the farm with a bomb and blows up the homestead—and Mrs. Samuels. Informed of the atrocity, Jesse enters the town saloon, guns down the cringing Barshee, and vows bloody vengeance against the St. Louis Midland Railroad. Hence, fifteen minutes into the film, audience sympathy for Jesse (whose Quantrell exploits are totally ignored) is assured.

Jesse soon becomes a folk hero, a delight to newspaper publisher Major Rufus Cobb (Henry Hull), whose editorial philosophy is simple: "If we are ever to have law and order in the West, the first thing we gotta do, is take all the lawyers and shoot 'em down like dogs!" Jesse's exploits are a nightmare for his sweetheart, Zee (Nancy Kelly), however; she warns him that "Shooting and robbing—it'll get in your blood, Jesse, you'll get like a wolf!" She promises to marry Jesse if he agrees to give himself up to United States Marshall Will Wright (Randolph Scott), Zee's unsuccessful suitor, who has been promised by the Railroad that it will prosecute Jesse gently if he surrenders. Jesse reluctantly agrees, and after he and Zee marry, he gives himself up. Once Jesse is in jail, however, Railroad president McCoy (Donald Meek) refuses to honor the bargain. "By the Almighty, he is going to hang!" announces McCoy. "Suppose Jesse don't *want* to be hanged?" asks Wright, and predictably, at midnight, Frank and the gang manage to free Jesse from jail, although not before Jesse makes the quivering McCoy literally eat his promise.

As the bitter Jesse's criminal career becomes increasingly wild and reckless, his marriage suffers; he is away when his baby boy is born, and the heartbroken Zee, tended to by the loyal Wright, moves back with her Uncle Rufus. Meanwhile, the governor offers amnesty and a reward to any member of the James gang who will assassinate the leader, and Pinkerton Detective Runyon (J.

Edward Bromberg) contacts Bob Ford (John Carradine) as a likely traitor. Ford agrees and informs Runyon of Jesse's plans to rob the First National Bank at Northfield, Minnesota. In a thrilling sequence, the James gang is blasted at Northfield, and a wild chase ensues after Frank and the wounded Jesse. In one of action cinema's most famous sequences, Frank propels Jesse's horse and rides his own horse over a towering cliff and into the river below (a stunt that inspired awed applause from audiences but unfortunately killed a horse). Frank escapes and is presumed drowned; Jesse makes his way back to his home where the loyal Zee and her son have set up watch for him.

Jesse, promising Zee he has forsaken crime forever, makes plans to move his family to California. On the day of their departure, however, Bob Ford and his brother Charlie (Charles Tannen) appear. Bob tries to lure Jesse out into the open by concocting a holdup trap; when the reformed Jesse refuses, the cowardly, perspiring Bob, his arm trembling, shoots Jesse in the back as the outlaw removes a "God Bless Our Home" sampler from the wall. At Jesse's funeral, as Zee and Marshall Wright listen, Major Cobb eulogizes Jesse: "Jesse was an outlaw, a bandit, a criminal. Even those that loved him ain't got no answer for that. But we *ain't* ashamed of him . . . I don't think even America is ashamed of Jesse James. . . ." Cobb unveils and reads the famous words of the grave marker: "In Loving Remembrance—Jesse W. James. . . . Murdered by a traitor and coward whose name is not worthy to appear here."

"About the only connection the film had with fact," said Miss Jo Frances James, a descendant of the outlaw, "was that there was once a man named James and he did ride a horse." Nevertheless, upon release on January 13, 1939, *Jesse James* was a box-office sensation. *The New York Times* praised the film as "Handsomely produced by Messrs. Darryl Zanuck and Nunnally Johnson, stirringly directed by Henry King, beautifully acted by its cast . . . an authentic American panorama." Many critics wailed that Power, who was at the peak of his considerable good looks, was miscast as Jesse, yet his performance won him new legions of fans, and *Jesse James* was largely responsible for his climbing from tenth place in the 1938 box-office polls to second place in 1939. The film was a special triumph for Fonda, whom Zanuck had labeled "a lousy actor" and was only cast at King's insistence. Kelly, who brought a dramatic intensity rare indeed in Western heroines, also excelled, although she never became a major star. There was glory for all the players, even though Carradine's portrayal of Bob Ford brought him perennial antipathy and typed him as a villain. Not long after *Jesse James*'s release, Carradine rode in a Hollywood parade and was booed and pelted with trash for two miles by "fans," many of whom squealed, "There's that sneak who shot Jesse James!"

The enormous success of *Jesse James* spawned a sequel, Fox's *The Return of Frank James* (1940). Directed by Fritz Lang, it featured role reprises by

Fonda, Hull, Carradine, Bromberg, Tannen, Ernest Whitman (as the James family's black laborer Pinky), and George Chandler (as Roy, Major Cobb's typesetter). The plot found Frank James out for vengeance against the Ford boys, but, due to censorship problems, he was not allowed to kill them. Charley fell from a cliff and Bob died from a bullet fired by Frank's sidekick Clem (Jackie Cooper). The script did allow Frank to terrorize both villains in crowd-pleasing fashion, however, and the finale found him exonerated of his crimes and free to start a new life.

In 1957, Fox released a remake of the saga entitled *The True Story of Jesse James*, starring Robert Wagner, Jeffrey Hunter, and Hope Lange as Jesse, Frank, and Zee, respectively. The only player retained from the 1939 version was Carradine, who here plays a preacher who baptizes Jesse. The film also contained the horse leap sequence from the original film. The film failed to match its predecessor, as have such other Jesse James movies as *I Shot Jesse James* (with Reed Hadley, 1948), *Kansas Raiders* (with Audie Murphy, 1950), *The Great Missouri Raid* (with MacDonald Carey, 1951), and *The Great Northfield, Minnesota Raid* (with Robert Duvall, 1972).

For all the glamorizing and distortions, the 1939 *Jesse James* remains the definitive saga of Jesse—melodramatic enough to build up sympathy for his adventures and honest enough to hammer home the crime-does-not-pay theme that makes the film a true tragedy. Indeed, in Pineville, Missouri, today, the locations where the stars played their roles are considered to be virtual shrines, still visited by pilgrims who have thrilled to *Jesse James* on their local late show.

Gregory William Mank

JESUS CHRIST SUPERSTAR

Released: 1973
Production: Norman Jewison and Robert Stigwood for Universal
Direction: Norman Jewison
Screenplay: Norman Jewison and Melvyn Bragg; based on the rock opera of
   the same name by Tim Rice and Andrew Lloyd Webber
Cinematography: Douglas Slocombe
Editing: Antony Gibbs
Music: Andrew Lloyd Webber
Running time: 108 minutes

> *Principal characters:*
> Jesus Christ .... Ted Neeley
> Judas Iscariot .... Carl Anderson
> Mary Magdalene .... Yvonne Elliman
> Pontius Pilate .... Barry Dennen
> Caiaphas .... Bob Bingham
> Simon Zealotes .... Larry T. Marshall
> King Herod .... Joshua Mostel
> Annas .... Kurt Yaghjian
> Peter .... Philip Toubus

In concept and presentation, *Jesus Christ Superstar*, which is based on a popular rock opera, defies the conventional telling of the Christ story. With its all-musical delivery resulting in the absence of dialogue, as well as in its story line's bizarre merging of ancient and contemporary strains, *Jesus Christ Superstar* ranks as perhaps the most innovative work about Jesus Christ ever made. It is also one of the most controversial.

The controversy is based on implications of the plot as perceived by some religious leaders and groups, who feel that the film suggests that Jews are collectively guilty of the death of Jesus. As a result, at the time of its release, *Jesus Christ Superstar* was embroiled in dispute. The $3.5 million production was condemned by the National Jewish Community Relations Advisory Council, which represents nearly every major Jewish organization in the United States. Calling the film a "catastrophe" to Christian-Jewish relations, the Council also singled out the film as a "singularly damaging setback in the struggle against the religious sources of anti-Semitism." The Israeli government also disassociated itself from the production, although the film had been made on location in Israel during a fourteen-week shooting period. Still other religious leaders approved of the film, as did many denizens of the so-called Jesus Movement, which was very active at the time of initial release.

The mixed reactions to the film—from critics as well as religious leaders—is in keeping with the history of the decidedly unique work. *Jesus Christ*

Superstar originated as a rock opera that was first released as a record in October, 1970. It later took the shape of a stage production in some sixteen countries, and of a concert attraction in America, where it has toured with regularity since July of 1971. Additionally, the production has been a rich source of recording material for singers and musicians—there have been more than fifty recorded versions of "I Don't Know How to Love Him" alone. Since its inception and throughout its evolution, *Jesus Christ Superstar* has generated discussion because of its very contemporary depiction of the last seven days of Christ's life.

The film's story line is certainly familiar, but the delivery is not. *Jesus Christ Superstar* opens against a panoramic landscape, as the camera moves across scaffolding that serves as a kind of stylized set and, finally, to a bus in the distance. The bus draws near, and stops. The passengers pile out, carrying props and the costumes they will don; thus *Jesus Christ Superstar* is presented as a play-within-a-play. Once the performers have put on their costumes, they prepare for the production.

The story itself opens with a segment involving Judas (black actor Carl Anderson), who is perched high atop a rocky landscape. After a series of zooms (with the camera in a slightly closer position with each zoom), the camera moves in for Judas's lament to Christ that "Your followers are blind—too much heaven on their minds." Jesus Christ (Ted Neeley), meanwhile, is with his followers, who clamor for his words with their question, "What's the buzz? Tell me what's happening?" As Jesus responds, Mary Magdalene (Yvonne Elliman) moves in to place dampened cloths on his brow, thus refreshing him from the desert heat. When Judas intercedes ("It seems to me a strange thing, mystifying, that a man like you can waste his time on women of her kind."), Jesus defends Mary and warns Judas and the others to curb their anger.

The High Priests, led by Caiaphas (Bob Bingham), are unable to control their concerns, for they are hearing too much about the man who is called King of the Jews. Assembled on the scaffolding, Caiaphas and the priests determine "This Jesus must die." The scene is marked by low camera angles which give a distorted view of the priests, who appear all the more ominous because they are attired in black flowing robes and strangely shaped hats. They watch in disapproving silence as Jesus and his followers make their way toward Jerusalem. The entry is marked by a celebration, which includes raised palm fronds and the song, "Hosanna." Jesus appears to have a premonition of what is to come, for when followers ask, "J. C., J. C., won't you die for me?" there is a brief freeze frame on his introspective face.

Led by Simon Zealotes (Larry T. Marshall), the followers then perform a frenzied dance of jubilation. It is an invigorating sequence marked by excessive use of freeze frames and slow motion. Camera trickery also has dancers appearing on the landscape seemingly out of nowhere. The celebration of love is contrasted by a brief glimpse of Pontius Pilate (Barry Dennen), who is troubled because he will have to deal with Jesus.

Jesus vents his own angers when he visits the temple that has been taken over by "money-lenders." This sequence may best exemplify the production's merging of modernism with antiquity, for temple racks are filled with products ranging from color postcards to machine guns. Dancing girls in evocative dress and poses taunt the buyers, the better to peddle their wares. After tipping over racks and turning on the crowd in a screaming rage, Jesus next finds himself in the midst of a leper colony, where the disfigured come at him in droves, begging to be healed. Jesus' shrieks drown out their cries.

That night, as an exhausted Jesus sleeps, Mary Magdalene questions her feelings for him in the song "I Don't Know How to Love Him." The scene contains exceptionally beautiful and intricately conceived photography. As it begins, Mary is in silhouette, walking against an orange-gold background, but as she passes a burning fire, there is a reversal, with the firelight casting an orange-glow on Mary's face against a black background. The betrayal by Judas follows, with Judas accepting gold from Caiaphas and the priest Annas (Kurt Yaghjian) in exchange for information about Jesus. Judas's actions are heightened by richly textured vistas of the desert, with its tranquillity shattered by the sudden appearance of modern jet fighters and tanks.

The Last Supper is reenacted in an outdoor, picnic setting. Afterward, Jesus reveals his own fears when he questions why he must die. His words are accompanied by a montage sequence that show's Christ's death as depicted by various works of art. The arrest of Jesus causes some supporters to turn away and to turn against him. Led by procession to Pilate, and later to King Herod (Joshua Mostel), Jesus is hounded by the crowd, many of whom ask jeering questions, with their hands held up to indicate the presence of microphones (giving the scene the look of a modern-day press conference). The encounter with Herod is particularly strange, with Herod, wearing Bermuda shorts, and his court lounging about on a raft in the Dead Sea. In challenging Jesus, Herod taunts, "Prove to me that you're no fool—walk across my swimming pool." Following a trial before Pilate (with Pilate washing his hands in what looks like a large glass salad bowl), Jesus is carried to the cross and crucified.

Judas hangs himself, but following the crucifixion, he reappears in a white fringed outfit for the film's rousing finale, "Jesus Christ Superstar." Performed amid temple ruins, the selection includes a host of heavenly singers, also wearing white fringe, who provide the chorus. When the number comes to a close, the viewer is reminded of the play-within-a-play format as the performers, more subdued than when first seen, reboard their bus. Neeley, who portrays Christ, is not among them. The film comes to a dramatic close with a glimpse of the cross against a burning sun. The figure of a single shepherd can also be seen against the darkened landscape.

Prior to establishing a reputation as the director of socially conscious films such as *In the Heat of the Night* (1967), Norman Jewison established himself as a television director and as the producer of eight Judy Garland television programs. Jewison, who also worked with performers such as Harry Belafonte and Danny Kaye, went on to direct the opulent *Fiddler on the Roof* (1971). It was during the filming of that spectacular musical that he first heard of, and committed himself to, the *Jesus Christ Superstar* project. Today it remains the most intriguing work of his diverse filmography.

In its initial release, and in subsequent rereleases, the film has become a major box-office hit. Sadly ignored by the film industry (only the musical score, conducted by Andre Previn, was Oscar-nominated), critics of the day gave the film only a tepid acceptance. Many complained about Neeley's performance as a shrieking and very human Jesus Christ, while others questioned the casting of a black man as Judas.

Pat H. Broeske

JOHNNY BELINDA

Released: 1948
Production: Jerry Wald for Warner Bros.
Direction: Jean Negulesco
Screenplay: Irmgard Von Cube and Allen Vincent; based on the play of the same name by Elmer Harris
Cinematography: Ted McCord
Editing: David Weisbart
Music: Max Steiner
Art direction: Robert Haas
Running time: 102 minutes

Principal characters:
Belinda McDonald	Jane Wyman (AA)
Dr. Robert Richardson	Lew Ayres
Black McDonald	Charles Bickford
Aggie McDonald	Agnes Moorehead
Locky McCormick	Stephen McNally
Stella McCormick	Jan Sterling
Mrs. Poggety	Rosalind Ivan
Pacquet	Dan Seymour

Johnny Belinda has a curious history. Jack Warner, head of Warner Bros. studio, for which it was made, disliked the film so much that he fired the director, Jean Negulesco, and shelved the movie. When it was finally released, Jane Wyman, the star, made Warner take out a trade advertisement apologizing to the cast and crew. Despite its forbidding subject matter, the film was a huge success and garnered raves from all the critics. Bosley Crowther of *The New York Times* called Wyman "sensitive and poignant," and Otis L. Guernsey, Jr., of *The New York Herald Tribune* said that her performance "is full of emotion . . . as genuine as pure gold."

Belinda McDonald (Jane Wyman), who is deaf and dumb, lives with her father, Black McDonald (Charles Bickford) and his sister Aggie (Agnes Moorehead) outside a small fishing village in Nova Scotia. While attending the birth of a calf, the local doctor, Robert Richardson (Lew Ayres), becomes interested in the girl, who works like a slave grinding grain and tending to the cattle on her father's farm. He teaches her sign language and lip reading and she begins to take an interest in learning more. After a village dance at which he gets drunk, Locky McCormick (Stephen McNally), one of the men who brings his grain to the McDonald mill, rapes Belinda. When Richardson takes Belinda to a specialist to find out more precisely how disabled she is, the doctor discovers she is pregnant. The baby, Johnny Belinda, is born with normal hearing. The villagers shun the McDonalds and refuse to bring their grain to the mill or to extend credit. Believing Richardson is the father, they also ostracize him and force him to look for a job elsewhere. Richardson realizes Belinda loves him and writes from Toronto that he will be sending for her and the baby soon.

When Locky brings grain to the mill, he sees the baby and comments, "You're the spittin' image of your father." When Black realizes that the child is his, he fights with Locky, who pushes him over the edge of a cliff, killing him. The townspeople convene and decide Johnny Belinda should be taken from his mother and aunt and given to a young couple. Locky and Stella (Jan Sterling) have just married, and when they drive out to the farm to get the child, Belinda protests, and Stella finds she does not have the heart to take the baby from her. When Locky admits he is the father and tries to force Belinda to surrender Johnny, she shoots him. During the trial which follows, Stella admits that Locky was the father, thus exonerating Belinda. Richardson, who has returned for the trial, takes Belinda and her baby back to the McDonald farm.

Johnny Belinda is not only an incisive picture of life on the rugged coast of Nova Scotia, it is also a perceptive dissection of a small town. Although not much time is spent detailing this aspect, a sharp indictment of the petty bigotry and hypocrisy endemic to most such villages emerges within the framework of Negulesco's melodrama. The director concentrates on the minutiae of rural existence—the long hours, the poverty, and drudgery—in contrast to which Richardson's sympathy and concern are a welcome change. Richardson opens a new world to Belinda; no longer "the dummy" as everyone unthinkingly calls her, she can communicate. Whereas previously she dressed in tatters, Belinda begins to take pride in her appearance, washing her face and wearing clean clothes.

Wyman is a pretty woman, but not a beauty, and she sensibly eschewed makeup, allowing the inner beauty of Belinda to shine through in her radiant expression. Her hair is roughly cut, her eyebrows are unplucked, and her dresses are ill-fitting, but when she taps her feet in time to a fiddler's music, her face is suffused with warmth and yearning. Wyman studied hard for this role, working with deaf mutes, learning sign language, and using earplugs to shut out sound during the filming, and she gives an affecting, understated performance. She never says a word, but with her wide-eyed innocence and shy smiles, she does not need speech.

Wyman had several Hollywood careers. She was a starlet, a "B"-picture star, glamour queen, brash blonde, second lead, and comedienne, and then, in the mid-1940's, she emerged as an actress of limited but undeniable gifts. She was Ray Milland's girl in *The Lost Weekend* (1945) and Gregory Peck's wife in *The Yearling* (1946), and she played opposite James Stewart in *Magic Town* (1947). Wyman won an Academy Award for *Johnny Belinda*, made a few more noteworthy films such as *Stage Fright* (1950), *The Glass Menagerie*

(1950), and *The Blue Veil* (1951), and even sang with Bing Crosby in *Here Comes the Groom* (1951); then, as quickly as her star had risen, it descended. She then did a few soap operas, had her own television series, and finally settled into semiretirement, emerging only for a few Disney films and her most recent movie, the Bob Hope comedy *How to Commit Marriage* (1969).

Ayres was the first Dr. Kildare; he had several good roles in the 1930's, most notably as the young German soldier in *All Quiet on the Western Front* (1930) and as Katharine Hepburn's drunken brother in *Holiday* (1938). The rest of his career was a disappointment. He took time out from films during World War II to do alternate service as a conscientious objector, but it was an unpopular stance. His films were boycotted, and when he returned to the screen, he was going gray and wore a mustache. In *The Dark Mirror* (1946) as in *Johnny Belinda*, he is a kindly, almost middle-aged man who takes an avuncular, sexless interest in the heroines. As Dr. Richardson he is concerned and patient; in fact, he almost exudes too much small-town saintliness, but he is quietly impressive, a convincing bedrock for the farm family to depend upon.

Bickford gives another kindly, gruff performance in a gallery of similar roles. Moorehead is yet again a spinster, this time somewhat less neurotic and strident than before, employing an effective Scots accent. Sterling makes a notable screen debut, toning down her doxie mannerisms and Brooklyn accent to render Stella as a sympathetic, if sluttish, village girl. McNally is rough and surly; it is unfortunate he is only allowed to play Locky as a villain. The role needs more than one dimension, but scriptwriters Irmgard Von Cube and Allen Vincent have not bothered to round it out.

The locales have a life of their own. Cinematographer Ted McCord had to substitute northern California for Nova Scotia, but he did a thoroughly convincing job of it, creating a rocky, bleak ambience from which the fisherfolk and the McDonalds cudgel an existence. The interiors, however, are his greatest achievement. McCord shoots them in high contrast with deep shadows, the light barely shining on the sparse decor, the homemade essentials of the cheerless farm. As Bickford waits for the birth of his grandchild, he is sunk in gloom, a distant light picking out the tears shining in his eyes. When he is laid out in the living room and the village men gather around the corpse, Wyman signs the Lord's Prayer. McCord keeps a key light on Wyman's face, while the others are scarcely illuminated at all, being rather a collection of lined, coarse countenances remarkable only for the manner in which they are moved by Wyman's unadorned piety.

For the most part, the film avoids pathos; Negulesco shoots the rape with commendable restraint, the light on Wyman's face, and her frightened eyes are the only sign of the enormity of what she is experiencing. Wyman's life is so brutalized anyway that, although she regresses briefly into her former slovenly state, the rape is just one more cruel event among many. Negulesco plays down both this and McNally's death, an occurence he does not even show directly. He prefers to concentrate on the homely details of farm life, the animals, bread-baking, and plowing. Most of all, however, he focuses on Wyman's growing awareness of her world, learning to write, to count, or to care for her child. Shut away from all but the most rudimentary civilization for so long, Wyman's blossoming capacities, her understanding of the variety and richness of life, is, as Bickford says, "like a miracle." Under the patient tutelage of Ayres, Wyman becomes a mature woman, not just a girl who stops wearing rags and puts on a flowered dress, but a responsible adult capable of loving a man, of killing to defend her child, and of taking her place in a society more complex and diverse than the one that has sheltered her for most of her life.

Judith M. Kass

JOHNNY EAGER

Released: 1941
Production: John W. Considine, Jr., for Metro-Goldwyn-Mayer
Direction: Mervyn LeRoy
Screenplay: John Lee Mahin and James Edward Grant; based on an original
  story by James Edward Grant
Cinematography: Harold Rosson
Editing: Albert Akst
Running time: 107 minutes

Principal characters:
Johnny Eager	Robert Taylor
Lisbeth Bard	Lana Turner
John Benson Farrell	Edward Arnold
Jeff Hartnett	Van Heflin (AA)
Mr. Verne	Henry O'Neill
Judy Sanford	Diana Lewis
Marco	Charles Dingle
Miss Mines	Leona Maricle
Peg Fowler	Connie Gilchrist
Mathilda	Robin Raymond
Jimmy Courtney	Robert Sterling
Floyd	Cliff Danielson
Tony	Nestor Paiva
Julio	Paul Stewart
Halligan	Cy Kendall
Lew Rankin	Barry Nelson
Policeman	Byron Shores

Johnny Eager is a gangster film, but it is also a film about ambition, obsession, love, and friendship. Although it is not a deep film, it does explore these themes in a tightly written script that is well-served by the star performances of Robert Taylor and Lana Turner as well as by the Academy Award-winning portrayal by Van Heflin in an important supporting role. The exposition is skillfully and quickly managed by the writers, John Lee Mahin and James Edward Grant, and the director, Mervyn LeRoy. Indeed, LeRoy's fine sense of pacing is evident throughout.

In the first sequence we meet Johnny Eager (Robert Taylor) and learn that he has served time in jail but is now out on parole. Working as a humble taxicab driver, living with his cousin, and reporting to his parole officer, Mr. Verne (Henry O'Neill), once a month, he is the ideal reformed criminal. Verne tells him that he wishes all his "boys" were as levelheaded as Johnny. Next, we are introduced to Lisbeth Bard (Lana Turner). She and her friend Judy Sanford (Diana Lewis) are upper-class young women taking a sociology class to see "how the other half lives." They are waiting outside Verne's office when Johnny leaves, and both stare at him with undisguised interest. When the two talk with Verne about Johnny, Lisbeth remarks that he looks too ambitious to be content as a cab driver, but Verne assures her that Johnny can be believed.

Next, however, we meet the real Johnny Eager. After he leaves Verne's office, he drives his cab to the Algonquin Park dog racing track where he has a luxurious suite and a large closet full of fine clothes. He changes his coat and tie and reveals his true self: he is the boss of a criminal gang that controls most of the gambling in the city. Using Marco (Charles Dingle) as his front and making payoffs to politicians, he is now trying to get city permission to open the dog track for business.

Then Verne's secretary, Miss Mines (Leona Maricle), who seemed to detest him when he was in the office, telephones to warn him that Verne is going to make a surprise visit to his supposed residence; so Johnny has to change back into his cab driver's clothes and go to a small apartment where his cousin Peg Fowler (Connie Gilchrist) and her daughter Mathilda (Robin Raymond) live. Peg is old enough to be Johnny's mother, and Mathilda is in high school. Johnny supports them so that he will have a residence acceptable to the parole officer. Judy has persuaded Lisbeth to accompany her and Verne on this visit to Johnny because it will be "exciting." It turns out to be more exciting for Lisbeth than for Judy, however, because during the perfunctory small talk of the visit she becomes quite intrigued with him, and he with her. Although neither realizes it, that meeting is the beginning of a relationship that is obsessive for Lisbeth and ambivalent for Johnny. It nearly destroys Lisbeth, and it causes Johnny's death, but on this afternoon it goes no further than Lisbeth's attempt to explain *Cyrano de Bergerac* to Johnny.

After Verne leaves with the young women, Mathilda remarks to Johnny, "That Miss Bard, anytime you want to whistle, she'll come running." Indeed, at that moment Lisbeth is discussing him with Judy. She is obviously fascinated with this man so different from anyone she has ever known; she says that she thinks he would beat a woman if she made him angry. Judy, on the other hand, has seen enough of how the other half lives. "There's a limit to this sociology business," she tells Lisbeth. Lisbeth, however, finds that there is now a limit to her tolerance of her upper-class friends and her too conventional fiancé, Jimmy Courtney (Robert Sterling). Instead of going to the art museum dinner with Jimmy that evening, she goes out with his alcoholic friend, Floyd (Cliff Danielson). That decision leads to her meeting Johnny again, for Floyd takes her to a drinking and gambling club, gets drunk, and disappears, leaving Lisbeth with a bill for eighty-five dollars. Lisbeth is in the office of the manager of the club, Tony (Nestor Paiva), trying to explain that Floyd will send him a check the next day when Johnny bursts in demanding an explanation of why Tony has been withholding money from him.

Johnny does not notice Lisbeth until he has finished his business with Tony. When he does notice her, he tries to explain his presence, but she looks at him intensely and says that she has no intention of reporting him. He offers to take her home, but once they are in his car, Johnny says, "You don't want me to take you home, and you know it." She replies, "Of course I don't," and soon they are locked in an embrace that will lead to the undoing of both.

When Johnny finally does take Lisbeth home that night, he finds waiting for her both Jimmy and Lisbeth's stepfather, John Benson Farrell (Edward Arnold). Farrell had helped send Johnny to jail and is now the city prosecutor so that he can help rid the city of "vermin" like Johnny. Jimmy merely warns Lisbeth that she will be hurt, but Farrell takes stronger action. After Johnny leaves, he tells his daughter never to see him again, and the next day he tells Johnny to have no contact with Lisbeth. Farrell says that he is an honest man, but he would go so far as to have Johnny framed on a false charge to keep him away from his daughter. All his efforts are in vain, however, for the next time we see Lisbeth she is in Johnny's luxurious suite.

Meanwhile we have met Jeff Hartnett (Van Heflin), an alcoholic intellectual who is Johnny's sidekick and only true friend. Jeff calls himself Johnny's "Boswell" in a reference to James Boswell, the eighteenth century biographer of Samuel Johnson. Because Jeff's mind is so different from those of his other associates, Johnny apparently feels that he can trust Jeff as he can trust no one else. The other gangsters simply dismiss Jeff as being "full of gin and big words," and even Johnny can get irritated with his continual analysis.

Jeff not only calls himself Johnny's Boswell but also makes frequent allusions to literature, history, and art. Some are offhand and appropriate; others are forced witticisms. For example, when Johnny knocks Tony down, Jeff remarks, "Michelangelo did his best work on his back." Jeff is, of course, dependent upon Johnny for his financial support and does feel a certain comradeship with and loyalty to him despite his unpleasant line of work. The virtue of Heflin's portrayal of Jeff is that he conveys the character's ambivalence about Johnny as well as his contempt for himself for being the alcoholic dependent of a gangster. Heflin also makes Jeff's intellectualism credible; too many actors playing intellectuals are too obviously reciting lines on subjects about which they have no knowledge. Heflin's Oscar for Best Supporting Actor was well-deserved.

After their first embrace, Lisbeth's feeling for Johnny is total devotion no matter what happens, but Johnny's feelings for her are more complex. Although he wants to believe that all women are alike and that none is special to him, occasionally he has to admit that Lisbeth might be an exception. His feelings for the young woman do not stop him, however, when he sees that he can use her.

When he is alone with Lisbeth, one of his henchmen, Julio (Paul Stewart), bursts into the room and attacks Johnny. In the ensuing struggle Johnny yells for Lisbeth to pick up a loose gun. She picks it up and shoots Julio. Immediately she wants to call for help, but Johnny tells her Julio is dying and she must leave quickly to keep from being charged with murder. Lisbeth is devastated by what she has done, but she is so concerned that Johnny's parole might be revoked that she agrees to do what he says. Then we find that the whole attack was an act; the gun held blanks and Julio is not even wounded. The reason for the act becomes clear a few scenes later when Johnny summons Farrell to his suite and tells him that Lisbeth has killed a man and that he (Johnny) is covering for her. Then he tells Farrell to arrange to have the injunction lifted so that his dog racing track can open. Farrell has no choice but to agree.

The whole episode, however, gives Johnny many puzzling moments. First, he finds himself feeling bad about what he has done to Lisbeth. Then, five days later, Jimmy comes to him to say that Lisbeth is in "frightful shape" and that for her sake he will give Johnny six hundred thousand dollars if he will take Lisbeth and leave town. After Jimmy leaves, Johnny asks Jeff, "What's the angle?" He cannot understand such behavior. Jeff says that no one could explain it to Johnny because it is unselfish. This remark enrages Johnny so much that he slugs Jeff. That blow is, for a few minutes, too much for Jeff to take. He says, "That broke it," and leaves. He is soon back, however, telling Johnny that he was going to tell all he knew and then kill himself, but he could not do it.

Finally, Johnny does feel that he should do something for Lisbeth, so he goes to see her and tells her that Julio was not killed, that it was a frame-up; but Lisbeth will not believe him and thinks that he is only telling her this "wonderful lie" so that she will not worry. She tells Johnny that she cannot live knowing what she has done without telling anyone but that she will wait a year until his parole is over and then confess to the police.

Johnny cannot understand her feelings, but he realizes that the only way he can help her is to show her Julio alive and well. It is here that a subplot which has been developing throughout the film intersects with the main plot. Halligan (Cy Kendall) has been trying to take over some of Johnny's men and some of his income. When an old friend of Johnny, Lew Rankin (Barry Nelson), defected to Halligan, Johnny killed him and made the death appear to be an automobile accident. Then, by the time Johnny wants to show Julio to Lisbeth, Julio has also defected. Johnny therefore has to endanger himself to accomplish his task.

Although he thinks he is a sucker to do so, he arranges for Jimmy to be there to take Lisbeth away after she sees Julio. Then he finds Julio alone on the street and takes him at gunpoint to the car where Lisbeth and Jimmy are waiting. She sees Julio and believes that she did not kill him, but now she cannot accept what Johnny has told her—that he is through with her. As she argues with him, Julio escapes. Because Johnny knows Halligan and his gang will soon be there, he hits Lisbeth and knocks her out when she will not get back in the car. Then he tells Jimmy to take her away and not to tell her about the tears falling down his cheeks. Then Halligan, Julio, and another of Halligan's men come after Johnny, and a fierce gun battle erupts. Johnny kills all three, but a policeman (Byron Shores) mortally wounds Johnny. Jeff arrives just in time for Johnny to die in his arms. Tearfully, Jeff says, "This guy could have climbed the highest mountain in the world if he'd just started up the right one."

At the time *Johnny Eager* was released, most of the interest in it was focused upon the romantic pairing of Turner and Taylor. Their fans were not disappointed, although the scene in which Taylor hits Turner in the face was a shock to most 1940's film viewers. Indeed, the film was reissued by M-G-M in 1949 and one of the love scenes was used in a later M-G-M film, *Watch the Birdie* (1950), in which Red Skelton studies the amorous techniques of movie stars by watching films. As has been noted, the Motion Picture Academy members rewarded Heflin's performance with an Oscar. Today, one can see beyond these three roles and note that virtually every part is superbly played and that the direction by LeRoy is particularly effective and well-paced without being showy or distracting.

Timothy W. Johnson

JOURNEY'S END

Released: 1930
Production: George Pearson for Gainsborough/Welsh-Pearson/Tiffany
Direction: James Whale
Screenplay: Joseph Moncure March and V. Gareth Gundrey; based on the
   play of the same name by R. C. Sherriff
Cinematography: Ben Kline
Editing: Claude Berkeley
Running time: 120 minutes

Principal characters:
Captain Denis Stanhope	Colin Clive
Lieutenant Osborne	Ian MacLaren
Second Lieutenant Raleigh	David Manners
Second Lieutenant Trotter	Billy Beven
Second Lieutenant Hibbert	Anthony Bushell
Captain Hardy	Robert Adair
Private Mason	Charles Gerrard
Sergeant Major	Tom Whiteley
Colonel	Jack Pitcairn
German Prisoner	Warner Klinger

Aside from being an impressive motion picture in its own right, *Journey's End* holds an important place in the history of the cinema. It was the first British-American talkie coproduction, albeit between a minor American studio, Tiffany, a minor British company, Welsh-Pearson, and a major British producer, Michael Balcon's Gainsborough Pictures. Although James Whale had worked as dialogue director on *Hell's Angels* (1930), *Journey's End* marked his first solo directorial effort and helped him on the road to being one of Hollywood's most stylish directors of the 1930's. In addition, *Journey's End* made movie stars of its two leading men, Colin Clive and David Manners.

As a play, *Journey's End* had been one of the surprise hits of the 1929 London season. D. W. Griffith wanted to buy and direct it for the screen. It was R. C. Sherriff's first play and undoubtedly helped him get a Hollywood screenwriting contract. It made a star of an unknown actor named Clive, and, without question, it helped its director, Whale, obtain the assignment on *Hell's Angels*, but only after he had successfully directed the New York production of the play.

George Pearson, one of Britain's best silent-film directors, acquired the screen rights for his small independent production company and worked out the arrangements for the coproduction. He came to Hollywood to supervise the filming, although there is no question that the direction was entirely handled by Whale. Pearson insisted that the film remain faithful to the stage-play, refusing, for example, all suggestions that the female element be represented at least by a photograph onscreen of Stanhope's sweetheart. Pearson did, however, agree to drop the original British screenplay and allow Joseph Moncure March, with whom Whale had worked on *Hell's Angels*, to write a new script.

Journey's End is the story of a group of British soldiers—it is probably the only war film in which no women ever appear—in a dugout on the Western Front at St. Quenton on Monday, March 18, 1918. The opening title announces "The Journey Begins." We see a group of troops entering the trenches, talking among themselves about where they would like to spend ten days leave, Australia or Margate. One soldier lights a cigarette and is told by his Sergeant Major to extinguish it. In these opening scenes, the filth and the camaraderie of life in the trenches is revealed, down to a shot of a cockroach running around a candle.

The principal players in the drama are Captain Stanhope (Colin Clive), who drinks too much and has been mentally destroyed by three years in the trenches; Second Lieutenant Raleigh (David Manners), fresh from college, who knew and idolized Stanhope at school and whose sister is engaged to him; Second Lieutenant Hibbert (Anthony Bushell), who is a coward; Lieutenant Osborne (Ian MacLaren), an ex-schoolmaster who remains calm and philosophical throughout; and Second Lieutenant Trotter (Billy Beven), who provides mild comic relief. To block out the horrors of war, these men talk of trivialities, quoting from *Alice in Wonderland* as if the war were hundreds of miles away and they were back in a green and peaceful England. Osborne and Raleigh lead a raiding party on the German trenches, during which the former is killed. As Stanhope drinks more heavily, he and Raleigh quarrel. Raleigh goes out on another raid and is killed, leaving the weary, lonely, and grieving Stanhope also to go out and be killed. The final shot is of the dugout collapsing. All that remains is one lighted candle and silence, except for the distant rumble of gunfire.

Much of the action takes place in the dugout—as did all the action in the play—with only occasional scenes elsewhere, such as two sequences of Raleigh and Trotter in the trenches and the raiding party going over the top. Basically, these scenes are superfluous, and one might wish the film had remained in the dugout with the horror of the raiding party existing only in one's imagination.

The acting at times verges on the melodramatic, but to criticize the film for this element is unfair. Under such circumstances, men would behave as do the characters in *Journey's End*. Clive as Stanhope appears neurotic and irrational, but who would not after three years in the trenches? Manners is perfectly cast as Raleigh, boyish and fresh-faced, innocent as to the horrors of war. Beven's comedy antics as Trotter do little to relieve the tension of the drama, however, and could just as well have been omitted. The only really questionable acting is from Bushell as Hibbert. In the sequence in which Stanhope turns down his request to go back down the lines, he clutches at his chest, breaks down in tears, and generally behaves in a pathetic, laughable fashion.

Journey's End has wrongly been described as an antiwar play and film. It is not. The film never criticizes the war chiefs who send these men out to die, and the men never question the futility of war. The film leaves no doubt that war is hell, but it does not come out and say that, as does Lewis Milestone's *All Quiet on the Western Front* (1930), which was filmed around the same time, and which makes an interesting comparison with *Journey's End*. *All Quiet on the Western Front* has impressive battle scenes with grandeur and scope, while *Journey's End* is quiet and intimate. *Journey's End* is not so much a film about war as a study of the reactions of a group of men to a specific event, an event which, as it happens, will end their lives. The men are enclosed in a British dugout only yards from the German lines, awaiting the final order to advance to Journey's End. They have no control of their destinies. From a fatalistic point of view, the lives of these five men have been long journeys to their dugout, which is a death trap. As one critic has pointed out, however, life itself is a similar journey. Perhaps the most amazing thing about *Journey's End*, as Hugh Walpole noted, is that Sherriff manages to tell his tale without once using a direct word of propaganda or rancor against any one individual or group of individuals.

There are moments in *Journey's End* which are unbearably moving. When Osborne leaves the dugout to go over the top, he puts down his smoking pipe on the table, remarking, "I hate leaving a pipe when it's got a good glow on the top like that." No actor ever had a finer exit line, and that pipe is a far more impressive memorial to the calm and quiet schoolmaster than any words.

The film cost $280,000 to make, the bulk of which money was for the screen rights to the play and for the salaries of its director and star. In the first ten months of release, *Journey's End* grossed two million dollars in the United States, a sure sign of popularity with both the critics and the public. From the former there was unanimous praise. "A picture of such poignant beauty that words can be but feeble praise," wrote *Photoplay* (June, 1930); *The Billboard* (April 19, 1930) announced, "It should be a box-office knockout"; *Variety* reviewed the film twice and called it a "gold mine" for its producers. The noted British critic, James Agate, wrote, "I hold *Journey's End* to be better as a film than as a play, because it begins to give an indication of that filth from which the glamour is not even yet departed."

Anthony Slide

JUAREZ

Released: 1939
Production: Hal B. Wallis for Warner Bros.
Direction: William Dieterle
Screenplay: John Huston, Wolfgang Reinhardt, and Aeneas MacKenzie;
based on the play *Juarez und Maximilian* by Franz Werfel and the novel
The Phantom Crown by Bertita Harding
Cinematography: Tony Gaudio
Editing: Warren Low
Music: Erich Wolfgang Korngold
Running time: 132 minutes

Principal characters:
Benito Pablo Juarez ....Paul Muni
Empress Carlota ....Bette Davis
Emperor Maximilian .... Brian Aherne
Porfirio Diaz .... John Garfield
Napoleon III .... Claude Rains
Marechal Bazaine .... Donald Crisp

During the 1930's and 1940's, of all the major studios, Warner Bros. was the quickest to spot a trend and the most adept at creating one. Busby Berkeley, James Cagney, and Errol Flynn are examples of artists around whom the studio constructed a whole line of films. Once a pattern was successfully established, few deviations were permitted. Their classiest genre, however, revolved around their most unlikely star, Paul Muni. Muni's historical dramas had started out more as prestige items than popular successes but had quickly become the latter as well. In 1938 the studio was looking for another suitably uplifting social topic involving a historical personage with which once again to tempt the award-winning team of Muni, director William Dieterle, and producer Henry Blanke.

They found it, surprisingly enough, in Mexico. Muni was offered the part of Benito Juarez, the phlegmatic Zapotecan Indian whose struggle to rid Mexico of foreign rule in the mid-1860's made him one of that country's great liberators. The planned film would deal not only with Juarez but also with King Maximilian, the Hapsburg prince whom Napoleon III had gulled into accepting the throne and then cruelly abandoned when it became politically necessary to do so. Largely because the role was so different from the vociferous and effusively talented men Muni had so often played, he accepted the part. For box-office insurance Warner Bros. then persuaded their top female star, Bette Davis, to take the role of Carlota, Maximilian's adoring wife whose last desperate attempt to avert Napoleon's treachery ends in her own madness. The part of Maximilian (by far the most interesting of the three) went to Brian Aherne, a rising screen actor who bore an uncanny resemblance to the real ruler.

With what it considered to be a powerhouse cast (John Garfield, Claude Rains, Gale Sondergaard, Donald Crisp, and Gilbert Roland all had strong supporting roles), the studio decided to spare no expense. The picture was alloted the then-incredible budget of $1,750,000, and the amount of work that went into its production reads like a press agent's dream. Muni was permitted some seven months to work up the part and was loaned more than two hundred works on Mexican history by the studio research department. An entire Mexican village was constructed on the Warners' ranch. 7,360 blueprints were required for the sets, fifty-four different actors had speaking roles, and the statistics go on and on.

There were also a few inherent problems as big as the budget. Like Elizabeth I and Mary Queen of Scots, who featured prominently in various films, the two main protagonists of this film never met in real life. This fact tended to turn the script into two separate stories, related in period and goal but not in outlook. Any one of them might have been fine film fare—indeed, it is surprising that the truly romantic tale of Maximilian and Carlota has never been remade. Of the two stories, the one on Juarez himself was the more straightforward, filled with sudden battles, peasant uprisings, freedom speeches, and plenty of action. The story of the two wayward Hapsburgs had much more pageantry, traditional romance, and, in its subplots, more confusion, but also more opportunities for character and personality to develop. For example, in his scenes with Juarez Mexican rebel Porfirio Diaz (John Garfield) is little more than an almost mute yes-man; in his two scenes with Maximilian, a nice and prickly personality begins to show through.

Despite the lavish display of money, the few quirks that developed during shooting were mostly the result of director Dieterle's overwhelming obsession with numerology. According to Muni's biographer Jerome Lawrence, Dieterle's wife, Charlotte,

> was delighted with the title; it contained six letters, a lucky omen. So much so, she claimed, that this magic number must be saved for the title alone and not wasted during the shooting of the picture with six-letter words like "Camera!" and "Action." Dieterle, brilliant in every department except this, agreed. Every shot began with his shouting an eight-letter direction: "Here . . . we . . . go!" [Charlotte] also decreed that the picture could not begin on the scheduled date of November 15. Dieterle obligingly shot one insert of a poster being ripped from a wall on October 29, 1938.

Despite Dieterle's care, the film was neither the critical nor financial hit the studio expected. Released in 1939, the year in which theaters were flooded with such films as *Gone with the Wind*, *Stagecoach*, *Wuthering Heights*, *Ninotchka*, and *Wizard of Oz*, the prevailing opinion about the film was a refined "so what?" There are various conclusions for why this was so. Davis in her autobiography advances the theory that the film would have been great if its long running time had not convinced the studio to make cuts. Muni saw the finished Carlota and Maximilian footage before his part had even begun shooting. Possibly because he felt, as his wife Bella did, that their portion of the film was a completed product, he added fifty pages to his part. Because of his power at the studio, when cuts had to be made in the overlong film, Davis' and Aherne's parts of the story suffered.

Other participants came in for censure as well. The New York-bred, Group Theatre-trained Garfield had obtained his role only through Muni's intercession, and once the studio got a look at him in the film, they never again allowed him to do a period role. It was not that he did not cut a dashing figure but that when he spoke, his accent sounded much more like South Brooklyn than south of the border; even he soon grew disenchanted with his performance, and his Jewish writer friends began addressing him as the "all-Mexican *schlemiel.* An even greater source of controversy was director Dieterle. Davis contends that the director was Muni's pawn: "I first made a picture with Dieterle called *Fog Over Frisco,* his first film at Warners. Then Muni found him, and Dieterle gave up his identity to Mr. Muni, and that was Dieterle's funeral. . . . Dieterle could have been one of the most important directors in Hollywood."

This is overstating the case; *Juarez* was the last film Dieterle made with Muni, and he still had the excellently atmospheric *The Devil and Daniel Webster* (*All That Money Can Buy,* 1941) and the exciting Charles Laughton version of *The Hunchback of Notre Dame* (1939) before him. He was in fact one of the few sound film masters of the crowd scene, of technical atmosphere and almost theatrical splendor. Not that this was in any way surprising: Dieterle had apprenticed under the German theatrical genius, Max Reinhardt, and had codirected *A Midsummer Night's Dream* (1935) with him. His best moments in *Juarez* were very much of this ripe school, sights that were wonderfully moody, as overdone as they were compelling: a bell tower that suddenly fills with snipers; Davis' frequently cited moment of madness when Rains's goateed Napoleon turns diabolic through clever lighting and the lady runs screaming into a black and fathomless void; and Muni's one-man assault on the rebel camp of a former lieutenant, his simple black-clad figure calmly moving among a mass of peons whose waving dust-white sombreros cannot quite obscure his stolid stove-pipe hat.

If on occasion Dieterle gets a little too atmospheric (Davis practically drapes herself about a statue of the Madonna), he does always keep a steady rein on the performers. Davis' stridency is muted into a poignant strain of loving concern mixed with neurotic fears of insufficiency. Aherne moves beneath Maximilian's frosty manner to reveal his genuine care for his adopted people and a sense of democracy that ironically rivals that of Juarez. Only Muni seems apart from it all, unresponsive to the mood. In the case of Juarez,

Muni completely submerged himself in the man, altering his appearance with heavy makeup and turning his light buiid into that of the heavy solid Indian leader.

As Jerome Lawrence puts it, "Muni chose to underplay the role totally . . . . Muni cut away all extraneous gestures or the flamboyant use of props. Later Muni felt he had been too faithful to the original, not allowing himself an artist's prerogative of adding coloration to the historical character." What neither Muni nor Dieterle seemed to realize was that Juarez was essentially a dull dramatic character, the cause of everyone else's dilemmas, but himself a man who changed not at all nor seemed to suffer much inner conflict. His lines were not very good to begin with—they ran to miniature civics lessons such as "When a monarch misrules, he changes the people; when a President misrules, the people change him"—and when played with no flamboyance, no humor, and little personality, those lines changed the great liberator into a pompous bore.

In the end, the reason for *Juarez*'s failure may be that it simply tried to do too much. Muni was too determined to submerge himself in the character, Warners threw in too much lavishness, and the script tried to tell too many stories. It was intended to be a crowning effort in the studio's series of prestige historical dramas; instead it became something of a Tower of Babel.

Lewis Archibald

JUDGE PRIEST

Released: 1934
Production: Sol Wurtzel for Fox
Direction: John Ford
Screenplay: Dudley Nichols and Lamar Trotti; based on original short stories
   by Irvin S. Cobb
Cinematography: Cyril J. Mockdirge
Editing: no listing
Running time: 79 minutes

Principal characters:
Judge Priest	Will Rogers
Jerome Priest	Tom Brown
Ellie May Gillespie	Anita Louise
Reverend Ashby Brand	Henry B. Walthall
Bob Gillis	David Landau
Virginia Maydew	Rochelle Hudson
Horace Maydew	Berton Churchill
Juror	Francis Ford
Jeff Poindexter	Stepin' Fetchit
Flem Tally	Frank Melton
Mrs. Priest	Brenda Fowler

Will Rogers, the homespun American humorist whose life ended in a tragic airplane crash in 1935, was an immensely popular film star in the early years of sound cinema. The film industry had tried to use him in silent films, but since his humor was largely verbal, the effort did not succeed. When sound came in, however, Rogers brought to a number of films the *persona* he had developed in nearly two decades of performing. Audiences responded enthusiastically.

One of his most popular films was *Judge Priest*. Although it was made in 1934, the film is set in 1890 in an old Kentucky town in which the Civil War is still very much alive in the memories of the residents. A shot of a man reading a newspaper opens the film, then the man lowers the paper and speaks directly to the camera. We soon learn that he is Judge William Pitman Priest (Will Rogers) and he is presiding over a court session. He is called "Billy" by nearly everyone, and it soon becomes evident that his character owes as much to the folksy personality of Rogers, who plays him, as it does to the script, which is based upon a series of Irvin S. Cobb short stories.

The slim plot is chiefly devoted to the successful efforts of the Judge to overcome various people who value power, appearances, and money above the more elemental virtues of goodness and honesty. The main focus of this plot is the romance of the Judge's nephew, Jerome (Tom Brown), who is just out of law school, and Ellie May Gillespie (Anita Louise), a young school-teacher. The chief obstacle to the romance is the fact that the identity of Ellie May's father is not known. Jerome's mother (Brenda Fowler) feels that Ellie May is not good enough for Jerome and tries to encourage a match between him and Virginia Maydew (Rochelle Hudson). Both Virginia and her father, Horace Maydew (Berton Churchill), are in favor of the match even though Maydew, a pompous politician, is a political opponent of Judge Priest and hopes to win his seat on the bench in the next election.

The other focus of the plot is a taciturn blacksmith in the town, Bob Gillis (David Landau). He keeps himself apart from the townspeople and their affairs, but when he hears a young barber make rude remarks about Ellie May, he slugs the young man. The barber, Flem Tally (Frank Melton), vows revenge and with two cohorts ambushes Gillis later. When Gillis responds with a knife, the three are defeated but claim that they were attacked without provocation.

Thus all the elements of the story are brought together for an emotional ending. Gillis becomes Jerome's first client, but he refuses to explain the real reason for his action—that he is Ellie May's father. Through the efforts of Judge Priest (who is forced to step down from the bench for the case because he has publicly supported Gillis before) and a minister, Ashby Brand (Henry B. Walthall), Gillis' entire story is told in the courtroom. During the Civil War Gillis had been released from a prison chain gang to fight for the Confederacy and had distinguished himself with many brave deeds. In addition he has provided for his daughter's education through the minister. This story is given added resonance by the fact that Walthall played the Little Colonel in D. W. Griffith's *Birth of a Nation* (1915). Once these details are told, the courtroom erupts in celebration. Gillis is now a hero, and the charges are forgotten. The film ends with a parade for which the townspeople insist that Gillis carry the flag.

The director of *Judge Priest*, John Ford, had already directed more than sixty silent and sound films by 1934 and was to become one of the most respected directors in American cinema. *Judge Priest*, however, was made just before the period in which Ford made his greatest films. Indeed, the film that many regard as the first of Ford's classic films, *The Informer*, was produced in the next year, 1935. *Judge Priest* does, however, bear some Ford trademarks, such as the protagonist addressing his dead wife at her grave, but the film overall is best regarded as a collaboration between Ford and Rogers rather than strictly as a Ford film. Indeed, Ford recognized the abilities of Rogers as an improviser and encouraged him to ad lib.

The Rogers/Judge Priest that is preserved in this film is folksy, unpretentious, and mildly iconoclastic. He remarks that the first thing he learned in politics was when to say "ain't," and after he got his law degree he "sat through two Republican administrations" before he got his first client. When the defendant in a case in his court is found to be sleeping, Priest states that no one but himself is allowed to sleep in his courtroom. Then he begins discussing fishing with the defendant until the scene dissolves to show the two going fishing together. Also, when he is asked to step down from the judge's bench for one case, Priest delivers a long, emotional monologue about his career and his dedication to the spirit rather than the letter of the law.

The defendant in the first case mentioned above is a black man, Jeff Poindexter, who is played by Stepin' Fetchit. His high-pitched, slow-paced voice, naïveté, shiftlessness, and love of flashy clothes all now seem the epitome of the unfavorable stereotype of blacks all too common in Hollywood at the time. Contemporary reviewers, however, saw him merely as an effective comic character, just as most of them also singled out a white performer, Francis Ford (John Ford's brother), for his broad comedy in his role as a tobacco-chewing juror.

All in all, *Judge Priest* gives us a look at the development of the career of John Ford and preserves for us one of the most popular cinematic performances of Rogers, the "cowboy Nietzsche" as *The New York Times* called him. In 1953 Ford reshaped the material of this film into *The Sun Shines Bright*, generally regarded as a deeper treatment of the themes of the earlier film, and including among its actors Fetchit reprising his role as Jeff Poindexter. The later film was regarded by Ford as one of his three best.

Timothy W. Johnson

JUDGMENT AT NUREMBERG

Released: 1961
Production: Stanley Kramer for United Artists
Direction: Stanley Kramer
Screenplay: Abby Mann (AA); based on his teleplay of the same name
Cinematography: Ernest Laszlo
Editing: Frederic Knudtson
Running time: 190 minutes

Principal characters:
Judge Dan Haywood	Spencer Tracy
Ernst Janning	Burt Lancaster
Colonel Tad Lawson	Richard Widmark
Madame Bertholt	Marlene Dietrich
Hans Rolfe	Maximilian Schell (AA)
Irene Hoffman	Judy Garland
Rudolf Peterson	Montgomery Clift

Judgment at Nuremberg is something of an oddity: it is one of the few films which had as its source material a teleplay. It had first been a drama produced for television's distinguished series, *Playhouse 90*. Abby Mann's script dramatizing the Nazi trials was then adapted by him for feature film production. The film added characters to the television play and restored much of Mann's stage directions, sidestepped in the television production. George Roy Hill, who would later direct a huge film hit, *Butch Cassidy and the Sundance Kid* (1969), directed the *Playhouse 90* dramatization. Stanley Kramer took on the director's role for the film version of *Judgment at Nuremberg*. Kramer had already established a reputation for liberal social drama films, so-called "message films." His previous films included *On the Beach* (1959), concerning the aftermath of a fictional nuclear war, and *The Defiant Ones* (1958), which followed the escape of two convicts, one black, the other white. Interestingly, although the script was rewritten and extended for the film, Kramer's direction retains the approach of a television drama, complete with logical moments for commercial breaks.

The story is based on information about the Nuremberg trials of Nazi war criminals, which were conducted by the Allies in the immediate postwar years. The first Nuremberg trials had had sensational Nazi criminals in the docks, key men famous for their role in the Third Reich. Mann's screenplay, however, focused on the men tried during the second Nuremberg trials, men to whom the proceedings of the court must have seemed very familiar. These Nazis were the judges. The bitter irony of judges on trial for their role in upholding the laws of their country, laws which involved patent abuses of human rights, was the subject of *Judgment at Nuremberg*.

The film is not confined to an exposé of Nazi legal atrocities. Mann's screenplay draws a parallel between the American judge Dan Haywood (Spencer Tracy), who comes to Nuremberg to preside over the trial, and the German Minister of Justice, Ernst Janning (Burt Lancaster), who is himself on trial. Both the American and the German are subjected to political pressure in their courtrooms from governments who see the outcome of the trials in terms of political expediency. The trials take place during the Berlin crisis of 1948, as American troops airlift supplies to Berlin. The American military occupation government foresees the need for a German ally in the face of a Russian threat, and they are therefore anxious to avoid antagonizing their ally with the Nuremberg trials. The German judges were only upholding their country's laws, argues the American military. The military leaders call in the American prosecutor, Colonel Tad Lawson (Richard Widmark), to point out the logic of "going easy" on the judges. "You don't get the support of the German people by sentencing their leaders to stiff prison sentences," Lawson is told. Eventually, Lawson gives in to the pressure. The question then is, will Judge Haywood allow the military to influence his decision in the case?

By putting the Nuremberg trial in the context of this political pressure from the occupation forces, Mann sets up a parallel between these Allied trials and the Nazi trials which are "on trial." The same sort of pressures which led Nazi judges to put "national interest" over justice are present at the Nuremberg trials. Justice can be made expedient in any society, especially in the guise of nationalism which sees justice as anything which is good for the country. *Judgment at Nuremberg* is a double-edged title which applies to the judgment of both the Nazis and Americans who each can be judged by different codes of justice and morality.

Ernst Janning, as played by Lancaster, is not a caricature of the evil Nazi. Rather, he is an extremely respected and learned man of law who agreed in the years just prior to the war to a temporary suspension of justice. He allowed his courtroom to be a forum for the erosion of human rights under inhumane Nazi laws. Why a judge of obvious integrity would agree to uphold immoral laws is a question which each of the other characters in the drama tries to answer.

Hans Rolfe (Maximilian Schell), a brilliant young German lawyer, takes on Janning's defense. Rolfe sees Janning as an unfairly maligned man, representing the best of Germany's tradition of justice, who is being punished for war crimes of which he knew nothing. As part of his argument, he points out the acceptance of Hitler during the 1930's by Allied leaders, who held a different opinion of Hitler before the war. "The Russians signed pacts with Hitler, Churchill praised him, American industrialists profited by him," Rolfe says. "Ernst Janning's guilt is the world's guilt. No more, no less."

To prove the immorality of Janning's judicial decisions, the American prosecutor decides to focus on one infamous prewar trial. The case involved a law prohibiting any sexual relations between Aryans and non-Aryans. Lawson persuades the then-star witness in the trial, a Jewish woman named Irene Hoffman (Judy Garland) who was thirteen at the time, to give up the privacy she has painfully established and once again give testimony at this trial.

Another character of the film, Rudolph Peterson (Montgomery Clift), gives perhaps the most touching moments to the film. Clift's part took only a few days to film and the role is small, but the impact on the audience is very moving. Playing a man judged to be "feeble-minded" by the Nazis and thus sterilized, Clift gives one of his most sensitive performances. The result of his testimony on those in the courtroom is equally moving. When that testimony proves to those in the court that Peterson is perhaps not of average intelligence, both the prosecutors and the defense attorneys are moved by the man's tragedy.

Rolfe is faced with proving that Janning's decision was just. In effect, the original trial is relived, with the lawyers replaying the roles and arguments of the original Nazi court. The similarity proves more than Janning can bear. For the first time during the trial, he speaks. "Enough," he says. The point is not whether the man was guilty of sexual relations with the girl. The point is that the law, forbidding Aryans to have relations with Jews, was immoral. Janning says that those who say "the law is the law" and that violators of *unjust* laws must be punished are those people no court can afford to condone.

Janning's eloquent speech traces the subversion of justice in his own court and the patriotism which motivated it, a patriotism which hindsight shows him is indefensible. Despite pressures from the military and the sympathy created by Janning's speech, Judge Haywood sentences Janning to the maximum term. Janning accepts the sentence, but later, in his cell, asks a departing Haywood if Haywood can personally understand why he went along with the Nazi laws. Referring to all the subsequent atrocities, Janning says, "I did not know it would come to that. You must believe it." Haywood responds, "It came to that the first time you sentenced to death a man you knew to be innocent."

One of the characters added to the screenplay for the movie was Mme. Bertholt, played by Marlene Dietrich. As a widow of a German general, Mme. Bertholt represents what Mann saw as an attitude of the German aristocracy. Bertholt cannot face the atrocities she knows her husband was a part of. Instead, she emphasizes the pride he took in being a good soldier and serving his country. Paraphrasing her husband's credo, she says, "I loathe the Nazi generals, but I serve them, because that's what the country wants." Haywood admires her as she admires him, but they cannot alter each other's opinions.

The film includes actual documentary footage of German concentration camps, including scenes of the gas ovens. Since the television production of *Judgment at Nuremberg* was sponsored by a gas company which demanded that the reference to the gas ovens be deleted, when the show aired, the audio was in fact deleted at that point, and audiences had to wait for the film to hear the description of that particular documentary scene. The concentration camp film is brief, however, as *Judgment at Nuremberg* shifts the balance of its trial away from Nazi atrocities to the corruption that can arise from nationalism.

Leslie Donaldson

JULIA

Released: 1977
Production: Richard Roth for Twentieth Century-Fox
Direction: Fred Zinnemann
Screenplay: Alvin Sargent (AA); based on the memoirs *Pentimento* by Lillian Hellman
Cinematography: Douglas Slocombe
Editing: Walter Murch
Production design: Gene Callahan, Willy Holt, and Carmen Dillon
Set decoration: Pierre Charron and Tessa Davies
Costume design: Anthea Sylbert
Music: George Delerue
Running time: 116 minutes

Principal characters:
Lillian Hellman .... Jane Fonda
Julia .... Vanessa Redgrave (AA)
Dashiell Hammett .... Jason Robards (AA)
Johann .... Maximilian Schell
Lillian (younger) .... Susan Jones
Julia (younger) .... Lisa Pelikan

Fred Zinnemann's remarkable *Julia* was released in 1977. In a year in which the science-fiction spectacular *Star Wars* became the greatest box-office success up to that time, it is both curious and astonishing that the thoughtful and austere *Julia* was a commercial and artistic success as well. Based on a chapter of playwright Lillian Hellman's memoirs *Pentimento*, the film is a graceful study of the deep friendship between two women: the liberated American playwright Lillian Hellman (Jane Fonda) and her longtime friend, the radical, regal, and mysterious Julia (Vanessa Redgrave). The plot revolves in a concise circular structure. Lillian lives in quiet privacy with her mentor and lover, the noted detective fiction writer Dashiell Hammett (Jason Robards). They share a remote beach cottage on the East Coast where they enjoy a modern unconditional relationship. In the opening frames of the film, Lillian is seen through a misty blue fog that places her in silhouette as she fishes in a boat by a jetty. This image is sustained as her voice-over narration begins the film's flashbacks. The same image is used at the conclusion of the drama, placing the story in a neat frame.

It is through this device that we learn of Lillian's relationship with Julia, the course this friendship takes, and the eventual resolution of the adventures and the tragedy that are a part of it. As young girls, Lillian (Susan Jones) and Julia (Lisa Pelikan) shared everything from Julia's stately family home to treasured secrets of girlhood, future hopes and dreams, intimate thoughts, and a close, almost physical love. This abiding friendship endures separation and trial and a rich maturing process that sees the women follow separate paths to personal fulfillment. Lillian begins their story by remembering their early years together. As we see them in flashback, we share Lillian's perspective and gaze into the past through a filter of tender memories.

Julia is seen growing up and developing an altruistic social consciousness. She has come from an enormously wealthy family, attended the finest schools, and lived in an ancestral home. Outside the opulent family circle, however, Julia sees the hardships and atrocities of real life. She becomes detached from the very society which has created her and zealously attempts to trace out and rectify the defects of that society through philanthropic and political activities. She becomes a self-avowed social reformer who would utilize her family fortune, influential acquaintances, dearest friends, and even her life for social causes. Lillian, on the other hand, matures also into a rugged nonconformist, but by comparison, her life style is remarkably passive. If she is concerned with the social and political chaos of her time, it will find expression only in her writing and in the camouflage of her symbiotic union with Julia. In Lillian we see a depth of understanding of others and a love that is entirely selfless. The thrust of the film is the elusive Julia's summons to Lillian to journey to Europe and Lillian's hesitant involvement with the other's cause.

Zinnemann has created *Julia* with a graceful delicacy of image and pace. For example, we share Lillian's anxieties and tremulously travel with her as she smuggles funds into wartorn Berlin. Production designers Gene Callahan, Willy Holt, and Carmen Dillon have diligently rendered the period trains, stations, cities, hotels, and restaurants into a wholly credible *mise-en-scène*. The costumes by Anthea Sylbert also are striking and complement the plot. The gray Persian lamb hat which conceals the cash is an important and beautifully striking image as it rests on Fonda's head, the central focus of the scene. Fonda gives an impeccable performance as Lillian. Her Lillian is the liberated playwright who drinks, smokes, is disciplined in her work, and makes the best of a given situation. Her preoccupation, bordering on obsessive fascination, with the haunting Julia is always convincing, and her faltering courage and momentary inertia expressed in the suspenseful train sequences are eloquently expressive.

The majestic Redgrave, who won the Best Supporting Actress Academy Award for her performance, plays the impassioned Julia with a controlled but lustrous warmth and peerless mystery. Robards, who also won an Oscar for his role, gives his usual fine performance as Hammett and plays well with Fonda. It is Maximilian Schell as the chilling Johann, however, who gives the film's stand-out performance. He is muted, compassionate, and concerned, a balanced zealot who convinces us of the righteousness of this cause. The smuggled funds Hellman must carry at her own personal risk will be well used to rescue suffering Jews from the Nazis. Schell expresses external detachment to a frightening degree; it seems he would sacrifice both Lillian and Julia for the cause. Yet beneath that cold detachment is a noble, loving heart which must stay repressed. The personality of Lillian is seen in sharp juxtaposition to the almost clinical Johann. Her great devotion to Julia is always defined in terms of love in action, understanding, and loyalty despite misunderstanding.

When Julia is beaten in a Viennese student uprising and lies almost completely bandaged in a dreary hospital, Lillian is there to protect and comfort her. After her sudden and baffling disappearance from the hosptial, Lillian waits in Vienna for word from her, which never comes. Later, when she returns to Paris to continue writing, she continues to wait for Julia or a message from her and dispels her loneliness with calls to Hammett and attempts to write. That Julia will call upon Lillian for help is implicit throughout the film. Lillian, out of love for Julia, consents to be used and embarks on a dangerous mission to transport money illegally to Julia through Germany. Their final reunion in a bleak German café is heartrending. The reunion is brief and, out of necessity, guarded, but the bond of affection between the women remains firm. Julia lost a leg in the Viennese hospital, but she has also given birth to a little daughter she calls "Lily." Hellman is deeply touched and hesitant to leave. Julia looks worn and haggard but her eyes sparkle affectionately. Unfortunately, the secrecy of their visit and the ominous threat of discovery impel them to separate quickly. Zinnemann has foreshadowed tragedy in the café scene. Lillian safely exits Germany only to learn later on a visit to Moscow that Julia has been killed. As if to keep a part of her close, Lillian searches fruitlessly and almost insanely for Julia's little daughter Lily throughout the baker's shops of Alsace, where Julia had mentioned offhandedly that her daughter had been in safe-keeping. Her search is in vain, however, and she returns to Hammett feeling totally defeated. His warmth and empathy for the impossibility of finding Lily provide a comforting conclusion to the narrative structure. That Hammett is sympathetic to Lillian's perilous journey and its tragic end is solacing. As Lillian explains in the final voice-over, Hammett sustained her through the days of melancholia that followed. The film ends with the opening shot of Lillian in hat and mackintosh fishing in the misty blue waters of her grief.

Zinnemann, who has ably demonstrated virtuosity and a full command of cinema techniques in his *oeuvre*, is often criticized for the dry detachment with which he tells his stories. He has been called dull by his harshest detractors and accused of superficiality in his directorial efforts at realism. His most acclaimed films, *High Noon* (1952), *From Here to Eternity* (1953), *The Nun's Story* (1959), and *A Man for All Seasons* (1966), reveal an adaptability to different genres. Some critics may call this a severe flaw that prevents him from consideration as an *auteur* in his own right; yet there are notable parallels in all of Zinnemann's films. The most striking parallel is between *The Nun's*

Story and *Julia*. In these films he deals with related themes of love and sacrifice, suffering and devotion. Both are moving and masterful works in which he expresses a causal ambivalence. In *Julia*, he deals with his characters and the story in an elliptical and characteristically restrained manner, leaving interpretation and emotion to the audience.

Julia did very well at the box office and was released in a particularly successful period of Fonda's career. There had been discussion at one time of Fonda appearing in the title role instead of Redgrave (although Julia's part is smaller). Fortunatley, she took on the role of Hellman instead, which was more suitable to her screen *persona* of recent years, that of a down-to-earth, yet idealless woman who undergoes a change of character and becomes dedicated to a new set of ideals. Redgrave is equally well cast as the ethereal Julia. Despite some criticism of her Oscar nomination by those who opposed her political beliefs, her award was well deserved for a beautiful performance.

Elizabeth McDermott

JUNIOR BONNER

Released: 1972
Production: Joe Wizan for ABC/Solar
Direction: Sam Peckinpah
Screenplay: Jeb Rosebrook
Cinematography: Lucien Ballard
Editing: Robert L. Wolfe
Running time: 100 minutes

Principal characters:
Junior Bonner	Steve McQueen
Ace Bonner	Robert Preston
Elvira Bonner	Ida Lupino
Buck Roan	Ben Johnson
Curley Bonner	Joe Don Baker
Charmagne	Barbara Leigh
Ruth Bonner	Mary Murphy
Nurse Arlis	Sandra Deel
Del	Dub Taylor
Red Terwiliger	William McKinney

It has been argued that of all the filmmakers to emerge from Hollywood during the 1960's, Sam Peckinpah is by far the most compelling. Indeed, the term *auteur*, which has been grossly mishandled by film critics over the past thirty years, can still be applied with more certainty to Peckinpah than to any other American director.

In its most basic form, *auteur* theory states that a true film author leaves an indelible personal attitude and vision on every frame of film he shoots, a stylistic and thematic signature that marks a film or group of films as having sprung from the world view of its creator. To proponents of this theory, every film produced by an *auteur* director is of great interest regardless of its artistic or commercial value. A genuine *auteur* can always rise above the limitations of a poor script, inferior subject matter, low budgets, and bad acting to convey consistently a personal statement which falls in line with attitudes expressed in each of his other films.

Like many *auteur* directors, Peckinpah is a genre director who works within the confines of the action-adventure film and the Western. Born and reared in California, he received a Master's degree in drama from the University of Southern California and worked as a theatrical actor and director before arriving at television station KLAC as a stagehand. Within two years, Peckinpah was working as filmmaker Don Siegal's dialogue director, and in one busy year, he worked on thirteen pictures for Allied Artists.

In the mid-1950's, Peckinpah labored extensively in television, almost exclusively within the Western format. He began on *Gunsmoke*, writing more than a dozen scripts for that distinguished series. He also wrote and directed many episodes of *The Rifleman*, *The Westerner*, *Klondike*, *Broken Arrow*, and the *Zane Grey Theater*. This experience provided a firm grounding in and mastery not only of the Western, but also of the technical concerns of scripting and directing.

Peckinpah's first film script was a rewrite of Siegal's science-fiction classic, *Invasion of the Body Snatchers* (1956). In 1961, he directed his first feature, *The Deadly Companions*, followed the next year by one of America's seminal postwar Westerns, *Ride the High Country*. *Major Dundee* (1965) was released after considerable difficulties, among them extensive recutting by the producing studio, Columbia. The next five years brought no new Peckinpah-directed films, although he provided scripts for *The Glory Guys* (1965) and *Villa Rides* (1968). In 1969, he wrote and directed *The Wild Bunch*, a film which is generally considered one of the best Westerns ever filmed, a remarkably evocative look at what happens when Western mythology is confronted with the progress of civilization.

All of Peckinpah's films reveal a preoccupation with losers, drifters, and social misfits, people who are emotionally and spiritually crippled, and who, above all, suffer from an intense lack of self-knowledge. Combined with this concern is a continual attempt to uncover the underlying roots of the American experience. The quest for personal definition which characterizes all of Peckinpah's heroes is firmly grounded in this concurrent and overriding theme of national identity. These thematic concerns are presented in a highly effective, almost surreal visual style, one which has become steadily more personal over the years.

Junior Bonner is Peckinpah's most low-key film to date. A subtle picture, it lacks the orchestrated mayhem and orgies of violence which have characterized much of his later work. Nevertheless, it is a true Peckinpah film, fitting comfortably within the larger framework of his *oeuvre*. As always, the director is occupied here with the theme of "reluctant past-primeness," of a hero growing old and not liking it at all.

Junior Bonner (Steve McQueen) is almost forty. No longer the top rodeo star he once was, Bonner is a man who has arrived at a critical point in life. He is broke, aware that his skills are fading, and fearful that the times are passing him by. He returns to his hometown of Prescott, Arizona, to compete in the annual Fourth of July Frontier Days rodeo, anxious to prove that he still has greatness in him. It is no accident that he is called "Junior," for that name has shaped his life as much as his personality has in turn given dimension to the name. Junior is the image of his father, Ace Bonner (Robert Preston), a former rodeo great now sixty years old, trapped by age, family ties, and faded dreams of glory. Ace seldom visits Junior's mother Elvira (Ida Lupino in her first screen appearance in sixteen years), has no job, boozes and womanizes continually, and is forever thinking up new get-rich-quick-schemes, the latest of which involves gold hunting in Australia.

Supporting this fragile family is Junior's brother, Curley (Joe Don Baker), a high-pressure real estate developer whose smiling, folksy commercials dominate local television screens. Curley's latest venture is a mobile-home retirement community, "Curley's Reata Ranchero." He has bought up his father's land for a pittance and is selling his mother's home so that she can live in the Ranchero and operate its curio shop. Curley is the new American entrepreneur, fast-talking, greedy, and unsympathetic to traditional values, values to which Junior and his father precariously cling.

Junior arrives home to find his family a shambles, his values uprooted, and his own life a series of broken dreams. As he prepares for the rodeo, in which he will attempt to ride Sunshine, a ferocious bull on whom no rider has lasted the required eight seconds, Junior is presented with two proposals, each of which could enable him to escape his tenuous existence. He meets with Curley, who, after distainfully labeling his brother a "motel cowboy," offers Junior a salesman's position at the Ranchero. Curley callously refuses to see Junior as anything other than a tool with which to lure potential buyers eager to meet a real rodeo star. Junior tells Curley his opinion of the offer by pushing him through a window. The next morning Junior meets with rodeo boss Buck Roan (Ben Johnson), who offers him yet another job, this one as Roan's assistant. Again, Junior refuses, both men realizing that Junior was born for only one occupation.

Junior fares well in the rodeo events, but finishes out of the money in almost every instance. When the bull-riding is completed, however, Junior has ridden Sunshine for the full eight seconds. He receives $950 in prize money, but more importantly, he has proven himself a winner once again. The film ends as Junior says his various good-byes in a manner which neatly sums up his own outlook. He bids farewell to Charmagne (Barbara Leigh), his latest one-night-stand, with the words, "Gotta go. It's rodeo time," thus confirming that he will never give up his nomadic life. His mother parts saying, "You had to win, didn't you?" and he agrees. Both recognize that proving one's self-worth is of the utmost importance in these confusing times. Finally, he uses his winnings to buy Ace an airline ticket to Australia, that last frontier. Junior has at last provided for his father, and he shows that he still shares in Ace's dreams, however wild they may be. The film ends as Junior Bonner climbs in his dirt-encrusted Cadillac and heads for the next rodeo.

Three scenes in *Junior Bonner* hit the heart of the film's thematic concerns and, by extension, the major interests of director Peckinpah. The first occurs toward the beginning of the film as Junior arrives at his father's ramshackle home. He drives up just in time to see the flimsy structure fall under Curley's land-clearing equipment, while in the distance, mobile homes spread over the silent hills. It is a masterful sequence. The destruction of the house is intercut with Junior's own attempt to steer clear of a monstrous tractor manned by a faceless operator. The cutting is extremely fast-paced. The viewer is bombarded with a cacophony of noise and visuals all of which point to the fact that Junior's past life and traditionalist values are being ripped apart by a new society that neither desires his participation nor cares for him in the least.

The second scene is significantly placed in the exact center of the film. It is the Fourth of July parade down Prescott's main street, a parade steeped in Americana and infused with a vision of the future. In quick succession Peckinpah treats us to images of our collective past moving side by side with those of the modern age. Antique cars rumble down the street, followed by a precision formation of motorcycles. Romantic images of the West (Indians in full regalia, wagon trains, and stagecoaches) pass before the crowd as Curley Bonner, atop his "Reata Ranchero" float, turns the corner to enter the procession. What Peckinpah has done here is to provide a loving look at small-town America, as well as a glimpse of our historical symbols combined with an off-center nod toward our country's destiny. In short, the parade becomes a gauge of America's self-image and another example of Peckinpah's search of meaning in the American experience.

The final of the three scenes takes place in the Palace Bar during the rodeo's intermission. As contestants and townspeople crowd the bar, the Bonner family holds an impromptu reunion. The Bonners gather together amid the confusion, a fragile group bound by family ties, tradition, and above all, genuine affection. Curley returns Junior's favor of the previous night by knocking him to the floor. Afterward the brothers share a drink, and Curley sums it all up, saying, "You're my brother and I guess I love you." Ace and Elvira meet for the first time in years and achieve a momentary reconciliation. Thus, amid the changing face and standards of American life, human bonds, even when stretched to the breaking point, can still survive.

Junior Bonner is a masterful film filled with thematic riches and cinematic delight. Peckinpah's firm hand is evident throughout, from the excellent performances delivered by his ensemble of players, to the wonderfully executed slow motion, quick cutting style of editing that has since *The Wild Bunch*, become his trademark. *Junior Bonner* stands as a poignant, elegiac, and humorous film, but above all, it will always be seen as an insightful look at America at a crossroads, surging toward an uncertain future, but with one eye glued to the past.

Daniel Einstein

THE KEYS OF THE KINGDOM

Released: 1944
Production: Joseph L. Mankiewicz for Twentieth Century-Fox
Direction: John M. Stahl
Screenplay: Joseph L. Mankiewicz and Nunnally Johnson; based on the novel
of the same name by A. J. Cronin
Cinematography: Arthur Miller
Editing: James B. Clark
Running time: 137 minutes

Principal characters:
Father Francis Chisholm	Gregory Peck
Dr. Willie Tulloch	Thomas Mitchell
Reverend Angus Mealy	Vincent Price
Mother Maria-Veronica	Rosa Stradner
Nora	Jane Ball
Aunt Polly	Edith Barrett
Francis Chisholm (younger)	Roddy McDowell
Joseph	Benson Fong
Monsignor Sleeth	Sir Cedric Hardwicke

In the 1940's, Hollywood produced a spate of religious films that were popular with the moviegoing public. Such films as *The Song of Bernadette* (1943) had demonstrated the viability of the religious theme at the box office. It was, therefore, not surprising that Joseph L. Mankiewicz would choose, as the first film he produced for Twentieth Century-Fox, a film with a religious theme, *The Keys of the Kingdom*, based on a 1941 best-selling novel by A. J. Cronin.

The story of a mildly iconoclastic Scottish priest, Father Francis Chisholm (Gregory Peck), *The Keys of the Kingdom* follows Chisholm from his unhappy boyhood and troubled young manhood to old age. To play the priest the studio selected Peck, who at the time had somehow become a star without ever having been seen in a film. In 1944 he had been in a few unsuccessful Broadway plays and had made one film, *Days of Glory*, which had not yet been released. Nevertheless, all the studios wanted to sign him, and in addition to his contract with Twentieth Century-Fox he also signed with M-G-M and David O. Selznick. It was an unprecedented beginning for an actor, but if there were any doubters about Peck's abilities as a motion-picture actor they were surely silenced by Peck's receiving an Academy Award nomination for *The Keys of the Kingdom* as well as by his decades of stardom since then.

The film uses a framing device to present the story of Father Chisholm's life. We first see him as an old, white-haired priest receiving Monsignor Sleeth (Sir Cedric Hardwicke) who has come to tell him that the bishop wants him to retire. Father Chisholm protests, but the Monsignor remains unconvinced. That night, however, he begins to read Chisholm's personal journal, which begins in 1878, and we see the priest's entire life through flashbacks.

As a boy (played by Roddy McDowell), Chisholm sees his happy childhood ended on a tragic night when his father is beaten by anti-Catholics, and then both his parents drowned in a storm-swollen river. He is reared by his aunt Polly (Edith Barrett), who wants him to become a priest, but he is determined to marry his childhood sweetheart Nora (Jane Ball) after he finishes college. Nora, however, believes that he will reject her for the priesthood, and Chisholm experiences his second tragedy when he arrives home from his last year at college to find that Nora has just died giving birth to an illegitimate child. Chisholm then does enter the priesthood, but he fails in his first two curacies, and it is not until he accepts a mission in China that he begins to find his way. It is a difficult, laborious process, however, in which he begins with little more than a ruined mission building and the help of a Chinese Christian convert named Joseph (Benson Fong). He decides that the only way he can combat the hostility of the local people is by offering to treat the sick. Even this brings little success until he saves the life of the son of a mandarin. In gratitude the mandarin gives him the property, materials, and workmen for building a fine new mission.

When the church sends three nuns to assist at the mission, Chisholm finds that their leader, the aristocratic Mother Maria-Veronica (Rosa Stradner), is disdainful of him as a "peasant priest" and keeps their relationship cold and distant. The arrival on a visit of Chisholm's lifelong friend, Willie Tulloch (Thomas Mitchell), who is a good doctor but also an atheist, does not increase the Reverend Mother's regard for Chisholm.

The mission soon finds itself in the middle of a civil war, and all the energies of Chisholm and Tulloch are devoted to treating the injured. Tulloch is fatally wounded, and, in a moving deathbed scene, thanks Chisholm for respecting his lack of belief and not trying to "bully" him into heaven. Chisholm then has to destroy a gun site personally to protect his mission. Later, Angus Mealy (Vincent Price), who was a seminarian with Chisholm and has become a bishop, visits the mission. His humiliating and patronizing treatment of Chisholm makes Mother Maria-Veronica realize that the peasant priest has true Christian virtues, and she apologizes to him for her arrogance. Many years of rewarding work in China follow before the church calls him back to Britain. After reading about all these events in Father Chisholm's journal, the Monsignor changes his mind and decides to recommend to the bishop that the old priest be allowed to keep his post in his native parish.

Throughout the film the basic theme is that Chisholm is a good and religious man but never an "ecclesiastical mechanic," as one bishop calls those who do not think for themselves but merely rigidly apply the doctrines they learn. Thus Chisholm never does harm to anyone, but he often gets in trouble with his superiors for not adhering strictly to church doctrine, especially in his continued friendship with Willie Tulloch despite the fact that he is an avowed atheist. Chisholm is also criticized for such lighthearted remarks as, "The good Christian is a good man, but I've found that the Confucianist has a better sense of humor." Indeed, some Catholic reviewers thought that the screenwriters had gone too far in their emphasis on the individual over the institution and doctrines of the Church.

Supporting Peck with fine acting performances are Mitchell as the priest's atheist friend who is full of life and humor, and Stradner as the Reverend Mother who is at last able to overcome her aristocratic prejudices and learn humility from the peasant priest. *The Keys of the Kingdom* was ably directed by John M. Stahl, who had been a Hollywood director since 1914 and who had the original versions of *Imitation of Life* (1934) and *Magnificent Obsession* (1935) to his credit. Perhaps the greatest overall influence on the film, however, was Mankiewicz, its producer and chief screenwriter. His imprint can be seen in the intelligence of the script as well as in its inclination toward talkative scenes and its lack of reverence for organized religion.

Judith A. Williams

THE KILLERS

Released: 1946
Production: Mark Hellinger for Universal
Direction: Robert Siodmak
Screenplay: Anthony Veiller and John Huston (uncredited); based on the short story of the same name by Ernest Hemingway
Cinematography: Elwood Bredell
Editing: Arthur Hilton
Running time: 105 minutes

Principal characters:
Ole Anderson (Swede)	Burt Lancaster
Kitty Collins	Ava Gardner
Reardon	Edmond O'Brien
Big Jim Colfax	Albert Dekker
Lubinsky	Sam Levene
Dum Dum	Jack Lambert
Blinky Franklin	Jeff Corey
Charleston	Vince Barnett
The Killers	Charles McGraw
	William Conrad

When former Broadway columnist-turned-film producer Mark Hellinger moved from Warner Bros. to Universal, he chose as his initial vehicle an adaptation of Ernest Hemingway's taut short story "The Killers." When it was released in 1946, the film marked one of the initial appearances of what came to be known as *film noir*, a new kind of film genre born out of the old established gangster film genre and the sense of general despair growing out of postwar disillusionment and Cold War fears. Heightened by a cynical script, uncredited but generally attributed to John Huston, and the brooding atmospheric direction of Robert Siodmak, *The Killers* proved an immediate success. The short story which forms the opening scenes of the film was wisely kept intact, with its ominously wisecracking killers (Charles McGraw and William Conrad) terrorizing a small-town diner and finally, inexplicably, gunning down a man known only as "the Swede" (Burt Lancaster). Siodmak's handling of these scenes is skillful and terrifying: the Swede knows the men are coming but no longer has the strength or will to run, and when the door to his cheap room bursts open, the two gunmen empty their weapons into a man who is already emotionally dead.

After such an auspicious beginning the film turns into a complex "whodunnit," relying heavily on flashback, detailing the dogged attempts of an insurance investigator named Reardon (Edmond O'Brien) to discover the key which would explain the Swede's refusal to run. It is a violent variation on *Citizen Kane* (1941). In the investigation, each person from the Swede's past supplies a piece in an intricate jigsaw puzzle of betrayal and death. The audience, knowing no more than Reardon, is implicated in the investigation and the growing danger which heightens with each new discovery.

Through flashback we see the Swede, a successful prizefighter, lose what is to be his last fight. As played by Lancaster, Swede is a sad, vulnerable figure. His childhood pal, Lubinsky (Sam Levene), has made a career on the police force and suggests that Swede do the same. Swede shrugs the notion off, however, because boxing is all he knows, and it has been taken away from him. Instead, he becomes involved in numbers racketeering and takes up with Kitty Collins (Ava Gardner), the girl friend of a gangster named Big Jim Colfax (Albert Dekker) who is serving a term in the penitentiary. The essential ineffectuality of the police in dealing with a criminal of Colfax's stature is suggested by showing that despite his incarceration, his gang remains free and his house is a sort of haven for criminals. Kitty compulsively steals a necklace, and when she is arrested by Lubinsky, Swede lies for her and takes the rap himself.

When he is released, he finds that Kitty has gone back to Colfax. She is able to convince Swede that it is he she really loves, however, and he is drawn into a factory robbery engineered by Colfax and his gang. Kitty and Colfax have been waiting for Swede's release. His blind trust in Kitty allows them to double-cross the gang by taking all the money and making Swede a fall-guy once more. It is his ultimate realization of this, and the audience's discovery of it, which makes the Swede's resignation to death in the opening scenes reverberate with new meaning.

As Reardon grows closer to the truth, Colfax and Kitty, realizing that their "perfect crime" is in danger of being exposed, attempt to set up Reardon for the killers. Once again, as with the Swede, it is Kitty who attempts to "seduce" Reardon into relaxing his guard. She meets him in a crowded restaurant and then manages to elude him just before the killers arrive. The plan fails, however, and the killers are gunned down by the police. Reardon and Lubinsky, knowing the whole story at last, race to Colfax's house only to find him dying, shot by yet another member of the old gang. Kitty begs Colfax to lie for her as Swede once did and declare her innocence to the police. Colfax, ironically, has reached the same point that Swede did. He stole not merely for money, but for Kitty; he even killed for her. His answer, the last words he will utter, is a request for a cigarette.

The Killers is an impressive film on several levels. It was a box-office and an artistic success (Hemingway himself considered the opening scenes to be the most faithful film adaptation of his work). The cast is uniformly excellent, from O'Brien as Reardon, driven more by compulsion than by duty, to Conrad and McGraw as the dispassionate messengers of death who give the film its name. Dekker's portrayal of Colfax is masterly. This fine actor, whose presence graced dozens of films in supporting roles, is able to lend a degree of sympathy to a character who might otherwise have been a conventional heavy. It is the chemistry between the two newcomers, Lancaster as Swede and Ava Gardner as Kitty, however, which puts the film over, making both actors enormous stars and prompting Universal to attempt a repeat performance three years later with *Crisscross*, again directed by Siodmak and starring Lancaster, with an appropriately overwrought score by Miklos Rosza, the favorite *film noir* composer.

The iconography of *film noir* is thoroughly represented in *The Killers*. Siodmak, a refugee from Nazi Germany, was perhaps the most skillful practioner of this kind of film, introducing themes and character types which would recur again and again with the regularity of a nightmare. In these films, the main character was an antihero: cynical, tough, often a private detective, and mistrustful of people, especially beautiful women who invariably, like Kitty Collins, have a compulsion to destroy their mates. The antihero must journey alone through a corrupt, urban night world, stalking his *Doppelgänger*, his darker side (Reardon/Swede), in order to unravel a mystery lost in the past, the understanding of which will enable him to understand himself. Thus, while it enjoyed enormous popularity as a slick, well-acted thriller, the film showed us that the American hero had become a psychological cripple, at the mercy of a world out of joint. Survival, it said, not peace, had become the order of the day.

Michael Shepler

KING AND COUNTRY

Released: 1964
Production: Joseph Losey and Norman Priggen for Allied Artists
Direction: Joseph Losey
Screenplay: Evan Jones; based on the play *Hamp* by John Wilson and on the
  novel *Return to the Wood* by James Lansdale Hodson
Cinematography: Denys Coop
Editing: Reginald Mills
Music: Larry Adler
Running time: 86 minutes

Principal characters:
Captain Hargreaves	Dirk Bogarde
Private Hamp	Tom Courtenay
Captain O'Sullivan	Leo McKern
Lieutenant Webb	Barry Foster
Colonel	Peter Copley
Captain Midgley	James Villiers
Chaplain	Vivian Matalon

Like many other films, *King and Country* has become a classic without ever
having been particularly successful—and without even recovering its costs.
Financed out of the surprise commercial success of *The Servant* (1963), it has
a great deal in common with Joseph Losey's previous film: the same producer,
Norman Priggen; the same star, Dirk Bogarde (for whom the two films represent something of a career watershed); and a similar fascination with the
British class system which finds its most obvious expression in *The Servant*
but is also central to *Accident* (1967) and *The Go-Between* (1971) as well as
to *King and Country*.

King and Country is an unrelenting antiwar film—not the kind that hedges
its bets by efficiently portraying the heroics it then goes on to condemn, but
a sparse, methodical indictment of the whole military structure. It is based
on a stage play which Losey claims simply gave him the starting point for his
film: the story of a young private who deserted from the British Army at
Passchendaele in 1917, was captured, returned to his unit, court-martialed,
and shot in the interests of "preserving morale." In terms of story, there is
little more to Losey's film. He does nothing to "open out" his theatrical
source. The film does not show Private Hamp (Tom Courtenay) "walking
away," for example, nor does it contain any action footage of the war. There
is also no tension as to the final outcome, since Hamp is first shown on screen
when a shot of a skeleton in a British army uniform slowly dissolves into
Courtenay's gaunt features.

King and Country is concerned, above all, with Hamp's court-martial and his encounter with Captain Hargreaves (Dirk Bogarde), the officer detailed against his will to defend him. At their first meeting, Hargreaves irritatedly brushes aside the accused's gratitude and makes him stand at attention while they talk. Hamp's story is simple enough. Having volunteered in 1914 as a result of a dare made by his wife and her mother, he has been on the front longer than almost anyone else in the company. He has watched most of those with whom he came out disappear, either dead or alive, into the mud, like 300,000 other soldiers during World War I, or like his friend from down the street who was blown apart by a shell—all over Hamp, who had to be given a new uniform. Finally, he simply cannot take any more of the mud, the rats, and the nonstop shelling on a front which has not moved more than a mile in either direction in three years. So he simply sets out to walk home, with no leave and no real hope of getting across the Channel to England.

Hamp's desertion is not properly thought out. He is certainly not protesting against the war, nor is he even particularly upset by the fact that his wife has left him. After three years in the trenches, he is no longer capable of feeling *anything*. In short, Hamp's actions are not heroic. Faced with his passivity, Hargreaves is forced to look at the war in a way in which he has never done before, and he gradually becomes obsessed with the need to defend and save Hamp. He is not only motivated out of sympathy for Hamp, but also out of a need to justify his own presence and behavior.

The court-martial is ruthlessly and militarily efficient. The main evidence is provided by the narrow-minded but desperately overworked Medical Officer, Captain O'Sullivan (Leo McKern). Hamp's desertion resulted from "sheer blue funk" (cowardice). Hargreaves, faced with Hamp's inability to give the "right" answers to the Court's questions since he is too trusting and too naïve to "play the game" in the way expected of him, launches into an impassioned defense. This prompts comment from the defending officer that "A proper court is concerned with law. It's a bit amateur to plead for justice." Hamp is sentenced to death, and the sentence is almost immediately confirmed by Headquarters with a terse dispatch: "Your batallion moving up tomorrow. Imperative to encourage morale. Sentence of death to be carried out immediately."

The night before the execution, Hamp's platoon mates get into his cell and make him paralytically drunk. Then, blindfolding him, they enact a cruel, heavily symbolic parody of the coming execution, although it is no crueler than the parody of justice that has led up to it. The chaplain (Vivian Matalon) comes to administer a last communion, but Hamp, drunk, vomits up the communion wafer. The next morning, the firing squad is still drunk and bungles the execution. Hargreaves walks over to the still breathing Hamp, who asks "Isn't it finished yet?" Hargreaves then shoots him in the mouth.

The excellence of *King and Country* lies in the unrelenting way it tells its appalling story. It is a film of mud, death, and despair. The film's visual texture is determined by the photographs from the Imperial War Museum which are cut into the action; in this sense, it is a realistic film. Made on a modest budget of £85,000 (about $220,000 at that time), *King and Country* was shot in only eighteen days, almost entirely on a single set which reproduced the conditions of the trenches to an occasionally alarming degree. Not only real mud and real rats were used, but also the carcass of a real horse. After the festival screenings in Venice, New York, and London in 1964, the company clearly did not know quite what to do with the film; they finally released it in Britain in December, 1964. Reviews were generally excellent—the *London Evening News* described it as "one of the half dozen greatest war films ever made"—but there were a number of reservations about Losey's stylized, theatrical treatment of his subject. Kenneth Tynan in the London *Observer* criticized the film's "emotive verbiage" and "italicized script," and Charles Barr, writing in *Movie*, commented: "I've met more people who just can't decide whether they like it than with any other film." When *King and Country* was finally released in the United States in January, 1966, similar reservations were expressed: while Bosley Crowther in *The New York Times* called it "an intense, compelling picture," *The New Yorker* found it "bold, challenging but curiously flawed."

Reservations about *King and Country* arise out of the feeling that Losey has overworked his material. Despite the sharply contrasted, documentary style of Denys Coop's black-and-white cinematography, the film is at times almost expressionistic in style. One series of still dissolves shows a body washed into the mud by the rain, then cuts to a Gainsborough painting in the Colonel's tent, contrasting the savagery of war with the civilized charade enacted by the officers. Another scene which illustrates this tendency shows Hargreaves carrying Hamp's death sentence; he stumbles and drops it and himself into the clinging mud. The most evidently theatrical device in the film, however, is Losey's use of a "Greek chorus" (his own phrase) of ordinary soldiers, speaking in something very close to verse. This chorus punctuates the action, comments on it, interjects ritual complaints, and even at times produces a low-level variation or parody of it, as in the mock execution of Hamp or the heavily symbolic scene in which they "try" a rat trapped in a tin helmet before executing it by stoning it to death in a pool of water.

Losey's touch is much surer with the rigid structure of the film, which dispenses entirely with fade-ins and fade-outs, and instead links scenes with inserts of stills. Posed Edwardian snapshots from Hamp's home life in London are used as "a combination of memory and fantasy and reality," in Losey's words. The harrowing official photographs from the Imperial War Museum are similarly used as the only "action footage" in the film.

King and Country is a symmetrical film, opening with an ironic shot of a war memorial with modern background traffic noise and an inscription praising "The Royal Fellowship. . . ." The camera pans around the base of the monument to complete the phrase with ". . . of Death," a grotesque phrase actually to be found on the Hyde Park Corner War Memorial in London. The opening sequence is reversed for the film's close. The camera pans down to Hamp's body in the mud, and the frame freezes, transfixing Hamp in a pose which is not royal and has very little to do with fellowship, but is undeniably dead. Thematically and formally the circle of the movie is complete.

In the final analysis, Losey does not attempt to make *King and Country* a realistic film, or one that appeals to our emotions. It is a cold, brilliant exercise in style, a formally perfect, theatrical, and even intellectual film. Reactions to it will be determined by the individual viewer's reaction to this kind of filmmaking. It is a powerful rarity in English-language cinema and deserves its reputation as such.

Nick Roddick

KING SOLOMON'S MINES

Released: 1950
Production: Sam Zimbalist for Metro-Goldwyn-Mayer
Direction: Compton Bennett and Andrew Marton
Screenplay: Helen Deutsch; based on the novel of the same name by H. Rider Haggard
Cinematography: Robert Surtees (AA)
Editing: Ralph E. Winters and Conrad A. Nervig (AA)
Running time: 102 minutes

Principal characters:
Elizabeth Curtis	Deborah Kerr
Allan Quatermain	Stewart Granger
John Goode	Richard Carlson
Smith	Hugo Haas
Eric Masters	Lowell Gilmore
Khiva	Kimursi
Umbopa	Siriaque
Chief Gagool	Sekaryongo
King Twala	Baziga

In 1950, M-G-M came up with a splashy Technicolor remake of *King Solomon's Mines* (1937), an outstanding adventure film which remains a classic of the genre. Codirected by Compton Bennett, the British director also responsible for *The Seventh Veil* (1945), *The Years Between* (1946), and *That Forsythe Woman* (1949), and Hungarian-born Andrew Marton, second-unit director on such action films as *The Red Badge of Courage* (1951), *A Farewell to Arms* (1957), *Ben-Hur* (1959), and *55 Days at Peking* (1962), *King Solomon's Mines* boasted the benefits of location filming. Only the third motion picture to be filmed entirely on location in Africa, it was the first to treat the African native with any measure of respect or dignity. Native Watussis were given major roles, and the African dialect spoken by Stewart Granger is actually excellent Swahili. A virtual travelogue, *King Solomon's Mines* leads the audience in the manner of a safari through myriad assorted wildlife. Included in the film is a marvelous stampede of hundreds of antelopes, zebras, and other African fauna. Cinematographer Robert Surtees, who won an Oscar for the film, does an outstanding job of capturing the vivid African landscape.

Critical response to the film was mixed, although the overall reaction was positive. The scenic novelty, teeming wildlife, and sheer spectacle were praised, but complaints about the script abounded. Considered too predictable, artificial, and melodramatic, *King Solomon's Mines* was likened to a low-budget Tarzan tale, although in actual fact, the book, written by H. Rider Haggard in 1885, was the first African adventure story and spawned the

Burroughs Tarzan series. An immensely popular novel, *King Solomon's Mines* was written on a bet that Haggard could not write anything half as good as Robert Louis Stevenson's *Treasure Island*. Whether he succeeded or not is debatable, but Stevenson himself was later to correspond with Haggard, offering praise of *King Solomon's Mines* and of Haggard's imagination, fine poetic usage, and "command of the savage way of talking." The film manages to capture all of these qualities.

Allan Quatermain, the main character of both the book and the film, is based on Haggard himself. A respected and honored English gentleman, Haggard was an Imperial politician and agricultural expert, knighted in 1912, who was also a mystic with a particular affinity for ancient Egypt, Iceland, and the Zulus. Working in Africa during the time of the Zulu war and the Boer Rebellion provided the background essential to Haggard's novels.

Cast as Allan Quatermain is British star Stewart Granger. Thirty-six-years old and one of England's most successful stars, Granger had been offered a seven-year contract by M-G-M, reportedly worth one-and-a-half-million dollars. Errol Flynn had been cast originally, but was shifted to the less illustrious *Kim* (1951), a rather disastrous step in his career. *King Solomon's Mines* was the first film of Granger's contract, one which would introduce him to American audiences, make him a star, and open the way to his future roles as a swashbuckler. As a relatively young, dashing, and virile hero, Granger was probably farther from the Quatermain of the book than was Sir Cedric Hardwicke, who played the character in the earlier Gaumont-British production of *King Solomon's Mines*, which also starred Paul Robeson as the native, Umbopa. An even earlier silent version was filmed in 1919 by a South African company. For the purposes of the 1950 Hollywood film, however, which deviated somewhat from the novel's original plot, Granger was eminently suitable. M-G-M took the bare essentials of the novel, a search for a lost diamond mine in the unexplored interior of Africa, and romanticized it for American audiences by adding Deborah Kerr as a love interest notably lacking in the book.

The film opens with a prim and rather oblique Elizabeth Curtis (Deborah Kerr) approaching Quatermain. Her husband, Sir Henry Curtis, has vanished on a search for the fabled diamond mines of King Solomon. Elizabeth wants to hire Quatermain to lead her on an expedition in search of the mines and her missing husband. She remains strangely evasive, however, as to the real reason for her insisted personal accompaniment. Quatermain, puzzled and contemptuous, refuses at first, relenting later upon being offered a sum substantial enough to provide for the future of his son. Additional members of the party are Elizabeth's brother, John Goode (Richard Carlson), and various native guides and pack-bearers. Immediately, an antipathy and competition can be sensed between the film's two main characters. Quatermain resents having a woman along on the safari, while Elizabeth, in her turn, is determined to keep up and present no additional difficulties. Quatermain's gruff, chauvinistic nature is unsettling to her.

Much of the first part of *King Solomon's Mines* deals merely with the emotional conflict between Elizabeth and Quatermain, the mystery surrounding Elizabeth's relationship with her husband, and the constant intrusion of the wildlife in the form of hairy spiders, pythons, stampeding animals, and a rampaging bull elephant who kills one of Granger's men. (This film, incidentally, treats animals with as much dignity as the natives and makes a good case against unnecessary killing.) The action picks up as the party is joined by the mysterious, seven-foot-tall Umbopa, played by the Watussi, Siriaque. Quatermain is immediately suspicious, but Elizabeth and her brother see no harm in him, and his presence as a guide is deemed necessary.

Eventually, a chance meeting with a solitary crazed white man named Smith (Hugo Haas), who claims to have seen Henry Curtis pass through and who is in league with the wicked Chief Gagool (Sekaryongo) and his tribe of cannibals, leads to a frantic chase scene through the jungle and the loss of Quatermain's best man, Khiva (Kimursi). A night spent together in a tree is the catalyst which finally brings Quatermain and Elizabeth together, their initial antipathy having masked a deeper mutual attraction. The search for Elizabeth's husband is resumed, but with a good deal less than the original enthusiasm.

Umbopa leads the group to his native land, a splendid place of mountains and plains, revealing, through a snake tattooed around his waist, that he is the rightful although dispossessed king of this land. Quatermain's suspicions have been groundless. Promising an old hag as guide to the diamond mines, Umbopa stays on in an attempt to secure his throne, while the rest continue their search. The mines, which are dazzling, are found, along with the skeletal remains of Elizabeth's husband. She now reveals that she had never really loved her husband and that her lack of affection had caused him to begin his quest for the mines; guilt had prompted her to search for him. Curtis' death, of course, clears the way for a romance between Elizabeth and Quatermain.

Just as everything seems happily settled, however, the old hag, on orders from the evil Watussi, King Twala (Baziga), has sealed the party into the mines. All hope seems lost, until an underground river is discovered which leads them to their eventual escape. Returning to the Watussi kingdom, they arrive in time to witness the contest between King Twala and Umbopa. Filmed with lavish spectacle and authenticity, their hand-to-hand combat is the visual and dramatic climax of the film. Umbopa is restored to his throne after winning the fight, and Quatermain, Elizabeth, and Goode set happily off on a comparatively safe and eventless return.

Perhaps as Hollywood contrived it the plot of *King Solomon's Mines* was rather traditional and melodramatic, but the entire film was made with such flair, color, authenticity, and enthusiasm that it comes across with a freshness, charm, and zest that is enormously appealing. Under the direction of Bennett and Marton, *King Solomon's Mines* moves with the crisp pace and suspense so essential to an adventure film, yet allows for depth and complexity of characterization.

As Quatermain, Granger dominates the film, expressing the competence and quiet efficiency of a capably renowned guide with years of experience behind him. Tough and tan, with silvered temples lending added maturity, Granger is the typical strong, handsome hero type. Not so typically, he is also a rather vulnerable and complex man whose difficulty in yielding to his softer emotions makes his capitulation all the more touching. As the spirited Elizabeth, Kerr is a satisfactory match for Granger, combining stubbornness and pluck with her own vulnerability. If predictable, their characters' gradual romance is nevertheless pleasing and exciting, and their successful pairing in this film led to two other films, *The Prisoner of Zenda* (1952) and *Young Bess* (1953), also for M-G-M.

The dominant feature of *King Solomon's Mines* remains the wildlife, spectacle, and authenticity rendered by the African location filming. It is this aspect above all which gives the film its freshness and makes it stand out as one of the best in a long line of similar African adventure films.

Grace Anne Morsberger

KING'S ROW

Released: 1941
Production: Hal B. Wallis for Warner Bros.
Direction: Sam Wood
Screenplay: Casey Robinson; based on the novel of the same name by Henry Bellamann
Cinematography: James Wong Howe
Editing: Ralph Dawson
Running time: 130 minutes

Principal characters:
Randy Monaghan	Ann Sheridan
Parris Mitchell	Robert Cummings
Drake McHugh	Ronald Reagan
Cassandra Tower	Betty Field
Dr. Henry Gordon	Charles Coburn
Dr. Alexander Tower	Claude Rains
Harriet Gordon	Judith Anderson
Madame Von Eln	Maria Ouspenskaya
Colonel Skeffington	Harry Davenport

Wartime films, in order to be successful, were often escapist comedies, but *King's Row* is the exact antithesis of the old formula which Hollywood has found to be so fruitful; it is a solid, thought-provoking film which brings much of Henry Bellamann's best-selling and controversial novel of 1940 to the screen. It succeeded in helping America momentarily forget the world conflict, and in the process became one of the best films produced during the war years. It was, in fact, somewhat of a surprise, for apparently few people expected it to rise above the mire of melodrama when transplanted from novel to film.

King's Row was the name of a small, turn-of-the-century town that could have been located almost anywhere in the Midwest, although Bellamann's hometown of Fulton, Missouri, saw too many similarities to believe that it could be any other place. The citizens of King's Row see their town as a good, clean place, a pleasant environment in which to rear children. Beneath the town's veneer, however, is a hidden element of sadism, cruelty, and insanity. Such is the stuff of which best-sellers are made, and the story was a natural for Hollywood to bring to the screen. Censorship and the difficulty of coping with a story that covered a thirty-year period presented serious problems for screenwriter Casey Robinson and director Sam Wood, but the end product is a film that captured the essence of the original novel. The plot of *King's Row* is filled with tragedy, cruelty, and suffering; it is a particularly absorbing tale which grips the viewer from beginning to end.

The story revolves around four young people in the town, and is in essence two intertwining love stories. Parris Mitchell (Robert Cummings) is a sensitive and intelligent boy who gives up the piano to become a world-famous psychiatrist; Drake McHugh (Ronald Reagan) is his carefree and worldly-wise friend who is brought down by personal tragedy; Cassandra Tower (Betty Field), the prettiest girl in town, becomes strange and baffling as she grows up; and Randy Monaghan (Ann Sheridan) is the girl from across the tracks. Their lives are altered and affected by other characters, such as Dr. Alexander Tower (Claude Rains), Cassandra's father; the sadistic Dr. Henry Gordon (Charles Coburn); Colonel Skeffington (Harry Davenport), friend and instructor of Parris, and Madame Von Eln (Maria Ouspenskaya), the grandmother and guardian of Parris. There are many other characters, of course, and enough incidents revolving around them to fill up several other films of more modest proportions, but since *King's Row* as a film did not share the novel's freedom from time constraints, the result is that some of the characters are only superficially developed.

The destiny of Parris Mitchell seems to be to try to untangle the web of madness and illness which pervades the small town. Before he is old enough to carry out his cherished dream of studying psychiatry in Vienna, he has had a thorough apprenticeship in King's Row. He has loved the beautiful and neurotic Cassandra, only to have her murdered by her father, who in turn kills himself. His friend Drake has had both legs amputated unnecessarily after being struck by a train; Dr. Gordon, who performed the operation, saw it as a way to punish Drake's wickedness. When Gordon's daughter, Louise (Jayne Meadows), who loves Drake, challenges his decision, she is given the choice of remaining silent or being committed to an insane asylum. The shocking events are an actor's field day, and the excellent cast makes the most of them without ever overdoing their parts. Even one bad portrayal of Bellamann's psychopathic characters would have made the whole film ludicrous, but fortunately that does not happen.

The story flows like halting, troubled speech at times, occasionally inarticulate and broken; yet at other moments the film has a compelling eloquence like that of Fyodor Dostoevski. It is an ugly and difficult story, mixed with pathos and nostalgia, which combine to form a story of considerable emotional power. While much of the film is undoubtedly gruesome and bleak, the total product is warm, inspiring, and believable. There is a feeling of likelihood and truth to the story which is never a coincidence; it is the result of fine writing, acting, and direction. The conclusion, although somewhat overdramatic, does not detract from the genuinely compassionate portrayal of life in a small town of not so long ago. In that it succeeds where a latter-day imitation called *Peyton Place* (1957) could only flounder in melodrama.

The high quality of *King's Row* as a film results from excellent directing and unusually good performances from a superb cast. Wood, who had previously directed *Goodbye, Mr. Chips* (1939), *Our Town* (1940), and *Kitty Foyle* (1940), achieves an excellent balance of drama, mood, and timing. The somber atmosphere pervades throughout, yet the viewer's interest is sustained. The screenplay by Robinson is a most competent job of a difficult task—that of toning down the sensational novel in order to get past the censor, without losing the story in the process. By and large he succeeds. The most controversial aspect of the novel, the incestuous feelings of Dr. Tower which lead to the death of his daughter Cassandra, is obviously a difficult area. The solution in the film is to have Tower observe insanity in his daughter. Rather than have her marry Parris and thereby destroy the young man's promising career, Tower kills her and himself. Cummings as Parris plays the role with a gentility which contrasts pleasantly with the brashness required of Reagan as Drake, the town's wild youngster. Future President Reagan, an ex-sports announcer who at the time was not particularly known for any great acting ability, nevertheless turned in a stellar performance which is the high point of his career. In fact, his most dramatic line, "Where's the rest of me," delivered when he discovers that his legs have been amputated, provided the title of his autobiography. As the two doctors of King's Row, Rains and Coburn contribute portraits that are memorable, the former for its constrained humanity and the latter for its sanctimonious exterior hiding of a vicious strain of sadism. The role of Cassandra is a difficult one to fill, since she is killed rather early in the story, and apparently many actresses, including Bette Davis, turned it down. The choice of Field was a fortuitous one, for she catches with haunting intensity the half-angelic, half-sensual quality of a girl whose life is overshadowed by the threat of insanity. Perhaps the finest performance, however, is that of Sheridan as Randy, the wholehearted girl from the wrong side of the tracks who rises magnificently above a crushing tragedy. Sheridan, better known as the "oomph girl" in previous roles, demonstrates that she did not have to rely only on her physical attributes; her performance is that of a seasoned, competent star. Supporting roles played by Anderson, Ouspenskaya, and Davenport contribute considerably to the overall effect and success of the story.

King's Row succeeds as an unusual wartime motion picture because of an artful blend of essential characteristics: a good script, excellent acting, superior directing, and careful attention to detail. It is believable, even with its presentation of what today appears to be an inordinate amount of madness and cruelty in a small town. In spite of overlength, the film has an excellent apportionment of dramatic qualities which succeed in capturing and holding the audience's attention from beginning to end. It was generally well received by the critics and by the public and was a hit at the box office, no doubt helped in part by the tremendous success of the best-selling novel. It was nominated for Academy Awards in three categories—Best Picture, Director, and Cinematography (black-and-white)—but failed to win when the Oscars were awarded. Nevertheless, *King's Row* has continued through the years to entertain and to impress audiences with its excellence and honesty. Although *King's Row* was seldom seen on television during the late 1960's and 1970's because of Ronald Reagan's political activities, since his election in 1980 it has been brought back frequently, a tribute to the popularity of the film itself, as much as to the popularity of the new President.

Dennis Thomison

KISS ME DEADLY

Released: 1955
Production: Robert Aldrich for United Artists
Direction: Robert Aldrich
Screenplay: A. I. Bezzerides; based on the novel of the same name by Mickey Spillane
Cinematography: Ernest Laszlo
Editing: Michael Luciano
Running time: 105 minutes

Principal characters:
Mike Hammer	Ralph Meeker
Velda	Maxine Cooper
Christina	Cloris Leachman
Lily Carver	Gaby Rodgers
Nick	Nick Dennis
Dr. Soberin	Albert Dekker

Kiss Me Deadly is one of the best of a group of films known as *film noir.* Literally translated as "black films" this American film movement was named by French critics (long admirers of American films) who, after not seeing imported films during World War II, noticed a visual and thematic darkness in a large proportion of the many years' worth of films that they saw after the war. *Film noir,* pervading many films produced from the early 1940's through the mid-1950's, is characterized by a dark view of the world which is reflected in both the narrative themes and the visual style of the films. This world view is paranoid, claustrophobic, hopeless, and without clear moral or personal identity. In it, man has been inexplicably uprooted from those values, beliefs, and endeavors that offer him a sense of meaning and stability, and nothing— friends, lovers, and even the natural world, according to *Kiss Me Deadly*— can be depended upon for direction. The visual style conveys this mood through expressive use of darkness which is both real, in the predominantly underlit and nighttime scenes, and also pyschological, in the shadows and claustrophobic compositions which overwhelm the character. *Film noir* is usually populated by fringe characters—small-time gangsters, poorly paid cops, and "B"-girls. In this sleazy environment, crime is almost a fact of life, and thus the detective film genre dominates *film noir* because it is perfectly suited to unfold the duplicity and hopelessness of the *noir* sensibility.

The roots and causes of *film noir* are many and diverse, but one important element is dime-novel detective fiction. The best of it is represented by the writing of Raymond Chandler, Dashiell Hammett, and James M. Cain; and one level lower is Mickey Spillane's Mike Hammer series, from which *Kiss Me Deadly* was taken. Hammer is not the romantic, chivalrous, doomed-to-disappointment idealist that Chandler's Philip Marlowe is. In *Kiss Me Deadly*, he is little more than a cheap hood, a private detective who specializes in divorce cases and is not above using his sensual assistant, the curvacious Velda (Maxine Cooper), who is in love with him, to set up husbands.

The film opens on a dark road at night with the white-coated figure of a woman running along the highway, the noise of her breath rasping loudly on the soundtrack. She stands in the middle of the road, forcing Mike Hammer (Ralph Meeker), who is driving by, to pull sharply off the road to avoid hitting her. She hitches a ride with him. Her name is Christina (Cloris Leachman) and she tells him that she has escaped from a mental institution where she was held because of information that she has. At a road block, he tells the officer that she is his wife when asked if they have seen a woman on the road. Further on, Mike and Christina are captured by the men who are after her. Mike is knocked out but comes to consciousness occasionally to see an expensive pair of shoes and Christina's feet dangling as she is tortured. When he wakes up, he is in the hospital, after barely surviving an "accident" in which his car was pushed over a cliff. Mike receives a new car and finds two bombs inside. He also gets a letter from Christina which simply says "Remember me." Over the objections of the police, he pursues some clues, which lead him to Lily Carver (Gaby Rogers), a gun-toting blond who is impersonating Christina's roommate. Mike gets the key to a locker by beating up the morgue attendant who found it during Christina's autopsy. Upon opening the locker, however, he is burned by a luminous substance that escapes before he can close the lid. In a series of complex plot developments, Lily Carver steals the box and Velda is captured by Lily's confederate, the mysterious Dr. Soberin (Albert Dekker). Mike finds them all in a house on the beach. Lily shoots both Dr. Soberin and Mike, however, and then opens the box to see her treasure. She cannot close the lid and is turned into a pillar of flame while apocalyptic, unearthly sounds dominate the soundtrack. The entire house erupts in an explosion which may be simply the first in an ever-growing series. There are two versions of this film, one in which the final shot of the exploding beach house is totally desolate, indicating the negative fate of the entire world, and the other in which two small figures (presumably Mike and Velda) are seen escaping down the beach.

Kiss Me Deadly is a fast-paced, brutal action film, as is quickly indicated when Mike's friend Nick (Nick Dennis) the mechanic is killed when the car under which he is working is lowered, crushing his body. The film received mixed reviews, some recognizing its excellence over other "B" detective films, but many not. A CBS-television censor (Ed Nathan) banned media ads for the film, claiming that it had "no purpose except to incite sadism and bestiality in human beings." Most agreed, however, that *Kiss Me Deadly* was the best of the Hammer films. Yet this did not exactly constitute thunderous applause in 1955. It took the perspective of history to give this little masterpiece its full due. Made in twenty-two days, it was not even economically profitable, although its director, Robert Aldrich, considered it one of his best films. Recent critics, writing in the 1970's on the genre of *film noir*, place *Kiss Me Deadly* in the circle of films that defined the movement.

In spite of the singular lack of appeal of every character (with the exception of the short-lived Christina and Nick), there are definite elements which raise *Kiss Me Deadly* above the average detective film. Character, in fact, figures very little. Mike is a contemptible, egotistical blunderer, and Velda is his narcissistic, manipulatively sexy partner. Lily Carver is a greedy "spider woman" who gets her just desserts; the police are unattractive and ineffectual; and the gangsters are mainly unseen evils. Christina, however, the victim that Hammer helps only when he is forced to, and then fails to protect, possesses cultural associations and insights that make her take on a much larger role than simply an excuse for the plot to get under way. She quotes poetry, is named for Christina Rossetti (whose poem gives Hammer the clues he needs), and listens to classical music. Her name is Berga Torn in the novel, lacking both the evocative sound and the culture which was added in the film.

Aldrich's film also expands the fear indicated in the novel into a broader catastrophe. Instead of the mafia of the novel, Hammer is fighting the international powers (always implied but only represented in the persons of the police and the urbane Dr. Soberin), all of whom are looking for the "great whatsit." What it is, is never specified but it appears to be an atomic device as is indicated both by its burning, explosive properties and by the words used to arouse fear about it: "Los Alamos," "Mahattan Project," and "Trinity." Lily Carver thus becomes, according to Dr. Soberin's literary metaphor, a modern-day Pandora instead of merely a greedy woman. When she opens the dreaded box, she is the first to turn into a pillar of fire, signaling the form by which the world will perish.

One of the primary obsessions of *film noir* is the destructive power of woman's sexuality. The "spider women" of these films lure men into danger and crime through their sexuality, before betraying and destroying them. There is less power in the sexuality of Velda than in many *film noir* heroines (Mike is "in love with himself" instead of her), but Lily Carver follows the archetype of destructive sexuality. In Spillane's novel she shoots Mike after exposing her mutilated body to him and becoming a metaphor for the filth and disease of women's sexuality. In the film, she is less sexual and more abstract, with no real attachment to anyone. She is primarily an angel of cosmic destruction. Aldrich considers *Kiss Me Deadly* a reflection of Cold War paranoia concerning the atomic bomb. It is also an excellent example of a film in which the source material—the Spillane novel—is expanded and improved upon.

Janey Place

KISS ME KATE

Released: 1953
Production: Jack Cummings for Metro-Goldwyn-Mayer
Direction: George Sidney
Screenplay: Dorothy Kingsley; based on the Broadway play of the same name by Sam Spewack and Bella Spewack and on the play *The Taming of the Shrew* by William Shakespeare
Cinematography: Charles Rosher
Editing: Ralph E. Winters
Art direction: Cedric Gibbons
Choreography: Hermes Pan
Song: Cole Porter
Running time: 109 minutes

Principal characters:
Lilli Vanessi	Kathryn Grayson
Fred Graham	Howard Keel
Lois Lane	Ann Miller
Bill Calhoun	Tommy Rall
Cole Porter	Himself
Hoodlums	Keenan Wynn
	James Whitmore
Bianca's suitors	Bobby Van
	Bob Fosse
	Kurt Kasznar

One of the handsomest, wittiest, and most colorful musicals of the 1950's, *Kiss Me Kate* was first a hit Broadway show based on William Shakespeare's *The Taming of the Shrew* (1593-1594), a play about a fortune-hunter, Petruchio, who chooses a shrewish woman, Katharina, for his wife because she is wealthy, and then makes her obedient to him. The story of the film is that of an egotistical producer-actor and his temperamental ex-wife, who are brought together to star in a musical version of *The Taming of the Shrew*. During the production of the play, the backstage scenes between the two parallel the tempestuous course of the onstage relationship of Katharina and Petruchio.

The parallelism between Shakespeare's play and the modern love affair is impressively underscored by Cole Porter's songs, which are smoothly integrated with the plot; in fact, many critics feel this is Porter's best score for a musical comedy. In the songs for the Shakespearean scenes Porter often effectively uses words, phrases, and lines taken directly from Shakespeare's play. In the others he uses his own sophisticated style for the lyrics, which include witty and often suggestive lines (cleaned up for the film), forced rhymes, and repetitive words.

In the film's opening sequence at the apartment of Fred Graham (Howard Keel), Fred is trying to persuade his ex-wife, Lilli Vanessi (Kathryn Grayson), to play opposite him in a musical version of *The Taming of the Shrew*. Lilli arrives bristling with hostility, but is persuaded by Cole Porter, who is also there, to sing a song with Fred, "So in Love." By the end of the duet the audience knows they are still in love with each other. Just when Lilli has relaxed her defenses, Lois Lane (Ann Miller)—Fred's latest flame—arrives to audition for the role of Bianca. Determined to win over Porter, Lois whips off her coat, revealing a skimpy costume, and launches into a sizzling rendition of "Too Darn Hot," in which she taps madly around Fred's living room, uses a black fan for a flirtatious effect, and shakes her hips outrageously. Lilli is vexed and says she cannot do the show because she will be on her honeymoon. She changes her mind, however, when it seems that the role will be offered to Lois.

During rehearsals Fred and Lilli continue to quarrel. Lilli is jealous of Lois, and Lois, for the sake of her career, pretends to be interested in Fred although she really loves Bill Calhoun (Tommy Rall), a dancer who likes to gamble and has signed Fred's name to an I.O.U. for ten thousand dollars. When Lois learns of this escapade, she sings "Why Can't You Behave?" to him, and the two do a fast, funny, and—on his part—flippant dance on the roof of the theater where they have gone to be alone.

Fred and Lilli bicker continually, with Fred domineering over her much as Petruchio domineers over Katharina in the play. He forbids her to eat before the performance because it gives her indigestion, and he bars her fiancé from the theater. In the middle of their sparring, however, they reminisce about the shows in which they have appeared together and then sing "Wunderbar," a lilting waltz that Porter intended as a satire on Viennese waltzes. Fred and Lilli waltz between their two dressing rooms and, when the music is over, kiss. It is now clear that the latent affection suggested in their first duet, "So in Love," has surfaced. Fred sends Lois a bouquet of flowers on opening night, but by mistake they are delivered to Lilli, who is touched and easily persuaded by Fred not to read the accompanying card.

The play within the film opens with the troupe singing "We Open in Venice" while throwing confetti at the audience. Fred, as Petruchio, then lounges against the proscenium arch and introduces the main characters in *The Taming of the Shrew*. As he introduces them, each character is individually picked out by a spotlight before the entire stage is illuminated. The techniques are stage devices, but they are clever and effective in the film as well.

Bianca then explains to Lucentio, one of her suitors, that she cannot marry until her older sister Kate finds a husband and then assures all three of her suitors (Bobby Van, Bob Fosse, and Kurt Kasznar) of her own eagerness to marry by singing "Tom, Dick, or Harry." Petruchio enters on a donkey and informs Bianca's suitors in song, "I've Come to Wive It Wealthily in Padua."

Katharina now struts about the stage, singing "I Hate Men," as she throws dishes and cutlery, now and then crashing a tankard on a table for added emphasis. During this number stage techniques are again used as a single spotlight picks her out on an otherwise darkened stage. At the end of the song she hurls the tankard straight at the camera, the lights come up, and she goes to the front of the stage to take her bows.

Indeed, in all of the scenes of the play within the film we are kept aware that the scene is being performed on a stage in front of an audience. Not only are there occasional shots which show the audience, but also the elegant scenery is designed as if for an actual theater stage to create the illusion of depth and perspective. As well as being excellently suited to creating the proper theatrical atmosphere, the scenery and costumes are visually attractive. Against the delicately colored backgrounds the costumes are sumptuous and rich: bright red is used for Katharina, black and white for Petruchio, and green and orange for Bianca. In addition, the design and staging reflect the fact that the film was shot using a three-dimensional technique called "3-D." With this in mind, some actions certain to startle the audience were used (such as Katharina's throwing the tankard), and other scenes, especially the musical numbers, were designed to use effectively the realistic depth produced by the technique. Although shot in 3-D, *Kiss Me Kate* has usually been shown in the standard flat form because of the complexities of projecting a 3-D film (including the necessity of having the audience wear special glasses). In 3-D the film is a great example of the dramatic and artistic capabilities of the process, and even in the standard form it reaps the benefits of the designers' emphasis on depth.

Petruchio agrees to marry Kate because of her large dowry, but he admits that she is not the kind of wife he had wished to marry as he sings "Were Thine That Special Face." This last song and "I've Come to Wive It Wealthily in Padua" combine several lines from Shakespeare's play with Porter's lyrics in a sophisticated blend. While Lilli, as Katharina, listens to Petruchio's song, she reads the card that accompanied Fred's bouquet. Enraged, she throws the bouquet at Fred on stage and tears the card up in his face, screaming that he is a louse. Fred threatens to spank her onstage if she does not behave, she slaps him, and he carries out his threat.

Lilli decides to leave in the middle of the show and marry her fiancé immediately, although Fred tries unsuccessfully to persuade her to stay. When two hoodlums (James Whitmore and Keenan Wynn) appear in his dressing room, however, demanding the money for the I.O.U. to which Bill signed his name, he tells them he will not have any if Lilli walks out of the show; so they persuade Lilli to stay by threatening her with a gun and end up onstage carrying the train of her wedding dress during the marriage of Kate and Petruchio. Once involved in the play, they function as clowns or fools do in Shakespeare's comedies—as comic relief. At one point a screen falls down, and the theater audience sees the two playing cards, oblivious of their surroundings.

Petruchio sings about his bachelor existence in "Where Is the Life That Late I Led" (another line from Shakespeare's play), as he thumbs through his little black book, remembering past girl friends. The action then shifts backstage as Tex (Lilli's fiancé) has arrived with an ambulance to take Lilli away; Lilli claims she cannot sit down since the spanking administered by Fred. Lois sees Tex and reminds him of the time she had something in her eye in Houston and he took her all the way to El Paso to get it out, but he pretends not to remember her. When Bill sees Lois talking to Tex he is jealous, but she pacifies him by singing a rollicking "Always True to You in My Fashion."

Meanwhile, the two hoodlums discover their boss has been killed and the I.O.U. cancelled. They allow Lilli to leave, although Fred continues to plead with her to stay. She drives off with Tex in a Rolls-Royce ornamented with a huge pair of steer horns. To cheer up a depressed Fred, the two gangsters sing "Brush Up Your Shakespeare" and do a soft-shoe dance. Fred smiles at their antics, but he is still despondent as the curtain opens for the last act of the play. The scene is Bianca's wedding, and she and her three suitors sing, "From This Moment On." The unsuccessful suitors are comforted by two other women and the result is a sizzling, colorful dance that is one of the film's high points. Finally, the three men drag the unresisting women off the stage. When the men return to take their bows they are in turn dragged off by the women.

As Petruchio, Fred wanders disconsolately onstage, waiting for Lilli's understudy to appear, but suddenly Lilli enters, in costume, and recites the lines "I Am Ashamed That Women Are So Simple." (The words are Shakespeare's and in the play they were sung rather than spoken.) They proclaim Lilli's submission to Fred as well as Kate's to Petruchio. The film ends as Fred/Petruchio picks up Lilli/Kate, saying "Kiss Me, Kate," and throwing away his little black book.

Kiss Me Kate is an elegant, sophisticated musical comedy with a witty Porter score and excellent acting and singing by Keel as Fred Graham and Grayson as Lilli Vanessi. Besides having wonderful singing voices, both show an unexpected flair for comedy. Tall, virile, and handsome, Keel fits the part of Fred/Petruchio perfectly; petite and fiery as Lilli/Kate, Grayson is equally well-cast. The supporting cast is excellent, particularly Miller's warm, good-natured Lois Lane, whose songs and dances are some of the best in the film. Whitmore and Wynn prove themselves adept comedians as the two hoodlums, and Van, Fosse, and Carol Haney are often electrifying in their dance routines. Under the brisk direction of George Sidney, *Kiss Me Kate* remains an outstanding musical comedy.

Julia Johnson

KITTY FOYLE

Released: 1940
Production: David Hempstead for RKO/Radio
Direction: Sam Wood
Screenplay: Dalton Trumbo, with additional dialogue by Donald Ogden Stewart; based on the novel of the same name by Christopher Morley
Cinematography: Robert de Grasse
Editing: Henry Berman
Art direction: Van Nest Polglase
Music: Roy Webb
Running time: 108 minutes

Principal characters:
Kitty Foyle .... Ginger Rogers (AA)
Wyn Strafford .... Dennis Morgan
Mark .... James Craig
Giono .... Edward Ciannelli
Pop .... Ernest Cossart
Mrs. Strafford .... Gladys Cooper
Delphine Detaille .... Odette Myrtil
Grandmother .... Cecil Cunningham

Ginger Rogers won an Academy Award for her performance in *Kitty Foyle* against such formidable opponents as Bette Davis, Joan Fontaine, and Katharine Hepburn, but today it is difficult to understand why. The movie has become dated. Its plucky, upwardly mobile heroine rapidly was becoming a stereotype in 1940, soon to be replaced by new female images—brash comediennes, the WACS and WAVES of World War II, and the neurotics who became more fashionable as Sigmund Freud's theories gained currency in Hollywood.

Rogers' Kitty Foyle is a very un-Freudian young woman from the wrong side of the Philadelphia tracks who meets and falls in love with a Main Line blueblood, Wyn Strafford (Dennis Morgan). When the magazine on which they work fails, Kitty goes to New York and finds a job in Delphine Detaille's exclusive department store. There she meets Mark (James Craig), a penniless intern who falls in love with her. On the night of the Philadelphia Assembly ball, a social event that Kitty has always wanted to attend, Wyn shows up to take her dancing, thereby evading the issue of presenting her to society in his home town. They elope, and Wyn takes Kitty home to meet his stuffy relatives. His mother talks about taking Kitty under her wing and preparing her for society, while his uncles explain that Wyn will lose his inheritance if he refused to live in Philadelphia. Realizing that she cannot compete with Wyn's heritage or his fortune, Kitty leaves him, only to discover that she is pregnant.

The baby is stillborn; Kitty gets her divorce and goes back to work at the store. Sent to open a branch store in Philadelphia, Kitty accidentally meets Wyn's wife and little boy, the child who could have been hers. She starts dating Mark again but the night he proposes, Wyn arrives to ask her to run away to Buenos Aires with him. After a lengthy internal debate Kitty chooses respectability and marries Mark.

The film takes the form of an extended flashback starting with Kitty's argument with herself over whether or not she should go off to live in sin with Wyn or wed her idealistic suitor. The discussion is between Kitty herself and her mirror image, which warns her of the risky social position she will be in as "Wyn's girl friend" and later, as she ages, as "that woman Wyn's involved with." Within the flashback, each new sequence begins by focusing on some landmark through the swirling snow of a glass paperweight, a talisman Kitty has kept with her since her youth. An additional device is employed which attempts to give Kitty a place in the political and social history of her time by alluding to Prohibition, the Depression, and Franklin D. Roosevelt's first election.

Aside from these devices, *Kitty Foyle* is a fairly straightforward film. As Rogers plays her, Kitty is not much different from the spunky heroines she had been portraying all along in such films as *Bachelor Mother* and the Fred Astaire musicals, and would continue to depict in *Tom, Dick and Harry* (1940) and *The Major and The Minor* (1942). She is the same self-sufficient, level-headed, optimistic young woman from the wrong side of the tracks that she plays in *The Primrose Path* (1940), which, along with *Kitty Foyle*, is one of her favorite roles and one for which the Academy briefly considered nominating her. Rogers is both glamorous and ordinary, a working girl who is both a "real" person and an inspiration to audiences who want to believe that her Cinderella story is within the realm of possibility.

Once Rogers got away from the coy hijinks of the Astaire musicals and into dramatic roles, the heroines she portrayed were typically straight shooters, moral, ambitious, and romantic. Even love does not prevent Kitty from doing the right thing. Even if she had wanted to, the Production Code would scarcely have allowed her to reside in a dubious social limbo with a still-married Wyn. Rogers' Kitty Foyle is a woman who aspires for love as much as she does for success in business. We see her as a fifteen-year-old girl in pigtails gawking at the socialites entering the Assembly ball, dreaming of "Cinderella stuff." Her favorite book is Tennyson's *The Lady of Shalott*, about the Arthurian damsel who dies of unrequited love.

Kitty, however, is made of sterner stuff. As Bosley Crowther pointed out in his *New York Times* review, comparing the screen Kitty with Christopher Morley's original: "His Kitty burned life's candle at both ends; this one burns two candles, and when one goes out she has the other handy." Crowther also complained that "the sharpness and contemporary significance of Mr. Morley's commentary are missing. His Kitty was of real flesh and blood; this one is persuasive but fictitious." The book decried the social inequality and frustration that were Kitty's lot; the screen Kitty listens to her father advise her against getting her heart broken, then she goes ahead and does what she wants, not out of egotism, but because she believes she is right. Romance and love must win out against snobbery and repression. This Kitty is not too stubborn to know when she is beaten, however, and she has the wisdom to settle for second best—the decent young man who offers her his name rather than adventure.

Rogers' leading men, Morgan and Craig, are such nonentities, that it is hard to understand what she sees in either of them. Morgan is clearly weak-willed, a handsome store-window dummy with little intellectual substance and no moral fiber. The actor is attractive, with his wavy-hair and engaging smile, but he was never a particularly notable performer. The part is so underwritten that even if Morgan were capable of delivering more, there is no meaningful context in which he could supply it. Craig is likewise personable but somewhat more substantial as a character. One of several Clark Gable look-alikes brought to Hollywood in the late 1930's and early 1940's, Craig never had much of a career. He was a capable actor, however, and here, despite being almost as pallid and inconsequential as Morgan, he is pleasant and reliable, almost a worthy rival to Morgan's social butterfly.

Sam Wood's direction is workmanlike and efficient, totally devoid (except for that portent-laden, snowy paperweight which means less than it implies) of visual style or any psychological import that would explain Kitty's romanticism or her underdeveloped professional ambitions.

Although *Kitty Foyle* is subtitled "The Natural History of a Woman," it is hardly that, either in what it says about white-collar heroines or daydreaming little girls who grow up to be equally fanciful career women. Kitty Foyle does not follow her "natural" inclinations; her head rules her heart. Common sense prevails, and Kitty, a prime illustration of Hollywood's notions of sentimental moral uplift, triumphs as an examplar of undaunted romantic rectitude.

Judith M. Kass

THE KNACK

Released: 1965
Production: Oscar Lewenstein for Woodfall
Direction: Richard Lester
Screenplay: Charles Wood; based on the play of the same name by Ann Jellicoe
Cinematography: David Watkin
Editing: Antony Gibbs
Running time: 84 minutes

Principal characters:
Nancy .... Rita Tushingham
Tolen .... Ray Brooks
Colin .... Michael Crawford
Tom .... Donal Donnelly

Director Richard Lester, who is well regarded for such early successes as the Beatle films *A Hard Day's Night* (1964) and *Help!* (1965), has gone on to make a number of well-known films, including *The Three Musketeers* (1974) and *Superman II* (1981). An often overlooked film of Lester, however, is the delightful one he made between the two Beatle films, *The Knack* (also released as *The Knack . . . And How To Get It*). *The Knack* shares with *A Hard Day's Night* the characteristics of cheerful irreverence, brisk pace, attention-getting editing, and an affinity to the spirit of youth.

Lester was born and educated in the United States, but after two years of directing live television in Philadelphia, he left for Europe. After a brief vagabond existence there, he settled in England where he resumed television directing and also made commercials. He also found himself working with a group of zany comedians called The Goons. This group, which included Peter Sellers and Spike Milligan, was to have a great influence on the style of his films, an influence that is quite discernible in *The Knack*. Indeed, Lester's first film was an eleven-minute short featuring The Goons and their ideas called *The Running, Jumping and Standing Still Film* (1959), which is a collection of visual gags. For example, a violinist reads his music (which is about one hundred yards away) through a telescope and rides a bicycle back and forth between the telescope and the music stand when it is necessary to turn the page.

Lester's style is to a great extent an editing style, and it was developed by his work in live television, in which there was no chance to cover mistakes or painstakingly work out effects, and his work in commercials, which require a message or an impression to be made quickly and economically. Even though for *The Knack* he had weeks for the filming and months for the editing, he still tried for, and achieved, a certain feeling of spontaneity reminiscent of that of live television.

Lester is not, however, undisciplined. For *The Knack*, as for most of his films, he chose a project that interested him and worked with a writer until he had a script that satisfied him. The writer was Charles Wood, and under Lester's supervision, "patting and prodding," he calls it, Wood wrote seven drafts of the screenplay. The first one Lester describes as a "total fantasy" using only the "mood" of the Ann Jellicoe stage play upon which it was based. Each draft of the screenplay, however, used more and more of the stage play, until the final version was a filmic adaptation of the play itself rather than of its mood only.

The film opens with its most striking and memorable image—a line of girls, wearing identical white sweaters, on the stairs leading to the door of Tolen (Ray Brooks). We soon find that this image is from the imagination of Colin (Michael Crawford), who is disheartened by his own lack of success with women—especially in comparison to Tolen, who has "The Knack." At the beginning of the film Colin hopes to learn the knack from Tolen, but by the end he discovers satisfaction and success in being himself rather than in an acquired technique. (This is the same theme that Woody Allen was to use some years later in *Play It Again, Sam*, 1972.)

Tolen and Tom (Donal Donnelly), a painter, live with Colin in a house that Colin owns. Their lives begin to change when a girl new to London asks them directions to the YWCA. She is Nancy (Rita Tushingham), and because she is rather plain and not stylishly dressed, she is not considered as a possible conquest by Tolen and Colin. She soon joins the others in a series of madcap adventures, the most elaborate and notable being the transporting of a large bed through the streets of London.

Throughout the film a device that was not in the stage play is used. Outsiders, usually older and rather staid-looking, watch and comment disapprovingly on the actions of the protagonists. "It will all end in tears," or "I blame it on the National Health," they remark. Lester says he actually photographed onlookers with disapproving expressions during the filming and then later put words in their mouths. Extremely effective in conveying Lester's avowed sympathy with the "youth revolution," this device gives an added dimension to the close of the film. During their adventures Nancy has become more attractive to the men, and when finally she chooses Colin and rejects Tolen's "knack," Tolen is left on the outside and joins the onlookers in clucking disapproval.

The Knack was made just as the media was discovering "swinging London" and has been called the first London picture. The filmmakers, however, got no support from the city, Lester reports. They frequently had to shoot hurriedly because the police usually stopped them whenever they were found on the city streets.

Tushingham, who plays Nancy, had won a British Academy Award with her first film role (in *A Taste of Honey*, 1962) and had played Nancy in the British production of the stage play. She conveys well the charm and attractiveness that do not depend upon the beauty or stylishness that Tolen and Colin think they want at the beginning of the film. Most of the actors and technicians who worked on *The Knack*, however, had not made a film before and were chosen by Lester because he knew them rather than because of their names or film experience. The gamble paid off, because the film, although it is not perfect, has no signs of amateurishness.

The Knack could not, of course, equal the success of *A Hard Day's Night*, but it did win the principal prize at the Cannes Film Festival in 1966 and was also successful at the box office.

Sharon Wiseman

LADIES IN RETIREMENT

Released: 1941
Production: Columbia
Direction: Charles Vidor
Screenplay: Garrett Fort and Reginald Denham; based on the play of the same name by Reginald Denham and Edward Percy
Cinematography: George Barnes
Editing: Al Clark
Running time: 91 minutes

Principal characters:
Ellen Creed .... Ida Lupino
Louisa Creed .... Edith Barrett
Emily Creed .... Elsa Lanchester
Leonora Fiske .... Isobel Elsom
Lucy .... Evelyn Keyes
Albert Feather .... Louis Hayward

When Bette Davis achieved her first important screen credit in *Of Human Bondage*, on loan-out from Warner Bros., to whom she was under contract, she paved the way for other actresses stifled in roles they were forced to play because they were contracted to do so. One of the most notable instances of this was the case of Ida Lupino, also under contract to Warner Bros. She went under contract to them in 1940 and got some important supporting roles the following year, opposite Humphrey Bogart in *High Sierra* and with Edward G. Robinson and John Garfield in Jack London's *The Sea Wolf*. She was an ambitious actress, however, and wanted to prove that she was a star in her own right, but the studio was not ready to promote her to that status; so she went on a loan-out to Columbia. There she starred in *Ladies in Retirement*, playing the same role that the fine middle-aged British actress Flora Robson had filled the previous year on Broadway.

At the time, Lupino was only twenty-three, but she possessed the intelligence and understanding of acting of a more mature actress, perhaps because she was a member of one of England's foremost theatrical families. Her role as Ellen Creed became a challenge, and she played it with little makeup and a severely dressed coiffure, suggesting the advanced years she did not have in fact, years that would make her credible as a sister to actresses Elsa Lanchester and Edith Barrett. Playing Ellen Creed gave Lupino the boost her career needed at the time, and when she returned to Warner Bros., they were willing to lend her out for leads at least twice again and finally to give her the role in *The Hard Way* (1943) that brought her a Best Film Actress of the Year Award from the New York Film Critics and led to her recognition as a Warner Bros. star.

Ladies in Retirement is set in late-Victorian England and is a psychological thriller, an English character study in the same vein as *Night Must Fall* (1939). Ellen Creed (Ida Lupino) works as companion-housekeeper to Leonora Fiske (Isobel Elsom), a retired actress who lives on a generous pension bestowed upon her by a onetime admirer. She owns a cottage on the lonely marshes of the Thames Estuary and is a stupid, frivolous old woman existing in gaudy memories of her own past. Ellen gets a reluctant permission from Leonora for her two sisters, Emily (Elsa Lanchester) and Louisa Creed (Edith Barrett), to visit her. They are mentally retarded and are in danger of being put away in a public institution.

Leonora is not very happy about playing hostess to two such dotty characters, and after a few weeks they get on her nerves to the point where she requests that they leave. Ellen pleads with her, but Leonora remains firm, and Ellen realizes she is being driven to a murderous decision. She sends her sisters away on a temporary holiday and gives Lucy (Evelyn Keyes), the kitchen maid, the day off. Then while Leonora is seated at her piano accompanying herself as she sings "Tit Willow," Ellen, with every ounce of strength at her call, calmly strangles her benefactress with the curtain cord and walls up the body behind the kitchen bake-oven.

There are few neighbors, and none of them ever knew Leonora Fiske well, so none doubts Ellen's story that Mrs. Fiske suddenly left England on a world tour, leaving her in charge of the house. Ellen recalls her two half-crazed sisters, and the three Creed women settle down to life in the house, the only other occupant of which is Lucy, the kitchen maid.

Into this house of women comes a male intruder, Leonora Fiske's wayward, handsome nephew, Albert Feather (Louis Hayward), who has come to get what money he can from his rich old aunt. Ellen is obliged to ask him to stay on, and in no time Albert begins an affair with Lucy, and they gradually dominate the house. Albert is suspicious of Ellen, and does not believe that his aunt has left the country alone on a world tour. He and Lucy suspect the worst of Ellen, and together they contrive a plan to terrorize her into revealing the truth about Leonora. Lucy puts on one of Leonora's wigs, and in the middle of the night Ellen discovers her at the piano, eerily playing "Tit Willow." Ellen, driven nearly insane with her own troubled conscience, is trapped into an admission of the crime to Albert. She is able to get some nuns to take over the care of her sisters. Albert realizes that, with the police coming to the house, he will probably be detained for some of his own past crimes, so he flees, leaving Ellen to confess to the police when they arrive to take her into custody.

Everyone connected with *Ladies in Retirement* gives his and her best. The picture deserved more honors than it got, being nominated for Academy Awards only in the categories of Interior Decoration (black and white) and Scoring of a Dramatic Picture. Charles Vidor, director, had been under contract to Columbia for two years before getting a chance to show how well he could direct a mood thriller, although he had given the studio a hint of what he could do as the director of *Blind Alley* (1939). He became known, however, for his direction of some of the studio's glamour girls, particularly Rita Hayworth. There is little question that *Ladies in Retirement* stands as his best work on the screen.

Isobel Elsom, who had played Leonora Fiske in the Broadway production of the play, re-creates the role for the film version, and is very effective. So are Elsa Lanchester and Edith Barrett as the half-witted sisters, and Evelyn Keyes gives one of her first outstanding performances at Columbia as Lucy. Louis Hayward, at that time married to Ida Lupino, plays Albert Feather to perfection; his scenes with Lupino are colorful and fraught with tension. They make a first-rate acting pair, and Lupino has always named Ellen Creed as her favorite screen role.

The story comes from the successful play by Reginald Denham and Edward Percy. Unacknowledged is the fact that the playwrights based the story on a horror tale to be found in H. B. Irving's *French Crime and Criminals*, a book containing a collection of studies of actual mental derangement. It provided a stunning evening in the theater in both its London and New York showings, and was a basis for this superior film which brought stardom to Ida Lupino. The film was remade in 1969 as *The Mad Room* starring Stella Stevens and Shelley Winters, but that version cannot compare with the original and was mediocre at best.

DeWitt Bodeen

LADY FOR A DAY

Released: 1933
Production: Harry Cohn for Columbia
Direction: Frank Capra
Screenplay: Robert Riskin; based on the short story "Madame La Gimp" by
  Damon Runyon
Cinematography: Joseph Walker
Editing: Gene Havlick
Running time: 88 minutes

Principal characters:

Dave the Dude	Warren William
Apple Annie	May Robson
Missouri Martin	Glenda Farrell
Judge Blake	Guy Kibbee
Happy	Ned Sparks
Louise	Jean Parker
Carlos Romero	Barry Norton
Count Romero	Walter Connolly
Governor	Hobart Bosworth
Butler	Halliwell Hobbes

Because it has not been widely seen in recent years (Frank Capra owns the rights and has not seen fit to reissue the film), *Lady for a Day* is not as highly regarded as it might be. For many reasons, it is an important film in the Capra canon. It was the first of an unbroken run of eleven hit features for the director, and it was the only one of his films that Capra himself remade. Most importantly, it was the first Capra film and the first Columbia production to be nominated for an Academy Award, and although it did not receive any Oscars, *Lady for a Day* garnered four nominations—for Best Actress, Best Direction, Best Picture, and Best Writing (adaptation).

Lady for a Day was the first of the successful Frank Capra-Robert Riskin productions to deal with the "little people" of the world, whose innate goodness allows them to succeed against adversity. It followed the unsuccessful but nevertheless magnificent *The Bitter Tea of General Yen* (1933) and is as far removed as possible from that film in look, style, dialogue, and plot. *Lady for a Day* was based on the short story "Madame La Gimp" by Damon Runyon, which deals with a downtrodden, gin-sodden "old haybag" who makes her living selling newspapers on a busy New York street corner. Capra changed the character's occupation to that of selling apples and provided her with the name of "Apple Annie." For the role, the director wanted Marie Dressler, but she was unavailable, being under contract to M-G-M. Luckily, however—for she was far more suited to the part than Dressler—May Robson was lured from the stage by Capra, and she provided a characterization of compassion and working-class strength. As *Motion Picture Herald* (July 6, 1933) noted, "May Robson has the difficult spot of carrying an emotional mood through rather broad comedy situations, but she manages this beautifully, and the picture is a personal triumph for her." *Lady for a Day* also established a new career as a film actress for Robson which lasted for the rest of her life.

Apple Annie (May Robson) is a typical Runyon character, as, for that matter, are all the New York types in the film. The only difference between them, for example, and the people of Runyon's *Guys and Dolls* is that they are as much the creations of Capra and Riskin as of Runyon.

Annie sells her apples in the Times Square area of New York, where all the gangsters and racketeers believe it is lucky to buy from her. Chief among her customers is Dave the Dude, gambler and petty gangster, played in his usual bland fashion by dapper Warren William. Unbeknown to Dave and her other clients, Apple Annie has used their money to send her illegitimate daughter, who knows nothing of her mother's occupation, to a convent school in Spain. Through the kindness of the lowly staff of a smart New York hotel, Annie is able to write and receive mail from her daughter and to pretend she is a prominent member of society, married to a wealthy husband.

One day, Annie receives word from her daughter Louise (Jean Parker) that she is onboard a ship bound for America, accompanied by her fiancé Carlos (Barry Norton) and his father, a Spanish count (Walter Connolly) who insists on checking into her family's social status. In despair and desperation, Annie turns to Dave the Dude, who, from fear that good luck will desert him at a crucial time in his career if he fails to help Annie, sets her up in the apartment of a wealthy friend who is out of town and finds her a husband in the shape of Judge Blake, a pool shark with an aristocratic manner, delightfully played by Guy Kibbee. Meanwhile, Dave's girl friend, Missouri Martin (Glenda Farrell), rounds up all the beauty experts that she knows, and the filthy old hag that was Apple Annie becomes the elegant society matron, Mrs. E. Worthington Manville. Dave the Dude's staff of "Muggs" are drafted as her domestic staff, while Missouri's nightclub chorus become society ladies.

All appears to be proceeding satisfactorily until three newspaper reporters, believing they have a great romantic story, become a little too curious and are kidnaped by Dave the Dude. Naturally, the newspapers pressure the city officials to take action on the disappearance. When Dave explains to the police chief, mayor, governor, and others in power the reason behind his action, they are sympathetic. In a wonderful sequence which could only happen in a Capra production, just when it looks as if Annie's final reception in honor of the Spanish count is to be a disaster, New York society, led by the governor (Hobart Bosworth) appears at her apartment *en masse*. The city provides a police escort to see the family off on their return to Spain, and there is the suggestion that Annie will not be returning to sell apples but will instead join her daughter in Spain at a later date.

Lady for a Day is one of those films that relies for its success not on flashy directorial techniques or camerawork, but on a simple plot and sincere acting. It has both. Particularly worthy of mention are many of the players in supporting roles: Ned Sparks as Happy (which, of course, he never is, with his eye-popping stare and sour look); Connolly as the Count; Bosworth, one of the cinema's most distinguished actors, as the governor; and Halliwell Hobbes as the butler. The scene in which Dave's gangster friends rehearse for their appearance at the reception for Annie's society friends succeeds in its broad comedy thanks entirely to the acting of a group of relatively unknown players.

The film opened at New York's Radio City Music Hall on September 7, 1933, and became an instant commercial and critical success. There were few who would have argued with *The New York Times*'s critic Mordaunt Hall, who described it as "a picture which evoked laughter and tears." When all is said and done, that is precisely what audiences in America at the height of the Depression expected, and needed, from a film.

In 1961, Capra remade the film as *A Pocketful of Miracles*, and, despite its poor press and disaster at the box office, the production is still very entertaining, thanks largely to the performances by Bette Davis and Edward Everett Horton.

Anthony Slide

THE LADY FROM SHANGHAI

Released: 1948
Production: Harry Cohn for Columbia
Direction: Orson Welles
Screenplay: Orson Welles; based on the novel *If I Die Before I Wake* by Sherwood King
Cinematography: Charles Lawton, Jr.
Editing: Viola Lawrence
Running time: 87 minutes

Principal characters:
Michael O'Hara	Orson Welles
Elsa "Rosalie" Bannister	Rita Hayworth
Arthur Bannister	Everett Sloane
Grisby	Glenn Anders

The Lady from Shanghai is a perfect example of *film noir* in that it draws the viewer into an atmosphere of dark shadows and uneasiness; we feel as unsettled and as confused as the hero. Orson Welles creates a moral labyrinth with his camera, and the hero struggles within this labyrinth, unaware that he is the pawn of evil. The film thus presents a basic Welles theme: the corruption and misery of the rich versus the struggle of the innocent for survival.

In the film, Michael O'Hara (Orson Welles), an Irish adventurer and sailor, meets a beautiful blond woman who is called Rosalie (Rita Hayworth) in a carraige in Central Park and manages to interest her enough that she deliberately drops her pocketbook for him to find. During the long carriage ride reminiscent of the one in Welle's *The Magnificent Ambersons* (1942), Rosalie tells Michael she was reared in the Orient, and the implication is one of mystery and a sordid past life. Michael later rescues her from thugs, escorts her to her car, and discovers from the parking lot attendant that she is the wife of Arthur Bannister (Everett Sloane), a famous criminal trial lawyer of whom Michael has spoken.

In Central Park, Rosalie tries to get Michael to accompany her and her husband on a Pacific cruise as part of the crew on their yacht. Michael declines, yet accepts the next day when Arthur Bannister himself comes to the seaman's hiring hall to find him. The first things we see when Bannister enters the hiring hall are his knotted canes, then his twisted limbs; they, along with his rasping voice, contrast with the simple men around him. In the bar sequence that follows, Bannister tells Michael that one has to have an edge; just what kind of an edge the rich have, Michael is soon to find out.

On the yacht, Elsa (Rosalie's real name) carries on the promise of a love affair with Michael, begging him to take her away, which soon seems possible through the vehicle of Grisby (Glenn Anders), Bannister's partner. Our first impression of Grisby is that of a voyeur as we look with the camera through his telescope at the seemingly vulnerable Elsa sunbathing. We immediately suspect the distorted way in which he views things. This is underlined by his leering face and verbal jabs at everyone around him, his expressions always badly lit to create a suspicious effect. As Elsa sings "Please Don't Kiss Me" on the yacht (suitably named *Circe*), she is the focal point, accentuated by the camera's view from above: Grisby and Bannister spoiling her singing with their nasty wisecracks, the maid worried about "that poor child he married," and Michael mesmerized, drawn on deck from below toward the female enchanteress, toward Circe. Welles, the master of sound, uses the song well; she is actually singing a song of compromise, deceit, power, and money, lulling Michael for the kill.

When they reach Acapulco, Grisby divulges a scheme to Michael: for five thousand dollars, he is to pretend to murder Grisby while the latter disappears from a world that he feels is threatened by not only a nagging wife but also an inevitable nuclear holocaust. Despite a signed confession, Michael will not be able to be convicted without a corpse. The Acapulco sequences are important to the establishment of the mood. Michael observes that "There's a fair face to the land, but you can't hide the hunger and the guilt"; Elsa in a white dress runs down a hillside in the dark (actually shot with a stand-in at the Fox ranch); and there is a tense cat-and-mouse game between Michael and Elsa and the detective she says her husband has hired to spy on her. All these things create a sense of foreboding in the night, a feeling that disaster is unavoidable. Elsa tells Michael that everyone returns to his original nature in the end. He wants to take her away from the evil of her surroundings, but she laughs at his innocence and speaks of money. She claims that the evil of the world must be dealt with; you must compromise, make deals, and come to terms with it.

Michael's narration continues as he tells us that Bannister gives his wife everything she wants, only in such a vulgar way that it would be better if he did not. The picnic Elsa wants, and gets, is a prime example, heavily laden with symbolism as it is. Snakes and alligators slither into the water as the Latin music pulses and the camera darts back and forth between the reptiles and the false faces in the rowboats. Later, Grisby and the Bannisters are sitting apart destroying each other verbally. Elsa wonders aloud who would want to live among them. Michael, summoned to relieve their boredom and provide new fuel for their venom, can only think of another horrible thing he has seen in his lifetime of wandering. He likens them to a group of sharks that went mad with the taste of their own blood, and in their frenzy began tearing themselves to pieces, feeding on one another's and their own flesh and blood. Michael tells his employers that not one of the sharks survived.

When they return to San Francisco, Michael seems determined to earn his five thousand dollars so that he can take Elsa away from the sea of blood. He meets her in the aquarium to tell her of the fake murder scheme. She warns him that there is something more behind Grisby's proposition, something evil. By now, we are sure of it, but Michael hears only her soft and passionate voice, breathlessly whispering her fear. Michael does not see her eyes. Welles again emphasizes the oceanic theme with the aquarium sequence. He deliberately used a wide angle lens to achieve the distortion he wants. The light comes from sources simulating the light from the fish tanks, but in fact the aquarium itself was shot separately and matted in after enlargement to achieve a more dramatic effect. In this way, the fish in the tank behind the faces of the lovers match the conversation: we see sharks and eels as a murder is planned.

On the night of the murder, Michael, as if in a trance, does exactly what Grisby tells him to do, but Grisby is forced to shoot the divorce detective hired by Bannister who has discovered the real plan. While Grisby supposedly disappears in his motor boat, the dying detective calls Michael and says Bannister is the real victim, the murder having been planned by Elsa and Grisby with Michael to take the blame. Michael rushes to Bannister's office to prevent the murder with the signed confession still in his pocket. As he arrives, the camera swoops down, catching the audience as offguard as Michael, just as Grisby's corpse is carried away. The lawyer and his wife stand by as Michael is arrested and put in prison.

Bannister now has to put his talents to use to defend Michael supposedly because he cannot let his wife think she is in love with a martyr. In reality he is her reluctant protector. The gun that killed Grisby cannot be found, and Michael's gun did not kill him. Moreover, the Irishman's story is weak and cannot hold up in court. Bannister goes even further and turns the courtroom into a theater for his own bizarre sense of humor, obviously losing Michael's case. The process of justice is made to be something ridiculous, the judge a total fool under Bannister's influence. While the jury is out, Elsa begs Michael with her eyes to swallow a bottle of her husband's pills, which he does, or pretends to, and escapes in the ensuing bedlam.

Michael flees through Chinatown, dodging into a theater, but Elsa in pursuit, with her fluent Chinese, has an easy time following. The Chinese theater sequence, with its quick, dynamic cutting and suspenseful music, brings the film to its climax. During their Judas embrace, Michael finds the gun that killed Grisby on Elsa. There is no longer any doubt about the blonde Circe or that Michael has been the dupe of all three of them in their efforts to destroy one another, like the sharks. Elsa had planned to kill Grisby and her husband for the money and then frame Michael. Michael, who has always been able to hold the evil of the world at bay with his humor, now finds himself in love with its incarnation.

He awakes in a funhouse, wondering who is crazy. The funhouse sequence was originally an entire reel long and is the most spectacular of all. Michael slides down a zig-zag slide, past a thirty-foot-high dragon's head into a pit where he sees Elsa and her husband, guns drawn, their rottenness and evil reflected in mirrors all around them. (Some of these myriad mirrors had two-way construction and holes drilled in them, so that the camera could shoot through them.) Bannister tells his wife he has written a letter to the district attorney explaining her guilt and Michael's innocence (she killed Grisby because he ruined their plans by shooting the detective). Elsa and Bannister shoot it out as Michael can only watch, fascinated and horrified, the mirrors breaking one after another as fake image after image splinters. The camera sinks down to Elsa's level as she is dying, pleading with Michael not to leave her; then it rises again to Michael as he walks away. We only lose if we quit, he counters to her philosophy of succumbing to evil. As he walks out in to the light, his final soliloquy upon his innocence is haunting: "A big word 'innocent'—stupid's more like it. Well, everybody's somebody's fool. . . . Maybe I'll live so long I'll forget her. Maybe I'll die trying."

The versions of Welles's decision to make *The Lady from Shanghai* vary each time they are told, but they all have several elements in common. Welles needed money to release the costumes for his New York show, *Around the World*. He called Harry Cohn of Columbia and got the money in return for a promise to direct a film for the studio. No one seems to know exactly the connection between this promise and Cohn's earlier "vow" that Welles would never work with him or Columbia again after he had married Hayworth, the studio's reigning star, thus reportedly ruining her sexual screen image. While Welles was on the phone to Cohn, however, he supposedly spied a girl at either a coat check or a newsstand or a film theater ticket booth reading a thriller about the murder of a millionaire attorney: Sherwood King's *If I Die Before I Wake* (1938). This story became *The Lady from Shanghai* with an enormously elaborated plot.

Shooting started in Mexico late in 1946 amid mightmarish difficulties. In typical fashion, Welles rode his actors hard, changing their lines from day to day. He never once saw rushes and ignored all studio telegrams. Hayworth's close-ups were all shot upon return to the studio because her husband could not wait for her makeup men to do their work on location. As a result, much of the Mexico footage was reshot. The final version of the film is a patchwork of retakes, dubbing, and rescoring. Cohn, upon seeing an early cut, reportedly stomped out of the screening room swearing he would give one thousand dollars to anyone who could explain the plot to him. The public preview was equally disastrous, and each time, further cutting resulted. Cohn also held up the film because he felt the public was not ready for Hayworth as an evil temptress. Undeservedly, the film was never a commercial success.

The Lady from Shanghai, however, remains one of Welles's most memorable films, and Hayworth's excellent performance is matched by his own.

Sloane and Anders are also superb, although their characters are more defined by exterior mannerisms. The use of sound underscored by Welles's unforgettable narration and the wry Irish accent creates an offkey minor mood. Despite the technical and political difficulties, the Welles mastery is at work in the notable sequences: the aquarium, the Chinese theater, the funhouse, and the hall of mirrors. The film is much more than a thriller. All the elements of filmmaking, lighting, sound, camera angles, and framing mesh with the acting and the story to create an atmosphere of unease and a feeling of disjointedness, of moral decay and corruption, of innocence, and of evil.

Gabrielle Ouellette

LADY IN THE DARK

Released: 1944
Production: Mitchell Leisen for Paramount
Direction: Mitchell Leisen
Screenplay: Frances Goodrich, Albert Hackett, and Mitchell Leisen (uncredited); based on the play of the same name by Moss Hart
Cinematography: Ray Rennahan
Editing: Alma Macrorie
Costume design: Raoul Pene de Bois, Edith Head, and Mitchell Leisen
Running time: 100 minutes

Principal characters:

Liza Elliott	Ginger Rogers
Charley Johnson	Ray Milland
Randy Curtis	Jon Hall
Kendall Nesbitt	Warner Baxter
Photographer	Mischa Auer
Dr. Brooks	Barry Sullivan
Mrs. Elliott	Kay Linaker
Mr. Elliott	Harvey Stephens

The play *Lady in the Dark* by Moss Hart, with music by Kurt Weill and lyrics by Ira Gershwin, was based upon Hart's own experience with psychoanalysis. The film based upon the play, however, minimizes the psychology and emphasizes the fantasy in three expensively produced dream sequences.

According to the director of the film, Mitchell Leisen, there was very little agreement among the principals involved in the adaptation. The executive producer, B. G. DeSylva, disliked Weill's music and any suggestion that the protagonist had an Electra complex; the writers, Frances Goodrich and Albert Hackett, wanted to make the dreams more fantastic and less connected to the plot than they were in the play; and the star, Ginger Rogers, wanted to play the part but had little understanding of it. Also according to Leisen's account, he had to accept DeSylva's ideas, but he (Leisen) was able to write a script that was fairly close to his conception of the Hart play, although Goodrich and Hackett received sole credit for the screenplay.

The basic plot is relatively simple. A successful editor of a fashion magazine, Liza Elliott (Ginger Rogers), is experiencing a puzzling crisis in her life. She has become afraid all the time and is unable to make decisions. Her doctor (Edward Fielding) assures her that there is no physical cause for her condition and suggests a psychoanalyst. Although disturbed by the idea of psychoanalysis, Liza soon becomes desperate enough to try therapy with Dr. Brooks (Barry Sullivan). The plot then moves both backward and forward as Liza tells Dr. Brooks of events in her past that have influenced her present behavior. The two threads are interwoven in the film, but the story that emerges is that as a young girl Liza was made to feel by her parents (Harvey Stephens and Kay Linaker) that she was not pretty enough. Then, when her mother died, she put on her mother's favorite blue dress and appeared before her father, thinking she would please him; instead, he became upset and demanded that she take it off. She therefore decided that she would ignore romance and concentrate on studying. This course of action was reinforced on the night of her high-school prom. She was spending the evening in the library, but she accepted a last-minute invitation to the prom from a boy (Rand Brooks) who was feuding with his girl friend, only to have him abandon her at the dance when the old girl friend demanded attention. From then on she concentrated on success in a career, with the only element of romance being a relationship with Kendall Nesbitt (Warner Baxter), an older married man who is the publisher of her magazine. He promises to divorce his wife and marry her, but we see that in the adulterous relationship he represents safety to her, not the romance possible in a serious commitment.

The thorn in Liza's side is her advertising manager, Charley Johnson (Ray Milland). He is brash and irritating, but she keeps him on her staff because he does his job so well. Charley is also irritated by Liza. He thinks that her being an executive is just a pose and is "flying in the face of nature," and he makes no effort to hide this opinion from Liza, derisively calling her "Boss Lady" quite frequently. The other ingredient that is mixed into the plot is a movie star, Randy Curtis (Jon Hall). He comes to the magazine office for a photography session and begins dating Liza.

In the simplified psychology of the film, it develops that the answer to Liza's problem is a man. He is, however, not the man we might expect. First Kendall Nesbitt announces that he is finally going to divorce his wife to marry Liza, but she has to admit she does not want to marry him. Then Randy Curtis proposes. Liza is delighted that she has succeeded in the world of glamor and romance and will have someone to lean on, but is disillusioned when she discovers that he is attracted to her because he perceives her as strong. "Don't worry," he tells her. "You're still going to be the boss." This changes Liza's mind immediately, for she has come to accept her psychiatrist's diagnosis: she has been dominating men most of her life, and what she needs is a man who will dominate her. Almost immediately after Randy leaves, Charley Johnson comes into her office to say good-bye; he is leaving for another job because he wants to be the boss. Liza says the two of them will run the magazine together if he will stay. He accepts and immediately begins explaining changes he wants to make in the magazine. Then he drops the business talk and turns to her. As they embrace, the magazine's photographer (Mischa Auer) bursts in and, astounded at what he sees, exclaims "This is the end, the absolute end"—and it is the end of the film.

The chief distinction of *Lady in the Dark* is not, however, its simplistic—

even reactionary—psychology, but the three dream production numbers that are used to illustrate the plot. The dream sequences illustrate facets of Liza's unconscious that affect her everyday life, especially the fact that she longs to be beautiful and glamorous even though she thinks she does not. To make the fantasy properly extravagant, the studio spent nearly three million dollars on the film, which was an enormous budget for that time, and which was mentioned by nearly every reviewer. Three hundred and fifty specially designed costumes were made, the most elaborate of which used hundreds of mink skins. Three quite talented people were responsible for the designs: Raoul Pene de Bois, Edith Head, and director Mitchell Leisen. De Bois was a stage designer; Head was near the beginning of a long and illustrious career that has brought her many Oscars; and Leisen was a costume designer for Cecil B. De Mille before he became a director.

Part of the effect of Liza's costumes in the dream sequences is derived from their contrast with the fairly severe, almost masculine-style clothes she wears at her office. Indeed, Charley looks at one of her suits and remarks that she must have the same tailor he does, for it is almost an exact duplicate of his own pinstripe suit. Also important is the color progression in the dreams. The first is done almost exclusively in blue, the second in white, gold, and rose, and the last in a whole array of vivid hues.

The "Blue Dream" begins with Liza talking to her psychoanalyst, and their conversation continues intermittently on the sound track as we see a very alluring and self-confident Liza. She has been chosen to have her portrait painted for a new two-cent postage stamp. The painter, however, is Charley Johnson, and when she sees the finished painting the illusion ends; Charley has portrayed her as an austere executive rather than as the seductive enchantress she has been in the dream. In the "Wedding Dream," which features a wedding gown designed by de Bois to suggest medieval costumes, we see that she really does not want to marry Kendall.

The most expansive and entertaining dream is the "Circus Dream." It begins with Liza in her office trying to decide whether to use a circus theme on the magazine's next cover. Suddenly, the proposed cover is a real circus and Liza is a young girl looking on. Then she sees that the ringmaster is Charley Johnson and in a cage is the adult Liza Elliott. Then the circus becomes a trial of Liza for not being able to make up her mind. She leaves the cage and defends herself by singing and dancing to a song, "The Saga of Jenny," the moral of which is "Don't make up your mind." She wears a fabulous dress with a long full skirt that is a dark mink on the outside but can be opened in the front to reveal Liza's legs and a dazzling red and gold sequined lining. (Leisen reports that Rogers thought the dance and the dress did not fit the refined image she was trying to cultivate.)

All in all, *Lady in the Dark* is a fairly ordinary film with some extraordinary moments. It is an ambitious film and was quite well-received at the time, especially at the box office; in fact, it was the highest-grossing film of Leisen's career, but it turned out to be the beginning of a decline in the careers of both Leisen and Rogers. It suffered from the fact that two of the best-known songs from the play were cut from the film after they had been shot. The two are "My Ship," which is heard throughout but is never sung, and "Tchaikovsky," a short patter song that had been made famous by Danny Kaye in the stage version. As it turned out, *Carefree* (1938)—although less ambitious than *Lady in the Dark*—was a more successful mixture of Rogers and psychiatry.

Sharon Wiseman

LADY IN THE LAKE

Released: 1947
Production: George Haight for Metro-Goldwyn-Mayer
Direction: Robert Montgomery
Screenplay: Steve Fisher; based on the novel of the same by Raymond Chandler
Cinematography: Paul C. Vogel
Editing: Gene Ruggiero
Running time: 105 minutes

Principal characters:
Philip Marlowe	Robert Montgomery
Lieutenant Degarmot	Lloyd Nolan
Adrienne Fromsett	Audrey Totter
Derace Kingsby	Leon Ames
Mildred Haveland	Jayne Meadows
Chris Lavery	Richard Simmons
Captain Kane	Tom Tully

Lady in the Lake was almost entirely photographed from a subjective point of view in which the camera serves as the actual eyes of detective Philip Marlowe. The only break from this personalized technique occurs in a prologue and at times when Marlowe sits behind his desk and introduces various confusing elements of the plot while encouraging the audience to unravel the mystery themselves and to "expect the unexpected." The other shots of director and star Robert Montgomery are an occasional mirror image of him as he fixes his tie or something equally trivial.

On the day before Christmas, Philip Marlowe (Robert Montgomery) is interviewed by Adrienne Fromsett (Audrey Totter). She is editor-in-chief of a series of crime magazines published by Derace Kingsby (Leon Ames) and is considering including one of Marlowe's own stories in its upcoming issues. Adrienne actually wants to hire Marlowe to find Kingsby's missing wife, Crystal, so that Kingsby's divorce proceedings can begin. The subjective camera records Marlowe's impressions while he listens to other characters speak. As the interview with Adrienne progresses, her alluring receptionist enters the room and Marlowe follows the newcomer's every move while she returns his stare with inviting, seductive expressions. Not only does this technique increase visual interest, but it also contrasts Adrienne's covert behavior with Marlowe's more candid personality and suggests that Marlowe is a man of action and is impatient with her intellectualism. Adrienne and Marlowe fight for control of their relationship, and in this visual translation of their conflict, Marlowe seems to possess more strength. The sequence also demonstrates that a completely visual activity in a film communicates a complex group of ideas more quickly and more powerfully than words can. Another film, *Dark Passage*, was made the following year also using a subjective camera for almost half of its length. Although the technique is more fully integrated into that film's plot, it lacks the consistent personalization of the camera as it is employed by director Montgomery in *Lady in the Lake*. *Dark Passage*'s camera never wanders meaningfully about a room or examines a character inch by inch.

In the first violent scene, when Marlowe questions Chris Lavery (Richard Simmons), Crystal Kingsby's lover, mirrors are used to add extra information to the audience's first-person point of view. Marlowe turns to look at a clock situated near a mirror and seems not to notice Lavery's reflection as the man prepares to hit the detective. The audience can anticipate the violent action before the actual blow lands, however, and the screen fills with darkness as Marlowe falls unconscious. Marlowe wakes up to find himself at the local police station, where he is warned by Captain Kane (Tom Tully) and the belligerent Lieutenant Degarmot (Lloyd Nolan) that they do not like private investigators harassing their citizens. When a corpse is found in the lake near Kingsby's vacation cabin, Marlowe suspects that it is Crystal but instead discovers that it is the wife of Kingsby's caretaker, Muriel Chess, whose real name is Mildred Haveland (Jayne Meadows). He returns to Lavery's house and is surprised by the scatterbrained landlady, who is just on her way out after killing Lavery. The police do not believe that the woman exists and think that Marlowe is the murderer. They are forced to release him, however, when his alibi checks out.

By restricting the field of vision to a purely subjective viewpoint and therefore making the audience the "co-protagonist," the film can heighten the tension and effectiveness of any unexpected violence connected with Marlowe. For example, when he is driving home along a deserted road after being freed from jail, another car forces him off the road and into a ditch. While he is barely conscious, liquor is poured over him by Lieutenant Degarmot, and Marlowe realizes that he is being framed for drunk driving. Later a celebrating passerby peeks from the top of the film's frame into Marlowe's car. A fist raises itself up from the lower right-hand portion of the frame and quickly knocks the man out. Marlowe saves himself by exchanging identification cards with this man. Again, the camera's point of view causes the audience to feel more like a participant than a mere observer. Marlowe struggles across the road to a telephone booth, crawling on his hands and knees; only his hands clawing at the asphalt are seen within the frame. Marlowe calls Adrienne from the phone booth for help, and they spend a quiet Christmas together during which they realize that they love each other. Their reverie is shattered, however, by Derace Kingsby's news that he has received a message from his wife. The mystery comes to a quick conclusion, with plot twists exposed and unraveled in the violent climax, when it is revealed that

Kingsby's wife is actually the woman in the lake, and Mildred Haveland, who was actually alive, reveals the answer to the mystery just before she is killed. Ultimately, however, what *happens* in the film is immaterial, since the visual discipline and suspension of conventional perception required of the viewer eliminate the necessity for complete dramatic development, just as the narrative confusion of *The Big Sleep* (1946) is functionally irrelevant.

Montgomery, *Lady in the Lake*'s director and star, sustains the film's one-dimensional style with numerous stylistic touches typical of the *film noir* genre, such as the gigolo found dead behind a bullet-shattered glass shower door, the oppressive antagonism of the police, and of course, Mildred's furtive behavior. Screenwriter Steve Fisher integrates his first-hand experience with pulp fiction to give Raymond Chandler's novel a new cinematic beginning. Fisher amusingly substitutes *Lurid Detective* and *True Horror* magazine (to which Marlowe has submitted a story entitled "If I Should Die Before I Wake") for the novel's "Gillerlain Regal, The Champagne of Perfumes" company and effectively transposes Chandler's environment of corrupt tycoons to a commercial literary establishment run by hypocrites. The dialogue is tough and gritty. Fisher retains much of Chandler's "Marlowe" speeches, as when Adrienne says, "I don't like your manner," and Marlowe replies, "I'm not selling it." Fisher makes Adrienne Fromsett into an important character who is initially Marlowe's chief antagonist, while Chandler kept her half-hidden as a devoted mistress to her boss. When the film's Marlowe breaks up Adrienne's mercenary wedding plans, she bitterly asks him, "On what corner do you want me to beat my tambourine?" Marlowe has little idea that it should be on his corner; and the screenplay keeps their verbal rivalry active until the mystery is almost concluded. When Marlowe and Adrienne admit their mutal attraction, it is a sentimental surprise dependent upon the film-maker's presumption that the audience demands a romantic, happy ending, no matter how contrived.

Elizabeth Ward

THE LANDLORD

Released: 1970
Production: Norman Jewison for United Artists
Direction: Hal Ashby
Screenplay: Bill Gunn; based on the novel of the same name by Kristin Hunter
Cinematography: Gordon Willis
Editing: William A. Sawyer
Running time: 114 minutes

Principal characters:

Elgar Enders	Beau Bridges
Marge	Pearl Bailey
Fanny	Diana Sands
Copee	Louis Gossett
Mrs. Enders	Lee Grant
Mr. Enders	Walter Brooke
Professor Duboise	Melvin Stewart
Walter Gee	Douglas Grant
Susan	Susan Anspach
Peter	Robert Klein
Lanie	Marki Bey

During the early 1970's, mainstream Hollywood belatedly acknowledged a mostly untapped segment of the American filmgoing populace: blacks. Dozens of films were released expressly for this "black market," from slick private eye-versus-gangster dramas such as *Shaft* (1971) to exploitative glorifications of drug pushers such as *Super Fly* (1972), from compassionate chronicles of life in the Deep South such as *Sounder* (1972) to violent, racist soap operas such as *Mandingo* (1975). Hollywood had finally realized that black audiences would bolster the box-office receipts of films featuring characters and plot lines which mirrored their ethnic experiences: *Shaft, Cotton Comes to Harlem* (1970), and the independently produced *Sweet Sweetback's Badasssss Song* (1971) were among the highest-grossing films of their years. One of the more perceptive, humanistic films of all is *The Landlord*, an intelligent, funny, although uneven portrait of the interrelationships between the races. Unfortunately, it did not find its audience and was a box-office disappointment.

The Landlord is directed by Hal Ashby and produced by Norman Jewison. Ashby, who made his directorial debut with the film, had previously won an Oscar as editor of the Jewison-directed *In the Heat of the Night* (1967). As in that Academy Award-winning film as well as *The Landlord*, it is a black—in this case, several blacks—who educates and expands the perceptions of a white.

The premise of *The Landlord*, although highly unlikely, is fascinating nevertheless. Twenty-nine-year-old Elgar Enders (Beau Bridges) is WASPish, wealthy, and white. His affluence has protected him from the very real pressures of survival in the outside world devoid of swimming pools, servants, and mansions. In his ignorance, he purchases a tenement brownstone in Brooklyn with the idea of evicting its black tenants and renovating it into his own psychedelic abode.

Instead, he becomes landlord to a group of whimsical tenants who are in no hurry to find new residences—or even to pay their rent. They include Marge (Pearl Bailey), a philosophical fortune-teller who introduces Elgar to soul food; Fanny (Diana Sands), a former Miss Sepia, now a hairdresser who eventually seduces Elgar; and Professor Duboise (Melvin Stewart), a teacher in a free school whose preachings are prosegregation. Elgar's snooty parents (Lee Grant and Walter Brooke) are appalled that their son would forsake the advantages of his upper-class status. Elgar, however, discovers that he is willing to listen to and understand his new acquaintances and learns to see them as human beings. He also, in the process, matures. He falls in love with a mulatto girl, Lanie (Marki Bey), an artist and part-time go-go dancer.

The Landlord is not without glaring deficiencies. Elgar is at the start far too innocent for a man approaching thirty. His naïve desire to swoop into a building inhabited by blacks, snap his fingers like a Southern plantation owner, and expect his tenants to pack their bags seems unbelievable now, just as it did in 1970. Bill Gunn's script veers from comedy to tragedy as the film erodes into a too-quickly paced farcical soap opera. Fanny becomes pregnant by Elgar. Elgar leaves Lanie to care for Fanny. Copee (Louis Gossett), Fanny's husband, is released from jail and attacks Elgar with an ax. Copee breaks down and is taken away to a hospital. Fanny gives birth and wants to put the child up for adoption. Instead, Elgar takes the baby and reconciles himself with Lanie.

Numerous sequences in *The Landlord* are riotously funny, however, such as when Elgar arrives at his new "home" as if he is a virginal bride at his wedding, dressed in a white suit and driving a white Volkswagen. The new landlord is dumbfounded as he is rapidly hustled into obedience by his tenants. Mrs. Enders visits the building, becomes drunk, and is transformed by Marge into a soul-food aficionado. In an unbelievably bizarre, satirical sequence, Elgar joins his family for a formal dinner. He follows his perpetually stoned sister (Susan Anspach) around the house with a can of airspray so that their mother will not catch on to her pot-smoking activities, even though she wears a roach clip in her hair. The family business of a suitor (Robert Klein) is "napalm, deodorant, and, uh . . . insecticide." Elgar, with his newfound consciousness, chastizes the subservient black butler by dumping a bowl of soup over his head.

The Landlord is quite eloquent in the sequences between Elgar and his tenants—particularly Fanny and Marge—and this is even more relevant than the humor. Elgar, white and rich, has never had to worry about money in his entire life, while the two women break the law in order to keep food on their tables: Fanny's beauty shop and Marge's fortune-telling business are both unlicensed. Elgar's appearance—he is the latest in the line of slumlords—is greeted with skepticism, but they all soon interrelate. Marge feeds him, while Fanny becomes his lover.

The blacks in *The Landlord* are presented as exploited and real and struggling with day-to-day survival. The black nationalist ravings of Professor Duboise are an angry although logical alternative to eking out existences in a white-controlled, white-dominated society. All the whites, including Elgar, are liberal clichés. *The Landlord* is not offensive to whites, however, in the same way as such "black-is-beautiful/whites-are-honkies" denunciations as *Mandingo*, *Mahogany* (1975), *Super Fly*, and dozens of bloody, "Z"-grade black exploitation films. In *The Landlord*, the characters and their interrelationships are warmly and fairly unravelled.

The performances in *The Landlord* are all top-notch. In a difficult role in which he must bridge the relationships and values in two entirely diverse environments, Bridges offers an engagingly deft delineation of Elgar. Bailey's Marge is a marvelous rendition of her earthy "Pearly Mae" *persona*. Aside from her role as Beneatha Younger in the film version of Lorraine Hansberry's *A Raisin in the Sun* (1961), Sand's Fanny is the only character of real substance in the actress' screen career. She is quite moving here: her last film was *Willie Dynamite* (1973), a pitiful eploitation film with a pimp as a protagonist. Tragically, Sands died of cancer in 1973 at the age of thirty-nine. The best performance is that of Grant, whose Mrs. Enders is a devastating caricature of a crazed, social-conscious suburban lady. She was nominated for a Best Supporting Actress Oscar, losing out with Karen Black (*Five Easy Pieces*), Sally Kellerman (*M.A.S.H.*), and Maureen Stapleton (*Airport*) to Helen Hayes in *Airport*.

Ashby's direction is slick. He is most outstanding when he contrasts visually the class and race of Elgar and his tenants. At the film's opening, for example, he alternates shots of Fanny's ghetto hairdressing shop with a white squash court. Elgar arrives in the dreary slum neighborhood to introduce himself to his tenants dressed in white and driving a white auto. The sequences in the Enders' home are overexposed and sundrenched, while the shots in the ghetto are almost brownish-yellow in tone. Gordon Willis' cinematography is stunning throughout.

Ashby had previously worked with Jewison on *The Russians Are Coming, The Russians Are Coming* (1966), *The Thomas Crown Affair* (1968), *The Cincinnati Kid* (1965), and *Gaily, Gaily*, 1969 (which starred Bridges as the young newspaper reporter Ben Hecht). His post-*Landlord* credits include some of the more controversial films of the 1970's: the cult film *Harold and*

Maude (1971), *The Last Detail* (1973), *Shampoo* (1975), and *Coming Home* (1978).

The Landlord was a box-office failure when initially released. It did slightly better when United Artists, the film's distributor, altered the ad campaign to resemble that of *Cotton Comes to Harlem*. It took in $1,580,898 in receipts, and was only the fifty-fifth highest grossing feature of its year. *The Landlord* may be flawed, but it is deserving of a far greater audience.

Rob Edelman

LARCENY, INC.

Released: 1942
Production: Jack Saper and Jerry Wald for Warner Bros.
Direction: Lloyd Bacon
Screenplay: Everett Freeman and Edwin Gilbert; based on the play *The Night Before Christmas* by Laura Perelman and S. J. Perelman
Cinematography: Tony Gaudio
Editing: Ralph Dawson
Running time: 95 minutes

Principal characters:
Pressure Maxwell .... Edward G. Robinson
Denny Costello .... Jane Wyman
Jug Martin .... Broderick Crawford
Jeff Randolph .... Jack Carson
Leo Dexter .... Anthony Quinn
Weepy Davis .... Edward Brophy
Homer Bigelow .... Harry Davenport
Sam Bachrach .... John Qualen
Hobart .... Jackie Gleason

The most prestigious role in the illustrious career of Edward G. Robinson is that of the vicious crime czar Cesare Enrico "Rico" Bandello in *Little Caesar* (1931). The film became one of the archetypes of all gangster motion pictures, and its star is best remembered for his portrayals of hoods from Rico up through Johnny Rocco in *Key Largo*, the Maxwell Anderson stage play filmed by John Huston in 1948. Warner Bros. produced more films of the genre than any other studio, with Robinson, James Cagney, George Raft, Humphrey Bogart, Allen Jenkins, John Garfield, and Frank McHugh among the stars and supporting players gracing the casts. By the late 1930's and early 1940's, however, audiences lost interest in these hard-boiled, "crime doesn't pay" melodramas. Robinson then acted in three Warner films which parodied the genre that made him famous. In *A Slight Case of Murder* (1938), based on a Damon Runyon story, he appears as a gangster attempting to go straight who discovers a corpse in his home; in *Brother Orchid* (1940), he is a racketeer who learns about the "true values of life" when he takes refuge in a monastery. The final film is *Larceny, Inc.*

Robinson stars in *Larceny, Inc.* as Pressure Maxwell, a glib hood who, with his muddle-headed crony Jug Martin (Broderick Crawford), is about to be paroled from Sing Sing. Leo Dexter (Anthony Quinn), a fellow inmate, wants them to assist him in a bank robbery as soon as he is released. The pair decline as they have decided to go straight. The lure of easy money is too intense, however, and Maxwell is soon plotting the heist. As a front, he purchases a small leather goods shop adjacent to the bank. His idea is to dig a tunnel from the basement of the storefront to the bank's vault. The store becomes a legitimate success, however, and Maxwell becomes a respected member of the community. The bank managers offer him a large sum of money to buy up the shop in order to expand bank operations. Maxwell decides to opt for honesty and accepts their offer, but Dexter, who has escaped from prison, turns up and attempts to carry out the original plan. Too many dynamite sticks are used to blow the tunnel wider, the shop is destroyed, and Dexter is returned to jail. Maxwell can now reopen the business—as an upstanding citizen.

Larceny, Inc. has several major deficiencies. The plot is predictable: Maxwell is so lightly likable that the audience knows he will be redeemed and will somehow not go through with his plan to rob the bank. Dexter, a one-dimensional villain, is sure to harass Maxwell and end up where he is at the beginning of the film—in Sing Sing. *Larceny, Inc.* is not without the usual trite romance which adds nothing to the film's enjoyment: Maxwell's adopted daughter Denny Costello (Jane Wyman), who operates the leather goods shop, is paired with aggressive luggage salesman Jeff Randolph (Jack Carson). The overall character of Maxwell is also questionable: if he had not become a successful, respected businessman—a plot device which insures that he will have the impetus to remain honest—would he have indeed gone through with his plan to plunder the bank? Maxwell is the hero and Dexter is the heavy, yet there seems to be little difference between their characters.

Larceny, Inc. is still breezily entertaining, however; Everett Freeman and Edwin Gilbert's slight script, based on Laura and S. J. Perelman's 1941 farce, *The Night Before Christmas*, is heightened by the crack performances of the cast. Robinson etches a polished, knowing parody of his *Little Caesar*. He is still hard-boiled, still talks tough, and still swaggers and gestures defiantly with his thumb, but he has added humor and even a bit of irony to his Maxwell; as he acts this alleged thug, his tongue is often in his cheek. Robinson is not only adept at portraying or parodying villains, however; he is also a marvelous character performer. Despite his short, stocky appearance and average looks, he managed to become a star in a variety of roles. In *The Whole Town's Talking* (1935), for example, he portrays a milquetoast clerk, the double of a notorious gangster named Killer Mannion. He is at home in roles from dedicated inventors (the title characters in *A Dispatch from Reuters*, 1940, and *Dr. Ehrlich's Magic Bullet*, 1940) to restrained sleuths (Inspector Wilson in Orson Welles's *The Stranger*, 1946) and unscrupulous businessmen (Joe Keller in Irving Reis' film of Arthur Miller's *All My Sons*, 1948).

In solid support of Robinson are several actors in the early stages of their careers. Wyman first started in films in 1936 as a light comedienne in "B," and then "A," productions, while Crawford was continually cast in unrewarding supporting roles as hoodlums or dim-witted henchmen. Before the

1940's would end, they each would be given the opportunity to display their talents in three-dimensional starring dramatic roles which would result in magnificent acting jobs and an Academy Award for each. Wyman won hers as a young deaf mute girl in *Johnny Belinda* (1948), Crawford as the conscienceless politician in *All the King's Men* (1949).

Quinn, in what is virtually a thankless part which could have been handled by any of numerous Warner Bros. contract players (he was freelancing from studio to studio at the time), later won fame for *La Strada* (1954), *Wild Is the Wind* (1957), *Zorba the Greek* (1964), and *Requiem for a Heavyweight* (1962), and Supporting Actor Oscars for *Viva Zapata!* (1952) and *Lust for Life* (1956). Carson, who like Wyman appeared in both "A"- and "B"-pictures for Warners, developed into a solid character actor (most notably in *Cat on a Hot Tin Roof*, 1958; *A Star is Born*, 1954, and *The Tarnished Angels*, 1957) and comedy lead. Edward Brophy humorously mugs as another of Maxwell's not-too-bright pals with the appropriate name of Weepy Davis. Cast in a minor role as a soda jerk is Jackie Gleason, minus pounds around his middle and a decade before his hit in television's *The Honeymooners*.

Larceny, Inc. was directed by Lloyd Bacon, a competent Warner Bros. contract director. Bacon is a craftsman as opposed to an artist. There is no continuity in the themes or visual structure of his works, and he is definitely no *auteur*. While there are no outstanding sequences in *Larceny, Inc.*, his work here is fast-paced and workmanlike. Bacon also directed Robinson in *A Slight Case of Murder* and *Brother Orchid*, and he did seventy-one other films for the studio, including such diverse films as *Marked Woman* (1937), *42nd Street* (1933), *Action in the North Atlantic* (1943), and *Knute Rockne, All American* (1940). It is easy to ignore the solid although unspectacular career of Bacon amidst the hoopla over more revered directors.

Larceny, Inc. received mixed reviews. Mostly, it was unfavorably compared to *A Slight Case of Murder*. These two, in addition to *Brother Orchid*, remain amusing examples of Hollywood—and, in particular, a specific studio—satirizing one of its film genres. In retrospect, *Larceny, Inc.* is the most diverting of the trio because of its cast of soon-to-be stars.

                                                                    Rob Edelman

LASSIE COME HOME

Released: 1943
Production: Samuel Marx for Metro-Goldwyn-Mayer
Direction: Fred McLeod Wilcox
Screenplay: Hugo Butler; based on the novel of the same name by Eric Knight
Cinematography: Leonard Smith
Editing: Ben Lewis
Running time: 88 minutes

Principal characters:
Joe Carraclough .... Roddy McDowall
Sam Carraclough .... Donald Crisp
Rowlie .... Edmund Gwenn
Dolly .... Dame May Whitty
Duke of Rudling .... Nigel Bruce
Mrs. Carraclough .... Elsa Lanchester
Priscilla .... Elizabeth Taylor
Dan'l Fadden .... Ben Webster

Lassie, a thirty-minute television program featuring a loyal, courageous collie who fords rivers, climbs mountains, and tussles with bad guys, was a Sunday night fixture on CBS television during the 1950's and 1960's. The dog, however, was not a television creation. She initially charmed film audiences in 1943 as the star of *Lassie Come Home*. Lassie, then a two-year-old brown-and-white collie, was purchased by trainer Rudd Weatherwax for ten dollars when she was a puppy. Weatherwax taught the dog, originally called "Pal," to respond to humans, and she was selected from hundreds of other dogs to follow Rin-Tin-Tin as a canine star. Weatherwax then trained the animal to perform the necessary feats required by the screenplay. Lassie, curiously, should really not be referred to as a "she"; the "she" required by the scenario was really a "he." A male collie was judged to be more suitable for the role, as females are smaller and generally more nervous, and their coats are thinner and less photogenic.

Lassie Come Home is proof of the old cliché that man's—in this case, boy's—best friend is his dog, presented as a simple, poignant tale of love and devotion between child and pet. In the film, Joe Carraclough (Roddy McDowall) lives in Greenal Bridge, Yorkshire, England, with his parents (Donald Crisp and Elsa Lanchester) and his collie. Mr. Carraclough is in need of money, so he must regretfully sell Lassie to the Duke of Rudling (Nigel Bruce). The dog does not appreciate her new owner, however, and she escapes several times from her kennel, forcing the Duke to take her to his estate in Scotland, where he plans to train her for showing. There the loyal collie breaks away from her trainer and heads home to Joe.

The estate in Scotland and the farm in Yorkshire are hundreds of miles apart, and Lassie's journey becomes the highlight of the film. Here, the film could be retitled *The Perils of Lassie*. She cuts her paw on a rock; she is caught in a terrible storm; she is shot at by sheepherders; and she fights a vicious sheepdog. She then swims a river and, disheveled, bleeding, and nearly dead from exhaustion, is found and tended to by a kindly old couple, Dolly and Dan'l Fadden (Dame May Whitty and Ben Webster). They let her go when she is well because they sense that she is not a stray but is on her way somewhere.

Lassie meets up with a traveling peddler named Rowlie (Edmund Gwenn) whom she saves from a robbery, and she assists him and his own dog Toots in putting on a show and selling pots and pans. The peddler also senses that Lassie is on a "mission," however, and they also part. She escapes from two dog catchers, and, finally, bedraggled and injured, she surprises Joe when she meets him at school at 4 P.M.—just as she always had done when she was his pet. The two live happily ever after.

Fourteen-year-old McDowall, most memorable as Huw in *How Green Was My Valley*, John Ford's Academy Award winner of 1941 (in which Crisp also portrayed his father and earned a Best Supporting Actor Oscar for his effort), is equally fine here as Joe. Lassie, however, is not McDowall's initial cinematic pet. Earlier in 1943, he had had great success playing opposite a rebellious horse in *My Friend Flicka*, and was thus the only actor considered by M-G-M to play opposite Lassie. The film is endowed with a sterling supporting cast: Gwenn, Bruce, Whitty, and Lanchester, in addition to Crisp.

Lassie Come Home is adequately directed by Fred M. Wilcox, whose career is undistinguished except for the intelligent science-fiction feature *Forbidden Planet* (1956). Leonard Smith's Technicolor cinematography is outstanding. The sequences in which Lassie romps through lush, pastoral settings as she returns to her true master are beautifully shot, with Washington State, Monterey, California, and the San Joaquin River substituting for Yorkshire and Scotland. Smith's work was nominated for an Academy Award, but he lost to Hal Mohr and W. Howard Green for *Phantom of the Opera*. The film opened to excellent reviews and was cited by the National Board of Review as one of the Ten Best Films of 1943. Even if *Lassie Come Home* were a clinker, however, it would be remembered today as the first notable screen appearance—in the role of Priscilla, the Duke of Rudling's granddaughter—of an eleven-year-old English girl named Elizabeth Taylor.

Lassie Come Home, based on the novel by Eric Knight, was dedicated to the late Major Knight, who was killed in early 1943 in a crash of an air transport bound for Africa. Sadly, Knight did not live to see the success of his work. The film did exceptionally good business, breaking the box-office record set by *Mrs. Miniver* (1942) at the Radio City Music Hall in New York City. The collie immediately attained a popularity comparable with that of

Rin-Tin-Tin, who had been a successful canine star during the 1920's. Lassie was ensconced in an air-conditioned kennel complete with private romping grounds, a hairdresser, and a chiropodist. The collie also appeared in a series of sentimental follow-ups to *Lassie Come Home*, but none was as entertaining as the original. The first, *Son of Lassie* (1945), featured Peter Lawford as a grown-up Joe Carraclough and June Lockhart, who for years was the mother on the *Lassie* television series, as the ingenue. Another, *The Son Comes Up* (1949), deserves only a footnote in film history because it was the final feature of M-G-M singing star Jeanette MacDonald.

The *Lassie* television series began in 1955, and enjoyed a remarkable seventeen-year run, and a five-part episode of the series was released theatrically in 1962 as *Lassie's Greatest Adventure*, but did poorly at the box office. A series of cartoon shorts titled "Lassie's Rescue Rangers" was televised beginning in 1973, after the live-action Lassie's demise. The most recent Lassie film is a musical, originally titled *Lassie, My Lassie* but released in 1978 as *The Magic of Lassie*. The film was coproduced by Bonita Granville Wrather (the former Bonita Granville, the adolescent actress of *These Three*, 1936, and *Hitler's Children*, 1942), associate producer and then-producer of the television series. The new Lassie was male—as were all the film and television collies—and a sixth-generation descendant of the original in *Lassie Come Home*. All Lassies have been trained by Rudd Weatherwax. *The Magic of Lassie* stars James Stewart, Mickey Rooney, Pernell Roberts, Stephanie Zimbalist, Michael Sharrett, and Alice Faye (her first screen appearance since *State Fair* in 1962). In the tradition of *Lassie Come Home*, it established a new box-office record for an opening day at the Radio City Music Hall.

Rob Edelman

THE LAST OF MRS. CHEYNEY

Released: 1929
Production: Metro-Goldwyn-Mayer
Direction: Sidney Franklin
Screenplay: Hans Kraly and Claudine West; based on the play of the same name by Frederick Lonsdale
Cinematography: William Daniels
Editing: Conrad A. Nervig
Running time: 94 minutes

Principal characters:

Mrs. Cheyney	Norma Shearer
Lord Arthur Dilling	Basil Rathbone
Charles	George Barraud
Lord Elton	Herbert Bunston
Lady Marie	Hedda Hopper
Willie Wynton	Cyril Chadwick
George	George K. Arthur
Mrs. Webley	Maude Turner Gordon

No screen star made the transition from silents to talkies with the ease that Norma Shearer evinced. It was one instance when being the wife of M-G-M production head Irving Thalberg paid off, for Thalberg handled his wife's career with intelligence and great taste. Her first talking film, *The Trial of Mary Dugan* (1929), was a courtroom melodrama and also M-G-M's first all-dialogue full-length feature. Shearer had never had the benefit of stage experience, but years of work as a silent actress had given her the advantage of building a performance based on listening and reacting, and now she showed that she was capable of building a denouement scene with professional finesse, building to a climax with all the expertise of a stage star. Censorship had forced the writer to change the speech in the film which Ann Harding had delivered with fine frenzy on the Broadway stage, a speech topped with angry defense, "It's a lie! It's a lie! It's a Goddamned lie!" Shearer, of course, had to gain the same dramatic effect by repeating "It's a lie!" three times, building her hysteria to near-breakdown without using even "damned." That she succeeded as well as she did is apt testimony to her skill as a speaking actress.

For a complete change of pace, demonstrating her versatility as an actress, Thalberg ordered a production of Frederick Lonsdale's drawing-room comedy, *The Last of Mrs. Cheyney*, as his wife's second talking venture. Released in the summer of 1929, it marked another first in M-G-M's film history, for it was the first feature with a soundtrack, those released previously having been recorded on accompanying discs. It was modern, full of witty characterizations and bright lines. On Broadway it had been one of Ina Claire's outstanding roles. As a film, it drew complete critical appreciation, even though its reception by the moviegoing public was not quite as popular as *The Trial of Mary Dugan*'s had been. Shearer was henceforth regarded, however, as a film star whose acting range was varied, whose future as an M-G-M player would be undisputed and bright, leading her the following year to an Academy Award as Best Actress for *The Divorcee*.

The Last of Mrs. Cheyney was also noted as being not only all-talking but more than a bit on the talkative side. It was almost a direct translation of the play, more than an hour-and-a-half long, and the screenplay writers, Hans Kraly and Claudine West, did little more than pare down the brilliant Lonsdale dialogue, leaving it to director Sidney Franklin to keep the actors so busy with interesting movement that the picture did not in the least resemble a talkathon. The actors were stylish and handsome, and they all delivered their lines with the consummate ease of complete professionals.

In the film, Mrs. Cheyney (Norma Shearer) has been accepted by London society as a very charming Australian widow whose late husband reputedly left her a handsome fortune. The opening scene finds her, as it did in the play, officiating as hostess at a charity concert being given in the gardens of the beautiful country home she has taken for the season. In the drawing room just off the gardens, Charles (George Barraud), Mrs. Cheyney's very able and distinguished butler, is discussing the concert party with George (George K. Arthur), the cockney page boy, who is very impressed with the gathering his mistress has collected. He has never seen so many "swells." "I've called everybody 'My lord,'" he confesses, "and I ain't been contradicted once!" Charles explains wisely that the English middle classes are much too well bred to argue, but he is pleased to agree that Mrs. Cheyney's guests do include "the social goods." There are two members of the nobility, two legitimate lords, who are especially taken with Mrs. Cheyney's charms: Lord Elton (Herbert Bunston) is a rich, eligible bachelor, but Lord Arthur Dilling (Basil Rathbone) is far more attractive and clever, and more popular with women. It is the opinion of Charles that Lord Dilling might be described as a man who has kept more husbands at home than any other man of modern times.

The charity concert is a great success, and Mrs. Cheyney is delighted. She has been deluged with invitations from the socially elite. Lord Elton, very much fascinated with Mrs. Cheyney, wants her to accept an invitation that his mother will issue her to visit them, and she confesses that she would be glad to come. Lord Dilling lingers after the other guests even though Mrs. Cheyney chides him, but he then leaves, realizing ruefully that she is going to be no easy conquest.

The moment he is gone, the mood changes in the drawing room to one of complete relaxation. Mrs. Cheyney pours herself a whiskey and soda and idly plays on the piano keys. The other servants enter, including Charles, who has changed to a velvet coat and is smoking a cigar. The air is one of informality. Gradually, it is learned that the relationship between Mrs. Cheyney and her servants is more than a little unconventional. They treat one another as equals, and Mrs. Cheyney confides that she is pleased to announce that she has got what she wanted—an invitation to stay with Mrs. Webley as an honored guest next Friday. Now the truth is divulged in full. Mrs. Cheyney and Charles are not lady and butler; Charles is only posing as her butler, and they are the nominal heads of a select band of jewel thieves who rob the rich of their treasures. Mrs. Cheyney knows nothing of Australia, confessing that Bloomsbury in London is more to her native taste. She is an adventuress who lives by her wits, and the band she and Charles have gathered together hope to make a killing at the forthcoming house party of Mrs. Webley (Maude Turner Gordon), for Mrs. Cheyney has her eye on Mrs. Webley's pearls as a future possession. They are worth twenty thousand pounds, and that is only the beginning. If they pull off this robbery, they could all retire, if they are so inclined.

There is only one problem, however, for Mrs. Cheyney confesses that while she may not have "fallen for the swells," she does find one of them, Lord Dilling, very much to her liking. This admission makes Charles realize that Mrs. Cheyney might be fantasizing, and he brings her back to earth by reminding her of her obligations.

On the next Friday at Mrs. Webley's house party, both Lord Elton and Lord Dilling pay suit to Mrs. Cheyney, who leads both of them on shamelessly. Charles has been a puzzlement to Lord Dilling, who is sure that he must have seen him somewhere in the past.

Later that night when Mrs. Cheyney steals into Mrs. Webley's room to get the pearls, she finds that Lord Dilling is its occupant. He has caught on to Mrs. Cheyney's real character because he has recognized Charles as a man he had once saved from a jail sentence in the courtroom and is convinced that Mrs. Cheyney and Charles now are working together. He has Mrs. Webley's pearls in hand and is now in a position to blackmail Mrs. Cheyney into becoming his mistress. Mrs. Cheyney, however, defiantly pushes the button which summons Mrs. Webley and her guests to the room in their nightwear; but before Mrs. Cheyney can confess her real identity, Lord Dilling confesses to all that it was he who persuaded Mrs. Cheyney to come to the room under false pretenses. Mrs. Cheyney, however, foils him, for she puts her hand in his dressing gown pocket, takes out the pearls, and restores them to Mrs. Webley, saying that she had liked them so much that she had to steal them. With the dawn comes a very neat and somewhat surprising solution of the predicament. It also brings the "last of Mrs. Cheyney" as she marries Lord Dilling.

As Mrs. Cheyney, Norma Shearer is at her best, and her scenes with Basil Rathbone as Lord Dilling are played expertly, with a sense of high comedy at its top best. The very next year, Shearer not only won a nomination for her performance in *Their Own Desire*, but won the Academy Award as Best Actress for 1929-1930 in *The Divorcee*, and she was nominated again the following year for her role in *A Free Soul*. Beginning with *The Last of Mrs. Cheyney*, Shearer established herself as the best interpreter of high comedy and stylish, even scandalous, modern drama. These were her best years, and during them she did her best-remembered work.

In 1937 *The Last of Mrs. Cheyney* was remade with Joan Crawford costarring with Robert Montgomery and William Powell, and it met with such success that in 1951 it was dusted off again, and a third version, this one called *The Law and the Lady*, was made with Greer Garson, starring with Michael Wilding in a dual role and Fernando Lamas. This version was not successful, with one critic stating that he hoped that this time it would *really* be the last of Mrs. Cheyney. To date *The Law and the Lady* has been the last English-language version of the film, although a German film, *Frau Cheney's Ende*, was made in 1962.

DeWitt Bodeen

THE LAST PICTURE SHOW

Released: 1971
Production: Stephen J. Friedman for Columbia
Direction: Peter Bogdanovich
Screenplay: Larry McMurtry and Peter Bogdanovich; based on the novel of the same name by Larry McMurtry
Cinematography: Robert Surtees
Editing: Donn Cambern
Production design: Polly Platt
Running time: 118 minutes

Principal characters:
Sonny Crawford	Timothy Bottoms
Duane Jackson	Jeff Bridges
Jacy Farrow	Cybill Shepherd
Sam the Lion	Ben Johnson (AA)
Ruth Popper	Cloris Leachman (AA)
Lois Farrow	Ellen Burstyn
Genevieve	Eileen Brennan
Coach Popper	Bill Thurman
Mr. Crawford	Grover Lewis

Peter Bogdanovich's elegy for a small Texas town in the 1950's was greeted with unanimous acclaim in 1971, and although, in retrospect, that acclaim was arguably out of proportion to the film's actual merits, the decline of the director's reputation following this early success seems rather cruel. Bogdanovich's most berated films, *Daisy Miller* (1974), and *At Long Last Love* (1975), are somewhat better than their reputations would indicate, while *The Last Picture Show* is not the flawless masterpiece it was taken to be. The film is distinguished by its neoclassicism and its relative maturity, however, qualities which remain impressive with the passing of time even if it is not taken into account that the director was a young man when he made the film. Retrospectively, it is possible to see the pessimism and lack of sentiment which have come to be characteristic of Bogdanovich, and it is also evident that he was always free of the desire to be modish, which makes the critical adulation which greeted him as a result of this film somewhat surprising.

As a film critic, Bogdanovich championed such veteran directors as John Ford, Howard Hawks, and Orson Welles, remaining scornful of the younger and more fashionable directors. He unhesitatingly betrays his admiration for classical directors and their works in *The Last Picture Show*, subtly enough that modern audiences who do not know the work of most of these men will not be distracted. For those who are familiar with and attached to the classical cinema, the film provides a somewhat different experience that is sometimes frustrating but ultimately rewarding.

Larry McMurtry's novel, which the author adapted for the screen in collaboration with Bogdanovich, describes growing up in a changing world, and the director has said that the closing of the town's only picture show and the advent of television marks the passing of an era as the advent of the automobile did in Welles's *The Magnificent Ambersons* (1942). Although there is a feeling of nostalgia in the film, the characters do not seem to be traumatized by it. The central character, Sonny Crawford (Timothy Bottoms), demonstrates a sensitivity to the values represented by the past, but he lives in the present, suffers within real rather than imagined relationships, and gives every indication that he will be able to adjust to being an adult. His alienation seems to be mostly self-imposed, especially in the climactic sequences, and his problems are actually timeless ones commonly associated with adolescence. Sonny is one of a group of characters who are involved with one another but also considered independently. They all change in the course of the story but there is no clear progression which would make it possible to define the story in terms of a beginning and end. As a result of being episodic and comparatively naturalistic, the narrative rambles along, sustained by the interest created by the characters more than by Bogdanovich's nostalgia for a vanished way of life, although it would be unfair not to note that the little town has been created with loving care by production designer Polly Platt.

In classical cinema, feelings are expressed through artificial narrative and visual structures, resulting in a greater intensity than is possible in a more naturalistic structure. The trap in concealing the contrivance necessary to produce a work of art is that ideas and feelings must be expressed discreetly, because the story may only proceed in the way life actually would, and *The Last Picture Show* does not entirely avoid this trap. Not wishing for the story to be boring, Bogdanovich goes from one essential scene to another, trying to have it both ways, consistently credible and consistently dramatic. As a consequence, the film betrays its weakness in the last few reels. Attempting to resolve the principal threads of the narrative in a realistic manner, but without permitting the film to drag out, Bogdanovich cannot avoid causing an impression of three successive climaxes, each of them given equal weight.

The film's structure is consistent with its style, which is both thoughtful and somewhat dispassionate. Bogdanovich has been fairly scrupulous in attempting to frame his compositions in a traditional manner, and there is little reliance on zoom lenses and other dubious devices. The characters are clearly and expressively placed in the scenes, and they are never obscured by pretentious camera angles. The lighting, however, is somewhat unimaginative, and as a consequence of this and the drab, cheerless setting, the film has a monotonously gray look that becomes depressing. Although the film was taken to be a glorious return to black-and-white cinematography, it has not proven to be influential, as most films continue to be made in color, and the work of veteran Robert Surtees on the film suffers in comparison to his earlier black-and-white work in films such as *The Bad and the Beautiful* (1952). From a technical point of view, Bogdanovich's greatest talent is in editing. The structural faults in the narrative are largely compensated for by the excellence of the editing within individual sequences. Bogdanovich never cuts to make an obvious point that is already apparent in a scene, with the result that when he chooses to isolate an important moment, as in the close-up which proves to be our last view of Sam the Lion, the moment is often effective.

What most distinguishes the film is Bogdanovich's genuine interest in the material itself. He makes each of the characters comprehensible and never condescends to any of them—in fact, his worshipful attitude toward Sam the Lion (Ben Johnson) shows the opposite tendency. Even in the case of Jacy Farrow (Cybill Shepherd), a character he clearly hates, he treats her with an awareness that his hatred is part of a fascination he feels for her, and appropriately, this fascination is shared by the two principal male characters. Bogdanovich is especially sympathetic to the two older women who figure prominently in the story, Jacy's mother, Lois (Ellen Burstyn), and Ruth Popper (Cloris Leachman), the unhappy wife of the high-school coach (Bill Thurman). The compassionate treatment accorded to these two characters, and the vivid and affecting performances of Burstyn and Leachman in the roles, deserve special praise because both characters could have easily degenerated into two-dimensional stereotypes.

Bogdanovich's nostalgia, although generally expressed with restraint, arouses contradictory emotions. It is difficult to resist the old songs employed in the film, especially those sung by the late Country Western star Hank Williams, and the movie posters announcing showings of such pictures as *Wagonmaster* (1950) and *Sands of Iwo Jima* (1949); but while it is not necessarily harmful to romanticize memories, both real and imagined, it can be harmful to dwell on them analytically. Much of what is reflected in the film as being past is still vivid in the old movies Bogdanovich mourns, with the result that he is compelled to create associations with ideas expressed in those classic movies. A clip from *Red River* (1952) is a reminder of the virtues of Hawksian friendships, and as the film is attended by Sonny and his friend Duane Jackson (Jeff Bridges) following their reconciliation after the disruptive influence of Jacy, we are encouraged to consider their relationship to be a Hawksian one which can transcend their mutual involvement with a shallow girl. This strained reflection is gratuitous because the relationship should be understood in terms of what is actually in the story or it is not worth understanding. Fortunately, we do have sufficient feeling for the two characters as friends without the *Red River* clip.

Sam the Lion, the old Westerner played by Johnson, is also a source of overcalculated emotion. Johnson was chosen, of course, because of his link to the films of John Ford (he was a member of Ford's stock company), and he has always been a genuine and natural screen personality. When he says, "Old times, I guess I'm just as sentimental as the next fellow about old times," however, and the character dies a few scenes later, it is difficult not to feel that the actor, in spite of his moving performance, has been exploited to indulge the director's grave wistfulness.

In one instance, Bogdanovich's predilection for mingling his material with cinematic memories is favorable to the film. This occurs in the Christmas dance sequence, which uses Country and Western renditions of such John Ford favorites as "Red River Valley" and "Golden Slippers," and opens with a tracking shot through a doorway copied from the one which initiates the famous ball sequence in *The Magnificent Ambersons*. This sequence, in which all of the major characters figure, has a beautifully complex mood, being at once sweet and melancholy. In the midst of the music and dancing, Sonny encounters his father (Grover Lewis), and a brief exchange betrays the awareness on the part of both characters that they are not very close and never will be, a moment which conveys with masterly precision the lack of a meaningful family existence in modern life. Later in the sequence, Sonny gravitates to an older woman, Ruth Popper, perhaps out of an unconscious awareness of his need for a relationship more substantial than that which can be offered by his friends. The dance sequence ends with Sonny and Ruth kissing outside, an intimation of a relationship that blossoms and dies in the course of the story. The treatment of the kiss and its attendant feelings on the part of both characters is touching and tender in comparison to the cynical and bloodless scenes of passion which dominate most contemporary films. In this moment, *The Last Picture Show* holds its own with the tradition it seeks to represent.

Fortunately, it is a moment not forgotten. The entire relationship between Ruth and Sonny, a potentially banal one which would be treated insensitively in most films, develops with total credibility and is handled with consistent skill and feeling. It is revealed that although the frustrated woman initiates the relationship, the boy is the one who behaves selfishly. She is willing to give her heart, and he never feels the need to consider the inadequacy of his own feelings. The scene in which he drives by her house, delayed as a result of spending time with Jacy, and fails to stop when he sees that her husband is home, is gripping because Sonny's expression makes evident that he will be too cowardly to face her later. The muted note of reconciliation between the two characters at the end of the film provides considerable emotional satisfaction. Ruth is allowed to reappear after a long absence from the story and to express her anger at having been rejected, and ultimately, she is able to forgive and comfort Sonny. Although the relationship is over, it is validated as the most meaningful one in the film. More significantly, this relationship lingers in memory as one of the most sensitively realized in American cinema of the 1970's.

Blake Lucas

LAST TANGO IN PARIS

Released: 1972
Production: Alberto Grimaldi; released by United Artists
Direction: Bernardo Bertolucci
Screenplay: Bernardo Bertolucci and Franco Arcalli
Cinematography: Vittorio Storaro
Editing: Franco Arcalli
Running time: 130 minutes

Principal characters:

Paul	Marlon Brando
Jeanne	Maria Schneider
Tom	Jean-Pierre Léaud
Rosa's mother	Maria Michi
Marcel	Massimo Girotti
Jeanne's mother	Gitt Magrini
Rosa	Veronica Lazare

Calling *Last Tango in Paris* "a film that has made the strongest impression on me in almost twenty years of reviewing," The *New Yorker*'s film critic Pauline Kael compared the evening Bernardo Bertolucci's film closed the 1972 New York Film Festival to the evening Igor Stravinsky's *The Rite of Spring* had its premiere. Both, she felt, were controversial cultural landmarks. Along with Kael's bold proclamation, there was the announcement of Bertolucci's Marxian politics, the revelation of the details of actress Maria Schneider's private life (illegitimate birth, miserable childhood, extensive drug use, bisexuality, and so forth), the return of Marlon Brando to center screen following his acclaimed performance in *The Godfather* (1972), and *Time* and *Newsweek* cover stories centering on the film's crude, graphic language and the powerful and erotic subject matter. In short, *Last Tango in Paris* became a *succès de scandale*, a five-dollar-per-ticket media event. The thirty-year-old Italian director gained wide-spread recognition, and like Federico Fellini after *La Dolce Vita* (1961), Françoise Truffaut after *Jules and Jim* (1962), Ingmar Bergman after *Wild Strawberries* (1957), Jean Luc Godard after *Breathless* (1959), and Michelangelo Antonioni after *L'Avventura* (1959), Bertolucci gained a heralded international reputation.

The film was released half in English and half in French with English subtitles. Written by Bertolucci and Franco Arcalli—who originally had Jean-Louis Trintignant and Dominique Sanda or Catherine Deneuve in mind—the X-rated film stars Brando as a former actor and journalist, a hulky, handsome, but aging forty-five-year-old American expatriate named Paul. He has spent seven wretched years in Paris living off his French wife Rosa (Veronica Lazare) and mother-in-law (Maria Michi), owners of a small, shabby residential flophouse.

Following the razor-induced suicide of his wife Rosa, the disheveled, red-eyed, and unshaven Paul wanders aimlessly, unseeing, passing by Jeanne (Maria Schneider), a twenty-year-old liberated French bourgeois girl. She is a parttime actress and model dressed in floppy hat, boots, and fur-trimmed coat which exposes her thighs under her miniskirt. Soon, looking at a peeling, dusty, but spacious apartment for rent in Passy, the two run into each other.

Sizing each other up and exchanging a few mild insults, they prowl around the bare premises; then, in less than five minutes, suddenly, violently, they find themselves furiously fornicating, fully clothed and standing up. Exhausted and satisfied, they decide to use the flat for further almost savage sexual encounters. He is a burnt-out man driven to assert his masculinity as he vents his frustration and aggression; she is the petulant, spoiled, modern hippie type indulging in her (perhaps Oedipal) fantasies with an older man. Although Jeanne wants to tell Paul about herself and wants to know his name and background, he insists that sex is all that matters, that it is the only mystery in life and that it is the only thing that makes life bearable. Thus, isolated in a dingy apartment, the self-loathing, profane man, making the ultimately personal into the ultimately impersonal, debases himself and her, demanding total subservience to his sexual wishes.

In the meantime, we see both of them (as they do not see each other) in their normal lives. We learn that the dark-eyed, sensual, baby-faced Jeanne lives with her mother (Gitt Magrini), the widow of a colonel, and that she is adored by Tom (Jean-Pierre Léaud), a location-scouting television director, more romantic than sexual, who is shooting a 16mm documentary about her. We see that Jeanne prefers Paul's closed world of the apartment to Tom's open world of the city. We see that she favors the man who debases her over the man who idealizes her.

We also see Paul visiting Marcel (Massimo Girotti), his dead wife's lover. The two aging men, in identical bathrobes (both given to them by Rosa), sit side by side, drink bourbon, and discuss the way they used to look. They also speak of Rosa as a calculating and willful "bitch." We see Paul visit his dead wife, who is laid out in a bed of flowers, and vent his grief and rage at the corpse. Shortly after, however, in an excess of tenderness, we see Paul as he tries to wipe away the cosmetic paint on her face.

Three days after his wife is buried, Paul is somewhat purged of his grief; he decides he wants to give up the flat, reveal more of himself, live, and love Jeanne as a normal person. By now, however, Tom has proposed to Jeanne, and when Paul fails to show up at the apartment, she thinks the affair is over. At this point in the relationship, the power changes into her hands as Paul tries to win her back. He chases her through the streets, getting her to agree to a drink at a 1920's-style tango palace. There, in a bizarre confrontation amidst the mannequinlike dancers engaged in a tango contest, a drunken Paul confesses his love and proposes a more conventional arrangement. He ends up, however, sprawled on the floor and baring his bottom to the woman official who asks him to leave. Jeanne flees, but he follows her toward her home. Panicking as he comes after her, she reaches for her father's revolver and fires bullets into her lover. Crying and claiming that he attempted to rape her, Jeanne insists that she does not know him, that she does not even know the man's name.

Like the film's opening shots of English artist Francis Bacon's paintings of tortured men and women with corroded faces, *Last Tango in Paris* deals with decadence, disintegration, and despair. The loneliness of the human condition is revealed and sexuality within relationships is explored. Stating that sexuality is a powerful drive in the human psyche, the film also explores the human needs behind the sex act. Sex, the film says, cannot merely be a refuge from, or an alternative to, more thorough relationships and responsibilities.

Brando adds yet another fascinating and controversial character to his gallery of screen roles. Bringing his own intensity to the script (it is said that Brando often insisted on posting his lines all over the set's walls and ceilings) and using improvisation as well, Brando's portrayal of the morose and tormented Paul is stunning. At one point Paul speaks in a long soliloquy about his early life: an alcoholic mother, a memory of going to a basketball game with cow dung on his shoes, and a memory of a hunting dog that could not catch rabbits. Later, seconds after he is shot, the gum-chewing Paul takes out the wad, sticks it under the balcony rail, and falls over and dies. Interestingly, the role of Paul in some ways reflects Brando's own life, for like Paul, he was an actor, had a Midwestern childhood, and spent much time in Tahiti in a kind of self-imposed exile. Using the system of acting that requires him to draw on his memory and use past experiences and emotions in preparation for the role, Brando's method acting makes interesting contrast to the French New Wave naturalistic acting of the actor who plays Tom (Léaud), François Truffaut's disciple cast in *The 400 Blows* (1959) and *Day for Night* (1972), among others.

Apparently satirizing himself with the role of Tom, the young foolish filmmaker, director Bertolucci (the son of a film critic) also alludes to movies of the past in *Last Tango in Paris*; as particular images appear, viewing the film often feels like enrolling in a course in cinema history. The tango scene evokes memories of the elegantly decadent tango sequence in Bertolucci's own *The Conformist* (1970); its extravagant look also reminds one of the films of German director Max Ophuls, with its use of light, glass, doorways, draperies, its long-graceful camera movements, and its scenes shot through frosted glass and against fractured mirrors. Paul, dressed in his T-shirt and silently brooding, reminds us of Brando's own Stanley Kowalski in *A Streetcar Named Desire* (1951), and Paul's quick soft-shoe recalls his Sky Masterson in *Guys and Dolls* (1955). A scene of Jeanne and Tom on a barge near a life preserver stamped "L'Atalante" reminds us of Jean Vigo's 1934 film of that name about a girl who experiences the excitement of Paris. The scene where Paul looks out on the roofs of Paris recalls René Clair's 1931 *Under Paris Rooftops*. Finally, when Jeanne takes out her gun and shoots Paul, it reminds us of the endings of many Hollywood films where the woman kills her lover, such as William Wyler's *The Letter* (1942), Michael Curtiz's *Mildred Pierce* (1945), and Irving Rapper's *Deception* (1946).

Last Tango in Paris is an enormously sensual film. There are constant references to smells (a dimension film cannot project, despite a brief attempt of some filmmakers at so-called "Smellovision" in the 1950's) as the ugly odor of the apartment is noted or when Paul speaks of the smell of manure on his shoes as a boy. The film is also beautifully shot, and cinematographer Vittorio Stovaro's camera captures the melancholy of autumnal afternoons with colors of oranges, beiges, browns, and pinks. Additionally, Armenian jazzman Gato Barbieri's music is feverish, making use of a sultry saxophone solo which enhances the mood.

Last Tango in Paris is not pornographic, although some might think it so. The sex is not particularly explicit, and although Schneider appears naked, we never see Brando without clothes. Instead, *Last Tango in Paris* is a stunning view of human relationships. Voted best film of the year (1972) by Italian cinema journalists, *Last Tango in Paris* received the group's annual Silver Ribbon Award.

Leslie J. Taubman

THE LAST TYCOON

Released: 1976
Production: Sam Spiegel for Paramount
Direction: Elia Kazan
Screenplay: Harold Pinter; based on the novel of the same name by F. Scott Fitzgerald
Cinematography: Victor J. Kemper
Editing: Richard Marks
Running time: 123 minutes

Principal characters:
Monroe Stahr	Robert De Niro
Rodriguez	Tony Curtis
Pat Brady	Robert Mitchum
Didi	Jeanne Moreau
Brimmer	Jack Nicholson
Boxley	Donald Pleasence
Kathleen Moore	Ingrid Boulting

During the 1970's, America was swept by a fervid nostalgia for F. Scott Fitzgerald and his era, and *The Last Tycoon* was one of two major films that were by-products of that nostalgia. Unlike *The Great Gatsby* (1974), which preceded it, however, Elia Kazan's film came closer to what the audience seemed to crave: not only a documentary of a bygone era's flamboyance and monied romanticism, but also a step-by-step description of how a filmmaker creates such a documentary. In essence, *The Last Tycoon* is a satisfying enough formula for how to make a movie *about* the sort of movie the audience craved.

If the film *The Last Tycoon* is a tribute to the old school of "escape" films which gave the people "what they need," as Monroe Stahr (Robert De Niro) explains to his love, Kathleen Moore (Ingrid Boulting), it is also the same for Fitzgerald's monumental unfinished novel, claimed by some critics to have been potentially his best work of fiction. Given this heritage, the film, with its screenplay written by Harold Pinter, has much to live up to.

Written during the last years of Fitzgerald's life, the novel is, when compared with biographies and Fitzgerald's own notes and letters, a painful rendering of the author's unsuccessful stint as a screenplay writer in Hollywood's feast-or-famine days of the 1930's. Perhaps a description of a perennially hopeful idea of what might have been had fortune treated him more kindly, Fitzgerald's story delineates the strange requirements expected of a certain group of people in their common effort to crank out successful films. To some, this meant turning out good films despite the audience's tastes; to others, the only criterion of success was box-office profits; to still others, it meant combining audience tastes with the industry's better capabilities and somehow reaching a happy medium that would ultimately elevate the audience's expectations as well as its tastes. Monroe Stahr belongs to this latter group.

Stahr, a quietly authoritative film executive, dictates the production of a large Hollywood studio from a respected vantage point of cool aloofness. One night while Stahr naps in his studio office, the area is shaken by a moderate earthquake. Jolted from sleep, Stahr rushes to the back lots of the studio to inspect for damage. One of the lots has flooded, and bizarre props from varied movies bob in the water before the lot's flood lights, floating with comic majesty down this newly formed river. Perched on a large, out-of-context pagan head is Kathleen Moore, whose own simple beauty is captivating enough, but whose striking similarity to Stahr's now deceased wife overpowers him. This half-comic, half-macabre first sighting begins for Stahr a consuming odyssey, not only of recapturing a part of his past, but also of relinquishing that self-contained, invulnerable status that affords him the strength and influence to accomplish what he does.

Regardless of the personal tuggings taking place in Stahr's private life, however, life at the movie factory is crumbling. It is the heyday of unionization, a situation ripe for infiltration of the studio by a Communist organizer (superbly played by Jack Nicholson). Much of what he professes is ideologically acceptable, but Stahr refuses to accept it. Rather than choose to thwart the organizer and the union efforts, Stahr for the most part elects to ignore them. This proves to be a crucial mistake. The film industry has chosen to ignore far too much of life, and its audience has grown to a certain sophistication that can no longer ignore itself and its real concerns in the entertainment it seeks.

This discrepancy between the making of films and the audience for whom the films are made is a pivotal issue upon which screenwriter Harold Pinter focuses much of his script. Each scene is crisp in its intention and in its movement from beginning to end, from premise to conclusion; and the series of scenes is held together by the thread of Stahr's varying functions in each of them. Creating these concise scenes is Pinter's strength, and it is ironically reflected in Stahr's repeated claims that only he is able to bring together all the components of similarly concise and worthy films. As the industry of filmmaking gradually rearranges itself more in keeping with the "real" world of the audience to whom the movies are directed, there is a direct strengthening of Stahr's belief in his own authority. To maintain this belief, however, Stahr isolates himself even more from his colleagues in the industry. This is what brings him to this end, what drove Fitzgerald down, and what brings the film to its perplexing conclusion.

Despite the power and influence Stahr wields in the film business, he grows to realize that he is not capable of manipulating either his own personal life or trends in audience taste with the same assuredness. Kathleen, proving either her willfulness or her weakness, decides not to change the prescribed course of her life, and abruptly announces in a letter to Stahr that she can no longer see him. In a brilliantly written and directed scene, Stahr in essence "makes a movie" in his mind to satisfy his need to understand and control what has happened, to discover what quirk of fate kept him from attaining this one goal. He stages the entire series of events leading not only to Kathleen's decision, but also to the execution of her decision. This is done with Stahr's obviously cinematic attention to even the smallest detail. Satisfied, Stahr assimilates what he has created into his own consciousness, accepting it, we suspect, with as much conviction as he would any other movie. The result is that Stahr is swallowed up by the very industry to which he once gave life and which now is the only force through which he can affirm his own existence. *The Last Tycoon*, then, is about a man who finds himself living in a world that can no longer accommodate him, estranged from society, and isolated by his own previously unquestioned power and his superb intellect and talent.

As Monroe Stahr, Robert De Niro gives one of his finest, and possibly most underrated, performances. The part is executed with a quiet deliberateness too often reserved for the cowboy heroes of Westerns rather than for the roles of the elegant intellectual. The understatement of De Niro's role is matched by Ingrid Boulting's portrayal of Kathleen Moore. If De Niro's role is governed by controlled aloofness, then Boulting's is marked by a wistful and profound resignation. The characters rendered by these actors are not superficial. Instead, they are intelligent, contemplative, and worthy of each other.

The Last Tycoon was not universally well received. Many notable critics objected to Kazan's treatment of the film industry, perhaps finding its approach somewhat ungrateful, if not hypocritical. It must be remembered, however, that few if any institutions are totally good, if they are good at all, and the same can be said for the film industry.

Bonnie Fraser

THE LAST WAVE

Released: 1979
Production: Hal McElroy and James McElroy for World Northal
Direction: Peter Weir
Screenplay: Peter Weir, Tony Morphett, and Peter Popescue
Cinematography: Russell Boyd
Editing: Max Lemon
Special effects: Neil Angwin and Monty Fieguth
Running time: 106 minutes

Principal characters:
David Burton	Richard Chamberlain
Annie Burton	Olivia Hamnett
Chris Lee	Gulpilil
Charlie	Nandjiwarra Amagula
Reverend Burton	Frederick Parslow
Gerry Lee	Walter Amagula
Larry	Roy Bara
Lindsey	Cedric Lalara
Jacko	Morris Lalara

Australian cinema came of age in the late 1970's. Buoyed by state support through an act passed by the Australian parliament in 1970, an industry that was once parochial and derivative burst onto the international scene in 1978 and 1979 via a handful of directors and films such as Gillian Armstrong's *My Brilliant Career* (1979), Fred Schepisi's controversial and—for Australia— relatively expensive ($1,200,000) *The Chant of Jimmie Blacksmith* (1978), and Philip Noyce's *Newsfront* (1979), which brought critical acclaim as well as financial success, particularly in the United States. The director who achieved the initial breakthrough, however, was Peter Weir, with *The Last Wave*.

It should come as no surprise that the initial focus of this new burst of creativity was Australia itself, its history and its mores. Armstrong's *My Brilliant Career*, Shcepisi's *The Chant of Jimmie Blacksmith*, and Weir's own *Picnic at Hanging Rock* (released in Australia in 1975 and in the United States in 1978) are all set in Australia around the turn of the century; Noyce's *Newsfront* is set in the Cold War era of the early 1950's. *The Last Wave*, which might be best described as an anthropological thriller, concerns an Australia that is both more contemporary and vastly more ancient than any of these other settings. Ostensibly set in modern-day Sydney, the film is in actuality completely outside of chronology, in the aboriginal Dreamtime. The Dreamtime contains the past, present, and future; it is the place where tribal consciousness is all-pervasive and unaffected by the white culture that came to dominate the continent in the nineteenth and twentieth centuries.

Weir immediately establishes the theme of cultures in conflict. As the film's credits roll, we see an aborigine sand painter constructing an intricate design. Thunder rolls ominously on the sound track, although the sky is clear. There is a quick shot of a group of aborigines acknowledging the omen and preparing to seek shelter, and then Weir cuts to a white schoolyard in the desert outback. The freak storm, foreseen by the aborigines, comes out of nowhere, dumping torrents of rain (and finally huge chunks of ice) on the terrified children and their equally terrified teachers. The scene is striking, and it also introduces the film's basic theme—that the white culture, for all its sophistication, lacks the ability to understand Nature, much less control it. It also introduces the principal image by which Weir conveys this theme: water.

Weir's use of the water image is one of the film's continuing fascinations. Water can be frightening, as in the opening scene in the schoolyard; but it can also be a thing of sensuous beauty, as in the next scene. We are introduced to David Burton (Richard Chamberlain), a handsome corporation lawyer in his late twenties, who is driving home in Sydney, Australia's largest city. He is on the eastern edge of that same rainstorm. Shots of the city through David's windshield, as the sheets of water are swept off by the windshield wipers, are lovely. It is water, too, via the suspicious drowning of a young aborigine whose accused killers Burton is asked to defend, that introduces us to the aboriginal myths that give the film its power. For the last wave of the film's title refers to nothing less than the destruction of the world by water—a variation on the flood myth that anthropologists reveal is very nearly universal among ancient cultures.

Weir spends the next twenty minutes of the film introducing us to David Burton and his family. He has a thriving career, a pretty wife named Annie (Olivia Hannett), two cute young children, and an impressive house with its own tennis court and a view of the ocean. Everything seems to give a portrait of a successful, upwardly mobile, and thoroughly conventional Australian WASP, until we learn that David has recently been troubled by mysterious dreams. His stepfather (Frederick Parslow), an Anglican minister, later reveals that he had similar nightmares as a child. David's dreams are obscure at first—dark, vaguely human shapes appearing out of the rainy night—but they gradually become clear. He is dreaming of aborigines, of wildly painted medicine men and stone amulets covered with indecipherable inscriptions and blood. It is not until he agrees to defend five indigent aborigines accused of murdering one of their friends tht he begins to understand the meaning of his dreams.

Meanwhile, Weir has shown us the supposed murder. Billy, a young aborigine, is chased through the maze of a subterranean power station and cornered by five of his tribesmen in a pub, where he has taken refuge. He runs into the street and appears to be well on the way to escaping until he sights a parked car containing an ancient bearded black man. The old man points a long thin bone at the fugitive, who pitches forward into a puddle, dead on the street. At the inquest, the coroner finds a small amount of water in the victim's lungs, but his verdict—death by drowning—seems clearly inadequate to explain what the audience has just seen.

David meets with the aborigines, Gerry Lee (Walter Amagula), Lindsey (Cedric Lalara), Larry (Roy Bara), and Jacko (Morris Lalara); the fifth defendant, Gerry's brother Chris Lee (Gulpilil), is absent. He discovers that his efforts on their behalf are complicated by their refusal to discuss the case with him. "Billy died, that's all," grunts Gerry Lee stolidly. Despite this lack of cooperation, however, David becomes fascinated with the case in particular and with aborigines in general. His wife is the first to suggest that tribal witchcraft might have been involved. The point is significant, since Australian law turns tribal offenses over to tribal authorities; but all evidence indicates that there are no tribal aborigines in the Sydney area. When David meets Chris Lee, the fifth defendant, however, he begins to wonder, for Chris is one of the figures out of his dreams, the man who appears to him every night offering him the bloody stone amulet. When that same amulet (complete with bloodstains) turns up in the effects of the dead aborigine, he is convinced. The aborigines are tribal. Getting them to admit it, however, is another question. The taboos against revealing tribal secrets are too strong.

Chris Lee stands out among the aborigines. He is more Westernized than they are; he is more articulate and more willing to talk with David, although he continues to deny the tribal status of his colleagues. When David tells Chris about his dreams, Chris merely nods, accepting the fact that their fates are linked somewhere in the Dreamtime. Chris brings Charlie (Nandjiwarra Amagula), the tribal medicine man, who is, unbeknown to David, the man who pointed the death bone at Billy, to the Burtons' house; Charlie is interested in David's ancestors. As Chris translates, they page through the Burton family album until Charlie stops, pointing at a picture and muttering "Mulcrul." The aborigines seem satisfied by the encounter, although David is thoroughly mystified.

A visit to a local anthropologist puts him back on the track. The amulet and the word "Mulcrul" are parts of the creation myth of a tribe of aborigines once based in the Sydney area, but now thought to be extinct. As David's excitement mounts, the anthropologist explains that the reappearance of the Mulcrul signifies the end of an age and the destruction of the world by some natural cataclysm.

David's dreams continue and now involve manifestations of Charlie as well as Chris. Mysterious and terrifying things begin happening in the Burton house; everything begins to take on the trancelike quality of David's dreams. Garish medicine men stalk the hallways, and David has visions of a world under water, full of floating corpses. He becomes convinced that he is the Mulcrul, as the torrential rains continue unabated.

Things begin to come to a head during the aborigines' trial. David is obsessed with proving that Chris and the rest are tribal and thus not subject to civil law. Under his questioning, Chris first concedes the group's tribal status, but when Charlie, a spectator in the courtroom, suddenly—and literally—disappears, Chris repudiates his testimony. "We got drunk. We had a fight. That's all," he insists stubbornly.

Still, Chris feels that he owes David a full accounting, partly out of friendship, but primarily because of their links in the Dreamtime. He leads David through the power station toward the inner sanctum; the complex machinery provides an ironic contrast to the primeval world they are about to enter. With Charlie (sometimes taking the form of an owl) monitoring their progress, they reach the underground cave that houses the tribal mysteries. Chris then leaves, saying "I'm going back to the Dreamtime."

David explores the cave alone. Many of the artifacts are suggestive of some universal ur-civilization, at once reminiscent of Egyptian, Mayan, and Easter Island cultures. There is a primitive calendar depicting the destruction of the Mulcrul civilization by a huge tidal wave, and a death mask of David's own face. His dreams are about to be realized: he is the Mulcrul come to bring the apocalypse.

David's initial impulse is to get out and warn Australia of its impending doom. Gathering up several of the artifacts as evidence, he attempts to retrace his steps, but discovers that he is trapped. He stumbles back into the cave and finally finds his way through a large sewer pipe to the beach. He staggers, exhausted, into the surf, and looks up. The last wave, hundreds of feet high, is on its way. All of Australia is returning to the Dreamtime.

The Last Wave is a taut, compelling film in which all of the parts fit together perfectly. The script, the cinematography and special effects, the acting—all are melded by Weir into a superbly entertaining piece of cinema. The film's script, by Weir, Tony Morphett, and Peter Popescue, contains a plot that, in the wrong hands, could have gone off onto any one of several counterproductive tangents. It might have turned into a morality play about the virtues of the noble savage and the villainy of the white race bent on destroying their way of life. Although Weir takes note of the racism in Australian society, he does not belabor the point. Although *The Last Wave* also shares many of the conventions of the thriller genre, the last thing in which Weir is interested is a cheap thrill or gratuitous shock. Restraint is the hallmark of the film's writing, directing, and acting.

Weir gets extraordinary performances out of his entire cast—not one character seems false or out of place—but four actors deserve special mention. In supporting roles, Hamnett as Annie Burton and Amagula as Charlie are outstanding. Annie is compassionate and intelligent, while at the same time confused and increasingly terrified at the events that have caught up her husband, and Hamnett aptly conveys all of these attributes. Charlie, the aborigine medicine man, is played with utter dignity and conviction by Amagula, who gives a thoroughly unnerving and convincing performance.

Similarly great performances are turned in by Chamberlain as David Burton and Gulpilil as Chris Lee, the two men linked by their dreams across an incredible cultural gulf. Chamberlain uses his matinee-idol looks and voice to good effect. Physically, he is every inch the part of an up-and-coming corporate lawyer. This is not to say that he relies on his "pretty boy" image from his television days as Dr. Kildare as a substitute for acting. He simply puts all of his gifts, physical and intellectual, to use. It is Chamberlain's intellect that most characterizes David Burton. Chamberlain plays him as restrained, even in the face of madness; urbane and civilized even in the face of the end of civilization. It is, perhaps, Chamberlain's finest performance.

David Burton's intellectual qualities are echoed by Chris Lee more than by any of the other aborigine characters in the film; but Chris is also in touch with his tribal consciousness. Gulpilil, a full-blooded aborigine who earned critical praise for his performance in Nicholas Roeg's *Walkabout* in 1971, turns in a bravura performance here. A man of tremendous dignity (like all of the aborigines in the film), his passionate portrayal of Chris Lee illuminates the special dilemma of a man caught between two worlds. Any number of black actors could have portrayed one side or another of Chris's character. Few could have showed us both as well as Gulpilil.

The success of *The Last Wave* also owes a great deal to the special effects of Neil Angwin and Monty Fiegutti and to the cinematography of Russell Boyd. It is through the efforts of Angwin and Fiegutti that the omnipresence of water is fully translated onto the screen, and it is Boyd's photography that gives *The Last Wave* much of its flavor. For, however terrifying the onslaught of water might have been, it was also quite lovely. This monumental irony— that the end of the world might be beautiful—heightens the tension in the film and at the same time gives it a dreamy, trancelike quality that perfectly suits the plot.

It is possible, of course, to overpraise *The Last Wave*. Ultimately, it is simply a thriller with exotic trappings. It is an extraordinarily well-made thriller, however; and the exotic (to non-Australian viewers) trappings are handled with such sensitivity that the audience never feels manipulated by the filmmaker. *The Last Wave* is clearly the product of a vastly talented director, cast, and crew. It is an excellent introduction to the new Australian cinema and to one of that cinema's leading lights, Peter Weir.

Robert Mitchell

THE LATE SHOW

Released: 1977
Production: Robert Altman for Warner Bros.
Direction: Robert Benton
Screenplay: Robert Benton
Cinematography: Charles Rosher
Editing: Lon Lombardo and Peter Appleton
Running time: 94 minutes

Principal characters:
Ira Wells	Art Carney
Margo Sperling	Lily Tomlin
Charlie Hatter	Bill Macy
Ron Birdwell	Eugene Roche
Laura Birdwell	Joanna Cassidy
Lamar	John Considine
Harry Regan	Howard Duff

If it had been written thirty years earlier, Robert Benton's screenplay for *The Late Show* could have been the basis for a stark melodrama, a stylish duel of deceptive women and dangerous tough guys played out in a setting of knife-edge shadows, extreme camera angles, and lonely cityscapes, where every street led to a dead end and the only glory lay in salvaging a shred of honor. Today, however, the loner with a gun and a "sense of honor" is more often seen as a Fascist or a sociopath than as a hero; and Benton has refashioned the elements of the genre into a bittersweet, slightly nostalgic, offbeat comedy.

The Late Show tries in many ways to span the years. The film's oddly resonant title suggests a relic, an old movie viewed on television, from a modern perspective. In another sense, the film truly details a "late" show. The great private eye Ira Wells (Art Carney) is in his sixties, overweight, with a hearing aid and a bad leg. He has already spent six months in a hospital with "tubes and stuff going every which way." Now Ira feels his own mortality. He knows that the case he is working on is his own late show. The case begins with the death of Ira's partner and with the seemingly insignificant theft of a cat. Its lonely owner, Margo Sperling (Lily Tomlin), is a fount of California clichés. An actress, talent manager, and astrologer, she also dabbles in dope-dealing to pay her "shrink." Margo fancies herself as hip, but to Ira she is an old story. "Back in the forties," he tells her, "this town was crawling with dollies like you, screwing up their lives just the same."

Working together in an uneasy alliance, Ira and Margo penetrate a maze of double- and triple-crosses. Indeed, the first pleasure of *The Late Show* is the logic and complexity of Benton's plotting. Margo's cat was stolen by her former "sexual interlude," Brian Henfield. At the time Ira's partner was shot, he was following that same Brian Henfield, having linked him to a big stamp theft and to the murder of the stamp collector's wife. The trail leads to Brian Henfield's fence, who has a wife who was having an affair with the stamp collector. She stole a gun from her husband (the fence) and gave it to her lover (the collector) for protection. That gun killed the collector's wife, and a fume of blackmail rises from it. Eventually it is found, hidden in the cage of the missing cat. Along the way, we see or hear about a gallery of murders and murderers. The story is carefully worked out and delightfully absurd. With nearly everyone in the film pickled in corruption, it hardly matters who killed whom; given half a chance, they are all potential killers.

The Late Show is most interesting in the ways it differs from classics of the genre. As director, Robert Benton never generates the narrative drive of the great private-eye films or their sense of life and death hanging in the balance. All the suspects are transparent crooks who never rise above their own venality. It is hard to care about them, or their guilt, except on the crossword-puzzle level of whodunit. The casting adds to the low-key feeling of the film. Carney never suggests that he might have had the wild, impulsive energy of a Humphrey Bogart or the acid sarcasm of a Robert Mitchum. He is an avuncular figure, never threatening or really threatened. Together, he and Tomlin do not generate the moral tensions of Bogart and Mary Astor in *The Maltese Falcon* (1941), let alone the sexual electricity of Bogart and Lauren Bacall in *The Big Sleep* (1946). Despite some vague dialogue about an attraction between them, Tomlin seems too cold and Carney too old.

Benton has treated the mythic aspects of the genre—the life-and-death melodrama, the moral ambiguities, the sexuality—as if they were clichés to be avoided. Instead, *The Late Show* dwells on the growing bond between a broken-down private eye and a Hollywood "kook." When Ira's partner dies at the opening of the film, Ira knows the man was foolish and greedy, but he was "good company." By the end of the film, Carney finds a new pal, a woman of courage and brains (when she chooses to use them). She is more good company, a fresh partner to fill the void.

The theme of "palship" as a redeeming consolation appears in the screenplays Benton coauthored with David Newman, notably *Bonnie and Clyde* (1967) and *Bad Company* (1972). In *The Late Show*, however, the quest for good company is the central action, and gives the film a surprising lyrical quality further enhanced by its muted, nostalgic colors.

To balance the film's wistful tone, Benton uses a memorably raffish supporting cast. Eugene Roche plays the fence with bloated self-satisfaction, surveying the world from a mount of stolen stereos and cameras. Bill Macy is deliciously oily as a low-rent informer; and Joanna Cassidy as the errant wife looks like a chorine and sounds like a Gothic heroine, proclaiming to Ira, "I'm going to be honest—lay myself naked before you." Ira reacts to them all with a funny, sniping invective. They are "nosepickers . . . without the sense God gave a common dog." His remarks are never moral or profound; he does not condemn the crooks so much as dismiss them. That, finally, is the tone of the film—less angry than amused.

Going for charm instead of guts, *The Late Show* was more successful critically than commercially. Produced by Robert Altman, it was even lighter in tone than Altman's own *The Long Goodbye* (1973). Perhaps audiences were unprepared for Benton's film, which may have been the first "liberal" private-eye movie. Regardless of what people expected, Ira Wells, like the genre itself, had reached an age of live-and-let-live. He could relax and enjoy the right and wrong in everyone, remembering his lost partner and looking forward to his new one. Depending on one's point of view, the loner with a gun had either grown old or grown up.

Ted Gershuny

LAUGHTER

Released: 1930
Production: Paramount
Direction: Harry d'Abbabie d'Arrast
Screenplay: Douglas Doty and Harry d'Abbabie d'Arrast, with additional dialogue by Donald Ogden Stewart
Cinematography: George J. Folsey
Editing: Helene Turner
Running time: 85 minutes

Principal characters:

Peggy Gibson	Nancy Carroll
Paul Lockridge	Fredric March
C. Morton Gibson	Frank Morgan
Ralph Le Sainte	Glenn Anders
Marjorie Gibson	Diane Ellis
Benham, the butler	Leonard Carey

Even without reading the credits, it was never difficult for the audience to know when Harry d'Abbabie d'Arrast had directed a picture. He was of the Ernst Lubitsch school, definitely having the celebrated master's "touch," but he was younger, like Mal St. Clair or Monta Bell, and the little worldly touches he had learned from Charles Chaplin were the real giveaways. D'Arrast had come to Hollywood to work with Chaplin. A Frenchman born in Argentina of aristocratic background, he had a taste for elegance and a gift for both casual and biting wit that was unmatched by any other man in Hollywood. He had a natural ability to charm, but unfortunately he was also indiscreet in his remarks; he earned a reputation for being able to make a friend and lose him on the same day simply by being unable to resist a wisecrack that was basically cruel and ungentlemanly. Samuel Goldwyn and David Selznick were only two producers who had been ready to swear by his talent, but who were offended by his wit and personal jibes, and so disdained him both socially and professionally. He ended by not being able to get a job as a film director in America.

D'Arrast had married actress Eleanor Boardman, who was well liked in Hollywood, and he took her back to his chateau in the French Basque country. They made what was purportedly a delightful color film of *The Three-Cornered Hat* (1935) in Spain. Douglas Fairbanks, Sr., saw it, and at his recommendation it was purchased for release by United Artists. Somehow the prints got lost, however, and nobody could find the negative. D'Arrast was apparently disliked by too many of importance, including United Artists' chairman, Joseph Schenck. Fairbanks was living in London, and so could not help when d'Arrast realized that somehow he had made enemies at United Artists who were successfully keeping his picture from being shown in the United States. Eventually, d'Arrast gave up trying; his wife returned to Hollywood, where there was a friendly divorce, and he spent the rest of his life quietly gambling in the Riviera casinos. He was one of the really talented early directors, but his own caustic personality destroyed his career.

It was a great waste of a very special talent. D'Arrast had a natural aptitude for film, and working with Chaplin on *A Woman of Paris* (1923) and *The Gold Rush* (1925) gave him a background for the comedic touch that was his own, but was also refined by his association with Chaplin. In 1927 he directed three urbane comedies for Paramount starring Adolphe Menjou, who had become a star because of Chaplin's *A Woman of Paris*. Menjou went on playing that same kind of polished man of the world for d'Arrast (*Service for Ladies, A Gentleman of Paris, Serenade*, all in 1927). D'Arrast stayed on at Paramount to direct the lovely Florence Vidor in *The Magnificent Flirt* (1928), and then went over to Fox to direct the equally lovely Mary Astor in *Dry Martini* (1928). He was definitely a director on his way up when Goldwyn signed him,

In a very short time, unable to resist the opportunity for an obvious retort, he had offended Goldwyn and was removed from the direction of Ronald Colman in *Raffles* (1930), a talkie, eventually sharing directorial credit for that film with George Fitzmaurice. Unable to get another job in Hollywood at the time, he went to New York, where Paramount officials, remembering the brilliant silent films he had directed for their company, bought an original screenplay written by him and Douglas Doty called *Laughter*. It also boasted some smart dialogue by Donald Ogden Stewart. D'Arrast was allowed to direct it because his producer was Herman Mankiewicz, who was liberal in thought, had a tongue as barbed as d'Arrast's and rather liked having someone around who could be as insulting and indiscreet as he.

Laughter is a gem of a comedy. It is ironic, bitter, funny, and sad. It is about rich Americans who have all the money in the world to spend, but do not know what it is to laugh. Released in 1930, *Laughter* looks back on the entire decade of the 1920's, and it is arguably one of the best cinematic presentations of the modes and manners of that time that has ever been made. The decade under consideration preceded the fateful stock market crash of October, 1929, which left few millionaires to laugh at anything.

Laughter's heroine is Peggy Gibson (Nancy Carroll), a onetime Follies girl who has married a multimillionaire, C. Morton Gibson (Frank Morgan), a glum Wall Street speculator who, when he makes $8,450,000 in one day, considers it a good day's work. There is nobody around to share his pleasure except his male secretary, for whom he buys a new typewriter and with whom he toasts his luck as a financier with champagne. Peggy has left their Long Island home for Manhattan, where she drops in on Ralph Le Sainte (Glenn Anders), a former suitor who is a successful sculptor, and who is still hopelessly in love with Peggy. She convinces him not to commit suicide, but has no intention of giving him love or anything else in return.

Peggy has come to the conclusion that money is far from being everything; in fact, it is a real handicap to happiness. She is ready to acknowledge that for her the ideal lover and constant companion is her music-composing friend who just returned from Paris, Paul Lockridge (Fredric March). Happy as a lark, he calls on Peggy and writes on the butler's shirtfront, "Peggy, I'm here"; Peggy sends the butler back with her message written below his, "I'm out." Of course, Peggy and Paul do get together again, and very soon. Marjorie (Diane Ellis), Gibson's daughter by a previous marriage, arrives home from Paris, and for a brief moment there is fun and laughter in the Gibson mansion, with Paul playing the piano, while the girls, stepmother and daughter, do a fancy Charleston before going in to dinner. Gibson returns home and is perplexed finding so much gaiety in his own home, a laughter that he cannot enjoy because it is the laughter of young people having fun and enjoying life for a change.

Peggy and Paul see a great deal of each other, and one day they are caught in a rainstorm with no gasoline in their car; they take refuge on the front porch of a Long Island cottage, and Paul, finding a window open, raises it, and they go inside and make themselves at home. The police patrol discovers them inside the house, and they are taken to the local station for questioning. When the police captain learns that Peggy is the wife of no less a figure than C. Morton Gibson, he sends them both home with a motorcycle police escort. Peggy begins to realize that she is nobody unless she is identified as Mrs. C. Morton Gibson; under that name she can get away with almost anything.

Her feeling of inadequacy is intensified when Ralph Le Sainte, who had been courting Marjorie, is disdained by her, and this time, clumsily and by accident, in trying to shoot Peggy, Ralph instead kills himself, whereupon Peggy is called upon by the police and questioned. More scandal threatens, until again, when it is discovered that Peggy is Mrs. C. Morton Gibson, apologies are forthcoming and she is immediately released. Gibson scolds her, however, and she decides that being his wife means that she belongs to him. She refuses to belong to anybody, however, and walks out in time to board the ocean liner *Rotterdam* and return with Paul to France, where she can hope to find a life of her own, sharing it with somebody who has a gift for laughter.

Laughter is only one of three films directed by d'Arrast that has not disappeared (*Raffles* and *Topaze* are the other two). D'Arrast himself, if lonely, was nevertheless free and independent; he not only had something brilliant to say when he wrote a scene, but he also directed his actors with rare skill so that they never seemed to be acting. Every player in *Laughter* turns in a stunning performance. Piquant Carroll as Peggy is absolutely delightful, and March has charm and insouciance as the carefree Paul, while Morgan gives one of the first of his many characterizations of a rich man bewildered and unhappy with all his wealth. The picture was shot at Paramount's Long Island studio and has a Manhattan Cartier brilliance rather than a Hollywood tinsel glitter.

DeWitt Bodeen

LAW AND ORDER

Released: 1932
Production: Universal
Direction: Edward L. Cahn
Screenplay: John Huston and Tom Reed; based on the novel *Saint Johnson* by W. R. Burnett
Cinematography: Jack Rose
Editing: Milton Carruth
Running time: 70 minutes

Principal characters:

Frame Johnson	Walter Huston
Ed Brant	Harry Carey
Deadwood	Raymond Hatton
Judge Williams	Russell Simpson
Poe Northrup	Ralph Ince
Luther Johnson	Russell Hopton
Walt Northrup	Harry Woods
Kurt Northrup	Richard Alexander
Johnny Kinsman	Andy Devine
Lanky Smith	Walter Brennan
Fin Elder	Alphonz Ethier

Before the popularity of the adult Western in the 1950's, Hollywood Westerns were no more than simplistic melodramas aimed at the imaginations of ten-year-old boys. Most sagas of the Old West featured heroes, heroines, and villains: handsome, clean-shaven cowboys galloping across the plains on white horses; pretty, virginal young girls whose rancher-fathers were heartlessly exploited and, in the last reel, replaced in their lives by the hero; and greedy, mustachioed chiselers garbed in black or savage, half-naked Indians. After a minimum amount of bloodletting, the bad guys ended up dead or behind bars, and the good guys and their true loves rode off into the sunset.

One glaring exception is a forgotten but nevertheless exceptional little film, *Law and Order.* On the surface, *Law and Order* is standard and clichéd; it even opens with stock footage from various Universal Westerns. Walter Huston stars as United States Marshal Frame Johnson, nicknamed "Saint" because of his reputation as a lawman. His cohorts are his brother Luther (Russell Hopton), Ed Brant (Harry Carey, Jr.), and Deadwood (Raymond Hatton); the quartet represents the real-life Earp brothers. Fresh from his job as peace officer in Wichita, Kansas, Frame Johnson rides into Tombstone, Arizona, with his companions. Tombstone is a lawless frontier town under the control of the selfish Northrup brothers (Ralph Ince, Harry Woods, Richard Alexander) who double for the Clanton gang. They are in charge of the election campaign of Fin Elder (Alphonz Ethier), who is running for town sheriff, and to insure that Elder will be victorious the ballot boxes will be stuffed.

Johnson and his friends head for the Golden Girl Saloon. They are recognized by the bartender and harassed by the Northrups, who resent their presence in Tombstone. That night, they hear shots in the saloon, where the votes are being counted: Jake Fawcett, who has objected to the dishonest election, has been murdered. The law-abiding citizens of the town then press Johnson into service to clean up Tombstone. With the support of his brother, Ed Brant, and Deadwood, he agrees. First, they take charge of Johnny Kinsman (Andy Devine), who is accused of murder, and then they stave off a mob which attempts to lynch him. He is an accidental killer, but he is guilty nevertheless. He is convicted of his crime and hanged, the first man legally executed in Tombstone. Johnson and his friends then tangle with the Northrups. Frame is determined to clean up Tombstone without gunplay. He and his companions go unarmed, but when they learn that the Northrups are planning to ambush them at the livery stable, they put on their guns again and a gunfight ensues.

Two sequences highlight *Law and Order*. The first is the pathetic hanging, when the honest lawmen are forced to put to death the likable Johnny Kinsman. The second is the finale, the shootout in the livery stable which could be a re-creation of the actual O.K. Corral gunfight. This sequence is spectacular, graphically brutal, and flawlessly directed and edited. The camera glides between the participants as if it somehow were actually involved in the action, not merely observing. At the end, "Saint" Johnson remains the only man standing. He turns in his badge and slowly rides out of Tombstone.

Law and Order is an outstanding film for more reasons than merely achievements. It is years before its time in that it stresses not only action and gunplay but psychological motivation and camaraderie as well. Rather than a one-dimensionally entertaining "shoot-'em-up" or a sanitized, stylized vision of the West, the film is a stark study of survival and good versus evil and a serious attempt to depict realistically the Western frontier. The saintly sheriff Johnson repeatedly remarks that the West really has no desire for law enforcement. By putting Kinsman to death, he serves notice that justice has no mercy and that the wild West will be tamed. The "bad guys" are brutal and contemptible, the "good guys" do their duty and eradicate the evil, and the Western landscape is harsh and uncompromising.

Law and Order is in no way as graphically bloody as Sam Peckinpah's *The Wild Bunch* (1969) or dozens of mysteries, melodramas, and Westerns released during the next decade. Still, for an early sound film, it is remarkably gory. Men do not die bloodlessly and corpses do not mysteriously disappear, as they do in other Westerns of the period. Also, incredibly, there is no love interest or feminine diversion in the film; the only noticeable woman in the scenario is a cynical dance-hall girl, and she is far down in the credits. "Saint" Johnson is a lawman, not a lover.

The film is also uniquely contemporary for a Western, that is, for a film set in a past century. There is an aura of despair in *Law and Order* that is similar to the gangster films of the day. The film is based on the novel *Saint Johnson*, which is the story of a renowned real-life lawman. The author is W. R. Burnett, who wrote *Little Caesar* (1930); and like that gangster classic, *Law and Order* is as much a comment on contemporary conditions and issues— rampant lawlessness and the need for it to be squelched—as a representation of a bygone era.

Huston gives his usual expert performance as Frame Johnson. He was very active in early sound films, appearing in more than a score of pictures during the late 1920's and early 1930's. In publicity blurbs for *Law and Order*, it was noted that Huston "has been hailed by many critics as this generation's greatest actor of stage and screen." He is ably backed up by a fine all-male supporting cast. Most familiar are Carey, a performer in films since the early part of the century and later an Academy Award nominee as Best Supporting Actor in *Mr. Smith Goes to Washington* (1939); Devine, co-star of television's *Wild Bill Hickock* and star of *Andy's Gang*; and Hatton, a staple in films for fifty years. Walter Brennan makes one of his earliest screen appearances in *Law and Order*; he is at the bottom of the credits, but in the next decade he went on to win three Best Supporting Actor Oscars, one each for *Come and Get It* (1936), *Kentucky* (1938), and *The Westerner* (1940).

One of *Law and Order*'s screenwriters is a *very* young John Huston, son of Walter and still almost a decade away from his directorial debut in the classic, *The Maltese Falcon* (1941). The younger Huston, of course, went on to become one of Hollywood's great directors, with credits ranging from *Treasure of the Sierra Madre* (1948) to *Wise Blood* (1979). In the former he directed his father to an Oscar for Best Supporting Actor, in addition to winning one himself for the same film.

The director of *Law and Order*, Edward L. Cahn, however, proved to be good in only this film. A former editor who worked for Hungarian director Paul Fejos, Cahn first turned his hand to directing in this film, and it is undeniably his best feature. His direction here is deliberately and effectively slow-paced. He later directed such second-line and forgettable features as *Radio Patrol* (1932), *Bad Guy* (1937), *Main Street After Dark* (1945), and *Secret of Deep Harbor* (1961).

Law and Order was remade by Universal in 1953 with Ronald Reagan as Frame Johnson; Nathan Juran directed this ponderous, undistinguished version. While the earlier film is devoid of women, this one features Dorothy Malone as Johnson's girl friend.

Rob Edelman

THE LEAGUE OF GENTLEMEN

Released: 1959
Production: Michael Relph for Allied Film Makers
Direction: Basil Dearden
Screenplay: Bryan Forbes; based on the novel of the same name by John Boland
Cinematography: Arthur Ibbetson
Editing: John D. Guthridge
Running time: 116 minutes

Principal characters:
Hyde .... Jack Hawkins
Race .... Nigel Patrick
Mycroft .... Roger Livesey
Lexy .... Richard Attenborough
Porthill .... Bryan Forbes
Stevens .... Kieron Moore
Rupert .... Terence Alexander
Weaver ....Norman Bird

Mainstream British cinema has always tended to have one eye on Hollywood, if only because the majority of films shown in British motion picture theaters are American and it is these which determine audience tastes and preferences. The result, inevitably and all too often, is hybrid films which have neither the character of British films nor even so much as the surface competence of American ones. *The League of Gentlemen,* for all its weaknesses, is one of the rare exceptions. It is a film which is undoubtedly, self-consciously, and even self-mockingly British, but which is still as exciting and as slickly put together as any American heist movie.

The screenplay by Bryan Forbes lay around on the shelves for a couple of years before it was finally picked up by a newly formed company, Allied Film Makers, made up of Forbes himself, producer Michael Relph, director Basil Dearden, and actors Jack Hawkins and Richard Attenborough—the "inmates taking over the asylum" once again. The idea of the military-style heist was, in many ways, a logical extension into peacetime of the played-out wartime dramas of 1950's British cinema, but it was not entirely an original one. Late 1950's cinema seems to be almost oversupplied with tales of Army veterans making unorthodox use of the skills taught them by a nation in need once the nation no longer needed them. As Hyde (Jack Hawkins) puts it in *The League of Gentlemen,* "I served my country well as a regular soldier and was suitably rewarded after twenty-five years by being declared redundant." In deciding to use his soldierly accomplishments for reasons of personal gain, Hyde was merely cast in the same mold as Frank Sinatra in *Ocean's Eleven* (1960),

Edward G. Robinson in *Seven Thieves* (1960), and even Vittorio Gassman in the Italian *Big Deal on Madonna Street* (1956, *Il soliti ignoti*).

Lieutenant-Colonel Hyde, or, to be more precise, *ex*-Lieutenant-Colonel Hyde, summons his team by sending out bait in the form of a number of copies of a cheap detective novel, *The Golden Fleece*, with the halves of ten five-pound notes and an invitation to lunch inside. The notes are signed 'Co-operative Removals Ltd.' The recipients are all ex-army officers who have fallen on hard times and are surviving on either side of the narrow borderline between opportunism and criminal endeavor: Race (Nigel Patrick), a top-class driver; Mycroft (Roger Livesey), an expert in disguises; Lexy (Richard Attenborough), a telegraph and radio wizard; Porthill (Bryan Forbes), a fearless con man; Stevens (Kieron Moore), a physical education instructor and combat expert; Rupert (Terence Alexander), a smokescreen specialist; and Weaver (Norman Bird), an explosives expert. When all seven of them turn up to lunch at the Café Royal, Hyde first more or less ensures their cooperation by revealing his knowledge of the various shady reasons for which their military careers were abruptly terminated. This knowledge was the fruit of his last six months in the service, spent searching diligently through War Office files. He then announces his plan to rob a London bank of one million pounds. "Think of it as a full-scale military operation. What chance has a bunch of civilians got?" All the men agree without much reluctance.

The first requirement is weapons, which are easily acquired through a raid on an army camp. Mycroft poses as a Brigadier sent down to inspect the cookhouse after a complaint about the food, while Lexy and Stevens break into the armory and carry off a quantity of machine guns and ammunition. They contrive to blame the raid on the Irish Republican Army.

Hyde is now able to reveal his target. Assembling the men in the basement of his suburban home, he shows them film, slides, maps, and a model of the bank with all the tactical analysis of an Air Force commander planning a bombing raid. "This," he tells them, "is the battlefield we shall fight on and enjoy our finest hour!" Preparations are completed by the theft of a large furniture truck to be used in the getaway. The raid goes almost entirely according to plan. The bank's alarm system is knocked out, the staff held up with machine guns, the area sealed off with smoke bombs, and the bullion delivery intercepted and loaded into the back of the truck. Film crooks, of course, cannot be allowed to get away with their crimes, however perfectly planned and executed. Thus Hyde's league of gentlemen is duly picked up by the police as a result of license plate's being spotted by one of those small boys who are the saviors both of law and order and of scriptwriters who have run short on ideas. Hyde, under the mistaken impression that he alone has been arrested, climbs into the back of the police wagon to find the rest of the gang sitting waiting for him: "All present and correct, sir," declares Race, saluting ironically.

Looking back at *The League of Gentlemen*, it is easy to pick out its faults and overlook its strengths. On the debit side, Forbes's screenplay seems more slick than ingenious, Dearden's direction too often seems stolid and unimaginative in the dialogue scenes which account for well over half the picture, and it would be as easy to be exasperated as entertained by the "old-boy" chumminess of the gang. The film takes far too long to get going, and makes particularly ponderous the introduction of each of the gang members in their civilian environment, a series of repetitive scenes differing only in their details. Forbes's attempts at finding an English equivalent for the sort of sharp talking that characterizes postwar American crime movies is also a little bit shaky. On the direction side, Dearden is perhaps unfairly hampered by a script which requires him to find ways of filming ten- or fifteen-minute scenes in which rarely less than six people discuss a subject in a single room. The action scenes of *The League of Gentlemen*, however, are genuinely gripping and even, in the case of the Army camp raid, gripping and comic, especially as "Brigadier" Mycroft forces his "junior officers" to sample the appalling food in the Army kitchen.

The film is frankly misogynist. Each of the "gents" has a lady companion whom he is pleased to be rid of, especially Rupert, whose wife phones her lover while soaping herself suggestively in a bubble bath. Hyde has a portrait of his wife illuminated on the stairs of his home in a way which encourages us to think he has suffered a tragic loss. "Is she dead?" asks Race discreetly. "No," replies Hyde, "I regret to say the bitch is still going strong." Their inability to deal with women, except in the case of Lexy, who simply treats them as commodities, and Stevens, who is homosexual, is what accounts for their nostalgia for the Army. It is a common enough theme in postwar cinema, American as well as British, and *The League of Gentlemen* treats it in an ironic way. The film is at its best when, in addition to being an incongruous transposition of an American genre, it is also parodying staples of postwar cinema, especially the heroic nostalgia of the British war film in which gangs of men almost indistinguishable from the "league of gentlemen" pool their wits and skills to defeat the Germans, or escape from a prisoner-of-war camp.

In this respect, *The League of Gentlemen* is never better than in its credit sequence. The shot is of a deserted, nighttime city street to the vague sound of the sort of strident jazz theme one associates with *film noir*. In the street, a manhole hatch begins to stir. We cut to a close-up of a pair of eyes, recognizable to any regular British moviegoer as those of Hawkins, peering over the rim. The figure ducks back out of sight when a streetwashing truck sweeps by, then reemerges. As the music track dissolves to a rousing military theme—instantly recognizable to a regular British cinemagoer as belonging to the same family as the themes from *The Dambusters* (1954), *Reach for the Sky* (1956), *The Cockleshell Heroes* (1955), and countless other wartime sagas—Hawkins, immaculate in evening dress, climbs out of the manhole, brushes himself off, strides across the street, and climbs into a Rolls-Royce parked at the curb. The credits continue to the same rousing theme, with the camera tracking back in front of the grill of the Rolls. It is a magnificent opening to which the rest of the film never quite lives up, an inspired blend of American thriller and British irony.

Nick Roddick

LENNY

Released: 1974
Production: Marvin Worth; released by United Artists
Direction: Bob Fosse
Screenplay: Julian Barry; based on his play of the same name
Cinematography: Bruce Surtees
Editing: Alan Heim
Running time: 111 minutes

Principal characters:

Lenny Bruce	Dustin Hoffman
Honey Bruce	Valerie Perrine
Sally Marr	Jan Miner
Artie Silver	Stanley Beck
Sherman Hart	Gary Morton

Lenny, based on a stage play by Julian Barry, tells its story through a series of flashbacks covering the rise, decline, and death of comedian Lenny Bruce (Dustin Hoffman) inserted into *cinema-verité* style interviews with his ex-wife Honey (Valerie Perrine), his mother Sally Marr (Jan Miner), and his agent Artie Silver (Stanley Beck). The bulk of the movie is made up of these flashbacks, with large sections of them given over to re-creations of Bruce's nightclub act.

The flashbacks start in 1951 when Lenny Bruce is working as a mediocre stand-up comedian at a club in Baltimore, while Hot Honey Harlow is doing her spectacular strip act at a small-time joint nearby. They meet, sleep together, and marry, but Lenny soon becomes possessive, and, resenting Honey stripping for other men, tries to get a double act together. Playing a club in the Catskills, Lenny is introduced to successful comic Sherman Hart (Gary Morton), "Mr. Entertainment" himself, who offers Lenny a spot on his television show but advises him to tone down his act: "Work clean, Lenny. With your talent, you don't need to come on with the filth." Lenny, even at this early stage, responds badly to criticism concerning his "obscenity." He starts his act by appearing to apologize and then begins to insult the audience. He is fired, and Honey is seriously hurt in an automobile accident caused by Lenny's emotional driving after the incident. The insurance money from the crash enables them to buy a second-hand Cadillac, and they set off for California. Lenny is by now quite heavily hooked on drugs. When they get to Los Angeles in 1954, Honey goes back to stripping while Lenny works some real dives. Nights are spent at dope parties including one at which Lenny forces Honey to make love to another woman in his presence and then taunts her for supposedly enjoying it. In November, 1955, a child, Kitty, is born to

Honey, but this does not save the relationship, and by 1957 the two are divorced.

Shortly after the divorce Honey is jailed in Hawaii for drug offenses and Lenny wins custody of Kitty. Lenny's material begins to get more sophisticated by the late 1950's, and he plays to hip audiences, arguing that "dirty words" are only offensive because they are suppressed. He is by now becoming a national celebrity and making big money, although a lot of the time audiences contain more policemen than paying customers. The latter are often there in the hope of seeing the police arrest the comedian for obscenity. He is arrested in Chicago, and finally New York, where he is cited for contempt of court when he tries to persuade the judge to let him demonstrate his act and to organize his own defense. By now obsessed with his legal battles, Lenny devotes large sections of his act to reading from trial transcripts, and audiences begin to dwindle. Finally, one night in 1966 he is found dead in his bathroom from an overdose of drugs, naked, with hypodermic needles lying nearby: the police let newspapermen in to photograph the corpse.

Lenny started life as a "small movie." Since director Bob Fosse had just received eight Oscars (including "Best Direction") for *Cabaret* (1972), United Artists was prepared to give him considerable leeway, and it was under these conditions that the film was prepared. The plan had always been to shoot the movie in black-and-white, but some of the "smallness" inevitably disappeared when Fosse decided on Dustin Hoffman for the title role, and the film eventually ended up costing $2,700,000. When the movie opened in New York on November 10, 1974, critical response was sharply divided. Even the normally singleminded trade papers were split down the middle. *The Hollywood Reporter* called it "a real downer" and described Fosse's direction as "sullen," while *Variety* termed it "a remarkable film." Vincent Canby in *The New York Times* gave a more carefully balanced consideration, deciding that it was "one-fourth brilliant"—the fourth concerned with re-creating Bruce's nightclub act—but was a good deal less enthusiastic about the three fourths containing the interviews (which "you never for a moment believe in") and the glimpses of Lenny's private life. To give some idea of how widely opinions varied, Gordon Gow in *Films and Filming* said that "it demands to be witnessed and marked as a human dilemma at which nobody on this earth has the right to sneer," while Joel E. Siegel of *The Washington Post* described it as "a simpering, simplistic white-wash in which the comedian literally dies for our sins."

Launched with high critical hopes, *Lenny* was nominated for four Oscars—Best Picture, Best Actor, Best Actress, and Best Direction—but won none, although Perrine received a couple of other richly deserved awards, including Best Actress at the Cannes Film Festival. Instead, the movie had to settle for a more than solid commercial success; by the end of 1975 it had easily recouped its costs with a gross of eleven million dollars. Obviously what had offended audiences in 1966 was standard box-office fare in 1975.

The question of whether the movie "represents" Lenny Bruce properly depends very much on what one means by represents. According to Fosse, most of the people who had known the real Lenny, including his family, felt that the movie captured him perfectly (scarcely surprising since three of them figure on the credits as "advisers"), although his friends thought it failed to show the "hostility and hate" that drove the man. At one level, that of the nightclub performances, *Lenny* is undoubtedly masterful. Hoffman may not resemble Bruce physically, but he captures perfectly the irregular machine-gun fire of Bruce's delivery as it is preserved on record and on Fred Baker's documentary portrait, *Lenny Bruce Without Tears*. Fosse's direction is at his best in these scenes. He manages, as he did so successfully in *Cabaret*, to create excitement out of something which is not in itself cinematic; his camera is never still, tracking through the audience, reframing the performer and cutting away to reaction shots. The parallel with *Cabaret*, however, is a slightly disturbing one. At times Lenny is a close cousin of Sally Bowles, and there is something about Hoffman's acting which creates a warmth and sympathy in Bruce which was never a part of his nightclub personality. Paradoxically, this comes across most strongly in what is in many ways the movie's—and Hoffman's—finest scene: his final, unfunny Chicago show. He stands, speared by the spotlight, apparently naked under his raincoat except for one black sock, unshaven, mumbling on for a seven-and-a-half-minute take as the audience begins to leave, before he finally gives up with the words: "I'm sorry. I'm just not funny tonight. Sometimes I'm not funny, I'm just Lenny Bruce."

The approach to Bruce which leads to his being portrayed as a victim is built into the movie's screenplay. It is a homage picture—"Lenny Bruce was the conscience of America," read the ads—and it is best seen in this way. It is a Hollywood biography for the 1970's, an updated portrait of a great artist helping society to destroy him. The performer's rise and fall is echoed in the flourishing and disintegration of a relationship—here, Lenny's with Honey. The *cinema-verité* interviews which provide the movie with its backbone, making it possible to link individual nightclub performances, trial appearances, and so on without lengthy dialogue scenes, accentuate rather than detract from the biographical atmosphere. They are a device, not a guarantee of realism, and this, surely, is all they were meant to be.

Hostility toward *Lenny* undoubtedly has arisen out of critics expecting something else from the movie—no doubt encouraged by studio publicity promising "the real Lenny Bruce." What we are given is a dramatized biography, truth enhanced by fiction, clearly designating Bruce as a moralist who told society things it did not want to know in 1965, but was quite ready for in 1975, and who was destroyed for his pains. The film presents Lenny Bruce *with* tears, in other words, although it does manage to suggest the vicious, self-destructive side of Lenny's nature—the side which destroyed Honey as well as himself. It also—and in this it departs from the standard film biography formula—pays an uncluttered, finely filmed, and brilliantly performed homage to what it was that made Bruce a great performer: his material.

Nick Roddick

LET GEORGE DO IT

Released: 1940
Production: Basil Dearden for Ealing Studios/Associated Talking Pictures
Direction: Marcel Varnel
Screenplay: John Dighton, Austin Melford, Angus Macphail, and Basil Dearden
Cinematography: Ronald Neane
Editing: Ray Pitt
Running time: 82 minutes

Principal characters:
George .... George Formby
Mary .... Phyllis Calvert
Mendez .... Garry Marsh
Slim .... Romney Brent
Nelson .... Bernard Lee
Ivy .... Coral Browne
Greta .... Diana Beaumont
U-Boat Commander .... Torin Thatcher
Arbuckle .... Hal Gordon
Strickland .... Donald Calthrop

George Formby (1904-1961) was a British music-hall comic and singer who made an easy transition to films in 1934, and who from that year until 1946 was starred in twenty features. These films were tremendously popular in England, where Formby was, for many years, voted *The Motion Picture Herald*'s number-one box-office star; unlike the films of other similar British music hall performers, the George Formby features were screened in other parts of the world. In 1944, Formby was awarded the Order of Lenin, being named the most popular man in Russia after Joseph Stalin. *Let George Do It* was the first Formby film to be released in the United States and paved the way for the distribution here of his other films; American critics on the whole liked George Formby and compared his comedy style to that of Harold Lloyd and Joe E. Brown.

There was a simple, unaffected, unsophisticated charm to George Formby. Without any provocation, he would pick up his ukelele and sing songs such as "When I'm Cleaning Windows," "Leaning on a Lamp Post," and "Mr. Wu's a Window Cleaner Now." The songs were saucy and a little bit vulgar, telling of what a window cleaner might see on his rounds or what portion of the human anatomy lurked underneath grandfather's nightshirt. Formby was once described as a "fellow with a face like a horse and teeth like tombstones," and in all his films he portrayed a gormless, likable idiot, an innocent in a world of sophisticates, but an innocent who, through his basic honesty and his clinging to old-fashioned moral and ethical values, always got the girl and always came out on top.

Let George Do It opens in Bergen, Norway, before the Nazi advance during World War II had led to the fall of that country. The Great Mendez and His Orchestra are broadcasting from a local hotel, and while playing "Don't the Wind Blow Cold," the ukelele player is shot and killed. It transpires that the Great Mendez, played with suavity and assurance by Garry Marsh, is a Nazi spy, somehow relaying messages, via his radio broadcasts, to Nazi U-Boats which then proceed to sink British shipping. The British are sending a ukelele-playing spy to infiltrate Mendez' orchestra, but in the confusion of a London black-out, the spy gets lost and is replaced by Formby, a ukelele player with a concert party called the Dinky Doos (also the name of the concert party in a popular British musical of the early 1930's, *The Good Companions*).

George arrives in Bergen and meets Mary (played by Phyllis Calvert, later to become a popular leading lady in British films of the 1940's produced by Gainsborough), who is a British agent posing as a receptionist at the hotel. Our hero, more through accident than design, discovers that Mendez is using a musical code, which he promptly proceeds to photograph in the orchestra leader's bedroom. The code is relayed to the British intelligence, and the tables are turned on the Nazis; British warships are waiting for the U-Boats when they go to search out British shipping.

Mendez suspects George of being the spy, and, by giving him a truth drug in his coffee, he finds out about George and Mary. George foils a plot to shoot him while the orchestra again plays "Don't the Wind Blow Cold," and follows Mendez on board a Nazi U-Boat, which is set to sink the *S.S. Macauley*, on which Mary is returning to England. Thanks to George's efforts, which include sending a wireless message to the *Macauley* and causing pandemonium onboard the U-boat, the British navy is able to capture the submarine. George is hiding in a torpedo shaft, and when Mendez fires off the torpedo in a last vain and desperate effort to destroy his adversary Mary, George is sent flying across the water, to land onboard the *S.S. Macauley* in the arms of his beloved Mary. He turns to the camera and delivers the catchphrase which had become his trademark, "Turned out nice again."

Let George Do It provides Formby with the opportunity to perform four songs, "Don't the Wind Blow Cold," "My Granddad's Flannelette Nightshirt," "Mr. Wu's a Window Cleaner Now," and "Count Your Blessings and Smile." The last is particularly charming in its lyrics and in its use. Mendez is using the song as a code for the Nazi U-Boats, but Formby is also using the song as a propaganda message to the English film audience. The number even features three British girls who give a passable imitation of the Andrews Sisters. Formby never misses an opportunity to perform a song, and always presents such songs in an ingratiating fashion. While singing "My Granddad's Flannelette Nightshirt," he actually does a double-take while looking at the camera, and then winks at the audience.

The comedy, on the whole, is fairly mild except for two outrageous sequences which do not entirely work. After photographing the musical code, Formby allows the camera to fall through a skylight into a bakery. His efforts to retrieve the camera result in a slapstick comedy routine, involving his being covered with flour and the like, which is childish in construction and more in the style of Mack Sennett than, say, Harold Lloyd, to whom Formby has a certain affinity. A continuing gag which has Formby getting himself into compromising situations with another man's wife is mildly amusing, but the audience is led to believe this couple will play some part in the plot when they do not. More unusual is a dream sequence, after Formby has been given the truth drug, in which he sees himself going to heaven, where the Pearly Gates have a sign saying "British passports only," and then dropping down from the sky (literally) on Adolf Hitler, whom he beats in a fistfight, to the delight of the dictator's followers.

Marcel Varnel, a French-born director, was responsible for *Let George Do It*. He was also responsible for a number of other Formby films as well as such popular British comedies as *Oh Mr. Porter* (1937), *Old Bones of the River* (1938), *Hi Gang* (1941), and *The Ghost of St. Michael's* (1941). Varnel had an extraordinary grasp of British comedy and what would appeal to a British audience, and it is unfortunate that Hollywood did not realize his potential.

Let George Do It typifies British comedies of World War II, in which music-hall performers, who had become British institutions, stood up to and defeated the Nazi terror. It shows the British "muddling through," and there is an endearing quality to the idea of British naïveté and innocence (in the form of Formby) overcoming total evil as represented by Nazi Germany. When the film opened at New York's Globe Theatre, *The New York Times* (October 14, 1940) noted, "*Let George Do It* is something of a phenomenon, interesting not so much as entertainment but as evidence of the Britisher's incorrigible 'thumbs up' attitude in the face of mortal danger." The *Hollywood Reporter* (October 28, 1940) commented, "It would be impossible to conceive of such a picture coming from a totalitarian studio. Hitler and Mussolini just wouldn't understand it."

When asked to explain his success, Formby said, "I wasn't very good, but I had something the public seemed to want." Precisely. It is perhaps this amateurish attitude toward himself, and an attitude that he exuded both on stage and screen, that made Formby the success that he was. To the working-class audiences of Britain, George Formby was one of them. He never forgot it; and they never forgot it.

Anthony Slide

THE LETTER

Released: 1940
Production: Hal B. Wallis and Jack L. Warner for Warner Bros.
Direction: William Wyler
Screenplay: Howard Koch; based on the play of the same name by W. Somerset Maugham
Cinematography: Tony Gaudio
Editing: George Amy and Warren Low
Costume design: Orry-Kelly
Music: Max Steiner
Running time: 97 minutes

Principal characters:
Leslie Crosbie	Bette Davis
Robert Crosbie	Herbert Marshall
Howard Joyce	James Stephenson
Dorothy Joyce	Frieda Inescort
Mrs. Hammond	Gale Sondergaard
John Withers	Bruce Lester
Ong Chi Seng	Victor Sen Yung
Head Boy	Tetsu Komai
Geoffrey Hammond	David Newell
Mrs. Cooper	Doris Lloyd
Adele Ainsworth	Elizabeth Earl
Chung Hi	Willie Fung

The Letter is one of the better-known Bette Davis vehicles filmed during her reign as the queen of the Warner Bros. studios in the 1930's and early 1940's. Made between *All This and Heaven Too* (1940) and *The Great Lie* (1941), *The Letter* came during one of Davis' most prolific periods. It proved once again that Davis fans could appreciate her talents even if she played a somewhat unsympathetic character. Her acting abilities made her equally believable as the slightly homely, pathetic governess in *All This and Heaven Too* and the glamorous adulterous *femme fatale* of *The Letter*.

The sign "L Rubber Company, Singapore, Plantation No. 1" sets the scene for the film as the camera tracks through a compound past Malaysian workers resting after their day's labor. A shot rings out, frightening a cockatoo and bringing a man staggering out of the main house and down the front steps as a woman empties a gun into his body. Unemotional, Leslie Crosbie (Bette Davis) is startled by the reappearance of the moon which had been hidden behind a cloud until that instant. The head boy (Tetsu Komai) recognizes the body of neighbor Geoffrey Hammond (David Newell), and Leslie orders him to get the district officer and her husband, Robert (Herbert Marshall), manager of the rubber plantation.

Robert arrives with his good friend Howard Joyce (Robert Stephenson), a lawyer, who is told by District Officer Withers (Bruce Lester) that all six chambers of the gun used in the killing are empty. Leslie then tells her story: she had been working on her lace when Hammond, whom she had not seen in some three months, had arrived, quietly and unexpectedly. He said he was lonely and then began enumerating her lovely features, drunkenly declaring that he was in love with her. With her back to her audience, Leslie goes on to declare that she had told Hammond that she loved Robert. At this, the intruder had acted like a madman and forced himself on her. The camera tracks up two steps, then to a chest and to the doors as she relates that she had remembered Robert's gun in the chest, taken it out, and begun firing.

Withers declares that she behaved magnificently and that Hammond got what he deserved. Robert comforts her as "my poor child" and states that most women would not have had her courage. Later, during a meal which Leslie prepares, she asks if she might be jailed, and Howard indicates that she will probably be out on bail, but that the charge could be murder. Withers discusses Hammond's character with Howard. As they leave, the departed head boy returns with Hammond's Eurasian wife (Gale Sondergaard), who looks at the body and cries.

At Howard's office, a distraught and disheveled Robert blames himself for leaving Leslie alone so much and welcomes Howard's offer to stay with him and his wife Dorothy (Frieda Inescort). The latter is enjoying a visit from her niece Adele Ainsworth (Elizabeth Earl), from England. After Robert leaves the office, Howard's efficient clerk Ong (Victor Sen Yung) tells his employer of the existence of a letter which a friend had made known to him. The letter proves conclusively that Leslie had invited Hammond to her house the night of the killing. The original of the letter is in the possession of Hammond's widow.

Howard confronts Leslie in prison with a copy of the letter which implored Hammond to come after parking his car some distance away, and assured him that Robert would be gone. Leslie tries to explain that she had forgotten about the note and had only wanted Hammond's advice on buying a gun for Robert's birthday. She faints and is assisted by sympathetic matron Mrs. Cooper (Doris Lloyd). Alone with Howard, Leslie asks his help in getting the original letter. Wrestling with his conscience, Howard talks of honesty, warning her not to tell him too much of the truth. Ong meets Howard outside the prison and says that Mrs. Hammond wants Leslie to bring ten thousand dollars to her for the damaging evidence. The assistant admits he is getting two thousand dollars and the "satisfaction of helping our client" for his trouble.

At his club, Robert learns of the letter and the "birthday present" and authorizes Howard to obtain the letter, if necessary. At the Joyces' home, Dorothy is already planning a party in honor of Leslie's acquittal. Robert,

Dorothy, and Adele are persuaded to go to the movies, so that Leslie and Howard can keep a rendezvous. Ong takes them to the Chinese quarter and the shop of Chung Hi (Willie Fung), a curio dealer. Leslie admires a pair of daggers before being escorted into an office where she meets Mrs. Hammond. With Ong interpreting, Leslie obeys her orders to remove her lace shawl and to approach her for the letter, which Mrs. Hammond drops to the floor. Leslie murmurs a thank you and leaves with Howard.

At the trial, Howard sweats, more from a guilty conscience than the oppressive heat, as he addresses the jury. At the end of the trial the head boy and Mrs. Hammond are visible as Leslie and Robert leave the courtroom following her acquittal. Back at the Joyce home, Robert cheerfully tells of his plans to take out his savings and obtain a loan to invest in the ownership of a rubber plantation in Sumatra. Learning that most of his money went to purchase the letter, however, Robert has Howard admit that buying such evidence is a criminal offense. For the first time, Leslie admits she loved Hammond and killed him because he preferred his wife to her, but both Howard and Leslie agree that Robert will forgive her.

During the Joyces' reception, Leslie finds a dagger outside her bedroom, and Robert drunkenly tells his planter friends of his now-shattered plans. Later he tells Leslie that if you love a person, you can forgive anything. Leslie betrays herself and him, however, by admitting that she still loves Hammond. Drawn into the garden as the moon is clouded, Leslie is grabbed by the house boy while Mrs. Hammond stabs her. Finally an officer takes the two away.

If the antihero has been a source of endless fascination, then the less-publicized but equally lethal antiheroine is just as fascinating. Few fill that classification as well as Leslie Crosbie, the creation of W. Somerset Maugham in 1925 for his stage play, *The Letter*. She is a creature of desire and vengeance, self-centered and anxious for self-preservation at all costs. Gladys Cooper first played her in England, followed by Katharine Cornell on Broadway in 1927. The first film version, which earned an Oscar nomination for its star, served as the talkie debut of the legendary Jeanne Eagels, who made only one other film, *Jealousy* (1929), before her untimely death in 1929. Both the 1929 and 1930 French-language film starring Marcelle Romee were made by Paramount. The definitive film of the play, however, was the Warner Bros. 1940 feature starring Davis. Warners also did a remake of sorts, *The Unfaithful* (1947), starring Ann Sheridan, which concerned the divorce faced by the indiscreet wife following her murder acquittal.

Earning her fourth Oscar nomination, Bette Davis does a memorable job of creating sympathy for a woman who kills in passion and lives to regret it. Considering that Leslie seems to feel more remorse for herself than for her dead lover, her husband, or the lawyer who compromises his ideals to save her, this is a tribute to the actress' skills and the sure hand of director William Wyler. Contemporary audiences tend to laugh at Leslie's blasting away at

Hammond, the lover, only because it seems natural for the strong-willed character which Davis epitomized to do such a thing.

Wyler uses the moon as a symbol of Leslie's guilt: it was the only witness, and she looks upon it with dread. The roving camera of Tony Gaudio and Max Steiner's superb score add to the effectiveness of the principally studio-bound production. Marshall had been the lover in the Eagels film, but this time he plays Robert Crosbie, the decent husband ready to forgive anything and incapable of believing his beloved wife could betray him. The face of the lover is never shown, making Hammond a mysterious character. As his Eurasian wife, Sondergaard exudes evil, almost without a word (except for a few lines in Chinese). Victor Sen Yung, then known mainly as Charlie Chan's Number Two Son, is completely believable as the assistant whose sincerity hides his sinister intent. Equaling Davis' performance is that of Stephenson as Howard Joyce; Stephenson was also nominated for an Academy Award, for Best Supporting Actor. This fine British actor died of a heart attack at fifty-three, a year after completing *The Letter*. Despite his excellence, his relatively brief career in American films has not made him a well-known actor.

There is an obvious indication of cutting just prior to the film's release: well-known character actor Cecil Kellaway is billed quite prominently, but has no part in the finished feature. He is, however, glimpsed in the courtroom scene and in the party sequence at the end. Another change was effected by the Hays Office, then guarding the morals of the public against excesses committed by Hollywood producers, who had to have Leslie pay for her crime. Mrs. Hammond therefore kills her in an artistic ending. Previously, the story had ended with Leslie's declaration that she still loved the man she killed, the indication being that her life now would be meaningless, providing a greater punishment, although a less satisfying one for the Hays Office.

John Cocchi

A LETTER TO THREE WIVES

Released: 1949
Production: Sol C. Siegel for Twentieth Century-Fox
Direction: Joseph L. Mankiewicz
Screenplay: Joseph L. Mankiewicz (AA); based on Vera Caspary's adaptation
of the novel *A Letter to Five Wives* by John Klempner
Cinematography: Arthur Miller
Editing: J. Watson Webb
Running time: 103 minutes

Principal characters:
Deborah Bishop	Jeanne Crain
Lora May Hollingsway	Linda Darnell
Rita Phipps	Ann Sothern
George Phipps	Kirk Douglas
Porter Hollingsway	Paul Douglas
Brad Bishop	Jeffrey Lynn
Sadie	Thelma Ritter
Voice of Addie Ross	Celeste Holm

William Wyler's *The Letter* (1940), Max Ophuls' *Letter from an Unknown Woman* (1948), Elia Kazan's *The Sea of Grass* (1947), and François Truffaut's *The Story of Adele H.* (1975) are films that are "epistolary" in style. Their plot lines are set in motion and advanced through the use of a letter. An outstanding example of the use of this device is found in Joseph L. Mankiewicz's *A Letter to Three Wives*. Set in a Middle-American suburb, the comedy-drama concerns three wives who receive a letter just as they are about to take their children on an annual all-day excursion and picnic. The letter is from their close friend Adele (Addie) Ross, the town's beautiful woman, who informs them that she has run off with one of their husbands. Since Addie does not specify *which* husband she has taken, all three women become heartbroken and terribly anxious. Because of this threat to their respective marriages, each begins to reflect upon her relationship with her spouse. Through a series of three extended flashbacks, we too, can examine the various marriages.

The first flashback deals with Deborah Bishop (Jeanne Crain), a young and eager though socially inept ex-farmgirl and former W.A.V.E., married to Brad (Jeffrey Lynn), a socialite. The somewhat gauche Deborah does not know how to talk to new people and consequently has great difficulty in handling herself at the local country club. The second flashback deals with Rita Phipps (Ann Sothern), a radio soap-opera writer who works partly because her schoolteacher husband, George (Kirk Douglas), does not bring home enough money. We see in one scene that Rita is so busy trying to impress the radio station's management that she forgets her husband's birth-day, giving an insight into their shaky relationship. The third flashback concerns Lora May Hollingsway (Linda Darnell), a beautiful golddigger from the "wrong side of the tracks" who plays hard-to-get. This ploy eventually wins Porter Hollingsway (Paul Douglas), a former boyfriend of Addie and one of the town's richest men, as her husband.

As the members of the group reflect on their respective relationships with their husbands, they gather for dinner at the country club. When they are seated for dinner it turns out that Brad is the only husband who does not show up. A broken, but surprisingly strong Deborah, helps to mend the relationship between Lora May and Porter by telling Porter that his supposedly fortune-hunting wife is actually deeply in love with him. Porter repays her kindness by telling the group that it was not Brad, but he himself, who had run off with Addie, but returned because he still loved his wife. The film ends when Brad walks innocently into the room, unaware of what has transpired, except for an oblique remark from Porter that "the kid" has had a hard time that day. The three couples remain together, happier than before because of the day's experiences and their own introspection.

A Letter to Three Wives is not only a psychological comedy, but also a critical look at contemporary society. The film was an early example of this type. While delving into the relationships of the principal characters, it also examines sex, money, class consciousness, and middle-class mores as they existed in postwar suburbia. Additionally, a criticism of the media is given by George when he attacks the tasteless programming on the station for which his wife works. While he is berating the station's use of commercials on laxatives and deodorants, however, his own character is also criticized. As a Shakespeare-quoting intellectual he at times appears ridiculously idealistic and hardly on the same plane as the other characters of the film. This is an intended device, however, not a flaw in the story. Most of the film's satire is not found in obvious humor, but in subtle insights into the lives of the characters, as seen in the flashbacks.

The character of Addie Ross is an example, also to be found in the films *Edward My Son* (1948) and *The Women* (1939), of a pivotal character who is never seen on screen, but who instigates most of the action. Although the woman does not appear on screen, her ubiquitous presence is felt just as keenly as if she did. The seductive voice-over narration for Addie was provided by Celeste Holm, whose own fine acting talents make even her small part of the film important. The acting is uniformly good in the film, with all of the actors, with the exception of Lynn, being well-known stars or character players. Darnell and Crain are particularly good and convey the most sympathy. Darnell, who was extremely beautiful, is effective especially as a woman who cannot admit that she loves her husband for fear that his own love for her is based solely on her elusive beauty.

Joseph L. Mankiewicz, the veteran writer/director/producer, proves himself to be a filmmaker worthy of the often-used term *auteur* in *A Letter to Three Wives*. Another of his films, *All About Eve* (1950), similarly shows him to be at his best when dealing with contemporary themes. These films, and his *The Barefoot Contessa* (1954), also do excellent jobs of portraying women in the midst of inner conflict. A writer more than a director, perhaps, Mankiewicz does not often try to use cinematic gimmicks to express his point; he relies more on the spoken word than on visual design. One exception to this rule, however, is the device of the flashback, which he uses effectively in these three films as well as in *The Quiet American* (1957). The voice-over narration, which combines a literary and cinematic technique, also lends itself very well to these films.

Mankiewicz won Academy Awards both for his screenplay and for his direction of *A Letter to Three Wives*, something which has rarely been done, except by himself the next year for *All About Eve*. *A Letter to Three Wives* was also nominated for Best Picture of the year, although it lost to *All the King's Men*.

Leslie Taubman

LIBELED LADY

Released: 1936
Production: Lawrence Weingarten for Metro-Goldwyn-Mayer
Direction: Jack Conway
Screenplay: Howard Emmett Rogers, Maurice Watkins, and George Oppenheimer; based on an original story of the same name by Wallace Sullivan
Cinematography: Norbert Brodine
Editing: Frederick Y. Smith
Running time: 98 minutes

Principal characters:
Gladys .... Jean Harlow
Bill Chandler .... William Powell
Connie Allenbury .... Myrna Loy
Warren Haggerty .... Spencer Tracy
Mr. Allenbury .... Walter Connolly

One of the most delightful cinematic inventions of the 1930's was the screwball comedy, a deft mixture of comedy and romance which features, in critic Molly Haskell's wonderful phrase, lovers who "seem to rub each other with and against the grain simultaneously." Although seldom explicitly feminist, these comedies are noteworthy for the fact that the men and women in them fight the battle of the sexes on virtually equal terms.

Jack Conway's *Libeled Lady*, written by Maurice Watkins, Howard Emmett Rogers, and George Oppenheimer, is an early example of the screwball comedy. *Libeled Lady*, however, differs from most films of its genre in two ways. First, the female leads are marginally less developed than their male counterparts; and second, the film features not one but two battling couples, thus showcasing four fine comic actors (Spencer Tracy, Jean Harlow, William Powell, and Myrna Loy) and giving the audience twice the opportunity for laughs.

Like one of Howard Hawks's great screwball comedies, *His Girl Friday* (1940), *Libeled Lady* is set in the world of journalism. As the film begins, printers are desperately trying to retrieve copies of a newspaper that contains a story which falsely accuses socialite Connie Allenbury (Myrna Loy) of having an affair with a married man. The author of the errant piece, reporter Warren Haggerty (Spencer Tracy), is about to get married to his long-suffering girl friend Gladys (Jean Harlow). Their wedding is interrupted by the news that a few copies of the paper have been distributed, and that one of them has fallen into the hands of Connie's wealthy father (Walter Connolly) in Europe. Haggerty's attempts to mollify Mr. Allenbury are to no avail. Allenbury announces that he is suing the paper for libel, for the sum of five million dollars. Meanwhile, Gladys, a divorcée, fumes at what is evidently another in a long line of nuptial interruptions. She is tired, she says, of playing second fiddle to a newspaper.

Desperate to avoid the lawsuit, Haggerty casts about for a plan to weaken the Allenburys' case. What if, he muses, he could prove that Connie Allenbury broke up another marriage? That would definitely weaken the Allenburys' contention that the first news story was false. He decides, therefore, to create a "happy" marriage that can conveniently be ruined by Miss Allenbury. The groom, he decides, should be Bill Chandler (William Powell), a former colleague on the paper and a man with whom Haggerty and Gladys have never gotten along. Chandler, however, has disappeared. Haggerty launches a worldwide search, and director Conway mocks Haggerty's desperation by showing radio announcers from all over the world broadcasting multilingual bulletins seeking to learn Chandler's whereabouts.

As it happens, Chandler is right there in New York City. He resides in a cheap hotel, where he is behind on his rent. Haggerty does not know that Chandler's fortunes have taken a turn for the worse, and when the two men meet, Chandler feigns disinterest in Haggerty's scheme, forcing the newsman to bid for his services. Chandler does not bite until Haggerty offers him five thousand dollars in advance and another twenty-five thousand when the mission is successfully accomplished. No sooner is the deal closed than Chandler's poverty is revealed, and Haggerty fumes as he realizes that he has been taken. The scene is funny, of course, but it also tells us something about the two men. Writers Watkins, Rogers, and Oppenheimer reveal early that while Haggerty is the more aggressive of the two men, Bill Chandler is by far more clever than Warren Haggerty. Conway and his colleagues will exploit this situation for laughs throughout the film.

Haggerty's plan is simple—and, of course, doomed to disaster. Chandler is to marry Gladys, and after a short interval, he will be mysteriously and publicly summoned to Europe, returning to America on the same ship with the Allenburys. In the five days that they are onboard together, Chandler is to lure Connie Allenbury into a compromising position, which will be photographed by Haggerty's men. The Allenburys will be shamed (or blackmailed) into dropping the libel suit, Chandler will divorce Gladys, who will then marry Haggerty, and everyone but the Allenburys will live happily ever after. Haggerty has trouble convincing Gladys to marry, however briefly, a man she despises, but she finally consents to the match. The marriage scene at the Justice of the Peace is a comic masterpiece, with Bill Chandler thoroughly enjoying himself, Gladys barely able to suppress her anger, and Haggerty standing around nervously, trying to keep the whole enterprise from blowing up in his face.

Chandler and Gladys spend their wedding night in separate bedrooms, and Gladys locks herself in her room. Later she will come to respect Chandler when she learns that he had a key to her room and could have used it; but for the moment, she is still hostile to her new husband. Another hilarious scene follows. In order to establish that the marriage is a happy one, Haggerty sets up the newlyweds in a hotel suite and arranges for the telegram summoning Bill to Europe to be delivered to their room. Chandler and Gladys bill and coo ferociously to impress the delivery boy, but as soon as he leaves, they resume their equally ferocious bickering. The cast handles the sudden reversals in mood with split-second timing, and the effect is hysterical.

On the oceanliner returning from England, Haggerty's plan begins to unravel. Chandler meets Miss Allenbury easily enough, but Connie, thinking him a fortune hunter, is determined to remain unimpressed by her suave new acquaintance; indeed, she is just as suave and witty as he. Mr. Allenbury is interested in only two things: trout fishing and talking about trout fishing. His immediate plans for seducing Connie foiled, Chandler resolves to get at her through her father. He reads every book on trout fishing in the ship's library, and is thus able to converse on the subject knowledgeably enough to wangle an invitation to the Allenbury lodge in New York for a weekend of fishing. Back home, Chandler's hapless attempts to learn fly casting wreak havoc inside his hotel room. "Too bad I'm not fishing for curtains," he quips. Paradoxically, the only cast he can master is the most difficult one in the book, which Chandler accomplishes only because of its similarity to a tennis stroke.

Haggerty's revised plan is for Chandler to lure Connie into the ever elusive compromising position at the lake where the fishing expedition will take place. Haggerty and Gladys will drive up unexpectedly, and there will be an embarrassing confrontation between the Allenburys and an aggrieved Gladys. As usual, things do not happen quite that way.

The scene shifts to the Allenburys' lake, where a sleepy Bill Chandler (sneaking surreptitious glances into a primer on trout fishing along the way) troops along the shore at dawn with Connie and her father. Chandler's mastery of the difficult fly cast surprises Connie and earns the hearty approval of Mr. Allenbury. Declining to press his luck, Chandler soon moves away from the Allenburys to avoid making a fool of himself in their presence. He promptly falls into the lake, where his thrashing about attracts the attention of a huge trout, which bites his hook and drags him through the water to the place where the Allenburys are fishing. They are immensely impressed with his "catch."

That night, after her father retires, Connie and Bill go for a moonlight swim. She is no longer flippant with him, his prowess as a fisherman having convinced her that he is not just a gigolo. She apologizes for her earlier behavior and admits to being fond of him. The heretofore hard-hearted Chandler suddenly melts. He hurries the confused Connie back to the lodge and runs out to intercept Haggerty and Gladys before they cause a scene.

The inevitable plot complication has arisen: Bill Chandler has fallen in love with Connie Allenbury. Now he must not only keep up his ruse with Connie, but he must also fool Haggerty and Gladys into thinking that he is still on their side. The filmmakers are not content to let matters rest there, however; in an additional plot twist, Gladys has developed a crush on Bill. Chandler's gentlemanly behavior coupled with Haggerty's boorishly singleminded dedication to squelching the libel suit have driven her into the arms of her "husband."

Chandler, desperately looking for a way to extricate everyone from the unpleasant situation, tries unsuccessfully to persuade Connie to drop the libel suit, and his efforts to convince Haggerty to forego his plan to embarrass Connie are equally unsuccessful. Meanwhile, Haggerty is angered by Gladys' increasingly obvious infatuation with Bill. "She may be his wife, but she's engaged to me," he complains. He drives to the Allenbury lodge to plead personally with Connie to drop the suit. She remains unmoved, but when Bill Chandler inadvertently walks in on the conversation, part of the deception is over. Haggerty recognizes what has happened and formulates another plan.

Complications come quickly after this point. Haggerty tells Gladys that Bill loves Connie, but Bill convinces Gladys that he is simply pretending to love Connie to further Haggerty's plot. Haggerty retaliates by printing up a dummy headline announcing Connie and Bill's marriage. Gladys is convinced, and heads off to the Allenburys for a showdown. Ironically, Haggerty's plans seem about to come off, only now no one is pretending.

At a swank party given by the Allenburys, Connie's father learns from a guest that Bill Chandler is married. He tells Connie, who confronts Bill. Rather than asking him directly, however, she decides to trap him by proposing. If he is already married, she reasons, he will not be able to accept. He does accept, however, and they leave hurriedly to find a Justice of the Peace. Close on their heels is Gladys, followed by Haggerty's newshounds.

Bill and Connie are married by a sleepy Justice of the Peace and return to his hotel room to await their pursuers. Gladys arrives first. Bill calmly explains that Connie knows about the whole plot, and that, because Gladys' Mexican divorce was not recognized in the United States, his marriage to Gladys was never legal in the first place. Gladys retorts that she was divorced in Peru and that his argument is therefore invalid. When Connie tries to mollify Gladys by offering to drop her libel suit, Gladys replies "My husband isn't for sale." Connie attempts to reason with Gladys. It was Haggerty's neglect, not love, that caused her to fall for Bill, she argues. In the other room, Haggerty has arrived, and he and Chandler soon come to blows. Gladys, finding herself rooting for Haggerty, realizes that Connie was right. When Chandler bloodies Haggerty's nose, Gladys returns the favor to Chandler. The women comfort their men, who, as the film ends, are standing around with handkerchiefs over their noses, looking exceedingly foolish.

Conway, a veteran M-G-M studio director who had been grinding out two or three largely undistinguished features a year since 1918, would continue to produce for Metro at a similar clip until 1948. Of the more than seventy films he directed, only a handful besides *Libeled Lady*, *Viva Villa!* (1934), *A Tale of Two Cities* (1935), and *A Yank at Oxford* (1938) merit any attention. On the basis of his record, critics have been forced to conclude that his few successes are due more to good scripts and serendipitous casting than to Conway's abilities as a director.

Certainly in *Libeled Lady*, Conway was blessed with both writers and actors of great accomplishment. The trio of writers gave him a script with four living, breathing characters; they embroiled these characters in humorous plot complications and gave them dialogue that was genuinely witty. *Libeled Lady* also benefited from a cast that was top-notch. The chemistry between Powell and Loy had already been demonstrated in W. S. Van Dyke's *The Thin Man* (1934) and its sequels, and the work of Powell and Loy in *Libeled Lady* proved that Nick and Nora Charles were not the only characters whom they could invest with their breezy charm. Harlow is delightful as Gladys, the girl who has been two-timed one time too often. Tracy, given the task of making us care about the least sympathetic of the film's major characters, was up to the task. The bumptious Warren Haggerty's perpetually backfiring schemes provide the impetus for much of the film's comedy.

While it would not do to overanalyze *Libeled Lady*, the film is a very entertaining variant of the screwball comedy. It is to be valued for its witty, well-conceived script and, most of all, for the marvelous cast that makes the whole thing work. M-G-M's attempt at a remake entitled *Easy to Wed* (1946) was a financial success due to its two stars, Van Johnson and Esther Williams, but it did not match the sophisticated charm of the earlier version.

Robert Mitchell

THE LIFE AND TIMES OF JUDGE ROY BEAN

Released: 1972
Production: John Foreman for Warner Bros.
Direction: John Huston
Screenplay: John Milius
Cinematography: Richard Moore
Editing: Hugh S. Fowler
Running time: 120 minutes

Principal characters:

Roy Bean	Paul Newman
Maria Elena	Victoria Principal
Frank Gass	Roddy McDowall
Lily Langtry	Ava Gardner
Rose Bean	Jacqueline Bisset
Reverend Mr. LaSalle	Anthony Perkins
Sam Dodd	Tab Hunter
Grizzly Adams	John Huston
Bad Bob	Stacy Keach
Tector Crites	Ned Beatty

The Life and Times of Judge Roy Bean, the only film directed by John Huston set in the Old West, combines two thematic perspectives. One is the commonplace theme, especially for Western films of the 1960's and 1970's, that the passing of the frontier and the coming of civilization exact a toll on the free-spirited frontiersmen who are at home in the wilderness environment, but whose own actions prepare the way for the civilized way of life to which they cannot adjust. The other one, which is recurrent in Huston's films, involves the plight of the dreamer pursuing an often tawdry ideal at the expense of a true appreciation of reality.

The film begins with the arrival of Roy Bean (Paul Newman) at Eagle's Nest, Vinegarroon County, Texas. As he boasts of his prowess as a bank robber, the outlaws and prostitutes at the local saloon beat and rob him. In one of several such scenes in the film, the characters, who are almost motionless, are viewed by cinematographer Richard Moore almost as figures in a Bosch or Breughel painting. Escaping death only when the rope which they loop about his neck breaks as his horse drags him through the sand and cactus, Bean returns to slaughter his persecutors. With an outdated lawbook, he sets himself up as the "Law West of the Pecos," his qualification for law enforcement being a life devoted to breaking the law. With a band of train robbers as his marshals, Judge Roy Bean becomes protector of the local citizens and sets out to establish a community devoted to law, order, progress, and the admiration of British actress Lily Langtry (Ava Gardner). Bean and the marshals purge the surrounding countryside of "varmints" and the town gradually prospers. The marshals marry and become family men, the railroad comes to town, and professionals such as lawyer Frank Gass (Roddy McDowall) open practices. Although Bean has dreamed of establishing a city in Lily Langtry's honor, he comes to realize that he will have no place in that civilized community. Unlike his marshals, he does not marry, but maintains a Mexican mistress, Maria Elena (Victoria Principal), despite the disapproval of the townspeople, especially the reformed prostitutes. Bean's summary brand of justice becomes more and more obsolete. The townsfolk begin to disapprove of the bodies of hanged outlaws being left on public display. When Maria Elena dies in childbirth, Bean attempts to hang the physician who was too drunk to care for her. The townspeople, led by lawyer Gass, now the mayor, prevent the execution. In disgust Bean leaves the town to Gass and the forces of civilization.

While most films which treat the disappearance of the frontier end with the death or exile of the character representing the old way of life—for example, the move to South America and deaths of the principals in *Butch Cassidy and the Sundance Kid* (1969), the retreat of Jeremiah Johnson into the farthest reaches of the mountains in the film of the same name (1972), and the massacre of the main characters in Sam Peckinpah's *The Wild Bunch* (1969)—*The Life and Times of Judge Roy Bean* ends with the triumph of frontier values. Twenty years after Bean has left, when Vinegarroon, under the control of Gass, is flourishing in an oil boom, Rose Bean (Jacqueline Bisset), the judge's daughter, tries to hold out against the lawyer's goons who want to evict her from her father's saloon. From out of the wilderness, Roy Bean reappears, regroups his marshals, who have lost their positions and dignity, and destroys all that the lawyer has created. Although Bean perishes in a final conflagration, his legend survives. Moreover, he returns Vinegarroon to the condition in which he found it, a desolate group of shacks in the Texas desert.

While the film deals with the passing of the Old West and the survival of its legends, *The Life and Times of Judge Roy Bean* also treats the vanity of illusions which blind people to reality. Like characters in many of Huston's other films (the conspirators plotting for the elusive statue in 1941's *The Maltese Falcon* or Fred C. Dobbs prospecting for gold in 1948's *The Treasure of the Sierra Madre*, for example), Roy Bean has a dream. His dream embodies itself in two ideals: Lily Langtry and the city which he wants to build in her honor. His idolatry of Lily Langtry manifests itself in the name chosen for his saloon ("The Jersey Lily"), the posters of her plastered ubiquitously on its walls, his frequent letters to her, his search through issues of *The New York Times* for mention of her, his "justifiable homicide" of a gunslinger who puts a bullet hole through one of her posters, and the oath required of his marshals ("To Texas and Miss Lily"). The ultimate evidence of his devotion to Miss Lily is his abandonment of civic and personal responsibilities as he leaves town and the pregnant Maria Elena to go to San Antonio to see the actress on tour. Bean never realizes his dream, however; tickets for her performance are sold out, and he is robbed and beaten in an alley in a scene reminiscent of his arrival at Vinegarroon. When he returns home, he finds Maria Elena dying and the town under the control of the newly elected mayor Frank Gass. Although the ideal of Miss Lily may not be as tawdry as a jewel-encrusted falcon, Bean's attempt to realize his dream backfires as surely as similar attempts do in other Huston films. Everything good in the unappreciated real world is destroyed in pursuit of the dream. Even Bean's dream of a progressive city proves empty as the civilization of Gass and the reformed whores demonstrates.

Although the character of Roy Bean dominates the film, several other characters, portrayed in cameo by well-known actors, add some color. The Reverend Mr. LaSalle (Anthony Perkins) is an itinerant preacher whose message of a righteous and wrathful God suggests to Bean that he should assume enforcement of the "Law West of the Pecos." Sam Dodd (Tab Hunter) demonstrates Bean's philosophy of the equality of justice. In an incident that contradicts legendary history about the actual Judge Roy Bean, Dodd is executed for the murder of a Chinese despite no law being found which expressly forbids killing a "Chinaman." Grizzly Adams, played by John Huston, who is a frequent actor as well as a director, is a mountain man, come down from the high country to die in the desert. His departure from the mountains which have lost their wilderness appeal foreshadows Bean's own exile from Vinegarroon. Watch-Bear (Bruno) becomes Bean's pet after being left behind by Grizzly Adams. The bear figures in an idyllic picnic scene with Bean and Maria Elena while Andy Williams croons "Marmalade, Molasses, and Honey" on the sound track. Bad Bob (Stacy Keach) is a flamboyant gunfighter who challenges Bean to a Main Street showdown, only to be shot in the back by the judge. Lily Langtry appears at the end of the film in a visit to the museum which is all that remains of Judge Roy Bean's dream.

The film utilizes several techniques of presentation beyond straight dialogue and action. Narration occurs from the point of view of several characters, especially Tector Crites (Ned Beatty), the bartender at the Jersey Lily who has reared Bean's daughter and has become curator of the museum. Transition between scenes in the film is often accomplished by the use of sepia-tinted stills. The tone of the film ranges from the seriocomic to the absurd, with Bean wisecracking as he condemns men to death.

Although *The Life and Times of Judge Roy Bean* involves a good deal in the way of intertwining themes and various characterizations, the film is a landmark for neither Huston nor Newman. Much of the acting is overstated, the picnic scene—as well as other elements in the film—seems directly derivative from *Butch Cassidy and the Sundance Kid*, and the film's serious themes become too encumbered by attempts at comic flourish. The film holds some interest for those concerned with recent developments in the Western movie, however, and with the recurrent ideas in Huston's directorial work. It has become a cult film which is shown frequently at revival houses.

Frances M. Malpezzi
William M. Clements

LIFE WITH FATHER

Released: 1947
Production: Robert Buckner for Warner Bros.
Direction: Michael Curtiz
Screenplay: Donald Ogden Stewart; based the play of the same name by Howard Lindsay and Russell Crouse and on the novels *God and My Father*, *Life with Father*, and *Life with Mother* by Clarence Day, Jr.
Cinematography: Peverell Marley and William V. Skall
Editing: George Amy
Costume design: Milo Anderson
Running time: 128 minutes

Principal characters:
Clarence Day, Sr. .... William Powell
Lavinia Day .... Irene Dunne
Mary Skinner .... Elizabeth Taylor
Cousin Cora .... Zasu Pitts
Clarence Day, Jr. .... Jimmy Lindon
Reverend Dr. Lloyd .... Edmund Gwenn
Whitney Day .... Martin Milner

Any producer who buys the screen rights to a famous Broadway play knows he is handling a two-edged sword. On the one hand, the play is famous and well loved; it has a presold title. On the other hand, the authors and the producers of the play extract a heavy price from the movie producer for that fame, perhaps more than it is really worth. With numerous road companies crossing the continent and the original Broadway company holding on, the public may be weary of it or have unrealistic expectations that the film cannot meet. Considering all these things, the fact that *Life with Father* was Broadway's longest-running play, and the fact that Warner Bros. paid the highest price to date for the screen rights, the filming of *Life with Father* was an enormous gamble. It was a challenge that studio head Jack Warner, with his producer Robert Buckner and director Michael Curtiz, met cautiously, and in the end, successfully.

When the play *Life with Father* opened on Broadway in 1939, no one predicted its enormous popularity. Written by Howard Lindsay and Russell Crouse and based primarily on Clarence Day, Jr.'s, autobiographical book, *God and My Father*, it told of Clarence Day, Sr., a wealthy stockbroker who lived with his wife Lavinia and their four sons in a comfortable townhouse on Upper Madison Avenue in the 1890's. The father swears a lot and one evening admits that he has never been baptized. Lavinia spends the rest of the play trying to persuade or trick him into a baptism and finally succeeds. Other plot elements were gleaned from Clarence Day, Jr.'s, other two books,

Life with Father and *Life with Mother*.

Clarence Day, Jr., was literally on his deathbed while writing these books, and, after their publication and moderate success, he almost sold the movie rights to Paramount, but changed his mind when he learned the studio intended them as vehicles for W. C. Fields. Day did not live to see the production of the play, *Life with Father*. After major actors and actresses had declined to play the leading roles, author Howard Lindsay and his wife, actress Dorothy Stickney, undertook them. The play finally opened, the critics raved, and it was an immediate hit. The Lindsays continued as Mother and Father for the next five years.

A Chicago company headed by Lillian Gish and a National Company starring her sister Dorothy Gish were soon sent out. Lillian Gish immediately advised her friend, silent star Mary Pickford, that the role of Lavinia would be perfect for Pickford's long-awaited movie comeback and urged her to buy the screen rights immediately. Pickford procrastinated, however, and soon all the major studios were trying to outbid one another for the rights. William Powell felt that the role of Clarence Day, Sr., could be the greatest of his entire career and urged his studio, M-G-M, to buy the rights. Rumor around M-G-M, however, had it that if the studio succeeded in buying *Life with Father*, the title role would go to Spencer Tracy, whose box-office following was better than Powell's. In the end, Warner Bros. outbid M-G-M, agreeing to give the authors and the original investors a down payment of $500,000, plus half of all profits. In addition, Lindsay and Crouse and the widow of Clarence Day, Jr., were to be brought to Hollywood to serve as technical advisers. No word of the play's text could be cut or changed without their permission; indeed, they were to have veto power over every aspect of the film.

The problems of casting began. Lindsay made a screen test, but disliked the way his voice sounded on the film and withdrew himself from consideration. Warner asked M-G-M to loan out Powell; the studio agreed and the public and the press voiced hearty approval.

Casting Lavinia proved more difficult. As the top Warner Bros. actress, Bette Davis had first refusal on any important female role. She worked hard on her makeup, hair, and characterization, but simply could not convey the daintiness and innocence that conceal Lavinia's will of iron. Pickford made several tests and all agreed that she would be perfect in the role since Lavinia was a somewhat older variant on Pickford's most popular silent screen roles. Warner wondered, however, whether Pickford had any following after a thirteen-year absence from acting.

Director Curtiz was holding out for Irene Dunne, whose *Anna and the King of Siam* (1946) had just been released to enormous success. Curtiz called on Dunne repeatedly, but she kept reading the script and refusing the role. She thought Lavinia was silly, and she did not see how she could make sympathetic a character who lied to and tricked her husband and who burst into tears when she did not get her way. Curtiz used all his powers of persuasion and finally, at the very last minute, Dunne called Warner to accept the role. Had she waited a few minutes longer, Pickford would have been signed.

Although Powell was playing the title role, Dunne was not about to concede top billing, so her agents met with his and a compromise was arranged: half the prints would bear her name first and the other half would have his. They would flip a coin for the New York premiere, with the loser getting first place for the Los Angeles premiere. First-run theaters would be required to alternate prints, with advertising alternating the same way.

The first chore was to dye all cast members' hair red. Genetics revealed that two red-headed parents would probably have all red-headed children, but each would be a different shade. Only Martin Milner, who was portraying Whitney, was a natural red-head, so the rest of the cast reported to the Westmore Beauty Parlour one Sunday morning to get their proper tints: Powell deep auburn, Dunne strawberry blonde and the children in various shades in between. When it came time to rinse the dye off, the beauticians found that the water had been turned off during street repairs. Panic set in as the operators struggled to remove the dye before it turned the hair vermillion. Finally one of them found a vat full of cold cream and applied it by the handful to inactivate the dye.

Shooting started in August of 1946 amidst much fanfare. At great cost, Warner Bros. tore down its largest exterior set, a Viennese street, and replaced it with a replica of Madison Avenue in the 1890's. The Day house was painted and furnished mostly in shades of green, mauve, and blue which made a becoming setting for the red hair. Milo Anderson, who designed the costumes, said that he was careful to use a green and blue plaid for the dress that Dunne wore through much of the film, and as Dunne was frequently required to run up and down flights of stairs, he kept the bustles on her skirts as small as possible while maintaining period accuracy.

On the stage, *Life with Father* takes place entirely in the Days' dining and drawing rooms. In writing the screenplay, Donald Ogden Stewart avoided changing the dialogue but, wherever possible, moved the action to other parts of the house, the street, and the back garden. He wrote brief scenes in the church, Delmonico's restaurant, and McCreeries' Department Store, playing out action which had only been referred to in the play. Lindsay and Crouse were on the set most of the time and occasionally reworded sentences to please Curtiz. They did not exercise their veto power unreasonably, nor did Mrs. Clarence Day. She approved of Dunne's characterization and even lent Dunne several pieces of jewelry that the real Lavinia Day had owned.

Curtiz had the reputation of working very fast, but the awesome reputation of *Life with Father* plus Warner's stated belief that the film would be "another *Gone with the Wind*" slowed him down. Powell and Dunne's reputations as comedians in the 1930's had come from quickly made comedies using much improvisation. Here the importance of *Life with Father* with its every almost holy word well known to the American public did not permit them to do anything off the cuff.

A simple story in few sets with a small cast which could have been filmed easily in six weeks was scheduled for twelve, then ran over into sixteen. Much of the delay was due to Powell's inexplicable absences from the set. The company would return after lunch, wait a few hours, then be told to go home. Although Powell never complained, he often seemed to be in great pain. It was not until many years later that he would reveal his history of cancer surgery during this period.

Once the film was cut and scored, the world premiere was delayed until August 15, 1947, the eighth anniversary of the Broadway premiere of the play. The reviews were good without being raves; most critics agreed that Clarence Day was a once-in-a-lifetime role for Powell, and although his frequent explosions of "damn" had to be toned down by movie censorship, the enormous energy Powell put into his substitute "Egads" compensated for the loss. Dunne, Elizabeth Taylor, Jimmy Lydon, and Edmund Gwenn, among others, all received favorable mention but not enthusiastic praise. Edwin Schallert of the *Los Angeles Times* was franker than most when he commented that *Life with Father* had a ". . . lack of spontaneity. . . ."

Life with Father, famous as it was, could not be another *Gone with the Wind* (1939). It was a simple little story, best told quickly and with affection. The massive production values dwarfed it. Nominated four times, it did not win any Oscars but it did respectably at the box office, placing well on *Variety*'s all-time highest-grossing film list. Warner Bros. made back their sizable outlay and a very good profit. *Life with Father* was given a major reissue in 1948 on the first anniversary of the initial release, but after that it faded away. When Warner Bros. films were first sold to television, *Life with Father* could not be included in the package because the studio had agreed not to distribute the film to any media after 1954. The film would remain in limbo for sixteen years, until a new agreement between Warner Bros. and the authors and producer made possible a network television sale. The story of *Life with Father* continued to be popular in a television series of the same name during the 1950's starring M-G-M character actor Leon Ames as Clarence Day, Sr.

David Chierichetti

LILI

Released: 1953
Production: Edwin H. Knopf for Metro-Goldwyn-Mayer
Direction: Charles Walters
Screenplay: Helen Deutsch; based on the short story "The Man Who Hated People" by Paul Gallico
Cinematography: Robert Planck
Editing: Ferris Webster
Music: Bronislau Kaper (AA)
Running time: 81 minutes

Principal characters:

Lili Daurier	Leslie Caron
Paul Berthalet	Mel Ferrer
Marc	Jean Pierre Aumont
Rosalie	Zsa Zsa Gabor
Jacquot	Kurt Kasznar

Musicals were in full bloom at Metro-Goldwyn-Mayer in the early 1950's. They ranged from elaborate versions of Broadway hits such as *Annie Get Your Gun* (1950) and *Kiss Me Kate* (1953) to original pieces such as *An American in Paris* (1951) and *Seven Brides for Seven Brothers* (1954), as well as revivals of such chestnuts as *Rose Marie* (1954) and such Esther Williams' aqua-extravaganzas as *Million Dollar Mermaid* (1952). Yet for all the spectacle of these grand entertainments, one of M-G-M's most fondly remembered musicals of that era is *Lili* (1953), the most quiet, low-key, and charming of them all. It is a love story filled with tender sentiment, containing the hauntingly pretty song "Hi-Lili-Hi-Lo," and featuring one of the finest screen performances of the beguiling Leslie Caron.

Filmed at M-G-M's Culver City studios, *Lili* was produced with little fanfare. It boasted no packaged prestige, lacking any Broadway origin or tune-crammed score. Its script, based on Paul Gallico's short story, did not even allow the chance for a high-kicking chorus to rush to the rescue to aid the pace and plot. When the studio's major musical director of the time, Vincente Minnelli, refused the job, it passed to Charles Walters, who had *Easter Parade* (1948) and *Summer Stock* (1950) among his credits. Caron, touted as a Metro star after her debut in *An American in Paris*, was challenged with her first major musical lead as Lili and was supported with a fine (but not "box-office") cast: Mel Ferrer as the crippled puppeteer Paul, Jean-Pierre Aumont as the dashing magician Marc, and Zsa Zsa Gabor as his wife Rosalie. Finally, the sentiment that was the backbone of *Lili* caused cynical skeptics to wince at its chances for commercial and critical success. Fortunately, all these concerns were cancelled out by the true artistry and emotion that made *Lili* a very special musical.

Lili tells the story of Lili Daurier (Leslie Caron), a French waif who seeks a job in a carnival. She is fascinated by the carnival's music, color, excitement—and especially its magician Marc (Jean Pierre Aumont), a dashing flirt who soon has the girl breathlessly infatuated. Lili is far less charmed by Paul Berthalet (Mel Ferrer), a former ballet dancer who now hides a crippled leg behind the curtain of a puppet booth. He is attracted to Lili's innocence and charm, but hides his sentiments behind a mask of scorn.

Working as a waitress, Lili soon loses her job when she becomes so mesmerized while watching Marc's magic act, performed with his assistant/secret wife Rosalie (Zsa Zsa Gabor), that she neglects her customers. Devastated and homeless, she sets out to leave the carnival that night. She passes the carnival's high-dive ladder, and the thought of suicide overtakes her; but as she begins to climb the ladder, a little voice calls her away. It belongs to Carrot-Top, a puppet who soon introduces the wonderstruck Lili to his friends: Marguerite, a vain prima donna; Renardo, a sly, flirtatious fox; and Golo, an awkward, soft-hearted giant. Lili pours out her emotions to these little friends, never realizing that Paul is really using the puppets to pour out his heart to her.

Lili subsequently joins the puppet act performed by Paul and his kind assistant Jacquot (Kurt Kasznar). She talks and sings "Hi-Lili-Hi-Lo" with Carrot-Top and company, and her winsome charm plays a major part in establishing the act as one of the carnival's most popular attractions. Paul finds himself increasingly drawn to Lili, but her continued infatuation with Marc causes him to treat her miserably. Although Marc reveals to Lili that Rosalie is his wife and leaves the carnival for a better offer, Paul's bitterness blocks his hopes of revealing his true emotions to her, and instead, he slaps her. Lily decides to leave the carnival again, and is once again stopped by Carrot-Top. All the puppets tell her of their love for her, and as she embraces them, she feels a trembling hand and pulls away the curtain to reveal Paul. The puppeteer confesses that he is all the puppets, the clever Carrot-Top, the lying Renardo, the vain Marguerite, and eager-to-be-loved giant. Confused and frightened, Lili runs away.

On the road, Lili dreams a beautiful ballet in which she dances with all the puppets, who have become life-size. Yet each one turns into Paul before her eyes, causing her to realize that the qualities she so loved in the puppets are all qualities of the man who really loves her. Wanting Paul, she runs back to the carnival and the two embrace as the puppets, via the magic of a love story's happy ending, peek approvingly around the curtain.

"You'll laugh, you'll cry, you'll love *Lili*," promised the advertisements when the musical premiered in March of 1953. *The New York Times* praised it as "a lovely and beguiling little film touched with the magic of romance and the shimmer of masquerade." *Lili* won an Academy Award for Bronislau Kaper ("Best Scoring of a Dramatic or Comedy Film"), an Oscar nomination for Caron, who lost to Audrey Hepburn (then wed to Ferrer) for *Roman Holiday*, and placed sixth on the *Film Daily* "Ten Best" poll of 1953.

M-G-M has re-released *Lili* over the years, always to warm reception. The gayly colored carnival sets in Technicolor, the splendid puppet work, and the melancholy accordian music are charmingly orchestrated by director Walters, and the entire case is delightful. As Jacquot, Kasznar plays with a patience and an understanding that helps create sympathy for Paul. Gabor is a true beauty, especially glamorous in the sequence in which her magician-husband "magically" causes her costume to fly off to reveal her in her black lingerie. Aumont plays with a true affection, not only a magician par excellence but also a man of real emotion which he conceals behind a wolfish façade. Ferrer, conversely, portrays a man who hides his sensitivity behind a façade of hate, and poignantly reveals the anguish and heartache of the puppeteer. Finally, Caron is a beautiful Lili, fully conveying the bewilderment and innocence of the naïve girl adrift in a complex world. The lovely ballet is a masterpiece of dance expressing emotion, and her reunion with Ferrer is truly rewarding to the audience, which has perceived their genuine emotions and applauds the love and protection they will give each other.

Finally, it should be noted that *Lili*, although it did not originate from a Broadway musical, did inspire one. The show was *Carnival*, with a book by Michael Stewart and music and lyrics by Robert Merrill. It opened on Broadway in 1961, with Anna Maria Alberghetti as Lili, Jerry Orbach as Paul, James Mitchell as Marc (here called Marco the Magnificent), and Kaye Ballard in the very augmented role of Rosalie. It ran for 719 performances, a testimony not only to the musical itself, but also to the charm, warmth, and reputation of its inspiration, *Lili*.

Gregory William Mank

LILIES OF THE FIELD

Released: 1963
Production: Ralph Nelson for United Artists
Direction: Ralph Nelson
Screenplay: James Poe; based on the novel of the same name by William E. Barrett
Cinematography: Ernest Haller
Editing: John McCafferty
Music: Jerry Goldsmith
Running time: 94 minutes

Principal characters:

Homer Smith	Sidney Poitier (AA)
Mother Maria	Lilia Skala
Sister Gertrude	Lisa Mann
Sister Agnes	Isa Crino
Sister Albertine	Francesca Jarvis
Sister Elizabeth	Pamela Branch
Juan Acalito	Stanley Adams
Father Murphy	Dan Frazer
Ashton	Ralph Nelson

"He was not of our faith or of our skin," says Mother Maria (Lilia Skala) of the itinerant black workman Homer Smith (Sidney Poitier), "but he was a man of greatness, of an utter devotion." Thus the Mother Superior pays tribute to the black Baptist man who helps a group of Roman Catholic nuns build a chapel for their town in the 1963 sleeper, *Lilies of the Field*. Filmed in the area surrounding Tucson, Arizona, the low budget, black-and-white film subtly and humorously depicts a small event which shows the goodness and selflessness of one man. The film concerns an ex-GI named Homer Smith, a laborer who has been touring the American Southwest in a stationwagon loaded down with camping equipment. On his way through the arid land of Arizona, he sees five nuns, all dressed in black, walking through the desert. When he stops to talk with the nuns he realizes that they are from East Germany and are refugees whose order has recently acquired an isolated farm as a bequest. Only one of the nuns, Mother Maria, speaks any English, and she tells Homer that the land which they now occupy is very barren and difficult to work.

The soft-hearted Homer takes pity on the nuns and begins to help them, but says that he only can stay for a few days. He works with them and receives food, but no money, as he gently reminds Mother Maria. She has no money to give him, but persuades him to stay with them anyway. Throughout the film Homer is constantly at loggerheads with Mother Maria, refusing to work and threatening to leave, but each time he says that he will leave, she convinces him to stay. Mother Maria thinks that Homer is the answer to their prayers, and she simply refuses to accept the fact that he will not work for them. Her faith, coupled with obstinancy, is impossible for Homer to fight, and he continually acquiesces to her "demands." He eventually bows to her wishes for a new chapel, because everytime he says "no chapel," she simply says, "yes, you build chapel." Homer never seems to know exactly why he follows Mother Maria's orders; he simply does.

Once the chapel is started, Homer takes a new protective interest in the nuns. In order to buy the supplies which are needed for the chapel, he even takes on extra jobs in the area to earn money for the project. The poverty-stricken Mexican-Americans in town do not understand Homer because they have refused to work for the sisters. Homer keeps working for the nuns, however, even after an argument with Mother Maria about wasting his money for lollipops for the nuns causes him to leave temporarily. Finally he gets a part-time job with a local contractor named Ashton (Ralph Nelson). With the extra money he is now earning he can buy more bricks for the chapel, and with the additional help of some of the Mexican-Americans, the chapel is soon completed. Unlike the selfless Homer, however, the local citizens seem to help because they feel that they will get some type of heavenly "insurance" for their good deeds.

Finally, when the chapel is completed and the traveling priest, Father Murphy (Dan Frazer), no longer has to use the back of his car for an altar, Homer decides to leave. Just as he arrived unceremoniously, he leaves in the same way, before the bishop is scheduled to arrive for the chapel's dedication; his task having been completed, he simply picks up and leaves. Only Sister Maria sadly notices that he is going, but she does not try to stop him. She knows that he was there to fulfill a special need, and now that that need has been taken care of, he cannot stay.

Although made on a miniscule budget (reportedly less than $300,000) and released without much publicity, *Lilies of the Field* became a success, both financially and critically. It earned five Academy Award nominations, winning one for Poitier for Best Actor. Poitier was perfect for the part, and the film brought him international stardom. He had previously been in a number of good films, but usually played the second or third lead. Most of these films, such as *Blackboard Jungle* (1955) and *No Way Out* (1950), had themes of social significance. It was not until the late 1950's, in *The Defiant Ones* (1958) and *Porgy and Bess* (1959), that he began to have starring roles; but after *Lilies of the Field*, he never went back to a costarring position, becoming the cinema's most popular black actor. He is also the only black man to have won an Oscar for Best Actor to date. Although many of his starring roles have been criticized for their "superblack" characterizations, his talent is undisputed. In the late 1970's he began directing his own films, and more recently he has done more directing than acting. His most successful film as a director so far has been *Stir Crazy* (1980), starring Gene Wilder and Richard Pryor, one of the largest-grossing films of all time.

In the understated role of Homer, Poitier is humorous and believable. He has no special talents or achievements; he is simply a nice man who has a big heart. He sees the need of the nuns and he helps them, despite the differences in their race and religion; in fact, the film shies away from many references to race. The most significant mention of Homer's race occurs when he is drinking with some of the Mexican-American workers by a campfire. They have come to admire him, and laughingly toast him as a "Gringo." Homer accepts their intended compliment with laughter, saying that he does not know whether Gringo is a step up or a step down from what he has been called most of his life. The fact that race is incidental to the plot actually makes more of a statement for understanding and love between the races than many social message films.

The cast has few professional actors, and none of them is well known. Skala, an Austrian actress who emigrated to the United States, has played a number of character parts over the years, but this is by far her best and most famous role, and one for which she received an Oscar nomination. Frazer as a bitter, frustrated priest is also quite good. The scene in which he tries to thank Homer by explaining to him how much it means for him to have his own church in which to say Mass, but winds up only embarrassing Homer, is one of the best in the film. Producer and director Ralph Nelson, who was more responsible than anyone else for the film, also has a small part as the contractor. Although he was not nominated for an Oscar for his direction, he did receive a nomination for the film in the Best Picture category, losing to *Tom Jones*.

For all of its fine performances and charming scenes, *Lilies of the Field* is probably remembered most often as the film that won Poitier his Oscar, and the one in which the up-beat Gospel favorite, "Amen," is sung. The scene in which Homer sings the verse and claps his hands as the nuns sing the chorus is delightful.

Janet St. Clair

LILITH

Released: 1964
Production: Robert Rossen for Columbia
Direction: Robert Rossen
Screenplay: Robert Rossen; based on the novel of the same name by J. R. Salamanca
Cinematography: Gene Shuftan
Editing: Aram Avakian
Running time: 112 minutes

Principal characters:
Vincent Bruce .... Warren Beatty
Lilith Arthur .... Jean Seberg
Stephen Evshevsky .... Peter Fonda
Bea Brice .... Kim Hunter
Laura ....Jessica Walter
Norman .... Gene Hackman

It is ironic that Robert Rossen's distinguished thirty-year career as a director, producer, and screenwriter was culminated with the controversy that met his final film, *Lilith*. Ill-treated by the critics and misunderstood by its releasing studio (which promoted the film as a "story of rapture, of a mad and limitless love"), *Lilith* also incurred the insult of being withdrawn from competition at the 1964 Venice Film Festival because festival organizers criticized the film's quality. That the film received such treatment at the time of its release is sadly ironic, since film scholars today view *Lilith* as a highly original and uncompromising work. Moreover, the film contains what is probably Jean Seberg's finest, most compelling work in an American film. The new esteem directed toward the film may also be due to changed times and attitudes. At the time of the film's release, the story line, involving sexual obsession and madness, was considered controversial and was not readily accepted by general audiences.

Filmed in black and white with an innovative camera, *Lilith* abounds in overlapping sounds and images, erratic editing, and scenes of heightened symbolism. Time relationships are shaky, and reality is frequently hazy and uncertain. These traits, and Seberg's ethereal performance as Lilith, amplify the viewer's descent into a world of madness. It is an often beautiful journey, as signified by the opening credits, which are seen over drawings of beautiful butterflies that become trapped in a spider's web. The merging of beauty and danger is but one of many dichotomies to be found in *Lilith*.

In Babylonian mythology, Lilith is the female embodiment of evil, and indeed, the Lilith of the film concurs that she "wants to leave the mark of her desire on every living thing." Her sexual desires become the catalyst for a series of tangled relationships. Among the resulting revelations is the fact that a seemingly normal person is quite mad.

Uncertainties are evident from the first scene, which finds a pensive Vincent Bruce (Warren Beatty) walking down a tree-lined path toward what is identified as Poplar Lodge. It seems an idyllic moment, but the tone abruptly shifts when a girl is viewed, from behind, as she peers out of bars at Vincent. (The viewer suspects the girl is Lilith.) Poplar Lodge is for the care and treatment of the insane, and Vincent has come to apply for work. He lives in the nearby town, and is just out of the Army. As he tells staff doctor Bea Brice (Kim Hunter), "I want to do some sort of work where I can be a direct help to people." His attitude pleases Brice, and she immediately hires him.

Returning home that night, Vincent has a chance encounter with his former girl friend, Laura (Jessica Walter). He is relaxed and friendly, but she is uneasy. Because the two never had "an agreement," she married someone else during his absence. She wonders, then, if he is angry, but he seems genuinely pleased for her. Before running to catch her bus, Laura makes a nebulous remark, saying she had heard Vincent had been "wounded or something." Throughout the film, much of Vincent's background is recounted by similarly blurred references. That night at his home, for example, he tells his grandmother about his new job, and she remarks that his "poor mother" would have been pleased.

When the story line shifts to Poplar Lodge, the viewer at last gets a satisfying look at the lovely Lilith. She is playing a flute, and another patient, Stephen Evshevsky (Peter Fonda), who is obviously attracted to the girl, stops a game of ping-pong so that Lilith's playing is uninterrupted. Lilith's ability to mesmerize becomes further apparent during a picnic outing for the patients. Lilith drops a paintbrush onto rocks above a rushing river, and Stephen valiantly tries to retrieve it. He comes dangerously close to falling, however, and Vincent has to save him. The near-accident angers Vincent, who suspects that Lilith dropped the brush in order to test Stephen, but it is also suggested that the brush was dropped to test Vincent.

During several casual discussions with staff members, Vincent learns about varying degrees of madness, and about Lilith. Like all the patients at Poplar Lodge, she is wealthy and intelligent. One staff member compares such patients to fine crystal that has shattered, noting, they are "the heroes of the universe . . . its finest product and its noblest casualty." When the talk shifts to schizophrenia, it is revealed that even spiders sometimes go mad. When they do, they spin webs that are nonsymmetrical and bizarrely beautiful. Vincent, who has had several unsettling experiences with Lilith, discusses his uncertainties about dealing with her. Questioning her motives—he wonders if she is trying to seduce him—he reasons, "It's almost like she wants to share this magic little world of hers." Without shame, he also confesses that there are times when he would welcome seduction by her.

Through the sessions, it is learned that Lilith's frail mental state—which includes a private world, complete with its own language—is due in part to the accidental death of her brother. It is later revealed that Lilith had enticed the boy. Her penchant for seduction surfaces during an afternoon bicycling trip with Vincent. After Lilith falls from her bike, he rushes to her aid. She embraces him, but he pulls away, insisting that she allow him to be honorable in his work. "I can't be saved by honor," she replies.

During another outing, which emerges as a pivotal point in the film, the two visit a nearby town where a famed jousting tournament is under way. There, Lilith's multifaceted personality surfaces. While watching a Punch and Judy show, her face glows like that of a child's. Moments later, she takes on a wicked repose, as she bends to give a small boy a suggestive, lingering kiss. After Vincent enters and wins the tournament, which requires riders to put their lances through small rings, she is luminous as she is crowned "Queen of Love and Beauty." It is, of course, a fitting title, for after riding into the countryside, Lilith and Vincent make love, after he has confessed his love for her. Afterward, Lilith asks, "If I died tonight, would it have been enough?"

A power play is now set in motion. At first it is Lilith who is eager to please Vincent, but later, she questions his love for her and shows her unwillingness to be possessed when she encourages the attention of one of the women patients. As the two walk hand-in-hand through the fields (they are walking alongside a lake, and the reflection shows them pressed together), Vincent follows. Aware of his presence, the women nevertheless enter a barn. They are undressing when Vincent bursts through the door. Although he turns on Lilith in disgust, she is unruffled. "I show my love to all of you, and you despise me for it," she says. Now it is Lilith who has power over Vincent, and she wields it cruelly, by continuing to see the woman patient. Vincent still follows them, but he now maintains some distance.

He is witness to another shaky relationship when he is again reunited with Laura. This time, it does not appear to be a chance encounter, for Vincent strolls across her front lawn early one evening. After inviting him inside, Laura introduces him to her dull husband, Norman (Gene Hackman). Norman is just about to leave for a meeting of the United Citizens Council (women, he tells Vincent, feel deserted by a man's civic obligations). First he politely chats with Vincent about mundane topics and questions him about his job, mentioning that Laura had said Vincent's mother used to be a bit crazy. He then leaves, encouraging Vincent to stay and visit with Laura. When her husband leaves, Laura wanders into another room to pour herself a drink. Marriage has changed her, she tells Vincent. She then invites him to make love to her ("Remember when I said I'd never really let you make love to me until I was married? Well, I am married now"), but Vincent is no longer interested.

Vincent's obsession with Lilith results in Stephen's tragic death. Stephen has carved a paint box for Lilith, and although the girl is delighted with the gift, Vincent will not admit to Stephen that she is pleased. With his delicate mental state shattered, Stephen commits suicide. Vincent, who is planning to move onto the hospital grounds because his jealousy of Lilith is becoming all-consuming, feels guilty about the death, but when he tries to relay his feelings to Lilith, she cannot comprehend them. She is once again slipping into her private world. Vincent's behavior, which has become increasingly erratic, compels Dr. Brice to pay a visit to his home. Vincent is not home, but the visit proves enlightening, for Dr. Brice sees a photograph of Vincent's mother—and she bears a striking resemblance to Lilith.

At film's end, Vincent becomes a patient when his own madness finally surpasses Lilith's, driving him to force his way into her room, apparently killing her. It is an uncertain point in the film; the scene showing Lilith's body is viewed only briefly, and critics were divided as to whether Lilith was dead or in a catatonic state. During the closing moments, Vincent approaches a knowing Dr. Brice with the words, "Help me."

Lilith's evocative sexuality and Vincent's disturbed state, which emerges slowly, dominate this study of sanity and madness. Through a myriad of mirror images—reflections seen in glass windows and in water—director Rossen dispenses clues about the madness at hand. The film also makes interesting use of bars, when at times it appears that Vincent is peering through bars, rather than Lilith. The fact that Lilith looks so much like Vincent's mother (who remains a mysterious figure) adds another interesting point, implying an incestuous interest. Vincent's own madness may be seen emerging, earlier in the film, when he asks, "What's so wonderful about reality?"

As for the complex and free-spirited character of Lilith, Rossen once said, she "is one of the honorable wounded in man's mortal struggle to understand." In keeping with the critical consensus of the film's performance, Rossen agreed that Beatty's work as Vincent was poor (there have been reports that the two did not get along during filming), but Seberg's performance as Lilith was highly praised. Seberg was the darling of French New Wave directors in the 1960's, appearing in films such as *Breathless* (1960) and *Time Out for Love* (1961). She was "discovered" at the age of seventeen, when Otto Preminger chose her for the much-publicized title role of *Saint Joan* in 1957. The film was a commercial failure, and Seberg's work was much ridiculed. As a result, she sought work in Europe, but later returned to the United States for roles in films such as *Paint Your Wagon* (1969) and *Airport* (1970). The actress's Cinderella-story origins and the respectability she finally secured within the film world made her suicide in Paris in 1979 appear all the more tragic. After her death, it was revealed that harassment by the F. B. I. (stemming from her work with the black nationalist party) had done much to injure her mental state. About the cool, collected image she always seemed to project, Seberg once stated, "People have a strange picture of me. I'm not at all the steady, calm person they seem to think I am. That's part of the masquerade that will never cease to amuse me. . . ."

For Rossen, *Lilith* capped off a prestigious career marked by his screenplays for socially conscious films of the 1930's, including *They Won't Forget* (1937) and *Dust Be My Destiny* (1939), and his direction of enduring films such as *Body and Soul* (1947), *All the King's Men* (1949), and *The Hustler* (1961).

Pat H. Broeske

THE LION IN WINTER

Released: 1968
Production: Martin Poll for Avco Ambassy
Direction: Anthony Harvey
Screenplay: James Goldman (AA); based on his play of the same name
Cinematography: Douglas Slocombe
Editing: John Bloom
Art direction: Peter Murton; set decoration, Peter James
Costume design: Margaret Furse
Music: John Barry (AA)
Running time: 134 minutes

Principal characters:
King Henry II ....Peter O'Toole
Queen Eleanor of Aquitaine ..... Katharine Hepburn (AA)
Princess Alais ....Jane Merrow
Prince Geoffrey ....John Castle
King Phillip of France .... Timothy Dalton
Prince Richard .... Anthony Hopkins
William Marshall .... Nigel Stock
Prince John .... Nigel Terry

The *Lion in Winter* falls into the same tradition as *Beckett* (1964) and *A Man for All Seasons* (1966), two earlier films which revived the historical drama. These films all had the general characteristic of taking actual historical incidents and characters and placing the circumstances into a modern perspective. All three present anachronistic speeches and insights in carefully reconstructed historical situations. *The Lion in Winter* is a companion piece and almost a sequel to *Beckett*, centering on King Henry II of England, who reigned from 1142 to 1189. In both films Peter O'Toole plays Henry, and although the two films are directed and written by different people, the same historical flavor and attention to detail is evident in both. The anachronistic aspect of these films is the dialogue, which seems too modern; yet it is the very contemporariness of the dialogue, coupled with the meticulous reconstruction of the historical setting, which makes both films excellent.

The *Lion in Winter* is based upon James Goldman's critically acclaimed 1966 Broadway play of the same name. The theme of the drama is family betrayal and intrigue, as illustrated by seven royal characters. All are intelligent and cunning, but also greedy and ambitious. Each one cheats and connives for personal gain and political power. The story takes place in the South of France at King Henry's Chinon Castle during the twenty-four-hour Christmas court held in 1183. The main character, Henry (Peter O'Toole), is a formidable monarch who has been on the throne for some years, feels his own mortality, and wants to select his successor. His eldest son and the natural successor, young Henry, died six months before the start of the action. Henry favors his youngest son John (Nigel Terry), a pimply-faced brat who merely uses his father's affection. Henry has a young mistress, Alais (Jane Merrow), who is the sister of the King of France, but he would like her to marry John in order to maintain England's holding in that country. She has no desire to do so, but Henry tries to persuade her that they will be able to remain lovers even if she does marry John.

For those conversant with the problems of medieval English and French history, the thrust of the film may be somewhat obscured. Although the film does give a great deal of historical background interspersed among the various speeches, it does not make clear the fact that in the twelfth century, the right of the English kings was still a fragile thing. Civil wars, murder, and pretenders to the throne could easily interfere with the type of hereditary succession which is now taken for granted in England. Additionally, England's holdings were not confined to the area now known as the British Isles; England also had extensive holdings on the Continent, principally in France, which caused great consternation in the dukes of the various French provinces, as well as in the kings themselves.

With this background in mind, the story makes more sense. The main part of the action begins when Henry's Queen, Eleanor (Katharine Hepburn), comes to the Court. Because she took part in civil wars against Henry and plots against his kingship, he has kept her under "house arrest" imprisoned in a tower in Salisbury, England, for the last ten years. Power, the thing which she values most, has been taken away from her. Henry and Eleanor are both strong-willed, and the film portrays them as having a love-hate relationship. They love, detest, fight, and sometimes protect each other.

When Eleanor discovers that Henry wants to name John to be his heir, she schemes to attain that honor for her chosen Richard (Anthony Hopkins), and eventually promises to yield her own territory, the Aquitaine, to Henry, if Richard is the heir. In their squabblings about Richard and John, their third surviving son, Geoffrey (John Castle), feels that he has been neglected, and he begins to undermine both of their plans. The final major character of the film, King Phillip II of France (Timothy Dalton), Alais' brother, comes to the Christmas Court after the others have arrived and begins his own plots. His aim is to rid France of any English holdings, and to this aim, he seduces (intellectually) John and Geoffrey in turn, after it is revealed that he had seduced (physically) Richard the summer before. Alais is merely a pawn of the others, being a prize because of her position, not herself.

Following Henry's abortive plan to annul his marriage to Eleanor and a failed attempt to kill Richard, the film ends with the main characters returning to the *status quo*. No heir has been selected, and Eleanor goes back to Salisbury. In the final scene, Eleanor and Henry part as lovers, although feuding ones. "You're still a marvel of a man," she says to Henry. "And you're still my Lady," he replies.

Although the film is one of the best representations of medieval life on film, some of the characters and details of the lives of the Plantagenets are altered for dramatic effect. The character of Alais does not have any historical basis, and it seems unlikely that a Christmas Court hosting King Phillip would have taken place at such a juncture. There were indeed fights and plots among the family members, but the question of succession as it is dissected in the film probably took place several years later, closer to Henry's death. The actual Henry and Eleanor, however, were involved in power struggles as portrayed in the film. Eleanor had previously been married to King Louis of France, and when she obtained a divorce from him because she failed to produce a male heir, she married Henry Plantagenet, who was considerably younger than she. This enabled Henry to consolidate her lands in France with his own. Eleanor did select Richard as her choice for king, but he later became disillusioned with her and fought against her. Geoffrey actually died before Henry and was therefore not in contention for the throne in 1189. Richard became King Richard I, the Lion-Hearted, and John was "bad King John Lackland," who succeeded his brother in 1204.

The film does an excellent job of showing the level of existence in the twelfth century. Although Henry is a King who can afford anything by twelfth century standards, his palace is cold, sparse, and dirty. The grounds, far from being the idyllic palaces seen in earlier films about medieval times, are dirty with peasants and animals sharing living space. The gracious banquets and jousting tournaments usually depicted are totally anachronistic, and this film does much to correct that erroneous picture.

Whatever the merits of the historicity of the film, however, the performances could hardly be improved upon. O'Toole and Hepburn are near-perfect in their roles. Although there is an age difference of twenty-five years between them, they seem perfectly matched. They snarl, cajole, bicker, and love in a way that excellently illustrates the strength of the actual characters whom they portray. O'Toole, who is playing the same character that he had played at a younger age in *Beckett*, gives one of the many fine performances of his career. He was nominated for an Oscar for his role, but lost to Cliff Robertson for his quiet, sensitive portrayal of a mentally retarded janitor in *Charly*. It is unfortunate that despite several Oscar nominations for some brilliant performances, O'Toole has never won the award. Hepburn equals O'Toole's brilliance, and she won her third Best Actress Oscar for the film, tying with Barbra Streisand for *Funny Girl*. Hepburn had also won the award the year before for her very different portrayal in *Guess Who's Coming to Dinner?* She is presently the only actress to have won three Oscars for Best Actress.

The others in the cast, including Hopkins, Castle, and Dalton in particular, are very good. Because the film is based on a play, it gives the actors many good opportunities to deliver speeches, which they do extremely well. In addition to Hepburn's award, James Goldman, for his very first screenplay, and John Barry, for the music, also won Oscars. Barry's music beautifully combines a new score with strains of authentic medieval music for the best possible effect. Goldman's screenplay, taking into account its historical anachronisms, is insightful and well drawn. The story provides a historical backdrop for a thematic study of familial relationships, and, in a certain sense, is a medieval reworking of Eugene O'Neill's *Long Day's Journey into Night* and other similar plays. At the end of the film, it is the love-hate relationships among the family members that come through as much as the historical aspects of the film.

Janet St. Clair

THE LIST OF ADRIAN MESSINGER

Released: 1963
Production: Edward Lewis for Universal
Direction: John Huston
Screenplay: Anthony Veiller; based on the novel of the same name by Philip MacDonald
Cinematography: Joe MacDonald and Edward Scaife
Editing: Terry Morse and Hugh S. Fowler
Makeup: Bud Westmore
Music: Jerry Goldsmith
Running time: 98 minutes

Principal characters:

George Brougham	Kirk Douglas
Anthony Gethryn	George C. Scott
Lady Jocelyn Bruttenholm	Dana Wynter
Marquis of Gleneyre	Clive Brook
Raoul Le Borg	Jacques Roux
Mrs. Karoudjian	Gladys Cooper
Sir Wilfred Lucas	Herbert Marshall
Derek	Walter Anthony Huston
Adrian Messinger	John Merivale

The List of Adrian Messinger was made by director John Huston during a period of his career when none of his films was either critically or financially successful. In the late 1950's and early 1960's, Huston had a period of unpopularity, producing such films as *The Unforgiven* (1960) and *The Misfits* (1961), which were panned at the time but have since been recognized as two of his better works. *The List of Adrian Messinger* was made at the end of this period, just before *The Night of the Iguana* (1964), which brought him back into favor. Although still not considered one of Huston's great works, *The List of Adrian Messinger* is a very good film and one which should not be dismissed.

The List of Adrian Messinger is a mystery which derives much of its suspense from the literal unmasking of several of the film's well-known stars. It utilizes a trick of filmmaking and publicity which creates a guessing game for the audience, which has to try to figure out what famous star was hiding behind what elaborate makeup design. Aside from the obvious publicity possibilities of featuring a number of prominent stars in disguise in the film, makeup is an important part of the main action of the story. Whatever the merits of the film on the levels of characterization and direction, its brilliance as a display of the art of makeup is without question. Usually films which are well known for superior makeup are horror or science-fiction films such as *Planet of the Apes* (1968) and *The Phantom of the Opera* (1943). Because such films as these are often recognized by the Motion Picture Academy with a special award, when merited, there has never been a need, according to the Academy board of governors, to establish a regular award category for makeup artists. The rationale for this is that makeup, like hair design, cannot be measured except in a film in which makeup is an important aspect of the production. The guild of makeup artists, however, feels that their work should be recognized in the same way that costumes are. Many films have been nominated in the category of costume design over the years which have modern dress settings and in which costumes are not an obviously integral part of the production. Whatever the resolution to this problem, it is unfortunate that films such as *The List of Adrian Messinger* in which makeup does add considerably to the story have not been recognized with an award by the motion picture industry as a whole.

As the story opens, we see an older man in a bowler hat rigging an elevator so that the next occupant will plummet down the elevator shaft and be killed. The audience does not know the reason for this murder or who the killer is. The action then shifts to the country estate of the Marquis of Gleneyre (Clive Brook), where Adrian Messinger (John Merivale), the Marquis' nephew, who is a writer, is having tea with the family and a good friend, Anthony Gethryn (George C. Scott), who is a retired British Intelligence Officer. Adrian asks Gethryn to check a list of eleven names for him, but he cannot tell him the reason why. Because Adrian is leaving on a transatlantic flight the next day, Gethryn promises to check on the names during Adrian's absence.

As Adrian checks his luggage at the airport, a heavy-set vicar discovers that his heavy suitcase is overweight, and Adrian graciously asks the ticket attendant to average out the weight between their two suitcases so that the vicar will not have to pay for excess baggage. After the vicar thanks Adrian, the bag goes onto the plane, but instead of boarding the plane himself, the vicar goes into the men's room and, in front of the camera, he removes heavy makeup, including plastic eye coverings, wig, and false nose, to reveal actor Kirk Douglas. Thus the audience now knows that Douglas is the person who killed the man in the elevator in the first scene, in another disguise.

The plane in which Adrian is traveling then explodes in midflight, and the only survivor is a Frenchman named Raoul Le Borg (Jacques Roux). Just before Adrian dies, Le Borg pulls him aboard a piece of the plane's floating debris, and Adrian deliriously utters a number of cryptic phrases. When Le Borg recuperates enough to receive visitors, Gethryn, who had known Le Borg by reputation because of their work in the underground during World War II, enlists his aid in finding the meaning of Adrian's list of names and the reasons for the plane crash.

The mystery becomes very complicated at this point, and, in fact, it is very hard to follow seeing the film only once. As it turns out in the investigation, all of the people on Adrian's list are dead, and an extraordinarily high number of them died from "accidental" deaths over a period of five years. Gethryn deduces that Adrian's name as well as the others was supposed to be on that list and he tries to find a common denominator between them. He eventually discovers that all had been prisoners-of-war in a Burmese prison camp during World War II, and that they had been betrayed by a Canadian officer. Gethryn then thinks that the man must be covering his past by murdering all of these people to protect his future.

When Gethryn and Le Borg are able to decipher Adrian's message, it is finally discovered that George Brougham (Kirk Douglas, not in disguise) is the heir to the Marquis of Gleneyre, with only the Marquis' young grandson Derek (Walter Anthony Huston) in line before him. Gleneyre and Le Borg set out to "unmask" George when he shows up at the country estate, and at a fox hunt in which George had hoped to kill Derek, he himself is killed instead. The end title then appears, but just after it does, Douglas yells "Stop, this isn't the end of the movie," and we see a parade of characters in disguise unmask themselves on camera: Tony Curtis as an organ grinder, Burt Lancaster as a husky woman who opposes fox hunts, Robert Mitchum as a gruff cockney, and Frank Sinatra as a gypsy. Then we see Kirk Douglas appear in all of his many disguises, finally unmask himself, and announce that this *really* is the end.

Theatrics aside, *The List of Adrian Messinger* is an excellent mystery in the Agatha Christie tradition. Based on Philip MacDonald's best-selling novel of the same name, the film uses many of the standard characteristics of the detective novel. Gethryn, well-portrayed by Scott, replete with mustache and English accent, is an old-fashioned detective who relies on his wits rather than guns. He is not the hard-boiled "gumshoe" type of many American detective novels, but instead a soft-spoken, plodding English gentleman. In truth, the entire film presents Gethryn and George as two opposites who have striking similarities. Both are plodders, both are patient, and both are very accomplished. The differences between the men lie in their moral stance: Gethryn is good, and George is evil. Perhaps a flaw of the novel and the film is the extreme evilness of George. There are no clues in the film concerning why George is so evil, only plenty of information about the evil things he has done. George simply states (like the murderer in Alfred Hitchcock's *Shadow of a Doubt*, 1943), that evil "does exist." This is perhaps acceptable in a mystery novel, but with today's emphasis on psychological motivation, it is less than satisfying.

Some sections of the film, particularly the romance between Le Borg and Jocelyn (Dana Wynter), Derek's widowed mother, actually detract from the main action, and the film could have been much tauter without it. It is the detection of the crime which is the strong point of the film. Douglas, an underrated actor, is very good as the steely George. The number of his disguises enables him to portray a wide variety of characters, and his own voices and movements make them as different as the makeup. He is hardly a likable villain, but at least he is a fascinating one.

The makeup tricks in the film are the creation of veteran artist Bud Westmore, a member of the famous Westmore family of makeup men. Bud and his brothers Frank and Perc were three members of a family of two generations of important makeup men who worked on countless films. Their craftsmanship made them the most important group of makeup men ever to work in the film industry. This was one of the last important films on which Bud worked because in the 1960's studios such as Universal were moving away from the big-name artists in favor of developing their own makeup departments.

For mystery fans, *The List of Adrian Messinger* is highly recommended. Although not one of Huston's important *auteur* films, it is very enjoyable. It is also interesting to try to guess which stars play which parts. As a footnote to the guessing game, Huston's son plays Derek in the film, and he himself has a bit part as one of the fox hunters; he is seen on horseback (Huston was a championship rider in his younger days) and utters a few words to hurry up the action of the hunt. This may have given Huston the idea to take up the acting profession again. While he had started as an actor on stage, following his father, Walter Huston, John gave up acting in films in 1930. After his brief appearance here, however, he began to act as often as he directed, and he has had major supporting roles in a number of films in the last twenty years.

Patricia King Hanson

LITTLE CAESAR

Released: 1930
Production: Hal B. Wallis for First National/Warner Bros.
Direction: Mervyn LeRoy
Screenplay: Francis Faragoh; based on the novel of the same name by W. R. Burnett
Cinematography: Tony Gaudio
Editing: no listing
Running time: 77 minutes

Principal characters:

Enrico Bandello (Little Caesar)	Edward G. Robinson
Joe Massara	Douglas Fairbanks, Jr.
Olga Strassoff	Glenda Farrell
Tony Passa	William Collier, Jr.
Diamond Pete Montana	Ralph Ince
Otero	George E. Stone
Ma Magdalena	Lucille LaVerne
Sergeant Flaherty	Thomas Jackson
Sam Vettori	Stanley Fields
Arnie Lorch	Maurice Black

As one of the earliest of the gangster sound films, *Little Caesar* seems somewhat clichéd, but it is certainly not as loaded with clichés as the talkies' first gangster film, *Lights of New York* (1928)—at least no one suggests taking anyone for a ride. Its performers, however, have that bad early talkie habit of staring at the camera and declaiming their lines. The film does introduce a number of clichés, such as the poor but honest Italian mother who wants her gangster son to go straight; the basically decent gangster who is turned off by the killings and the violence and who meets the girl who will try to save him; and the gangster who turns "yellow" and is wiped out by the mob.

Little Caesar must take responsibility for the popularity of the gangster films in the 1930's. It is the natural precursor of two of the greatest gangster films of all time, *The Public Enemy* (1931) and *Scarface: The Shame of the Nation* (1932). In fact, the author of the novel on which *Little Caesar* is based, W. R. Burnett, was coscriptwriter of *Scarface*. Surprisingly, Edward G. Robinson did not become typecast as a gangster after this film. He did play gangster roles in *Smart Money* (1931), *The Little Giant* (1933), *Brother Orchid* (1940), and *Key Largo* (1948), but he is not as closely associated with the genre as, for example, is Humphrey Bogart.

While glorifying the gangster despite its best intentions, *Little Caesar* does try to preach against the crimes and criminals it depicts in such graphic detail.

The opening title is a quote from St. Matthew, "For all them that take the sword shall perish by the sword."

Enrico Bandello (Edward G. Robinson) and his partner, Joe Massara (Douglas Fairbanks, Jr.) are introduced as two small-town gangsters. Bandello is a punk in every sense of the word, and, despite his rise to power, he never comes across to the audience as anything else but a punk. The two men go to the big city—never identified, but presumably either Chicago or New York—where Bandello becomes a member of Sam Vettori's gang, while Joe becomes a dancing partner to Olga Strassoff (Glenda Farrell) at a smart nightclub. Olga tries to help Joe get away from his gangland connections, but, as he tells her, "Once in a gang—you know the rest. . . . You can't go back on a gang."

Joe is correct, for when Vettori's gang plans a robbery of the nightclub on New Year's Eve, Joe is forced to act as their "inside man." In so doing, he sees Enrico shoot and kill the crime commissioner, who is leaving the club in disgust having discovered that it is partly financed by gangster Arnie Lorch (Maurice Black). Instead of becoming scared at what he has done, the murder makes Enrico brave, and he takes over the gang from Vettori. One gang member, however, Tony Passa (William Collier, Jr.), who had driven the getaway car, becomes terrified. Collier's performance as Passa is the worst in the film; his nervous histrionics are totally unbelievable. His mother reminds him, "You used to be a good boy, Antonio. Remember when you sang in the church." He does remember, and it is to the church he goes, but as he climbs its steps in the snow to Italian lullabies playing on the sound track, he is gunned down by Enrico. It is a powerful moment in the film—it has no dialogue, just music and gunshots—made more powerful by the melodramatic speeches which have preceded it.

In true gangland fashion, Tony Passa is given a hero's funeral, which is followed, the same evening, by a dinner in honor of Enrico. At the dinner, Enrico receives a gold watch—which proves to have been stolen from his fellow gangsters—receives a visit from Sergeant Flaherty (Thomas Jackson) of the police department, and has his photograph taken for the newspapers. Enrico has become "Little Caesar," and the other gangster bosses have reason to be concerned. Arnie Lorch plans to have him killed, but Enrico is only shot in the arm. Now that Vettori has been pushed to one side, Lorch is next. Enrico visits him at his headquarters and persuades the gangster to leave town and return to Detroit; he even plants a gossip item in the newspaper about Lorch's departure.

"The Big Boy," who runs the city and all the gangsters in it, invites Enrico to his home, and hands over Lorch's territory to him. Enrico is obviously impressed by "The Big Boy" and his style of living, which he soon attempts to ape. Just as "The Big Boy" offered him cocktails or a splash of brandy, he offers the same to Joe. He wears jewelry—a diamond tie pin and rings—

like fellow gangster "Diamond" Pete Montana (Ralph Ince). The trappings, however, mean little, for beneath them, Enrico is still crude, vulgar, and cheap, a product of the gutter. As he stands before a full-length mirror dressed in all his finery while one of his henchmen, Otero (George E. Stone), applauds his appearance, all we see is a little man who has grown too big for his boots, a minor crook who is out of his league.

In the end, it is Joe who brings about Enrico's downfall. To save himself and Olga, he turns Enrico in to the police, and, for once, Enrico cannot kill, even though Joe's death might mean his escape. Some critics have suggested that there might be a homosexual relationship between Enrico and Joe, and there is, perhaps, a vague hint of this. Enrico is certainly never seen with women and seems to have no need of their company.

Enrico is no longer the bigshot; he came from the gutter, and now he returns to it. He is forced to hand over his money to an old hag, Ma Magdalena, wonderfully played by veteran character actress Lucille LaVerne, in return for her hiding him from the police. The man who could order the death of anyone in the city must now rely for the safety of his own life on an old woman. We next see Enrico in a flophouse, dirty and unshaven; he snarls—sounding like what he is, nothing more than a dog—as he listens to an old man reading from the newspaper in which Sergeant Flaherty calls Enrico a coward. Just as Flaherty had known he would, Enrico telephones him, the call is traced, and the police go after Enrico. As he walks, a slight, lonely figure, down a dirty, windswept city street, the police track him down. Behind a gigantic poster advertising Joe Massara and Olga Strassoff in a new show, *Tipsy, Topsy, Turvy*, Enrico hides. The police spray the poster with machine-gun fire, and Enrico falls. His last words are, "Mother of mercy, is this the end of Rico?" He dies in the gutter.

From a technical point of view, *Little Caesar* is competently directed, but it lacks something; at times, it almost drags, with the camera usually remaining static. As critics at the time of its release noted, the production might well be described as ordinary were it not for Burnett's story and Edward G. Robinson's magnificent portrayal of the central character.

Anthony Slide

THE LITTLE MINISTER

Released: 1934
Production: Pandro S. Berman for RKO/Radio
Direction: Richard Wallace
Screenplay: Jane Murfin, Sarah Y. Mason, and Victor Heerman; based on the play and novel of the same name by James M. Barrie
Cinematography: Henry W. Gerrard
Editing: William Hamilton
Running time: 110 minutes

Principal characters:
Babbie	Katharine Hepburn
Gavin Dishart	John Beal
Rob Dow	Alan Hale
Wearyworld	Andy Clyde
Mrs. Dishart	Beryl Mercer
Lord Rintoul	Frank Conroy

The Little Minister was an extremely popular vehicle for five decades. Sir James M. Barrie first wrote it as a novel in 1891 and eight years later turned it into a play. The play was a huge success in both England and America, with Maude Adams playing the lead role of Lady Babbie in the American production. The work was also produced as a silent film at least twice, most notably with Betty Compson in 1921. Ruth Chatterton revived the play on Broadway in the 1920's, and Adams returned to it in a radio performance in the 1930's. Katharine Hepburn, a great admirer of Adams, wanted to play Lady Babbie also and in 1934 starred in the RKO production of the work.

Despite its long history and many productions, *The Little Minister* presented difficulties for the screenwriters assigned by RKO, with at least five different writers working on it at one time or another, the principal work being done by the husband and wife team of Victor Heerman and Sarah Y. Mason— winners of an Oscar the previous year for their script for *Little Women.* Fortunately, these difficulties are not evident in the finished film, which is a charming tale of the romance between a minister and an aristocratic young woman in nineteenth century Scotland.

There are, in fact, three stories interwoven in *The Little Minister*: the minister's efforts to establish himself in a new church and a new village, the poor weavers' rebellion against the authorities, and the romance between the minister and the young woman who appears to be a gypsy. Each story complicates the other two, and near the end all three seem destined for catastrophe, but by the end most of the problems are solved and Babbie and the little minister are happy together.

We first learn about the minister and his situation. After the title has established that we are in the village of Thrums in 1840, we soon see a crowd awaiting the arrival of the new minister, Gavin Dishart (John Beal). When he arrives, many people remark on his short stature, a fact of which he is painfully aware and which he tries to minimize by wearing a tall hat whenever possible. (When Hepburn first met Beal, she reportedly told him he was too tall for the role, but for the filming he wore shoes with very thin heels, which made him short enough to satisfy her.) He has brought his mother (Beryl Mercer) to live with him, and we find that both are depending on this position to give them an income above the bare minimum upon which they have been subsisting. In addition, it is Gavin's chance to prove himself, and his mother's happiness, it is made clear, depends upon her son becoming a respected member of the community. Gavin passes his first test when he is heckled during a church service by Rob Dow (Alan Hale, Sr.), a huge, uncouth drunkard. Gavin shows no fear in facing down the challenger and, in fact, persuades him to quit his drinking. Gavin gains the respect of his parishioners for his courage as well as the devotion of Rob Dow.

The little minister first meets Babbie (Katharine Hepburn), the young gypsy woman, when he hears her singing, an intrusion upon the traditional propriety of the Scottish sabbath. Gavin, who has earlier been tolerant of villagers who are not members of his church, shows no such tolerance for this gypsy, whom he regards as simply too much of an outsider. He reads her the warning to gypsies posted by the village and tries to get her to go away. The weavers, we learn, are not at all satisfied with their lot and frequently try to rebel. Their rebellions, however, are put down by soldiers sent by Lord Rintoul (Frank Conroy). Babbie tries, usually quite successfully, to protect the weavers by warning them when the soldiers are coming.

The three parts of the story come together as Gavin, against his will, begins to fall in love with Babbie. The romance threatens to destroy his position in the community because his parishioners are no more tolerant of gypsies than he was at first, so his love for Babbie could cost him all he has worked for, both for himself and for his mother. Indeed, even Rob Dow, Gavin finds, is disillusioned and will go back to drinking if he does not give up Babbie. We also learn of a further complication; Babbie is not the gypsy she seems to be but the ward and fiancée of Lord Rintoul. At one point she resolves to give up Gavin for the good of himself, his mother, and his parishioners. She writes him a note saying that she will not be back, burns her gypsy clothes, and prepares to marry Lord Rintoul.

Babbie and Gavin do get back together, however, and the climax comes on a dark and stormy night after the little minister forgets to attend a prayer meeting because he is with Babbie. A delegation of elders goes to the manse to dismiss him while Gavin goes to church. When he tries to enter, he is prevented and then is accidentally stabbed with a knife by Rob Dow in the ensuing scuffle. He is carried home unconscious but revives enough to declare his love for Babbie in the presence of the elders, the villagers, and his mother. Babbie's true identity is then revealed and her engagement to Lord Rintoul canceled, clearing the way for her acceptance by all and a happy ending uniting her with the little minister.

Although it is reported that Hepburn was satisfied with neither the director, Richard Wallace, nor the finished film, both she and Beal, as Gavin Dishart, do a fine job with the material. Hepburn conveys both the lightheartedness of the gypsy role and the intensity of her love for the little minister. Mercer handles as well as possible the overly sentimental role of the minister's mother, and Andy Clyde gives a delightful performance as Wearyworld, the comic policeman who is, because of his position, befriended by no one and is given to such pronouncements as, "It's a wary world, and women is the most un-canniest things in it." All in all, *The Little Minister* emerges as an enjoyably entertaining work that shows none of the problems and doubts that beset its production.

Marilynn Wilson

THE LITTLE SHOP OF HORRORS

Released: 1960
Production: Roger Corman for Santa Clara; released by Filmgroup
Direction: Roger Corman
Screenplay: Charles B. Griffith
Cinematography: Archie Dalzell
Editing: Marshall Neilan, Jr.
Art direction: Daniel Haller
Running time: 70 minutes

Principal characters:
Seymour Krelboin .... Jonathan Haze
Audrey .... Jackie Joseph
Gravas Mushnik .... Mel Welles
Dental patient .... Jack Nicholson

To appreciate fully the work of Roger Corman, often referred to as "King of the 'B's," it is first necessary to cast aside that misleading title, which simplifies and somewhat obscures his accomplishments as a filmmaker. Strictly speaking, Corman never made "B"-films. He began his career in the early 1950's, at a time when the traditional "B"-film, the staple of double bills and Saturday matinees, was nearing its demise. For more than two decades, the low-budget feature film served a particular function for its audiences and occupied a well-defined position within the economic structure of the motion picture industry. "B"-films were the "junk food" of Hollywood, usually competently made and easily digestible, but rarely exceptional. They were manufactured according to a strict formula—limited budgets, tight shooting schedules, familiar plots, stereotyped characters, and even a scaled-down "star system" consisting of hundreds of Hollywood's lesser lights who were no less beloved by their fans than the more famous ones.

During the 1930's and 1940's, when motion pictures were still the preeminent form of mass entertainment in America and Hollywood the principal supplier, the production and distribution of the "B"-films was so carefully tailored for the relatively stable market that their profitability, while modest, was virtually assured. The major producers relied on their "B"-programs as a solid backup for the somewhat riskier big-budget ventures, while many other companies—known collectively as Hollywood's "poverty row" studios—turned out low-budget programmers exclusively. The advent of television in the late 1940's, however, precipitated a radical reordering of the film industry, and the traditional "B"-film was one of the primary casualties. There were, of course, many other contributing factors, but it was television that most directly usurped the form and function of the "B"-film—and at no cost to its audiences. This did not mean the death of low-budget filmmaking, but it did signal the need for a redefinition of methods and objectives. The career of Corman, more than that of any other individual, reflects the new direction the makers of such films would take.

The changes in the motion picture business during the 1950's—decreased attendance, the breakdown of the previously set differentiation between "A"-films and "B"-films, the breakup of the vertical integration of the industry (that is, ownership of theaters by production companies) by Federal court order in 1948—all added up to increased competition for a diminished box-office dollar. In the mad scramble for public favor, producers of big-budget films opted for technological extravagance—the wide-screen, color, cast-of-thousands approach that was obviously beyond the resources of all but the major studios. For their part, low-budget filmmakers cannily directed their product toward one particular segment of American society which was not interested in staying at home and watching television—teenagers. The films that pointed the way toward the developing "youth market" were major Hollywood productions such as *The Wild One* (1954), *Blackboard Jungle* (1955), *Rebel Without a Cause* (1956), and others—but it was the independent producers who exploited this market to the fullest. While they did not necessarily invent the most popular genres of the 1950's—science fiction, motorcycle and hot-rod films, dramas of troubled youth, and rock 'n' roll musicals—they exploited them shamelessly. Topicality and sensation were the hallmarks, and advertising became even more important than before. To lure their audiences, films had to promise something special—exotic, daring, exciting, shocking—and unavailable on television. The basis of the traditional "B"-film—the careful preplanning and relatively reliable financial outcome—was gone; the high-risk atmosphere made low-budget filmmaking a much more adventurous enterprise than in previous years. Budgets were squeezed even more tightly, shooting schedules more breakneck than ever; producers, with one eye on the headlines and the other on box-office receipts, tried to read the public pulse, rushing to capitalize on anything that smelled like a popular trend. In such a highly competitive milieu, quality was usually a minor consideration.

It was in this atmosphere that Corman's career began. Following a few odd jobs in the industry, he made his first script sale, a crime melodrama called *Highway Dragnet*, in 1953; combining the proceeds from that enterprise with his other meager resources, he formed his own company and produced *Monster from the Ocean Floor* (1954). This science-fiction "epic," in a clear presaging of his later career, was shot in six days on a miniscule twelve-thousand-dollar budget. His next production, another criminal-on-the-lam story entitled *The Fast and the Furious* (1954), became the first film to be released by James H. Nicholson and his partner Samuel Z. Arkoff; it provided the basis for their formation of American International Pictures, the first notable corporate success in the "new" Hollywood. The early fortunes of AIP and of Corman were almost inseparable. Corman's output over the next fifteen years totaled sixty-eight films, most of which he produced, and forty-eight of which he directed; all but a few of these were profitable, and most were released by AIP.

Corman began directing with *Five Guns West* (1955). While some of his early efforts were in the more traditional genres such as Westerns and gangster films, by the end of the decade he had tried his hand at many others—science fiction (*It Conquered the World*, 1956, and *War of the Satellites*, 1957), rock music dramas (*Rock All Night*, 1957), teen melodramas (*Teenage Doll*, 1957, and *Sorority Girl*, 1957), black comedy (*A Bucket of Blood*, 1959), and a few films which defy generic classification (*Teenage Caveman*, 1958, and *Viking Women and the Sea Serpent*, 1957). Many of the twenty-three films of Corman's first five years as a director were crudely exploitative, but few are unwatchably bad, and a handful are remarkably good—notably *Machine Gun Kelly* (1958), *Teenage Doll*, and *A Bucket of Blood*. Corman was obviously feeling his way, learning his craft under the adverse circumstances imposed by severe budgetary limitations, and the overall quality of his work is only a modest cut above that of other low-budget directors of the period. His work during this period, however, does show the development of a fluid, striking visual style— clear, dynamic, and occasionally graceful—that would flower more fully in his post-1960 films. His early films, particularly those in collaboration with cinematographer Floyd Crosby, display an intelligent, inventive use of the black-and-white, wide-screen format—and a consistent avoidance of the static, visually awkward quality of many wide-screen Hollywood productions of the decade.

The Little Shop of Horrors (1960) is one of Corman's most remarkable films, not merely because it was shot in the phenomenal time of only two days (and a night), but because it manages, in spite of its extremely limited material resources, to be funny, imaginative, and entertaining. It is black comedy of the purest sort and lends itself as well to serious analysis of its social satire. The story concerns simple-minded schlemiel Seymour Krelboin (Jonathan Haze, in a performance clearly derivative of Jerry Lewis), who works in a Skid Row flower shop as an assistant to greedy florist Gravas Mushnik (Mel Welles) and is in love with Mushnik's daughter Audrey (Jackie Joseph). Seymour is frustrated at his lot in life and at his inability to gain respect and social acceptance. One night, while in the shop tending to a mysterious young Venus flytraplike plant that seems near death, Seymour accidentally cuts his finger. His blood then drips onto the plant, which is immediately revitalized. It slurps up the spilled blood, all the while grunting and groaning ecstatically. Appalled by his discovery of the fern's grisley diet, Seymour is nevertheless gratified by the praise he receives when others witness the miraculous recovery of the unusual plant. Sensing the great potential of his chance notoriety, Seymour christens the plant "Audrey, Jr.," in honor of

Miss Mushnik, and in secret continues to appease its morbid appetite by squeezing his other nine fingers dry. Realizing that he cannot himself give blood indefinitely, he agonizes over a substitute. Audrey, Jr., meanwhile, begins to speak! "Feeeeeeed me! I'm huuuuuungry!" it implores.

That night, wandering the streets in despair, Seymour startles a tramp, who in his panic stumbles into the path of an oncoming train and is killed. Although at first Seymour is upset and guilt-stricken over his role in the man's death, it soon occurs to him that the problem of sustenance for Audrey, Jr., has been solved, albeit temporarily. He feeds the body, piece by piece, to the voracious plant. Spurred by this extravagant feast, the fiendish fern begins to grow at a phenomenal rate, attracting even more attention from the local community; Seymour, taking credit for the plant's prodigious development is at last winning the affections of Audrey and the admiration of her fame-starved father. The ravenous plant, however, becomes increasingly demanding—and vocal. Driven by a desperate need to maintain his tenuous grip on his newfound fame, Seymour embarks on a series of murders—a streetwalker, an obnoxious neighbor, and a sadistic dentist—to provide food for Audrey, Jr. As the plant grows to gigantic proportions, Seymour is presented with a trophy from a local organization, and a horticultural magazine expresses an interest in photographing the gruesome greenery. Mushnik holds an exhibition to celebrate these events, but at the most inopportune moment, the plant blooms—revealing in each of its enormous flowers the terrified face of one of Seymour's victims. A wild chase ensues; eluding his pursuers, Seymour returns to the shop that night and confronts his creation. Despondent at his dead-end situation, he blames the plant and suicidally attacks it; the next morning, Mushnik and Audrey discover Seymour's face in one of the plant's flowers.

Corman says that *The Little Shop of Horrors* "was the film that in the long run has made me whatever legend I am." He recalls that it was made as a kind of "joking challenge" when a studio manager offered him the use of a store set. Working with writer Charles B. Griffith, a frequent collaborator, he developed a rough outline, which Griffith turned into a script in a week; the film was then shot at breakneck speed. Corman and Griffith used the premise of an earlier collaboration, *A Bucket of Blood*, as a taking-off point. In that film, aspiring artist Walter Paisley (Dick Miller), working as a busboy in a beatnik coffee house, discovers that the corpse of his accidentally slain pet cat—covered in clay—is hailed by the beat crowd as a brilliant work of sculpture. Eventually, as in *The Little Shop of Horrors*, he is forced to go on a murder spree to supply "models," and when discovered, he creates his ultimate "work of art" by covering his body with clay and hanging himself. *A Bucket of Blood* was also a horror comedy; it was shot on the relatively expansive schedule of five days, yet *The Little Shop of Horrors* is a superior film.

Both films have an undercurrent of biting social satire, but the particular ethnic flavor of *The Little Shop of Horrors* lends its some additional weight. Seymour Krelboin and the Mushniks are lower-middle-class Jews in a generalized urban ghetto milieu; Seymour's innocence quickly succumbs to his literally murderous social climbing. He sacrifices his humanity in order to increase his social status; ultimately, the source of his success becomes the instrument of his destruction. The film is implicitly critical of this sort of ambition, portraying it as physically and morally destructive. Serious considerations aside, however, the film is frequently hilarious—the repartee between Seymour and Audrey, Jr., is priceless (the plant's vocabulary consisting entirely of variously modulated pleas for more food), and among other small delights, the goings-on include a bizarre cameo appearance by a young Jack Nicholson as a masochistic dental patient. *The Little Shop of Horrors* has quite deservedly gained a cult following among film buffs.

   The Little Shop of Horrors, in the circumstances and spirit of its production, is the crowning achievement of Corman's early directorial career. It comes significantly in the middle of an important transitional period. That same year, he also produced and directed *House of Usher*, the first in his series of Edgar Allan Poe "adaptations," a few of which were reasonably faithful to their sources, others being mere borrowings of titles. It is for this group of films that Corman is most widely known as a director; during the next several years, he directed *The Pit and the Pendulum* (1961), *The Premature Burial* (1961), *Tales of Terror* (1961), *The Raven* (1962), *The Haunted Palace* (1963), *Tomb of Ligeia* (1964), and *The Masque of the Red Death* (1964). Shot on comparatively extravagant three-week schedules, in color, and with budgets that could have financed a half-dozen of his earlier films (although still quite low by general Hollywood standards), the Poe films were extremely profitable. They also exhibited an increasingly complex and ambitious visual style and gained Corman some slight attention in critical circles. (British critic Penelope Houston referred to them as "Roger Corman's elegant arabesques of horror. ") The mainstay of the series was Vincent Price, who starred in all except *The Premature Burial*, but the films' appeal was enhanced by the occasional presence of such charismatic veterans as Ray Milland, Boris Karloff, Peter Lorre, Basil Rathbone, and Lon Chaney, Jr. Several of the Poe films—particulary *The Pit and the Pendulum* and *Tomb of Ligeia*—rank among Corman's best work as a director.

   It was also during this period that Corman made his only foray into "serious" filmmaking with *The Intruder* (1961), a drama of racial tension in the American South, adapted by Charles Beaumont from his own novel. Its impact enhanced by location shooting (on a typically low budget), *The Intruder* was a solid and compelling film, featuring a superb performance by William Shatner as a rabble-rousing bigot. As socially conscious melodrama in the Stanley Kramer vein, it is superior to many better-know essays on the same theme, as well as being several years ahead of its time in its cinematic treatment of school desegregation in the Deep South. The film received excellent reviews and won prizes at several film festivals, but at the box office it was a dismal failure, one of only a small handful in Corman's career. While he remains justifiably proud of *The Intruder*, it was probably this factor that dissuaded him from similar ventures after that time. For the rest of his directorial career, while hardly avoiding themes and subject of social importance—*The Wild Angels* (1966), *The Trip* (1967), and *Gas-s-s-s* (1969) are valuable reflections of contemporary American society, regardless of their strengths or weaknesses as films—Corman generally couched his "statements" more firmly in the context of entertainment. In retrospect, it is interesting to speculate on the quite different direction his career might have taken had *The Intruder* been a box-office hit.

In 1970, following several years of decreased activity as a director and bad experiences with the distribution of his last few films, Corman abandoned the director's chair to form his own production and distribution organization, New World Pictures. Essentially, New World is a corporate extension of Corman—not only in his continuation, from an executive position, of the same well-honed principles of budgetary tightness and no-nonsense commercialism that contributed significantly to the success of American International, but in his more serious aspirations as well. In this sense, New World is a somewhat schizophrenic operation. From *The Student Nurses* (1970) and *Women in Cages* (1971) through *Grand Theft Auto* (1977) and *Humanoids From the Deep* (1980), Corman's mainstay remains the low-budget, trend-following, profit-making "exploitation" films which he pioneered in the 1950's. Yet his company has also imported and distributed such films as Ingmar Bergman's *Cries and Whispers* (1976) and *Autumn Sonata* (1978), Federico Fellini's *Amarcord* (1974), François Truffaut's *The Story of Adele H.* (1975), Akira Kurosawa's *Dersu Uzala* (1978), and Volker Schlöndorff's *The Tin Drum* (1979), as well as backing "prestige" films such as *I Never Promised You a Rose Garden* (1977) and Peter Bogdanovich's *Saint Jack* (1979). Artistic considerations aside, however, Corman has always been a canny businessman, and under his guiding hand New World has become one of the most successful Hollywood ventures of the 1970's. His success, coupled with the degree of control he exercises over his production program, makes him the spiritual heir to such old-time Hollywood moguls as Jack Warner, Darryl F. Zanuck, and Louis B. Mayer.

In addition to Corman the director and Corman the producer/studio head, there is a third Corman: the mentor. His nurturing of potentially important film talent is another key element of his status in the film industry; he has long been known for his willingness to give young, untested filmmakers an opportunity to learn their craft as he once did, toiling under the pressures imposed by tight schedules and small budgets. His motives for this policy are perhaps more economic than altruistic, but the list of Corman "alumni" is nevertheless impressive: Francis Ford Coppola, Martin Scorsese, Peter Bog-danovich, Robert Towne, Jack Nicholson, Jonathan Demme, Bruce Dern, and Peter Fonda, among others, all received valuable experience working for Corman early in their careers—experience without which there may never have been films such as *The Godfather* (1972), *The Last Picture Show* (1971), *Mean Streets* (1973), *Easy Rider* (1969), and *Chinatown* (1974), all important, influential films. With all his activities taken into account, Corman emerges as far more than "King of the 'B's"; he has obviously had a major influence, directly and indirectly, on both the commercial and artistic shape of the American cinema for more than two decades.

Corman as a director, however, is a figure of critical controversy. Consideration of his films as cinematic art invariably leads directly into the "art versus money" argument which pervades much film criticism. Unable to come to grips with the concept of a true "commercial art form," many critics cannot see—or refuse to look—beyond the generally exploitative surfaces of Corman's films. Indeed, their perception is easily clouded by the titles alone: can the creator of such lurid-sounding films as *Teenage Doll*, *The Wasp Woman* (1959), *A Bucket of Blood*, *The Trip*, *The Man with the X-ray Eyes* (1963), and dozens of others be taken seriously as an artist? The official tastemakers tend to say no, although they may nod in Corman's direction out of sociological interest—a fertile, although obvious, field for exploration of his prolific output.

As a reaction to this narrow, elitist attitude, there have been attempts to elevate Corman to the status of a full-fledged *auteur*, postulating (to quote one example) that his body of work is "a series of comments and variations on the theme of sacred time, largely expressed in terms of the Myth of the Eternal Return." This position seems equally extremist, a manifestaiton of the generally undisciplined nature of film criticism and of the often perverse desire to elevate the obscure at the expense of the established. While the first approach demonstrates a blindness to the complex nature of film as an art form, the latter displays a riotous lack of perspective on Corman's work. It is obvious from Corman's own statements that he is primarily a businessman with a constant eye on a film's finances; as a director (a position he seems in no hurry to resume after a decade in the executive's chair), he regards himself as an entertainer, not an artist. It should be remembered, however, that the American cinema's main purpose has always been entertainment, and that some of the directors who are now acknowledged to be among our greatest film artists—such as Howard Hawks and Alfred Hitchcock—were equally modest about their achievements and were overlooked or denigrated as "mere" entertainers by many critics.

At the very least, Corman's films exhibit a prodigious financial resource-fulness that is in itself a form of virtuosity, a cinematic grace that often belies the film's tawdry subject matter, a compelling dynamism that easily eclipses the work of many better-known filmmakers, and a keen awareness of the currents and rhythms of American life. Perhaps one day the influence and quality of Corman's work will be fully appreciated by critics and historians—as they always have been, anonymously, by film audiences.

Howard H. Prouty

LIVES OF A BENGAL LANCER

Released: 1935
Production: Louis D. Lighton for Paramount
Direction: Henry Hathaway
Screenplay: Waldemar Young, John L. Balderston, and Achmed Abdullah; based on Grover Jones and William Slavens McNutt's adaptation of the novel of the same name by Major Francis Yeats-Brown
Cinematography: Charles Lang
Editing: Ellsworth Hoagland
Running time: 109 minutes

Principal characters:
Captain McGregor	Gary Cooper
Lieutenant Forsythe	Franchot Tone
Lieutenant Stone	Richard Cromwell
Colonel Stone	Sir Guy Standing
Major Hamilton	C. Aubrey Smith
Mohammed Khan	Douglas Dumbrille
Emir	Akim Tamiroff
Hamzulla Khan	Monte Blue
Tania Volkanskaya	Kathleen Burke
Lieutenant Barrett	Colin Tapley
Grand Vizier	J. Carrol Naish

From 1935 to 1939, there flourished a species of motion picture dealing with imperialism in India, Africa, and in one instance the Philippines. There had been a few forerunners *Beau Geste*, 1926; (*Beau Sabreur*, 1928; and *Four Feathers*, 1929); but the genre really started with *Lives of a Bengal Lancer*, released by Paramount in January, 1935. A week later, Fox released *Olive of India*. These inspired a number of others during the next four years, among them *The Last Outpost* (1935), *The Charge of the Light Brigade* (1936), *Wee Willie Winkie* (1937), *Gunga Din, The Sun Never Sets*, and remakes of *Four Feathers* and *Beau Geste*, all in 1939. Although two of these were set in the French Foreign Legion and one other dealt with Americans during the Filipino insurrection—*The Real Glory* (1939)—all of them were basically Kipling-esque, that is, inspired by the works of Rudyard Kipling. Their appeal lay in a combination of swashbuckling adventure, exotic locales, swarming hordes of dark-skinned antagonists, and a celebration of the alleged military virtues of comradeship, loyalty, stiff-upper-lip courage, self-sacrifice, and duty to the service and one's country. Never were the pith helmet and the kepi so prominent in Hollywood. The cast of these films became almost a stock company, with Ronald Colman, Gary Cooper, Douglas Fairbanks, Jr., David Niven, Cary Grant, Victor McLaglen, Errol Flynn, Nigel Bruce, and C. Aubrey

Smith all doing their best for the cause of the Empire.

Lives of a Bengal Lancer is not only the first of these films, but also one of the best. Often rated as one of the great adventure films of all time, it is based very loosely upon a book of the same title by Major Francis Yeats-Brown, but the screenplay by Waldemar Young, John Balderston, and Achmed Abdullah is essentially an original work of fiction. Set in India's northwest frontier in the vicinity of the Khyber Pass, it begins when two new officers, Lieutenants Forsythe (Franchot Tone) and Stone (Richard Cromwell), are assigned to the 41st Regiment of the Bengal Lancers, commanded by Colonel Stone (Sir Guy Standing). The Colonel is a completely professional soldier, a fair but rigid disciplinarian. Although Lieutenant Stone is his only son whom he has not seen for years, he receives him with the same cold, official courtesy with which he treats the other officers. Young Stone, on his first assignment, is crushed at what he takes to be a total rejection by his father, but the Colonel insists that there is no place for sentiment in the army. His sterness toward his son is actually a neurotic fear of appearing weak by letting his genuine emotions show. He is deeply moved at meeting his son again but cannot let himself appear vulnerable.

The two new officers are assigned to share quarters with Captain McGregor (Gary Cooper), a veteran of frontier warfare. A Canadian of Scottish descent, McGregor has a gruff exterior that masks a warm and humorous personality. Lieutenant Forsythe, a dapper sophisticate, enjoys baiting McGregor with his flippant wit, but Forsythe is also a superb horseman and a dashing soldier; he and McGregor respect each other and strike up a comradeship that consists on the surface of their trying to one-up each other. McGregor is a crotchety individualist, and his frequent defiance of authority appeals to an irreverent streak in Forsythe. Lieutenant Stone, on the other hand, is a baby-faced novice. Not only is he embittered by his father's aloofness, he also lacks the toughness necessary if he is to survive in the Bengal Lancers. The two older, more experienced officers take him under their wing; and although Forsythe taunts the Captain with being "Mother McGregor," he too acts like a father or at least a big brother to the fledgling Stone.

McGregor is given command of a detachment to find Lieutenant Barrett (Colin Tapley), who has gone undercover to gather intelligence about the mountain tribes. He learns from Barrett that Mohammed Khan (Douglass Dumbrille), a supposed ally of the British, has been organizing the tribes into a mutinous confederacy. Mohammed Khan has promised them two million rounds of ammunition to use in the planned uprising. When McGregor reports to the Colonel, the latter informs him that the precise amount of ammunition is to be delivered to the friendly Emir of Gopal (Akim Tamiroff), who is about to have a week of boar-hunting to which Mohammed Khan is invited. The Colonel arranges for the regiment to attend as well; after all, the hunters go after the boars with lances, and he wants to show what the Lancers can do.

During the hunt, Lieutenant Stone in unhorsed and endangered by a charging boar. The Colonel tries to rescue his son and is wounded before Captain McGregor kills the boar. Even though he has risked his life for his son, the Colonel continues to treat him with official detachment, and the immature lieutenant only becomes more resentful. During the festivities at the Emir's palace, a ravishing *femme fatale* (Kathleen Burke) flirts with all the younger officers but succeeds in snaring only Lieutenant Stone. She turns out to be a Russian spy named Tania Volkanskaya in league with Mohammed Khan; together, they kidnap Stone and carry him off as a hostage to the Khan's mountain fortress. Expecting a trap and refusing to risk the lives of his men out of sentimental concern for his son, Colonel Stone refuses to send a rescue expedition.

Thereupon McGregor and Forsythe go A.W.O.L. to rescue Lieutenant Stone themselves. Disguised as bearded pilgrims, they succeed in entering the fort but are discovered and captured. Mohammed Khan demands that they tell him the route of the ammunition train; when they refuse, he has them tortured with burning splinters placed beneath their fingernails. They endure the pain with stoic fortitude and refuse to speak, but Lieutenant Stone, feeling betrayed by the father who will not try to rescue him, lets anger toward the Colonel and fear of torture outweigh the honor of the regiment and gives Mohammed Khan the information. The Khan successfully ambushes the ammunition train, and from the window of their dungeon, the prisoners see it arrive in the fort.

Although he would not go to rescue his son, Colonel Stone responds to military necessity and sends the regiment to attack the fort. The prisoners realize that the Khan has baited a trap for the Lancers. As the attack begins, they succeed in breaking out of the dungeon. McGregor and Forsythe plan to blow up the ammunition dump, and because they know it is a suicidal mission, each man volunteers to do it alone. In a moment of *noblesse oblige*, McGregor knocks Forsythe out, sacrifices himself for his friend, blows up the arsenal, and dies in the action. Lieutenant Stone, now repentant for his cowardice, redeems himself by fighting his way to the fortress wall and diving off it onto Mohammed Khan as he is about to gallop out of the great gate. He stabs the Khan to death, and the mutineers surrender. Father and son are reunited and come to understand each other. At a regimental parade several weeks later, the Colonel awards the D.S.O. to Lieutenants Forsythe and Stone and pins the Victoria Cross on the saddle of Captain McGregor's horse.

Lives of a Bengal Lancer was distinguished by superior direction, script, performances, and production values. Director Henry Hathaway blended extensive footage shot several years earlier in India by a documentary film expedition headed by Ernest Schoedsack with elaborate studio sets and outdoor action scenes shot at the Paramount ranch. The extravagant sets were so impressive that Cecil B. De Mille used them again later that year for *The Crusades*. *Lives of a Bengal Lancer* was nominated for six Academy Awards; best picture, director, editor, scenario, sound recording, and second unit direction; it won in the last category. None of the performers was nominated, but the cast is outstanding. As Captain McGregor, Cooper cuts a dashing figure with a thin mustache (Cooper wore a mustache in only one other film, *Peter Ibbetson*, also made in 1935), a turban, and colorful uniforms. Since Cooper's American speech would be implausible for an Englishman, McGregor was made a Canadian. Cooper's laconic, tight-lipped character and Tone's suave, smirking satirist were effective foils to each other and to the immature vulnerability of Cromwell's unseasoned lieutenant. Their friction generates a good deal of humor throughout the film. As Colonel Stone, Standing is the incarnation of the stiff-upper-lip Victorian officer.

Reviewers praised the picture for its virility; the *London Daily Telegraph* called it "the best army picture ever made." Its portrayal of the comradeship of three men recalls both Kipling's *Soldiers Three* stories and the three brothers in *Beau Geste*; in turn, it anticipates *Gunga Din*, *The Real Glory*, and the remake of *Beau Geste*. All are basically stories of men without women.

Critics observed that the Kiplingesque adventure film set in India or the Sudan had a great deal in common with the American cavalry Western: outdoor military adventure in similar mountain and desert settings, with dark-skinned tribesmen as the enemy. Actually, the Kiplingesque films are more spectacular; the locations and costumes are more exotic, and the forts and palaces make the Western sets look shabby by contrast. Nevertheless, *Lives of a Bengal Lancer* was redone in 1939 as a low-budget Western entitled *Geronimo*; the basic plot was kept intact and only the setting changed.

The cycle of adventure films celebrating imperialism peaked in 1939 with six films; then it abruptly disappeared for eleven years. In the early 1950's, the genre was resurrected briefly with *Kim* (1951), *Soldiers Three* (1951), *Bengal Brigade* (1954), and *King of the Khyber Rifles* (1954), but these lacked the vigor and panache of the 1930's films. *Zulu* (1964), *Khartoum* (1966), *The Wind and the Lion* (1975), and *The Man Who Would Be King* (1975) were worthy successors, with more complex characterizations and a more complex view of history, but they were labeled anachronistic. The glories of the British Empire have departed, and we no longer respond to the strains of "The British Grenadiers." In the period during and after the Vietnamese War, military glory in general and imperialism in particular have been distinctly out of fashion and no longer appeal to a disenchanted public. A review of *Zulu Dawn* (1980) called it a film that should not have been made. *The Man Who Would Be King* succeeded because its adventurers failed; the story could be seen as a criticism of imperial conquest.

During its heyday, however, the spectacular adventure film set in the far-flung reaches of empire offered stirring escapist fare; and if one discounted the politics of imperialism—which were not the films' major concern in any case—they extolled the virtues of *noblesse oblige*, honor, comradeship, and courage. These values too are no longer universally in fashion, and we might do well to be reminded of them.

Robert E. Morsberger

THE LODGER

Released: 1944
Production: Robert Bassler for Twentieth Century-Fox
Direction: John Brahm
Screenplay: Barre Lyndon; based on the novel of the same name by Marie
Belloc-Lowndes
Cinematography: Lucien Ballard
Editing: J. Watson Webb, Jr.
Running time: 83 minutes

Principal characters:
Kitty Langley	Merle Oberon
John Warwick	George Sanders
The Lodger	Laird Cregar
Robert Burton	Sir Cedric Hardwicke
Ellen Burton	Sara Allgood

The ghoulish career of England's Jack the Ripper, who butchered five prostitutes in the alleys of Whitechapel between August 31 and November 9, 1888, has proven a subject of a bizarre but perpetual fascination for cinemagoers. Indeed, the Ripper's celluloid slaughters have been international, be he raving through an expressionistic landscape in the German *Waxworks* of 1924 or battling Sherlock Holmes in 1965's British *A Study in Terror*. There have been no less than five screen versions of *The Lodger*, Marie Belloc-Lowndes' novel based on the murderer's atrocities. Although Alfred Hitchcock's offbeat silent version in 1926, with Ivor Novello as a Christlike red herring, has proven to be of the most interest to scholars since it was Hitchcock's first feature-length effort, the most famous, striking, and best-remembered screen treatment of the Ripper's bloody reign is Twentieth Century-Fox's 1944 version of *The Lodger*. It is a florid, chilling costume melodrama with Laird Cregar as the most mad, most anguished, and most fascinating of screen Rippers.

Fox began production on *The Lodger* during an interesting transitional period in Hollywood in which sex was becoming an increasingly obvious factor in cinema melodrama. Even in the "B" thrillers cranked out at Universal, a werewolf, mummy, or ape woman rarely capered about without a nightgown-clad heroine nearby to scream and swoon at its perfidy. *The Lodger*'s scriptwriter Barre Lyndon devoted the most screen time to the charms of music-hall actress Kitty Langley, played by a tempting and rouged Merle Oberon, sporting a spicy array of tights and lacy pants. The role of the Lodger—depicted as a shy, Bible-quoting zealot whose brother's ruin caused by an actress has triggered his insanity—was entrusted to Fox's ace character star,

Cregar. This six-foot, three-inch, thirty-year-old actor, weighing three hundred and twenty-eight pounds, had won a peculiar stardom as the perverted cop who kept his apartment as a shrine to dead Carole Landis in Fox's *I Wake Up Screaming* (1941). Since that triumph, he had appeared time and again as an obese ogre, displaying intriguing sexual nuances as he menaced such alluring ladies as Veronica Lake in Paramount's *This Gun for Hire* and Michele Morgan in RKO's *Joan of Paris* (both 1942). His most recent part had been in Fox's *Heaven Can Wait* (1943), as Lucifer himself. In *The Lodger*, however, Cregar had to accept third billing under Oberon and George Sanders, who suavely plays the Scotland Yard Inspector who becomes Kitty's beau and the Ripper's nemesis.

Under the direction of the underrated John Brahm, *The Lodger* opens on a dreary Whitechapel street, where an old floozy is singing her way out of a tavern. She passes into an alley. We hear her exchange a few pleasantries with a stranger; and then her bloodcurdling scream echoes through the cobbled streets. Shortly afterward, as a newsboy spreads the news of the Ripper's latest murder, a stranger (Laird Cregar) calls at the home of Robert Burton (Sir Cedric Hardwicke) and his wife Ellen (Sara Allgood), who have a room to rent. The audience knows immediately, through Brahm's ominous angles and Cregar's hypnotic acting, that this tenant is the Ripper—especially after his face subtly contorts at the sight of the Burtons' niece, Kitty Langley (Merle Oberon), whose French Can-Can dance act in the Whitechapel music hall is making her the rage of London.

The Lodger soon reveals his various neuroses. He turns the portraits of actresses which hang on his wall around backwards, claiming that their eyes appear to be mocking him. He is discovered burning his bag and a strangely stained cloak in the furnace, and, in a beautifully played scene, he reveals to Mrs. Burton the story of his brother's demise, almost surrendering to hysteria as he stares lovingly at his portrait and asks her, "Have you ever seen eyes like that on a man?" He has strange and morbid conversations with Kitty, staring at her as he condemns the evil of actresses who "exhibit the loveliness of their body on the stage as a lure . . . leading men on. . . ."

The film's climax takes place in the music hall. After watching Kitty and her girls perform their Can-Can, the Lodger furtively enters Kitty's dressing room: "Men will not look at you again as they did tonight!," he states. Before his knife can strike, however, Scotland Yard Inspector John Warwick (George Sanders) crashes into the room, wounding the wildly insane Ripper, who then leads the police in a mad chase throughout the catwalks and eaves of the theater before plunging out of an attic window and crashing into the river below.

All of the ingredients of the *The Lodger* mesh perfectly. Brahm's direction is superb. His gloomy interpretation of the seedy Whitechapel district (the same backlot set used by Fox in 1943's *The Song of Bernadette*) creates an atmosphere of decay and evil, as if the decayed area is a panorama of the Ripper's decayed soul. In one unforgettable vignette, the camera *becomes* the Ripper, approaching with quavering hysteria an aged prostitute who becomes paralyzed with fright. Oberon, always an exquisite beauty, makes a lovely Kitty, possessed of charm and theatrical allure. Sanders, of course, is suavely authoritative as the Inspector and Hardwicke and Allgood are authentically apprehensive as the landlord and landlady. It is Cregar, however, who is the great asset of *The Lodger*. With his silky voice and tormented eyes, he gives a magnificent performance, building from the shy, Bible-quoting Lodger to the manic-eyed, knife-slashing, gasping fiend. He even manages, with disturbing pathos and an inoffensive sensationalism, to suggest perversities in his madness that were only faintly suggested in Lyndon's original script. The pathetic longing in his eyes as he gapes at the portrait of his dead brother suggests a tragic theme of incest. The peaceful lilt in his voice as he assures Kitty that the beauty of a woman improves when the evil is cut out—". . . Then it is still. . . . Then it is even more beautiful. . . ."—intimates a chilling necrophilia. With such macabre garnishments, Cregar creates a truly haunting and terrifying character.

Released in January of 1944, *The Lodger* proved a great success. *New York Newspaper PM* called it ". . . undoubtedly the best Jack-the-Ripper movie ever made," while the *New York Herald Tribune* praised the film's ". . . grim psychopathic underlining . . . ," noting that ". . . it becomes something of a Kraft-Ebbing case history of a sex maniac." A small minority of critics opined that the piece was too theatrical and Cregar's performance too flamboyant, and a few sages unsportingly pointed out that fingerprinting, used in the film to clinch the Ripper's identity, was not yet a practice with Scotland Yard in 1888. Nevertheless, such carping was lost in the applause that greeted *The Lodger*, which became a box-office hit and established Cregar as a major star.

In reality Cregar was a tormented homosexual with a longing to play romantic leads, and he had strenuously dieted during the filming of *The Lodger* in hopes of realizing this dream. He was also disturbed by the "sick" fan mail he received from psychopaths who either perversely congratulated him on his screen insanities or sadistically detailed with self-righteous glee the methods by which they would like to kill him. His next and last film was the melodrama *Hangover Square* (1944), also with Robert Bassler, Brahm, Lyndon, and Sanders. After dieting to lose more than one hundred pounds and undergoing an abdominal operation to control his food intake, Cregar suffered two heart attacks and died on December 9, 1944, at the age of thirty-one.

Whatever private demons Cregar brought to *The Lodger* still serve the film powerfully today. *The Lodger* remains the Jack-the-Ripper film par excellence—a gloriously theatrical, genuinely frightening, and ultimately moving exploration of the evil that can infect and destroy the human soul.

Gregory William Mank

LOLITA

Released: 1962
Production: James B. Harris for Metro-Goldwyn-Mayer
Direction: Stanley Kubrick
Screenplay: Vladimir Nabokov; based on his novel of the same name
Cinematography: Oswald Morris
Editing: Anthony Harvey
Music: Nelson Riddle
Running time: 152 minutes

Principal characters:
Humbert Humbert .... James Mason
Lolita Haze ....Sue Lyon
Charlotte Haze ....Shelley Winters
Clare Quilty ....Peter Sellers
Dick (Lolita's husband) .... Gary Cockrell

The story of *Lolita* begins at the end. Humbert Humbert (James Mason), a middle-aged British scholar, arrives at the baroque mansion of television writer, Clare Quilty (Peter Sellers), with whom he engages in cryptic banter before pulling a gun and shooting him. The rest of the film recalls the events, beginning four years earlier, that have led to this bizarre killing.

During his tenure at a small New England college, Humbert rents a room in the house of Charlotte Haze (Shelley Winters), a sex-starved widow with an alluring young daughter, Lolita (Sue Lyon). Humbert's passions are so aroused by Lolita that he marries Charlotte simply to be near the child. Charlotte's nagging possessiveness soon awakens murderous instincts in Humbert, but he is saved the trouble of killing her when she discovers his secret passion for Lolita by reading his diary and then hysterically runs into the path of an oncoming automobile. Following her death, Humbert finally seduces the not-so-naïve Lolita; they become lovers and begin a nomadic existence, but their affair quickly disintegrates because of Humbert's jealous nature, which is fueled by the intrusion of Clare Quilty in various disguises. Finally, Lolita disappears; some time later, Humbert receives word that she is married and pregnant and goes to visit her. She tells him that she had left him for Quilty, who had in turn abandoned her. Humbert begs her to come back to him, but she prefers instead to remain with her husband (Gary Cockrell), a dull but good-hearted young man. A broken man, Humbert gives her all his money and then sets off to find and kill Quilty. A final title informs us that Humbert died in prison while awaiting trial for Quilty's murder.

The key line in the publicity for *Lolita* was "How did they ever make a movie out of *Lolita*?," and most discussions of director Stanley Kubrick's adaptation of Vladimir Nabokov's celebrated novel of a middle-aged man's sexual obsession with a prepubescent girl seem to begin by questioning the film's faithfulness to its source. This, in fact, was a matter of widespread speculation from the moment the project was announced, at which time the book was still recognized more because of its "sensational" subject matter than its considerable literary value. The problem of realistically portraying Humbert Humbert's pursuit and seduction of the nymphet Lolita while also satisfying censorship requirements was, of course, one of Kubrick's prime concerns. He engaged Nabokov to adapt his own work for the screen, and after six months of work, the author produced a four-hundred-page screenplay which would have run seven hours on the screen. Kubrick understandably rejected it, and Nabokov wrote a much shorter version, which was in turn extensively revised by Kubrick and producer James B. Harris. The final screenplay was only about twenty percent Nabokov's, although he received sole screen credit for the adaptation.

Ultimately, Kubrick's answer to the problem was found in a combination of treatment and casting—the book's twelve-year-old Lolita became a girl of no specific age in the film, and was played by fourteen-year-old Sue Lyon, whom most critics felt seemed closer to seventeen. Not only was Lolita thus made to seem more of a woman than a child, but also Kubrick's handling of the Humbert-Lolita relationship makes it seem that Humbert's initial and primary motivation is not so much lust as "love," in a more or less traditional movie sense. This aspect is emphasized by Nelson Riddle's musical score.

Another major alteration was the transposition of the murder of Quilty from the end of the novel to the opening of the film. This has two major effects—since the chain of events leading to the shooting is presented in a single long flashback, the movie takes on something of the nature of a mystery story which is visually reinforced by the excellent low-key black-and-white cinematography of Oswald Morris. Also, as at least one critic has noted, Humbert Humbert is thus initially introduced to the viewer in the *persona* of killer/avenging lover rather than pervert—the former apparently more acceptable to the censors.

Many of the film's critics, misunderstanding the essential problem of adaptation, are unable to see beyond such thematic and structural alterations as those discussed above. Their furor over the "betrayal" of Nabokov's work has blinded them to the considerable merits of *Lolita* as a film. It is also relevant in this context to note that Nabokov himself has called *Lolita* "a first-rate film with magnificent actors" and Kubrick "a great director," and that the placing of Quilty's murder at the beginning of the film was a point of agreement between him and Kubrick early in their collaboration. Taken on its own terms, Kubrick's film is as thoroughly engaging and witty a black comedy as has ever graced the screen. He plays the Humbert-mother-daughter triangle for all its delicious, offbeat, and occasionally morbid humor and obtains a great deal of bizarre comic mileage out of the various permutations of the Clare Quilty character. Irony is strong throughout, particularly in the manner in which Humbert's Lolita is finally delivered to him just when things look darkest, via her mother's freakish death.

Mason is excellent as Humbert Humbert, whose obsession destroys his pride and ultimately his life. Winters vividly portrays the hilariously (and unconsciously) provincial Mrs. Haze, whose shrewishness and whining stupidity are matched only by her sexual hunger. Lyon, despite the carping of contemporary critics, is perfect as Kubrick's Lolita (as distinct from Nabokov's), her performance managing to suggest much of the woman-child sexual appeal which motivates Humbert, and capturing what Nabokov described as Lolita's "eerie vulgarity."

The real standout of the film, however, is Sellers in the role (or roles) of the eccentric, scheming Clare Quilty. The part is a *tour de force* for Sellers, since Quilty bedevils Humbert throughout the film in various forms, including two entirely fabricated personalities (a conventioneering police detective and a school psychologist, "Dr. Zemph"), and at one point he is merely a mysterious voice over the telephone. For each role, Quilty employs a different set of physical and vocal disguises designed to conceal his identity from Humbert while at the same time disturbing him in ways which ultimately contribute to his breakup with Lolita—which is, of course, Quilty's goal all along. Sellers' portrayals are astounding in their versatility—so distinctive and bizarre that they are often both hilarious and unsettling to watch, thus strongly suggesting the discomfort felt by Humbert who does not have the viewer's advantage of being able to see the humor in the situation. Reportedly, much of Quilty's dialogue and business were improvised by Sellers and Kubrick. The result is one of the most amazing multiple performances in cinema history, perfectly in tune with Lolita's final summation of Quilty: "He wasn't like you and me. He wasn't a normal person."

Because of the critical shortsightedness mentioned above, *Lolita* is one of Kubrick's most underrated films. It maintains the viewer's interest throughout its running time of more than two-and-one-half hours, no mean feat in itself, and succeeds in being unfailingly entertaining and original. In some ways, it may be seen as a warmup for Kubrick's next film, the black comedy masterpiece *Dr. Strangelove* (1964), in which Sellers repeats his multiple role-playing, again proving his genius.

Although set in America, *Lolita* was Kubrick's first film to be produced in England. All his subsequent projects have been filmed there also, although he still considers himself an American director. *Lolita* was also the first of an unbroken string of films over which he has had complete artistic control; he had resolved to insist upon such control following his unpleasant experience with the producers of his previous film, *Spartacus* (1960). To this day, whether in triumph as with *2001: A Space Odyssey* (1968) or folly with *Barry Lyndon* (1975), Kubrick has maintained his independence and remains one of the most distinctive talents at work in motion pictures. Although the film *Lolita* has been thought by many critics to lack the depth of Nabokov's original novel, it still shines as a cinematic work of art and in retrospect is far better an interpretation of the story than Edward Albee's 1981 Broadway adaptation which closed shortly after its premiere.

Howard H. Prouty

LONELY ARE THE BRAVE

Released: 1962
Production: Edward Lewis for Universal
Direction: David Miller
Screenplay: Dalton Trumbo; based on the novel *Brave Cowboy* by Edward
  Abbey
Cinematography: Philip H. Lathrop
Editing: Leon Barsha
Running time: 107 minutes

Principal characters:
Jack Burns	Kirk Douglas
Jerri Bondi	Gena Rowlands
Sheriff Johnson	Walter Matthau
Paul Bondi	Michael Kane
Truck Driver	Carroll O'Connor
Gutierrez	George Kennedy

Lonely Are the Brave is a moving film about a man who is unable to adapt to the world in which he finds himself. He is a loner unable to accommodate his desires to other people's needs, a cowboy in a time when cowboys are almost obsolete. He is a free spirit unfit for a world of fences and of laws, a child unable, or perhaps unwilling, to grow up. Jack Burns has our admiration throughout, because we share his desire to be independent and because he seems completely free of malice. The film, however, is not simply an exercise in fantasy. Life is not easy for Jack Burns or for the people who are his friends. We see that his way is unworkable, no matter how much we might want it to succeed.

Lonely Are the Brave is a Western, but it is a Western with a difference. The classical Western, such as *High Noon* (1952), is set in the past and presents a conflict between outlaws and civilized people. In such a film the outlaws represent an almost complete anarchy while the townspeople stand for order or civilization. The hero, often a lawman, is a middleman who has some of the same skills and drives as do the outlaws but who uses them for the benefit of the town—of civilization. *Lonely Are the Brave*, however, is set in the present, and the old categories of outlaw, hero, and civilization are difficult to apply. It is a time and a film in which the old values and skills are out of place, in which the "hero" no longer fights for civilization, but instead finds it to be his antagonist. Two other Westerns in the early 1960's explore similar themes. In *The Misfits* (1961), modern "cowboys" are reduced to capturing wild horses for dog food, and in *Ride the High Country* (1962) two aging exlawmen try to cope with a West in which they have become irrelevant.

The basic conflict of *Lonely Are the Brave* is established in the opening

Are the Brave*

sequence. We see the barren landscape of New Mexico and Jack Burns (Kirk Douglas) waking up beside a campfire as jets fly overhead. He regards them without anger although they represent the forces which will soon defeat him. Jack mounts his horse, Whisky, and rides to the house of Paul (Michael Kane) and Jerri Bondi (Gena Rowlands). His friend Paul has been convicted of helping illegal Mexican immigrants and is in the local jail awaiting his transfer to the penitentiary. Jack has come to help him break out of jail. To Jack the situation is simple; he hides two hacksaw blades in his boots and gets himself thrown into jail so that he and Paul can then escape. The situation is not so simple to Paul, however, and he refuses to leave; Jack escapes alone. He is then pursued by the local sheriff and other lawmen as he tries to reach the Mexican border.

By the time of the jailbreak we know what kind of a man Jack Burns is. We have seen him, as he rides across the range, cutting a barbed wire fence and going through it rather than around it. We have seen that he, unlike everyone else, rides a horse and has no driver's licence, no social security card, no identification at all, much to the surprise and displeasure of the police who book him. Perhaps most importantly we have seen that he is loyal to a friend. We have also seen the manner in which he is different from his friends Jerri and Paul. Jerri does not understand Jack's defiance of laws and limits. For her the issue is simple: "You go by the rules or you lose." This Jack dismisses as merely an "Eastern" attitude. Indeed, it is a standard theme of the Western that women represent the values of civilization and the family. Paul, however, has Jack's independent spirit but is trying to come to terms with the world in which he lives. It is an effective scene in the jail cell as the two old friends argue about whether Paul will escape with Jack. Paul and Jerri can go with him, Jack argues, and rear their son, Seth, as a natural man—an idea he and Paul have often discussed. Paul, however, has decided that he can endure jail because Jerri and Seth are waiting for him, and he does not want them to have to run or hide—ever. "You grew up on me, didn't you?" asks Jack. Jack, however, remains determined to go his own way regardless of the consequences and escapes from the jail.

After the jailbreak Jack has to cross a mountain ridge and a highway to reach a forest which will hide him en route to Mexico. He gets started well ahead of the lawmen, but we soon see the inequality of the contest as Sheriff Johnson (Walter Matthau) goes after him in a jeep with a two-way radio. Other lawmen, including Gutierrez (George Kennedy), a sadistic policeman who beat him up while he was in jail, are hunting him from other directions. Even a jeep cannot follow a horse in the rugged terrain, and Jack keeps out of sight of the men who are hunting him. Then, a military general from a nearby Airbase sends two men in a helicopter to give them some practical experience in pursuing criminals.

Jack Burns, then, is facing three quite different opponents. Gutierrez is driven by pure hatred, while the men in the helicopter have the arrogant feeling that their machine can conquer any problem; they claim they have the ability to pick the fugitive off a treetop if they want to. Less intense and more human is the sheriff. He knows that his job is to capture Jack, and he performs that job as well as he can, but he does so without arrogance or animosity. In fact, more than once he reveals his admiration for Jack as well as his disdain for the attitude of the other lawmen. "For two bits I'd call the whole thing off," he says at one point, and when Jack makes it to the top of the mountain ridge, the sheriff says, "You son of a gun, you did it." When the men in the helicopter try a foolish tactic and are shot down, the sheriff remarks sarcastically that they got a "bellyful" of practical experience.

Jack never shows hatred in this contest with the lawmen. Indeed, he goes out of his way to be considerate of his pursuers. When the helicopter men see him and one of them starts down a rope ladder to capture him, he does not shoot to kill but merely shoots the tail rudder of the craft so that it goes down slowly. Later, Gutierrez comes down a rope from the top of the ridge, thinking he has trapped Jack. When Jack comes out of hiding, he has a perfect chance to take revenge on the man who beat him up in the jail; instead, he merely knocks him out and throws away his guns. In fact, it is the innate kindness of Jack Burns that is his undoing almost as much as the technological advantages of his pursuers. His horse Whisky helps him until he is near the top of the ridge, but as the slope gets steeper, Whisky becomes more hindrance than help. Jack briefly considers abandoning him, but instead laboriously pulls the animal up to the rim.

When he mounts Whisky and rides down the other side of the mountain, he has only to cross a highway to reach the forest and almost certain freedom. The weather, however, decides Jack's fate as rain begins to fall, soon becoming a downpour. Trying to cross the highway, Whisky becomes confused by the lights and cars; he stops, and is struck by a huge diesel truck. In the confusion that follows we see Jack Burns lying at the side of the road, alive, but unable to move or speak. His eyes tell us eloquently, however, that he feels like a wild animal that has been wounded and captured. When he hears the pistol shot which puts Whisky out of his misery, Jack's spirit seems to ebb. The only discernible emotion in his eyes is one of fear. We know that this is the end of Jack Burns even though he is still alive when an ambulance comes and takes him away. In the last image of the film we see its whole theme: Jack's cowboy hat lying on the highway in the rain. The anachronistic free spirit has lost to the new technological world.

It is easy to see why this is one of the films of which Douglas is most proud. Indeed, he chose the story and put up part of the money to have it made. His portrayal of Jack Burns is the greatest strength of this strong film. Douglas delineates a character who is kind, likable, and open. His performance contains no showy emotional scenes, yet his artistry is evident, particularly in the final sequence, in which he conveys deep emotion by using only his eyes.

The rest of the cast contains many actors who would later become famous: Matthau as Sheriff Johnson, Rowlands as Jerri Bondi, Kennedy as Gutierrez, and Carroll O'Connor as the truck driver. Along with Kane as Paul Bondi, they provide excellent support. The script by Dalton Trumbo, from the novel *Brave Cowboy* by Edward Abbey, has excellent dialogue, especially in the scenes between Jack and Jerri and Jack and Paul. An unnecessary contrivance in the script, although it does not mar the film as a whole, is the appearance throughout the film of the truck which eventually hits Burns and his horse. At the beginning of the film this is merely confusing, and near the end it is too obvious.

Credit for the quality of *Lonely Are the Brave* must go not only to the acting and the script but also to the cinematography of Philip H. Lathrop. The black-and-white compositions forcefully depict both the sunny, nearly barren New Mexico landscape at the beginning and the later scenes in the bar, the jail, and finally in the rain. Even though it was praised by nearly all reviewers, the film was not commercially successful. Through the years, however, it has acquired a large following of people who recognize the well-written and well-acted treatment of the theme of the individual against society and its rules.

Timothy W. Johnson

THE LONG, HOT SUMMER

Released: 1958
Production: Jerry Wald for Twentieth Century-Fox
Direction: Martin Ritt
Screenplay: Irving Ravetch and Harriet Frank, Jr.; based on the short stories,
   "Barn Burning" and "Spotted Horses," and a part of the novel *The Hamlet*,
   all by William Faulkner
Cinematography: Joseph LaShelle
Editing: Louis R. Loeffler
Running time: 115 minutes

Principal characters:

Ben Quick	Paul Newman
Clara Varner	Joanne Woodward
Jody Varner	Anthony Franciosa
Varner	Orson Welles
Eula Varner	Lee Remick
Minnie Littlejohn	Angela Lansbury
Alan Stewart	Richard Anderson

Martin Ritt's films usually evoke strong, lasting characterizations and place an emphasis on personal relationships. Ritt is especially skillful in dealing with love and conflict, which are the key elements of *The Long, Hot Summer*, a melodramatic Tennessee Williams-flavored tale based on three works by William Faulkner and sporting hearty doses of melodrama and sex. Critics of the day compared the film to *Peyton Place*; both pictures were produced by Jerry Wald.

What distinguishes *The Long, Hot Summer* are its vivid, larger-than-life characters; the film is an exceptional ensemble piece. It also marks the first collaboration between Ritt and Paul Newman, cast here as Mississippi vagabond Ben Quick. In this film, Newman makes his first screen appearance opposite his wife Joanne Woodward, with whom he has since frequently costarred. Two short stories by William Faulkner, as well as a portion of his novel *The Hamlet* are the basis for this episodic motion picture. At the core of the production is brash Will Varner (Orson Welles), a Southern patriarch reminiscent of Big Daddy from Williams' *Cat on a Hot Tin Roof*, which was released as a film the same year as *The Long, Hot Summer*.

Varner is a crusty manipulator; he controls the county, owning the biggest farm, the town bank, and the hardware store, among other things, and he controls his family as well. From his first moments onscreen (he arrives in a siren-screaming ambulance, following recuperation from an operation in a manner again reminiscent of *Cat on a Hot Tin Roof*), to the closing scenes filled with his laughter, Varner is a hulking, dominating figure. He has a mistress, Minnie Littlejohn (Angela Lansbury), whom he will not marry, a son Jody (Anthony Franciosa) who fears him, and a daughter Clara (Joanne Woodward), who is his adversary. Jody nearly crumbles in his presence. During Varner's absence, Jody and his sexy, playful wife, Eula (Lee Remick), enjoy a much-needed bit of freedom, but upon his father's return, Jody once again becomes a mass of nerves. "Look at my hands, Papa," he laments, his voice shaking, "and all the time you were away they didn't sweat—not once." Clara, whom Varner calls Sister, is the object of her father's reproach because, at the age of twenty-three, she remains unmarried. A prim schoolteacher, she can nevertheless display a sly, sensual quality. This quality goes unnoticed by her sweetheart of five years, Alan Stewart (Richard Anderson), who is pale, well-bred, dignified, and extremely mother-dominated.

Into the already shaky lives of the Varners comes outsider Ben Quick. He is a man with a reputation as a barnburner—a serious offense—as well as a conniving spirit. He is the perfect match for Varner. The two embark on a wonderful battle of wits, with Clara and Jody their unfortunate pawns. While Varner and Quick are two of a kind, Varner is, initially, angered to learn that, in his absence, Jody rented the newcomer a small sharecropper farm. Varner does not want a barnburner on his grounds. After meeting Quick, however, Varner sees in him a mirror image. Impressed with what he sees, he puts Quick to a test by having him auction off a bunch of bad (wild) horses. Quick pulls it off, selling the horses to a group of gullible farmers. Varner, who applauds Quick's con-man spirit, invites him to dinner. Later, Varner invites Quick to live on Varner land—a farming area rumored to be the site of a cache of treasure dating to the Civil War.

When Varner takes to Quick, both Jody and Clara feel threatened. Clara dislikes Quick because, in mannerisms, he reminds her of her father. The weak-willed Jody envies Quick and is also hurt that his father seems to favor Quick over him. Jody's concerns are well-founded, because Varner gives the newcomer Jody's job as manager of the main store. With the aggressive Quick (with his intriguing reputation) running the store, business picks up. In a depressed state, Jody begins spending his days at home, much to the irritation of his wife.

Thick with Southern drawls (it is sometimes hard to decipher Varner's dialogue), *The Long, Hot Summer* evokes a dusty, humid backdrop, complete with such familiar Southern trappings as the big white mansion, the homespun general store, and the box-lunch picnic. The script's dialogue also smolders with sexual passion; Varner alludes to it boldly; Clara's sly humor also suggests it. Jody and Eula cavort on the porch on sultry summer nights; Varner pays visits to Minnie; and Clara feels her sexual responses being awakened because of Quick. Confused by her feelings, she cruelly lashes out at Quick about his barnburning reputation.

Varner, who has witnessed anger between the two, also senses a chemistry between them. Desperate for a grandchild, he gives Clara an edict—get married, or else. He tells her she can marry either Quick or Alan, although he would prefer Quick. Infuriated and bewildered, Clara musters up the nerve to ask Alan about his feelings toward her. Awkwardly, he confesses that, although he is "extremely fond" of her, his devotion belongs to his mother. Clara is left to reexamine her thoughts about Quick.

Jody, in the meantime, still angry about being usurped, threatens to shoot Quick. Retaliating with a cruel tactic, Quick salts his land with a bag of silver dollars and insists they are part of the legendary buried treasure. Jody, hungry for recognition, pays Quick a thousand dollars for the land. He is still digging and hunting when his father comes upon him around midnight. Varner, who immediately spots Quick's scheme, humiliates his son, and Jody's hatred then shifts to his father. Jody wants to kill Varner, and he gets his chance when Varner goes into the barn to check on a mare that has foaled. Closing the doors, Jody starts a fire. News of a burning barn sends a lynch mob after Quick, but Clara comes to his defense. She has discovered that he inherited his reputation—a reputation that really belonged to his father. Jody also has second thoughts, and releases his father from the fiery barn.

During the film's final moments, relationships fall happily into place. Jody's defiant act makes his father see him with renewed respect, and Jody and Eula's marriage, which had begun to fall apart, is saved. Clara and Quick also reveal their love for each other. Varner, who smugly believes he has manipulated these moves, is also tricked into a marriage proposal by his longtime love, Minnie.

The Long, Hot Summer was popular with audiences, but it did not generate any Oscar nominations, although Newman won the Best Actor Award at Cannes that year. The Ritt-Newman collaboration was now under way, and among their work is the poorly received but intriguing *The Outrage* (1964), based on Japanese director Akira Kurosawa's *Rashoman* (1951), as well as *Hombre* (1967), a study of a white man reared with Indians. Their most celebrated effort is *Hud*, the 1963 film in which Newman effectively interprets the role of an enigmatic Texas heel. In addition to initiating the Ritt-Newman collaboration, *The Long, Hot Summer* showcased the work of then relative newcomers Woodward, Franciosa, and Remick. Lansbury is delightful as the clever Minnie Littlejohn, and Welles, who was then, at age forty-two, a staggering 275 pounds, had a field day with the colorful role of Will Varner.

Pat H. Broeske

THE LONGEST DAY

Released: 1962
Production: Darryl F. Zanuck for Twentieth Century-Fox
Direction: Ken Annakin, Andrew Marton, and Bernhard Wicki
Screenplay: Cornelius Ryan, Romain Gary, James Jones, David Pursall, and Jack Sedden
Cinematography: Henri Persin, Walter Wottitz, Pierre Levent, and Jean Bourgoin
Editing: Samuel E. Beetley
Music: Maurice Jarre
Running time: 180 minutes

Principal characters:
Lieutenant Colonel
Benjamin Vandervoort .... John Wayne
Brigadier General Norman Cota .... Robert Mitchum
Brigadier General James M. Gavin ...... Robert Ryan
Private Dutch Schultz .... Richard Beymer
Private John Steele .... Red Buttons

Like the Allied success on D-Day, *The Longest Day* succeeded in spite of great obstacles and occasionally in spite of itself to become the greatest war film of all time. Described by its producer, Darryl Zanuck, as the "most ambitious undertaking since *Gone with the Wind* and *Birth of a Nation*," it was indeed the largest, most expensive war film produced up to that time. In fact, even Zanuck's son, who would later go on to fame as the producer of *Jaws* (1975), begged his father not to embark on the project. Although he would later spend at least as much money constructing and filming a mechanical shark, the younger Zanuck was nervous about spending several million dollars on a film. "What scared me," he said, "was that we were getting into an eight- or an eight-and-a-half-million-dollar picture, which at that time was really fantastic." Another problem was that Darryl Zanuck was considered almost washed-up in Hollywood. His son thought that going ahead with *The Longest Day* in an era when World War II was no longer relevant was "liable to really be the end of the line" since a major percentage of the 1960's moviegoing public had not even been born at that time.

The older Zanuck, never one to back away from a challenge, decided to go ahead with the production; indeed, he never expressed any doubts even when presented with almost insurmountable problems, and he purchased the film rights to Cornelius Ryan's book for $175,000. Since no films of the actual 1944 Normandy landings were available from military archives, no stock footage was available; thus, the entire invasion had to be staged. Further complicating this problem was a shortage of World War II vintage vehicles and equipment. Other films dealing with the invasion—such as *D-Day the Sixth of June* (1956), and *The Americanization of Emily* (1964)—surmounted the problem by emphasizing only small unit assaults and filming them on beaches north of Los Angeles. Zanuck would have none of this, however, insisting upon a documentary realism for his film. That he achieved this realism was attested to several years later when experts found that still photographs taken during the shooting were virtually indistinguishable from actual photos taken during the June 6, 1944, assault on the beaches of Normandy.

Putting together a filmable screenplay was the first major battle of the production. Zanuck was primarily interested in following "the brave, funny, bewildering, human and tragic events of the day," since he felt it was those characteristics that made Ryan's book rise above mere history. Additionally, the director wanted to recount the events on the enemy side during the invasion in order to avoid "a rosy, star-spangled-banner drawing of D-Day" which would inevitably make the film a failure. To accomplish his many objectives for the film, Zanuck hired Ryan himself to write the screenplay. This seemingly logical decision led to some unanticipated problems since Ryan had no experience working in film. He did know what happened on D-Day, however, and he wanted *The Longest Day* to portray precisely and completely all of the events that he had written about. As a writer, he could not appreciate the tyranny of the camera and did not recognize the need for some degree of compromise to ensure the dramatic visual impact vital to a motion picture.

Despite many changes in direction and a number of running battles between Zanuck and Ryan, the author turned in an extremely thick script; Zanuck was unhappy with it and redid the entire screenplay to suit his own needs. He also sought additional advice from writers in the major countries involved in the invasion, including Romain Gary and James Jones, the author of *From Here to Eternity*, who was employed specifically to make the GI dialogue sound more authentic. Jones's additions, like Ryan's, proved to be a double-edged sword. Although his dialogue was realistic, the Production Code Office would not approve its "casual profanity" as well as some of the obvious substitutions of euphemistic terms which still retained the ring and the spirit of the more vulgar words used by actual soldiers. The censors objected to "crap, muck it, mother lover, bastards, damn, and hell," as well as the lines such as "they couldn't sink this clucking can if they tried to." To complicate matters further, the Production Code Office objected to what they considered to be "an excessive amount of slaughter in the story." For the most part, Zanuck quietly ignored these concerns, but Jones reacted violently—"What did they think Omaha was, if not a bloodbath?" Faced with these problems and a continuing dialogue not only with his writers but also with the Pentagon, the revision of the script went slowly.

This delay in fact may have been providential since it gave the producer time to conduct a vast scavenger hunt across Europe to track down the scarce World War II matériel that he needed to depict the war. Many German weapons, particularly tanks, were uncovered in Spain, and a British tank buried for seventeen years in the sands of Normandy was exhumed and made serviceable. Guns were easier to come by and were collected all over Europe. A British company was located that had built the original gliders for the invasion, and they contributed two replicas for the film. Zanuck also found three British Spitfires in Belgium and two German Messerschmitts in Spain. This small air force proved to be enough since the coast of Europe was heavily overcast on D-Day and few planes could be seen. Thus Zanuck could still maintain a degree of accuracy without creating a massive flying force. Uniforms were also less of a problem since Allied costumes have changed little to this day, although the German uniforms had to be re-created from scratch.

By this point in the production, Zanuck had virtually assumed the role of supreme commander in supervising all aspects of the preparations. Yet there was one element beyond his control—the cooperation of the military forces of the countries involved in the original invasion. In order to save money, Zanuck had arranged to borrow a British fleet to re-create the original invasion task force. When British authorities informed him that a $300,000 fuel bill would have to be paid by the studio, however, the producer turned to the United States Sixth Fleet, which had amphibious maneuvers scheduled for Corsica.

Zanuck sent his associate, director Elma Williams, and six camera crews to the Mediterranean to attempt to film these maneuvers for use in the film; the commander of the marine assault force, however, expressed serious reservations based upon the relative inexperience of his men in performing beach assaults. Williams, in the best Hollywood tradition, convinced the marines that it would be better and more realistic for training purposes if the film crews re-created the Normandy beaches and set off explosive charges. Thus, by the time that the fleet arrived, the film crew had constructed obstacles along a two-mile stretch of beach, buried explosives, and erected machine-gun emplacements so that the shoreline looked like Omaha Beach as it had been on D-Day. At the same time, Zanuck had another crew, armed with the permission of the French authorities, burning the beach at Pointe du Hoc next to the real Omaha Beach landing area. (The actual site could not be used because of a prominent monument and buried live ammunition.) Film crews fortified the entire beach, fabricated shell holes, and built fortifications, sandbagging monuments in the process to look like bunkers.

The American Command in Germany supplied a battalion of Army Rangers and a unit of the 505th Infantry Battle Group to comprise the assault force and to prepare the film's actors for the cliff assault. Zanuck complicated their task by hiring Paul Anka, Tommy Sands, and Fabian, three rock-and-roll singers, along with veteran actor Robert Wagner, to portray soldiers in the four-minute sequence. Although this casting was calculated to bring younger viewers into the theater, the film crews on location were horrified at these selections for roles that would be physically difficult even for trained soldiers. This feeling was justified when Anka was immediately immobilized, first by sand in his eye and later by a torn fingernail. Eventually, however, the entire cast performed so perfectly that they actually had to be reminded to make some mistakes since things had definitely not gone perfectly on D-Day.

At this point in the production, Zanuck, in the minds of some military experts, was ranked ninth as a world power. He had at his disposal thirty-seven military advisers, thousands of United States servicemen, and twenty-two ships of the United States Sixth Fleet. In addition, he had one thousand British Paratroopers and two thousand French regulars (filming was done at the height of the Algerian crisis). To move all of these troops, he put together a fleet of jeeps, tanks, and halftracks as well as a large personal navy of assorted landing craft. "My job was even tougher than Ike's," Zanuck claimed. "He had the men and he had the equipment. I had to find both."

The men chosen for the film's leading roles included forty-two of the biggest names in motion pictures. The most prominent were John Wayne, Robert Mitchum, Henry Fonda, Richard Burton, Curt Jurgens, Robert Ryan, Rod Steiger, Robert Wagner, Richard Beymer, Mel Ferrer, Jeffrey Hunter, Peter Lawford, Kenneth More, Richard Todd, Eddie Albert, Edmund O'Brien, Red Buttons, Sal Mineo, Tommy Sands, and Fabian. They were supported by five scriptwriters and an equal number of directors. Some idea of the epic scale of *The Longest Day* can be gleaned from the fact that these different directors specialized in "British Exterior Episodes," "American Exterior Episodes," and "German Episodes." Additional episodes were added to Ryan's and Zanuck's original script by writers Gary, Jones, David Pursall, and Jack Seddon. Also prominent among the other advisers who worked on the film was Frau Rommel, whose husband Field Marshal Erwin Rommel, had first coined the phrase "the longest day" when he said, "The first twenty-four hours of the invasion will be decisive. For the Allies as well as Germany, it will be the longest day."

The Longest Day begins with the concentration of Allied forces along the coast of Britain. An air of nervousness reflects itself in the impatience of officers awaiting the fateful decision to attack and in the time-killing pastimes of sharply honed soldiers with nerves stretched to the breaking point, poised to go. Then comes the highly suspenseful moment when General Eisenhower has to make the critical decision whether the invasion will go or be postponed. The word comes to go, and Pathfinders are sent by air to parachute into Normandy at midnight and light the way for the paratroops to follow.

With the coming of daylight, there is the dull drone of the first landing craft piling in on the fortress-fringed Normandy beaches; then the artillery adds its thunder to the air, and bloody battles erupt along the bullet-strafed sands of the Utah and Omaha beaches as the Americans attack. Simultaneously, Sword, June, and Gold sectors are invaded by the British and Canadians. The camera captures the large-scale sweep of the operation by jumping back and forth from Britain to occupied France to the French Resistance fighters and finally to the paratroops in action behind the German lines. Thus, the film has no plot in the traditional sense. The invasion of the coast is depicted in vast panoramas as the camera sweeps from beach to beach. This technique captures the onslaught as a whole before the camera focuses on individual scenes of bloody combat both on the shore and in the interior. There is the fight of the French resistance fighters to capture the seaside town of Ouistreham and the rugged climb by American Rangers up the sheer face of the cliffs at Pointe du Hoc before the Germans realize what is happening. On the German side of the conflict, the camera captures the anxieties and activities of the troops behind the Atlantic Wall as they wait for the expected attack without knowing where it will come. All the way through the film the bickering and bunglings of the German generals are dramatically interspersed.

Again and again, *The Longest Day* portrays, with photographic realism, the confusion of battle and the horror of death. Some of the conflicts, particularly those that flare up in the darkness, are picturesque and exciting, while others provide a sense of comic relief from the tensions of combat. For example, one paratrooper falls from the skies and lands beside an old lady on her way to the outhouse; another visitor from the air lands in a well. Still other scenes, such as those of paratroops still in their chutes and harnesses swinging lifeless from battle-ravaged trees, lend a note of almost haunting poignancy.

While *The Longest Day* has no regular plot as does a typical dramatic film, Zanuck did not consider his film to be a documentary, but, rather, "the story of little people, of the underground and of general confusion." No one character is singled out as being more important, heroic, or cowardly than anyone else. Among the actors, Buttons is convincing in his portrayal of John Steele, who must watch the wholesale murders of his buddies in the town square of Sainte-Mere-Eglise while hanging from the church steeple by the entangled harness of his parachute. Beymer ably portrays a young soldier who wanders in a daze through the entire day separated from his outfit and never firing a shot. He has a poignant episode beside the body of a dead German and a badly wounded RAF pilot (Richard Burton). As the day is ending, the pilot says, "Funny isn't it? He's dead, I'm crippled, you're lost." Beymer replies, "I wonder who won." Wayne is appropriately rugged as Colonel Vandervoort, the tough officer of the 82nd division who hobbled through D-Day on a broken ankle using his rifle as a crutch. Mitchum does an equally convincing job in his portrayal of General Cota, who led his men of the 29th Division from the boats onto Omaha Beach and then off of it after a day of heavy pounding by the enemy. The tough officer led his men in a breach of the Vierville road-blocks.

The film's use of an elaborate cast of well-known actors has a structural value beyond the obvious one of publicity and star attraction. The familiar faces help the audience to identify the characters during battles and constantly changing scenes. Although some critics found these faces, particularly that of Wayne, a jarring experience that conjured up memories of other films, the average theatergoer found that these very memories added to the character-izations that Zanuck could not devote sufficient time to construct in detail. In other words, since the filmmakers could not go behind the scenes, indulge in incidental flashbacks, or establish character, if the audience could transfer its collective images of the Wayne *persona* from the Ringo Kid in *Stagecoach* (1939) to Sergeant Stryker in *The Sands of Iwo Jima* (1949), that is exactly the characterization that Zanuck wanted to imply. The same is true of his use of Mitchum, Ryan, and the rest.

The total effect, then, is one of an enormous documentary report colored by personal details; yet the film is not a documentary but a re-creation of the events of June 6, 1944. It may lack the feeling of a complete or definitive view of the event, but its job of exposition of a complex and sprawling subject is remarkably clear and exciting. Its realism is heightened by having the actors speak in their own languages with subtitles for the French and German ones instead of Hollywood's version of foreign accents. The use of different direc-tors for the national sequences keeps these episodes coherent and swiftly paced. The best scenes of this type are the ones of the German high command directed by Bernhard Wicki. These scenes avoid the pitfalls of making the Germans foils for the high comedy of D-Day and instead re-create an atmo-sphere of confusion and factual reaction to the momentous events of the day.

The action scenes are some of the most authentic and exciting ever filmed. While the motion picture is not necessarily a tribute to courage or a diatribe against war, the screen swarms with men and equipment, and the action is frenetic. D-Day was a long day and a large day; it was also a terrible and a necessary one. The film confronts this truth but makes no conclusive obser-vation other than the obvious one that the longest day was a gallant though costly triumph for the Allied forces. Zanuck saw the film as

> the story of David and Goliath, the triumph of the seemingly weak over the seemingly invincible. There were the Allies, weary of long years of war, of humiliating defeats, divided, uncertain, the knife at their throats, uniting in a combined attack that first broke the hold of Nazism and then broke its neck.

The Longest Day returned more than $17,500,000 in domestic rentals on an investment of close to $10,000,000, the most expensive black-and-white film ever made. The black-and-white cinematography gives it a virtual newsreel authenticity, particularly in the vivid, realistic battle scenes. Its success meant not only the rebirth of Zanuck's career but also the financial salvation of Twentieth Century-Fox. *The Longest Day* was to be the producer's last film. Shortly after its completion, he wrested control of the studio from Spyros Skouras and was elected president, a position he held until 1971. He died in retirement in 1979.

The Longest Day presents many aspects to its viewers. It is on the one hand a commercial drama, yet it is also a pseudodocumentary. Zanuck said that "If anybody acts in *The Longest Day*, it is unintentional. My job was to prevent actors from acting—to encourage them to play their individual roles realistically and without camera awareness." This technique worked because, as one of its writers stated, the film's production thoroughly resembled the war that it was attempting to portray. The film succeeds in spite of great obstacles. It would have failed, for example, if it had limited its focus to two or three characters; instead, it has no stars, but forty-two major cameo roles. It has no plot, and its portrayal emphasizes a particular moment in time. It has no beginning and no middle, and everyone knows the end; it builds no tension as the action unfolds. *The Longest Day* is the definitive combat film because of the authenticity of its action scenes and because Zanuck, like Cornelius Ryan before him, focuses on the men who fought the battles and their fears and miseries as well as on the courage that enabled the human spirit to survive the horror of war.

Stephen L. Hanson

THE LONGEST YARD

Released: 1974
Production: Albert S. Ruddy for Paramount
Direction: Robert Aldrich
Screenplay: Tracy Keenan Wynn; based on an original story by Albert S. Ruddy
Cinematography: Joseph Biroc
Editing: Michael Luciano
Running time: 120 minutes

Principal characters:

Paul Crewe	Burt Reynolds
Warden Hazen	Eddie Albert
Captain Knauer	Ed Lauter
Nate Scarboro	Michael Conrad
Caretaker	Jim Hampton
Granville	Harry Caesar
Pop	John Steadman
Unger	Charles Tyner
Rassmeusen	Mike Henry
Warden's Secretary	Bernadette Peters

The Longest Yard is a film which many have labeled sadistic, vicious, and totally manipulative. It is also very funny, however, which in the context of the other adjectives used to describe it seems comething of a dichotomy. Nevertheless, for all its violence, the film is entertaining, uplifting, and exhilarating.

The plot is simple: Paul Crewe (Burt Reynolds), is an ex-professional football player who lands in jail after stealing his wealthy girl friend's car and leading the police on a wild chase. While there seems to be no motivation for his totally irresponsible behavior, it does make for some exciting car stunts, and it sets the main character up for his changes in prison. When he arrives at the prison, he is presented to Warden Hazen (Eddie Albert), whose superficial friendliness covers a sadistic streak; actually, Hazen prides himself on maintaining a highly disciplined prison. Hazen, knowing of Crewe's football past, wants him to train the prison football team, made up of his guards, whom he wants to win a state prize. Crewe refuses because he does not want to get involved, and because the captain of the prison team, Knauer (Ed Lauter), beats him. Knauer is jealous of Crewe's former professional status.

Crewe soon learns that life in a prison can be hard and decides to play ball, figuratively and literally, with the warden. With the aid of an industrious inmate named Caretaker (Jim Hampton) and an aging ex-player, Nate Scarboro (Michael Conrad), they set out to organize a football team made up of prisoners with whom the guards can.practice. At first, the prisoners' reaction to Crewe and his aids is one of suspicion. Then they learn that Crewe was kicked out of professional football for point-shaving—an act which does not sit well with the primarily black population of the prison who love football. Nevertheless, Crewe convinces them of his sincerity and is soon on his way to the formation of a football team. He has also started his change of personality, moving toward involvement and self-respect. In the process of bolstering his team and providing it with more of a winning attitude, Crewe discovers that prisons are full of psychopaths and killers who find the idea of playing football against the guards very appealing.

With the team finally formed, Crewe, Caretaker, and Scarboro set out to train and prepare the men for their big game. Caretaker is particularly resourceful in this area, coming up with game films, medical records, x-rays of the guards' previous injuries (to help in the planning of new ones), food, vitamins, and equipment and uniforms originally earmarked for the guards but diverted to what is now known as "The Mean Machine." Not everyone is happy with what Crewe is doing for the prisoners. A stoolie named Unger (Charles Tyner), resentful of the way Crewe has snubbed him and isolated him from the team, mistakenly kills Caretaker in a trap designed for Crewe. Now dedicated to winning one for Caretaker, The Mean Machine is ready for the big game.

Hazen's plan of soundly defeating the prisoners is quickly destroyed as The Mean Machine, with Crewe as quarterback, jumps ahead in the first half. Hazen, fearful that the guards might lose and destroy his plan for humiliating the prisoners, sets out to insure a guard victory. When he threatens Crewe with trumped-up charges which would further lengthen his stay in prison, Crewe agrees to throw the game on the condition that when the guards are twenty-one points ahead they will lighten up on the prisoners. As the second half begins, it becomes clear to everyone that Crewe is giving the game away; the guards begin to score, and soon The Mean Machine is more than twenty-one points behind. Faking an injury, Crewe removes himself from the game only to be rejected by the other members of the team on the bench. Sitting virtually alone on the bench with no one but Pop (John Steadman), the trainer, he watches as the guards, following the direct order of Hazen, subject the prisoners to as much physical abuse as possible.

Soon, unable to stand the abuse being handed his teammates, and finally becoming committed, Crewe reenters the game. The other members of the team, however, are not eager to see him and allow the guards repeated chances to destroy him. Eventually recognizing his desire to make amends, however, they once again play as they did in the first half. Inspired by Crewe's incredible determination, they come within a few points of the guards' score. With only seconds remaining and a yard to go for victory, Crewe begins the quest for the "longest yard," the difference between victory and defeat.

Utilizing slow motion and extended time, the audience holds its collective breath as Crewe makes his way laterally across the backfield before turning in and diving over the goal line for victory. He has finally become the man he always wanted to be.

The stands, consisting mostly of prisoners, go wild. They have overcome the odds and won a great moral victory—a victory which Warden Hazen cannot forgive. Seeing Crewe walking in what appears to be a direction of escape, Hazen orders Knauer to shoot him. Knauer, however, hesitates, feeling that something is not right. Crewe stops, bends over and picks up the game ball. As he passes the speechless and embarrassed Hazen, he laughs, knowing that the prisoners have won the ultimate victory. They have not only defeated the Warden's football team but also his philosophy; they have shown themselves to be stronger than him both physically and emotionally.

The film is both vicious and violent. The guards are characterized as mean and sadistic, with not one of them having the slightest redeeming quality. Thus when one of them is injured, the audience cheers. Some of the violence in the game is excessive, but because it represents on the playing field what the prisoners have experienced on a daily basis from the guards, the audience finds itself rooting for the prisoners no matter what they do. In any film in which divisions are clearly made as to who the good guys are and who the bad guys are, the success of the film is dependent upon the representatives of each side. Crewe, for all his moral ambiguities, is nevertheless likable. He continually comes across as a victim who does not belong in such a terrible place. Warden Hazen is exactly the opposite. He is so despicable, in fact, that from the very beginning he is the object of the audience's hatred, and not for even the slightest moment does it seem that his motives are justified. By the end of the film, after he has lost not only the game but also the respect of his supporters, one can only feel contempt for him. Most film "villains" evoke some sympathy, but Hazen as expertly played by Albert has not the least human foible which might endear him to the audience.

Written by Tracy Keenan Wynn and directed by Robert Aldrich in his typically dynamic style, *The Longest Yard* is filled with a plentiful array of psychopaths and sadists who somehow become likable by the end of the film. Aldrich's style, previously established in such films as *The Big Knife* (1955), *Whatever Happened to Baby Jane?* (1962), and *Too Late the Hero* (1970), is characterized by an effective use of seeming contradiction and violence. His characters are not what they seem, and although changed by the end of the film, their "moral victories" are ambiguous. Thus when Crewe has the satisfaction of putting Hazen in a position of ridicule, the audience knows (or they should know) that Crewe will ultimately suffer because he is still a prisoner. The violence in *The Longest Yard* may seem gratuitous, but it is not. It has a cathartic effect on the characters and the audience, but as in many of Aldrich's other films, it brings no final resolution to the problem.

The film did quite well at the box office despite its "R" rating. It was released in the early period of Reynolds' popularity and helped to establish him as a major star. Although critically panned by some reviewers, at the time of its release, it is now recognized as one of both Aldrich's and Reynolds' best films.

James J. Desmarais

LOOK BACK IN ANGER

Released: 1959
Production: Harry Saltzman for ABP/Woodfall; released by Warner Bros.
Direction: Tony Richardson
Screenplay: Nigel Kneale, with additional dialogue by John Osborne; based on the play of the same name by John Osborne
Cinematography: Oswald Morris
Editing: Bert Bates and Richard Best
Music: Chris Barber
Running time: 100 minutes

Principal characters:
Jimmy Porter	Richard Burton
Alison Porter	Mary Ure
Helena Charles	Claire Bloom
Mrs. Tanner	Dame Edith Evans
Cliff Lewis	Gary Raymond
Colonel Redfern	Glen Byam Shaw
Mrs. Redfern	Phyllis Neilson-Terry
Hurst	Donald Pleasance
Mrs. Drury	Jane Eccles
Kapoor	S. P. Kapoor

Three years after its sensational debut in May, 1956, on the stage of the Royal Court Theatre in London, John Osborne's caustic diatribe on life in Britain's welfare-state society, *Look Back in Anger*, reappeared as a film. Tony Richardson, who directed the stage version, Nigel Kneale, who adapted the play for the screen, and Osborne, who contributed additional dialogue, transferred the work to film with rare fidelity, retaining the play's integrity and preserving the texture and substance of its scourging honesty.

Critics have agreed that *Look Back in Anger* began a new era in British drama. The play ran for months in London, sending shock waves through the British cultural establishment. It touched the exposed nerves of the post-World War II generation and was very popular with the young. In New York the play ran for more than a year on Broadway and won the Drama Critics Circle Award as Best Play of the season. Journalists, always ready to tag a new trend, quickly joined three dissimilar writers—Kingsley Amis, John Wain, and Osborne—in a new literary movement and dubbed them "the Angry Young Men."

The trendy label caught the mood of the time and became permanently associated with Osborne, perhaps because his work was the angriest. There is no doubt that he was considered the most representative of the new lashing spirit which was then beginning to stir the arts in Britain. What was new to

British drama was the realistic portrayal of a flailing, disgruntled sensitivity. The striking rudeness and the animating force of uncontained disgust directed at the entrenched middle class was deliberately provocative and unsettling. Above all, the frank, brutal speeches of Jimmy Porter, the antihero par excellence, struck down conventional barriers and opened an exciting range of new subject areas for dramatists. *Look Back in Anger* was indeed angry, and loudly so; it was direct and personal, filled with bitter sarcasm couched in terms seldom if ever heard before in contemporary British drama.

The film, like the play, centers upon the relationship of Jimmy Porter (Richard Burton) with his wife, Alison (Mary Ure). Jimmy comes from lower-class stock, but he has an education from one of the new stylish universities, and he has married above his station. Alison was reared in a background of privilege, and her parents not only objected to the marriage, but also tried to prevent it. Alison's mother found Jimmy uncouth, and, suspecting he was engaged in criminal activities, she hired detectives to follow him, hoping to reveal his unsavory connections. Jimmy virtually stole Alison from her home, but her parents discovered the plot and met the young couple in the church. These details are not acted, however; they are spewed out in Jimmy's probing, spite-filled harangues directed at Alison to test her loyalty, to uncover her feelings, and to make her sever all connections with the past and belong entirely to him.

Most of the action occurs in the cramped attic apartment that Jimmy and Alison share with Cliff Lewis (Gary Raymond), Jimmy's best friend and business partner. The small, unattractive apartment underscores the pinched style of life they lead and reflects the limited scope of British life after World War II as Jimmy sees it. The narrow, restricted style, deprived of charm and imagination, is also expertly rendered in the documentarylike shots of the provincial, gray Midlands town where Jimmy and Cliff operate a candy stall in the market center. Views of working-class children playing in the uninviting streets and people walking to church in the rain, of rows of ugly houses, and of the drabness of the market all add clinical details to Porter's unrelenting, vitriolic attack on his wife, her parents, their politics, and a variety of other woes that strike his febrile mind. Oswald Morris' cinematography provides a credible, authentic milieu and sustains the tone of Jimmy's righteous invective.

The action of *Look Back in Anger* is ordinary melodrama. Jimmy succeeds in driving his wife back to the arms of her family without learning that she is pregnant. He has an affair with Helena (Claire Bloom), an actress friend of Alison who has come to live in the same house while she appears in a play that is touring. At first Jimmy and Helena spar with each other, but after Alison leaves they discover a strong sexual attraction for each other and Helena moves in and takes Alison's place in the household. Cliff, who adores Alison, does not really like Helena and decides to move away and to give up his share in the business. At the end Alison returns, weak and dispirited. She has lost the baby and feels out of place with her parents. Helena decides her relationship with Jimmy is wrong and returns to London. Alison pleads with Jimmy to let her stay with him, abasing herself in the way he had said he wanted to see her, on her knees "in the mud." He relents and they embrace.

While the plot of *Look Back in Anger* is, in summary at least, trite and melodramatic, the writing is alive and vital and the characters searingly real. The creation of Jimmy Porter is filled with energy and freshness; he vibrates with passion like a dangerous electric wire down in a storm. His lack of restraint and detachment in expressing his feelings provides a revelation that is discomforting because it confronts deep pain and humiliation. Burton plays Jimmy Porter with an unrelenting intensity. His familiar ringing, slightly frontal tones at full pitch ably characterize Jimmy's anger, but he also conveys the nasty, often juvenile temper at its most unattractive. In the film Jimmy becomes a petulant child who refuses to accept any compromise with his own vision of reality. He is egocentered, full of self-pity, and, except for his lacerating intelligence, lacking in appeal. It is a brilliant characterization, beautifully and intensely played.

The rest of the cast is uniformly excellent. Ure re-creates the role of Alison which she had successfully played in the original British stage production. The character of Alison is less commanding than that of Jimmy, but the ambivalence of her feelings regarding Jimmy and her ultimate capitulation to him and his world offer a demanding challenge. Ure meets the challenge of the role with total conviction. In the first half of the film she conveys both the charm and the weakness of Alison with consummate skill, and at the end when she begs Jimmy to take her back, she presents a pathetic, lonely, and beaten creature with an anguished dignity. Bloom is perfect as the sophisticated, disapproving actress friend of Alison who succumbs to the physical and mental attractions of Jimmy. Helena's swings to and from Jimmy are entirely credible because of Bloom's acting skill. In contrast to Jimmy, his friend Cliff Lewis is a friendly, likable man, and Raymond invests the part with a rare naturalness. The role is a dramatic necessity as a counterbalance to Jimmy, and Raymond manages to distinguish the part with a genuine humanity, compelling and attractive in its own right. Dame Edith Evans rounds out the cast in the part of Mrs. Tanner, the mother of one of Jimmy's friends; in addition, she provides the funds that enable Jimmy to set up his candy-stall business. Evans in this cameo role adds star luster to the cast and lends a needed touch of quiet pathos to an otherwise noisy, strident tirade of a film.

Look Back in Anger was Richardson's first effort at directing a feature film. The film was generally well-received, and while it did not create the same impact on the film public that it made on the theater audience, it did win a place for itself in film history. The National Board of Review of Motion Pictures named it Number Six in its list of best foreign films of the year.

Although at close range Jimmy Porter's rantings appear to be merely the articulate aches of an immature but vociferous young man, the energy of the creation is galvanic, and the film conveys his youthful pangs with an electric excitement.

William T. Stanley

THE LOOKING GLASS WAR

Released: 1970
Production: John Box for Columbia
Direction: Frank R. Pierson
Screenplay: Frank R. Pierson; based on the novel of the same name by John LeCarré
Cinematography: Austin Dempster
Editing: Willy Kemplen
Running time: 108 minutes

Principal characters:
Leiser	Christopher Jones
Leclerc	Ralph Richardson
Haldane	Paul Rogers
Avery	Anthony Hopkins
Susan	Susan George
The Girl	Pia Degermark

The 1960's marked the era of the spy film; both the best and the worst of the genre were made then. The times were extraordinary—social and military revolutions the world over, assassinations, wars in Southeast Asia and the Middle East—and they seemed to call for extraordinary men to fight the good fight on behalf of the free world. The best of the spy films were based on novels, and the best of these novels were written by Englishmen. Ian Fleming's James Bond, the indestructible 007, was the exemplar of one pole of this movement—the superhero—and the success of the Bond films spawned a virtual cottage industry of imitations and parodies.

There were writers, however, who adopted a more realistic view of the business of espionage. Their protagonists were often reluctant spies, and often discovered that a doublecross rather than a blonde awaited them at the end of the line. Len Deighton's *The Ipcress File* (filmed by Sidney J. Furie in 1965,) *Funeral in Berlin* (directed by Guy Hamilton in 1966), John LeCarré's *The Spy Who Came in from the Cold* (Martin Ritt, 1965), and *The Looking Glass War* (Frank R. Pierson, 1970) were the best of these more realistic filmed novels.

Pierson directed *The Looking Glass War* in a different manner from the others. He retains LeCarré's antiheroic characters and pessimistic world view, but, unlike other directors working in this genre, he adopts a narrative structure that is as fragmented as the subculture it portrays. Instead of a neat linear plot, Pierson offers us a jagged series of scenes that add up to an impressionistic view of Cold War espionage. The film's title alludes to Lewis Carroll's *Through the Looking Glass* (1871), a place where logic is irrelevant and nothing is as it seems. Pierson uses a number of odd camera angles in the first scene, with many shots of mirrors and other reflective surfaces, suggesting the looking glass of the title. Subsequent events reveal that the metaphor is apt.

The film opens at an airport in Finland, where we witness a furtive conversation between a pilot and another man, obviously some sort of a spy. A reel of microfilm changes hands; shortly thereafter the spy is murdered, although his anonymous killers lose the microfilm in the snow near the airport.

The scene shifts to Geneva, where two men, officials in the British secret service, discuss the spy's death. Their conversation is dry and utterly businesslike. The only hint of animation comes with their decision to abandon modern cloak-and-dagger wizardry such as satellites and infiltrate a man into East Germany to reacquire the information lost (to both sides) on the microfilm. "Like the old days," one of them remarks. In London, the two men are given names: Leclerc (Ralph Richardson) and Haldane (Paul Rogers). They are middle-aged, middle-class, and as Pierson shows us, thoroughly businesslike. They are bored men whose only passion is espionage; although they approach it with a pretense of ennui, they grow increasingly excited by the prospect of sending a live agent across the German border.

Leclerc and Haldane recruit a young Pole named Leiser (Christopher Jones) to do their dirty work for them. A steward on a Polish ocean liner, Leiser has jumped ship and sought asylum in England. The reasons he offers are initially frivolous—"to be a millionaire and sleep with movie stars"—but he finally admits the reason behind his desertion. He has impregnated an English girl and wants to be near the baby. He insists that it is his future child, and not the girl, that is the main focus of his interest. Leclerc and Haldane offer him a deal—asylum in return for his services as a spy. Amused by their offer, he accepts.

From this point on, Leiser becomes the focus of the film. In a series of short scenes, we learn a good deal about him. He is aggressive, with a palpable mean streak—he beats up his girl friend Susan (Susan George) when he learns that she has aborted their child; he is neither stupid nor particulary bright; and he rather enjoys his espionage training.

The only person in Leiser's life who has any particular affection for him is Avery (Anthony Hopkins), one of the men training him for his mission (which, it develops, is to confirm, either by photograph or wireless radio, the presence of a new Soviet rocket in East Germany). When Avery suggests to his colleagues that they are needlessly risking Leiser's life, Leclerc retorts "We aren't risking his life. He is. We had scruples like you. We learned to overcome them." Thus does Pierson sum up the amorality of the spy's credo.

Leiser crosses into East Berlin, and, in the film's most exciting sequence, kills a border guard. Shortly thereafter, however, the pace of the film begins to slow a bit. As the scenes lengthen, the impressionistic flow of the film ceases, and its focus shifts from the espionage process to the misadventures of Leiser. Since he is neither particulary sympathetic nor, in and of himself, particularly interesting, the film suffers as a consequence. Things begin to go very badly for Leiser. The murder of the guard alerts the East German police to his presence in the area; and he seriously injures his hand making good his entry into the country. Although they are initially confused at the thought of someone trying to break *into* the Iron Curtain country, the Communist police quickly decide to follow the fugitive and see what use they can make of him before they kill him.

Leiser is picked up by a truck driver who offers him a ride to his destination, but when the driver makes a homosexual advance, Leiser kills him. Commandeering the truck, he meets a beautiful girl (Pia Degermark) his own age. We learn very little abut the girl—not even her name—but she becomes attached to Leiser. She helps him elude a police roadblock, and they make love; but Leiser's dedication to his mission drives him on to the city of Kriegstad, where the Soviet rocket awaits. Leiser and the girl are no sooner ensconced in a hotel room than a rocket is trundled through the street in plain sight—a suspiciously easy intelligence coup indeed. Leiser suspects nothing, however, and quickly begins to transmit his message back to London.

The mystery is cleared up, however, as Pierson intercuts Leiser's death at the hands of the East German police with an argument between Leclerc and Avery. Leclerc explains the situation in this way: Leiser compromised his mission by killing the guard, thus revealing his existence to the Communist authorities. They responded by showing Leiser the wrong rocket and letting him live just long enough to send the misinformation back to his English masters. Leclerc and Haldane, however, are aware that Leiser had tipped his hand, and thus know to disregard any message he might send back. Leclerc is obviously enormously pleased with his analysis of the situation. Avery, infuriated by the smugness of Leclerc and Haldane, excoriates them. "This is better than monkey glands for you, isn't it," he sneers, putting his finger on the unwholesome satisfaction the two men have extracted from the incident. The fact that the mission was a failure and that their operative died clearly pales in the light of the pleasure of matching wits with their Communist counterparts. They have rejuvenated their spirits at the cost of Leiser's life.

The film ends where it began, at the airstrip in Finland. Some children are playing along the runway, and one of them discovers the missing roll of microfilm that has cost Leiser his life. To them it is a toy, something to play with just as Leiser's life was a plaything to Leclerc and Haldane.

The Looking Glass War is a far from perfect film. Its major flaw is Pierson's inability or unwillingness to sustain the impressionistic flow of the film's first half. When his narrative becomes more conventionally linear, it makes the innovations in the early part of the film seem willfully obscure. Indeed, critical reception to *The Looking Glass War* was lukewarm at best, and much of the negative reaction to the film dwelt on its elliptical and often murky plot.

Although Pierson's writing and directing abilities are not without merit—individual scenes in the film are outstanding—the film as a whole does not hang together.

Nevertheless, *The Looking Glass War* is not without redeeming characteristics. The acting in the film—particularly on the part of Richardson, Hopkins, Rogers, and Jones—is first-rate. The female roles in the film are poorly developed. George is pretty and sluttish as Susan, Leiser's first girl friend, and Degermark is pretty and ethereal as his unnamed second girl friend; but espionage is a man's world, at least in this film. All of the important male characters are reasonably well thought out; and these characters are illuminated by the actors who bring them to the screen. Richardson and Rogers, as Leclerc and Haldane, complement each other perfectly as the two aging spooks (as professional spies call each other) whose vicarious urge to get back in the thick of things leads to Leiser's death. Their quiet smugness, always well-modulated yet increasingly apparent, provides an effective counterpoint to the more violent exertions of Hopkins and Jones.

Hopkins is outstanding as the disillusioned Avery. We can see the desperation and betrayal in his eyes as the machinations of his colleagues come to a head. Jones does well in the difficult role of Leiser. The character is singularly unappealing—violent, impulsive, and not very bright—but Jones humanizes him a bit. Although we never actually come to like him, we can share Avery's disgust at his senseless death.

The Looking Glass War, then, provides a convincing if sometimes perplexing look into the unglamorous aspects of Cold War espionage. Although flawed, the film is noteworthy for several fine performances and as an anodyne to the James Bond films of its era.

Robert Mitchell

THE LOST PATROL

Released: 1934
Production: Merian C. Cooper for RKO/Radio
Direction: John Ford
Screenplay: Dudley Nichols; based on Garrett Fort's adaptation of the novel
  Patrol by Philip MacDonald
Cinematography: Harold Wenstrom
Editing: Paul Weatherwax
Music: Max Steiner
Running time: 74 minutes

Principal characters:

The Sergeant	Victor McLaglen
Sanders	Boris Karloff
Morelli	Wallace Ford
George Brown	Reginald Denny
Quincannon	J. M. Kerrigan
Herbert Hale	Billy Beven

Although the topic of death has usually been treated by Hollywood as an excuse for maudlin soap opera or lurid escapism, the subject of how men and women *face* and *accept* death has produced some outstanding screen dramas. The ideal genre for such a topic is, of course, the war film. Cinemagoers have pitied the anguish of Colin Clive's liquor-ridden, soul-shocked Captain of James Whale's *Journey's End* (1930), laughed in jubilant admiration at the doomed but wisecracking Robert Preston and William Bendix of John Farrow's *Wake Island* (1942), and winced in shock at the fatal atrocities of Michael Cimino's *The Deer Hunter* (1978). One of the most famous films to explore this sombre theme was RKO's *The Lost Patrol*, a blend of John Ford's terse direction, Harold Wenstrom's sullen camera, Victor McLaglen's stiff upper lip, Boris Karloff's spewing lunacy, and Max Steiner's thundering score all contributed to a somewhat dated but tense melodrama which still retains moments of the raw power indicative of Ford's greater works.

Based on Philip MacDonald's novel *Patrol*, which had already inspired a 1929 English film, *The Lost Patrol* proved to be an offbeat project and production. RKO produced the film with reluctance. There was not a single female in the cast, in the vein of the aforementioned *Journey's End*, and the entire tale transpired in the dreary wilds of the desert. There was also serious script trouble causing Ford to ask his trusted colleague Dudley Nichols to perform an emergency rewrite. Nichols did so in an astonishing eight days, and Ford took his cast and crew into the hellish desert dunes near Yuma, Arizona, for the filming. The temperature soared almost daily past the 110 degree mark, and the company swooned with sunstroke attacks and heat prostration. Ford rapidly shot the picture in two grueling weeks.

The Lost Patrol opens in the Mesopotamia Desert. An Arab sniper has killed a British cavalry officer. His soldiers are now lost, for the officer carried his orders and map "in his head." The Sergeant (Victor McLaglen) takes command of the twelve men. The group includes such characters as the glib, clever, amoral Brown (Reginald Denny), tough trooper Morelli (Wallace Ford), and demented religious fanatic Sanders (Boris Karloff). Their horses are parched and their canteens almost empty when the men jubilantly discover an oasis, complete with a pool, date trees, and an abandoned mosque.

All this time, the soldiers have been trailed by Arabs who have contrived to cause the men to camp at the oasis and thus be at their mercy. By night, as the exhausted soldiers sleep, the Arabs kill a sentry and steal the horses. Then begins a terrible ritual as the unseen Arabs, lurking within the undulating dunes, shoot the men one by one. When two of the soldiers try to escape to bring back help, their bodies are returned tied to their horses. Finally, only Morelli, the Sergeant, and the increasingly raving Sanders are alive. Just when all seems lost, a British aviator circles the area. He sees the men, lands his plane, and, despite the warnings shouted by the men, is shot through the heart.

Hysteria finally triumphs. Sanders, now wildly insane, must be bound and tied for his own safety and that of his compatriots. Yet he escapes, and, garbed in the rags of an Old Testament prophet and carrying a makeshift cross, he madly marches over the dunes, directly into the fire of the enemy. Morelli gallantly races to rescue him, and both men are killed. Now the Sergeant cracks, and, bearing a machine gun from the downed plane, guns down the advancing Arabs with laughs of vengeful glee. Only now does a rescuing cavalry arrive. The Sergeant is asked where his men are, and he points, in a sad daze, to the sword-marked graves in the sand.

The Lost Patrol was released February 16, 1934. The *Motion Picture Herald* praised the picture as "a courageous picture; one that courageous, resourceful showmen should welcome." The film placed sixth on the very discriminating National Board of Review's "Ten Best" list, and delighted RKO by becoming one of the top money-making movies of 1934. The score by Steiner, which strikes many today as excessive and intrusive, earned the distinction of becoming the first film score to be nominated for an Academy Award. It was defeated by *One Night of Love*.

There is much still of value in *The Lost Patrol*. Ford's direction, seemingly simplistic, actually becomes strikingly emotional. He splendidly evokes the thirst, hunger, and doom of the soldiers with the aid of Wenstrom's cinematography, with its gloomy scanning of the oppressive dunes and glaring sky. So powerfully does Ford build his film that many audiences cheered in vicarious and violent release as McLaglen viciously and maniacally slaughtered the Arabs who finally revealed themselves. McLaglen (whose brother

Cyril played the Sergeant in the 1929 British version) plays with great authority, free of the raucous vulgarity that often blemished his performances. Such Ford favorites as Wallace Ford, J. M. Kerrigan, and Reginald Denny also make solid dramatic contributions.

Nevertheless, as was noted by *The New York Times* in 1934, *The Lost Patrol* suffers as a whole because ". . . the incidents are often strained" and "the dialogue is too forced and often far from natural." These flaws are all too obvious when *The Lost Patrol* plays today. The film benefits greatly, however, from the performance of Karloff. Fresh from his triumphs at Universal City in *Frankenstein* (1932), *The Old Dark House* (1932), and *The Mummy* (1932), the Englishman cherished this opportunity to play in the film and unleashed a performance of hysterical bravado, transcending the stilted situations and wooden dialogue that chokes much of the pace of the picture. As the pathetic Sanders, Karloff shrieks, screams, leers, pouts, and cackles, and his climactic madness as he marches, as if to Calvary, into the Arab bullets in rags and with his cross, gives the film its most memorable episode. As with Thomas Mitchell in *Stagecoach* (1939), Ford, who usually detested and ridiculed theatricality in his actors, encouraged Karloff's flamboyance, and its result makes *The Lost Patrol* memorable even today.

The Lost Patrol remains a milestone in Ford's career. Its huge critical and box-office success prompted RKO to allow Ford to direct *The Informer* (1935), which would win Academy Awards for Nichols, McLaglen, and Ford, clinching the director's reputation. On its own merits, *The Lost Patrol* remains a quite fascinating albeit flawed film—a great director's treatment of the classic theme of the acceptance of death and the human passion for survival.

Gregory William Mank

LOVE AFFAIR

Released: 1939
Production: Leo McCarey for RKO/Radio
Direction: Leo McCarey
Screenplay: Delmer Daves and Donald Ogden Stewart; based on an original story of the same name by Mildred Cram and Leo McCarey
Cinematography: Rudolph Maté
Editing: Edward Dmytryk and George Hiveley
Song: B. G. DeSylva, "Wishing" and Harold Arlen and Ted Koehler, "Sing My Heart"
Running time: 87 minutes

> *Principal characters:*
> Terry MacKay .... Irene Dunne
> Michel Marna .... Charles Boyer
> Grandmother Janou .... Maria Ouspenskaya

Romantic comedies such as *It Happened One Night* (1934) are always cited as being among the most popular and enduring films of the 1930's, and an equal number of romantic melodramas such as *Back Street* (1932) are similarly remembered with respect and affection. Through a special alchemy, some films of the period manage to succeed in both modes at once, and foremost among these is *Love Affair*, which has a magic all its own.

Leo McCarey was essentially a comedy director who had made an initial reputation supervising some of the most memorable silent films of Laurel and Hardy, and who had later guided the Marx Brothers in what is widely considered to be their best film, *Duck Soup* (1933). In subsequent films, McCarey did not lose touch with his talent for whimsical improvisation, but he also added sentiment, very appealing in its genuineness, which enriches the tone of such classics as *Ruggles of Red Gap* (1935) and *The Awful Truth* (1937), while *Make Way for Tomorrow* (1937) is an unexpected and fully realized tragedy of a man and wife cruelly separated in their twilight years. These varied earlier films give a context for the balance between laughter and tears which McCarey achieves in *Love Affair*. It is a film which relies strongly on his gift for making his material both entertaining and believable, because the story is structured to depend on chance for several reversals in the central relationship. As a result of the love and understanding McCarey has for the characters, and the intelligence and warmth with which Irene Dunne and Charles Boyer respond to his direction, the audience readily yields to these improbabilities.

When Terry (Irene Dunne) and Michel (Charles Boyer) meet on shipboard, their initial attraction for each other is complicated by their engagements to others. Perceiving themselves as sophisticated people, however, they believe their friendship can remain harmless as long as it centers on the witty repartee for which they both have considerable talent. What is so charming about this initial stage of their relationship is that both of them continually allow their true feelings to be revealed. When Terry accompanies Michel to see his grandmother Janou (Maria Ouspenskaya), she learns in a direct way of his tenderness and sensitivity and of his denial of his promise as a painter. A spiritual harmony is achieved as they pray together in Janou's little chapel, and Terry is linked to Janou herself as she sings "Plaisir D'Amour" while Janou plays the piano. Janou's deep love for her late husband is felt as an intimation that the love of Terry and Michel will be of the same kind.

To appreciate the extent of their love, Michel and Terry must test it, and true to the traditions of melodrama, their meeting at the top of the Empire State Building, described in the film as "the nearest thing to heaven," is thwarted not by lack of feeling but by a tragic caprice of fate. Paralyzed in an automobile accident as she rushes to the appointed meeting, Terry is unwilling to see Michel and tell him the truth, while he becomes bitter in his belief that her love was less true than his own. The memory painting of Terry with Janou, vibrant with Michel's undying love for both women after Janou has died and he has "lost" Terry, reconciles the lovers when Michel discovers it in Terry's apartment at the last possible moment.

There is a belief that a make-believe world of the kind found in a film like *Love Affair* depends too strongly on melodramatic conventions which willfully deny reality as it is actually experienced. This belief fails to take into account the fact that men and women often see their own lives in terms of these melodramatic conventions and allow many of their actions to be ruled by romantic and fatalistic concepts. A film which implicitly acknowledges this may be profound in an especially moving way, if the characters convince that their emotions are true, and if their experiences find counterpoint and an aesthetic release in certain inventions of image and sound. *Love Affair* has these inventions in abundance.

Although McCarey's style often appears to be relatively simple, distinguished by its gracefulness and generosity to the actors, he finds certain images which have a direct visual expressiveness. The scene of Terry and Michel in the chapel, beautifully lit by Rudolph Maté, is one example, conveying a warm and exquisite empathy between the characters as they kneel in wordless communion. Another example is Terry's happiness over her expected meeting with Michel, as she speaks on the telephone and opens her window to reveal a reflection of the Empire State Building. The most forceful image occurs when Michel opens the door of Terry's bedroom in the final sequence and the camera whips over to a mirror reflecting the painting, causing the audience to share the shock of Michel's realization of Terry's paralysis.

Love Affair also benefits immeasurably from the presence of three wonderful songs, each of which expresses some aspect of the film's meaning. The first song, the haunting "Plaisir D'Amour," poignantly intimates the possibility of a sad conclusion to the story before there is any indication of what could go wrong for the couple. The second song, composed by Harold Arlen, is sung by Terry when she has a job in a nightclub during the six months prior to the appointed meeting, and in it she sings with a dramatic exhilaration of "that happy ending," words which become ironic a few scenes later but retrospectively appropriate at the fadeout. The final song is performed after Terry has become crippled and has taken a job in a school, and the song beautifully expresses what the audience wants to believe and what the film wills to be truth, that "wishing will make it so." It is this song, charmingly performed *twice* by children and heard again offscreen during the final image, which is the most lovely manifestation of the spirit which distinguishes *Love Affair*.

Blake Lucas

LOVE AND DEATH

Released: 1975
Production: Charles H. Joffe for United Artists
Direction: Woody Allen
Screenplay: Woody Allen
Cinematography: Ghislain Cloquet
Editing: Ralph Rosenblum
Running time: 85 minutes

Principal characters:
Boris	Woody Allen
Sonja	Diane Keaton
Countess Alexandrovna	Olga Georges-Picot
Count Anton Ivanovitch	Harold Gould
Napoleon	James Tolkan
Ivan	Henry Czarniak

A film by Woody Allen is likely to be a collection of jokes or variations on a theme rather than a chronological narrative, and *Love and Death*—which Allen wrote, directed, and starred in—is no exception. He uses the film's nineteenth century Russian setting not to present a Russian story but rather as a background for his humor, which ranges over many subjects but focuses on Russia (or at least Russian literature and the films based on it), on love, and on death.

Love and Death does have a definite story, but that story is sometimes silly, sometimes inconsistent, and many times unimportant. It is about Boris (Woody Allen), a nineteenth century Russian who does not fit into the crude rural society in which he grows up. Instead of boisterous drinking and dancing, he prefers "deep conversations" with his cousin Sonja (Diane Keaton)—conversations which start as a discussion of a serious subject such as the existence of God and then disintegrate into abstruse double talk. Boris finds, however, that Sonja wants to marry his brother Ivan (Henry Czarniak), who—Boris says—can barely write his own name.

When Napoleon invades Austria, all the young men enthusiastically join the army except Boris, who is forced to join. Rejected by Ivan, Sonja marries a smelly herring merchant, leaving Boris to go to war with only his butterfly collection for comfort. When he returns from the front, however, he meets the beautiful Countess Alexandrovna (Olga Georges-Picot), who invites him to her room. He happily accepts even though he has been warned that she is the mistress of the jealous Count Anton (Harold Gould). The Countess is delighted with Boris, but Anton is furious and challenges him to a duel. Having learned that Sonja is now a widow, Boris persuades her to marry him if he escapes his almost certain death in the duel. When Boris survives the duel, Sonja is forced to accept Boris as her husband although she does not love him. She eventually grows to love him, however, and they have a happy life until Napoleon invades Russia. Sonja then decides that she and Boris must save Russia by assassinating Napoleon (James Tolkan). This idea provokes much intellectual discussion about violence and murder before Boris finally agrees, although when they eventually find Napoleon, he cannot go through with the assassination. When someone else shoots Napoleon, however, Boris is charged with the murder, and Sonja escapes. A further complication is the fact that the dead man is not actually Napoleon but a man impersonating him. Sentenced to death for a crime he did not commit, Boris is assured by an angel that he will be reprieved. The angel is wrong, however, and Boris is executed. After his death he appears to Sonja, tells her what has happened, then turns and talks to the audience about love and death.

The plot's variety of romantic situations provides great scope for Allen's humorous consideration of love, both requited and unrequited. In a scene somewhat reminiscent of the famous eating scene in *Tom Jones* (1963), Boris and the Countess—in separate boxes at the opera—exchange amorous looks. She underscores her meaning with the deft use of a white fan. He responds by using first his white glove, then a black fan, then his sword, and finally his tongue. When the two next meet, she invites him to come to her room at midnight. He arrives exactly at the appointed hour. Six minutes later (according to the ornate clock on the wall), the room is a shambles and she is telling him that he is the greatest lover she has ever had.

With Sonja, on the other hand, Boris is less successful. Early in the film when she describes her ideal man as intellectual, sensual, and spiritual, Boris assumes she is describing him and is astounded to find that she is in love with his loutish brother Ivan. When Ivan marries someone else, Sonja, instead of turning to Boris, marries a herring merchant whom she does not love. When he is challenged to a duel and asks her to marry him if "by some miracle" he is not killed, her first response is, "What do you think the odds are?," but she does consent. The duel, however, does not go as expected; Anton misses Boris, so Sonja has to marry him. All she can say at the wedding is "he missed." Later when the two are in bed, Boris starts to touch her arm and she snaps, "Don't—not here." As time passes, however, he wins her heart and the two are happy.

Love and Death contains many humorous references to films and literature. Near the end Sonja is talking with a woman friend and we suddenly see the faces of the two together in a famous composition used by Ingmar Bergman in *Persona* (1966). The figure of death also makes several appearances in *Love and Death*, usually suggestive of images in Bergman's *Seventh Seal* (1956), and in a battle scene a man's eyeglasses are shattered in a shot which recalls a famous image in Sergei Eisenstein's *The Battleship Potemkin* (1925). Early in the film Boris and Sonja have a conversation consisting of virtually nothing but titles of books by Fyodor Dostoevski. Having decided to become a great poet, Boris writes two lines which are actually from T. S. Eliot's *The Love Song of J. Alfred Prufrock* ("I should have been a pair of ragged claws/ Scuttling across the floors of silent seas") but rejects them as being too sentimental.

In its treatment of war, *Love and Death* is never completely serious or completely humorous. The main battle is portrayed with a mixture of the realistic, the surrealistic, and the absurdly comic. We see long shots of soldiers marching toward one another, close-ups of fury of the battle, and shots of men lying dead. These are intermixed with shots of cheerleaders for Russia and a concessionaire selling food during the battle. After it is over and only fourteen out of twelve thousand have survived, a religious man tells Boris he is thankful that God is on the side of the Russians, but Boris is not cheered. "I'm sure things could have gone a lot worse if he wasn't; it might've rained." Although he is a thoroughly inept soldier, Boris later becomes a hero because he hides in a cannon which is fired before he can get out. He lands in a group of French generals, causing their immediate surrender.

The script of *Love and Death* might seem to be merely a collection of fairly clever gags, but the film is truly greater that the sum of its parts. It is unified by Allen's direction and the acting of Allen as Boris and Keaton as Sonja. As the director, Allen's main virtues are effective camera placement and a brisk pacing which keeps the strong scenes sharp and the weak ones from seriously harming the film. Keaton possesses an undeniable screen presence which enables her to make every scene interesting, and Allen plays a mock Russian version of the screen *persona* he uses to some extent in all his films— the lustful, incompetent, neurotic intellectual. This characterization requires Allen to convey enough charm that we accept him as the hero even when he seems incapable of succeeding at anything, and—although he sometimes overdoes the clumsiness—Allen accomplishes this feat admirably. Indeed, the talent of Allen—the film's writer, director, and costar—has made *Love and Death* an achievement of film comedy to which a viewer can turn with pleasure again and again.

Timothy W. Johnson

LOVE IS A MANY-SPLENDORED THING

Released: 1955
Production: Buddy Adler for Twentieth Century-Fox
Direction: Henry King
Screenplay: John Patrick; based on the novel of the same name by Han Suyin
Cinematography: Leon Shamroy
Editing: William Reynolds
Costume design: Charles Le Maire (AA)
Music: Alfred Newman (AA)
Song: Sammy Fain and Paul Francis Webster, "Love Is a Many-Splendored Thing" (AA)

> *Principal characters:*
> Han Suyin .... Jennifer Jones
> Mark Elliott .... William Holden

Stars Jennifer Jones and William Holden, the exotic backdrop of Hong Kong, and the lyrics of the title song by Sammy Fain and Paul Francis Webster indicate that *Love Is a Many-Splendored Thing* is first and foremost a love story. Although Han Suyin's novel of the same name was more concerned with the heroine's Eurasian background and devotion to the medical profession, the film subjugates these themes and concentrates on the ill-fated affair between Han Suyin (Jennifer Jones) and Mark Elliott (William Holden). The growing threat of Communism on mainland China and the personal problems that the new government causes Suyin's family are less important in the film than the romantic scenery Hong Kong provides since the film is centered on the developing love between two people.

Han Suyin is a widowed Eurasian doctor. Her husband, who was a general in the Nationalist army, was killed by the Communists. Her mother's family was English and thus Suyin was educated in European schools, but her father's family is mainland Chinese and she still maintains close ties with her Chinese relatives. Unlike the novel, in the film Suyin's mixed blood seems more of an asset than a hindrance as it gives her an air of romantic mystery. Jones beautifully captures the stature and serenity of a Western educated Eurasian woman.

Suyin's seriousness and distaste for the frivolous Americans who have invaded Hong Kong is evident from the film's opening scenes. Mark Elliott is the complete opposite of the serious Suyin. A brash, cocky American journalist, Elliott's first action in the film is to try to "pick up" the beautiful Suyin. "I really can't believe that you're a doctor, Doctor," Elliott quips in cocktail-party fashion. "What a shame we haven't a scalpel with us," Suyin responds coolly, "I'd make a slight incision to convince you."

Before the end of the party, however, Suyin is finally charmed by Elliott.

Although she knows that he is married, she accepts his invitation to dinner, convinced that she could have no lasting interest in such a man. They attend the Moon Festival celebration, where the atmosphere, candles, and rituals encourage intimate conversation, and the essential and extreme differences in their heritage, philosophy, and nature become apparent.

Suyin is deeply superstitious, a strange trait in a person steeped in science. Since her husband's death, she has devoted herself to medicine, and she sees herself as a woman of duty and composure. Elliott observes that her isolation is as much protection from suffering as it is a dedication to stopping it. Elliott views her "ivory tower" attitude as a challenge. His persistence and growing love for Suyin eventually break down the artifice of her isolation from the world of romantic love. Although she warns him not to wake a "sleeping tiger," his confidence breaks down her resistance. When Suyin must return to mainland China in order to counsel her sister, who is living with a "foreigner," she must at the same time confront her own decision to continue with Mark. It is a complicated issue. There is not only their cultural difference to consider, but also the fact that Mark is still a married man whose wife refuses to give him a divorce.

In love with Suyin, Mark travels to see his estranged wife and press for a divorce. His affection for Suyin is touchingly represented. Nervous and ill-at-ease when they first met, Mark had bitten his nails constantly. Suyin tells him, "when you stop biting your nails it will mean you are completely at peace and completely mine." While Mark is away a telegram arrives for Suyin announcing, "I have stopped biting my nails." Overjoyed at the news that Mark's wife has agreed to a divorce, Suyin finally fully commits herself to love.

As in the case of many lovers, especially on the screen, as soon as happiness is extended it is taken away. Mrs. Elliott changes her mind, and the couple's patience is tested. Suyin is fired from the hospital staff because of her affair with Mark and moves in with friends. Mark is called to Korea to cover the impending war, and Suyin is left behind to wait for him and for a change of heart from his wife. Their cultural differences are paralleled beautifully in his absence. Scenes of Mark sitting at his typewriter composing love letters are juxtaposed nicely with scenes of Suyin painting a Chinese good luck prayer for his safety.

A memorable cut captures the moment of Mark's death. As the bomb that kills him drops in the Korean wilderness, it metamorphoses into a shattering india ink bottle that has been knocked from Suyin's table; Suyin has been "widowed" again. Tragically, even after the news of his death, his last letters arrive one by one. The pain is almost more than she can stand, and she runs through the crowded Hong Kong streets to their meeting place, a hill that overlooks the enormous bay. Their private sanctuary that was her "secret garden" and his "mountain" offers her strength instead of sadness. Suyin imagines Mark's presence, and the memory of his belief in love comforts her. "Tis ye" echoes Elliott's quote from Thompson, "tis your estranged face that miss the many splendored thing." Renewed by his love, Suyin has grown past the pain of isolation she felt when they met. She has learned the truth in Thompson's poem; she has not missed the many splendored thing.

The characters are impressively nonstereotyped in a film which could easily have deteriorated with less talented acting. Mark, while thoroughly masculine and often brash, quotes poetry and writes love letters. More pensive than many of his contemporaries, he is not afraid to say "I love you"; his masculinity is expressed through tenderness and understanding. Holden sparkles with an American confidence and easily captures the youthful energy of the bright, endearing journalist.

The character of Suyin is equally out of step with her peers. She is strong, but not masculine, and has a genuine rapport with children. Her Eastern silk dresses are the epitome of femininity, just as her physician's garb symbolize her intelligence and dedication. Suyin is a scientist who has retained her humanity, a woman who embodies the wisdom of ancient cultures as well as modern ideals.

The depth of these two characters makes the film successful. At the same time, *Love Is a Many-Splendored Thing* typifies the type of slick postwar romance on which American audiences thrived. Henry King, who directed Jones in her Academy Award-winning performance in *The Song of Bernadette* (1943), has imparted a great sensitivity to the film, and as a result of his competent direction, both Jones and the film were nominated for Oscars. Although neither won, the film took three other Academy Awards, for Best Costume (Color) for Charles Le Maire, Best Song for Fain and Webster, and Best Scoring of a Dramatic Picture for Alfred Newman.

Joanne L. Yeck

LOVE ME OR LEAVE ME

Released: 1955
Production: Joe Pasternak for Metro-Goldwyn-Mayer
Direction: Charles Vidor
Screenplay: Daniel Fuchs and Isobel Lennart (AA); based on an original story
  by Daniel Fuchs
Cinematography: Arthur E. Arling
Editing: Ralph E. Winters
Running time: 122 minutes

Principal characters:
Ruth Etting	Doris Day
Martin "The Gimp" Snyder	James Cagney
Johnny Alderman	Cameron Mitchell
Bernard V. Loomis	Robert Keith
Frobisher	Tom Tully

Love Me or Leave Me is the story of Ruth Etting, popular singing star of the 1930's, and of her tempestuous relationship with gangster Marty Snyder, better known as "The Gimp." Producer Joe Pasternak realized the box-office potential of the story, because it contained drama, music, romance, and a revealing look at Chicago gangsterland in the 1920's and 1930's. With James Cagney already signed to play "The Gimp," it was doubly important to find a Ruth Etting who would not be overshadowed by the strength of Cagney's gangster portrayal. Pasternak sent the script to Doris Day—a strange choice on the surface, since Day had previously specialized in playing clean-cut young ingenues. In this film, she would be required to be a rather cheap, ambitious dance-hall girl. Day hesitated but she finally accepted the role and later felt that it was the greatest challenge of her career. She listened to Ruth Etting records and tried to capture the values and inflections of the singer's voice rather than to imitate it exactly. Many feel that Day has never been in better voice, and she proved to herself and to her audiences that she was capable of a serious, thoughtful performance and need not restrict herself to the light-hearted parts that she had been playing in the past.

With a fine script by Daniel Fuchs and Isobel Lennart, and with the full cooperation of the real Ruth Etting and Marty Snyder, the film succeeded in realistically capturing the essence of the strange saga of Ruth Etting and "The Gimp" Snyder. Cagney threw himself completely into the role, even to the extent of working for weeks on his limp so that it would feel right. He submerged his own personality into that of the crippled Snyder and comes off in the film as a brutal, power-loving person. Yet as Cagney plays him, there is a pathetic side to Snyder that adds another dimension to the role.

As the film opens, Ruth Etting is working in a Chicago dance hall as a dime-a-dance girl. It is the glamorous 1920's when jazz is king. Young Ruth dreams of success and of bright lights as she struggles to become a singer. She has a hard time in the dance hall and is forced finally to kick a customer in the shins for making a pass at her. She is promptly fired for insubordination, but not before she catches the eye of Marty Snyder, a racketeering laundryman who gives her a job in the chorus at one of his clubs. Snyder (known as "The Gimp" for his pronounced limp) becomes Ruth's manager and encourages and helps her in her career as a singer. In the process, he attempts to take over every aspect of Ruth's life. As she becomes more and more successful, she becomes increasingly aware of what a boor Snyder is. His uncouth manners succeed in alienating just about everyone with whom she wants to cultivate a relationship. Still, she keeps on singing and eventually becomes a radio and recording star, and plays in the Ziegfeld Follies. Behind her every step of the way is "Gimp" Snyder, who battles viciously over contracts and is jealous of any relationship that Ruth makes on her own. Ruth falls in love with pianist Johnny Alderman (Cameron Mitchell) and tries to break the hold that Snyder has over her. When she attempts to tell the gangster that she wants to be free of him, he slaps her around, nearly rapes her, and scares her so much that she agrees to marry him.

The married life of the pair is a disaster. Ruth continues to grow as a singer, but is miserable every moment that she is with Snyder. Several years pass, and the two go to Hollywood where Ruth is to do a film. The studio musical director turns out to be Johnny, whom Ruth still loves. Knowing that her life with Snyder is a big mistake, she demands a divorce. Maddened with jealousy, Snyder shoots Johnny, wounding him severely. Ruth finally leaves Snyder after bailing him out of jail, stays with Alderman throughout his recovery, and eventually marries him. The film has a sentimental but effective climax as Ruth, for old times sake, sings at the opening of a new club owned by "The Gimp."

The film was a critical and popular success, with Day and Cagney both receiving much credit. Cagney was nominated for an Academy Award but lost to Ernest Borgnine for his performance in *Marty*. The film did, however, receive an Oscar for Best Motion Picture story, by Daniel Fuchs and Isobel Lennart. The only person who objected to the film was the real Ruth Etting Alderman, who was retired and living in Colorado. She felt that the film distorted her character and made her come across as an opportunist. In truth, because of the strange nature of her relationship with Marty "Gimp" Snyder, Etting led a protected, almost sheltered life during her singing career, strangely isolated from her contemporaries. Some legal action was taken by Etting, but nothing came of it.

Love Me or Leave Me brought Day some dramatic roles. She starred for Alfred Hitchcock in *The Man Who Knew Too Much* in 1956 and followed that with *Julie* in the same year. Both roles demanded intensive dramatic acting from her, but she was unable to sustain her career with that kind of part. For the next ten years, Day cornered the market on another kind of heroine—the professional virgin. With such films as *Pillow Talk* (1959), *Lover Come Back* (1961), and *That Touch of Mink* (1962), her career got further and further away from roles like that of Ruth Etting. As for Cagney, "The Gimp" was really his last serious portrayal of a gangster. In *Love Me or Leave Me* he proved that the years had not slowed him down—he could handle criminal roles every bit as masterfully as he did in *The Public Enemy* (1931) or *White Heat* (1949). Cagney enjoyed playing "The Gimp" and remarked in an interview that he realized that gangsters are what people wanted him to play. "But," he added, "Some day I'd like to make one picture that the kids could go see."

Joan Cohen

THE LOVED ONE

Released: 1965
Production: John Calley and Haskell Wexler for Metro-Goldwyn-Mayer
Direction: Tony Richardson
Screenplay: Terry Southern and Christopher Isherwood; based on the novel of the same name by Evelyn Waugh
Cinematography: Haskell Wexler
Editing: Antony Gibbs and Brian Smedley-Aston
Running time: 116 minutes

Principal characters:

Dennis Barlow	Robert Morse
Wilbur Glenworthy/ Henry Glenworthy	Jonathan Winters
Aimee Thanatogenos	Anjanette Comer
Mr. Joyboy	Rod Steiger
Mr. Kenton	Milton Berle
Mrs. Kenton	Margaret Leighton
Sir Francis Hinsley	John Gielgud
Sir Ambrose Ambercrombie	Robert Morley
General Brinkman	Dana Andrews
Immigration Officer	James Coburn
Gunther Fry	Paul Williams
Brahmin	Lionel Stander

The Loved One, filmed in 1965, is a prototype for cinematic black humor. It was advertised as the "motion picture with something to offend everyone," and it succeeded remarkably well, taking as its setting and principal topic one with the greatest taboo of all: death. It is set in a Los Angeles Forest Lawn-type memorial cemetery (dubbed Whispering Glades in the film) where the hero, Dennis Barlow, falls in love with a beautiful, mad, necrophilic cosmetician, Aimee Thanatogenos. Because the film takes aim at funeral parlors, California, and in particular Los Angeles as its satirical targets, it is thought to be making a philosophical statement about the meaning of life (or death) in America as embodied by California. This intent is made even more pointed by the playing of "America the Beautiful" on the soundtrack at the film's beginning and end.

The idea for the film came from British novelist Evelyn Waugh, who wrote about his experiences as a Hollywood screenwriter in the short satirical novel *The Loved One*, published in 1948. Using this novel and Waugh's *Life* magazine essay "Death in Hollywood," playwright Christopher Isherwood and scenarist Terry Southern (who wrote *Dr. Strangelove*, 1963) wrote the screenplay. While the burial customs of Los Angeles County are the main satirical focus, potshots are also taken at the military bureaucracy, overeating, and the film business.

Many major stars play relatively small roles in *The Loved One*, including Jonathan Winters, John Gielgud, Rod Steiger (particularly memorable as the macabre Mr. Joyboy, an embalmer), Robert Morley, Liberace, Margaret Leighton, Milton Berle, James Coburn, Roddy McDowell, Tab Hunter, and a very young Paul Williams. The main characters are the Waugh character, Dennis Barlow (Robert Morse), and his love object, Aimee (Anjanette Comer).

Barlow is a young English poet whose writing style relies heavily on plagiarism. At the beginning of the film he arrives in Hollywood to visit his uncle, Sir Francis Hinsley (John Gielgud), who has worked for many years as an art director for a major studio. Sir Francis has recently been fired by the studio in an economy drive, however, and he becomes increasingly despondent, finally committing suicide by hanging himself. Sir Ambrose Abercrombie (Robert Morley), a leader among the British community of actors, writers, and artists employed in the film colony, asks Barlow to arrange a dignified funeral for his uncle at Whispering Glades Memorial Park, Hollywood's most exclusive cemetery. Whispering Glades is run by the Reverend Wilbur Glenworthy (Jonathan Winters), who also has a twin brother operating a similar business. Harry Glenworthy (also Jonathan Winters) is the owner of the Happier Hunting Grounds, a pet cemetery. Because he needs a job after his uncle's burial, Barlow gets a job as a preacher working for Harry.

Barlow meets and quickly falls in love with Aimee Thanatogenos, a cosmetologist at Whispering Glades. She is also being wooed by Mr. Joyboy (Rod Steiger), however, the effeminate chief embalmer. Aimee rejects both of them, because, although she is disappointed to learn that Barlow's poems are all plagiarized, she is completely disgusted when she meets Mr. Joyboy's gluttonous mother. She consults a guru named Brahmin (Lionel Stander) but remains deeply confused about what to do with her two lovers. She finally asks for advice from the Reverend Glenworthy, but is horrified when he, too, makes advances toward her. Unable to cope any longer, she commits suicide by embalming herself.

In doing this, however, Aimee plays right into the Reverend's schemes. He has been planning to turn the cemetery into a senior citizens' home, but in order to do this he must disinter all of the caskets and move them some place. His idea is to launch them into outer space in a burial concept entitled "Celestial Rest." He had planned to initiate this program with the assistance of Air Force General Brinkman (Dana Andrews) by using the body of an astronaut. Aimee's body is substituted for the dead astronaut and is lifted into space on a rocket developed by a child prodigy named Gunther Fry (Paul Williams). A considerably dejected Barlow returns to England as the film ends.

Most critics seem to agree that the screenplay takes on too many satirical topics, particularly after the first half of the film which is primarily concerned with the outlandish state of the Los Angeles funeral business. It gets too far afield, perhaps, in its attempt to satirize real estate developments, homes for senior citizens, and almost the entire Southern California life-style. Moreover, some critics and audiences found the combined comedy about dead bodies and food simply too offensive in an era before *Animal House* (1979) invented the "food fight," as well as a bit overplayed. One reason for this heavy-handedness may be that screenwriter Southern's specialty, ridiculous bad taste, did not entirely jell with director Tony Richardson's favorite metaphor as seen in *Tom Jones* (1963)—eating as sexual symbolism.

Very fast-paced editing does much to cover up some of these structural incongruities, however; *The Loved One* originally ran five hours before being cut down to its more manageable two-hour length. The fine cinematography by Haskell Wexler adds to the mood of the film, reflecting the macabre surroundings. The climax of the film presents a very baroque travesty of the religious theme of resurrection of the soul. Here the talents of Southern mix well with Richardson's to make some comments that go beyond the ridiculous brand of California Christianity satirized, and are about American life as well.

Marsha McCreadie

LOVERS AND OTHER STRANGERS

Released: 1969
Production: David Susskind for A.B.C. Pictures
Direction: Cy Howard
Screenplay: Renee Taylor, Joseph Bologna, and David Zelag Goodman;
  based on the play of the same name by Renee Taylor and Joseph Bologna
Cinematography: Andrew Laszlo
Editing: David Bretherton and Sidney Kats
Song: Fred Karlin and Robb Wilson
Running time: 104 minutes

Principal characters:
Bea Vecchio	Beatrice Arthur
Susan Henderson	Bonnie Bedelia
Hal Henderson	Gig Young
Mike Vecchio	Michael Brandon
Frank Vecchio	Richard Castellano
Jerry	Robert Dishy
Johnny	Harry Guardino
Brenda	Marian Hailey
Richie Vecchio	Joseph Hindy
Cathy	Anne Jackson
Joan Vecchio	Diane Keaton
Bernice Henderson	Cloris Leachman
Wilma	Anne Meara

"So, what's da story?" dentalizes Italian-American papa Frank Vecchio (Richard Castellano) throughout *Lovers and Other Strangers*, providing a hilarious running gag that certainly helped word-of-mouth advertising in 1970 for this marital comedy. A wise, witty, and well-acted farce about love and marriage, sex, divorce, freedom, and happiness, the movie presents a cross-section of touching and comic couples as they prepare for the wedding of Susan Henderson (Bonnie Bedelia) and Mike Vecchio (Michael Brandon). Having secretly lived together for more than a year, and despite Mike's fears that a marriage license will diminish their present excitement and romance, the two begin to plan for the ritual. Soon, the best, worst, and funniest of both of their families is brought out in a series of revealing vignettes, loosely held together by the wedding preparations.

Susan is the daughter of upper-middle-class parents, Hal (Gig Young) and Bernice Henderson (Cloris Leachman). Although the parents are in love, Hal, it turns out, has also been clandestinely involved for ten years with Bernice's equally middle-aged sister Cathy (Anne Jackson). At the same time, we learn that Susan's older, very domineering sister Wilma (Anne Meara) and her husband Johnny (Harry Guardino), a former Marine, are having sexual problems. Arguing over who is boss in the family and forever questioning Johnny's masculinity, Wilma is perturbed because Johnny is not romantic enough. Confused and upset during one of their arguments, Wilma ends up shrieking, "I'm more feminine than you'll ever be!"

In another subplot, Susan's whining cousin and bridesmaid, Brenda (Marian Hailey), does not have an escort for the wedding, and so Mike calls up his unattached buddy and bridal party usher Jerry (Robert Dishy). Reluctant at first, the swinging single agrees to meet the girl at a local bar. She wants a meaningful relationship and spends much time quoting poet Kahlil Gibran, whereas he wants to get her straight into bed.

Mike's side of the wedding family is equally crazy. Coming from a more religious, lower-middle-class background, Mike's father is an Italian-American blue-collar worker. For Frank and his wife Bea (Beatrice Arthur), marriage has always been one long compromise full of conventions. Upon learning that his older, more serious brother Richie (Joseph Hindy) is planning a divorce from his wife Joan (Diane Keaton), Mike becomes scared about his own future marriage. With ensuing arguments that the wedding arrangements are all made, however, Susan and Mike's father manage temporarily to calm the youth down.

As the various foibles of all concerned unfold, the ceremony and reception soon get under way; the thirteen principal characters, however, continue to work out their assorted relationships amidst the festivities. Bernice's philandering husband consoles Cathy on his knee, usually in a free bathroom. Forever promising Cathy that he will get a divorce, Hal never makes good his word. When she finally states that she is going to marry another man, the hurt and angry Hal accuses her of playing around.

Wilma and Johnny are still at each other's throat, but they end up happily in bed. Richie and Joan attempt to patch up their differences, but apparently do not reconcile (although this point is ambiguous at the end). Jerry does manage to bed the virginal Brenda, but later reads her book. Hal and Bernice remain together, and only poor Cathy, holding the bridal bouquet and crying while resting in still another bathroom, seems to have a sad end. As the emotional crises swirl all around them, the oblivious newlyweds go off on their honeymoon, another husband and wife ready to begin conjugal life.

A sort of Italian *Goodbye Columbus* (1969), *Lovers and Other Strangers* not only has ethnic appeal but also has universality. As gentle satire on the self-deceiving side of human nature, the comedy manages to show us the tears beneath the raucous laughter. In a scene both funny and heart-wrenching, the groom's inarticulate father converses with his son; Frank admits to Mike that his own marriage has been joyless and that it has suffered greatly because the prudish Bea never provided any sexual satisfaction. "I'm content," he says, because he and Bea have things in common—like food and "the relatives."

As the befuddled, heavy-set, middle-class Italian, Richard Castellano is wonderfully endearing. It was this funny-sad portrayal that won the actor an Academy Award nomination for Best Supporting Actor, and led to his highly praised role as Clemenza in *The Godfather* (1972). As for the father of the bride, Gig Young is quite good as the husband Hal, in his first role since his Oscar-winning performance as the heartless promoter in *They Shoot Horses Don't They?* (1969). As the disenchanted wife Wilma, Anne Meara is also excellent, as usual. Jerry Stiller, her husband and comedy partner, is not billed in the credits, but we catch a glimpse of him and their daughter among the wedding guests. Another actress, Diane Keaton, in the small role of Joan, went on to stardom and an Oscar for her role in *Annie Hall* (1977).

Nominated for best screenplay, *Lovers and Other Strangers* was based on the play written by (and adapted to the screen by) Renee Taylor and Joseph Bologna; the husband-and-wife team later wrote and starred in another comedy about relationships, *Made for Each Other* (1971), which was not as successful as this film, although they have collaborated on several other successful films and teleplays. With its insightful script, bright characterizations, excellent casting, and crackling dialogue, the film was a big success at the box office. Although there are no "main characters" per se, each character (and actor) comes across believably. The mixture of humor and sadness makes a very entertaining film.

Leslie J. Taubman

THE LUCK OF GINGER COFFEY

Released: 1964
Production: Leon Roth for Walter Read-Sterling
Direction: Irvin Kershner
Screenplay: Brian Moore; based on his novel of the same name
Cinematography: Manny Wynn
Editing: Antony Gibbs
Running time: 100 minutes

> *Principal characters:*
> Ginger Coffey .... Robert Shaw
> Vera Coffey .... Mary Ure
> Paulie Coffey .... Libby McClintock
> Joe McGlade ....Tom Harvey
> McGregor .... Liam Redmond

The Luck of Ginger Coffey is one of those rare films that does not seem to be a film at all. It is a slice of life in which actors never appear to be acting and in which only the essentials of their daily lives are retained. The film is about accepting life as it is rather than as one wishes or dreams it to be. The title character slowly awakens to the realization that his dreams will only come true when he learns the power of assertion and the wisdom of compromise.

Ginger Coffey (Robert Shaw) is an Irish immigrant who moves to Canada with his wife Vera (Mary Ure, in real life, Shaw's wife) and daughter Paulie (Libby McClintock) in the hope of making a better life for them. Like many, he is convinced that his "ship will come in" any day now. As a result, he becomes ineffectual, making only half-hearted attempts at landing a job, and alienates his wife and potential employers in the process. Vera finally leaves him when it becomes clear that she and her daughter will starve otherwise. Ginger must be made to come to his senses.

Faced with the reality of his wife's departure, Ginger lands a meager job proofreading for a newspaper, and then only because an old friend named Joe McGlade (Tom Harvey) works there as a reporter. Even this menial labor with its equally menial wages, is not enough to deter Ginger from pursuing impossible dreams. He yearns to be a reporter, although he has no qualification whatsoever for the job.

The luck of the title comes into play when Ginger is working as a driver for a diaper service and suggests to his boss that the company might do well to rent baby cribs. The boss likes this idea and gives Ginger a bonus, as well as an offer of a higher position with the company. Ginger, however, clinging to the newspaper editor's phony promise of a job as a reporter, stupidly refuses the diaper service offer. He has come a long way since the first reel, but not quite far enough in terms of letting go of elusive dreams for a more profitable reality.

As played by Shaw, Ginger Coffey is both an individual and a recognizable type: the man or woman who chases dreams in an obstacle-strewn world. The fact that he never gets anywhere, he is convinced, is everyone's fault but his. There are millions like Coffey, building mountains out of fruitless dreams or the empty promises of others, never coming to terms with themselves. They usually end up slaving away at demeaning jobs because they lack the initiative or common sense to better themselves. *The Luck of Ginger Coffey* improves the inevitable fate of such losers by allowing the protagonist to wake up to what he must do for himself. In the process a more intelligent, resourcefully assertive man emerges. During the last half hour especially, we can see his intelligence sharpen, as though necessity has become the mother of cunning.

Shaw's performance as Coffey is like a bolt of quiet lightning. He opens the character by degrees, exposing the sympathetic pain as well as the folly. Although Shaw will probably be best remembered for his shark hunter in *Jaws* (1975), Ginger Coffey is his triumph as a film actor. He builds a characterization that catches the viewer short with the changes that have subtly occurred by the last reel. He is never an actor acting, always a real man living out his real life for the camera.

This is not to deny the excellence of the other actors. Ure, McClintock, Harvey, and Liam Redmond all turn in sharply realized performances. Ure, in particular, makes the audience feel the pain of Vera Coffey's hard time with Ginger. When she sleeps with him one last time toward the end, we know it is probably the end and that there is no going back to the marriage as it once was.

Director Irvin Kershner is best known for films such as *The Flim Flam Man* (1967), *Loving* (1970), and the excellent *Raid on Entebbe* (1977); later he turned to such trivia as *Eyes of Laura Mars* (1978). *The Luck of Ginger Coffey* was a turning point in his career, establishing his reputation for hard-edged dramas about the grittier aspects of life. Films such as *The Hoodlum Priest* (1961) and *Face in the Rain* (1963) purportedly demonstrated his ability to rise above the hackneyed level of his previous low-budget melodramas. With *The Luck of Ginger Coffey*, he perfected the cinema of naturalism that had been his trademark, displaying a knack for drawing from actors performances that convey a compelling reality rather than recycled Hollywood formulas.

Kershner also has the benefit of Brian Moore's incisive screenplay, Manny Winn's clear-eyed, flawlessly intuitive cinematography, and Antony Gibbs's talents as editor. Because of this fine ensemble artistry, the viewer ceases to be aware of *The Luck of Ginger Coffey* as a film within the first half hour. It is as though we are eavesdropping on a real family in which the father is having trouble coming to terms with the responsibilities of adulthood.

Along the way, we do wonder what life was like for the Coffeys before they moved to Canada. Obviously Vera was attracted to the dreamer in Ginger, tolerating his wild fancies as long as they were rooted to their homeland. Once uprooted, however, the dreams become nightmares, forcing Vera to some hard decisions.

The turning point in the film occurs when Vera tells Ginger that she will not come back to him unless he becomes financially stable and holds down a better job than that of proofreader. This convinces Ginger to make a better life for himself and his family. He gets that better job, provides a single-parent home for his daughter (although she would rather live with her mother), and begins to make something of himself. Although he regresses at the end by refusing the job with the diaper service, we feel as Vera does that things will turn out all right. He has lost his wife and daughter for the time being, but gained a new and better sense of himself.

The Luck of Ginger Coffey is classical theater, enacting a universal type of drama that inspires us to better ourselves as the title character has done. We may start out pitying Ginger's lack of self-realization but we certainly end up feeling that there, but for the grace of God, go we. We have all surely held childhood ideals, only to see many of them shattered upon growing up. The trick is to compromise with life in such a way that those ideals are realized to the extent of one's potential. This, according to the film, is the "luck" we are provided with, the luck that we make for ourselves in dealing with the world so that it gives us what we want. *The Luck of Ginger Coffey* is a film that makes us care about its people, makes us think about ourselves in relation to them, and gives us hope for making a better life when we take up where it leaves off.

Sam Frank